HOT WACKS BOOK

Supplement 3

THE HOT WACKS PRESS

PO BOX 544, OWEN SOUND, ONTARIO, CANADA N4K 5R1

FAX 519-376-9449

Dedicated to Kurt Cobain who left too soon.

Also dedicated to producers of fine recordings the world over and collectors who take the time to write
and share information on these recordings.

With thanks to:
Beanie for patience. Mom for encouragement. Kurt for feeding the monster. Elvis for the attitude.
And Ed Sullivan for February 9 1964.

© 1995

HOT WACKS BOOK
Supplement 3

is a copyright protected publication of

THE HOT WACKS PRESS™

P.O. Box 544
Owen Sound, Ontario
N4K 5R1 CANADA
24 Hour FAX 519-376-9449

PRINTED IN CANADA
ISBN 0-96980 80-2-X

Front cover photo by Julian Beveridge, Halifax, Nova Scotia.

Intro: Future Wacks

HOT WACKS BOOK XV (1992 - see page 203) was the last complete bootleg discography. Up until Book XV, each edition contained the information from the previous book plus any new releases. However, the book was becoming too big. BOOK XIV was 496 pages and, with the explosion of new releases on both vinyl and CD, BOOK XV was more than 800 pages. This was not only a monster to produce but expensive to ship. On top of that, it became a bit redundant and expensive for those of you who bought every edition of the book to have to buy the old information with the new.

HOT WACKS BOOK SUPPLEMENT 1 was released in 1993 and was designed to keep you on top of the bootleg world. It contained only new releases and a few old listings not found in Hot Wacks Book XV. HOT WACKS BOOK SUPPLEMENT 2 (1994) continued this format as does SUPPLEMENT 3.

Future plans call for THE ULTIMATE WACKS to be published in 1996. This will be a hard-cover, large-format book jam-packed with: interviews with bootleggers, photo discographies, bootleg memoribilia as well as the most complete bootleg listings ever.

As many of you well know, Hot Wacks does not include every bootleg that has ever been released. Not everything that comes out is available here in Canada because of the limited runs of some items and because contacts with some producers or distributors have not been established. While we have access to a great number of items through various collections, there are still some things that get by.

With this in mind, The Hot Wacks Press asks for your help to keep future books up to date. If you have some things in your collection that do not appear in BOOK XV, SUPPLEMENTS 1, 2 or 3 please write with the information about these items. Please send a picture or photocopy of the cover(s) along with song listings, the source and sound quality of the recording. Feel free to include any comments you want about the recording, performance, or cover.

If you have a collection that you feel is unique and would care to share it with the rest of the world please write or FAX (519-376-9449) with information about your collection.

If you are a producer of bootlegs, vinyl or CD, please send sample copies or information about your product. We don't need your address or number, just the tracks facts.

A History Of Bootlegs

(Editor's note: The following may seem familiar to some of you who have seen all or portions of it elsewhere. If you've read any articles or books that focus on bootlegs, most use this source (often uncredited) as a basis for their histories and definitions of boots. Future historians note - give credit where credit is due.)

In 1969 bootleg rock records made their appearance in the United States and Europe. Previously bootlegs consisted mainly of Jazz and Blues artists. These, however, did not receive the attention that rock bootlegs did as the artists were not big money-makers. Dean Meador, writing in HOT WACKS QUARTERLY (A History Of Bootleg Recordings, Issue #4), traced bootlegs back to the turn of the century.

"Mapleson, the librarian of the Metropolitan Opera at that time, received a cylinder recorder from Thomas Edison. He took his gift up into the fly-loft on several occasions during the Met's 1901-03 seasons and recorded bits and pieces of performances. Even though Mapleson had his machine a long way from the stage area and his medium had limitations (his cylinders ran for only a few minutes at a time, making it impossible to capture all of a long aria or duet), he produced an astonishing number of unique recording documents."

"Mapleson and his cylinders provided a taste of actual performances during that period. Mapleson gave collectors a chance to obtain and hear performers, singers, artists and speakers of that era who never appeared on commercial recordings, others in roles they didn't duplicate on authorized discs."

The record that started it all for rock boots was Bob Dylan's GREAT WHITE WONDER. This double album originally came in a plain white jacket without any printed label or title. Since sound recordings did not receive copyright protection in the USA until February 15, 1972, GWW received wider distribution than the bootlegs of today. However, claims that it sold some 350,000 copies are extremely unlikely. It is further interesting to note that when Columbia Records released the same material in authorized form years later as THE BASEMENT TAPES the official version sold quite well.

A distinction had best be made at this point between bootleg, pirate and counterfeit records. A bootleg consists of unreleased material recorded at concerts, studio outtakes, and radio or TV broadcasts. A pirate album consists of released material without attempting to make the LP look like an original. A counterfeit album is an exact copy of an officially released album.

Record industry spokespeople often include bootlegs with counterfeit and pirate recordings when making statements about the loss of revenue from record piracy. Bootlegs, with their small pressings, should not be included in this figure as the record labels do not lose revenue from a recording which is not in their catalog.

These same spokespeople completely overlook the historical significance of bootlegs as well. While this is obvious when speaking in terms of opera, jazz and blues boots, rock has not been around for the same amount of time. With rock's seemingly unending loss of performers due to untimely deaths, this will soon become evident. Albert Goldman, in his bestseller ELVIS, is one of the first biographers to appreciate the historical significance bootlegs have.

"Not just the man but the performer continued to emerge after his death. Though RCA had nothing better to offer than gleanings from its soon-exhausted archives, the record bootleggers, those great friends of the fans, cut the legal knots that had long restrained the release of Elvis's most significant live sessions. The legendary Elvis of the Louisiana Hayride, the Dorsey Brothers shows and the Hawaiian benefits appeared. All the jams from the Singer Special were offered in two beautifully-packaged albums from California that far surpassed both in interest and in appearance any legitimate offerings of RCA Victor. In yet another illicit release came at last the most sought-after tape in the history of rock 'n' roll: the fabled 'Million Dollar Quartet,' an impromptu sing in the Sun Studio around Christmas 1956, by the three greatest heroes of rockabilly: Elvis, Jerry Lee Lewis and Carl Perkins (minus the anticipated fourth voice, Johnny Cash). Though in this instance the reality of the recording hardly matched the glamour of its legend, the value of the disc as a document was enormous. At last you were inside the Sun Studio listening attentively as Sam Phillips' greatest singers did what they most enjoyed doing: pickin' and singin' their favorite rock songs and hymns."

Currently the average pressing in the USA of a bootleg is 1,000 copies; in Europe 500 to 1,000 copies; and a few hundred copies in Japan. Australia, which just recently became a steady source of supply, quite likely has runs as small as Japan. Canada deserves mention if only for the fact that an entire run of Bruce Springsteen boxed sets was seized before they could be distributed. With that exception, Canada is not a bootleg-producing country.

All of the early American bootleg labels have ceased operating. This is the case with RUBBER DUBBER, IMMACULATE CONCEPTION RECORDS (ICR), CONTRABAND MUSIC (CBM), DITTOLINO DISCS, KUSTOM RECORDS, TRADE MARK OF QUALITY (TMOQ), PIG'S EYE, HIGHWAY HI FI (HHCER), PHONYGRAF and one outfit that used a different name for each release (Hen, Steel Led, etc.). Their product was a thick, black record in a white jacket. To simplify matters they are referred to in this text as White Cover Folks (WCF).

The second generation of bootleggers, which includes WIZARDO RECORDS (WRMB), IDLE MIND PRODUCTIONS (IMP), HOFFMAN AVENUE RECORDS (HAR), K&S RECORDS and THE AMAZING KORNYFONE RECORD LABEL (TAKRL), is also out of business.

At the present time the vast majority of releases is coming out of Europe. If anything, the Europeans have improved on their sound quality and packaging, both of which they have been leaders in for years. Most of their product matches, and in some cases surpasses, legitimate record releases.

(December 22 1985 Kurt Glemser - Editor of HOT WACKS - Books I thru XI)

1986 saw the rise and fall of BOX TOP RECORDS. This label re-released many old classics, most on colored vinyl, from original plates. These came in a thin cover with a color snap-shot of the artist on the front and a sticker with the song listings on the back. Titles were rubber-stamped on the front. In the spring of 1987, after two years of production, ROCK SOLID RECORDS/INTERNATIONAL RECORDS (RSR/International) also went out of business.

1988 witnessed the short-lived return of the TRADE MARK OF QUALITY (TMOQ or TMQ) and THE AMAZING KORNYPHONE RECORD LABEL (TAKRL) labels working together to provide 'A High Standard Of Standardness'. Records came in one-color covers with the artists' name and the album title on the front and a jacket-sized label logo on the back. There were two separate batches of releases and each had the song listings for albums in that batch on sheets enclosed in the record jackets. Each release was limited to 500 copies.

1989 brought the introduction of the bootleg CD and the demise of vinyl. In some cases bootleg CDs are a waste of technology since these are taken from the original boots of the same name, not new or better sources. After all, who wants a bad recording containing pops and crackles that'll last forever. In other instances when a good source is available, such as with ULTRA RARE TRAX VOLUMES 1&2 (The Beatles) or DALLAS '75 VOLUMES 1&2 (Led Zeppelin), the results are incredible.

1990 through 1995 can only be described as the era of the bootleg CD. Using loopholes in the copyright laws of some European, Far East countries and Australia bootleggers flooded the market with CD re-issues of old boots as well as a wealth of new, often soundboard, recordings. Many of these items are available in North America through mail-order and in stores in Europe, Japan and Australia.

There is some speculation that this will all come to an end soon because of recent changes in some copyright laws but I suggest that the action will just relocate. As long as fans crave the live and unusual, the bootlegger and bootlegs will exist.

Please note, THE HOT WACKS PRESS does not sell the records or CDs listed in this book, this is a discography not a catalog. Most of these items are long out of circulation and not available.

(May 1995 Bob Walker - Editor/Publisher of HOT WACKS Books XII to SUPPLEMENT 3).

STOP AND READ THIS

Abbreviations

Abbreviations have been used in order to save space, making Hot Wacks more compact and easier to use. These are as follows:
R = Recording: Ex = excellent, Vg = very good, G = good, s = stereo, m = mono.
S = Source (recording location and/or date of recording).
C = Comments: Eb = European bootleg*, ECD = European CD*, ACD = Asian CD*,
Dcc = deluxe color cover/insert, Dbw = deluxe black & white cover/insert, GF = gatefold,
DL = deluxe label, CV = colored vinyl, MCV = multi-colored vinyl, SS = song separation.
*(source of development, manufacture or distribution)

Sound Quality

The HOT WACKS rating system is based on the sound quality of bootleg releases, not legitimate albums and CDs. Sound quality has come a long way since the old days of boots in the early 70s. We were very forgiving in those days, simply amazed that we could hear our faves live and ignoring some of the less than perfect recordings. So what if it was an audience recording from the back of a stadium with some drunken lout yelling for "Hard Rain", "Heart Breaker" or "Whipping Post". It was our band LIVE.

The introduction of high quality bootleg CDs has spoiled us. No longer will collectors accept less than perfect recordings. I've talked to some collectors who will not even consider an audience recording. How soon we forget.

Sure, excellent sound quality is desirable but sometimes it's just not available. Do we ignore the Australian Zep shows or Quarrymen rehearsals because of the less than perfect quality? I think not. I hope not. When we start putting the sound quality of recordings ahead of historic importance we are buying bootlegs for the wrong reasons.

Enough soapboxing, let's look at how things are graded for this edition of THE HOT WACKS BOOK SUPPLEMENT. The big thing to keep in mind is the state of live recording at the time of the performance. Remember, DAT portables did not always exist.

Excellent (Ex): Everything is nice and clear - instruments and voice(s) are well defined.
Very Good (Vg): Lacks the edge of an Ex recording.
Good (G): Still quite listenable but not for everyone.
Poor: For the hard-core collector.

Soundboard Recording (Soundboard): Professional recording from the mixing board at a concert, a recording studio source or from a radio or television broadcast.

Audience Recording (Audience): Amateur recording on portable audio or video equipment.

An Ex Soundboard recording more often than not differs from an Ex Audience recording and this should be kept in mind when looking at the gradings. Soundboard recordings tend to provide an even balanced recording while Audience recordings rely on the quality of the sound system, the recording equipment and the position of the recorder.

Equalizing Bootlegs
Getting The Most Out Of Unauthorized Audio

By Hugh Jones
© 1995 Hugh Jones & HJR/Proximity Productions
(Hugh Jones is the editor and publisher of the esteemed Led Zeppelin fanzine PROXIMITY, and has been collecting live tapes since 1972. He also operates a home recording studio and spends much of his time in the company of decibels, hertz and kilohertz.)

For many collectors, unauthorized recordings of their favorite bands comprise the most enjoyable and challenging area of collecting. The vast majority of recordings making the rounds in trading and bootleg circles are live concert material, in most cases recorded by someone in the crowd with considerably less than state-of-the-art equipment (fondly referred to as 'audience tapes'). In the last ten years or so the technology of portable audio equipment has increased dramatically, first with the advent of high-quality yet tiny decks like the Sony D50 (virtually designed with bootleg recording in mind) and more recently, DAT recorders. Prior to this, however, compact recording devices were low quality and about the size of your average hardcover book, thus very difficult to smuggle into tight-security concerts.

Of course, concert security wasn't very tight until around 1972, and some of the early tapes of 'classic' bands were actually recorded on reel-to-reel decks using good studio microphones, lugged down to the hall and brought inside via a sympathetic roadie or event staffer. The excellent quality Led Zeppelin recording from the LA Forum 9/4/70 (the source for the famous LIVE ON BLUEBERRY HILL bootleg) was recorded this way, as were several other well-known tapes.

None the less, many of the tapes in circulation are poor sound quality, ranging from mildly tinny, distorted or unbalanced to virtually unlistenable. In many cases, the listenability of a tape can be improved by equalization, and the purpose of this article is to introduce this concept to those of you who are not familiar with it, and to pass along some tips to those of you who are.

Equalization is a tool for enhancing (or 'treating') sound, not creating it. The degree of improvement possible on any given tape is directly related to the raw materials at hand. In other words, if the basic elements of the music are audible on a tape to begin with, then equalizing it can sometimes make a big improvement. On the other hand, if a tape is totally muddy, distorted, and sounds terrible to begin with, no amount of equalization or treatment is really going to help - you simply cannot turn mud to gold!

In theory, a good microphone strategically placed in relation to a sound source will yield a good recording - this is a basic tenet of recording music. A classic (albeit misguided) view of this comes from Robert Plant in a 1970 interview for the British paper MUSIC NOW. Talking about the then-brand-new LED ZEPPELIN III album, Plant says, ". . . 'Since I've Been Loving You' is virtually a live track recorded in the studio. The sound is great. If pirate [bootleg] albums got it together, instead of waving evil mikes [sic] on the end of broomsticks, that is the kind of sound they could get at a live concert."

What Plant fails to acknowledge here is that the recording of 'Since I've Been Loving You' was done in a controlled environment (Island Studios in London), a room isolated from outside sound and designed for recording music with the aid of a skilled sound engineer and producer (in this case Andy Johns and Jimmy Page). No matter how good the equipment is, an individual recording a live concert from the crowd is subject to the problems inherent in an uncontrolled environment—crowd noise, the acoustics of the hall, the quality of the sound mix, hostile security guards, and any number of other factors. And, they only get one chance to make their recording, with no opportunity to monitor the results until it's completed!

That said, it is possible to get a good quality recording at a live show with the right combination of luck and skill. Standing in the right position (near a PA speaker or, in some cases, the mixing board), being around people who are willing to keep quiet and using good recording equipment are all important factors.

UNDERSTANDING EQUALIZATION

What is equalization all about? Well, I've heard equalizers described as 'glorified tone controls', but it's probably more accurate to say that the tone controls on your stereo are a simplified (or very limited) form of equalization. The human ear is theoretically capable of hearing frequencies from 20 hertz (Hz) on the low end up to 200 kilohertz (KHz) on the high end. Somewhere within this range are the sounds we hear every day: noises, conversation, music and what-not. In music, certain instruments tend to fall within a given range of frequencies (high, mid or low-range) and equalization allows one to manipulate the level of those frequencies and change the perceived sound of various instruments and/or the overall sound of a recording.

The more isolated a frequency is in the spectrum, the more control one has over it via equalization. For example, the majority of tones generated by a bass guitar occupy the lower frequencies of the spectrum, usually in the 60Hz to 100Hz range. On your average audience tape of a rock band, the bass is the most prominent sound in that range, thus it is easy to increase or decrease the overall bass level on the tape by drawing it out or burying it with equalization. Conversely, vocals and guitars often fall right into the same high to mid-range frequencies, making it difficult to isolate one from the other and adjust one without affecting both.

THE TWO TYPES OF EQUALIZERS

A graphic equalizer has individual slider controls that can cut and boost the decibel (db) level of a specific part of the audio spectrum. This type of unit may have as few as 10 or as many as 30 (or more) different sliders, each one controlling a different portion of the audio spectrum between 20Hz and 200KHz. When this type of equalizer's settings are placed in a specific pattern, they visually approximate a graph of the sound, thus the name graphic equalizer.

A parametric equalizer, though harder to use and usually more expensive than a graphic, provides more precise control over the sound since it allows you to 'dial in' specific frequency ranges. This type of unit has three controls that set the frequency at which the filter operates, the degree of cut or boost and the width of the area being treated. When properly used, a parametric can really zero in on certain frequencies and effectively enable one to bring them out of (or subdue them in) the mix.

CHOOSING YOUR EQUIPMENT

Most people's budgets limit their options to the graphic variety of equalizer, and this type of unit is quite satisfactory for equalizing the sound on bootlegs. One of the best deals on the market right now is the ALESIS M-EQ 230, a 30-band stereo graphic equalizer that sells for around $300.00. With 30 bands of EQ for each channel, this unit provides the most bang for the buck available, and it's a reliable, easy to use machine.

This is the equalizer used in the examples and illustrations in this article, but that doesn't mean that a cheaper unit with less bands won't also be effective; I've seen 15-band stereo equalizers advertised for under $100—it's worth shopping around, and keeping an eye on the used market as well. I've seen the

Alesis unit in the classifieds for as low as $175.00.

While a single-channel equalizer will work for most bootleg tapes, since they're generally mono recordings, the average person will find a stereo (2-channel) unit like the MEQ-230 most desirable. Another feature that is absolutely essential in an equalizer is a mute, or 'in/out' switch, which allows you to switch back and forth between the equalized ('treated') sound and the unequalized ('dry') sound at any time, without moving the sliders back to zero. A/B comparison with the original sound of your tape is essential to maintain perspective when equalizing, so that you can hear the effect of your settings at any time.

EQUALIZING METHODS

Usually when I get a tape that's in serious need of EQ, I make a dub of it, running the signal through the equalizer and creating a new master tape. Of course, this reduces the overall quality by one generation, and one must weigh the positives of improving the tonal characteristics of the recording against the negatives of losing one generation. Boosting the high and/or midrange frequencies slightly and using good tape decks with Dolby C or S on the dub will keep generational loss to a minimum; still, this is a factor to consider.

Another way to go is to take notes and keep track of how each tape in your collection may be EQ'd for optimum quality, and then reset the equalizer each time you play or dub the recordings. This requires a lot more energy setting up for each listening, but saves the generational loss, and keeps your tape costs down.

One important word to the wise: NEVER GET RID OF YOUR MASTER TAPES! No matter how much improvement you feel you've made by equalizing a dub, it's a bad idea to erase or let go of the original source recording. For one thing, if you do a lot of trading, some collectors prefer an unequalized original so that they can do their own treatment of it. Even more important, equalizing is such a subjective thing that your own opinion of an EQ'd dub's sound quality might change, or your skill and your equipment might improve over time to the point where you want to go back to the drawing board and create a new and better equalized version of a tape.

MISCELLANEOUS TIPS

• Never equalize a tape starting with the first song of the concert; generally sound improves as a show progresses, since the sound crew are also twiddling dials and experimenting with equalization and other effects as they go. Usually by the second or third song things have stabilized, and the sound quality remains constant for the rest of the performance.

• It helps to equalize at several points on the tape and try to achieve an average using different types of songs as reference points. I find that it also helps to do the equalizing in a song that has loud and quiet passages, or perhaps solo vocal and/or instrumental passages as well as all band members playing at once.

• Start by making a sample tape using a few different settings. Listen to it in the car, at work, with a walkman; on as many different stereos as possible. This can give you insight into other ways to improve the recording. I find it very valuable to listen to tapes on my main home stereo and then on a cheap blaster, and evaluate them from opposite ends of the spectrum.

• When equalizing a tape, don't monitor at excessively high volumes. You'll make better judgements if it's playing at a lower volume, and anything that sounds good quiet will only be improved by cranking it up later.

• Don't spend hours and hours equalizing; you'll start to get noise fatigue and lose perspective. It's amazing how a poor-sounding recording will start to sound better as you get used to it, and it's also easy to lose objectivity if you're listening to a really great show and get caught up in the music. Take your time, do several different versions, and go back to the process after a break and some objective listenings on different systems.

• Most audio engineers will tell you that equalization should always be done on a smooth curve, and while this is often true when dealing with musical sounds, it does not always apply to dealing with bootlegs. When trying to get rid of hiss or certain annoying sounds, it can be very effective to drastically cut a single frequency, as on some of the examples here.

SPECIFIC EXAMPLES

Described here are four shows by three different artists and how I EQ'd them. The Zeppelin Melbourne tape benefitted the most, the Who and the Zep Stoke concerts the least, but all sound better (to my ears) after careful equalization adjustments.

Remember, sound quality is an extremely subjective thing. Using the settings described here will give you a starting point, but they may or may not be as pleasing to your ears as they are to mine. Some people like a lot of bass, some people like less; some can listen to endless variations of 'Dazed & Confused,'others prefer 'Are You Experienced' or 'Substitute.' That's what makes horse races! Like anything else, practice makes perfect, and once you're familiar with your equipment and go through the process a few times, the results can be very satisfying.

NOTE: On the diagrams, where no setting is indicated, the fader remains at 0db. Also, each diagram illustrates only one channel of a two-channel mixer. Assuming a mono recording, your settings should be the same on both channels.

LED ZEPPELIN: Melbourne, Australia February 20, 1971

This recording is a prime candidate for equalizing. The untreated sound is very tinny, with almost no bass frequencies and an annoying ring in the high end, but all the components of the band are audible, and, as is common with outdoor recordings, there is no reverberation to make the sound turn into mush. Jones' bass notes can be heard, they just don't possess the powerful low frequencies characteristic of electric bass guitar, and while the high end tinniness is exacerbated by Plant's already high voice, this is a recording that can be vastly improved by equalizing.

Starting with the bass, we find that its presence is strongest in the 80Hz to 200Hz range. Boosting at 200Hz brings out the melodic aspects of the instrument, while boosting at 160Hz and 125Hz gives us more of the tonal qualities—that low end warmth that is often felt as much as heard. Since this tape is so severely lacking in the bass department, a steep curve starting with a 2db boost at 80Hz, a10db peak at 160Hz and a 2db boost at 320Hz to finish takes care of the bass sound.

At the other end of the spectrum, the high end tinniness that our ears interpret as annoying falls into a narrow range between 5 and 8KHz. Cutting 8KHz a full -12db removes the worst of the tinny drone, but moving the faders too far down at 5 and 6KHz has a detrimental effect on the music; some of the clarity of Plant's voice is lost, and the guitar is affected as well. My solution here is to drop in a gradual curve from 4 to 6.2KHz, cutting no more than 3 or 4db, then plunge down on the 8KHz fader to -12db. An A/B comparison reveals the tinniness is gone while the highs remain crisp.

At this point the tape has already been greatly improved, and one might choose to leave well enough alone, however, I still desired a bit more volume and punch out of Jimmy Page's guitar. Most of the guitar sound is in the same spectrum as the highend elements that we have already cut back, though key guitar frequencies also exist in the 500Hz to 1KHz range. The trick here is to enhance the guitar without bringing back the tinniness in the 3 to 4KHz range, and without over-boosting the bass in the 500 to 800Hz range. With some judicious tweaking, I ended up with a gentle curve, starting with a 2db boost at 640Hz, peaking with a 4db boost at 800Hz fader, and ending with a 2db boost at 1KHz; which put more balls into the guitar's sound. To give the effect of raising its volume and punchiness, I also put a curve in starting with 2db at 2KHz, peaking at 4db at 2.5KHz, ending with 2db at 3.1KHz.

Now the A/B comparison is like night and day; a noisy audience tape that might rate a 6 or a 7 on the average taper's list becomes a very listenable recording worthy of an 8 or even 9.

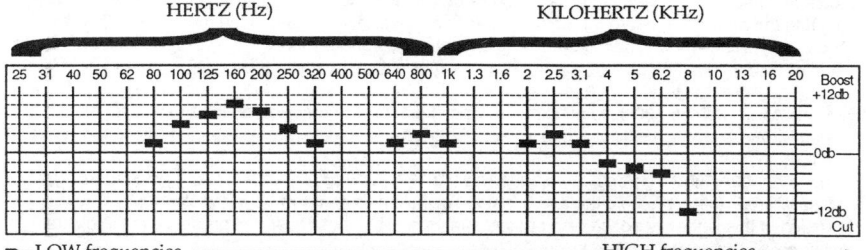

EQ Chart for LED ZEPPELIN, MELBOURNE, AUSTRALIA, 2/20/72

JIMI HENDRIX EXPERIENCE: Singer Bowl, Flushing NY, August 23, 1968

This performance, while perhaps not one of Jimi's best, is a high-energy set from the peak of the Experience's popularity. No doubt recorded on a primitive cassette deck, there is lots of enthusiastic crowd noise and a fair amount of distortion in the actual recording (not to mention the high-volume playing itself!) While equalization can't do much to solve these inherent problems, this tape certainly benefits from some judicious tweaking.

My tape of this came directly from a bootleg LP, and it's sonic problems stem mainly from too much hiss and not enough bass. To deal with the hiss effectively, a dramatic plunge of -12db at 6.2KHz and 8KHz seems to do the job without undermining the midrange and high frequencies that comprise the majority of the sound—and Jimi's guitar and vocals.

The bass on this recording is fairly buried, and difficult to isolate into a frequency that is easy to control. I got the biggest improvement by creating a gradual curve from 62Hz to 160Hz, with a very high peak of 12db on the 100Hz fader. This still doesn't give Noel Redding's instrument much clarity, but it brings it out a bit and unquestionably adds some overall low end balls to the sound. The drums are pretty much a lost cause on this recording, as is true on many audience tapes from the early days of rock. In most cases they were not mic'ed well through the PA system to begin with, and what drum sound does come through is in the same mid-to-high range that contains the guitar frequencies (and hiss).

Some tweaking in the midrange area does improve Hendrix' guitar sound considerably here—again, a gradual curve from 1.6KHz to 5KHz, peaking with a solid 10db boost at 3.1KHz, seems to have the best effect. Note the sharper curve going down on the high frequencies than going up on the midrange here—this is needed to keep too much hiss from creeping back in, and while it does add some hiss to bring out the guitar, it's not the same grating sound that we eliminated at the beginning of the process with this tape.

While not as big an improvement as the previous Zeppelin tape, this Hendrix recording goes from perhaps a 5 rating for sound up to a 6 or 7.

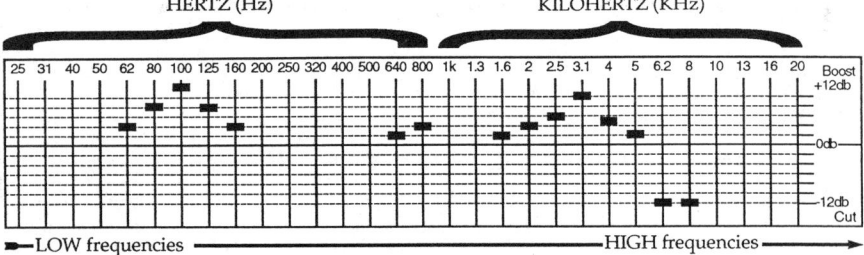

EQ Chart for JIMI HENDRIX, SINGER BOWL, NYC, 8/23/68

THE WHO: Anaheim Stadium, Los Angeles, March 21, 1976

Also recorded at an open-air venue (which often yields above-average audience tape results), this is a decent audience recording with all the elements of the band more or less audible. While equalization can't add too much to a recording like this, there is a flat quality to it due to the majority of the sound frequencies falling in the middle range of the spectrum. By boosting things at each end, more presence is added, and at least the illusion of more clarity, especially to Townshend's guitar.

Boosting a full 12db on 100Hz fader is the only point that has much effect on the bass guitar, but curving upwards on each side to a max of about 7db warms up the overall recording on the low end.

On the other hand, the high end curve added from 3.1KHz to 6.2KHz really livens up the recording, adding cymbals to the drum sound and bringing Townshend's guitar more to the forefront. The downside of this is that audience also becomes more audible, but the added presence to the overall sound makes this a small compromise.

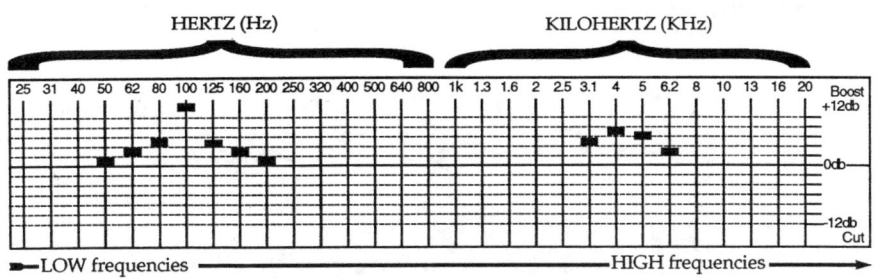

EQ Chart for THE WHO, ANAHEIM STADIUM, 3/21/76

LED ZEPPELIN: Trentham Gardens, Stoke, January 15, 1973

This is one of those infuriating soundboard recordings where everything came through loud and clear except the guitar! On this particular tape the bass is also too loud, but Bonzo's drums sound very good and Plant's vocal is right up front, if a bit 'dry'. Again, all the elements are here, but with a graphic equalizer it is very difficult to pull the select frequencies of Page's guitar out and raise them to a satisfactory level; a parametric might be more up to this task.

Even so, a wide curve that boosts the frequencies from 800Hz to 3.1KHz (peaking with a 10db boost at 1.6KHz) brings the guitar out considerably. The down side of this is it also affects the vocals and drums, making them a bit harsher and also proportionately louder; a slight dip of about 4db at 8 to 10KHz provides a little compensation, but at this point how much equalization is used becomes a matter of personal taste.

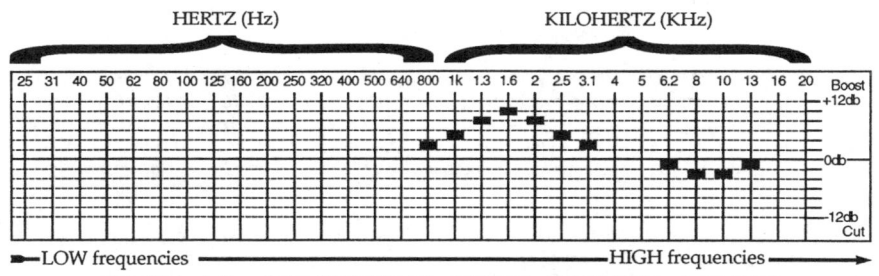

EQ Chart for LED ZEPPELIN, STOKE, ENGLAND, 1/15/73

Legal Issues

The following has been reprinted with permission from the February 1995 issue of
ICE - THE MONTHLY CD NEWSLETTER
(PO Box 3043, Santa Monica, CA 90408 USA)

The end is near in Italy, probably the most prolific country in the world for producing underground CDs. According to one well-placed source, Italian pressing plants have told the "live" labels to submit their final titles this month. After one last run, the factories will no longer press CDs that previously fell into the copyright protection gap. The gap allowed labels to release recent recordings without artist permission, as long as they paid royalties through the SIAE (the Italian equivalent of BMI or ASCAP) and received that organization's authorization (usually shown as a rubber stamp on many Italian CDs). Pressure from the major labels and other interests has finally caused the SIAE to stop putting its blessing on live CDs. In the last few months, some factories have allowed labels to sign "documents of responsibility" in lieu of SIAE approval, but apparently that final loophole is about to close. Recordings made more than 20 years ago remain temporarily in the clear, but that could change as soon as July and certainly by the end of the year. ...As for the future, our source hints that some labels plan to relocate - with Australia and the Far East mentioned prominently - or to go underground a la British and American labels. Regardless, the end of an era is upon us.

Bootlegs Keep
Music Kicking

By Tony Parsons
The following has been reprinted with permission of the author from the November 25th 1994 issue of
THE DAILY TELEGRAPH (1 Canada Square, London E14 5DT England)

A Toast. Charge your glasses with moonshine and let us drink to Prince's THE BLACK ALBUM. On Monday the biggest-selling bootleg album of all time (global sales are estimated at 200,000) finally appeared in the record shops.

I know that many readers will join me in toasting the release of this previously-proscribed classic because a column I wrote earlier this year urging the music business to differentiate between pirate or counterfeit records (official record company releases, illegally duplicated) and bootlegs (an artist's live recordings or unofficial studio material, illegally released) produced a phenomenal response.

"Counterfeit records and CDs are produced to deceive the public into thinking that they are buying the genuine article," wrote two committed bootleg buyers from Hertfordshire. "However, the same cannot be said for bootleg recordings, which are generally made by people who love the music for people who love the music. Long live the bootleggers! Long live music!"

The bootleg industry is a twilight zone full of treasures that are unknown to the general public. The discovery of early Beatles sessions, recorded for the BBC, has been compared by EMI with finding Tutankhamen's tomb. But this material - soon to be officially released by the company as LIVE AT THE BBC - has been knocking around for years on bootleg, albeit in vastly inferior sound quality, so there are footprints all over Tutankhamen's tomb. And anyway, does the world really need another version of 'Long Tall Sally?'

THE BLACK ALBUM is a perfect example of why the music business will never beat the bootleggers. It is the missing piece of Prince's purple jigsaw. Originally meant to be Prince's followup to SIGN O' THE TIMES in Christmas 1987, THE BLACK ALBUM was withdrawn at the last moment, although not before CDs had been pressed and review tapes sent out. A bootleg bonanza was inevitable.

Why did Prince suppress THE BLACK ALBUM? It has been said that he was worried about sexually explicit nature of the record, which would surely be like Megadeath withdrawing an album because they thought it was a bit noisy. Apart from a song about tying someone to a chair, THE BLACK ALBUM is probably Prince's least libidinous record. "All sisters like it when you lick them - on the knees," he smirks at one point. That's pretty tame for someone with songs like 'Head', 'Sexy MF' and 'Darling Nikki' in his canon of debauchery.

Still, there is some dubious lyrical content on THE BLACK ALBUM. On 'Cindy C', allegedly a song about Mrs. Richard Gere, Prince goes way beyond his usual Benny Hill type banner. "Cindy C - I will pay the usual fee," Prince leers repeatedly. Not the kind of thing a gentleman says to a lady. But perhaps the kind of thing that a rabid sex dwarf would like to whisper to a luscious young supermodel.

Although THE BLACK ALBUM is Prince's heaviest dance record, it reveals an ambivalent attitude to the hip-hop community. '2 Nigs United 4 West Compton' pours scorn on bad-ass dudes with their hats on back to front, while elsewhere Prince sneers, "Rappers' problems usually stem from being tone-deaf."

Whatever the reason for its premature withdrawal, THE BLACK ALBUM is certainly a very fine Prince album, containing 'Bob George', one of his greatest songs, and oodles of funky goodness. Although not quite in the same league as PURPLE RAIN, 1999 or SIGN O' THE TIMES, it is infinitely superior to the dreary LOVE-SEXY, the record that eventually appeared in its place.

Ironically, three days before THE BLACK ALBUM was released, police, customs officers and members of the BPI anti-piracy unit seized 25,000 illegally produced CDs valued at £300,000 from an address in south London, the biggest ever haul of musical contraband. The story made the cover of MUSIC WEEK, but we were not told how many of the records seized were pirates and how many were bootlegs. The music business still can't tell the difference. But the public can.

"Owning a bootleg tape or CD if a live concert wouldn't stop either of us buying an official live recording, usually on release date", write my correspondents from Hertfordshire, surely speaking for all bootleg fans.

The kind of people who buy bootlegs are not killing the music industry. They are keeping it alive.

From The Trenches

The following articles are written by people in the trenches... collectors. Some say that we at HOT WACKS are (or should be) the experts. The way I see it, it's you the collectors compiling that seemingly never-ending collection that are the real experts. Sure, we listen and document a lot of the material that goes into HOT WACKS but It's the collectors who write with new information and information missing from past editions that make the book as complete as it is. Please feel free to send in any information you may have or an article about your favorite group.

The Beatles
BELMO'S BEATLEG VIEWS

(BELMO is founder/editor/publisher of the international newsletter for collectors, BELMO'S BEATLEG NEWS. Belmo is a frequent contributor to BEATLEFAN and GOLDMINE and a long-time collector of Beatlegs. Belmo and co-author Jim Berkenstadt recently completed their book on the history of The Beatles underground recordings which will be published sometime in 1995.
Belmo can be reached at: Belmo's Beatleg News, P.O. Box 17163, Ft. Mitchell, KY 41017.
Send $3 for a sample copy of Belmo's newsletter.)

The question I'm most often asked by the readers of my newsletter, BELMO'S BEATLEG NEWS, is: "What are the best and most essential bootlegs that I should have in my Beatles collection?".

The answer, of course, changes year to year and sometimes month to month. The past few years have seen a tremendous surge of new releases with fantastic sound quality and many rare and unreleased songs. The major bootleg companies (such as YELLOW DOG, VIGOTONE, BIG MUSIC and GREAT DANE) have taken bootlegs to new heights in terms of musical selection, sound quality and packaging - sometimes even outdoing the legitimate companies. The BBC BOX SET by Great Dane is an excellent example of this. Their 9-CD boxed set and accompanying deluxe book puts to shame the recent EMI release of THE BEATLES LIVE AT THE BBC.

The criteria for selecting THE BEST OF THE BEATLEGS is based on the following:
A) Rarity of material/Historical importance
B) Sound quality
C) Packaging
D) The enjoyment factor

There have been well over 2000 (!) Beatles bootlegs (group & solo) manufactured since 1970 and there is no end in sight. Most of these are no longer available, but not to worry because most were crap anyway. The early vinyl releases suffered from shoddy mastering and horrid packaging. With the advent of compact discs these poorly pressed recordings became obsolete. In addition this new technology made bootlegging more profitable. Thus a lot of new material and improved tapes were unleashed on the market. And thanks to some loopholes in the European copyright laws, the products found a mass market they might not have enjoyed previously.

So most of what I have selected as essential for Beatles collectors should be currently available if you know where to go to locate them. (And, no, I'm not going to help you find any. You are on your own.) Bootleg compact discs generally cost $20 - 25 apiece and box set prices depend on the number of discs and the packaging. Should you purchase everything on my list, expect to shell out over $ 800!

With that said let's get on with it. Here, then, are THE BEST OF THE BEATLEGS:

(1) THE COMPLETE BBC SESSIONS (Great Dane, GDRCD 9326/9)
This nine-CD boxed set is phenomenal. It features 247 chronologically-ordered tracks from the Beatles' BBC performances. The sound quality is mostly superb and the accompanying full-color album size booklet details the recordings with a complete sessionography and bootleg history. It easily wins my vote for the BEST BEATLES BOOTLEG EVER MADE! The Beatles' live performances were captured best during their BBC sessions - no screaming fans, just great rock and roll performed by the world's most exciting band. This fantastic bootleg preserves these important shows with style and respect. Certainly a MUST HAVE.

(2) AS NATURE INTENDED (Vigotone, VT-122)
There have been a glut of GET BACK releases over the years, but this one stands heads and shoulders above them. The first nine songs on this CD are from the Rooftop Performance and the sound quality has never been better. The rest of the disc is from tape source and is of Glyn John's first master tape compilation of GET BACK. This disc is highly enjoyable to listen to and certainly much better than the legit LET IT BE album. It is also much better than all the discs of the Twickenham sessions combined. If you are a collector of those painful sessions, then seek out the GET BACK JOURNALS (Vigotone, Vigo 101/108). This eight-CD collection is housed in a hard-case film box and a reproduction of the original GET BACK book. Or you can seek out ROCKIN' MOVIE STARS on the ORANGE label. There are eight volumes so far and counting.

(3) SESSIONS (Disques Du Monde SS87 1967)
This is a splendid copy of the nearly-released 1983 EMI compilation of unreleased Beatles music. Though the songs on the record have subsequently appeared on ULTRA RARE TRAX and others, this bootleg is the only way to own a replica of what was to be a ground-breaking release - the first of its kind for a major rock group. Highlights include Paul's demo of 'Come And Get It', 'That Means A Lot', 'Not Guilty' and George's acoustic demo of 'While My Guitar Gently Weeps'.

(4) THE COMPLETE CHRISTMAS COLLECTION (Yellow Dog YD 031)
If you missed out on the Beatles' fan club Christmas flexies (seven in all), then here is your chance to catch up on some highly enjoyable listening. The Boys always seemed to be having a great time when recording their annual Christmas messages and some of the skits are truly weird. The sound here is 'best yet' and as a bonus we are treated to some 1964 Christmas message outtakes. Merry Gimble and Happy Michaelmaus.

(5) UNSURPASSED DEMOS (Yellow Dog YD 008)
The quest by fans for WHITE ALBUM outtakes and demos is legendary. Thanks to the LOST LENNON TAPES, various bootlegs and private tape sources, the demos have finally come to us. Twenty four tracks are included here, making this an excellent buy. Appearing for the first time are demos of 'Singalong Junk', 'Sour Milk Sea' and Harrison's 'Colliding Circles'. Conspicuous by their absence are demos of 'Glass Onion', 'Sexy Sadie' (with expletives) and the holy grail of all outtakes, the 18-minute version of "Helter Skelter'.

(6) THE QUARRYMEN 58 TO 62 (Middle Record Company QMCD 593)
There have been a number of bootlegs of the Quarrymen's earliest recordings through the years, and this CD is about as good as any you'll find. Besides the 19 tracks from 1960, the disc also includes the 1958 acetate of 'That'll Be The Day' (incomplete) and the Cavern Club Rehearsals from Liverpool 1962. The music and the recordings are rough, but as historical artifacts they are a MUST HAVE.

(7) CANDLESTICK PARK (Masterdisc MDCD - 007)
Any serious Beatles collection must contain The Beatles' last concert appearance. There are many bootlegs of this material, but this CD produced by Masterdisc of Japan is by far superior to any previous releases. The sound is crisp and even the drums have punch. Tony Barrow's tape ran out during the final number ('Long Tall Sally'), but even that short piece is included here. Another piece of history.

(8) THE ULTIMATE COLLECTION (Yellow Dog YDB 101-104)
While this four-CD boxed set contains some non-essential material, it is what IS included that sets it apart from previous releases. The fifteen DECCA TAPES are all here and at the correct speed and in best sound quality yet. All the ED SULLIVAN SHOWS are here and the quality is superb. We are also treated to new versions of 'Blackbird' and 'Helter Skelter' and the complete recordings of 'Aerial Tour Instrumental'. The final disc in the set is the first recorded hour of the LET IT BE sessions. A very satisfying collection.

(9) ULTRA RARE TRAX: VOLUMES 1&2 (Swingin' Pig TSP-CD-001/2) and VOLUMES 3&4 (Swingin'

Pig TR 2190) and VOLUMES 5&6 (Swingin' Pig TR 2191)
These ground-breaking bootlegs were released in 1988 and 1989 to great acclaim among collectors. These master tape quality studio outtakes set the music business on its ear and sent EMI executives scurrying. Suddenly we had amazing-sounding outtakes complete with false starts and studio chat. Not only that but many of the songs on the bootlegs were in stereo (unlike their mono counterparts on the first four Beatles albums.) In total there are over 70 songs on these two compact discs and four LPs.

(10) UNSURPASSED MASTERS: VOLUMES 1-4 (Yellow Dog YD 001-004)
Following closely on the heels of the ULTRA RARE series came the aptly-titled UNSURPASSED MASTERS from Yellow Dog. These CDs picked up where ULTRA RARE left off. There is some duplication of material, but for the most part these contain exciting new outtakes and demos in master tape quality. Yellow Dog's ACETATE (YD 009) is also worth mentioning. It contains a great collection of acetates in best quality yet.

(11) STARS OF '63 (Swingin' Pig TSP-CD-005)
John Lennon's favourite Beatles concert was recorded October 24, 1963, at Karlaplansstudio for a Swedish radio program called 'Pop '63'. The Beatles performed 'I Saw Her Standing There', 'From Me To You', 'Money', 'Roll Over Beethoven', 'You Really Got A Hold On Me', 'She Loves You' and 'Twist and Shout'. Lennon felt this was the Beatles at their best and I agree. The energy and enthusiasm flows from this record and you can't help but feel some of that old 'Beatlemania'.

(12) ARTIFACTS (Big Music BIG 4018-22)
For collectors who want the best of the unreleased Beatles music, look no further than this ambitious five-CD boxed set of rarities. Big Music has gathered the best of the rarities and produced this fine, chronologically-arranged set. The set is augmented by highly informative liner notes and rare photos. Each of the five discs represents an 'era' in Beatles history: THE EARLY YEARS (Quarrymen, Decca, early demos and studio outtakes, and BBC tracks from 1958-63), BEATLEMANIA (demos, studio outtakes, Ed Sullivan, BBC and live cuts from 1964-65), THE PSYCHEDELIC YEARS (demos, studio outtakes, mono mixes, live cuts from 1966-67), INNER REVOLUTION (demos, alternate takes, India songs from 1968) and GET BACK TO ABBEY ROAD (Twickenham tracks, rooftop performances, Abbey Road outtakes and demos from 1969-70). Seasoned collectors may want to pass this set up, but newcomers will certainly want to begin with this set. ARTIFACTS II on Big Music is the follow-up to the highly successful first set. While not as essential, it does include what I call 'the best of the rest' available rarities.

While there is not enough room in this article to review the best bootlegs of The Beatles as solo artists, let me suggest ARTIFACTS III : THE SOLO YEARS on the Big Music label. It is a four-CD boxed set of the best of the unreleased music spanning the years of The Beatles solo careers (1969 through 1994). It is chronologically arranged and comes complete with liner notes and rare photos. All the good stuff is here as well as some never-before-released rarities. It even has Lennon's demo of 'Free As A Bird' which the surviving Beatles re-recorded for their rarities boxed set.

Led Zeppelin
THE TARANTURA SERIES:
By Dave Lewis
(Dave Lewis is the editor/publisher of the Led Zeppelin magazine TIGHT BUT LOOSE
You can write Mr. Lewis at 14 Totnes Close, Bedford MK40, England.)

This is a reproduction of a feature that I recently compiled for my TIGHT BUT LOOSE magazine. The TARANTURA series of CDs began to emerge over the past 18 months. The source is a Japanese outlet committed to presenting key Zepp performances on multi-disc CD sets in deluxe packaging. The majority of them are issued in cardboard gatefold sleeves (non jewel boxed) with elaborate artwork. They are highly-limited runs; indeed many of them have already exhausted their supply and are very expensive at around £30 (editor's note: around $45.00 US) for a single disc, £60 doubles and over £100 for the triple sets.

In general they are superb collectors' items with packaging unsurpassed in the annals of underground releases by any artist. The downside is that some of them (particularly the more recent issues) are sourced from average and sometimes below-average audience tapes, and it can be an expensive method of investing in CD sets of dubious sound reproduction. That said when they come up with the goods (ie FREEZE!, BLUEBERRY HILL) these TARANTURA releases are some of the best CD sets produced.

What follows is a round up of the TARANTURA catalogue with TIGHT BUT LOOSE performance and sound-quality ratings. If you're feeling particularly affluent and can manage to search out an outlet that deals in these rare issues, this should provide an overview of what to expect from this elite series of CDs.

Dave Lewis / January 1995.

LIVE ON BLUEBERRY HILL - ORIGINAL MASTER BOOTLEG (TARANTURA T2 CD4)
Performance ***** Sound Quality *****
Packaged in a long box format that parodies the legitimate Audio Fidelity Master artwork, this is a seminal presentation of the famous LA Forum Sept. 4 1970 show. Two CDs in better-than-ever quality from the original Rubber Dubber label tapes in the correct order. One for my desert island.

BONZO'S BIRTHDAY PARTY (TARANTURA TCD 72007)
Performance **** Sound Quality ***1/2
Another famous TMQ vinyl bootleg given the TARANTURA once-over. This is the full concert spread over three CDs. The sound quality is a little flat and slightly inferior to the original vinyl version. The packaging however is out-standing. Picture disc CDs with a full colour cover version of the famous William Stout cover complete with raised relief on strategic parts of Miss Piggy's ample frame! Has to be seen to be believed.

BBC ZEPP (TARANTURA T2CD 7 12)
Performance **** Sound Quality ****
Gatefold yellow sleeve depicting the flying pig containing a two-CD version of the 1971 April 1 BBC show. The cover states it's from the original master - unfortunately this is not so and gets the date wrong. It's actually from the same source of the THANK YOU IT'S COMPLETE CD set and retains the background interference that can be heard periodically - and it's still not complete with no 'Bridget The Midget' speech prior to Whole Lotta Love. Still a great artifact of Zepp bootleg history, but something of a luxury purchase.

EYE THANK YOU (TARANTURA T4CD 4)
Performance *** Sound Quality ****
Deluxe 4-CD set packaged in a fold-out sleeve depicting the 'Over Europe' look-out logo. This contains most of the Mannheim show on July 3 and the July 2 show up to 'Kashmir'. Both these nights were previously out on FLYING DISC's 'Motivated Dinosaurs' - 'Dinosaur Watching' sets. Sound is from a rather flat soundboard and there are some clumsy edits. I personally find some of the 1980 performances very stiff and soulless. It's not how I remember the shows at the time when I was actually there (see THE FINAL ACCLAIM for the way it was then) and hearing them in the cold light of day fourteen years on there are some nice moments but not much excitement. As a bonus there is a good audience recording of the Munich July 5 'Rock And Roll/Whole Lotta Love' Simon Kirke jam. Overall this is a brilliantly-packaged souvenir of the tour but hardly essential performances.

PRETTY WOMAN (TARANTURA T3CD30)
Performance **** Sound Quality **
3-CD set from the Budokan Sept. 24 1871 show. Excellent black and white fold-out sleeve with photos from the gig and press conference. Never less than interesting Japanese show marred by a frankly poor recording - no better that the Mud Dogs AFTERNOON DAZE version. This is most unfortunate as the set is full of highlights, notably the 'Whole Lotta Love' medley which includes 'Your Time Is Gonna Come'.

THE DARK TOWER (TARANTURA T70CDD 3/4)
Performance **** Sound Quality **
2-CD set packaged in a weird futuristic tower design reproduced on the discs themselves, plus inner photos of the Oct. 1970 Board of Trade disc awards ceremony. This is another version of the Montreux March 14 1970 appearance already out on the single disc WE'RE GONNA GROOVE. This TARANTURA version is slightly inferior sound but does include 'Moby Dick.' At the going price definitely for completists only.

FREEZE! (TARANTURA T3C2)
Performance **** Sound Quality *****
3-CD package available in two versions - one with a Page Oakland shot, and incorrectly dated (Feb. 13), the other with a Plant '75 shot and bearing the correct date of recording. This is a complete performance from Baton Rouge Feb. 28 1975 on a very clear audience tape. I have no hesitation in recommending this one - it captures the band just as they were really getting into their stride on the '75

tour after a difficult start. One of the very best complete performances from this era.

BLITZKRIEG OVER EUROPE (TARANTURA T3CD 5)
Performance **** Sound Quality ****
Superb souvenir of the 1980 tour spread over a 3-CD set. This has the full Frankfurt show from June 30, plus an extra CD featuring the curtailed Nuremberg set plus cuts from Cologne. Worth the price for the Frankfurt show which is far better than the Mannheim showing - in fact perhaps the best 1980 performance and has the 'Money' encore with Phil Carson on bass.

LOOVE (TARANTURA TCD9)
Performance **** Sound Quality ****
New 2-CD gatefold presentation of the famous 'Pole And Sticks' performance at the KB Hallen Copenhagen May 3 1971. Improved sound quality to previous versions.

WALK DON'T RUN (LA 2 DAYS) (TARANTURA T4CD)
Performance **** Sound Quality ***1/2
Lavish fold-out 4-CD set covering two nights on the 1971 US tour from LA Aug. 21/22. The 22nd show is the same as the Mud Dogs WALK DON'T RUN - the 21st is much scarcer and only to be found on CD here at the time of writing. An expensive but comprehensive souvenir of the era.

FRONT ROW (TARANTURA T3CD)
Performance **** Sound Quality ****
Superb deluxe long box 2-CD package of the Budokan Sept. 21 1971 set. Slightly upgraded sound to the TALES OF STORMS and STORM OF FANATICS versions.

THE HAMMER OF THE GODS (TARANTURA T3CD 1/3)
Performance **** Sound Quality ****
Triple fold-out sleeve with various '75 US tour pics and an impressive blow up of the arena shot used in the A CELEBRATION introduction page (all the pics are reproduced from the book). The source is two shows from Seattle in March 1975. Tracks 1 to 5 duplicate the SEATTLE SUPERSONIC CD from March 21. The rest is made up from the impressive sound. Plant can be heard to shout "Who is Karen Carpenter?" after 'Moby Dick' - a subtle reference to Bonzo being placed below her in that year's Playboy musicians poll. Overall an interesting package but inferior to the other '75 TARANTURA - FREEZE!.

A LAST TWO NIGHTS (TARANTURA T2CD5)
Performance **** Sound Quality ****
2-CD set in a rare Tarantura jewel box. This has ten rather average-sounding soundboard cuts from the July 29 Madison show in 1973 and 'Kashmir', 'No Quarter' and 'Tangerine' from a slightly inconsistent video soundtrack source from Earls Court May 25. These 1975 tracks have now surfaced on the SHAKE FOR ME BABY Missing Link single CD. A full tape from this source would be most welcome! Some tracks here suffer from edits and fades.

ROUTE 66: SILENTLY RAVAGING AMERICA 1972 (CALIFORNIA 2 DAYS) (TARANTURA T4CD3)
Performance ***** Sound Quality ***
Quad-fold-out 4 CD set with black and white shots from the June 6 Cobo Hall Detroit show. The CDs themselves house two audience-recorded 1972 shows: San Bernadino from June 22 (first time on disc) and the LA June 25 show already out as BURN LIKE A CANDLE and HEARTBREAK HOTEL. This version is missing some of the encores to be found on the earlier version discs. Nonetheless an impressive if again expensive chronicle of the 1972 era.

THE NOBS (TARANTURA T70CD 1/2)
Performance **** Sound Quality ***
Two-disc version of the celebrated KB Hallen Feb. 28 1970 show where they appeared as The Nobs due to complaints from Countess Von Zeppelin. Gatefold sleeve with Plant submerged-in-water photo shot on the cover. Average sound and performance.

THE DESTROYERS/CLEVELAND 2 DAYS (TARANTURA T6CD 1/2)
Performance ***/**** Sound Quality *****/***
Amazing 6-CD luxury CD-size box set - containing a pair of superbly-packaged triple-CD sets in fold-out sleeves. Set one is the April 27 1977 soundboard recording (including 'Moby Dick/Over The Top' which is missing from the standard 2-CD versions), while set two reproduces the fine audience tape from April 28. Limited to 600 individually-numbered copies, at around £300 this is a luxury package but already is very rare.

PLEASE PLEASE ME, WITH FROM ME TO YOU AND 19 OTHER SONGS (TARANTURA T3CD4)
Performance **** Sound Quality **1/2
2-disc set capturing another enjoyable 1971 Japanese show - this time the Sept. 28 Osaka set. Also
out on Mud Dogs as C'MON EVERYBODY. Sound quality is consistently hard work but this particular
TARANTURA's attraction lies firmly with the packaging. It comes in a thin square box and the cover
parodies the style of The Beatles' PLEASE PLEASE ME 1960s-style cover with cunning accuracy. A
quite beautiful artifact.

PB (TARANTURA PB 1001)
Performance **** Sound Quality *****
Authentic artwork adorns this attempted re-issue of the early TMQ bootleg taken from the Vancouver
March '70 broadcast. The effect is spoiled slightly by the addition of tracks from Winterland and BBC
'69 mislabelled.

SECOND NIGHT IN A JUDO ARENA (TARANTURA T2CD6)
Performance *** Sound Quality ***
2-CD presentation of the Budokan Oct. 3 show previously available on THE SECOND DAZE from Mud
Dogs. Average performance and okay sound. Nice to hear 'The Ocean' encore.

COPENHAGEN WARM UPS (TARANTURA T4CD2)
Performance *** Sound Quality ****
4-disc set in fold-out sleeve with Knebworth pics. This is a straight re-issue of the familiar 1979
Copenhagen warm-up shows from July 23/4 already available. Again this is a luxury souvenir package
of another two nights in the life of.

PEACE (TARANTURA/PEACE 1A 2A)
Unheard - no rating available. One of the forerunners in the TARANTURA series. This is a two-disc
jewel-cased set with outer box featuring the Sept. 27 1971 Hiroshima charity show.

LIVE (LIVE 1/20)
Unheard - no rating available. 2-CD set from October 9 1972 Osaka show.

THE LOST GEISHA TAPE (TARANTURA TS1)
Unheard - no rating available. Single disc extracts from the Oct. 29 1971 Osaka show plus 'The Ocean'
from Oct. 2 1972.

LONG TALL SALLY
Performance **** Sound Quality ***
2-CD jewel-case presentation. This has the August 18 1969 Rockpile show (available on Hideaway)
plus the Buffalo Oct. 30 1969 tape out on the single disc Buffalo '69.

TIGHT BUT LOOSE (TARANTURA T2CD20)
Unheard - no rating available. 2-CD set with material from the Jan 26 1969 Boston show.

TULSA HILLBILLY (TARANTURA T2CD)
Performance **** Sound Quality ***
2-CD set in gatefold sleeve - no different from the Tulsa August 21 1970 show previously available as
BOTTLE UP AND GO.

DANGEROUS RELATIONS (MEDUSA JP 2/1/2)
Performance **** Sound Quality ***1/2
2-CD jewel-case packaging, this Page showcase features THE OUTRIDER outtakes in good quality -
plus the MIDNIGHT MOONLIGHT Swan Song instrumental demos from late '73 - early '74 in fair
quality. A fascinating Page profile.

COVERDALE PAGE: ONE MORE CHECK (TARANTURA T1CD 001)
Performance **** Sound Quality ****
Single CD offering the soundcheck extracts from Tokyo, Osaka and Nagoya on the 1993 tour. Good to
hear Jimmy flexing out on various Zepp riffs - e.g. 'Heartbreaker', 'For Your Life' and 'Whole Lotta Love'.
These run-throughs do pale a little on repeated listenings and are curios more than playlist faves.
Packaged in a hilarious William Stout spoof depicting dear David and Sir Jim.

LED ZEPPELIN (TARANTURA 19128)
Performance **** Sound Quality ***
Beautifully-packaged new collection of the Zepp 3 rehearsals. See elsewhere for full review.

PUNK (TARANTURA T2CD 81-2)
Performance *** Sound Quality **1/2
Fold-out sleeve housing a two-disc audience tape of the Nov. 6 1969 Winterland San Francisco appearance.

NO USE GRECO (GRECO 1 001/2)
Performance *** Sound Quality ****
Tokyo Oct. 2 1972 - 2 CDs from an improved audience tape source than that employed for the APHRODITE label DANCING DAYS version. Packaged in a stylish PVC wallet with rare '72 era Japan tour visuals.

PUSSY AND COCK (TARANTURA T3CD 6)
Performance **** Sound Quality ****
The familiar Long Beach March 11 1975 set (out before on Flying Disc and Red Line) - this time though as the complete show on a lavishly-packaged 2-CD fold set (great pics), and improved sound. The drawback is that it's mastered just slightly fast but not enough to spoil the overall enjoyment of a happening night on the '75 tour.

MAGICAL MYSTERY TAPES (TARANTURA)
Performance **** Sound Quality ***
Another version of the July 6 Chicago soundcheck from 1973. The packaging though is as the title suggests, another very clever Beatles pastiche - this time based on their MAGICAL MYSTERY TOUR album.

GET BACK TO LA (TARANTURA - T9CD1)
Performance **** Sound Quality ***
An incredible package - 9 CDs comprising the complete shows (audience sourced and out previously in other versions across various sets) from their LA Forum stint of March 24, 25, 27 1975. All presented in a special square box container with rare '75 black and white photo sleeves. The ultimate status CD package! Vastly expensive and already very scarce.

Postscript: Also just through from Japan: DESTROYER 3 - (Largo Maryland May 30 1977), JUMP LEG (Madison Sound Square Garden February 12 1975), HOLY GRAIL (Munich March 1973) plus STUDIO WORKS ('Death Wish' outtakes) and YELLOW ZEPPELIN (Image Club Miami 1969 on 2 CDs).

On a final note - the TARANTURA series, whilst clearly the best packaged of any label, does not seem to have run short of good sources on its more recent batch of releases. To justify the often vast investment, collectors will surely be hoping for improved quality source tapes for future releases.

(Mr. Lewis would like to thank RH, Julian Walker, Phil Tattershall, Paul Sheppard and Simon Pallett for additional information and research.)

Nirvana

NIRVANA BOOTLEGS
By Lori from Chicago.

By its very nature, punk rock undermined the traditional channels of rock music production, distribution and profit. Early punks (1977-early 1980s) were completely cut off from the mainstream music industry both by necessity and design. Believing (quite correctly) that once financial greed enters the picture music itself suffers greatly, the punk rock scene released its records in much the same way bootleggers released their product: small pressings on tiny, self-manned labels, funded by somebody's day job, sold by mail order to a widely enthusiastic, albeit fractional, audience.

Punk musicians were much freer than their mainstream counterparts. Very few were bound by contract to a single record label; they could do whatever they wanted, and many bands released singles, EPs and LPs on several labels.

Beginning in 1985, when Husker Du signed to Warner Brothers and the Replacements and Sonic Youth attracted major label attention, murmurs of shock and apprehension went through the punk world as formerly unknown, beloved musicians were sucked into The Biz.

That was the beginning of the end of the tight community documenting largely ignored-bands very few cared about, but punk rock did not go mainstream in the United States until 1991, when a band called Nirvana released NEVERMIND, which is currently at quintuple-platinum status and counting. Nirvana was a punk band at its core, with nominal doses of 70s pop and Beatles influences peppered within. Throughout their career, fans and opportunists alike documented their performances on bootleg CD and vinyl.

Nirvana vocalist Kurt Cobain's suicide in April of 1994 underscores bootlegging's importance. First it often provides a more complete, interesting, revealing history of a band: from garage nothings to multimillionaires. Secondly, it allows fans who never experienced the band live to have a document of what an actual performance was like (Nirvana's later shows often featured unreleased songs and cover versions not available legitimately as of this writing). Bootlegs preserve the energy and emotion of the artist in a way the majors have never been able to do (note the disgustingly trite 'tributes', a.k.a. greatest hit repackages, to Jim Morrison and the Doors, Jimi Hendrix and other artists offered by major labels through the years).

The following Nirvana bootlegs were chosen based on sound quality, track selection and band performance. Enjoy.

(1) D.U.M.B. (KISS THE STONE KTS 133) (Europe 1992) - Early, rough performances of 'All Apologies' (different lyrics) and 'Dumb,' rare live 'Stay Away'. Throughout there's excellent sound quality, musical improvisation by the band and KTS liner notes reminiscent of the old days of TAKRL vinyl.

(2) IN THE BLOOM (Europe 1990) - Extremely high sound quality 'Bleach' era performance with lots of energy. Highlights: 'Spank Through', 'Dive', very rare 'Paper Cuts'.

(3) I HATE MYSELF AND WANT TO DIE (METAL CRASH MECD 1146) - Only CD-quality live performances (as of this writing) of 'Milk It' and 'Tourette's'. Only alternative live performance of 'Where Did You Sleep Last Night', even more intense the the Unplugged version. Also available as I LOVE MYSELF AND WANT TO LIVE.

(4) WIPEOUT (LP) - Jack Endino demos 1990 including the infamous NEVERMIND demos with Chad Channing. Includes a beautiful early version of 'Verse Chorus Verse' (then titled 'Everything & Nothing'), 'Pay To Play,' electric 'Poly' plus alternate takes of 'Love Buzz' and 'Spank Through.' Excellent stereo, some hiss.

(5) ALL ACOUSTICALLY (KISS THE STONE KTS 253) - The American MTV Unplugged performance has appeared on countless bootleg CDs. This one makes the list because of its high quality and because it is coupled with Nirvana's electric performance on MTV New Years' Eve.

(6) SEATTLE SOUND SOUNDS GREAT (INSECT IST 23) - Stupid title, excellent performance. Rome 1991. Includes early, unfinished live version of 'Rape Me' and all the essential NEVERMIND material live.

(7) DEEP - Germany, 1989. Raw and extremely loud. Includes live 'Mr. Moustache.' Excellent sound quality.

(8) HARDCORE ACT - Along with some legitimate material (HOARMOANING songs) the compilers of this CD came up with the only live version of 'Oh The Guilt' (titled here 'It Takes A Time') I have ever heard, along with a song entitled 'Talk To Me' that is equally mysterious. Quality varies throughout. Last 10 tracks from Amsterdam 1991 in excellent quality.

(9) AMSTERDAM 91 (STENTOR STEN 91.012) - Infectious performance, superb (broadcast) sound quality. If you own one NEVERMIND show this should be the one.

(10) ROMA (KISS THE STONE KTS 284) (also available as 'XXII II MCMXCIV' on OCTOPUS OCTO 001) - Fitting that the final Top Ten entry is one of Nirvana's final performances, one and a half weeks before Kurt Cobain overdosed on champagne and tranquillisers in his (Roman) hotel room. Over eighty minutes of superb sound and an unbelievably tight, enthusiastic performance covering all three studio LPs. 'XXII II MCMXCIV' also includes 'The Man Who Sold The World' from the MTV Unplugged show.

A word of caution: Nirvana bootleg CDs are beginning to be copied at an alarmingly rate. The number of actual shows circulating at this writing is far less than the number of CDs. Caveat emptor.

Pink Floyd

MORE FLOYD MUSINGS BY KEITH FROM TORONTO

"The band is just fantastic, that is really what I think. Oh by the way which one's Pink?"
Roger Waters, "Have a Cigar" 1975.

Hey Floydaholics! Who really is the genius of Pink Floyd? Roger, Syd or David? Since no one ever mentions Nick or Rick in the debate, let me throw their names in the mix too.

While I declared a bias for the Gilmour–led–Floyd in HOT WACKS SUPPLEMENT 2, the topic this time around is different. Fundamentally, like the Beatles, there is more to the total than the sum of the parts. Oddly, this is where bootlegs come in. The wealth of underground material represents an historical time machine. Fans can hop aboard and go back and visit places (sounds) otherwise not possible. (Check out September 1994's MUSICIAN for more comments about this from bootleggers and artists.)

As for the "who's PINK" question, bootlegs are all we have to objectify the debate (although sound quality may muddy some opinions). In–studio wizardry, guest musicians, post–concert over–dubs and sweetening make Floyd's legit catalogue suspect. After all, Dave Gilmour (Roger doesn't deny it) says he played much of the bass parts on Floyd records while Roger won all the polls.

Consider this as well. Few of us have actually seen the band in all their incarnations. Even if you have, can you ever re–capture the effect of seeing the group LIVE for the first time? As one virgin–Floyd–concert–goer from Ottawa said to me at the end of the band's first '94 Toronto show, "I'll never be the same again." Well, that's true! So let's take away the visual and studio experiences altogether and focus only on the LIVE playing through the years.

Members of Pink Floyd may wish we'd use something other than bootlegs to do this. Nick Mason says as much on the LIMITED INTERVIEW DISC (CBAK 4013 Baktabak Records)... "It's a rip off! ..., if people want those sort of souvenirs then I suppose you can't stop them from buying it but I'd rather they'd buy a T–shirt". But, unfortunately, Floyd hasn't provided any commercial alternatives for us – certainly their box set wasn't generous in the outtake or live context was it? Sorry Nick – we're talking about much more than souvenirs here.

So, let's fire up as many of these suckers as we can find and check out some LIVE solo performances and select Syd, Roger and David–led group shows. They'll help us decide who's PINKing who. By the way, the opinions expressed here come from listens to CD boots only (one exception where noted) with titles available through the late 1980s up to Fall, 1994). Get your other HOT WACKS books ready too. In the LAST WACKS, turn to pages P–Q, 21, 268–269, 459–478 and 715–716. In SUPPLEMENT 1, turn to pages 5, 48 and 108–110. In SUPPLEMENT 2, turn to pages H–K, 5 and 108–110. And read pages 139-142 in this book for further reference.

TOP 10 "WHO'S PINK" BOOTS

(1) NEW GAME (Aulica A.2135 1992 double CD) /
IN FLOYD WE TRUST (Beech Marten BM 054 1992)
Finding any Gilmour solo product is rare. NEW GAME has more material on it than IN FLOYD WE TRUST but has poorer sound quality (IN FLOYD... is from a July 12, 1984 radio broadcast of a performance in Pennsylvania U.S.A. ergo, the better sound).

Both CDs have Gilmour renditions of 'Money', 'Comfortably Numb' and 'Run Like Hell'. The Roger-less Floyd version of 'Comfortably Numb' featured on the MOMENTARY LAPSE and DIVISION BELL tours starts here. Unfortunately, the playing of this song on both CDs is a bit ragged and lacks the depth featured on the Floyd tours. This isn't a surprise though, since the Gilmour touring band was not as deep as the current Floyd version – both in instruments and musicians on stage.

Separate interviews with Roger Waters, Bob Ezrin and David Gilmour focus on 'Comfortably Numb' as one of the songs that generated major arguments between Gilmour and Waters. Listen to Gilmour's version here and you get a far different vocal line on the verses than during the WALL tour and Roger's Berlin Wall WALL performance. Also, you'll be tempted to fill in the keyboard plink on the "just a little pin prick" line – could its absence be a dig at Roger? After all, on the WALL tour and the Berlin Wall WALL performance, the "pin–prick plink" is most definitely in. I, for one, miss it.

Roger has also said the band obviously "just doesn't get it" by featuring songs from the WALL on the post–Roger, huge stadium Floyd tours. In spite of Roger's feelings, the guitar playing and the extended solos on this song have become one of the new Floyd's signature tunes. I'm just sorry the original WALL tour featured such an abbreviated version of the song. Chalk up points for Gilmour's version over Waters', "plink" in or not.

The NEW GAME CD also features the song 'Near The End'. While Gilmour no doubt played the extended electric guitar part on his solo studio recording, it's Mick Ralphs (Bad Company) who gets the workout here. He does a great job capturing Gilmour's style. Contrast this to Tim Renwick's (Sutherland Brothers, Quiver, Mike and the Mechanics) playing with the Roger–less Floyd.

Refer to any of the MOMENTARY LAPSE OF REASON or DIVISION BELL boots featuring 'Learning to Fly' or 'Another Brick In The Wall Part 2'. You can tell when Gilmour is not playing lead (he doesn't play the solos at all in 'Learning to Fly'). Renwick says he deliberately tries to stay away from playing other people's licks including Gilmour's.

Is Tim the source for the brief lead guitar riff just after the line "he played a mean guitar" from 'Welcome to the Machine'? Check out THANKS FOR THE RIDE (see entry 3) and compare with NOTHING IS CHANGED (Red Phantom RPCD 2026 2027, 1991). You'll note Roger's version includes this riff as well.

Roger's PROS AND CONS tour featured Eric Clapton but also one Mr. Tim Renwick. Coincidence? I think not. Especially since you don't hear this bit of electric guitar when last performed by the Roger–with Floyd on the ANIMALS tour (check out IN THE FLESH Great Dane Records GDR CD 9103/A 9103/B, 1991 also released as OAKLAND CALIFORNIA 5–9–77 Stonehenge STCD 2017/A 2017/B or, better yet, CAUGHT IN THE CROSSFIRE Neutral Zone NZCD 89017, 1989 also released as WELCOME TO THE MACHINE Swingin' Pig TSP–CD–061, 1992 and NEW YORK '77.

The Gilmour tour for his ABOUT FACE album took place in 1984, a good three years before the MOMENTARY LAPSE OF REASON tour. Waters also toured in '84 with PROS AND CONS then hit the road again in 1987 with RADIO K.A.O.S. – the same time as Floyd's MOMENTARY LAPSE OF REASON. Even separated, the urge to work within the same timeframes is intwined between Waters and Gilmour. It wasn't until 1994 when the Roger–less Floyd released the DIVISION BELL (and toured) that we see a solo playing filed for one or the other. As this article is being written there's only one statement from Waters. When asked about THE DIVISION BELL he cut off conversation after admitting he'd heard the album and said, "I'm not prepared to get involved in that [discussion of Floyd] again." Maybe this is just as well. But, oddly, many of the performances on the DIVISION BELL tour echo (intentional pun) what Waters did on his RADIO K.A.O.S. tour.

(2) ROGER WATERS & BLEEDING HEART BAND (Beech Marten Records BM 074, 1992)
The jacket says this is from a May 2, 1987 show in Quebec but it's actually from a November 7 Quebec show that year. The source is a radio broadcast and, like IN FLOYD WE TRUST, doesn't feature the full show. This is unfortunate for lovers of Roger's new work since most of the RADIO K.A.O.S. material is also missing.

What's interesting here are Roger's versions of 'Wish You Were Here' and 'Another Brick In The Wall'. While Roger can't hope to capture the sound of Gilmour's voice (he doesn't even try on 'Money' giving Paul Carrack, of Squeeze and Mike and The Mechanics fame, the vocal opportunity on this tour), he does some wonderful things to 'Wish You Were Here'. Song-writer's prerogative but let's remember this is also a "words by Waters, music by Gilmour" song. Actually, if you go back to the ANIMALS tour (see IN THE FLESH or CROSSFIRE referred to above), you'll hear a similar sounding version - much more emphasis on the piano and a repeat of the chorus not found on the studio record. To be fair to Roger, it is more an entirely new version than old, with sax fills and, of course, Waters and female back-up vocals instead of Gilmour.

'Another Brick In The Wall' (actually Parts 1 and 2 with 'Happiest Days of Our Lives') blends vocals between female and male voices and is similar in many ways to what we heard on the DIVISION BELL tour – especially with the addition of the instrumental lead-up (minus Roger's 'Stand Still Laddie' with Floyd) to the vocals and dual guitar solos (Gilmour and Renwick in Floyd and Andy Fairweather–Low and Jay Staplay in the Bleeding Heart Band).

While Roger criticizes the Roger–less Floyd for doing some sort of sacrilege to the concept of the WALL by performing selections from it in their stadium shows, it is odd that he funks the music up as much as he does here. Not the kinds of changes you'd expect from a man who Tim Renwick says "wanted everything exactly the same as the record".

A final note on Renwick before we move on. Roger Waters asked him to catalogue the arrangements for all of Floyd's material in preparation for the PROS AND CONS tour. It's no wonder, then, why he's been so valuable to both the Floyd and Waters' camps. And probably the reason why he isn't a part of Roger's Bleeding Heart Band today – his presence on the MOMENTARY LAPSE tour being the wrong side to support. Either way, there's a pretty good argument to dub Tim the fifth Floyd (or would it be sixth if you count Syd?) – he's also a contemporary of the band, hailing from the same place – Syd once being his Scout leader.

(3) ROGER WATERS THE PROS AND CONS OF LIVE HITCH HIKING (Silver O Rarities SIRA 45/46 1992) / THANKS FOR THE RIDE (Golden Stars GSCD 1018 and 1019 1990) also available separately as THANKS... Part 1 and Part 2.
Important, because both feature Eric Clapton. (The PROS AND CONS LIVE ... is listed as a June 27, 1984 show in Birmingham (Solihull), England but it's actually a July 27 performance.) Consider Roger's use of what I call the 'guitar Gods' – Clapton, Beck (AMUSED TO DEATH) and, of course, Gilmour. (There's also Snowy White who helped out a solo Peter Green of early Fleetwood Mac fame, played on the ANIMALS and WALL tours and was a special guest lead guitar player at the Berlin Wall WALL performance.) These guitar-God performances show a reliance on a certain kind of guitar sound. (Andy Fairweather–Low, who toured with Clapton, doesn't get many high-profile solos and we have yet to see Eddie Van Halen or Slash have we?)

Think about it. There is no doubt Waters hears soaring guitar parts in his head and requires the guitar Gods to help paint his aural masterpieces. But this is why a Roger Waters LIVE performance is somewhat less fulfilling than a Floyd show. While Gilmour can sing and play his way to the recorded Floyd sound, Roger has the disadvantage (some would say advantage if video and radio programmers would let him have it) of sounding different. Whatever. With Clapton on the early part of the PROS AND CONS tour, Roger certainly came closest to sounding like the Roger–led Floyd.

His versions here of 'Set The Controls For The Heart Of The Sun', 'Money', 'Have a Cigar', 'Hey You', even 'Wish You Were Here' are standouts in the Floyd tradition. Keep in mind though, this was an expensive arena tour (Gilmour was content to go for smaller theatres for ABOUT FACE) using the full quad Floyd sound system and projections. The band was comparable in size to the new Gilmour–led Floyd as well.

Listening to the show you can't help think how important a strong lead guitarist is to the Floyd mystic. Chalk up points to the Gilmour–led Floyd for going full out. Hard to beat when you have the strongest vocalist and guitar soloist in charge and the fan support to do it big. Give the people what they want.

Speaking of which, this is where the "who's PINK" argument takes a turn against Waters. He admits he's in competition with himself and losing. The only factor in his favour is his ability to pen Floyd's best lyrics. He wrote the book, eclipsing even Syd (it's interesting, however, that the Roger–less Floyd keeps panning their early work including 'Astronomy Domine' and 'Echoes' as having embarrassing lyrics – so much for "Floyd in space").

This too is why the DIVISION BELL album and tour prove so interesting. With the Gilmour–led Floyd having a solo playing field this time around, fans (new ones anyway) won't even know about Roger's contributions. There is nobody to announce "words and music by Roger Waters" (unlike the computer screen readouts and accolades from Jim Ladd as the DJ during the RADIO K.A.O.S. tour).

(4) THE LIVE BELL (Kiss The Stone KTS 294/95, 1994) / YOUR FAVOURITE DISEASE (Capricorn Records CR–20018/19, 1994) / THE GIANTS AT THE GIANTS (Octopus 033–044, 1994)
At the same time, can you excuse the Roger–less, Gilmour–led Floyd for putting so much emphasis on the same material as during the '87–'88 tour? What we got in '94 was disappointingly close to the MOMENTARY LAPSE tour. While there were a very few select '94 performances (Detroit and East Rutherford, New Jersey – see below)) that featured all of DARK SIDE OF THE MOON, we never, anywhere, got all of the new album.

The question is why not? It's particularly odd that the Gilmour–led Floyd would come up with a set virtually the same as the '87–'88 tour. This comes after Gilmour stated emphatically they were overly generous last time out and would have trouble deciding what to do next time ("... having moved from a Pink Floyd that did basically the newest album on all our old tours to a sort of greatest-hits show last time, I couldn't do that same show"). Well, maybe it was easiest to do it again after all. This was even more a greatest-hits version featuring many MOMENTARY LAPSE songs instead of DIVISION BELL material.

The addition of 'Astronomy Domine', although welcome, can't make up for passes on some really strong new stuff. Give Roger points for integrity in playing all of the PROS AND CONS material even when nobody really wanted it. Take the absence of the first Richard Wright vocal and song material in years – 'Wearing The Inside Out'. Which PINK decided to leave this out?

The song itself is classic Floyd with lyrics comparable to the Roger dynasty (as Waters said about the MOMENTARY LAPSE album but applicable here too – "a pretty fair forgery"). Does this show a lack of appreciation for Rick? While it's great to hear him sing on 'Time', his new material is fresh and good! PINK may not have thought so. Oddly, in an interview with Rick just before the Miami opening of the '94 tour, he said how much he was looking forward to singing.

Some may argue that the performances of 'Shine On', 'Wish You Were Here', 'Money', etc. are actually different from '87–'88 and this is true. (The tour also featured the original sax man from these recordings, Dick Parry.) But go back to the ANIMALS tour (see IN THE FLESH above also featuring Mr. Parry) and you'll hear the same approach as '94.

The start of the 1987 tour also featured a version of 'Money' akin to '94's. Proof comes from the as-yet-to-make-it-onto CD, NEW MACHINE LIVE (Rock Solid Records RSR – LP 1987). As an aside, and in regards to the note about 'Echoes' not making it to CD on anything but HAND OF FATE (see Hot Wacks SUPPLEMENT 2, page J), this LP, taken from a September 21, 1987 Toronto performance, has a full version.

You also should note that later bootlegs and the DELICATE SOUND OF THUNDER commercial release feature an extended 'Money'. As the Floyd '94 tour moves to Europe, you might find the same evolution happening to the same song. Maybe it's the way the band keeps fresh night after night and gets beyond the safety of tour rehearsals.

But there is good news. David Gilmour's (and the band's) playing is as good, melodic and confident as ever. The three CDs listed above provide the most significant record from the North American leg of the tour to date. THE LIVE BELL is from the first show and it's amazing that the performance is as good as it is. These are professional musicians all around and the extensive rehearsal time in Miami pays off for a crowd too excited to even notice. There is also a bonus sound check included on disc 2. Very interesting run offs of 'Astronomy Domine' and a clear example of Gilmour leading the band.

It falls to YOUR FAVOURITE DISEASE (excellent sound quality and playing) however to capture the essence of what fans got on the '94 tour. There is no indication of where this show is from (I suspect mid–tour judging from the CD's release in mid September '94) but maybe that's appropriate – Anywhere U.S.A.! Includes 'Poles Apart' and 'On The Turning Away', not played in Miami on THE LIVE BELL. ('Coming Back To Life', not played at every concert, can be found on both THE BELL GETS LOUDER (Kiss The Stone KTS 339/40, 1994) and THE GIANTS AT THE GIANTS noted above. (THE BELL GETS LOUDER is from Floyd's New York City shows and also includes 'Eclipse' but from the second night's-show in New Jersey (July 18), not the same performance as found on THE GIANTS AT THE GIANTS.) The GIANTS AT THE GIANTS (East Rutherford, New Jersey on July 17) is the most surprising of all the '94-tour CDs. (Gilmour actually says in his introduction that the audience may be in for a few surprises. You can hear a guy in the audience closest to the bootlegger's mic say: "Hear what he said right? A few surprises later. That's that airplane right there." Little did this guy know at the time it would be DARK SIDE!

The tell-tale sign starts with 'Shine On' as the band varies its first set to feature the full DARK SIDE OF THE MOON in set 2. Now, indeed, this is different to '87–'88 and the show we all wanted to see. The sound quality is outstanding (but, as you may have gathered from above, it's an audience recording). Again, the playing is fantastic. Most of the original sound effects are included (compare to BRAIN DAMAGE Capricorn Records CR–1001, 1994 – from the BBC tapes of the November London shows during the 1974 tour – there is a difference between the playing of the four–piece Floyd in 1974 and the augmented Floyd of 1994). Gilmour also thanks Roger "for the words" after finishing 'Eclipse'. Nice gesture for those who know who Roger is, or was!

All of DARK SIDE was featured in very few other places in North America. Some articles covering the tour mention the band rehearsing 'Eclipse' at soundchecks while in Montreal (in late May). It is likely the pre–tour agenda did not allow enough time to get a DARK SIDE set fully established until late in the actual tour. Rumour had it of course that the band would indeed be playing all of DARK SIDE at least once in places where they were appearing for more than one evening. Guess Toronto didn't qualify.

Rumour also has it that the Floyd London shows will feature the same show as East Rutherford. Can a commercial video of this be far behind? And stay tuned for material from the European leg of the tour.

As this article was going to press the Floyd single release for 'High Hopes'/'Keep Talking' (EMI CDEM 342/7243.8.81772.2.1) included a live performance of 'One of These Days' (from an August show in Germany) that is decidedly different to what we heard in North America!

(5) THE WALL REHEARSALS (Rotation Rota 04 1993) / BEHIND THE WALL BOX SET (Stonehenge STBX 022, 023, 024).
Speaking of tour rehearsals and different performances, this package was mentioned in the top 10 list in the last supplement (note BEHIND THE WALL BOX SET features better sound). What's interesting here is the insight into the Roger–led Floyd. You'll hear him barking out orders and commands ("Stop building the WALL please, thank you. Is there somebody on the headset at the desk? 'Cause there should be - always! Answer me now please!! Send it now!!! You're fucking cheating you WALL builders; stop!!!!")

Let me also clear up a small typo found in SUPPLEMENT 2 – the line talking about Roger's control should read: "There's no doubt he's in charge" instead of "there's doubt he's in charge".

Other than Roger as task master, what is most noticeable about the rehearsal is the free and easy playing – a lot less tight than the actual show. Give points to Gilmour for extending material when it's up to him (giving a little more headroom night after night). Collectors take note – if you have one boot of the WALL LIVE, you have all you need. This is why the box set, including both the rehearsals and show performance, is so satisfying.

It would be interesting to hear rehearsals for the DIVISION BELL for comparison (including DARK SIDE). Certainly the DIVISION BELL sounds the most traditionally Floyd–like in years (return to a melody balance over lyrical emphasis). That's got to be because of the higher contribution Rick Wright made during rehearsals and writing the album. Something just not as clear on MOMENTARY LAPSE OF REASON and openly admitted by the band in interviews. This also makes the in–concert absence of 'Wearing The Inside Out', 'Cluster One' and 'Marooned' that much more disappointing.

As for Nick Mason, go back to number (1) and note how different Gilmour sounds with a different drummer. Chris Slade (Gilmour drummer on the 1984 tour) plays well to be sure but there is a noticeable lack of, I don't know, let's call it mood evident without Mason. Mason himself plays laid back – behind the beat and he really isn't a great "technical drummer". But he's a great "mood drummer"! Maybe that's why from the WALL tour on, Floyd features two drummers on stage. One for frills and vital timing and Mason for the mood. I don't say this as an insult. (Ex–Beatle Ringo does the same thing on his tours).

By the way, during the WALL rehearsals, there is a sudden stop by the band during 'Hey You' where Roger questions David about why he stopped. David says defensively, "I didn't. Nick did."

Speaking of 'Hey You', the Gilmour–led Floyd performed the song as an encore during the DIVISION BELL tour. It's interesting how close the band comes to the original version. Jon Carin's (who also played keyboards with Bryan Ferry) vocal sounds exactly like Roger Waters, screaming voice and all. There's no doubt Gilmour could capitalise on this should he ever decide to do more songs originally having Roger singing lead (and, unlike Roger's decision, not to mimic Gilmour.) Note, this doesn't happen on the '94 version of DARK SIDE OF THE MOON with Gilmour handling the lead vocals on 'Eclipse'. Actually a fair impersonation of Waters' style by Gilmour himself!

(6) TOTAL ECLIPSE (Great Dane Records GDR CD 9320 4 CD box set)
For one–stop shopping and true insight (and, for those who are keeping track, this should be the real number one on the top 10 of any Floyd list), there is this outstanding four–CD trip covering Floyd throughout the years. As the liner notes say, much of this material should have been included in the grand box set put out by the band. Not everything is LIVE but there's enough here to graduate as a Pink Floyd expert. In particular, for our "who's PINK" argument, you'll find the acoustic demo for 'Money' featuring a great vocal by Waters. Ironically, this "unplugged" and raw version makes me think how good a Floyd or Roger UNPLUGGED would be.

'Money' really works acoustically and Roger can sing this song well. The same holds true for the acoustic demo (strumming mostly) featuring the core for 'Comfortably Numb'. Both segments show the strengths (words and music) of the individual members, while the group performances reveal how important arrangements (and contributions) can be. Take some bows Nick Mason and Richard Wright. But what about Syd?

(7) MAGNESIUM PROVERBS (the Gold Standard NIGHT TRIPPER GD – 10, 1994) / A SAUCERFUL

OF OUTTAKES (Chapter One CO 25195, 1994) and STONED ALONE (the Gold Standard NIGHT TRIPPER AST – 552, 1994)
Unfortunately, we have very little we can listen to featuring the Syd–led Floyd LIVE. There is an abundance of Top Gear performances (some on TOTAL ECLIPSE, see above) and, allegedly, some other very rare but horrific recordings. STONED ALONE features a 1967 performance. 'Arnold Layne' appears with hard to hear vocals and 'Matilda Mother' could be Roger or Rick singing for all you can tell. Regardless, any of the first Syd-penned singles really do not represent Floyd's LIVE work or band essence anyway.

A radio interviewer clipped on MAGNESIUM PROVERBS, says he thinks it all a bit too much for him but maybe, as a musician, he just can't appreciate the band with "long stretches of material repeated endlessly and loud". Any Syd–with–Floyd bootlegs show some of the long stretches alright. They can't do justice to "loud" however.

Is Syd PINK? Well, hearing the first Floyd recorded material – 'Lucy Leave' and 'King Bee' (on both MAGNESIUM PROVERBS and A SAUCERFUL OF OUTTAKES) is telling. Anyone who doubts Syd Barrett's potential and R&B mettle (or should I say Meddle?) may have to re-evaluate. While Syd didn't write the material (the songs are not performed LIVE here but were featured in early shows – see note below), they are our first taste of Floyd.

Dramatically, 'Interstellar Overdrive' and 'Astronomy Dominie' are in a completely different universe to 'Lucy' or 'King Bee' (maybe 'See Emily Play' and 'Arnold Layne' are a wormhole). Perhaps it's a mark of Syd's vision that he could have the band cross space and time so quickly.

Certainly Floyd's early stuff, their LIVE set, foreshadows the soon–to–be–familiar "concept" piece. Songs running over thirty minutes moving in and out, over and under a musical signature, were not the norm for beat group performances. Different, yes!

When you listen to Syd's collected work, what stands out is the bending of rock music (neither heavy metal or pop). 'Scream Thy Last Scream Old Woman With A Casket', 'Pow R Toc H' and 'Dominoes' evoke a far different feeling from their titles alone than songs by the other groups and writers of the time.

By the way, a set list included in the Omnibus Press book PINK FLOYD A VISUAL DOCUMENTARY by Miles (published 1980, updated in 1988), shows an October 1966 gig run-down that includes the song 'Lucy Leave' with other titles: 'Flapdoodle Dealing', 'I Can Tell', 'Gimmie A Break', 'Piggy Back', 'Snowing', 'Pink', 'Let's Roll Another' (the future 'Candy And A Current Bun'), 'Stoned Alone', 'The Gnome', 'Interstellar Overdrive', 'Stethascope' (sic), 'Matilda Mother', 'Pow R Toc H' and 'Astronomy Dominie'. Would Gilmour or Waters choose such a set now?

As for the transition from Syd to Roger and the others' leadership? Gilmour states they played very few gigs as a five-piece. I would suspect any bootleg that claims to be one of these. The five-piece never actually recorded together in the studio either.

MAGNESIUM PROVERBS does include Syd's only live solo appearance at the Olympia in London (the boot says the Royal Festival Hall) June 6, 1970 (not June 1 as listed and for the Music and Fashion Festival known as Extravaganza 70). David Gilmour is on hand to play bass. (Not really a legit reunion is it? All we've got though.)

And don't forget to check out the mystery riff – a backwards tape message from the song 'Empty Spaces' (THE WALL): "Congratulations. You have just discovered the secret message. Please send your answer to Old Pink, care of the Funny Farm, Chalfont." No kidding.

A final word on Syd. Phil Smee, in the liner notes to the Syd tribute, BEYOND THE WILD WOOD A TRIBUTE TO SYD BARRETT (Imaginary Records ILLCD 100, 1989), writes: "The Floyd without Syd produced some brilliant music immediately after his departure – but it would seem they were running on his momentum and inspiration because as his influence faded they were left stranded, and produced more and more self parodying mega–pomp opuses aimed at hi–fi–lifestyle boves and supported by record company executives with a pitiful knowledge of music and short memories." Guess he won't agree with my opinions huh? It's ironic how critics who weren't even born when Syd was in charge now accuse the Roger–less Floyd of the same thing.

(8) DESK TAPE (Darkside ll HBO2 1994) / TIME (Great Dane Records
GDR CD SAT 4 1994) / DARK SIDE OF THE SKY (Chapter One CO 25117 1990)

For performances well after Syd's reign, check out these items. The first features material from the ANIMALS tour while the latter is an early DARK SIDE OF THE MOON show. 'Pigs (3 Different Ones)' in particular is a stand-out on DESK TAPE (also features the version of 'Wish You Were Here' mentioned earlier on IN THE FLESH, CROSSFIRE, etc.). The recordings on both TIME and DARK SIDE OF THE SKY are from the famous Rainbow Theatre show from 1972. Outstanding sound on both captures what surely was a magic night for fans. There is a group punch in performance that makes you take notice. The show epitomises what's been called "Gilmour's languid blues guitar and alienation effects" and that's PINK enough for me.

(9) and (10)?
Well, we don't actually get to nine and 10 on this list (I've cheated anyway by listing more than one selection in other places). I do offer three honourable mentions to complete the "who's PINK" assessment however. (A) MOONLIGHT TUNES (Pig Records Pig 01, MT1994), (B) BRITISH TEMPTATION (World Productions of Compact Music WPOCM CD IO90F059-2, 1990) and (C) LIVE AT WINTERLAND (Swingin' Pig Records TSP-CD-170-2, 1994).

(A) shows a very cool Gilmour and band working under less-than-ideal conditions. This is from a Houston, Texas April 1994 concert (third stop on the '94 tour) during a rainstorm. Grab the June 16, 1994 ROLLING STONE and you can read about the band's feelings around this particular show and the DIVISION BELL tour. What's interesting about the rain-shortened second set is audience reaction to the potential early departure of the band. You can hear several bummed out fans (?) crying "bullshit", "bullshit" as Gilmour concedes the weather is a problem.

Notably, the song 'What Do You Want From Me', from the DIVISION BELL, asks the right question. Perhaps the fans (?) would want to say they attended the show where the band got killed. Certainly it's unfortunate the show was cut back but what can you do? Compare Gilmour's relative calm here to Roger Waters patter heard on BLACK HOLES IN THE SKY (Great Dane Records GDR CD 9101/A 9101/B, 1991) or, though we don't have this on bootleg, the WALL inspiring spitting incident that took place at Olympic Stadium during the ANIMALS tour in 1977. At least the fans in Houston were already wet.

One final note. The band's quick end to 'Run Like Hell' makes you wonder if Las Vegas is in their future with a very musak–like finish. Of course most of the instruments have conked out by this time. Their blowing off 'Great Gig In The Sky' and move to 'Money' also shows flexibility – who says they can't be spontaneous?

(B) BRITISH TEMPTATION also highlights equipment trouble on the song 'Astronomy Domine'. Worth checking out since it goes back to 1970 and you can compare this version with that of 1994. Three attempts get you through the song (sort of) and it is a far different version to the DIVISION BELL tour opener. Also features a kinder, gentler Roger Waters as host explaining (questioning the roadies about) the problem. Some great drumming from Nick too.

(C) LIVE AT WINTERLAND, featuring excellent sound quality from a show in October 1970, offers a rare 'Granchester Meadows' LIVE (beautifully segueing into 'Astronomy Domine' with no breakdown here). Again, going for the UNPLUGGED analogy, it shows the band doesn't have to rely on pyrotechnics for effect. 'Granchester Meadows' is a gorgeous song pure and simple. Makes you long to hear 'Fearless' from MEDDLE in performance. The song also demonstrates the great vocal interplay between Waters and Gilmour. And this is something both the new Floyd and Roger Waters' tours lack: full Floyd sound systems, Jon Carin and Paul Carrack extra vocals aside!

So who's really PINK? Well, in the end, maybe another Roger lyric says it best – "If you want to find out what's behind these cold eyes? You'll just have to claw your way through this disguise." And that's why I'll still be found clawing around the trenches. See you there!

RIP OFF ALERT part 2...
If you are collecting, don't get too caught up and lay out good money for false claims listed on many bootleg CD covers. A prime example is the London Rainbow show from 1972 (see above reference). Many CD boots claim they are from this show but very few actually are. A clue? If it's got back-up female vocals and sax, you ain't hearing the early LIVE performance of DARK SIDE.

In addition, don't be taken in by longer versions and new or different names for song titles. The Floyd (unlike Led Zeppelin) stay pretty time-consistent through tour performances. And other than early performances of songs and what's called 'Blues Jam', 'Floyd's Blues' or 'Blues' by bootleggers (TOTAL ECLIPSE features this), there isn't anything new or different in concert.

At one memorabilia show a new Floyd collector got me thinking about this when he said he was avidly searching out PINK ELEPHANTS FLEW OVER TORINO (Cocayne Records ENT YNE 102.2.1/102.2.2.) His reason? HOT WACKS lists the CD (accurately) as listing an 8:12 version of 'Round & Round' – way longer than on MOMENTARY LAPSE. On the boot though, like the whole tour, you get 'Round & Round' as on record followed by 'A New Machine Pt 1', 'Terminal Frost' and 'A New Machine Pt 2'.

These simply aren't listed on the jacket but make up the added time. They also list Roger Waters as playing bass on this CD. Do you want to believe this one too?

The tradition continues on boots from the new tour as well. JURASSIK SPARKS (Red Phantom RPCD 2165–2166, 1994 and very poor sound) lists 'A New Machine Part 2' but it's actually 'Sorrow'. (See SUPPLEMENT 2, page F for an explanation why so many boots have inaccurate information on them.)

The point is folks, don't trust the jackets, liner notes or anything else – just your ears! Any of the "not–in–it–solely–for–whatever–profit–can–be–made" dealers will let you preview material first. Anything less and it's buyer beware – making Nick Mason's point about bootlegs right after all!

FOR THE FANS
By Ron (Chicago) February 1995

I discovered bootleg albums in the late 1970's, and in the ensuing years have acquired a quite respectable collection. Bootleg albums and tapes gave me the ability to hear concerts that were before my time and listen to current shows I could not attend.

PINK FLOYD has always been my favourite band; from way back to the Barrett years, through its current incarnation almost 30 years later, the Floyd's music has been a major part of my life's soundtrack. Bootleg recordings allowed me to explore Barrett's musical genius at its rise and peak, as well as his rapid demise into mental illness, The band's evolution proceeded in a new direction with the induction of guitarist David Gilmour, accompanying the Floyd through an experimental, and understandably unfocused period.

Early recordings have captured classic moments such as the band's appearances on BBC radio and TV. Unlike many bands, Pink Floyd performed new raw material in front of live audiences, slowly developing them into well-known classics. Bootlegs allowed me to hear early versions of 'Echoes', 'Dark Side of the Moon' (a year before it was recorded), 'Shine On You Crazy Diamond', and 'Raving And Drooling' and 'Gotta Be Crazy' (before Waters molded them into 'Sheep' and 'Dogs supplementing the 'Animals' trilogy).

For the past 18 years, I have established a very respectable reputation amongst the hierarchy of Floyd collectors. By no means am I an 'obsessive' or 'completest', mind you. My original goal has always been to obtain the best possible sound recordings representing each of the Floyd's major tours. Besides, with my connections I have access to virtually every gig the band ever played (thanks to my obsessive and completest friends).

In early 1990, I picked up my first bootleg CD, GREAT DANE's ECLIPSE (a combination of 2 early BBC broadcasts) and had the insight to see the tidal wave of bootleg CDs that would soon hit the market. After reading an interview with Rinaldo Tagliabue (GREAT DANE's CEO) in ICE magazine, explaining the legality of these recordings in his country, I decided to contact him to see if he was interested in any of my material. I figured that if all these CD companies were just going to rehash old material that everyone already had on vinyl, then at least there should be someone in the quality-control department that gave a shit about what was being produced.

So I set out to fulfil and surpass my original goal by producing the best recordings representing each of Pink Floyd's major tours. With each release I supplied extensive liner notes covering the band at that period of time, and the songs and performance as will. I also supplied GREAT DANE with relevant photos from that tour as well as choosing (and sometimes designing) cover artwork, and having the fun of naming each title. GREAT DANE put all of the pieces together and have gotten more professional-looking over the years. They have earned themselves the reputation for producing a very high-quality product, as critics and fans alike have raved about their CD's.

I am proud to have produced these CDs for the fans like myself, who care about the music and want to buy a product that has some intelligence and creativity applied to it. And as crazy as this may seem, I never received a penny from GREAT DANE for my efforts. My rewards came from seeing the CDs I produced appreciated by the fans who bought them, and from knowing that I was proud of what I had done. The only thing I received was a limited number of the titles I produced and access to anything else I might want from the GDR catalogue.

With copyright laws recently going through some drastic reforms, I am proud to have been able to produce the following titles for GDR over the past 5 years:

THE MAN AND THE JOURNEY (GDR CD 9207) Concertgebow, Amsterdam 9/17/69
The Floyd's first 'conceptual' piece combing early material with sections of improvisation. This Dutch radio broadcast was never issued in its entirety and has never sounded as good as this.

THE COMPLETE TOP GEAR SESSIONS 1967-1969 (GDR CD 9206)
Once again, these famous BBC sessions were never packaged under the same title and I was able to track down the sources to represent the best sound quality from each.

STAYING HOME TO WATCH THE RAIN (GDR CD 9013) HOLLYWOOD BOWL 9/22/72
Originally issued on vinyl as the famous CRACKERS boot, I obtained a very low-generation recording that not only sounded much better, but also included material that was supposedly 'lost'. This CD features many of Floyd's early standards as well as an embryonic version of 'Dark Side...', known at the time as 'Eclipsed'.

BLACK HOLES IN THE SKY (GDR CD 9101) Wembley, London 11/16/74
The best-sounding complete recording from the 1974 tour heralding the birth of 'Shine On', 'Raving and Droolin', and 'Gotta Be Crazy'.

RANDOM PRECISION (GDR CD) Nassau Coliseum, New York 6/16/75
This previously-unreleased recording rates up there with the best boots from the 1975 tour (IVOR WYNNE, PIGS WISHES AND MOONS, & PRISM).

IN THE FLESH (GDR CD 9103) Oakland Coliseum, CA 5/9/77
My personal favourite CD, featuring the complete WISH YOU WERE HERE and ANIMALS LPs performed live. The Floyd's performance is right on the money (no pun intended), and the show includes the encore of 'Careful With That Axe, Eugene', the only time it was performed on that tour. This low-generation recording doesn't have the musical 'dropouts' you'll find on the other boots.

BRICK BY BRICK (GDR CD 9313) Nassau Coliseum, New York 2/28/80
After researching every known recorded performance of THE WALL, I came to the much-chastised conclusion that the best recording from this tour was the one that was most reproduced on vinyl. Since that was the case, I took on the laborious task of hunting down a 1st-generation tape to insure that the quality would be unchallenged. I also included a CD of the band rehearsing THE WALL (at Paramount Studios in L.A., 2/1/80), just days before its premier. The sound on this CD is far superior to Stonehenge Records BEHIND THE WALL box, which is much 'hissier' and has long gaps of silence between verbal banter. And although BEHIND THE WALL is packaged with a very nice booklet. it's information is limited to a short paragraph on the back cover, and incorrect tour dates scattered throughout.

FOR WHOM THE BELL TOLLS (PLR CD 9413) Jack Murphy Stadium 4/14/94
This was released on GDR's subsidiary label PLUTO RECORDS (probably because of the recent date), and is one of the best DAT audience tapes I've ever heard. Originally packaged in a 'digi-pack' format, a second pressing (in the slim line double jewel case) is already almost sold out.

TOTAL ECLIPSE (GDR CD 9320) 4CD (52 song) Retrospective
My piece de resistance. GDR released this box set in a 'book-style' format, with a 32-page full-color booklet including liner notes on the band's history and a track-by-track description. When Floyd released their much-awaited box set SHINE ON they refused their fans what every other major artist had supplied; outtakes, live recordings, demos, B-sides, etc. Instead, Gilmour responded, "You'll just have to buy the boots". TOTAL ECLIPSE is my response to what the fan's would have wanted and deserved.

My special thanks to Rinaldo for making it all happen. And my deepest apologies to my close friends, who liked Pink Floyd a lot more before they met me. Shine On!

Book Reviews

Explanation-Turned-Into-A-Review

By HOT WACKS editor and publisher Bob Walker

Last fall, many of you received a flyer or saw an ad in GOLDMINE for the book THE GREAT WHITE WONDERS and many of you ordered it. But, none of you received it... at least not from The Hot Wacks Press. Here's why.

I originally heard about the book from people who'd been interviewed by author Clinton Heylin. The project sounded exciting and I contacted Heylin to see if I could help. I sent him copies of HOT WACKS and HOT WACKS QUARTERLIES for background and we talked a number of times. I was looking forward to having another book, this time a history, to offer HOT WACKS readers.

After the book was published (September 1994 in the U.K.), I contacted the publisher (Penguin Books Ltd., England) who arranged shipment to me through Penguin Canada. I was told my 500-book order would be delivered to me on or before November 14th in time to distribute for Christmas 1994.

However, before the books could be delivered, a lawsuit was launched against THE GREAT WHITE WONDERS by the founder and original publisher of HOT WACKS, Kurt Glemser. The author of THE GREAT WHITE WONDERS came to certain conclusions and made false statements about Glemser based on poor information and research.

After assessing the situation, Penguin agreed to withdraw the book and change the passages-in-question in future editions of THE GREAT WHITE WONDERS. This left me without a book to sell, cheques to return and apologies to make.

There's no question that researching a book like THE GREAT WHITE WONDERS would be difficult because of the underground nature of the bootleg business. However, getting facts wrong that are a matter of public record might lead one to question other areas of the book. This may be a bit hypocritical because HOT WACKS is far from perfect. Mistakes have been made and continue (thankfully) to be corrected by readers and bootleggers.

There is also an element of sour grapes involved in this explanation-turned-into-a-review. There's very little mention of HOT WACKS and its role in the history of bootlegs. Bruised ego?! I don't think so. It's my opinion (and that of many readers who write to tell me how important the book is to their collecting) that HOT WACKS was and is an integral part of the bootleg world.

And, at the risk of tooting the HOT WACKS horn, there is no other publication that provides the amount of bootleg information found in HW. There are books that focus on the bootlegs of specific artists but not one that looks at the whole picture the way HW does. HOT WACKS has been around for over 20 years and I suggest that these other books, and THE GREAT WHITE WONDERS, grew out of a need for information created by HOT WACKS. It's also interesting to see how some of the boot histories, definitions (of boots, pirates and counterfeits) and listing formats used in these books are similar to what's found in HOT WACKS.

All that said, would I recommend THE GREAT WHITE WONDERS? Yes. It's the only book on the market at this time that gives an inside look at the workings of the bootleg industry past and present. Heylin's examination of the legal aspects is particularly good and the interviews with bootleggers are interesting. There are gaps in the overall history (see the following article) but, if you're interested in bootlegs, you'll enjoy the book. I've been told by Penguin Canada that the revised edition of THE GREAT WHITE WONDERS will be available this summer.

LiverR Than You'll Ever Be:
A Critical Review Of "The Great White Wonders"

By former HOT WACKS editor and publisher Kurt Glemser

The average reader of THE GREAT WHITE WONDERS, which claims to be the "full history" of rock bootleg recordings, will undoubtedly read the book and think it is just that; an accurate history from the beginnings of bootleg records to the current glut of bootleg CDs. Nothing could be further from the truth.

My own involvement in writing about bootleg records since 1973 attests to that. While I cannot comment on the bootleg CDs, having handed the reins of HOT WACKS to Bob Walker in 1986, I question if a book can be so wrong about the bootleg records and then be right when it comes to CDs.

The book tells some of the story, but only a part, certainly not "the whole fascinating story". It also is full of errors, poor research and false statements.

Some of the weakness of the book is due to the fact that its author, Clinton Heylin, seemed unable to find most of the bootleggers and quite probably others refused to be interviewed.

Considering that dozens of bootleggers were active during the record period in North America alone, he was able to interview only a few of note. Dub, who was there in the late 1960's when it all began, was the only major source for the author. While this laid a good foundation to build on, sadly, it is also the book's high point. Hardly what the dust jacket promises - "most of the important individuals involved in the business since 1969".

The two bootleggers identified as Peter and Richard are worthwhile subjects and deserve credit for some of the best packaged bootlegs coming out of North America. Both of them spent enormous amounts of time, money and effort on cover art and presentation.

As far as North America is concerned, however, the top bootleg labels were TRADE MARK OF QUALITY (TMOQ) - co-founded by Dub and Ken - and THE AMAZING KORNYFONE RECORD LABEL (TAKRL). The latter is the work of Ken along with several partners. Ken was also responsible for quite a number of other labels such as IMPOSSIBLE RECORDWORKS.

When the author does offer some inside information on KORNYFONE he does so by quoting HOT WACKS QUARTERLY. The author states on page 111: "In a letter to Hot Wacks Quarterly in 1980, the circumstances of TAKRL's formal closure were related by 'Art Gnuvo'."

Actually, the letter was published in HWQ #1 which is from 1979 and this is not the only instance of misidentifying source material. The reader may say this is a minor matter of getting dates wrong but if you can make mistakes of this nature you are also undoubtedly making others that are not as apparent. It also goes to the heart of research and checking your facts.

Instead of Ken we are treated to the rambling of one Eric Bristow. Unfortunately for history and the readers, this person did not enter the bootleg field until the mid-1980's. Eric made the ROCK SOLID RECORDS bootlegs, and with Ken made bootleg CDs in the 1980's, but this alone hardly qualifies Eric as a reliable source on TMOQ or TAKRL or the history of bootleg records for that matter.

Eric, who I've known for years, makes so many serious errors in the book that his entire contribution comes into question. At this point it's only fair to say that, largely as a result of what was attributed to him in the book, I took legal action against THE GREAT WHITE WONDERS.

Having written and published HOT WACKS I came into contact with a considerable number of bootleggers. In a large part in order not to put myself in a position where if this went to trial I would be forced to answer questions about them I did not take any action against the book for statements made about myself and bootlegging. If you don't contest it they cannot ask questions about it. Also, after reading the book I was hardly interested in giving Heylin information which he could use in a new edition. Let me state quite clearly, however, that every single thing written in the first hardcover British edition about myself, not dealing with bootlegs, was completely false. This is what I took legal action against and this is what will be missing from the US edition and all future editions. These statements, made on three different pages, were false. The end result was that PENGUIN BOOKS withdrew the book from distribution worldwide without my having to take them to court.

Eric, who knew me quite well at the time I was raided in 1980, gave a most outrageous account of that event amongst other things. Without repeating the false statements let me say that his account of the raid and its aftermath was completely wrong. Eric incorrectly stated what was seized, what the charges were (four very serious criminal charges were named none of which, in fact, I was charged with), and how the charges were resolved. In reality, the charges were stayed by the prosecution before even having a preliminary hearing. Not only that but all the items seized from me, including bootlegs, were returned by the RCMP (Royal Canadian Mounted Police).

The author, more so than Eric, deserves to take the blame for this bizarre state of affairs. If Heylin had bothered to do even the smallest amount of research he would have saved himself the embarrassment. Heylin quotes a number of times from HOT WACKS QUARTERLY including from issue #6 in regards to the Vicky Vinyl bust. On the same page he quotes from is a paragraph in regards to my bust. It refers back to issue #5 which lists all the charges. Certainly Heylin was aware of the magazine. It would have been one source of information. Another source would have been the courts. Criminal charges, after all, are a matter of public record. Any self-respecting author, much less a historian, must verify his sources. The accepted norm is that three sources are required to protect a publication from possible legal action. It would be the least the readers of this book could expect from a "history".

Eric, in another part of the book, is also quoted as saying that the 1980 raid "was a massive organizational accomplishment for the RIAA, the FBI and the RCMP in Canada. They managed to swoop down on 150 people on the same day, everywhere from Georgia to California to Ontario, Canada. The only people that they missed in this big swoop were Ken and Mike, because they were in Spain".

In reality, a total of eight people were raided in Canada and none in the USA. Therefore not only did Ken and Mike escape this dragnet but so did every other US bootlegger. While a number of locations in the US (none in California) were raided, these locations, like the seven Canadians beside myself, were alleged to be part of the bootleg ring "masterminded" by yours truly. The exaggeration is mind-boggling. Again Heylin didn't avail himself of the accurate information in court records or HOT WACKS QUARTERLY. We wouldn't want the facts to get in the way of a good story after all.

Unfortunately, the reader cannot be expected to know that these kinds of statements are totally false. That is the author's job. The reader is left with the feeling of getting the inside story from Eric Bristow. Knowing the real facts would certainly have any reader wondering about the accuracy of anything attributed to Eric.

Heylin himself makes numerous statements without foundation. He refers to BERKELEY and CONTRABAND MUSIC (CBM) as copycat bootleg labels. While this is true of BERKELEY's releases with only a few exceptions the vast majority of CBM's releases were original to CBM. If CBM can be knocked for anything it is for how few of its records were of excellent sound quality.

He further states that K&S RECORDS and WIZARDO (WRMB) "continued this shoddy tradition". This incredibly stupid comment can only come from someone who knows little about bootlegs. If a person were inclined to do research they could take HOT WACKS and go to the back where there is an appendix of bootleg labels. If you then look up the WIZARDO titles individually you'll see how very few are indeed copies. Several of the actual copies are of European bootlegs which were largely unavailable in the USA and several were made by someone using the WRMB logo.

As far as K&S is concerned, the only true copy was SIN CITY SOCIAL, its first release. K&S RECORDS issued numerous original bootlegs as well as represses of out-of-print bootlegs. The latter were very limited ranging from 50 to 200 copies and were made from the original plates and pressed on colored vinyl. Now when you use the original plates and titles that simply does not qualify as a copycat bootleg. The value of the colored vinyl K&S releases in today's collector's market attests to that. So either the collectors have got it all wrong or Heylin is wrong. Take your pick.

K&S RECORDS' swan song the Rolling Stones TRIDENT MIXES makes it into Heylin's list of all-time great bootlegs at the back of his book. This double album with a deluxe colour cover certainly deserves this honor yet this doesn't gibe with Heylin's criticism of K&S. I wonder if it's only his lack of research that comes through or if Heylin has been influenced by some bootlegger who's ego leads him to knock anything that he didn't have a hand in. Either way the author must take the blame.

Vicky Vinyl also came in for what by now seems the standard "copycat" bootleg charge from the author. On page 139 he writes: "Vicki (sic) Vinyl had wisely refrained from putting either of the Springsteen sets on her most regular outlet for product, IDLE MIND PRODUCTIONS, which would almost certainly have involved her in further litigation."

Now hold on a minute. She was taken to court for exactly those two record sets - LIVE IN THE PROMISED LAND and PIECE DE RESISTANCE. Does this guy know what he's writing about?

Heylin continues, "An infuriating mish-mash of original and copycat releases, Idle Mind was one of the last labels to abandon its paper-insert origins."

Far from being an "infuriating mish-mash" the following are the copies - Led Zeppelin EARL'S COURT (copy of a European boot of the same name), Dylan NOTHING IS REVEALED (from original K&S plates of TAPES FROM SHERRY'S ATTIC), Eagles WELCOME TO THE LATE SHOW (copy of the ANTI-GRAVITY boot of the same name), Rolling Stones BRING IT BACK ALIVE (from original K&S plates of the same title) , Queen MERCURY POISONING (copy of the Japanese boot INVITE YOU TO A NIGHT AT THE BUDO KAN), and Rolling Stones BILL WYMAN'S ROLLING STONES (from the original plates of the BRR boot BILL WYMAN AND THE ROLLING STONES).

Neither European nor Japanese bootlegs had any distribution to speak of in the USA. Therefore, the release of two of the above titles does not warrant an attack on their release. The others, with the exception of the Dylan title, were released under their original titles or close to in the case of the second Stones boot. I just don't see the problem. Anyone can easily pick up HOT WACKS and get the above information.

Heylin also seems unaware of Vicky's many other efforts which did not appear on the IMP label. Furthermore, having known Vicky for a number of years unlike Heylin who did not interview her, I don't know where he gets off stating that her issuing of the Springsteen bootlegs was "purely a commercial release" and that she was "in it for the money". Vicky was hardly a crass commercial operator when she was averaging some 50 cents per disc in profit. Noticeably, Eric didn't get labeled in the same fashion yet on page 296 the author himself points out that he was selling his CDs for $10 wholesale while the manufacturing cost was roughly $1.22. As Eric himself points out, "We made more money out of CDs in ten months than we had in the previous four of five years out of records." Bootleg record producers surely made their product to make some money but it was hardly the primary reason.

Are these digs at bootleggers who did not agree to be interviewed or does the author lack a grasp of the subject matter he's writing about?

The latter may well be the case. On page 114 he writes: "K&S was always destined to remain a small-time operation selling primarily to a market (Canada) where discrimination was not always an option."

The "colonies" remain to be sneered at in true British fashion. What a pompous ass! Canada, in fact, had the best selection of any country when it came to bootleg records. Japanese, European and American bootlegs were readily available from the usual sources. American dealers often got their European boots through Canada which served as a crossroads. Furthermore, K&S product remained mainly in the USA with only a portion being imported into Canada.

Oddly enough, the author seemingly contradicts his dig at Canada on page 131 when he states "Toronto had been one of the first cities in North America to sell GREAT WHITE WONDER... [editor's note: this refers to the Dylan boot GREAT WHITE WONDER] remaining a major outlet for bootleg titles throughout the seventies." What an infuriating mish-mash of fact and fantasy.

Even his obsession with copycat bootlegs deserves another point of view. Bootleg records were an underground endeavor. Each bootlegger had his distributors, some of which were exclusive to him. Therefore, if a particular bootleg was in demand in a large enough quantity, it made sense for the bootlegger to make his own copy. This satisfied that demand. It wasn't a deliberate attempt in most cases to sell the same product again under another title.

In actual fact, THE GREAT WHITE WONDERS primarily is the story of a number of California-based bootleggers. Even so, quite a number of notable California bootleggers are never mentioned. One example, and there are others, is the person behind JAMES PATRICK PAGE: SESSION MAN, another bootleg that makes it into Heylin's list of top 100. This bootlegger also released the classic Rolling Stones boot GARDEN STATE amongst numerous other titles.

From reading the book you wouldn't know that the East Coast also had a large bootleg contingent. At times in the 1970's there were more bootleg releases on the East Coast, with Springsteen and the Grateful Dead being particular favorites, than on the West Coast. With the exception of the Elvis Presley bootleg busts and interviews with one bootlegger (who, however, was active only in the 1980's) these are missing from "the history".

Japanese bootlegs, of which there were many, get practically no mention. It doesn't suffice to write a couple of sentences when you claim to be a "full history".

European bootleg records certainly got better coverage than the Japanese but it was mainly the British scene that was covered. The much more prolific German and Italian bootleggers were largely ignored. Let's face it, the vast majority of European bootlegs had excellent sound quality and deluxe covers which surpassed most of what was coming out in North America. It would therefore make sense to give equal or better coverage to the European bootlegs. Also lacking completely is any information on the many mail order outfits and wholesalers who made their own contributions to the history of bootleg records. They had a large part in getting the music to the people.

These Heylin must have been aware of. After all, a number of them are listed in the FBI reports he refers to on page 139. Again the reader must think that if Heylin went so far as to get FBI reports he must have really been digging and doing his research. In fact, these reports of interviews with a Michel Meese, have been circulating in bootleg circles ever since the Vicky Vinyl case where they were first revealed.

Meese (referred to in FBI reports as "Mess") was interviewed by Special Agent James M. Dietzen and Special Agent David A. Heinle on January 12, 17 and 19, 1979, in Los Angeles. The agents contacted him "regarding his knowledge of and involvement in the sale of bootlegged, long playing albums".

While admitting his "previous involvement in the sale of bootlegged records" he went on to claim "he no longer deals in records in any manner and has not done so for a year and a half".

The reports continues, "Mess related that he was currently facing charges in Canada for a shipment of bootlegged albums from Los Angeles to Montreal. He claims another person is responsible for this shipment but he refused to identify him."

In the January 12, 1979, interview Meese "advised that he has never personally known anyone in the Los Angeles area dealing in bootlegged albums". It appears obvious to me the FBI agents found much of this hard to believe which led to two additional visits.

It is from the January 19, 1979, interview with the same FBI agents that Heylin quotes Meese in regards to myself. Once again, research falls to the wayside as another story is related by the author. For starters, according to Meese I find that I reside in Toronto. At that time I lived in Kitchener which is a good 60 miles from Toronto. Heylin could have easily researched this. It leaves me with the feeling that the reader is not being treated to a history of bootlegs but rather a hearsay of bootlegs. There is a difference. The author apparently feels it is enough if anyone makes a statement to put it to print.

Careful reading of the FBI reports, even without the apparent unwelcome effort of research, suggests the agents themselves are less than believing of Mr. Meese. The report is full of such words as "Mess claims" and further points out that: "It should be noted that some of these addresses were different than provided on January 17, 1979".

It seems that by the l7th Meese, in fact, did know people in the Los Angeles area involved in bootlegs contrary to his statement of the 12th. By January 19th some of their addresses had changed! Chalk up another reliable source for the history of bootlegs according to Heylin.

The January 19th report ends with: "Finally, Mess agreed to contact the Plattsburg, New York Resident Agency of the Federal Bureau of Investigation to further discuss his activities and to assist them in any way possible."

Heylin writes: "It would take a year for the FBI and RCMP to organize a coordinated attack on the manufacturer-producers named by Mess". In fact, only two of the nine named individuals were raided - Vicky Vinyl in June 1979 and myself in February 1980

....

Kurt Glemser began documenting bootleg records in 1973 with the release of BOOTLEGS. His next effort entitled UNDERGROUND SOUNDS was published in 1974. These discographies led to HOT WACKS in 1975. Kurt was the author and publisher of this book up to and including HOT WACKS BOOK XI.

From 1979 until 1985 he was editor and publisher of the collectors' magazine HOT WACKS QUARTERLY. HWQ dealt with all aspects of music collecting, especially bootleg records.

At the present his writing is very much of a historical nature. He has authored two books and several articles on military history. His third book on that subject is now in the works.

A

ABBA

CD - MADE IN SWEDEN
MISTRAL MUSIC MM 9336
Greeting From Sweden (Abba)/ When I Kissed The Teacher (live)/ Being A Hipster (Benny)/ Hovas Vittne (promo)/ Working Together (Bjorn)/ Gimme! Gimme! Gimme! (live)/ Super Trouper (live)/ The Start Of Abba (Frida)/ Slipping Through My Fingers (instrumental)/ Eurovision Song Contest (Bjorn)/ Under Attack (live-Saarbrucken TV show)/ The Influences (Bjorn)/ Dreamworld (unreleased)/ Frida's Childhood (Frida)/ I Have A Dream (Japan)/ Agnetha's Early Years (Agnetha)/ On Top Of Old Smokey (full version)/ Abba On Tour (Benny)/ The Day Before You Came (live-Saarbrucken TV show)/ Divorce (Bjorn)/ When All Is Said And Done (instrumental)/ The Magic Of A Song (Bjorn)/ Tiveds Hambo (Abba's last performance)/ The End (Stig)/ Dancing Queen (live-U2, Bjorn, & Benny)
R: Exs. Soundboard.
S: Various.   C: ECD. Dcc. Interview clips mixed in-between cuts. Time 57:24.

CD - SWEET DREAMS ARE MADE OF THIS
BIG MUSIC BIG 094
Voulez Vous (4:44)/ Knowing Me, Knowing You (4:30)/ Chiquitita (5:29)/ Gimme, Gimme, Gimme (5:06)/ Super Trouper (4:31)/ I Have A Dream (6:35)/ The Name Of The Game, Eagle (9:26)/ Thank You For The Music (3:40)/ Two For The Price Of One (3:10)/ Slipping Through Your Soul (4:04)/ Me And I (4:19)/ Summer Night City (5:29)/ Take A Chance On Me (4:33)/ The Way Old Friends Do (3:06)/ Waterloo (3:31)/ Dancing Queen (3:45)
R: Exs. Soundboard.   S: '81.   C: ECD. Dcc. Pic CD.

CD - VOULEZ VOUS
PIPELINE PPL531
Voulez Vous (3:01)/ Knowing Me, Knowing You (2:04)/ Dancing Queen (3:55)/ Chiquitita (3:47)/ Gimme! Gimme! Gimme!, A Man After Midnight (5:09)/ Summer Night City (5:51)/ I Have A Dream (4:28)/ Does Your Mother Know (3:58)/ Hole In Your Soul (4:37)
R: Vg-Ex. Soundboard.   S: Las Vegas Aug. 1 '80.   C: ECD. Dcc. Time 36:55.

ADAMS, BRYAN

CD - GREATEST HITS
EVE 44
Summer Of '69/ It's Only Love/ Can't Stop This Thing We Started/ Straight From The Heart/ Somebody/ Into The Fire/ Heaven/ Heat Of The Night/ Run To You/ One Night Love Affair/ (Everything I Do) I Do It For You/ Cuts Like A Knife/ Lonely Nights/ Kids Wanna Rock/ Hearts On Fire/ House Arrest/ There Will Never Be Another Tonight
S: USA, Canada & Belgium, '85-'93.

CD - THE SECRET SHOW
BLUE CAT RECORDS 111 193
Intro/ La Bamba/ Satisfaction/ Gloria/ Wild Thing/ I Feel Good/ It's Only Rock'N Roll/ Born To Be Wild/ You Can't Judge A Book By Looking At Its Cover/ Come Together/ I Fought The Law/ Y.M.C.A./ Rebel Rebel/ I'm Going Down/ Summer of '69/ Twist & Shout/ Good Golly Miss Molly/ When The Night Comes/ Diana
R: G-Vg. Audience. *G.   S: Secret Gig, La Tierra Night Club, Barcelona Nov. 11 '93. *Tracks 18-19 Conopy Stage, Roskilde, Denmark July 1 '90.
C: ECD. Color cardboard folder with disc in white paper sleeve. Time 77:51.

AEROSMITH

CD - BIG-MAMMED WOMAN
TEDDY BEAR RECORDS TB43
Eat The Rich (4:43)/ Toys In The Attic (4:04)/ Draw The Line (9:36)/ Monkey On My Back (4:54)/ Messin' Round (5:55)/ Janie's Got A Gun (5:14)/ Love In An Elevator (6:09)/ Dude (Looks Like A Lady) (4:01)/ Come Together (4:22)/ Dream On (4:50)/ She Cried - Livin' On The Edge (7:04)/ Walk This Way (6:45)
R: Exs. Soundboard.   S: Woodstock, Saugerties, NY Aug. 13 '94.   C: ECD. Dcc. Pic CD.

CD - CASTLE KINGS 1994
OCTOPUS OCTO 022/023
CD1: Intro - Eat The Reach (5:15)/ Toys In The Attic (4:04)/ Get A Grip (4:52)/ Fever (4:20)/ Monkey On My Back (5:26)/ Amazing (5:18)/ Mama Kin (4:34)/ Cryin' (5:03)/ Rats In The Cellar (8:04)/ Boogie Man (2:31)/ Shut Up And Dance (7:09)/ Bright Light Fright (2:29)
CD2: Walk On Down (4:01)/ Janie's Got A Gun (6:07)/ Kings And Queens (5:44)/ Love In An Elevator (6:42)/ Sweet Emotion (6:34)/ Dude (Looks Like A Lady) (4:33)/ Train Kept A Rollin' (4:12)/ Dream On (5:07)/ Livin' On The Edge (5:47)/ Walk This Way (6:06)
R: Exs. Audience.   S: Castle Donnington '94.
C: ECD. Dcc. Pic CDs.

CD - EAT THE FUCKIN' RICH
ZEPPELIN ZEP 0013
Love In An Elevator/ Back In The Saddle/ Flesh/ Rag Doll/ Cryin'/ Eat The Rich/ Toys In The Attic/ Janie's Got A Gun/ Dude (Looks Like A Lady)/ Dream On/ Walk This Way/ Livin' On The Edge/ Sweet Emotion/ What It Takes
R: Poor-G. Audience.   S: Biloxi July 15 '93.
C: ECD. Dcc. Time 75:07.

CD - FEVER
ROYAL SOUND MUSIC RSM 049
Love In An Elevator/ Back In The Saddle/ Fever/ What It Takes/ Rag Doll/ Last Child/ Cryin'/ Shut Up And Dance/ The Other Side/ Janie's Got A Gun/ Dude (Looks Like A Lady)/ Dream On/ Walk This Way/ Livin' On The Edge
S: Mansfield, MA '93.   C: ECD.

CD - GET A FUCKIN' LAST
REAL LIVE CO. AJ-940517 A/B
CD1: Eat The Rich/ Toys In The Attic/ Rag Doll/ Fever/ What It Takes/ Shut Up And Dance, Boogie Man, Drum Solo/ Mama Kin/ Cryin'/ Lord Of The Thighs/ Flesh
CD2: Stop Messin' Around/ Blight Light Flight/ Janie's Got A Gun/ Love In An Elevator/ Dude (Looks Like A Lady)/ Walk This Way/ Dream On/ Living On The Edge/ Sweet Emotion, Bass Solo/ Dazed And Confused - Peter Gunn
R: G-Vg. Audience.   S: Budokan, Tokyo, Japan May 17 '94.   C: Japanese CD. 12" X 12" B&w cardboard gatefold cover. CDs in full color sleeves.

CD - GET THE HEAVENLY LIPS OFF...
RARE RECORDING COLLECTION RRC 044
Fever/ Draw The Line/ What It Takes/ Last Child/ The Other Side/ Cryin'/ Shut Up And Dance/ Stop Messin 'Round/ Rag Doll/ Janie's Got A Gun/ Walk This Way/ Living On The Edge/ Sweet Emotions/ Peter Gunn Theme/ Train Kept A 'Rollin'
R: Vg. Soundboard.   S: Brussels '93.   C: ECD. Time 78:30.

CD - LIVE AND F.I.N.E.
SOUNDS ALIVE CD 2400110

Same Old Song And Dance/ F.I.N.E./ Monkey On My Back/ Permanent Vacation/ Janie's Got A Gun/ Mama Kin/ Voodoo Medicine Man/ Red House/ Rag Doll/ Draw The Line/ Dream On/ Love In An Elevator/ Dude (Looks Like a Lady)/ Sweet Emotion/ Walk This Way
S: Boston, MA Apr. '90.   C: ECD.

CD - LIVIN' ON THE EDGE
GRAPEFRUIT GRA-029-A
Livin' On The Edge (4:46)/ Janie's Got A Gun (5:08)/ Dude (Looks Like A Lady) (4:35)/ Love In An Elevator (4:43)/ Train Kept A Rollin' (3:50)/ Ragdoll (4:15)/ Dream On (4:55)/ The Other Side (3:58)/ Walk This Way (3:25)/ Amazing (4:17)/ Toys In The Attic (4:06)/ Cryin' (4:11)/ Young Lust (3:42)/ Sweet Emotion (3:10)
R: Exs. Soundboard.   S: USA '93.
C: Australian CD. Dcc.

CD - NIGHT AT THE RAINBOW
16 MRH/26MRH
CD1: Intro/ Eat The Rich/ Toys In The Attic/ Fever/ Same Old Song And Dance/ What It Takes/ Mama Kin/ Rag Doll/ Monkey On My Back/ Crying/ Blues - Draw The Line
CD2: Stop Messin' Around/ Walk On Down/ Janie's Got A Gun/ Love In An Elevator/ Dude (Looks Like A Lady)/ Sweet Emotion - Peter Gunn/ Dream On/ Living On The Edge/ Walk This Way
R: G-Vg. Audience.   S: Rainbow Hall, Nagoya, Japan May 6 '94.   C: Japanese CD.

CD - OUT OF CONTROL
NIKKO NK 010/11
CD1: Eat The Rich (5:14)/ Toys In The Attic (4:04)/ Get A Grip (4:27)/ Fever (4:45)/ Monkey On My Back (5:28)/ Amazing (5:20)/ Mama Kin (4:34)/ Cryin (5:00)/ Rat In The Cellar (8:15)/ Intro - Shut Up And Dance (9:06)
CD2: Bright Light Fright (2:37)/ Walk On Down (3:49)/ Janie Got A Gun (6:07)/ Kings And Queen (5:42)/ Love In An Elevator (5:55)/ Bass Solo, Sweet Emotion, Guitar Solo, Peter Gunn, Sweet Emotion Reprise (9:13)/ Dude, Looks Like A Lady (4:33)/ Train Kept A Rollin' (5:08)/ Dream On (5:05)/ Living On The Edge (5:48)/ Drum Solo, Walk This Way (5:19)
R: Exs. Soundboard.   S: Europe '94.   C: ECD. Dcc. Digi-pack. Pic CDs.

CD - RIGHT PLACE, RIGHT TIME
VIVID SOUND PRODUCTIONS VSP 51016/17
CD1: Eat the Rich (5:45)/ Young Lust (4:21)/ F.I.N.E. (4:12)/ Love In An Elevator (5:37)/ Fever (4:29)/ Draw The Line (6:36)/ What it Takes (4:58)/ Last Child (4:52)/ The Other Side (4:37)/ Cryin' (5:00)/ Boogie Man (2:14)/ Shut Up And Dance (3:29)
CD2: Rag Doll (4:05)/ Janie's Got A Gun (4:05)/ Dude (Looks Like A Lady) (4:34)/ Dream On (4:42)/ Drum Solo (3:58)/ Walk This Way (4:18)/ Living On The Edge (5:16)/ Sweet Emotion (6:37)/ Peter Gunn (2:01)/ Train Kept A-Rollin' (3:59)/

Same Old Song And Dance (5:32)/ Red House (5:14)
R: Vg-Ex.   S: Brussels Oct. 31 '93. CD 2 tracks 11,12 Spectrum, Philadelphia Apr. '90.   C: ECD. Dcc.

CD - ROAD TO HEAVEN-PAVED IN HELL 1
ALL ABOUT FAME AAF 030 CD
Young Lust/ F.I.N.E./ Love In A Elevator/ Fever/ Draw The Line/ What It Takes/ Last Child/ The Other Side/ Cryin'/ Shut Up And Dance/ Stop Messin' Round/ Rag Doll/ Janie's Got A Gun
R: Exs. Soundboard.   S: Europe '93.   C: ECD. Dcc. Time 68:30.

CD - ROAD TO HEAVEN-PAVED IN HELL 2
ALL ABOUT FAME AAF 031
Dude Looks Like A Lady/ Dreams On/ Joey Kramer Drum Solo/ Walk This Way/ Living On The Edge/ Sweet Emotion/ Peter Gunn Theme/ Train Kept A' Rollin'/ Dream On/ Train Kept A' Rollin'/ Walking The Dog/ Toys In The Attic
R: Exs. Soundboard.   S: Europe '93.   C: ECD. Dcc. Time 55:00.

CD - SKIN AND BONES
BACK STAGE BKCD065/66
CD1: Eat The Rich/ Young Lust/ F.I.N.E./ Love In An Elevator/ Fever/ Draw The Line/ What It Takes/ Last Child/ The Other Side/ Cryin'/ Boogie Man/ Shut Up And Dance
CD2: Shut Up And Dance/ Stop Messin' Around/ Rag Doll/ Janie's Got A Gone/ Dude (Looks Like A Lady)/ Dream On/ J. Kramer Drum Solo/ Walk This Way/ Sweet Emotion/ Perry Mason Theme/ Train Kept A Rollin'
S: European leg of the 'Get A Grip' tour '93.
C: ECD.

CD - STRUTTIN' MY STUFF
KISS THE STONE KTS 292/93
CD1: Young Lust (4:27)/ Rag Doll (4:22)/ (Tell Me) What It Takes (5:19)/ Fever (4:22)/ Monkey On My Back (4:32)/ Amazing (5:06)/ The Other Side (4:24)/ Cryin' (5:04)/ Shut Up And Dance, Drum Solo (12:19)
CD2: Walk On Down (3:44)/ Mama Kin (4:25)/ Janie's Got A Gun (5:25)/ Love In An Elevator (5:00)/ Dude (Looks Like A Lady) (4:18)/ Sweet Emotion (7:07)/ Dream On (4:47)/ Living On The Edge (4:59)/ Walk This Way (4:03)
R: Exs. Soundboard.   S: Brazil Jan. '94.
C: ECD. Dcc. Pic CDs.

CD - TOXIC GRAFFITI
KISS THE STONE KTS222
Toys In The Attic (4:35)/ Medley: Sweet Emotion, Peter Gunn Theme (6:42)/ Cryin' (5:30)/ Dude (Looks Like A Lady) (4:51)/ Living On The Edge (6:23)/ Walk This Way (4:21)/ Love Comes Tumbling Down (6:18)/ Big Ten Inch (Record) (3:56)/ Dream On (5:05)/ Train Kept A Rollin' (3:12)/ Walkin' The Dog (3:49)/ Toys In The Attic (4:05)/ Cryin' (5:03)/ Walk This Way (3:52)

R: Exs. Soundboard.   S: Foxboro Stadium Aug. 6 '93.   C: ECD. Dcc. Pic CD.

CD - WOODSTOCK 1994
OCTOBER OCTO 040/041
CD1: Hangman Jury (6:16)/ Big Ten Inch Record (4:07)/ Dream On (5:05)/ Train Kept A Rollin' (3:07)/ Walkin' The Dog (3:51)/ Toys In The Attic (4:06)/ Eat The Rich (4:56)/ Toys In The Attic (4:28)/ Fever (4:33)/ Draw The Line (9:37)/ Rag Doll (4:53)/ Crying (5:22)/ Crazy (5:35)/ Monkey On My Back (5:07)/ Mama Kin (4:10)
CD2: Boogie Man (2:59)/ Shut Up And Dance (5:19)/ Stop Messin' Around (4:11)/ Walk On Down (4:07)/ Janie's Got A Gun (5:32)/ Love In An Elevator (6:07)/ Dude (Looks Like A Lady) (4:41)/ Sweet Emotion (9:56)/ Come Together (4:48)/ Dream On (4:56)/ Living On The Edge (7:32)/ Walk This Way (7:01)
R: Exs. Soundboard.   S: Woodstock Festival, Saugerties, New York Aug. 13-14 '94.   C: ECD. Dcc. Pic CDs.

AFGHAN WHIGS

CD - BLACK SOUL GENTLEMEN
OCTOPUS OCTO 011
If I Were Going (3:35)/ Debonair (4:28)/ Turn On The Water (8:04)/ Gentlemen (4:36)/ Be Sweet (3:39)/ My World Is Empty Without You (6:45)/ When We Two Parted (6:45)/ Retarded (3:50)/ Fountain And Fairfax (3:54)/ Come See About Me (5:02)/ You My Flower (3:49)/ What Jail Is Like (3:45)/ Tonight (3:22)/ Miles Is Dead (5:1?)
R: Exs Soundboard.   S: 'Gentlemen' tour Europe '94.   C: ECD. Dcc.

CD - FLIP YOUR WHIGS
KISS THE STONE KTS 333
If I Were Going (3:33)/ Debonair (4:29)/ Turn On The Water (8:04)/ Gentlemen (4:36)/ Be Sweet (3:38)/ My World Is Empty Without You (6:30)/ When We Two Parted (6:45)/ Retarded (3:45)/ Fountain And Fairfax (3:59)/ Come See About Me (5:05)/ You My Flower (8:46)/ What Jail Is Like (3:45)/ Tonight (3:22)/ Miles Iz Dead (5:13)/ The Back Beat Band: Money (2:25)/ Long Tall Sally (1:56)
R: Exs. Soundboard.   S: Europe spring '94. Tracks 15-16 Los Angeles 6 '94.   C: ECD. Dcc. Pic CD. Time 75:56.

ALICE IN CHAINS

CD - JOHNNY STEROID'S LAST SHOW
BLUE KNIGHT RECORDS BKR 27
Dam That River (3:20)/ We Die Young (2:32)/ Them Bones (3:06)/ Would (4:11)/ Rooster (6:51)/ Sick Man (5:49)/ It Ain't Like That (5:07)/ Dirt (6:20)/ Hate To Feel (5:54)/ Fuck You, Fuck You, Where' My Dick (3:14)/ Angry Chair (4:22)/ Man In The Box (4:54)/ Put You Down (3:55)/ Rain When I Die (6:38)/ Love, Hate, Love (7:24)

R: G. Audience.   S: Europe '93.   C: ECD.

CD - TIE ME UP
HOME RECORDS HR 5920 6
Dam That River (3:24)/ Them Bones (2:35)/ Would
(3:41)/ Love Hate Love (6:58)/ God Smack (4:79)/
Junkhead (6:29)/ A Little Bitter (4:06)/ Rain When I
Die (4:05)/ Hate To Feel (5:32)/ Rooster (7:02)/
Would (3:42)/ Angry Chair (3:43)/ Sickman (4:09)
R: G-Vg. Audience.   S: Tracks 1-10 Portland,
Oregon June. 20 '93. Tracks 11-13 'Rock For The
Environment'.   C: ECD. Dcc. Pic CD.

ALLMAN BROTHERS BAND, THE

CD - A HOT STEAMY SUMMER NIGHT
ROYAL SOUND MUSIC RSM 044 CD
Blue Sky/ All Night Train/ Same Thing/ Seven
Turns/ Jessica/ No One To Run With/ Back Where
It All Begins/ Whipping Post
S: The Walnut Creek Amphitheater Raleigh, NC
'94.   C: ECD.

CD - BACK IN NEW YORK CITY '94
FRONT ROW FRONT FM 2101/2/3
CD1: Sailing (5:49)/ Statesboro Blues (7:11)/ Blue
Sky (8:37)/ All Night Train (5:32)/ Same Thing
(9:00)/ Soulshine (6:49)/ Seven Turns (5:46)/
Medley: Jessica, Mountain Jam, Jessica (15:56)/
Midnight Rider (3:23)
CD2: Temptation Is A Gun (6:09)/ One Way Out
(13:22)/ Change My Way Of Living (8:18)/ You
Don't Love Me (7:27)/ Dreams (15:19)/ Back
Where It All Begins (11:44)
CD3: Medley: In Memory Of Elizabeth Reed,
Drums, In Memory Of Elizabeth Reed (37:10)/
Nobody Left (6:06)/ Whipping Post (16:22)
R: Ex. Audience.   S: Beacon Theatre, New York
City Apr. 1 '94.   C: ECD. Dcc.

CD - DIXIE FLAG
TEDDY BEAR RECORDS TB 42
Statesboro Blues (5:42)/ Blue Sky (6:56)/
Soulshine (7:01)/ Midnight Rider (4:15)/ Melissa
(11:54)/ No One To Run With (6:24)/ Back Where
It All Begins (10:45)/ One Way Out (11:16)/
Whipping Post (11:49)
R: Exs. Soundboard.   S: Woodstock, Saugerties,
NY Aug. 13 '94.   C: ECD. Pic CD.

CD - NEW YORK CITY BLUES
GOLD STANDARD AB-22-94-06
Introduction/ Statesboro Blues/ Trouble No More/
Don't Keep Me Wondering/ Did Somebody Wrong/
One Way Out/ Tuning Up/ (In Memory Of)
Elizabeth Reed/ Stormy Monday/ You Don't Love
Me
R: Exs. Soundboard.   S: A & R Studios, NYC
Apr. '71.   C: ECD. Dcc. Time 72:43.

CD - SOUTHERN REVENGE
TEDDY BEAR RECORDS TB30
Intro (0:57)/ Statesboro Blues (4:09)/ One Way
Out (4:56)/ In Memory Of Elizabeth Reed (12:32)/

Whipping Post (19:00)/ You Don't Love Me, Soul
Serenade (17:25)
R: Vg-Exs. Soundboard.   S: Fillmore East, New
York City June 26 '71 (closing night).   C: ECD.
Dcc. Pic CD.

CD - SWEET MELISSA - AN ACOUSTIC EVENING
KISS THE STONE KTS 286
Come Into My Kitchen (5:29)/ Seven Turns (4:18)/
Goin' Down The Road (5:22)/ Midnight Rider
(3:00)/ Southbound (5:36)/ In Memory Of Elizabeth
Reed (9:34)/ Melissa (5:03)/ Come Into My
Kitchen (5:12)/ Come And Go Blues (5:13)/
Melissa (3:33)
R: Ex.   S: Track 1-7 Los Angeles June. 11 '92.
Track 8 USA Oct. '91. Tracks 9-10 USA Dec. 27
'81.   C: ECD. Pic CD.

AMOS, TORI

CD - AFTER BURN
HAWK 036
Tear In Your Hand (6:01)/ Silent All These Years
(4:31)/ Upside Down (4:39)/ Mary (4:31)/ Girl
(4:25)/ Whole Lotta Love (1:51)/ Thank You (2:24)/
Leather (3:24)/ Precious Things (5:06)/ Sugar
(3:48)/ Love Song (4:37)/ Little Drummer Boy
(4:34)/ Crucify (3:25)/ Winter (4:28)/ Love Line
(12:44)
R: Ex. Audience/Soundboard.   S: Track 1
Backstage Tavern, Ballard, WA May 6 '92. Track 2
The Dennis Miller Show '92. Track 3 Carefree
Theatre, West Palm Beach, FL Aug. 16 '92. Track
4 Henry Theatre, Hollywood, CA Aug. 24 '92.
Tracks 5-8 Coach House, San Juan Capistrano
Sept. '92. Track 9 'Kevin And Bean' Show, KROQ
Radio Pasadena, CA Sept. 10 '92. Tracks 10-11
KROQ Radio, Pasadena, CA Jan 19 '93. Track 12
Baltimore, Maryland Nov. 12 '92. Tracks 13-14
The Tonight Show Jan. 11 '93. Track 15 KROQ
Radio Studio, Pasadena, CA Sept. '92.   C: ECD.
Dcc. Pic CD.

CD - ANYTHING BUT HONEY
OCTOPUS OCTO 061
American Pie (2:35)/ Smells Like A Teen Spirit
(4:31)/ Icicle (4:55)/ Crucify (6:36)/ Happy
Phantom (4:02)/ God (4:15)/ Silent All These
Years (5:44)/ Bells For Her (6:06)/ Winter (8:34)/
Cornflake Girl (5:12)/ China (6:16)/ Wrapped
Around Your Finger (6:37)/ Cloud On My Tongue
(5:35)/ Sugar (6:42)
R: Ex. Audience.   S: Tracks 1-11 Palladium,
London Apr. 29 '94. Tracks 12-14 Tampa Theater,
Tampa Aug. 3 '94.   C: ECD. Dcc. Pic CD.
Time 77:45.

CD - BACK TO BASICS
BLUE MOON RECORDS BMCD 19/20
CD1: Intro/ Home On The Range/ Crucify*/ Pretty
Good Year*/ Precious Things*/ Icicle/ Happy
Phantom/ God/ Silent All The Years/ Past The
Mission/ The Waitress*/ Leather/ Smells Like Teen

Spirit
CD2: Tear In Your Hand*/ Bells For Her/ Me And A Gun/ Winter/ Cornflake Girl/ Famous Blue Raincoat/ Upside Down/ China/ Space Dog*/ A Case Of You*/ Yes Anastasia*/ Song For Eric*/ Ain't No Sunshine**/ Imagine**
R: Ex. Audience.   S: Her Majesty's Theatre, Haymarket, London, England Mar. 6 '94. *Cambridge Corn Exchange Mar. 4 '94. ** Toscas, Switzerland '91.   C: ECD. Dcc.

CD - CANADIAN SPRING
ANGRY DINO AD 1012
Smells Like Teen Spirit (4:04)/ Icicle (4:25)/ Precious Things (6:04)/ Happy Phantom (3:58)/ Pretty Good Year (4:04)/ God (4:12)/ Silent All These Years (5:14)/ Leather (3:40)/ Upside Down (6:30)/ Me And A Gun (6:30)/ Winter (6:20)/ A Case Of You (5:20)/ Here In My Head (5:25)/ Angie (5:50)/ Cornflake Girl (5:30)
R: Vg. Audience.   S: The Olympic Theatre, Montreal Apr. 2 '94.   C: ECD. Dcc.

CD - CHILDHOOD MEMORIES
INSECT IST 62/63
CD1: Intro - Space Dog/ Crucify/ Icicle/ Precious Things/ Leather/ God/ Silent All These Years/ Upside Down/ The Waitress
CD2: Bells For Her/ Me And A Gun/ Cornflake Girl/ American Pie/ Smells Like A Teen Spirit/ Cloud On My Tongue/ A Case Of You/ Winter/ Baker Baker/ Pretty Good Year
R: Ex. Audience.   S: Raleigh, North Carolina July 29 '94.   C: ECD. Dcc. Pic CDs. Time CD1 51:02. CD2 51:42.

CD - CORNFLAKE GIRL
GRAPEFRUIT GRA-009-A
Crucify (6:08)/ Silent All These Years (5:16)/ Happy Phantom (3:43)/ Girl (4:25)/ Whole Lotta Love (4:12)/ Leather (3:36)/ Smells Like Teen Spirit (3:44)/ China (5:44) Cornflake Girl (3:16)/ Pretty Good Year (2:36)/ Baker Baker (3:16)/ God (3:37)/ Sugar (5:45)/ Precious Things (5:45)/ Tear In Your Hand (5:19)/ Winter (7:02)
R: Ex.   S: San Juan '92. New York '94. Toronto, Canada '92.   C: Australian CD. Dcc.

CD - CORNFLAKE GIRL
NOT GUILTY NG 490794
Sugar (4:01)/ Precious Things (5:52)/ Icicle (4:40)/ Crucify (6:19)/ Leather (3:46)/ God (4:00)/ Upside Down (5:14)/ Waitress (3:20)/ Bells For Her (5:41)/ Winter (6:51)/ Cornflake Girl (6:03)/ Landslide (4:18)/ Yes, Anastasia (6:22)/ China (5:46)
R: Ex. Audience.   S: New Haven, Conn. June '94.   C: ECD. Dbw. Orange type.

CD - EUROPE 1992
RARITIES & FEW RFCD 1314
New Shoes, Flying Dutchman (8:05)/ Crucify (6:26)/ Silent All These Years (4:57)/ Precious Things (5:08)/ Leather (4:11)/ Whole Lotta Love (3:43)/ Thank You (4:53)/ Happy Phantom (3:21)/

China (5:25)/ Tear In Your Hand (4:58)/ Me And A Gun (5:18)/ Winter (6:23)/ Smells Like Teen Spirit (3:14)/ Mother (6:47)/ Sugar (5:21)
R: Ex. Audience.   S: Frankfurt, Germany June '92.   C: ECD. Dbw.

CD - FAIRY TALES
KISS THE STONE KTS 353
American Pie (2:32)/ Smells Like Teen Spirit (4:30)/ Icicle (4:56)/ Crucify (6:20)/ The Happy Phantom (4:18)/ God (4:15)/ Silent All These Years (5:44)/ Bells For Her (6:06)/ Winter (7:48)/ Cornflake Girl (5:11)/ China (6:01)/ Leather (4:09)/ Upside Down (6:08)/ Cloud On My Tongue (5:28)/ A Case Of You (5:41)
R: Ex. Audience.   S: Tracks 1-11 Europe Apr. 29 '94. Tracks 12-15 USA July 29 '94.   C: ECD. Dcc. Pic CD.

CD - I LIKE LED ZEPPELIN AND I LOVE THE STONES
SUGARCANE RECORDS SC 52017/18
CD1: Crucify (5:11)/ Leather (3:21)/ Silent All These Years (5:30)/ Winter (5:58)/ Crucify (6:11)/ Silent All These Years (4:51)/ Happy Phantom (3:25)/ Me And A Gun (5:06)/ Winter (6:34)/ Smells Like Teen Spirit (3:10)
CD2: Crucify (6:20)/ Silent All These Years (5:19)/ Precious Things (5:19)/ Happy Phantom (4:01)/ Leather (3:33)/ Tear In Your Hand (5:20)/ Whole Lotta Love (2:03)/ Thank You (2:24)/ Me And A Gun (5:54)/ Winter (6:58)/ Smells Like Teen Spirit (3:40)/ China (5:48)/ Angie (5:28)
R: Ex.   S: CD1 tracks 1-4 Chicago Mar. 3 '93. Tracks 5-10 Charleston July '92. CD2 Albany Nov. 8 '92.   C: ECD. Dcc.

CD - I LOVE TOFFEE APPLES
MOAS MUSIC 001
Crucify (8:16)/ Icicle (4:42)/ Precious Things (6:22)/ Leather (3:41)/ God (4:08)/ Silent All These Years (5:57)/ The Waitress (4:24)/ Honey (4:15)/ Bells For Her (6:18)/ Me And A Gun (6:04)/ Cornflake Girl (5:14)/ Here In My Head (5:06)/ The Wrong Band (4:16)/ Sister Janet (4:09)/ Case Of You (5:25)
R: Ex. Audience.   S: Wolverhampton Civic Hall Apr. 30 '94.   C: ECD. Dcc. Pic CD.

CD - L'AFFAIRE D'AMOREUSE
MONTANTA MO 10005
C: See 'The Piano' (LU 2005) for songs and source.

CD - LAST TEMPTATION OF TORI
ALLEY CAT 051
American Pie/ Smells Like Teen Spirit/ Pretty Good Year/ Crucify/ Icicle/ Happy Phantom/ God/ Bells For Her/ Me And A Gun/ Baker Baker/ Cornflake Girl/ Tear In Your Hand/ Summertime/ Winter
R: Ex. Audience.   S: Trinitatiskrin Cathedral Berlin, Germany '94.   C: ECD. Dcc. Pic CD. Time 75:26.

CD - LITTLE EARTHQUAKES, DEMOS & OUTTAKES

COLLECTORS PLEASURE COP 011
Crucify (outtake) (4:14)/ Winter (percussion mix) (5:30)/ Happy Phantom (outtake) (3:20)/ Take To The Sky (demo) (4:20)/ Leather (demo) (3:16)/ Sarah Sylvia Cynthia Stout (outtake) (2:34)/ Little Drummer Boy (radio promo) (3:05)/ Crucify (solo piano demo) (5:23)/ Thoughts (solo piano demo) (2:46)/ Song For Eric (outtake) (1:13)/ Mary (demo) (4:20)/ Silent All These Years (solo piano demo) (3:55)/ Leather (solo piano demo) (3:14)/ The Pool (demo) (2:51)/ China (solo piano demo) (5:54)
R: Exs. Soundboard.   C: ECD. Dcc. Pic CD.

CD - LITTLE RARITIES

PIANO CLASSICS PIC01
Upside Down/ Here In My Head/ Thank You/ Angie/ Flying Dutchman/ Sugar/ Sweet Dreams/ Take To The Sky/ Mary/ Smells Like Teen Spirit/ Humpty Dumpty/ Thoughts/ Song For Eric/ Ode To The Banana King/ The Pool/ The Happy Worker, Happy Phantom (live)/ Precious Things (live)/ Mother (live)
R: Exs. Soundboard.   C: ECD. Dcc.

CD - ME AND A PIANO

FLASHBACK 01 940227
Numbness (1:38)/ Crucify (5:54)/ These Precious Things (5:26)/ Happy Phantom (3:35)/ Leather (3:26)/ In My Head (4:37)/ Little Earthquakes (8:32)/ Whole Lotta Love (1:49)/ Welcome (2:48)/ Me And A Gun (5:45)/ Winter (5:45)/ Smells Like Teen Spirit (3:28)/ Mother (6:51)/ Tear In Your Hand (5:16)/ Song For Eric (2:31)
R: Vgs. Audience.   S: Moore Theatre, Seattle Aug. 29 '92.   C: ECD. Dcc.

CD - A MESSAGE FOR YOUR HEART

RED PHANTOM RPCD 1154
Happy Phantom (4:11)/ Crucify (8:50)/ Silent All These Years (5:18)/ Precious Thing (5:44)/ Tear In Your Hand (7:33)/ Whole Lotta Love (4:45)/ Winter (6:48)/ Smells Like Teen Spirit (3:38)/ Silent All These Years (4:41)
R: Exs. Soundboard.   S: Phoenix Club, Toronto Oct. '92.   C: ECD.

CD - MILAN 1994

LIVE STORM LSCD 51572
Crucify (3:28)/ Icicle (4:50)/ Precious Things (5:55)/ Leather (4:23)/ God (8:25)/ Silent All These Years (5:33)/ The Waitress (4:27)/ Here In My Head (5:09)/ Baker Baker (5:04)/ Cornflake Girl (6:15)/ American Pie (2:55)/ Smells Like Teen Spirit (4:05)/ Past The Mission (4:26)/ Winter (7:18)
R: Ex. Audience.   S: Milan, Italy Apr. 18 '94.
C: ECD. Dbw.

CD - THE PIANO

LUNATIC LU 2005
Smells Like Teen Spirit/ Happy Phantom/ Crucify/ Silent All These Years/ Precious Thing/ Leather/ Tear In Your Hand/ Whole Lotta Love/ Little Earthquakes/ Angie/ Me And A Gun/ China/ Mother
R: Ex.   S: Toronto '93.   C: ECD. Dcc. CD looks like a record. Time 67:43.

CD - POPCORN GIRL

SHINOLA SH 69011
Hopeless (5:34)/ Crucify (6:20)/ Tear It Down (3:02)/ You (3:43)/ Precious Thing (5:57)/ Josie's Arms (7:57)/ I Believe In Peace (3:34)/ Steps (5:58)/ Leather (3:45)/ Silent All These Years (5:33)/ Burnin' Inside (7:32)/ Cloudy Sky (4:24)/ Cornflake Girl (1:59)
R: Vg. Audience.   S: Live USA '94.   C: ECD. Dcc.

CD - RHAPSODY IN PINK

ALLEY KAT 040/41
CD1: Sugar/ Crucify/ Icicle/ Precious Things/ Happy Phantom/ Pretty Good Year/ God/ Silent All These Years/ Past The Mission/ The Waitress/ Leather/ Smells Like Teen Spirit/ Me And A Gun/ Baker Baker
CD2: Cornflake Girl/ Tear In Your Hand/ Winter/ Song For Eric/ Flying Dutchman (Edinburgh, Scotland Feb. 28 '94)/ Mother (Eugene, OR. Aug. 30 '92)/ Bells For Her (Glasgow, Scotland Feb. 27 '94)/ Little Earthquakes (Eugene, OR. Aug. 30 '94)/ Upside Down (Eugene, OR. Aug. 30 '94)/ A Case For You (LA Mar. 22 '94)/ China (Newcastle, England Feb. '94)/ God (LA Mar. '94)/ Icicle (LA Mar. '94)/ Baker Baker (LA Feb. '94)
R: Ex. Audience.   S: UW Meany Hall, Seattle Mar. 20 '94.   C: ECD. Dcc. Pic CDs. Time CD1 67:31. CD2 74:35.

CD - SPIRIT IN THE SKY

KISS THE STONE KTS325
Flying Dutchman (6:15)/ Crucify (6:24)/ Icicle (4:11)/ Precious Things (5:50)/ Happy Phantom (5:48)/ Pretty Good Years (4:09)/ God (4:13)/ Silent All These Years (5:28)/ The Waitress (3:29)/ Smells Like Teen Spirit (4:09)/ Baker Baker (3:36)/ Cornflake Girl (5:23)/ Here In My Head (4:55)/ God (3:44)/ Baker Baker (3:14)/ Cornflake Girl (3:22)/ Pretty Good Year (2:49)
R: Ex. Audience.   S: Symphony Space, NYC Mar. 29 '94.   C: ECD. Dcc. Pic CD.

CD - SUGAR BABY

BANZI BZCD 042
Crucify/ Space Dog/ Precious Things/ Icicle/ God/ China/ The Waitress/ Bells For Her/ Baker, Baker/ Cornflake Girl/ Silent All These Years/ Past The Mission/ A Case Of You/ American Pie/ Smells Like Teen Spirit
R: Ex. Audience.   S: Orpheum Theatre, San Francisco Sept. '94.   C: ECD. Dcc. Pic CD. Time 77:17.

CD - TEEN SPIRIT

INTERNATIONAL BROADCAST RECORDINGS

IBR 2335
Crucify (5:11)/ Leather (3:21)/ Silent All These
Years (5:30)/ Winter (5:58)/ Crucify (6:11)/ Silent
All These Years (4:51)/ Happy Phantom (3:25)/
Me And A Gun (5:06) Winter (6:34)/ Smells Like
Teen Spirit (3:10)
R: Exs. Soundboard.   S: Tracks 1-4 WKQX,
Chicago Mar. 3 '93. Tracks 5-10 Mountain Stage,
Charleston July '92.   C: ECD. Dcc.

CD - TORI THE FOX
ROCKS 92129
Sugar (4:26)/ Crucify (9:33)/ Icicle (4:30)/ Precious
Things (6:06)/ Happy Phantom (6:39)/ Pretty Good
Year (4:06)/ God (4:27)/ Silent All These Years
(5:13)/ The Waitress (3:30)/ Leather (3:32)/ Me
And A Gun (6:32)/ Baker Baker (4:37)/ Cornflake
Girl (5:22)/ Winter (7:40)
R: G. Audience.   S: New Orleans '94.   C: ECD.
Dcc.

CD - WINTER
TEDDY BEAR RECORDS TB44
Crucify (6:08)/ Silent All These Years (5:18)/
Precious Things (5:40)/ Happy Phantom (3:42)/
Leather (3:31)/ Upside Down (5:08)/ Little
Earthquakes (7:50)/ Whole Lotta Love (4:22)/
Winter (7:15)/ Smells Like Teen Spirit (3:42)/
Mother (7:33)/ China (5:52)/ Song For Eric (2:29)
R: Exs. Soundboard.   S: Boulder, Colorado
Sept. 9 '92.   C: ECD. Pic CD.

CD - WHOLE LOTTA TEEN SPIRIT
ROYAL SOUND MUSIC RSM 024
Crucify/ Silent All These Days/ The Happy
Phantom/ Girl/ Whole Lotta Love/ Leather/ Smells
Like Teen Spirit/ China
R: Ex.   S: Coach House, San Juan Capistrano
'93.   C: ECD. Time 39:03.

CD - A WOMAN ON A MISSION
HOME RECORDS - HR 5931 - 8
American Pie (2:02)/ Smells Like Teen Spirit
(4:00)/ Crucify (6:30)/ Icicle (6:39)/ Precious
Things (5:53)/ Leather (3:39)/ God (3:38)/
Cornflake Girl (1:42)/ Pretty Good Year (3:46)/
Flying Dutchman (6:56)/ China (6:00)/ Angie
(4:39)/ Me And A Gun (5:26)/ Mother (6:18)/
Happy Phantom (3:47)
R: Vg. Audience.   S: Palladium, Rome Apr. 19
'94.   C: ECD. Dcc. Pic CD.

ANDERSON, JON

CD - ALONE ON THE EDGE
COSMIC TRILLS PRODUCTION CT 50001
I've Seen All Good People (4:16)/ Yours Is No
Disgrace (2:36)/ Starship Trooper (7:53)/ All In A
Matter Of Time (3:20)/ Animation (9:02)/ Long
Distance Runaround (2:44)/ Close To The Edge
(2:57)/ Olympia (4:56)/ The Friends Of Mr. Cairo
(4:25)/ Roundabout (8:08)*
R: Vg-Ex. Soundboard.   S: Pittsburgh '82. *USA
'74 with Yes.   C: ECD. Dcc.

ATLANTA RHYTHM SECTION

CD - OUTLAW MUSIC
ROYAL SOUND MUSIC RSM 022SQ CD
Champagne Jam/ I'm Not Gonna Let It Bother Me
Tonight/ Imaginary Lover/ Interpolating/ Miss You/
So Into You/ Homesick/ Alien/ Large Time/
Spooky/ Long Tall Sally/ Doraville/ Angel/ Jukin'/
Interpolating/ San Antonio Rose
S: Savoy, New York '81 and Japan.   C: ECD.

B

BABES IN TOYLAND

CD - MOCKING BIRDS
HAWK 016
Swamp Pussy/ Ripe/ Blue Bell/ Right Now/ Pearl/
Blood/ Mother/ Magick Flute/ Won't Tell/ Real
Eyes/ Spun/ Bruise Violet/ Jungle Train/
Handsome & Gretel/ Catatonic/ He's My Thing
R: G-Vg. Audience.   S: LA, CA '92.   C: ECD.
Pic CD.

BAD RELIGION

CD - U.S.A. 1993
LIVE STORM LSCD 51621
Turn On The Light (1:50)/ Suffer (1:50)/ Generator
(3:09)/ Anesthesia (2:36)/ Flat Earth Society
(2:22)/ Modern Man (1:50)/ No Control (1:48)/ You
Are The Government (1:50)/ 21th Century Digital
Man (2:47)/ Only Entertainmont (3.03)/ No
Direction (3:06)/ Atomic Garden (2:43)/ I Want To
Conquer The World (2:18)/ Best For You (2:04)/
The Answer (1:50)/ Fuck Armageddon (2:06)/
Babies In The Dark (2:06)/ Get Off (1:50)/ Too
Much To Ask (2:45)/ Operation Rescue (1:50)/
Along The Way (1:52)/ Do What You Want (1:53)/
Change Of Ideas (1:55)/ Heaven Is Falling (1:50)/
Tomorrow (1:56)/ Automatic Man (1:50)/ We're
Gonna Die (2:17)
R: Exs. Soundboard.   C: ECD. Dcc.

BEACH BOYS, THE

CD - ALL SUMMER LONG
TRIANGLE PYCD083
California Girls (3:34)/ I Can Hear Music (2:24)/
Sloop John (2:39)/ Darlin' (1:59)/ Wouldn't It Be
Nice (2:49)/ Wouldn't It Be Nice/ In My Room
(2:20)/ Do It Again (4:19)/ 409 (1:56)/ Shut You
Down/ Little Old Lady From Pasadena (0:44)/ Little
Deuce Coupe (1:44)/ I Get Around (1:57)/
Runaway (2:41)/ God Only Knows (2:36)/ Come
And Go With Me (2:37)/ Be True To Your School
(2:35)/ Surfer Girl (2:27)/ All Summer Long (1:13)/
Help Me Rhonda (2:10)/ Rockin' All Over The
World (2:44)
R: Ex.   S: Jamaica World Music Festival,
Montego Bay, Jamaica Nov. 26 '82.   C: ECD.

CD - IT'S ABOUT TIME
CAPRICORN RECORDS CR 2004
Heroes And Villains/ Do It Again/ Darling/ Aren't
You Glad/ Cotton Fields/ Vegetables/ Okie From
Muskogee/ Cool Cool Water/ Help Me Rhonda/
Student Demonstration Time/ Caroline No/ You
Still Believe In Me/ Sloop John B./ Wouldn't It Be
Nice/ God Only Knows/ Good Vibrations/
California Girls/ Surfer Girl/ I Get Around/ It's
About Time
R: Vg. Disturbing static. S: Syracuse University,
New York May 1 '71. C: ECD. Time 69:32.

CD - PET SOUNDS REHEARSALS
YELLOW DOG YD 029
Wouldn't It Be Nice (1:54)/ I Just Wasn't Made
For These Times (takes 1-5) (15:45)/ Studio
Chatter (dialogue) (3:36)/ Piano Practices (You
Still Believe In Me) (10:33)/ I Just Wasn't Made
For These Times (takes 6-23) (17:33)/ You Still
Believe In Me (2:46)/ I'm Waiting For The Day
(3:03)
R: Vg-Ex. S: Studio rehearsals. C: ECD. Dcc.

CD - SUMMER SOUNDS (& PET SESSIONS!!)
INVASION UNLIMITED IU 9410-1
Help Me Rhonda (vocals only)/ A 'Real' Big
Session With The 'Very' Bull Daddy (a painful
confrontation between father and son during 'Help
Me Rhonda' vocals)/ Help Me Rhonda (stereo
mix)/ In The Back Of My Mind (stereo backing
track)/ Please Let Me Wonder (rough mix)/ Good
To My Baby (stereo backing track)/ Good To My
Baby (stereo mix)/ Do You Wanna Dance (vocal
session)/ I'm So Young (stereo mix)/ You've Got
To Hide Your Love Away (unreleased)/ Be My
Baby (unreleased)*/ The Little Girl I Once Knew
(stereo backing track)/ Wouldn't It Be Nice (early
backing track)/ Wouldn't It Be Nice (different
vocal)/ I Just Wasn't Made For These Times
(different vocal)/ I'm Waiting For The Day (backing
track)/ I'm Waiting For The Day (different vocal)/
You Still Believe In Me (early stereo backing
tracks - 3 takes)/ You Still Believe In Me (different
vocal, stereo mix)/ Don't Talk (Put Your Head On
My Shoulder) (backing track)/ Holy Holy
(unreleased)/ Time To Get Alone (produced by
Brian Wilson for vocal group 'Redwood' which
became 'Three Dog Night'. The same backing
track was later used for The Beach Boys version)
R: Ex. Some Vg. *G. All soundboard. S: All
songs recorded at Western Studios, LA. Tracks 1-
9 'Beach Boys Today' session outtakes '65.
Tracks 10-11 'Beach Boys Party' session outtakes
Oct. '65. Track 12 single autumn '65. Tracks 13-21
'Pet Sounds' session outtakes early '66. Tracks
22-23 '67. C: ECD. Dcc. Time 75:39.

CD - TIME TO GET ALONE
SILVER SHADOW CD 9316-2
CD1: Help Me Rhonda Sessions/ Mountain Of
Love/ You've Got To Hide Love Away/ Ticket To
Ride/ Student Demonstration Time/ Laugh At Me
CD2: I'm So Young/ Help Me Rhonda/ Good To

My Baby (instrumental)/ Good To My Baby/ In The
Back Of My Mind/ Little Girl I Once Know/ Holy
Holy/ Time To Get Alone/ Wouldn't It Be Nice/ You
Still Believe In Me
R: G. S: CD1 track 1 'Help Me Rhonda'
sessions '65. Tracks 2-10 rehearsals '65 ('Party
Session' tapes). CD2 tracks 1-7 demos '65. Track
8 demo '67. Tracks 9-17 'Pet Sounds' demos '66.

BEASTIE BOYS, THE

CD - BEASTIE SONGS
ANGRY DINO AD 1013
Sure Shot (2:51)/ Shake Your Rump (4:31)/ Tough
Guy (1:03)/ Time For Living 2:44)/ The Update
(4:08)/ Allright, Hear This (4:41)/ Rhyming &
Stealing (5:35)/ Sabotage (3:01)/ Flute Loop
(2:03)/ Heart Attack Man (1:56)/ Sabotage (2:56)/
The Update (4:20)/ Drifter (1:43)/ Stand
Together/Root Down (6:07)/ Time to Get III/The
Scoop (6:20)/ Posse In Effect (3:02)/ Ricky's
Theme (2:40)/ Somethings Got To Give (4:02)/
Flutterman's Rule (2:45)/ Slow And Low
R: G-Vg. Audience. S: III Communication Tour,
USA '94. C: ECD. Dcc.

CD - GOOFIN' AROUND
HOME RECORDS HR5958-1
Pass The Mic (4:36)/ Do It (3:17)/ Finger Lickin'
Good (Mix) (2:56)/ Tough Guy (1:00)/ Time For
Livin' (1:49)/ Pow (1:45)/ Sabrosa (3:21)/ The
Maestro (3:21)/ Allright Hear This (3:16)/ Drifter
(1:43)/ Stand Together Root Down (6:07)/ Time To
Get III The Scoop (6:20)/ Posse In Effect (3:02)/
Ricky's Theme (2:40)/ Elbow Room (3:26)/
Freebird (4:18)/ Transit Cop (1:54)/ Heart Attack
Man (2:38)/ Something's Got To Give (4:02)/
Sabotage (3:06)/ Flutterman's Rule (2:45)/ Slow
And Low (2:18)/ So What'Cha Want (3:27)
R: G-Vg. Audience. S: City Square, Milan June
'94. C: ECD. Dcc. Pic CD.

CD - RABID
KISS THE STONE KTS 364
Egg Man (2:35)/ Do It (3:16)/ Pass The Mic (4:31)/
Tough Guy (1:29)/ Futtermans Rule, The Update
(7:36)/ Pow (1:53)/ The Maestro (4:02)/ Allright
Hear This (2:59)/ Time To Get III (2:24)/ Stand
Together (2:20)/ Boot Down (3:17)/ Bodhisativa
Row (2:46)/ Elbow Room (2:38)/ Heart Attack Man
(2:02)/ Sabotage (2:55)/ Sabotage (3:50)/ Sure
Shot (2:56)
R: Ex. S: Paradiso, Amsterdam, Holland June
21 '94. Tracks 16-17 MTV Video Music Awards,
Radio City Music Hall, NYC Sept. 8 '94. Track 18
NYC Aug. '94. C: ECD. Dcc. Pic CD.

CD - SEVEN DAY WEEKEND
KISS THE STONE KTS 320
Sure Shot (2:51)/ Shake Your Rump (4:31)/ Tough
Guy (1:03)/ Time For Living (2:44)/ The Update
(4:08)/ Allright, Hear This (4:41)/ Rhyming And
Stealing (5:35)/ Sabotage (3:01)/ Flute Loop
(2:03)/ Heart Attack Man (1:56)/ Sabotage (2:56)/

The Update (special effects version) (4:20)
R: Ex. Audience.   S: Europe '94.   R: ECD.
Dcc. Pic CD.

BEATLES, THE

CD - ACROSS THE UNIVERSE
OIL WELL RSC 032 CD
Ob La Di, Ob La Da/ Tomorrow Never Knows/ A
Day In The Life/ Yes It Is/ I Saw Her Standing
There/ Norwegian Wood/ Not Guilty #1/ Across
The Universe/ While My Guitar Gently Weeps/
Ticket To Ride/ One After 909/ A Taste Of Honey/
I Feel Fine/ Yer Blues/ Blues Jam/ Not Guilty #2/
Get Back/ Mailman Bring Me No More Blues/ Do
You Want To Know A Secret/ All You Need Is
Love
R: Ex. Soundboard.   S: Outtakes. All is not all
well at Oil Well if they think this 'Live in Sheffield
Mar. 3 '64' as declared on the cover.   C: ECD.
Dcc. Time 65:46.

CD - ALL MY LOVING
GRAPEFRUIT GRA-001-C
'From Us To You' (From Me To You) 1:03)/ Roll
Over Beethoven (2:16)/ Johnny B Goode (2:49)/ I
Wanna Be Your Man (2:08)/ All My Loving (2:08)/ I
Call Your Name (2:03)/ Can't Buy Me Love (2:13)/
Medley: Love Me Do, Please Please Me, From Me
To You, She Loves You/ I Want To Hold Your
Hand (4:01)/ Shout (2:03)/ 'With Monday To You'
(Happy Birthday) (:21)/ I Forget To Remember To
Forget (2:07)/ You Can't Do That (2:32)/ Matchbox
(1:56)/ Long Tall Sally (1:59)/ Things We Said
Today (2:21)/ And I Love Her (2:21)/ If I Fell
(2:11)/ I'm Happy Just To Dance With You (1:59)/ I
Should Have Known Better (2:38)/ Kansas City,
Hey! Hey! Hey! Hey! (2:47)/ A Hard Day's Night
(2:29)/ Honey Don't (2:27)/ I'll Follow The Sun
(1:53)/ Rock And Roll Music (2:09)/ Everybody Is
Trying To Be My Baby (2:26)/ I Feel Fine (2:07)/
R: G-Vg.   S: Chronology part 3 - '63-'64. See
'From Me To You', 'She Loves You' and
'Yesterday'.   C: Australian CD. Dcc.

CD - ALL THINGS MUST PASS (PART 2: ACOUSTIC SET)
YELLOW DOG YD 053
Dialogue, All Things Must Pass/ Dialogue, Isn't It a
Pity/ Window Window/ For You Blue/ Please Mrs.
Henry/ Rambling Woman Vol. 1/ Rambling
Woman Vol. 2/ I Threw It All Away Mama, You
Been On My Mind/ Old Brown Shoe/ Dialogue, For
You Blue
R: Ex.   S: 'Let It Be' rehearsals.   C: ECD. Dcc.
Time 51:59.

CD - ARTIFACTS II (THE DEFINITIVE COLLECTION OF BEATLES RARITIES 1960-69)
BIG MUSIC BIG BX 008
CD1: YOUNGBLOOD 1960-63: Hallelujah I Love
Her So (2:20), Wildcat (2:29), Movin' And Groovin'
(2:13), Hello Little Girl (1:54) (Hamburg '60)/ Ain't
She Sweet (2:14), Cry For a Shadow (2:23)

(Hamburg, June 22 '61)/ What'd I Say
(1:34)(Cavern Club Summer '62)/ Love of The
Loved (1:48), The Sheik Of Araby (1:39), Three
Cool Cats (2:19) (London '62)/ Dream Baby (2:01),
Please Mr. Postman (2:22) (BBC 'Teenager's
Turn' Mar. 7 '62)/ Besame Mucho (2:37) (EMI,
June. 6 '62)/ First Radio Interview (7:21) (Oct. 27
'62)/ I Saw Her Standing There (2:45), Lend Me
Your Comb (1:53) (Star Club, Hamburg Dec. 31
'62)/ Love Me Do (1:24) (home tape Jan. '63)/
There's A Place (2:05) (EMI take Feb. 11 '63)/ A
Taste Of Honey (2:15) (EMI take Feb. 11 '63)/ I
Saw Her Standing There (4:57) (EMI takes Feb.
11 '63)/ Do You Want To Know a Secret (2:05)
(EMI takes Feb. 11 '63)/ The One After 909 (4:24)
(EMI takes Mar. 5 '63)/ Thank You Girl (2:10) (EMI
takes Mar. 5 '63)/ The Hippy Hippy Shake (1:47)
(BBC Saturday Club Mar. 16 '63)/ Youngblood
(2:07) (BBC 'Pop Go The Beatles' June 1 '63)/
Soldier Of Love (2:36) (BBC 'Pop Go The Beatles'
July 2 '63)/ From Me To You (1:12) (Liverpool
Dec. 7 '63)/ The Beatles Christmas Record (4:59)
(EMI Dec. '63)/ All I Want For Christmas, Crimble
Medley (1:21) (BBC 'Saturday Club' Dec. 21 '63)
CD2: TICKET TO RIDE 1964-65: Guitar Blues
(1:06) (NYC Feb. 21 '64)/ I Wanna Be Your Man
(2:34) (BBC 'From Us To You' Feb. 28 '64)/ I Call
Your Name (2:11), I Got A Woman (2:35) (BBC
'Saturday Club' Mar. 31 '64)/ Hard Days Night
(2:38) (EMI take Ap. 16 '64)/ Honey Don't (2:22)
(BBC 'From Us To You' May 1 '64)/ From Us To
You (:58), I'm Happy Just To Dance With You
(1:59), I Should Have Known Better (3:08) (BBC
'From Us To You' July 17 '64)/ Leave My Kitten
Alone (2:55) (EMI take 4 Aug. 14 '64)/ I'm A Loser
(2:51) (EMI take 3 Aug. 14 '64)/ Twist And Shout
(1:23) (Hollywood Bowl Aug. 23 '64)/ She's A
Woman (3:19) (EMI take 2 Oct. 8 '64)/ I Feel Fine
(2:25) (EMI take 5 Oct. 18 '64)/ Another Beatles
Christmas Record (4:01) (EMI Oct. 26 '64)/
Christmas Outtake (3:25) (EMI Oct. 26 '64)/ Ticket
To Ride (3:25) (EMI take 5 Feb. 15 '65)/ Yes It Is
(4:27) (EMI takes 1&2 Feb. 16 '65)/ Help (3:10)
(EMI, Takes 6, 7 Apr. 16 '65)/ Ticket To Ride
(3:04) (BBC 'The Beatles' May 20 '65)/ Waltzing In
Matilda (:37) (Australian interview June. 15 '65)/
We Must Not Forget The General Erection, The
Wumberlog (Or, Magic Dog) (1:11) (BBC 'Tonight'
June 18 '65)/ We Can Work It Out (4:34) (EMI
takes 1 and 2 Oct. 20 '65)/ Run For Your Life
(1:16) (EMI take 5 Oct. 20 '65)/ Norwegian Wood
(2:28) (EMI take 4 Oct. 21 '65)/ Michelle (1:05)
(home demo Nov. '65)/ Think For Yourself (3:02)
(EMI take 1 Nov. 8 '65)/ The Beatles Third
Christmas Record (6:24) (EMI Nov. 8 '65
CD3: NORTHERN SONGS 1966-67: Rain (3:07)
(EMI take 7 Apr. 7 '66)/ Backwards Speech (1:00)
(EMI Apr. '66)/ Tomorrow Never Knows (2:56)
(EMI mono mix Apr. 27 '66)/ I'm Only Sleeping
(3:00) (EMI mono mix May 6 '66)/ For No One
(10:18) (EMI monitor mixes May 9-16 '66)/ Here,
There And Everywhere (5:55) (EMI monitor June
16 '66)/ Got To Get You Into My Life (2:39) (EMI
mono mixes June 20 '66)/ Backwards Speech

(:41) (Lennon tape Nov. 66)/ Strawberry Fields Forever (6:10) (EMI take 7 Nov. 28 '66)/ Strawberry Fields Forever (3:10) (EMI remix Dec. 15 '66)/ Pantomime: Everywhere It's Christmas (6:37) (Dick James House Nov. 25 '66)/ You Know My Name (1:02) (Lennon demo Jan. '67)/ A Day In The Life (4:52) (EMI reduction mix Jan. 19 '67)/ Penny Lane (2:55) (EMI mono mix Jan. 25 '67)/ Only A Northern Song (3:20) (EMI mono mix Apr. 21 '67)/ Magical Mystery Tour (2:46) (EMI mono mix May 4 '67)/ I Am The Walrus (4:12) (EMI Take 9 Sept. 5 '67)/ Christmas Time (Is Here Again) (5:46) (EMI complete version Nov. 28 '67)/ All Together On The Wireless Machine (:58) (BBC Dec. 12 '67)
CD4: ALONE TOGETHER 1968: Lady Madonna (1:18) (EMI monitor Feb. 3 '68)/ Across The Universe (3:43) (EMI alternative mix Feb. 4 '68)/ Step Inside Love (2:21) (McCartney demo Feb. '68)/ Act Naturally (2:15) (BBC TV Feb. 6 '68)/ The Continuing Story OF Bungalow Bill (2:33), While My Guitar Gently Weeps (2:33), Rocky Raccoon (2:43), Not Guilty (3:07), Yer Blues (3:26), Revolution (3:58), Cry Baby Cry (2:24) (Esher demos May '68)/ Julia (2:56), The Maharishi Song (3:11) (Lennon demos May '68)/ Blackbird (2:24) (EMI take 32 June. 11 '68)/ Everybody's Got Something To Hide Except For Me And My Monkey (2:36) (EMI alternative mix June 27 '68)/ Ob-La-Di, Ob-La-Da (3:14) (EMI take 23 July 15 '68)/ Don't Pass Me By (6:44) (EMI take 7 '68)/ Sexy Sadie (2:43) (EMI monitor mix July '68)/ Dear Prudence (3:48) (EMI alternate take Aug. 28 '68)/ Revolution (3:23) (promo film Sept. 4 '68)/ Helter Skelter (3:37) (EMI mono mix Sept. 17 '68)/ I'm So Tired (2:01) (EMI remix Oct. 8 '68)/ The Beatles 1968 Christmas Record (7:54) (home recordings Nov. '68)
CD5: THE LONGEST ROAD 1969: Up Against The Wall (4:20), Medley: Across The Universe, Rock'n Roll Music (2:45), Not Fade Away (2:54), When I'm 64 (1:26), Gimme Some Truth (:54), Polythene Pam (1:45), Medley, Take Me Home, A Quick One (3:39), Gilly Gilly Ossenfeffer Katzeneleen Bogen By The Sea (1:13), House Of The Rising Sun (3:03) (Twickenham Studios Jan. '69)/ Get Back (2:14), Let It Be (2:50) (Twickenham Studios Jan. '69)/ Hole In The Heart (:41) (Twickenham Studios Jan. '69)/ Two Of Us (6:56) (Twickenham Studios Jan. '69)/ All Things Must Pass (3:06) (Twickenham Studios Jan. '69)/ Rocker (2:24), Don't Let Me Down (3:46) (Apple Studios Jan. 22 '69)/ Teddy Boy (3:34) (Apple Studio Jan. 27 '69)/ The Walk (4:05) (Apple Studios Jan. 27 '69)/ Mailman Bring Me No More Blues (1:55) (Apple Studios Jan. 29 '69)/ The Long And Winding Road (3:44) (Apple Studios Jan. 31 '69)/ You Never Give Me Your Money (5:53) (Apple Studio May 6 '69)/ Something (5:41) (Apple Studios take 37 July 11 '69)/ The Beatles Seventh Christmas Record (7:43) (home recordings fall '69) R: Vg-Ex. Some good.   C: ECD. Box set. Jewel cases have Dcc. Pic CDs. Full color booklet. The second of the 'Artifacts' series brings more

important pieces of the puzzle together with excellent documentation. I predict these will become the sets to have for the best overview of the Fabs' unreleased.

CD - ARTIFACTS III (THE DEFINITIVE COLLECTION OF BEATLES RARITIES 1969-94) BIG MUSIC BIG BX 009
CD1: NOT FADE AWAY 1969-1971: Cold Turkey (3:32), Give Peace A Chance (:28) (demos fall '69)/ Only You Know And I Know (4:34) (Denmark Dec. 10 '69)/ Instant Karma (3:02) (BBC-TV Feb. 11 '70)/ Sentimental Journey (3:11) (promo film Mar. 15 '70)/ Every Time Somebody Comes To Town (1:22), I'd Have You Anytime (1:51), If Not For You (3:33) (studio sessions May '70)/ God (2:12), Well Well Well (1:10), My Mummy's Dead (1:14) (demos summer '70)/ Happy Birthday John (1:13) (private tape fall '70)/ I'm The Greatest (1:19) (demo fall '70)/ Oh Woman Oh Why (4:11) (promo single Jan. '71)/ God Save Us (1:56) (demo June '71)/ Imagine (3:06), I Don't Want To Be A Soldier (5:47), How Do You Sleep? (5:46) (early takes summer '71)/ McCartney Interview (2:36) (summer '71)/ Tragedy (3:10) (Sept. '71)/ Rave On, Not Fade Away (2:10) (Sept. '71)/ John's 31st Birthday (2:47) (Oct. 9 '71)/ Happy Xmas (War Is Over) (3:20) (alternate mix Oct. '71)/ Luck Of The Irish (3:13) (demo Nov. '71)/ Two Faced Man (3:40) (Dec. '71)/ Attica State (3:23) (Ann Arbor Dec. 10 '71)
CD2: SUE ME SUE YOU 1972-1975: Johnny B. Goode (3:10) (Feb. 16 '72)/ Don't Be Cruel (1:27), Hound Dog (2:57) (rehearsals Mar '72)/ 1882 (6:39) (Rotterdam Aug. 17 '72)/ Mother (4:55) (Aug. 30 '72)/ Sue Me Sue You Blues (2:52) (demo Dec. '72)/ Miss O'Dell (2:28) (acetate Jan. 73)/ Maybe I'm Amazed (3:38) (Mar. 73)/ Six O'Clock (4:57) (alternate take Apr. '73)/ Make Love Not War (3:17) (spring '73 demo)/ Lucille (5:55) (Mar. '74)/ Venus And Mars (2:16) (alternate mix summer '74)/ Hey Diddle (3:43) (Nashville June '74)/ Only You (3:11) (demo summer '74)/ Move Over Ms. L. (2:55) (outtake July '74)/ On Hand Clapping (1:15) (summer '74)/ I Lost My Little Girl (2:35) (summer '74)/ Dark Horse (4:20) (demo Sept. '74)/ I Saw Her Standing There (2:54) (rehearsal Nov. 24 '74)/ My Carnival (2:04) (Feb. 75)/ No No Song (2:09) (Apr. 28 '75)/ Hi Hi Hi (3:12) (Melbourne Nov. 13 '75)/ The Pirate Song (2:07) (Dec. 26 '75)
CD3: AS TIME GOES BY 1976-1980: As Time Goes By (:14)/ Mucho Mungo (:47) (early '76)/ I'm Gonna Love You Too (2:14) (summer '76)/ Rock Island Line (2:00), Bye Bye Love (2:55) (Nov. 19 '76)/ Boil Crisis (3:47) (spring '77)/ I Love My Suit (:54), Simple Life (:58) (summer '77)/ Scouse The Mouse (2:41) (fall '77)/ You're 16 (2:26) (Apr. 26 '78)/ Spin It On (2:15), Old Siam Sir (4:08), Robber's Ball (3:54) (summer '78)/ News Of The Day (4:32) (Nov. '78)/ Flying Hour (4:05) (Dec. '78)/ Mr. H. Atom (2:18), Summer's Day Song (3:16) (summer '79)/ Tears Of The World (3:50) (fall '79)/ Flying Horses (2:10), We All Stand

Together (3:54) (fall '79)/ My Life (3:11) (fall '79)/ With A Little Help From My Friends (:38) (winter '79)/ Beautiful Boy (2:46), Watching The Wheels (3:00) (summer '80)/ I'm Losing You (4:21) (summer '80)/ Serve Yourself (3:38) (fall '80)/ Dear John (4:17) (Nov. '80)
CD4: FREE AS A BIRD 1981-1994: My Old Friend (3:22) (Feb. '81)/ For No One (2:04) (winter '82)/ Twice In A Lifetime (2:21) (spring '83)/ On The Wings Of A Nightingale (2:27) (demo summer '84)/ Abandoned Love (4:11) (winter '84)/ Yvonne (4:17), Hanglide (5:18) (spring '85)/ Nonsense (2:28) (May '85)/ Everybody's Trying To Be My Baby (2:16), Honey Don't (3:00) (Oct. 21 '85)/ Love Is Strange (1:54) (summer '86)/ Hottest Gong In Town (3:39) (July '86)/ Peggy Sue (2:54) (Feb. 19 '87)/ Cut Across Shorty (2:15) (July '87)/ Every Grain Of Sand (1:36) (Feb. 10 '88)/ End Of The Line (3:14) (alternate take May '88)/ Put It There (2:03) (May 18 '89)/ Get Back (4:43) (Aug. 11 '89)/ I Call Your Name (2:43) (Mar. '90)/ Lennon Medley (4:30) (June 28 '90)/ Maxine (3:11) (summer '90)/ Between The Devil And The Deep Blue Sea (2:24) (June '91)/ Payment (1:20) (spring '92)/ Ride Rajbun (5:02) (summer '93)/ Free As A Bird (3:25) (demo '80)
R: Vg-Ex. Some good.   C: ECD. Box set. Jewel cases have Dcc. Pic CDs. Full color 24 page booklet. The third of the 'Artifacts' focuses on rare material from the solo years. Excellent documentation.

CD - AS NATURE INTENDED
VIGOTONE VT 122
Get Back/ Get Back/ Don't Let Me Down/ I've Got A Feeling/ The One After/ Dig A Pony/ I've Got A Feeling/ Don't Let Me Down/ Get Back/ Rocker/ Save The Last Dance For Me/ Don't Let Me Down/ Dig A Pony/ I've Got A Feeling/ For You Blue/ Teddy Bear/ Two Of Us/ Maggie Mae/ Dig It/ Let It Be/ The Long Winding Road/ Get Back
R: Ex. Soundboard.   S: Tracks 1-9 Apple Corps rooftop performance Dec. 30 '69. Tracks 10-22 Glyn John's first master tape compilation of 'Get Back' mixed Mar. 10-11, May 7, 9 Olympic Sound Studios, London.   C: ECD. Dcc. Time 71:54.

CD - CANDLESTICK PARK
MASTERDISC MCD 007
Rock & Roll Music/ She's A Woman/ If I Needed Someone/ Day Tripper/ Baby's In Black/ I Feel Fine/ Yesterday/ I Wanna Be Your Man/ Nowhere Man/ Paperback Writer/ Long Tall Sally (incomplete)
R: G.   S: Candlestick Park, San Francisco Aug. 29 '66. Direct from the Tony Barlow tape.
C: Japanese CD. Dbw. Numbered limited edition. Time 27:26.

CD - CONQUER THE WORLD (VOL. 1)
BANANA BAN-001-A
Introduction (0:47)/ I Saw Her Standing There (2:49)/ From Me To You (2:07)/ Money (2:51)/ Roll Over Beethoven (2:27)/ You Really Got A Hold On Me (3:05)/ She Loves You (2:30)/ Twist And Shout (2:46)/ Introduction (0:25)*/ She Loves You Version #2 (2:52)*/ Twist And Shout Version #2 (2:44)*/ I Saw Her Standing There Version #2 (2:53)*/ Long Tall Sally (1:48)*/ Interview (11:24)*
R: Vg. Soundboard. *G. Soundboard.   S: Europe '64.   C: Australian CD. Dcc.

CD - CONQUER THE WORLD (VOL. 2)
BANANA BAN-001-B
I Saw Her Standing There (4:39)/ I Want To Hold Your Hand (3:06)/ All My Loving (2:14)/ She Loves You (2:37)/ Till There Was You (2:15)/ Roll Over Beethoven (3:20)/ Can't Buy Me Love (2:30)/ This Boy (2:29)/ Twist And Shout (3:00)/ Long Tall Sally (4:18)/ You Can't Do That (3:02)/ All My Loving (2:18)/ She Loves You (3:07)/ Can't Buy Me Love (2:07)/ Twist And Shout (3:48)/ Long Tall Sally (2:10)
R: G-Vg. Soundboard. Some hiss.   S: Tracks 1-10 Adelaide, Australia June 12 '64. Tracks 11-16 Melbourne, Australia July 1 '64.   C: Australian CD. Dcc.

CD - CONQUER THE WORLD (VOL. 3)
BANANA BAN-001-C
Twist And Shout (1:37)/ She's A Woman (3:00)/ Can't Buy Me Love (2:42)/ I'm A Loser (2:55)/ I Wanna Be Your Man (2:31)/ A Hard Day's Night (2:41)/ Baby's In Black (2:32)/ Rock And Roll Music (2:05)/ Everybody's Trying To Be My Baby (2:32)/ I Feel Fine (2:25)/ Ticket To Ride (3:58)/ Long Tall Sally (2:05)/ Twist And Shout (1:28)/ She's A Woman (3:14)/ I'm A Loser (3:07)/ Can't Buy Me Love (2:27)/ Baby's In Black (2:49)/ I Wanna Be Your Man (2:26)/ A Hard Day's Night (2:53)/ Everybody's Trying To Be My Baby (2:38)/ Rock And Roll Music (2:22)/ I Feel Fine (2:13)/ Ticket To Ride (3:25)/ Long Tall Sally (2:09)
R: G. Soundboard.   S: France '65 - Tracks 1-12 afternoon show. Tracks 13-24 evening show.
C: Australian CD. Dcc.

CD - CONQUER THE WORLD (VOL. 4)
BANANA BAN-001-D
Introduction (1:12)/ Rock And Roll Music (1:36)/ She's A Woman (3:22)/ If I Needed Someone (3:03)/ Day Tripper (3:10)/ Baby's In Black (2:43)/ I Feel Fine (2:37)/ Yesterday (2:31)/ I Wanna Be Your Man (2:34)/ Nowhere Man (2:31)/ Paperback Writer (2:47)/ I'm Down (3:03)/ Introduction (1:12)/ Rock And Roll Music (1:35)/ She's A Woman (3:15)/ If I Needed Someone (2:48)/ Day Tripper (3:11)/ Baby's In Black (2:43)/ I Feel Fine (2:26)/ Yesterday (2:31)/ I Wanna Be Your Man (2:36)/ Nowhere Man (2:40)/ Paperback Writer (2:43)/ I'm Down (2:42)
R: G-Vg. Soundboard. Tracks 13-24 G. Soundboard.   S: Japan '66 - Tracks 1-12 June 30. Tracks 13-24 July 1.   C: Australian CD. Dcc.

CD - CONTROL ROOM MONITOR MIXES
YELLOW DOG YD 032
Across The Universe (outtake Feb. 4 '68)/ For No

One (take 1, take 2 May 9 '66)/ I'm The Walrus (take 7, 8 and 9 Sept. 5 '67)/ For No One (May 16 vocal overdub)/ Here There And Everywhere (June 16 '66)/ Sexie Sadie (bits and pieces July 19 '68)/ Brain Epstein Blues (July 19 '68)/ Sexie Sadie/ Lady Madonna (from unidentified session)/ Happiness Is A Warm Gun (single track from remix session Oct. 15 '68)/ I'm So Tired (backing track)/ I'm So Tired 1, I'm So Tired 2, I'm So Tired 3 (remixes)/ I'm So Tired 4 (incomplete)
R: Vg-Ex.   S: Off-line recording taped from studio monitors during the preliminary mix.
C: ECD. Dcc. Time 49:58.

CD - FIRST N' LAST
TRADE SECRETS ATLCD6593
Like Dreamers Do (2:33)/ Money (2:22)/ 'Till There Was You (2:58)/ The Sheik Of Arabia (1:40)/ To Know Her Is To Love Her (2:34)/ Take Good Care Of My Baby (2:26)/ Memphis, Tennessee (2:20)/ Sure To Fall (2:01)/ Hello Little Girl (1:38)/ Three Cool Cats (2:23)/ Crying, Waiting, Hoping (2:00)/ Love Of The Loved (1:50)/ September In The Rain (1:53)/ Besame Mucho (2:38)/ Searchin' (3:02)/ Let It Be (4:00)/ Don't Let Me Down (3:49)/ For You Blue (3:01)/ Get Back (2:54)/ The Walk (0:54)/ WBCN Dialogue (1:01)/ Get Back (2:37)/ I've Got A Feeling (0:09)/ Teddy Boy (5:47)/ Two Of Us (3:48)/ Dig A Pony (4:00)/ I've Got A Feeling (2:52)/ The Long And Winding Road (3:39)
R: Ex. Soundboard.   S: Tracks 1-15 Decca demo tapes, Decca Studios, London Jan. 1 '62. Tracks 16-28 reference acetate Mar. 10 '69 aired on radio station WBCN, Boston.   C: ECD. Dcc. Time 73:46.

CD - FROM ME TO YOU
GRAPEFRUIT GRA-001-A
Dream Baby (1:49)/ Memphis Tennessee (2:14)/ Please, Mr. Postman (2:04)/ Ask Me Why (2:17)/ Besame Mucho (2:25)/ A Picture Of You (2:17)/ Keep Your Hand Off My Baby (2:43)/ Beautiful Dreamer (1:58)/ I'm Talking About You (1:59)/ A Taste Of Honey (2:04)/ Thank You Girl (2:04)/ Side By Side (:44)/ Too Much Monkey Business (2:06)/ I'll Be On My Way (2:00)/ A Shot Of Rhythm And Blues/ Sure To Fall (In Love With You) (2:12)/ Money (That's What I Want) (2:41)/ I Got To Find My Baby (1:58)/ Youngblood (2:00)/ Till There Was You (2:15)/ Baby It's You (2:45)/ Anna (Go To Him) (3:02)/ Boys (2:31)/ Chains (2:18)/ P.S. I Love You (2:02)/ Some Other Guy (2:03)/ Memphis, Tennessee (2:22)/ From Me To You (1:53)/ That's All Right Mama (3:02)/ Carol 2:43)/ Soldier Of Love (2:03)/ Lend Me Your Comb (1:52)/ Clarabella (2:47)
R: G-Vg. Some poor - G.   S: Chronology part 1 - '62-'63. See 'All My Loving', 'She Loves You' and 'Yesterday'.   C: Australian CD. Dcc.

CD - HAIL, HAIL ROCK N' ROLL
OCTOPUSS OCT 001
Something/ Get Back/ Schooldays/ Stand By Me/ I've Got (Another) Feeling/ Two Of Us/ For You

Blue (false start)/ For You Blue/ Let It Be/ Take This Hammer/ Instrumental, Johnny Be Good/ Get Back (rock version)/ For You Blue/ Two Of Us/ Maggie Mae/ Dig It/ Dig It (long version)/ Let It Be/ It's Just For You/ I've Got A Feeling
R: Ex. Soundboard.   S: 'Let It Be' outtakes, Twikenham Studios.   C: ECD. Dcc. Time 58:08.

CD - HELLO GOODBYE (ONE DAY AT THE ABBEY ROAD STUDIOS)
LUNA RECORDS LU 9425-2
CD1: Intro - Revolution (:17)/ I Shall Be Released (1:48)/ Sun King, Don't Let Me Down (8:22)/ 'The Teacher Was A Looking' (1:42)/ Sun King (1:08)/ Two Of Us (11:18)/ Crackin' Up (:31)/ All Shook Up (1:05)/ Your True Love (1:43)/ Blue Suede Shoes (1:38)/ Three Cool Cats (2:43)/ Blowin' In The Wind (:32)/ Lucille (2:20)/ I'm So Tired (2:35)/ Ob-La-Di, Ob-La-Da (1:18)/ Third Man Theme (1:45)/ Negro In Reverse (:37)/ Because I Know You Love Me So (2:27)/ If Tomorrow Ever Comes (:59)/ I've Been Tickled That You Love Me So (:30)/ Won't You Please Say Goodbye (1:00)/ Bring It On Home To Me (1:52)/ Hitch Hike (1:51)/ You Can't Do That (2:26)/ Hippy Hippy Shake (2:29)/ Instrumental (:38)/ Short Fat Fanny (2:45)/ Midnight Special (2:08)/ When Your Drunk Think Of Me (:12)/ What's The Use Of Getting Sober (:08)/ What Do You Want To Make Those Eyes At Me For? (1:41)/ Money That's What I Want (1:16)/ Give Me Some Truth (1:58)/ Speak To Me (riff) When I'm Sixty-Four (2:01)/ Instrumental (:40)/ Oh! Darling (:37)/ From Me To You (:28)/ Don't Let Me Down, Devil In Her Heart (7:07)
CD2: Common Wealth (4:15)/ Get Off White Power (7:00)/ Honey Hush (2:11)/ For You Blue (2:09)/ Let It Be (2:49)/ Medley: Ramblin' Woman, I Threw It All Away, Mama You've Been On My Mind (7:14)/ Let It Be (rehearsal session) (8:31)/ Two Of Us (2:04)/ Hi Heeled Sneakers (2:40)/ Get Back (2:04)/ Get Back (rehearsal session) (5:00)/ Instrumental (:35)/ Lady Jane (:39)/ Jazz Piano Song (1:19)/ Piano Instrumental (:26)/ Woman (1:16)/ The Back Seat Of My Car (3:05)/ It's Just For You (rehearsal session) (5:41)/ Tea For Two (1:33)/ Chopsticks (:22)/ Whole Lotta Shakin' Goin' On (:47)/ Bad Boy (4:23)/ Sweet Little Sixteen, Around And Around (2:52)/ Almost Grown (1:47)/ Schooldays (1:36)/ Postcard Dialogue (2:42)/ All Along The Watchtower (:11)
R: Vg-Ex. Soundboard. Some hiss.   S: Abbey Road Studios '69.   C: ECD. Dcc.

CD - HERE WE GO
GREAT DANE RECORDS GDRCD 9326/10
The Trad Lads: Instrumental/ The Beatles: Misery, Do You Want To Know A Secret, Please Please Me/ Ben Richmond: Warmed Over Kisses (Left-Over Love)/ The Northern Dance Orchestra: Waltz In Jazz Time/ The Trad Lads: Unknown Song
R: Vg-Ex.   S: BBC radio show 'Here We Go' recorded at the Playhouse Theatre, Manchester Mar. 12 '63. Broadcast Mar. 12 '63.   C: ECD. Fold-open cardboard sleeve with background on

the material. Found just after the 'Complete BBC Sessions' box was released.

CD - HOT AS SUN
EMI PARLOPHONE CD PCS 7088 2
Hot As The Sun (1:27)/ Across The Universe (3:44)/ Come And Get It (2:27)/ I Mean Mine (1:41)/ Octopus's Garden (2:47)/ Maxwell's Silver Hammer (3:34)/ Oh! Darling (3:25)/ Something (5:28)/ Because (2:13)/ You Never Give Me Your Money (3:51)/ Sun King (2:27)/ Mean Mr. Mustard (1:07)/ Her Majesty (0:23)/ Polythene Pam (1:18)/ She Came In Through The Bathroom Window (1:51)/ Golden Slumbers (1:31)/ Carry That Weight (1:36)/ The End (1:55)
R: Ex. Soundboard. Some distortion.
S: Original sound recordings '69.   C: Japanese CD. Cardboard sleeve with B&w picture of group.

CD - HYSTERICAL ADELAIDE FULL SHOW
THE MASTER WORKS PCS-1964-DU-2
Opening/ I Saw Her Standing There/ I Want To Hold Your Hand/ Introduction By Paul/ All My Loving/ She Loves You/ Till There Was You/ Roll Over Beethoven/ Introduction By Paul/ Can't Buy Me Love/ Introduction By George/ This Boy/ Twist And Shout/ Long Tall Sally/ Ending Emcee
R: Vg. Soundboard. Some break-up.
S: Centennial Hall, Adelaide, Australia June 12 '64.   C: Japanese CD. Dbw. Yellow background. Red Type. Pic CD. Time 29:36.

CD - THE 'LET IT BE' REHEARSALS VOL. 4 (ROCK AND ROLL)
YELLOW DOG YD 054
Rock & Roll Music, Lucille, Thirty Days, Be-Bop-A-Lula/ Hail Hail Rock & Roll, Crackin' Up, All Shook Up, Your True Love, Blue Suede Shoes, Three Cool Cats, Blowing In The Wind, Lucille/ Negro In Reverse, If Tomorrow Ever Comes, Won't You Please Say Goodbye, Bring It On Home To Me, Hitch-Hike, You Can't Do That, The Hippy Hippy Shake/ Short Fat Fanny, Midnight Special, Drunk Again, What Do You Wanna Make Those Eyes At Me For?/ Let's Dance, Digging My Potatoes, Rock Island Line, Michael Row The Boat Ashore, Singing The Blues/ Maybelline, Brown-Eyed Handsome Man/ Short Fat Fanny/ Sweet Little Sixteen, Almost Grown, Schooldays, Hail, Hail, Rock & Roll/ Stand By Me/ I'm Talking About You, Highschool Rock, Great Balls Of Fire, Blue Suede Shoes/ I Got To Find My Baby, Vacation Has Just Begun, Maybe Baby, Peggy Sue Got Married, Thinking Of Linking, Crying Waiting Hoping, Mailman Bring Me No More Blues/ Low-Down Blues Machine, Hi Heel Sneakers
R: Exs/m. Soundboard.   C: ECD. Dcc. 74:11.

CD - THE 'LET IT BE' REHEARSALS VOL. 5 (THE AUCTION TAPES)
YELLOW DOG YD 055
She Came In Through The Bathroom Window, Sausages And French Fries, Hi Ho Silver, Stand By Me/ Harry Pinsker, Hare Krishna Mantra, Two

Of Us, You Got Me Going, Don't Let Me Down/ I've Got A Feeling, The One After 909/ All Things Must Pass, Mean Mr. Mustard, Don't Let Me Down, All Things Must Pass, Fools Like Me, You Win Again/ She Came In Through The Bathroom Window, Baa Baa Black Sheep/ Don't Let The Sun Catch You Crying, Sexy Sadie, Blue Suede Shoes, Hava Nagila, Movin' Along The River Rhine, The Long And Winding Road/ If Tomorrow Ever Comes, What Do You Wanna Make Those Eyes At Me For?/ Don't Be Cruel, Costa Del Sol, My One And Only Prayer, My Baby Left Me
R: Exs/m. Soundboard.   C: ECD. Dcc. Time 74:53.

CD - LIVE AT ATLANTA WHISKEY FLAT 65 AND WASHINGTON DC 64
ADAM V111 LTD CD 49-017
Intro/ Twist And Shout/ You Can't Do That/ Paul Intro/ All My Loving/ John Intro/ She Loves You/ George Intro/ Things We Said Today/ Roll Over Beethoven/ Paul Intro/ Can't Buy Me Love/ John Intro/ If I Fell/ I Want To Hold Your Hand/ Paul Intro/ Boys/ John Intro/ A Hard Day's Night/ Paul Outro/ Long Tall Sally/ She Loves You/ I Saw Her Standing There/ Paul Intro (John's 'Shut Up' Quote)/ I Want To Hold Your Hand/ (Ed Sullivan Show Feb. 23 '64)/ Roll Over Beethoven/ From Me To You/ Paul Intro/ I Saw Her Standing There/ Paul Intro/ Twist And Shout/ Paul Intro/ I Wanna Be Your Man/ Paul Intro/ Please Please Me/ George Intro/ This Boy/ Paul Intro/ All My Loving/ Paul Intro/ Till There Was You/ She Loves You/ Paul Intro/ I Want To Hold Your Hand
R: G. Some poor.   S: Tracks 1-21 Atlanta Whiskey Flat '65. Tracks 22-25 Ed Sullivan Show Feb. 16 '64. Tracks 27-45 Washington, DC Feb. 11 '64.   C: ACD. Dcc. Time 71:03.

CD - NO. 3 ABBEY ROAD N.W.8
VIGOTONE VT 116
How Do You Do/ Blackbird/ The Unicorn/ Lalena/ Heather/ Mr. Wind/ The Walrus And The Carpenter/ Land Of Gish/ Octopus's Garden/ Her Majesty/ Golden Slumbers, Carry That Weight/ You Never Give Me Your Money/ Oh! Darling/ Maxwell's Silver Hammer/ Something/ Because/ A Huge Melody/ A Huge Melody
R: Vg-Ex.   S: Tracks 1-8 Paul and Donovan during sessions for Mary Hopkin's 'Postcard' LP Nov. '68 - Jan. '69. Tracks 9-18 early mono mixes and takes recorded between Apr. and Aug. 1 '69.
*Early version Aug. 1-4 '69.   C: Japanese CD. Dcc. Time 58:00.

CD - POSTERS, INCENSE, AND STROBE CANDLES
VIGOTONE VTCD-07
WBCN Station ID/ Chess King Ad/ DJ Monologue/ Let It Be/ Don't Let Me Down/ For You Blue/ Get Back/ The Walk/ DJ Monologue/ Arlo Guthrie Concert Ad/ DJ Monologue/ Hey Jude Tap (by Harry Zonk)/ Golden Slumbers, Carry That Weight (incomplete)/ DJ Monologue/ Get Back Honk/ Get

Back/ I've Got A Feeling (fragment)/ Teddy Boy/ Two Of Us/ Dig A Pony/ DJ Monologue/ I've Got A Feeling/ The Long And Winding Road/ The One After 909/ Two Of Us (cut)
R: Exs. Soundboard. Some surface noise.
S: 'Get Back' reference acetate broadcast on WBCN FM Boston Sept. 22 '69.   C: Japanese CD. Dcc. Time 50:20.

CD - REVOLUTION
VIGOTONE VT 117
Mellotron Music No. 1 (mellotron experiment Weybridge '68)/ Girl (mono mix Nov. 11 '65)/ We Can Work It Out, Lucy From Little Town (Paul's acoustic home demo '65 with John's spoken word play)/ Michelle (acoustic home demo '65)/ We Can Work It Out (rough mono mix Oct. '65)/ It's Not Too Bad (three composing demos for 'Strawberry Fields Forever' Spain '66)/ Good Morning Good Morning (home demo '67)/ Mellotron Music No. 2 (mellotron experiment Weybridge '68)/ Revolution (alternate mix '68)/ Across The Universe (alternate mix Feb. '68)/ Revolution 9 (alternate mono mix June '68)/ Mellotron Music No. 3 (mellotron experiment Weybridge '68)/ Julia (acoustic demo Weybridge May '68)/ Stranger In My Arms (unfinished Weybridge May '68)/ Revolution 1 (Yoko's observations)/ Hey Jude (promo film soundtrack)/ Revolution (promo film soundtrack)
R: Vg-Ex. Some G. Some hiss. Some surface noise.   C: Japanese CD. Dbw. Time 71:27.

CD - THE ROAD TO FAME 1961 TO 1962
STAR CLUB RECORDS HADCD241
My Bonnie (German intro) (2:41)/ My Bonnie (English intro) (2.41)/ When The Saints Go Marching In (3:18)/ Why (2:58)/ Cry For A Shadow (2:23)/ If You Love Me Baby (2:53)/ Sweet Georgia Brown (overdubbed changed lyrics) (2:04)/ Sweet Georgia Brown (original version)/ Nobody's Child (3:54)/ Ain't She Sweet (2:11)/ Like Dreamers Do (2:34)/ Money (2:22)/ 'Till There Was You (2:58)/ The Sheik Of Araby (1:40)/ To Know Her Is To Love Her (2:34)/ Take Good Care Of My Baby (2:26)/ Memphis, Tennessee (2:20)/ Sure To Fall (2:01)/ Hello Little Girl (1:38)/ Three Cool Cats (2:23)/ Crying, Waiting, Hoping (2:00)/ Love Of The Loved (1:50)/ September In The Rain (1:53)/ Besame Mucho (2:38)/ Searchin' (3:02)
R: Ex. Soundboard.   S: Tracks 1-6 and 8-10 Freidrich Ebert Halle, Hamburg, Germany June 22 and 23 June '61. Track 7 re-recorded by Tony Sheridan in 1963. Tracks 11-25 original Decca tapes recorded Monday Jan. 1 '62 at the Decca Studios, London England. True speed.   C: ECD. Dbw. Orange type.

CD - SECRET SONGS IN PEPPERLAND
MASTERDISC MDCD006
All You Need Is Love (long ending - no fade)/ Lucy In The Sky With Diamonds (first verse sung by the Blue Meanie)/ Sound Effects Only for 'Good Morning Good Morning'/ Audience Sounds Intro To 'Sgt. Pepper'/ Billy Shears Applause 'Sgt.

Pepper' to 'From My Friends'/ Yellow Submarine (mono take)/ It's All Too Much (extended version)/ All Together Now (best mono take)/ Only A Northern Song (best mono take)
R: Exs/m. From the original EMI recordings.
C: Japanese CD. Dcc. Time 28:25.

CD - SHE LOVES YOU
GRAPEFRUIT GRA-001-B
So How Come (No One Love Me) (1:47)/ Nothin' Shakin' (But Leaves On The Trees) (3:00)/ Lonesome Tears In My Eyes (2:44)/ Sweet Little Sixteen (2:20)/ Do You Want To Know A Secret? (1:49)/ Please Mr. Postman (2:18)/ Hippy Hippy Shake (1:51)/ I'm Gonna Sit Right Down And Cry (Over You) (2:03)/ Crying, Waiting, Hoping (2:09)/ To Know Her Is To Love Her (2:52)/ The Honeymoon Song (1:43)/ Pop Goes The Beatles (1:11)/ Please Please Me (1:57)/ I Got A Woman (2:49)/ She Loves You (2:23)/ Words Of Love (1:51)/ Glad All Over (1:58)/ I Just Don't Understand (2:49)/ Slow Down (2:45)/ Ooh! My Soul (1:35)/ Don't Ever Change (1:59)/ There's A Place (1:51)/ Love Me Do (2:26)/ I'll Get You (2:06)/ You Really Got A Hold On Me (2:53)/ Misery (1:53)/ Lucille (2:31)/ Ask Me Why (1:55)/ Devil In Her Heart (2:21)/ I Saw Her Standing There (2:42)/ Twist And Shout (2:37)/ Happy Birthday 'Saturday Club' (:32)/ This Boy (2:19)/ I Want To Hold Your Hand (2:17)/ Xmas Medley: 'Crimble' (:33)
R: G-Vg.   S: Chronology part 2 - '63. See 'From Me To You', 'All My Loving' and 'Yesterday'.
C: Australian CD. Dcc.   C: Australian CD. Dcc.

CD - SO TIRED (ANOTHER DAY AT THE ABBEY ROAD STUDIOS)
LUNA RECORDS LU 9426-2
CD1: Intro - To Kingdom Come (2:01)/ Boat Show Dialogue (10:01)/ Don't Let Me Down (3:37)/ Two Of Us (4:18)/ Baa Baa Black Sheep (1:34)/ Suzy's Parlour (2:34)/ One After 909 (2:14)/ Norwegian Wood, This Bird Has Flown (:39)/ She Came In Through The Bathroom Window (rehearsal session) (2:46)/ Be-Bop-A-Lula (1:06)/ She Came In Through The Bathroom Window (rehearsal session) (5:22)/ Get Back, A.K.A: 'No Pakistanis' (3:50)/ La Peninia (1:06)/ Across The Universe (3:34)/ 'Shakin In The Sixties' (:40)/ Move It (:52)/ Good Rockin' Tonight (:59)/ Tennessee (2:03)/ Across The Universe (:12)/ House Of The Rising Sun (3:11)/ Madman (7:19)/ Mean Mr. Mustard, 'Madman' (3:57)/ 'Watching Rainbows' (5:08)/ Instrumental (2:21)/ Take This Hammer (3:38)/ Johnny B. Goode (1:38)/ I Shall Be Released (1:20)/ Instrumental (1:16)
CD2: Early In The Morning, Honey Hush (2:20)/ Stand By Me (2:19)/ Hari Krishna (:58)/ Instrumental (:34)/ Hari Krishna (Reprise) (:40)/ Two Of Us (3:30)/ You Got Me Going (:23)/ Twist And Shout (:22)/ Don't Let Me Down (3:06)/ I've Got A Feeling (3:45)/ One After 909 (3:43)/ Too Bad About Sorrows (:43)/ Just Fun (:28)/ She Said, She Said (:31)/ Mean Mr. Mustard (3:24)/

Don't Let Me Down (1:05)/ All Things Must Pass (3:19)/ Fools Like Me (2:15)/ You Win Again (1:41)/ Instrumental (1:08)/ She Came Through The Bathroom Window (2:27)/ I Me Mine (rehearsal session) (9:29)/ Almost Grown (:55)/ Norwegian Wood, This Bird Has Flown (:22)/ What Am I Living For (:37)/ Rock 'N' Roll Music (:51)/ I Me Mine (rehearsal session) (4:53)/ Her Majesty (2:24)/ There You Are Eddie (4:16)/ Every Night, Pillow For Your Head (5:55)/ Hot As Sun (1:40)/ Two Of Us, Hello Goodbye (rehearsal session) (:31)/ Diggin' My Potatoes, Rock Island Line (2:37)/ Singin' The Blues, Knee Deep In Blues (2:43)
R: Ex. Soundboard.   S: Abbey Road Studios '69.
C: ECD. Dcc.

CD - TWIST AND SHOUT
GRAPEFRUIT GRA-001-E
Intro (1:20)/ Twist And Shout (1:22)/ You Can't Do That (3:12)/ All My Loving (2:17)/ She Loves You (2:41)/ Things We Said Today (2:17)/ Roll Over Beethoven (3:16)/ Can't Buy Me Love (2:41)/ If I Fell (2:13)/ I Want to Hold Your Hand (3:14)/ Boys (2:30)/ A Hard Days Night (3:05)/ Long Tall Sally (:53)/ Intro (:31)/ Twist and Shout (1:19)/ You Can't Do That (3:16)/ All My Loving (2:22)/ She Loves You (2:34)/ Things We Said Today (2:11)/ Roll Over Beethoven (3:10)/ Can't Buy Me Love (2:41)/ If I Fell (2:10)/ I Want To Hold Your Hand (3:00)/ Boys (2:32)/ A Hard Days Night (2:53)/ Long Tall Sally (2:02)/
R: G-Vg. Soundboard.   S: Tracks 1-13 Indiana '64. Tracks 14-26 Philadelphia '64.   C: Australian CD. Dcc.

CD - THE ULTIMATE COLLECTION VOL. 1
YELLOW DOG YDB 101/2/3/4
CD1: Intro - Like Dreamers Do (2:38)/ Money That's What I Want (2:25)/ 'Till There Was You (3:01)/ The Sheik Of Araby (1:43)/ To Know Her Is To Love Her (2:37)/ Take Good Care Of My Baby (2:29)/ Memphis Tennessee (2:22)/ Sure To Fall In Love With You (2:04)/ Hello Little Girl (1:41)/ Three Cool Cats (2:26)/ Crying Waiting Hoping (2:04)/ Love Of The Loved (1:53)/ September In The Rain (1:57)/ Besame Mucho (2:41)/ Searchin' (3:05)/ I Saw Her Standing There (3:11)/ The One After 909 (3:13)/ The One After 909 (3:18)/ Catswalk (1:24)/ Catswalk (1:24)/ Some Other Guy (2:12)
R: Ex. Soundboard. Tracks 16-20 G-Vg. Audience. Track 21 G.   S: Tracks 1-15 Decca Tapes at right speed - Decca Studios Jan. 12 '62. Track 16-20 rehearsal at The Cavern early '62. Track 21 de-clicked acetate.
CD2: Intro, All My Loving (3:44)/ 'Till There Was You (2:11)/ She Loves You (2:54)/ Intro, I Saw Her Standing There (2:52)/ I Want To Hold Your Hand, Outro (3:31)/ She Loves You (2:22)/ This Boy (2:39)/ All My Loving (2:23)/ Intro, I Saw Her Standing There (2:50)/ From Me To You (2:34)/ I Want To Hold Your Hand, Outro (3:19)/ Intro,

Twist And Shout (3:04)/ Please Please Me, Speech (2:01)/ I Want To Hold Your Hand (3:02)/ Interview, You Can't Do That (4:40)/ Intro, I Feel Fine (3:22)/ I'm Down (2:25)/ Act Naturally, Speech, Intro (3:01)/ Ticket To Ride (2:46)/ Yesterday (2:26)/ Help, Outro (3:01)/ Ed Sullivan intro without songs (:42)/ She Loves You (2:32)/ This Boy (2:49)/ All My Loving, Intro (3:10)/ I Saw Her Standing There (2:39)/ From Me To You (2:08)/ I Want To Hold Your Hand, Outro (2:34)
R: Vg-Ex. Some G. Soundboard.   S: Ed Sullivan Shows Tracks 1-5 Feb. 9 '64. Tracks 6-11 rehearsal show Miami Feb. 15 '64. Tracks 12-13 NYC Feb. 23 '64. Tracks 14-15 AHDN outtakes May 24 '64. Tracks 16-21 NYC Sept. 12 '65. Tracks 22 '66. Tracks 23-28 Miami Feb. 16 '64.
CD3: Inspite Of All The Danger ('93 Version) (:49)/ The First Sounds Of Strawberry Fields Forever (:36)/ We Love You Beatles (1:07)/ Twist And Shout (2:30)/ Roll Over Beethoven (1:48)/ I Wanna Be Your Man (1:44)/ Long Tall Sally (1:41)/ Medley: Love Me Do, Please Please Me, From Me To You, She Loves You, I Want To Hold Your Hand (3:56)/ Can't Buy Me Love (2:03)/ Shout (1:59)/ Girl (backing track - 2:20)*/ We Can Work It Out (:31)/ Obladi Oblada (2:35)/ Blackbird (demo - 1:48)/ Helter Skelter (demo - :55)/ Oh Darling (vocals only - 8:27)/ Think For Yourself (studio talk - 5:04)/ Ariel Tour Instrumental - Flying (complete long version - 9:39)/ Ariel Tour Instrumental (reversed - 9:39)
R: Vg-Ex. Some G. *Poor.   S: Tracks 3-10 'Around The Beatles' recorded Apr. 27-28 '64. Aired May 6. '64. Here without audience.
CD4: Footsteps (setting up), Don't Let Me Down, Dig A Pony, Don't Let Me Down (15:47)/ Let It Down, Brown-Eyed Handsome Man, I've Got A Feeling, Child Of Nature, I Shall Be Released (16:07)/ Don't Let Me Down Dialogue, I've Got A Feeling (14:51)/ I've Got A Feeling (1:18)/ I've Got A Feeling (16:16)
R: Ex. Soundboard.   S: The first recorded hour of the 'Let It Be' sessions Twickenham Jan. 2 '69. Film roll numbers 1A, 2A, 3A and 4A.
C: ECD. Box set with full color cover. Contains two full color inserts - one with set's listings and sources and a second with listings of remaining two boxes in this series. Pic CDs.

CD - THE ULTIMATE COLLECTION VOL. 2
YELLOW DOG YDB 201/2/3/4
CD1: Intro - Interview Swedish Radio (1:48)/ Intro, I Saw Her Standing There (3:31)/ From Me To You (2:08)/ Money (2:48)/ Roll Over Beethoven (2:28)/ She Really Got A Hold On Me (3:05)/ She Loves You (2:32)/ Twist And Shout (2:46)/ I'm A Loser (3:06)/ Can't Buy Me Love (2:42)/ I Wanna Be Your Man (2:45)/ A Hard Day's Night (2:48)/ Rock And Roll Music (2:19)/ I Feel Fine (2:36)/ Ticket To Ride (3:30)/ Long Tall Sally (2:02)/ Intro (1:20)/ Rock And Roll Music (1:36)/ She's A Woman (3:16)/ If I Needed Someone (2:58)/ Day Tripper (3:16)/ Baby's In Black (2:42)/ I Feel Fine (2:31)/

Yesterday (2:32)/ I Wanna Be Your Man (2:37)/ Nowhere Man (2:47)/ Paperback Writer (2:45)/ I'm Down (2:42)
R: Tracks 1-8 Vg. Tracks 9-16 G-Vg. Tracks 17-28 G.   S: Tracks 1-8 Stockholm Oct. 24 '63. Tracks 9-16 Paris June 20 '65. Tracks 17-28 Tokyo July 1 '66.

CD2: There's A Place (take 1) (2:10)/ There's A Place (take 2) (2:07)/ There's A Place (takes 3, 4) (2:13)/ There's A Place (takes 5, 6) (2:21)/ There's A Place (takes 7, 8) (2:46)/ There's A Place (take 9) (2:06)/ There's A Place (take 10) (2:03)/ I Saw Her Standing There (take 1) (3:05)/ I Saw Her Standing There (take 2) (3:12)/ I Saw Her Standing There (take 3) I Saw Her Standing There (take 4), I Saw Her Standing There (take 5) (2:42)/ I Saw Her Standing There (takes 6-9) (4:57)/ Do You Want To Know A Secret (take 7) (2:40)/ Do You Want To Know A Secret (take 8) (2:06)/ A Taste Of Honey (take 6) (2:12)/ A Taste Of Honey (take 7) (2:13)/ There's A Place (take 11) (2:07)/ There's A Place (take 12) (2:29)/ I Saw Her Standing There (take 10) (3:03)/ I Saw Her Standing There (take 11) (3:41)/ Misery (take 1) (2:02)/ Misery (takes 2-6) (4:51)/ Misery (takes 7, 8) (2:24)
R: Ex. Soundboard.   S: Recording of 'Please Please Me' LP Feb. 11 '63. Tracks 1-11 morning session. Tracks 12-22 afternoon session.

CD3: From Me To You (takes 1, 2) (3:32)/ From Me To You (take 3) (1:57)/ From Me To You (take 4) (1:54)/ From Me To You (take 5) (2:18)/ From Me To You (takes 6, 7) (2:19)/ Thank You Girl (take 1) (2:12) Thank You Girl (takes 2-4) (2:37)/ Thank You Girl (take 5) (2:08)/ Thank You Girl (take 6) (2:23)/ Thank You Girl (edit pieces takes 7-13) (4:07)/ From Me To You (take 8) (2:13)/ From Me To You (edit piece takes 9-13) (1:55)/ One After 909 (takes 1, 2) (4:27)/ One After 909 (takes 3-5) (5:41)/ Hold Me Tight (track 2 - take 21) (2:44)/ Hold Me Tight (track 2 - takes 22, 23, 24) (4:04)/ Hold Me Tight (track 2 - takes 25, 26) (3:03)/ Hold Me Tight (track 2 - takes 27, 28) (1:56)/ Hold Me Tight (track 2 - take 29) (2:52)/ Don't Bother Me (remake take 10) (2:52)/ Don't Bother Me (remake takes 11-13) (3:55)
R: Ex. Soundboard.   S: Tracks 1-14 Abbey Road Studios Mar. 5 '63. Tracks 15-21 Abbey Road Studios Sept. 12 '63.

CD4: Speak To Me, I've Got A Feeling, I've Got A Feeling (16:06)/ Dialogue, I've Got A Feeling (16:19)/ Dialogue, I've Got A Feeling, Don't Let Me Down (16:16)/ Don't Let Me Down, Dialogue, Don't Let Me Down (16:19)
R: Ex. Soundboard.   S: The second recorded hour of the 'Let It Be' sessions Twickenham Jan. 2 '69. Film roll numbers 5A, 6A, 7A and 8A.
C: ECD. Box set with full color cover. Contains color booklet with listings and sources. Pic CDs.

CD - THE ULTIMATE COLLECTION VOL. 3
YELLOW DOG YDB 301/2/3/4
CD1: Intro - To Much Monkey Business (2:19)/ I

Got To Find My Baby (2:19)/ Young Blood (2:26)/ Baby It's You (2:44)/ A Shot Of Rhythm And Blues (2:29)/ Happy Birthday, A Taste Of Honey (2:24)/ Sure To Fall In Love With You (2:11)/ Money (3:17)/ Twist And Shout (3:02)/ Memphis Tennessee (2:18)/ That's All Right Mama (3:06)*/ Carol (3:08)/ Soldier Of Love (2:09)/ Lend Me Your Comb (2:20)/ Clarabella (3:05)*/ Matchbox (2:28)/ Please, Mr. Postman (2:17)/ Hippy Hippy Shake (1:50)/ I'm Gonna Sit Right Down And Cry, Over You (2:31)/ Crying, Waiting, Hoping (2:09)/ Kansas City (2:46)/ To Know Her Is To Love Her (3:22)/ The Honeymoon Song (1:46)/ Long Tall Sally (2:37)/ You Really Got A Hold On Me (3:00)/ I Got A Woman (2:53)/ Honey Don't (2:53)/ Roll Over Beethoven (2:21)
R: Vg-Ex. *G.   S: 'Pop Goes The Beatles' BBC '63 .

CD2: A Hard Day's Night (take 2) (2:34)/ A Hard Day's Night (take 3) (2:37)/ A Hard Day's Night (take 4) (2:42)/ A Hard Day's Night (takes 6, 7) (4:36)/ A Hard Day's Night (takes 8-9)/ (2:34)/ I'm A Loser (takes 1, 2) (2:38)/ I'm A Loser (take 3) (2:55)/ I'm A Loser (takes 4-6) (4:43)/ I'm A Loser (takes 7, 8) (1:16)/ She's A Woman (take 2) (3:22)/ She's A Woman (takes 3-5) (3:46)/ She's A Woman (take 7) (6:32)/ I Feel Fine (takes 1, 2) (3:17)/ I Feel Fine (take 5) (2:27)/ I Feel Fine (take 6) (2:49)/ I Feel Fine (take 7) (2:47)
R: Ex. Soundboard.   S: Studios sessions. Tracks 1-5 Mar. 16 '64. Tracks 6-9 Aug. 14 '64. Tracks 10-12 Oct. 8 '64. Track 13-16 Oct. 18 '64.

CD3: Yes It Is (take 1) (3:01)/ Yes It Is (takes 2-7) (4:05)/ Yes It Is (takes 8, 9) (3:09)/ Yes It Is (takes 10, 11 and 14 (3:15)/ Help (takes 1-4) (3:31)/ Help (take 5) (2:52)/ Help (takes 6-7) (3:19)/ Help (takes 8, 9) (2:46)/ Help (take 10) (2:35)/ Help (takes 11, 12 (2:46)/ Help (take 13) (2:25)/ Run For Your Life (take 1) (:17)/ Day Tripper (take 1) (2:08)/ Day Tripper (takes 2, 3) (4:16)/ We Can Work It Out (take 1) (2:03)/ We Can Work It Out (take 2) (2:30)/ Paperback Writer (tracks 1, 2) (4:08)/ Rain (3:07)
R: Ex. Soundboard.   S: Studio sessions. Tracks 1-4 Feb. 16 '65. Tracks 5-11 Apr. 13 '65. Tracks 12 Oct. 12 '65. Tracks 13-14 Oct. 16 '65. Tracks 15-16 Oct. 20 '65. Track 17 Apr. 13 '66. Track 18 Apr. 14 '66.

CD4: Eating Sandwiches, Well All Right, All Things Must Pass, Two Of Us, Two Of Us (16:20)/ Two Of Us, Two Of Us (15:34)/ Paul's Piano Tune, Whole Lotta Shakin' Goin' On, Let It Be, Taking A Trip To Carolina (15:50)/ Please Mrs. Henry, Ramblin' Woman, Talking About The Band, I Bought A Picasso, Taking A Trip To Carolina, Hey Jude, Thinking Of All The Tunes I Got, All Things Must Pass, Ringo Testing Drums (16:15)
R: Ex. Soundboard.   S: The third recorded hour of the 'Let It Be' sessions Twickenham. Tracks 1-2 film roll numbers 9A-10A Jan. 2 '69. Tracks 3-4 film roll numbers 11A-12A Jan. 3 '69.
C: ECD. Box set with full color cover. Contains color booklet with listings and sources. Pic CDs.

CD - WBCN GET BACK REFERENCE ACETATE
YELLOW DOG RECORDS YD 035
DJ Announcement Side B (0:48)/ Let It Be (4:02)/
Don't Let Me Down (3:45)/ For You Blue (3:09)/
Get Back (2:53)/ The Walk (0:58)/ DJ
Announcement / DJ Announcement Side A (0:34)/
Get Back (2:49)/ Teddy Boy (5:54)/ Two Of Us
(3:57)/ Dig A Pony (4:47)/ I've Got A Feeling
(3:02)/ The Long And Winding Road (3:42)/ Let It
Be Dialogue (33:58)
R: Exs. Soundboard.   S: Broadcast Sept. 22 '69.
C: ECD. Dcc.

CD - YESTERDAY
GRAPEFRUIT GRA-001-D
Ticket To Ride (3:00)/ I'm A Loser (2:19)/ The
Night Before (2:23)/ Dizzy Miss Lizzy (2:46)/ She's
A Woman (2:47)/ I'm Down (2:11)/ Act Naturally
(2:27)/ Yesterday (1:58)/ Help! (2:14)/ Baby's In
Black (2:11)/ If I Needed Someone (2:30)/ Day
Tripper (3:05)/ Nowhere Man (2:11)/ Paperback
Writer (2:23)/ Roll Over Beethoven (2:40)/ From
Me To You (2:39)/ I Saw Her Standing There
(3:41)/ Twist And Shout (1:54)/ I Wanna Be Your
Man (2:59)/ Please Please Me (2:14)/ This Boy
(2:45)/ All My Loving (2:28)/ Till There Was You
(2:06)/ She Loves You (3:36)/ I Want To Hold Your
Hand (2:23)/ Kansas City, Hey! Hey! Hey! (2:27)/
I'm A Loser (2:22)/ Boys (2:13)/
R: G-Vg. Soundboard.   S: Chronology part 4 -
'65-'66 plus 1 track from '64. See 'From Me To
You', 'All My Loving' and 'She Loves You'.
C: Australian CD. Dcc.

CD - YOUNGBLOOD
THE MASTER WORKS CD PCS-1960
One After 909/ Waiting For The Sunrise/ What'd I
Say/ Some Other Guy/ Some Other Guy/ Twist
And Shout/ Please Mr. Postman/ P.S. I Love You/
Besame Mucho/ Picture Of You/ From Me To You/
Ticket To Ride/ All My Loving/ Seventeen/ Kansas
City, Hey! Hey! Hey!/ Simmy Simmy/
Unknown Song/ Roll Over Beethoven
R: Poor to G.   S: Cover says 'Lost BBC tapes,
lost Star Club tapes and more'.   C: Japanese
CD. Unflattering drawings of the band. Yellow
background. Red Type. Pic CD. Time 39:11.

BECK, JEFF

CD - AS 19
MINOTAURO RECORDS
Guitar Shop/ Slingshot/ Big Block/ Behind The
Veil/ Freeway Jam/ Where Were You/ Stand On It/
Pork Pie Hat/ Day In The House/ Train/ Two
Rivers/ Blue Wind/ People Get Ready/ Goin' Down
R: Vg. Audience.   S: Italy '90.   C: ECD. Dcc.
Pic CD. Time 70:39.

B-52'S

CD - BOMB AWAY THE M.E.
RAID MASTERS CD 910701
52 Girls (3:21)/ 6060-842 (2:13)/ Lava (4:21)/

Private Idaho (3:22)/ Hero Worship (3:46)/ Devil's
In My Car (5:03)/ Dance This Mess Around (4:05)/
Running Around (2:55)/ Strobe Light (3:57)/ Rock
Lobster (4:39)
R: Vg. Soundboard.   S: Boston '79.   C: ECD.
Dcc.

BEE GEES, THE

CD - A KICK IN THE HEAD IS WORTH EIGHT IN THE PANTS
BROTHERS GIBB RECORDS BGR 003
A Lonely Violin/ Losers And Lovers/ Home Again
Rivers/ Dear Mr. Kissinger/ Jesus In Heaven/
Harry's Gate/ Rocky L.A./ Castles In The Air/
Where Is Your Sister?/ Life, Am I Wasting My
Time?/ Money/ Alexander's Ragtime Band/ Hey
Jude/ Beatles Medley/ Bye Bye Blackbird
R: Tracks 1-10 Vg. Tracks 11-15 Poor.
S: Tracks 1-10 studio. Tracks 11-15 'Midnight
Special' NBC TV '73.   C: ECD. Dcc. Time 48:43.

CD - FROM THE ARCHIVES
BROTHERS GIBB RECORDS BGR 001
All The King's Horses/ Mrs. Gillespies
Refrigerator/ Deeply Deeply Me/ Mr. Wallers
Wailing Wall/ Every Morning Every Night/
Irresponsible Unreliable Indispensable Blues/
Distant Relationship/ Merrily Merry Eyes/ If I Were
The Sky/ Everytime I See You Smile/ End Of My
Song/ Who Knows What A Room Is/ Don't Forget
Me Ida/ Nobody Someone/ Ellen Vallin (Manx
National Anthem)/ Ring My Bell/ We Can Lift A
Mountain (1st version)/ We Can Lift A Mountain
(2nd version)/ God's Good Grace/ Give A Hand
Take A Hand ('69 version)/ Jumbo (instrumental
version)/ Another Cold And Windy Day (Coca Cola
jingle)/ Sitting In The Meadow (Coca Cola jingle)
R: G-Vg. Some surface noise.   S: Previously
unreleased tracks '66-'72.   C: ECD. Dcc. Time
62:51.

CD - JIVE TALKIN'
THAT'S LIFE TL 930009
How Deep Is Your Love (4:16)/ It's My
Neighborhood (3:30)/ How Can You Mend A
Broken Heart? (3:27)/ House Of Shame (4:38)/ I
Started A Joke (2:50)/ Massachusetts (2:53)/
Stayin' Alive (3:59)/ Nights On Broadway (4:12)/
Jive Talkin' (8:57)/ You Win Again (3:26)/ You
Should Be Dancin' (6:03)
R: Exs. Soundboard.   S: Live Melbourne,
Australia.   C: ECD. Dcc.

CD - LIVE AT THE BEEB
BROTHERS GIBB RECORDS BGR 002
New York Mining Disaster 1941/ Holiday/ To Love
Somebody/ I Can't See Nobody/ In My Own Time/
Mrs. Gillespies Refrigerator/ I Close My Eyes/
Cucumber Castle/ In My Own Time/ One Minute
Woman/ (The Lights Went Out In) Massachusetts/
Birdie Told Me/ And The Sun Will Shine/ Words/
Worlds/ Man For All Seasons/ Lonely Days/ Alone
Again/ Every Second Every Minute/ Saved By The

Bell/ August October/ Weekend
R: Vg.   S: BBC Radio - Tracks 1-10 '67. Tracks
11-15 '68. Tracks 16-22 '70. Tracks 20-22 Robin
Gibb '70.   C: ECD. Dcc. Time 59:17.

CD - ORDINARY LIVES
THAT'S LIFE TL 930008
Ordinary Lives (5:31)/ Givin' Up The Ghost (3:48)/
To Love Somebody (3:39)/ I've Gotta Get A
Message To You (3:52)/ One (5:01)/ Tokyo Nights
(3:50)/ Words (5:27)/ Juliet (3:24)/ Lonely Days
(3:28)/ New York Mining Disaster 1941 (2:06)/
Holiday (1:32)/ Too Much Heaven (1:46)/
Heartbreaker (0:56)/ Islands In The Stream (1:27)/
Run To Me (1:02)/ World (1:26)/ Spicks & Specks
(2:45)
R: Exs. Soundboard.   S: Live Melbourne,
Australia.   C: ECD. Dcc.

BEE GEES, THE - FEATURING BARRY GIBB

CD - GUILTY DEMOS
YELLOW CAT YC 005
Run Wild/ Promises/ Woman In Love/ What Kind
Of Fool/ The Love Inside/ Carried Away*/ Life
Story/ Guilty/ Make It Like A Memory/ The Wishes
We Share
R: Exs. Soundboard.   S: Unreleased studio
demos for Barbara Streisand and *Olivia Newton-
John.   C: ECD. Dcc. Time 43:08.

BELLY

CD - GUT FEELING
KISS THE STONE KTS 235
Low Red Moon (6:41)/ Duster (3:35)/ Angel (3:09)/
Full Moon, Empty Heart (3:16)/ Star (2:58)/ Dream
On Me (5:28)/ White Belly (3:53)/ Gepetto (3:33)/
Sexy F. (4:01)/ Feed The Tree (3:32)/ Slow Dog
(4:05)/ Stay (7:59)/ Low Red Moon (8:43)/ Full
Moon, Empty Heart (3:22)/ Gepetto (3:40)/ Angel
(3:09)/ Dream On Me (5:05)/ Star (2:57)
R: Exs. Soundboard.   S: Tracks 1-12 Grant
Park, Chicago July 4 '93. Tracks 13-18 Apr. 26
'93.   C: ECD. Dcc. Pic CD.

BIOHAZARD

CD - FAST FUSE BURNING
ROCKS 92132
Black And White And Red All Over (4:37)/ Urban
Discipline (5:53)/ Business (4:07)/ Wrong Side Of
The Tracks (4:25)/ Shades Of Grey (4:25)/ We're
Only Gonna Die (From Our Own Arrogance)
(3:42)/ Hold My Own (3:36)/ Chamber Spins Three
(4:13)/ Business (4:04)/ Black And White And Red
All Over (4:57)/ Shades Of Grey (4:00)/ Wrong
Side Of The Tracks (3:59)
R: Ex. Soundboard.   S: Tour '93.   C: ECD.
Orange cover. B&w picture.

CD - 100% ASS-KICKING LIVE
DEAD DOG RECORDS SE 447
Shades Of Grey/ What Makes Us Tick/ Chambers

Spins Three/ Survival For The Fittest/ State Of
The World Address/ Black And White And Red All
Over/ Down For Life/ Wrong Side Of The Tracks/
Love Denied/ We're Only Gonna Die/ Tears Of
Blood/ Tales From The Hard Side/ Business/ Five
Blocks To The Subway/ I Ain't Going Out Like
That/ Punishment/ Peace Out
R: G-Vg.   S: Belgium Dienze, May 12 '94.
C: ECD. Time 61:24.

CD - RUN FOR COVER
KISS THE STONE KTS 372
Black And White And Red All Over (6:42)/ Lost
(7:21)/ Lack There Of (4:25)/ Punishment (5:25)/
Black And White And Red All Over (4:36)/ Army
Disappear (5:40)/ Newton (4:06)/ Wrong Side Of
The Track (4:59)/ Shades Of Grey (4:07)/ We're
Only Gonna Die, From Our Own Arrogance (3:28)/
Hold My Own (3:39)
R: Ex. Audience.   S: Tracks 1-4 Dronden,
Holland Aug. '94. Tracks 5-11 Sweden June '94.
C: ECD. Pic CD.

CD - WRONG SIDE OF THE STAGE
DEAD DOG RECORDS SE 420
In Your Face/ Chamber Spins Three/ Survival Of
The Fittest/ Business/ Black And White And Red
All Over/ Shades Of Grey/ Wrong Side Of The
Tracks/ Urban Discipline/ Punishment/ We're Only
Gonna Die/ Peace Out
R: G. Audience.   S: 'Dynamo Open Air'
Eindhoven May 29 '93.   C: ECD. Comes with
round 'Biohazard' sticker. Time 47:37.

BJORK

CD - BJORK AND THE SUGARCUBES
LIVE STORM LSCD 51542
C: ECD. Dbw. See 'Bjork And The Sugarcubes'
(MO 10014) for songs and source.

CD - BJORK AND THE SUGARCUBES
MONTANA MO 10014
Birthday (3:54)/ Hit (3:47)/ Deus (3:33)/ Leash
Called Love/ Finish Traditional (4:05)/ Pump
(4:22)/ Dear Plastic (3:25)/ Coldsweat (3:37)/
Mama (2:59)/ Regina (3:33)/ Tidal Wave (2:54)/
Sick For Toys (3:05)/ A Day Called Zero (2:44)/
Chihuahua (3:40)/ Walkabout (3:50)/ Blue Eyed
Pop (2:43)/ Motorcrash (2:21)/ Motorcycle Mama
(4:11)/ Delicious Demon (3:01)
R: Vg-Ex.   S: Ohio '91. Toronto '92.   C: ECD.
Dcc. Time 62:02.

CD - COMEBACK
HOME RECORDS - HR 5944-6
Human Behavior (5:27)/ One Day (5:28)/ Venus
As A Boy (5:51)/ Play Dead (3:16)/ Crying (5:03)/
Violently Happy (5:17)/ There's More To Life Than
This (3:39)/ Big Time Sensuality (3:42)/ Tidal
Wave (2:57)/ Deus (3:36)/ Coldsweat (3:39)/
Delicious Demon (3:03)/ Walkabout (3:52)/ A Day
Called Zero (2:46)/ Birthday (3:57)/ Blue Eyed Pop
(2:45)/ Pump (3:16)/ Regina (3:59)/ Violently

Happy (acoustic) (4:45)
R: Exs. Soundboard.   S: Tracks 1-8 USA '94.
Tracks 9-18 USA '91.   C: ECD. Dcc. Pic CD.

CD - THE GIRL FROM OUTERSPACE
HAWK 047
Human Behavior (4:07)/ The Happy Song (3:08)/
One Day (5:15)/ Venus As A Boy (4:34)/ Come To
Me (4:29)/ The Anchor Song (3:25)/ Aeroplane
(4:17)/ Down The Line (3:14)/ Violently Happy
(6:15)/ There's More To Life Than This (3:42)/ Big
Time Sensuality (5:31)/ Unlovely (4:08)/ Other
Things (4:35)
R: Vg. Audience.   S: Wiltern Theatre, LA Nov. 19
'93.   C: ECD. Dcc. Pic CD.

CD - SUGAR CANDY KISSES
KISS THE STONE KTS 268
Human Behavior/ The Harbour/ One Day/ Venus
As A Boy/ Come To Me/ Aeroplane/ Play Dead/
Crying/ Violently Happy/ There's More To Life
Than This/ Big Time Sensuality/ If You Complain
Once More/ Modern Things/ Human Behavior/ The
Harbour/ One Day/ Come To Me/ The Anchor
Song
R: Exs. Soundboard.   S: Kosmopolitan, Aarhus,
Denmark Sept. 9 '93.   C: ECD. Dcc. Pic CD.

BLACK, FRANK

CD - BLACK IS BEAUTIFUL
FLASHBACK 09 93 0217
Intro (2:47)/ Professor's Theme (2:08)/ Fear
(1:38)/ War (5:28)/ I Heard Romona Sing (3:44)/
Los Angeles (3:44)/ Places Named After Numboro
(2:57)/ Fu Manchu (3:21)/ Everytime I Go Around
Here (3:47)/ Adda Lee (2:34)/ Hang On Your Ego
(3:21)/ Freedom Rock (5:50)/ Parry The Wind High
(5:20)/ Ten Percenter (3:37)/ Two Spaces (3:37)/
Old Black Dawning (2:02)/ Don't Ya Rile'Em
(3:17)/ This Is Where I Belong (2:26)/ Czar (3:37)
R: Exs. Soundboard.   S: Houston, Texas July 5
'93.   C: ECD.

CD - THE RETURN OF FU MANCHU
HAWK 019
Intro (2:17)/ One Step Beyond (2:36)/ I Heard
Ramona Sing (3:55)/ Fu Manchu (2:21)/ Los
Angeles (4:33)/ Tossed (4:38)/ Places Named
After Number (2:46)/ Two Spaces (2:38)/ Old
Black Drawing (2:02)/ Parry The Wind High, Low
(3:41)/ Ten Percenter (3:54)/ Czar (3:56)
R: Ex. Audience.   S: USA July 15 '93.
C: ECD. Dbw. Pic CD.

BLACK CROWES, THE

CD - AS THE CROWES FLY
RARE RECORDING COLLECTION RRC 041
No Speak No Slave/ Sting Me/ Hard To Handle/
My Morning Song/ Whatever Is Under The Pillow
Jam/ Thorn In My Pride/ Black Moon Creeping/
Thick N' Thin/ Hotel Illness/ Stare It Cold/ Three
Little Birds/ Sometimes Salvation

R: Exs. Soundboard.   S: Houston, Texas '93.
C: ECD. Dcc. Time 75:20.

CD - FIVE LITTLE BIRDS
HAPPY RECORD SK 2
Sting Me/ Sister Luck/ Bad Moon Creeping/ Twice
As Hard/ Thick & Thin/ Hotel Illness/ Stare It Cold/
Three Little Birds/ Jealous Again/ Remedy/ Thick
& Thin/ She Talks To Angels/ Interview/ Hard To
Handle/ Jealous Again
R: *G-Vgs. Audience. Rest Vg. Soundboard.
S: *Tracks 1-10 Europe Dec. 6 '92. Tracks 11-12
Saturday Night Live Jan. 23 '93. Track 13 Good
Rockin' Tonite Show '90. Track 14 David
Letterman Show Oct. 9 '90. Track 15 Arsenio Hall
Show Nov. 2 '90.   C: ECD. Dcc. Pic CD.
Time 73:14.

CD - HIGHER THAN THE MOON
ROCKS OF ROCK ROR 001
My Morning Song/ Hotel Illness/ Sting Me/ Seeing
Things/ Band Intros/ Twice As Hard/ Black Moon
Creeping/ Sometimes Salvation/ Hard To Handle/
Remedy/ Shake 'Em On Down
R: Vg. Soundboard.   S: London Nov. 28-29 '92.
C: ECD.

CD - TALLER
KISS THE STONE KTS 376
Conspiracy/ P. 25 London/ Wiser Time/ She Talks
To Angels/ Remedy/ Nonfiction/ Long Time Gone/
Jealous Again/ Thorn In My Pride/ Intro/ Black
Moon Creeping/ Twice As Hard/ Thick N' Thin/
Stare It Cold
R. Ex. Audience.   S: Europe 1994.   C: ECD.
Dcc. Pic CD. Time 77:24.

BLACK FLAG

CD - LAST SHOW
HAWK 065
Retired At 21/ Annihilate This Week/ Bastard In
Love/ Drinking And Driving/ Paralyzed/ In My
Head/ White Hot/ Black Love/ Kickin' And Stickin'/
Society's Tease/ This Is Good/ I Can See You/
Nothing Left Inside/ Gimme Gimme Gimme/ Louie
Louie
R: Ex. Audience.   S: Detroit, MI '86.   C: ECD.
Dcc. Pic CD. Time 69:05.

BLACK SABBATH

CD - IRON MAN (VOL. 3)
BANANA BAN-053-C
War Pigs (7:10)/ Neon Knights (5:15)/ Children Of
The Sea (5:46)/ Heaven And Hell (12:26)/ Die
Young (4:37)/ Children Of The Grave (5:24)/ Hot
Line (5:01)/ Zero The Hero (7:47)/ Smoke On The
Water (5:12)/ Paranoid (3:35)
R: Ex. Soundboard.   S: USA '89 & '83. Tracks 1-
5 with Ronnie James Dio. Tracks 6-10 with Ian
Gillan.   C: Australian CD. Dcc.

CD - IRON MEN
HOME RECORDS HR 5936/37
CD1: Time Machine (4:24)/ Children Of The Grave (5:19)/ Children Of The Sea (6:17)/ I Witness (5:38)/ Mob Rules (4:06)/ Into The Void (7:07)/ Psychophobia (2:59)/ Black Sabbath (8:12)/ Neon Knights (5:27)
CD2: Immaculate Deception (4:42)/ The Wizard (4:16)/ Cross Of Thorns (9:33)/ Headless Cross (5:45)/ Paranoid (4:54)/ Iron Man - Sabbath Bloody Sabbath (3:48)/ The Mob Rules (6:00)/ Computer God (9:04)
R: Vg. Audience.   S: Universal Amphitheater '94.
C: ECD. Dcc. Pic CDs.

BLIND FAITH

CD - CAN'T FIND MY WAY HOME
RED LIGHT RL-1003
Can't Find My Way Home/ Had To Cry Today/ Untitled Number/ Cross Roads/ Presence Of The Lord/ Means To An End/ Do What You Like
R: G. Audience.   S: UCLA Puley Pavilion, LA Aug. 26 '69.

BLIND MELON

CD - A SWEET SLICE OF BLIND MELON
HOME RECORDS HR 5911-1
Tones Of Home (4:26)/ Soak The Sin (3:40)/ Deserted (7:21)/ No Rain (4:59)/ Drive (5:02)/ No Bidness (2:25)/ Paper Scratcher (3:55)/ Change (3:22)/ Time To Go (6:12)/ No Rain (4:52)/ Paper Scratcher (3:23)/ No Rain (acoustic - 3:46)
R: G-Vg. Audience.   S: Tracks 1-9 USA '93. Tracks 10-11 Saturday Night Live Jan. '94. Track 12 acoustic version.   C: ECD. Dcc.

CD - HIGH TIMES
HAWK 024
Tones Of Home (5:05)/ Soak The Sin (3:59)/ No Rain (5:24)/ Drive (5:12)/ Change (3:47) Time (7:05)/ Time (10:28)/ I Wonder (6:50)/ Tones Of Home (4:51)
R: Ex. Audience.   S: USA '93.   C: ECD. Dcc.

CD - SCREAMIN' AT THE SUN
ROCKS 92121
Tones Of Home (5:02)/ Soak The Sin (3:41)/ No Rain (5:40)/ Drive (5:08)/ Change (3:32)/ Time (6:32)/ Tones Of Home (5:00)/ Paper Scratcher (3:35)
R: Exs. Soundboard.   S: Tracks 1-6 Hollywood '93 Tracks 7, 8 Saturday Night Live Jan. 8 '94.
C: ECD. Dcc.

CD - STING ME
KISS THE STONE KTS 254
Tones Of Home/ Soak The Sin/ No Rain/ Drive/ No Rain/ Change/ Candy Says/ Paper Scratcher/ Twenty Below (The Boston Song)/ Change/ No Rain
R: Exs. Soundboard.   S: USA '93.   C: ECD. Dcc. Pic CD. Time 52:14.

BLONDE

CD - HEART OF GLASS
GRAPEFRUIT GRA-019-A
Dreaming (3:20)/ In The Sun (2:56)/ Die Young Stay Pretty (3:22)/ Slow Motion (3:01)/ Shayla (4:00)/ Union City Blue (3:20)/ Hardest Part (3:28)/ Atomic (6:07)/ Denise (2:55)/ Picture This (2:45)/ Louie Louie (4:07)/ Heart Of Glass (4:48)/ Hanging On The Telephone (2:35)/ I Feel Love (6:37)/ Heroes (6:19)/ I Got You (I Feel Good) (2:45)/ Sunday Girl (4:06)/ Pretty Baby (4:43)/ In The Flesh (3:01)
R: Vg. Soundboard.   S: Hammersmith Odeon, London, UK '80.   C: Australian CD. Dcc.

BLUE MURDER

CD - MURDER LICENSE
CRYSTAL SOUND CS-005
Out Of Love/ Boogie On A Good Foot/ Tony Franklin Bass Solo (includes Purple Haze)/ Billy/ Ptolemy/ Carmine Appice drum solo/ Jelly Roll/ Still Of The Night
S: Toronto, Canada Sept. 19 '89.

BLUES TRAVELLER

CD - ROADSHOW
BLUE KNIGHT RECORDS BKR 34
Mullin It Over (8:22)/ Warmer Days (8:47)/ Droppin Some NYC (9:50)/ What's For Breakfast (4:58)/ But Anyway (8:17)/ Crystal Time (14:46)/ Gina (7:26)
R: Exs. Soundboard.   S: Cabaret Metro, Chicago Mar. 3 '91.   C: ECD. Dcc.

BLUR

CD - MODROPHENIA
KISS THE STONE KTS 302
Girls & Boys/ Park Life/ Bank Holiday/ London Loves/ Chemical World/ Advert/ Jubilee/ Pop Scene/ Girls & Boys/ For Tomorrow/ Sunday, Sunday/ Park Life/ Jubilee/ For Tomorrow
R: Exs. Soundboard.   S: Tracks 1-10 electric set '94. Tracks 11-14 acoustic set '94.   C: ECD. Dcc. Pic CD.

CD - SAWDUST SEIZURES
KISS THE STONE KTS 338
Jubilee/ Tracy Jacks/ Magic America/ End Of A Century/ For Tomorrow/ There's No Other Way/ To The End/ Advert/ Parklife/ Girls & Boys/ Bank Holiday/ This Is A Law/ Lot 105/ Jubilee/ Girls & Boys/ Pop Scene/ Advert/ End Of A Century/ Parklife/ Parklife/ Bank Holiday/ This Is A Law
R: Ex. Audience.   S: Live in Europe '94.
C: ECD. Dcc. Pic CD. Time 77:32.

BODY COUNT

CD - THE HOUSE
BUNDY RECORDS SE 323

Power (4:40)/ 6 AM In The Morning (5:01)/ Body Count's In The House (3:45)/ Halb (1:45)/ Body Count (4:29)/ Bowels Of The Devil (6:03)/ KKK Bitch (3:15)/ Voodoo (3:20)/ There Goes The Neighborhood/ Evil Dick (5:26)/ Mommos Gotta Die Tonight (7:34)
R: G-Vg. Audience.   S: Live.   C: ECD. Dbw.

CD - SURVIVING THE GIG... LIVE
OLYMPUS RECORDS 0R 001
Body Count's In The House, Masters Of Revenge (9:49)/ Killin' Floor, Necessary Evil (8:03)/ Body Count (6:31)/ KKK Bitch (3:58)/ Who Are You (3:46)/ Surviving The Game (5:53)/ Drive By, Voodoo (4:48)/ There Goes The Neighborhood (6:31)/ Evil Dick (3:24)/ Street Labotomy (3:24)/ Last Breath (3:36)/ Born Dead (8:32)/ Copkiller (6:20)
R: G-Vg. Audience.   S: Europe '94.   C: ECD. Dcc. With ICE T.

BOGUSS, SUZY

CD - WHAT'S THE STORY ALL ABOUT
ROYAL SOUND MUSIC RSM 062SQ CD
Someday Soon/ Other Side Of The Hill/ Drive South/ Cross My Broken Heart/ Save Yourself/ Heartache/ Letting Go/ I'm Home On The Range/ Just Like The Weather/ Outbound Plane/ Hey Cinderella/ Aces/ I Want To Be A Cowboy Sweetheart
S: 'Something Up My Sleeve' tour USA '94.
C: ECD.

BOLTON, MICHAEL

CD - LIVE VOL. 1
JOKER JOK-052-A
That's What Love Is All About (4:54)/ Sittin' On The Dock Of The Bay (4:17)/ How Am I Supposed To Live Without You (3:22)/ I Found Someone (3:35)/ Steel Bars (4:07)/ Time, Love And Tenderness (5:30)/ When A Man Loves A Woman (6:28)/ We're Not Making Love Anymore (6:14)/ Georgia On My Mind (7:23)
R: Exs. Soundboard.   S: Europe '91.
C: Australian CD. Dcc.

BON JOVI

CD - BED OF ROSES
GRAPEFRUIT GRA-002-A
I Believe (5:15)/ Wild In The Streets (4:54)/ You Give Love A Bad Name (3:41)/ Born to Be My Baby (5:27)/ Medley: Can't Help Falling In Love/ Bed Of Roses (8:50)/ Keep The Faith (7:43)/ I'd Die For You (4:41)/ Blaze Of Glory (6:14)/ Lay Your Hands On Me (9:21)
R: Exs. Soundboard.   S: New Jersey, USA '93 part one. See 'In These Arms' (GRA-002-B) for part two.   C: Australian CD. Dcc.

CD - IN THESE ARMS
GRAPEFRUIT GRA-002-B

Medley: I'll Sleep When I'm Dead, Jumping Jack Flash (8:23)/ Medley: Bad Medicine, Shout (10:55)/ Help! (3:13)/ Medley: Little Wing, Wanted Dead Or Alive (10:27)/ Medley: In These Arms, Livin' On A Prayer (14:47)/ I'll Be There For You (9:56)
R: Exs. Soundboard.   S: New Jersey, USA '93 part two. See 'Bed Of Roses' (GRA-002-A) for part one.   C: Australian CD. Dcc.

CD - LIVE VOL. 1
JOKER JOK-045-A
I'll Sleep When I'm Dead/ Lay Your Hands On Me/ Bed Of Roses/ Bad Medicine/ Blaze Of Glory/ I'll Be There For You/ You Give Love A Bad Name/ Wanted Dead Or Alive/ Livin' On A Prayer/ Runaway/ Burning For Love/ Only Lonely/ Shot Through The Heart
R: Exs. Soundboard.   S: Tokyo, Japan '85. New Jersey '87 - '90.   C: Australian CD. Dcc.

CD - ONLY FOR YOU (VOL. 1)
BANANA BAN-002-A
Tokyo Road (5:55)/ Breakout (6:21)/ Only Lonely (5:52)/ She Don't Know Me (6:40)/ Bang Bang (My Baby Shot Me Down) (1:32)/ Shot Through The Heart (5:04)/ Silent Night (6:28)/ The Hardest Part Is The Night (5:03)/ In And Out Of Love (8:38)/ Runaway (5:05)/ Burning For Love (5:19)/ Get Ready (7:00)
R: Ex. Soundboard.   S: Japan '85.
C: Australian CD. Dcc.

CD - ONLY FOR YOU (VOL. 2)
BANANA BAN-002-B
You Give Love A Bad Name (3:44)/ Wild In The Streets (5:22)/ Wanted Dead Or Alive (8:34)/ Silent Night (10:37)/ Let It Rock (11:34)/ In And Out Of Love (9:04)/ Drift Away (5:42)/ Get Ready (8:32)/ Livin' On A Prayer (5:24)/ Runaway (5:24)
R: Ex. Soundboard.   S: USA '87.   C: Australian CD. Dcc.

CD - ONLY FOR YOU (VOL. 3)
BANANA BAN-002-C
Lay Your Hands On Me (5:28)/ I'd Die For You (4:29)/ Wild In The Streets (5:03)/ You Give Love A Bad Name (3:39)/ Fever (2:03)/ Born To Be My Baby (6:58)/ Let It Rock (10:04)/ I'll Be There For You (9:00)/ Blood On Blood (12:17)/ Livin' On A Prayer (5:45)/ Living In Sin (10:36)
R: Vg-Ex. Soundboard.   S: USA '90.
C: Australian CD. Dcc.

CD - SEATTLE SURVIVORS
WHY NOT BKCD 080
Lay Your Hands On Me/ Tokyo Road/ I'll Be There For You/ I'll Sleep When I'm Dead/ Living On A Prayer/ Wanted Dead Or Alive/ You Give Love A Bad Name/ Keep The Faith/ Blaze Of Glory/ In These Arms/ Bad Medicine/ Shout
R: Exs - FM.   S: Tempe, AZ '93.   C: ECD. Time 74:00.

CD - SHOUT
HAMMERJACK HJ 011
I Believe (5:20)/ Walking Street (6:15)/ You Give
Love A Bad Name (3:31)/ Can't Help Falling In
Love (1:59)/ Bed Of Roses (6:32)/ Keep The Faith
(7:29)/ Blaze Of Glory (5:54)/ Dry County (11:25)/
Lay Your Hands On Me (8:31)/ I'll Sleep When I'm
Dead (6:41)/ Shout (1:59)/ With A Little Help From
My Friends (6:13)/ Living On A Prayer (4:39)*
R: G. Audience. *Ex. Soundboard.   S: Ahoy,
Rotterdam Apr. 23 '93. Track 13 From MTV.
C: ECD. Dcc.

BOSTON

CD - FROM HERE TO ETERNITY
SHINOLA SH 69018
More Than A Feeling/ It Isn't Easy/ A Man I'll
Never Be/ Smokin'/ Peace Of Mind/ Foreplay/
Long Time/ Rock 'N' Roll Band/ Help Me
R: G-Vgs. Soundboard.   S: Live California.
C: ECD. Dcc. Time 47:56.

BOWIE, DAVID

CD - A CAT FROM LONDON
JUP CD J-003
Hang On To Yourself/ Ziggy Stardust/ Changes/
Moonage Daydream/ John I'm Only Dancing/
Watch That Man/ The Jean Genie/ Time/ Five
Years/ Let's Spend The Night Together/ Starman/
Suffragette City/ Rock'N'Roll Suicide/ 'Round And
'Round
R: Audience.   S: Sibuya Public Hall, Tokyo,
Japan Apr. 20 '73.

CD - THE JEAN GENIE (VOL. 1)
BANANA BAN-004-A
White Light, White Heat (3:38)/ Let Me Sleep
Beside You (3:13)/ Unwashed And Somewhat
Slightly Dazed (3:55)/ Wild Eyed Boy From
Freecloud (4:33)/ Bombers (2:42)/ Looking For A
Friend (2:55)/ Almost Grown (2:06)/ Kooks (3:01)/
The Supermen (2:47)/ Ziggy Stardust (3:17)/ Five
Years (4:19)/ Starman (3:59)/ Rock 'N' Roll
Suicide (3:04)/ Hang On To Yourself (2:39)/ I'm
Waiting for The Man (4:56)
R: Ex. Soundboard.   S: Europe '69-'72.
C: Australian CD. Dcc.

CD - THE JEAN GENIE (VOL. 2)
BANANA BAN-004-B
Hang On To Yourself (2:47)/ Ziggy Stardust (3:24)/
Changes (3:32)/ The Supermen (2:56)/ Life On
Mars? (3:28)/ Five Years (5:20)/ Space Oddity
(4:57)/ Andy Warhol (4:11)/ My Death (5:44)/ The
Width Of A Circle (10:38)/ Queen Bitch (3:00)/
Moonage Daydream (4:36)/ John I'm Only
Dancing (3:03)/ Introduction To The Band (0:31)/
I'm Waiting For The Man (5:43)/ Jean Genie
(4:15)/ Suffragette City (3:33)/ Rock'N'Roll Suicide
(3:10)
R: Ex. Soundboard.   S: USA '72.
C: Australian CD. Dcc.

CD - THE JEAN GENIE (VOL. 3)
BANANA BAN-004-C
Look Back In Anger (3:04)/ Scary Monsters (And
Super Creeps) (3:27)/ Rebel Rebel (2:17)/ Heroes
(4:51)/ What In The World (3:27)/ Life On Mars?
(4:08)/ Sorrow (2:08)/ Fashion (2:38)/ Let's Dance
(4:36)/ Red Sails (3:17)/ China Girl (4:52)/ White
Light White Heart (4:55)/ Station To Station (8:39)/
Cracked Actor (3:08)
R: Ex. Soundboard.   S: USA '84.
C: Australian CD. Dcc.

CD - THE JEAN GENIE (VOL. 4)
BANANA BAN-004-D
Ashes To Ashes (3:48)/ Space Oddity (5:05)/
Introduction To The Band (1:50)/ Young American
(5:00)/ Cat People (Putting Out Fire) (4:04)/ Fame
(3:55)/ Star (2:29)/ Jean Genie (5:53)/ I Can't
Explain (2:48)/ Breaking Glass (2:46)/ Golden
Years (3:24)/ TVC 15 (3:36)/ Stay (8:02)/ Modern
Love (3:46)
R: Ex. Soundboard.   S: USA '84.   C: Australian
CD. Dcc.

CD - NAKED & WIRED
BOW 005
Space Oddity/ Rupert The Riley/ Changes/ Kooks/
Amsterdam/ Star Man/ Jean Genie/ A Lad In Vain/
All The Young Dudes/ Tired Of My Life/ Who Can I
Be Now?/ London Bye Ta Ta/ The Chingaling
Song/ Lover To The Dawn/ The Man Who Sold
The World/ Boys Keep Swinging/ Ashes To Ashes/
Space Oddity
S: Tracks 1-13 demos and outtakes. Track 14
unreleased. Tracks 15,16 and 18 Saturday Night
Live. Track 17 Johnny Carson Show.

CD - STARMAN IN SESSION
SILVER RARITIES 93
Love You Till Tuesday/ When I Live My Dream/
The Little Bombadier/ Silly Box Blue/ In The Heat
Of The Morning/ Waiting For The Man/ Width Of A
Circle/ Wild Eyed Boy From Free Cloud/
Suffragette City/ Hang On To Yourself/ White Light
White Heat/ Moonage Day Dream/ Ziggy Stardust/
John I'm Only Dancing/ Lady Stardust/ Starman/
Changes
R: Exs. Soundboard.   S: BBC Session 1969-72.
C: ECD. Dcc. Time 65:51.

THE BREEDERS

CD - DON'T NEED NO FAT MAN
BLUE MOON BMCD9
Divine Hammer (2:34)/ Cannonball (3:30)/ Doe
(1:59)/ Limehouse (1:34)/ Divine Hammer (2:32)/
No Aloha (2:22)/ Cannonball (3:20)/ Flipside
(1:52)/ Iris (3:21)/ Hag (2:29)/ Divine Hammer
(2:35)/ No Aloha (2:19)/ Cannonball (acoustic)
(3:14)/ Hellbound (2:09)/ When I Was A Painter
(2:53)/ Fortunately Gone (1:37)/ Iris (3:09)/ I Just
Wanna Get Along (1:43)/ Safari (3:11)/ Don't Call
Home (3:44)/ Fortunately Gone (1:39)/ Iris (3:38)/
Opened (2:18)/ Do You Love Me Now? (2:46)/

Happiness Is A Warm Gun (2:33)
R: Exs. Soundboard.   S: Tracks 1-2 Seattle winter '93. Tracks 3-4 'Last Splash' tour fall '93. Tracks 5-9 MTV Studios, Camden, London, England winter '93. Tracks 10-13 alternate studios versions summer '93. Tracks 14-18 Palladium Studio demos spring '90. Tracks 19-25 Glastonbury Festival summer '92.   C: ECD. Dcc.

CD - DOUBLE-TROUBLE
KISS THE STONE KTS223
Iris (3:11)/ Cannonball (3:35)/ Saints (2:34)/ Hag (2:25)/ Fortunately Gone (1:50)/ When I Was A Painter (2:46)/ Doe (2:06)/ Limehouse (1:54)/ Only In 3's (3:39)/ Doe (2:05)/ Hellbound (2:46)/ Safari (3:13)/ Happiness Is A Warm Gun (2:40)/ Glorious (2:38)/ Do You Love Me Now? (3:02)/ Don't Call Home (4:01)/ Fortunately Gone (2:00)/ I Just Wanna Get Along (1:54)/ When I Was A Painter (3:57)/ Limehouse (1:59)/ Iris (3:33)/ Opened (2:22)
R: Exs. Soundboard.   S: Live '93.   C: ECD. Yellow cover. Red text. Pic CD.

CD - NEVER MIND THE BREEDERS - HERE'S THE BREEDERS
MIND THE MAGIC MTM 038
Devine Hammer/ No Aloha/ Flipside/ Saints/ Hag/ Cannonball/ Iris/ Don't Call Home/ Fortunately Gone/ When I Was A Painter/ Doe/ Limehouse/ Invisible Man/ I Just Wanna Get Along/ Iris/ Cannonball/ Saints/ Hag/ Fortunately Gone/ When I Was A Painter/ Doe/ Limehouse/ Hag/ Iris
R: Exs. Soundboard.   S: Europe '93.   C: ECD. Dbw. Red type. Time 61:30.

CD - SONIC ECSTASY
OCTOPUS OCTO 015
SOS (1:53)/ New Year (1:56)/ Hellbound (2:25)/ When I Was A Painter (3:19)/ No Aloha (2:21)/ Flipside (2:08)/ Never Call Home (3:31)/ Iris (3:34)/ Lord Of The Thighs (3:32)/ Fortunately (2:02)/ Cannonball (3:32)/ Invisible Man (3:04)/ Roi (3:02)/ Hag (2:55)/ Devine Hammer (2:41)/ Safari (3:21)/ Saints (4:42)/ Doe (2:14)
R: Exs. Soundboard.   S: Metro Club, Chicago June 6 '94.   C: ECD. Dcc. Pic CD.

BROWNE, JACKSON

CD - EVERYMAN'S ALIVE
WESTERN BEAT RSM RSM 047 2
CD1: Doctor My Eyes (4:46)/ I'm Alive (5:17)/ World In Motion (5:02)/ Everywhere I Go (6:46)/ My Problem Is You (5:04)/ In The Shape Of A Heart (6:26)/ Late For The Sky (6:19)/ Your Bright Baby Blues (6:29)/ Miles Away (4:36)/ Too Many Angels (8:11)/ For Everyman (7:10)/ Boulevard (3:52)/ That Girl Could Sing (5:33)
CD2: Sky Blue And Black (8:01)/ The Pretender (6:58)/ Running On Empty (4:48)/ The Load-Out (5:06)/ Stay (3:34)/ Linda Paloma (4:52)/ Two Of Me Two Of You (2:49)/ For America (5:50)/ Tender Is The Night (4:24)/ Chasing You Into The Light

(5:19)/ Anything Can Happen (6:26)/ For A Dancer (5:55)/ Lawless Avenues (7:33)/ The Word Justice (5:06)
R: Exs. Soundboard.   S: CD1 &CD2 Tracks 1-6 Eugene, Oregon '94. CD2 Track 7 solo acoustic studio performance '94. Tracks 8-14 USA '89 Tour.   C: ECD. Dcc.

CD - TOO MANY ANGELS
KISS THE STONE KTS 258
Too Late For The Sky (5:59)/ World In Motion (4:40)/ My Problem Is You (6:17)/ Two Of Me, Two Of You (3:08)/ Miles Away (4:07)/ Too Many Angels (6:32)/ For Everyman (6:16)/ Sky Blue And Black (7:10)/ The Pretender (6:39)/ Before The Deluge (7:43)
S: '93.   C: ECD. Dcc. Pic CD.

BUFFALO, GRANT LEE

CD - LIKE A SHOT
KISS THE STONE KTS 320
The Shining Hour (4:26)/ Drag (4:25)/ Jupiter And Teardrop (5:21)/ Soft Wolf Tread (2:56)/ Fuzzy (5:54)/ America Snoring (4:02)/ For The Turnstiles (4:17)/ The Shining Hour (2) (4:05)/ Wish You Well, Jupiter And Teardrop (6:40)
R: Exs.   S: Live on tour '94.   C: ECD. Dcc. Pic CD.

BUFFALO TOM

CD - LUPO'S HEARTBREAK HOTEL
TRIANGLE RECORDS PYCD 092
Velvet Roof (4:42)/ Latest Monkey (2:45)/ I Am Allowed (4:19)/ Suppose (3:10)/ Late At Night (4:07)/ Soda Jerk (4:32)/ Taillights (3:50)/ Flushing Star (3:48)/ Mineral (5:28)/ Tree House (4:13)/ Larry (5:48)/ Darl (3:28)/ Staples (3:47)/ Brain (3:39)/ Frozen Lake (4:01)/ Torch Singer (3:09)/ Butterscotch (3:52)/ The Bus (5:48)
R: Vg-Ex. Audience.   S: Lupo's Heartbreak Hotel Mar. 3 '94.   C: ECD. Dcc.

BUSH, KATE

CD - BACK SIDES
OBSERVATION RECORDS OB 002
December Will Be Magic/ Warm And Soothing/ Ran Tan Waltz/ Full House/ The Empty Building/ Burning Bridge/ Not This Time/ The Handsome Cabin Boy/ Under The Ivy/ The Big Sky
R: Exs. Soundboard. Some surface noise.
C: ECD. Dbw. Time 36:90.

CD - HOME DEMOS
THE GENUINE PIG RECORDS TGP-CD-093
Babooshka (2:04)/ Kashka From Baghdad (2:00)/ Coming Up (2:30)/ Oh, To Be In Love (1:50)/ Playing Canasta (3:10)/ Snow (4:00)/ Ferry Me Over (2:30)/ Lionhearts (3:04)/ Violin (2:22)/ The Craft Of Love (2:02)/ Queen Eddie (2:55)/ In My Garden (2:30)/ Frightened Eyes (2:10)/ Never The Less (3:15)/ Goodnight Baby (2:55)/ So Soft

(3:50)/ I Don't See Why I Shouldn't (2:50)/ Babooshka (2:50)/ The Kick Inside (3:46)/ Hammer Horror (2:46)/ A Rose Growing Old (2:58)/ Keep Me Waiting (2:55)/ Davy (3:10)/ Disbelieving Angel (2:15)/ Don't Push Your Foot On The Heart Brake (2:51)/ Kite (2:47)/ L'Amour Looks Something Like You (2:12)/ Strange Phenomena (2:44)/ Really Gets Me Going (3:14)
R: G-Vg. Some surface noise.   S: Tracks 1-24 home demos '74. Tracks 25-29 studio outtakes '75.   C: ECD. Dcc.

CD - THIS WOMAN'S WORK - EXTENDED EDITION I

The Empty Bullring/ Ran Tan Waltz/ Passing Through Air/ December Will Be Magic Again/ Warm And Soothing/ Lord Of The Reedy River/ Ne T'en Fui Pas/ Un Baiser D'Un Enfant/ Under The Ivy/ Burning The Ivy/ Burning Bridge/ My Lagan Love/ The Handsome Cabin Boy/ Not This Time/ Walk Straight Down The Middle/ Be Kind To My Mistakes/ Rocket Man/ Candle In The Wind
R: Exs. Soundboard.   C: ECD. Black/red cover. White type. Time 56:00.

CD - THIS WOMAN'S WORK - EXTENDED EDITION II

I'm Still Waiting/ Ken/ One Last Look Around The House Before We Go/ Wuthering Heights (new vocals)/ Experiment IV/ Them Heavy People/ Don't Put Your Foot On The Heartbreak/ James And The Cold Gun/ L'Amour Looks Something Like You/ Running Up That Hill/ Cloudbusting (organon mix)/ Hounds Of Love (alternative)/ The Big Sky (meteorological mix)/ Experiment IV (12" mix)/ Rubberband Girl
R: Exs. Soundboard.   C: ECD. Black/red cover. White type. Time 73:45.

THE BYRDS

CD - BOSTON TEA PARTY

YELLOW DOG YD 045
You Ain't Going Nowhere (3:24)/ He Was A Friend Of Mine (3:22)/ Old Blue (3:35)/ Long Black Veil (3:27)/ Goin' Back (3:46)/ Get Outta My Life Woman (3:21)/ Ballad Of Easy Rider (2:48)/ Jesus Is Just Allright (3:22)/ Mr. Spaceman (3:04)/ This Wheel's On Fire (4:42)/ Lay Lady Lay (3:22)/ The Time Between (2:08)/ My Back Pages (2:33)/ Whacha Want Me To Do (3:24)/ Big City Bride (2:13)/ It's All Over Now, Baby Blue (4:19)/ Way Beyond The Sun (2:55)/ Way Beyond The Sun (2:55)/ Turn, Turn, Turn (1:52)/ Mr. Tambourine Man (2:30)/ I Shall Be Released (3:16)/ Drug Store Truckdrivin' Man (3:23)/ Nashville West (2:01)
R: Exs. Soundboard.   S: Feb. 22 '69.   C: ECD. Dcc.

CD - NEVER EVER BEFORE

WHOOPY CAT WKP 0020
Mr. Tambourine Man/ I Knew I'd Want You/ It's No Use/ The Bells Of Rhymney/ Feel A Whole Lot Better/ You Won't Have To Cry/ We'll Meet Again/

She Don't Care About Time/ Set Me Free This Time/ It's All Over Now Baby Blue/ The World Turns All Around Her/ She Has A Way/ Turn Turn Turn/ Eight Miles High/ Why
R: Ex. Soundboard.   S: Studio outtakes.
C: Japanese CD. Dcc. Time 70:10

CD - REUNION SPECIAL

NIGHTINGALE ELECTRIC RECORDS BYR 78
CD1: Lover Of The Bayou/ American Girl/ Mr. Spaceman/ Why Baby Why/ Tiffany Queen/ Golden Loom/ It's Gone/ Chestnut Mare/ Dixie Highway/ Shoot 'Em/ So You Want To Be A Rock'N Roll Star/ Mr. Tambourine Man/ Eight Miles High
CD2: Kansas City Southern/ Denver Or Wherever/ Release Me Girl/ Hula Hula Man/ We Know It's Wrong/ Rise And Fall/ Nothing Gets Through To You/ Rollin' And Tumblin'/ No Reason To Cry/ Quits/ The Witching Hour/ It Doesn't Matter
R: Exm. Soundboard.   S: Hammersmith Odeon, London '78.   C: ECD. Dcc. Discs mislabelled - 1 is 'Disc 2' and 2 is 'Disc 1'. Time CD1 57:06. CD2 54:44.

CD - TAMBOURINES AND 12-STRINGS

GOLD STANDARD 32
I Knew I'd Want You #1/ It's No Use #6/ The Bells Of Rhymney #2/ I'll Feel A Whole Lot Better #2/ It Won't Be Long #8/ The World Turns All Around Her #15/ Satisfied Mind/ Set You Free This Time #1, 2, 3, 4, 8/ Stranger In A Strange Land #1, 2/ Wait And See #25, 26/ Oh Susanna #1/ 5D #1-7/ 5D #12/ It's All Over Now Baby Blue #4, 5/ Tambourines And 12-Strings/ Mr. Tambourine Man #4, 5, 6/ Goin' Back/ Don't Make Waves/ He Was A Friend Of Mine/ My Back Pages/ Baby What You Want Me To Do?/ Byrds Chyrp
R: Ex. Soundboard.   S: Tracks 1-18 alternate studio versions, Columbia Studios, CA. Tracks 19-20 Avalon Ballroom, San Francisco, CA Nov. 2 '68. Track 21 interview '65.   C: Dcc. Time 77:13.

BYRNE, DAVID

CD - UNPLUGGED + MORE

KISS THE STONE KTS 247
The Cowboy Mambo (Hey Look At Me Now) (3:58)/ (Nothing But) Flowers (4:38)/ Naked (3:53)/ The Future (4:11)/ Gypsy Woman (3:44)/ Girls On My Mind (4:18)/ Wall Of Death (2:17)/ Road To Nowhere (3:24)/ Rockin' In The Free World (3:40)/ Psyco Killer (4:37)/ Something Ain't Right (3:38)/ Man Without Name (2:23)/ Green-Back Dollar (1:52)/ A Walk In The Dark (4:21)/ Girls On My Mind (3:52)/ Tiny Town (4:50)/ Dirty Old Town (4:23)/ Last Night (2:11)/ (Nothing But) Flowers (4:36)/ Naked (3:34)/ Dallas (3:54)*
R: Exs. Soundboard.   S: San Francisco, CA Dec. 13 '92. *with 10,000 Maniacs.   C: ECD. Dcc. Pic CD.

C

CAN

CD - RADIO WAVES
GOLD STANDARD FIC-929
Up The Bakerloo (with Anne Nightengale Mar. 16
'72)/ Paperhouse (Beat Club spring '71 for
German TV)/ Entropy (Germany '70)/ Little Star
(studio recordings, Schloss Norvenich Apr.
'69)/ Turtles Have Short Legs (LP B-side of the single
'Spoon' '71)/ Shikaku Maru Ten (non-LP B-side of
the single 'Halleluwah' '71)
R: Vg-Ex. Soundboard.   C: ECD. Dcc. Gold disc.
Time 71:16.

CANDLEBOX

CD - BOTH ENDS BURNING
KISS THE STONE KTS 355
Cover Me, Bothered (acoustic versions USA Aug.
17 '94)/ Change, No Sense, Far Behind, Cover
Me, You (Whiskey A Go Go, LA '94)/ Change, No
Sense, Embryo, Far Behind, You (Boston Mar. 12
'94)
R: Exs. Soundboard.   C: ECD. Dcc. Pic CD.

CD - INTO THE FLAME
ALLEY KAT AK 440
Pull Away/ Change Is Gonna Come/ Far Behind/
Can't Give In/ Cover Me/ Time/ Lonely People/
Run/ In My Memory/ Listen (take 2)/ Strapped/
Listen (take 1)/ Change Is Gonna Come*/ Far
Behind*
R: Exs. Soundboard.   S: Tracks 1-12 studio
demos. *Los Angeles, CA USA 02/05/94.
C: ECD. Dcc. Pic CD. Time 69:05.

CD - THE LAST GREAT SEATTLE BAND
HOME RECORDS HR5970-7
Change (6:06)/ No Sense (2:23)/ Far Behind
(6:10)/ Cover Me (4:57)/ You (4:51)/ Change
(6:43)/ No Sense (5:29)/ Embryo (4:40)/ Far
Behind (8:54)/ You (5:15)
R: Ex. Audience. Tracks 6-10 poor-G. Audience.
S: Tracks 1-5 Whiskey A Go Go, Los Angeles '94.
Tracks 6-10 Centrum, Mass. Mar. 12 '94.
C: ECD. Dcc.

CALE, J.J.

CD - J.J. DOES!
RARE RECORDING COLLECTION RRC 039
After Midnight/ River Boat Song/ Mama Don't/
Humdinger/ Hold On Baby/ New Orleans/ Lickin'
Stick/ Disadvantage/ Hard Times/ Movin' Blues/
Magnolia/ Call Me The Breeze/ Cocaine/ Money
Talks/ Crazy Mama/ Ride Me High
R: Exs. Soundboard.   S: Minneapolis Apr. 18
'91.   C: ECD. Dcc. Time 78:25.

CALE, JOHN & CHRIS SPEDDING

CD - DOWN AT THE END OF LONELY
STREET...HARD ROCK CAFE
ARCHIVIO ARC CD 006
Autobiography (4:46)/ Mercenaries (9:18)/ Love
Me Two Times (2:34)/ The Hunt (3:55)/ Paris 1919
(3:44)/ Helen Of Troy (4:21)/ Guts (4:22)/
Heartbreak Hotel (3:43)/ Pablo Picasso (3:08)/
Cable Hogue (3:32)/ Dying On The Vine (4:28)
R: Vg-Ex. Audience.   S: Stockholm '75.
C: ECD. Dcc.

CAPTAIN BEEFHEART

CD - DON'S BIRTHDAY PARTY
TUFF BITES T.B. 94.1008
Suction Prints (2:36)/ My Human Gets Be Blues
(3:27)/ Nowadays A Woman's Got To Hit A Man
(4:15)/ Hot Head (3:36)/ Ashtray Heart (4:09)/ Dirty
Blue Gene (4:24)/ Best Batch Yet (6:13)/ Safe As
Milk (5:23)/ A Carrot Is As Close As A Rabbit Gets
To A Diamond (2:12)/ One Red Rose That I Mean
(2:27)/ Dr. Dark (3:01)/ Bat Chain Puller (8:24)/
Sugar 'N Spikes (3:23)/ Veteran's Day Poppy
(4:34)/ Sheriff Of Hong Kong (6:53)/ Suction Prints
(5:21)/ Big Eyed Beans From Venus (4:46)
R: G-Vg. Audience.   S: Showbox, Seattle Jan.
15 '81.   C: ECD. Dcc. Digi-pack. Pic CD.

CD - THE EARLY YEARS 1959-1969
BEEF MUSIC CDBF 5969
Lost In A Whirlpool (2:21)#/ Teenage Maltshop
(1:13)/ Metal Man Has Lost His Wings (3:25)/
Tupelo Mississippi (4:11)*/ Somebody's Walking
(2:46)*/ Old Folks Boogie (3:17)*/ Evil (2:23)*/
Blues Jam (3:10)*/ Out Of The Frying Pan
(alternate version (1:57)/ Almost Grown (2:08)/
Call On Me (slow version) (2:57)/ Sure Nuff And
Yes I Do (2:33)/ Moody Liz (rare acetate version)
(4:38)/ Korn Ring Finger (7:38)/ Frownland (1:50)/
Ella Guru (2:33)/ Hair Pie-Bake 1, Hair Pie-Bake 2
(5:33)/ Pachuco Cadaver (4:01)/ Sugar 'N Spikes
(2:37)/ Neon Meat Dream Of A Octofish (2:28)/
The Blimp-Edit, Candy Man, China Pig (5:40)/
Well Well Well (1:58)
R: G-Vg. #Poor.   S: *Avalon Ballroom '68.
C: ECD. Dcc. Very rare stuff. Pic CD.

CAPTAIN BEYOND

CD - IT'S OUR LIFE
TNT STUDIO 940138
Distant Sun/ Dancing Madly Backwards (On A Sea
Of Air)/ Armsworth/ Myopic Void/ Drifting In Space/
Thousand Days Of Yesterdays/ Frozen Over/
Guitar Solo/ Mesmerization Eclipse/ Stone Free
R: Ex. Audience.   S: Texas '73.   C: Japanese
CD. Dcc. Time 70:19.

CAREY, MARIAH

CD - SOMEDAY
KISS THE STONE KTS 335

Emotions/ Hero/ Someday/ Without You/ Make It
Happen/ Dreamlover/ Love Takes Time/ Anytime
You Need A Friend/ Vision Of Love/ I'll Be There
R: Exs. Soundboard.   S: USA '94.   C: ECD.
Dcc. Pic CD. Time 40:20.

CARPENTERS, THE

CD - CLOSE TO YOU
GRAPEFRUIT GRA-018-A
Only Yesterday (:50)/ There's A Kind Of A Hush
(2:21)/ Yesterday Once More (3:19)/ Superstar
(1:38)/ Rainy Days And Mondays (1:57)/ Goodbye
To Love (3:30)/ We've Only Just Begun (2:57)/
Jambalaya (3:18)/ For All We Know (2:37)/ Top Of
The World (2:45)/ Close To You (3:29)/ Sing
(3:27)/ Sometimes (2:26)/ Help (3:23)/ Mr. Guder
(3:44)/ I Need To Be In Love (3:45)/ Don't Be
Afraid (1:06)/ From This Moment On (1:59)/ Thank
You For The Music (3:26)/ Medley: Close To You,
For All We Know, Top Of The World, Ticket To
Ride, Only Yesterday, I Won't Last A Day Without
You, Hurting Each Other, Please Mr. Postman
(9:37)
R: Vg. Soundboard.   S: Tokyo, Japan & New
York '76.   C: Australian CD. Dcc.

CATHEDRAL

CD - COSMIC FUNERAL
KISS THE STONE KTS 390
Enter Worms/ Autumn Twilight/ Cosmic Funeral/
Midnight Mountain/ A Funeral Request/ Ride
R: Exs. Soundboard.   S: May 24 '94.   C: ECD.
Dcc. Pic CD. Time 38:59.

CAVE, NICK

CD - VIVA LAS VEGAS
MONTANA MO 10012
I Put A Spell On You (5:12)/ Knocking On Joe part
1/2 (7:42)/ City Of Refuge (4:11)/ From Here To
Eternity (1:59)/ Well Of Misery (6:47)/ Sad Dark
Eyes (3:00)/ Blind Lemon (7:56)/ Wanted Man
(4:31)/ Your Funeral My Trail (3:55)/ She Fell
Away (4:15)/ Train Long Suffering (4:13)/ St. Huck
(7:06)/ All Tomorrows Parties (6:11)/ The Carnival
Is Over (3:00)/ Little Girl Tree (5:17)
R: Exs. Soundboard.   S: USA. Australia.
C: ECD. Dcc.

CHAPIN CARPENTER, MARY

CD - PASSIONATE KISSES FROM AUSTIN
ROYAL SOUND MUSIC RSM 033 SQ
Never Had It So Good/ You Win Again/ Going Out
Tonight/ Rhythm Of The Blues/ Passionate Kisses/
Read My Lips/ Only A Dream/ Come On Come
On/ He Thinks He'll Keep Her/ The Moon And St.
Christopher/ I Feel Lucky/ Never Had It So Good
(Pete Kennedy on guitar)
S: Austin, Texas '92.   C: ECD.

CLAPTON, ERIC

CD - BIG BLUE
HAWK 049/50
CD1: Intro - White Room (6:10)/ Pretending (6:48)/
I Shot The Sheriff (9:03)/ Running On Faith (8:00)/
Another Love (6:05)/ Tears In Heaven (4:52)/
Before You Accuse Me (9:26)/ Old Love (11:15)
CD2: Badge (7:05)/ Wonderful Tonight (9:10)/
Layla (8:01)/ Crossroads (10:58)/ Sunshine Of
Your Life (5:11)
R: G-Vg. Audience.   S: Los Angeles '92.
C: ECD. Dcc. Pic CD.

CD - BLUES POWER
GOLD STANDARD
Presence Of The Lord/ Blues Power/ Have You
Ever Loved A Woman/ Bottle Of Red Wine/
Comin' Home (BBC '70 with Delaney & Bonnie)*/
Jam With Peter Green's Fleetwood Mac (Boston
Tea Party '70)/ I Want To Know/ Crossroads/
Powerhouse Blues/ Stevie's Takeaway/ Spoonful
With Cream (Club 'Revolution' London '67)
R: G-Vg. * Poor-G.   S: Tracks 1-4 BBC '70.
Tracks 7-8 '66 with Powerhouse. Tracks 9-10
unknown source.   C: ECD. Dcc. Gold disc.
Time 73:45.

CD - BLUES REHEARSALS
KISS THE STONE KTS 382
Hootchie Coochie Man/ I'm Tore Down/ Sinner's
Prayer/ Motherless Child/ Malted Milk/ Born Under
A Bad Sign/ Someday After A While/ It Hurts Me
Too/ 44/ Five Long Years/ Crossroads/ Ain't
Nobody's Business/ Bonus Tracks: I'm Tore
Down/ Five Long Years
R: Exs. Soundboard.   S: NYC Sept. 28 '94.
C: ECD. Pic CD.

CD - COMPLETE UNPLUGGED
EC RARITIES ECR 001, 002
CD1: Signe #1/ Before You Accuse Me/ Hey Hey/
Tears In Heaven # 1/ Circus Left Town/ Lonely
Stranger/ Nobody Knows You When You're Down
And Out/ Layla/ My Father's Eye #1/ Running On
Faith #1/ Walking Blues #1/ Alberta/ San
Francisco Bay Blues #1/ Malted Milk #1
CD2: Signe #2/ Tears In Heaven #2/ My Father's
Eye #2/ Rollin' And Tumblin'/ Running On Faith
#2/ Walking Blues #2/ San Francisco Bay Blues
#2/ Malted Milk #2/ Worried Life Blues/ Old Love/
Tears In Heaven (MTV Awards '92)/ Tears In
Heaven (Grammy Awards '93)
R: Ex. Soundboard.   S: Jan. 16 '92.
C: Japanese CD.

CD - THE END OF SUMMER NIGHT
DYNAMITE STUDIO DS 92N043/44
CD1: Layla/ Bell Bottom Blues/ Key To The
Highway/ Mainline Florida/ Can't Find My Way
Home/ Further On Up The Road/ Knockin' On
Heaven's Door/ Blues Power
CD2: Teach Me To Be Your Man/ Stormy Monday/
Badge/ Carnival/ Little Wing/ Eyesight To The

Blind
R: Poor.   S: Scope Arena, Norfolk, VA Aug. 30
'75.   C: Japanese CD.

CD - FEELIN' ALRIGHT
EMILLE LUSKEN EMLK 18793
CD1: White Room/ Badge/ Wonderful Tonight/
Stone Free/ Burning The Midnight Lamp/ Circus
Left Town/ Tears In Heaven/ Feelin' Allright/ Love
Me Like You Do/ You Can Leave Your Hat On/
Hard Times
CD2: Unchain My Heart/ Groaning The Blues/
Crossroads/ Ain't Nobody's Business/ Layla/
Stone Free/ Old Love/ Gimme Some Loving/ Can I
Get A Witness
R: G-Vgs. Audience.   S: NEC Arena Oct. 1 '93.
Tracks 7-11 and CD2 track 1 vocals Joe Cocker.
CD2 tracks 6-9 Cowdry Park, Sussex Sept. 18 '93.
C: Japanese CD. Dcc. Time CD1 52:43.
CD2 56:42.

CD - INFLUENTIAL BLUES
LORDS OF ARCHIVE RECORDS L.A.R. 5
Keep On Drinking/ How Long?/ Kidman Blues/
County Jail/ Room #44/ Blues All Day Long/ Going
Away/ Standin' Round Cryin'/ Hootchie Coochie
Man/ It Hurts Me Too/ Five Long Years/ The Third
Degree/ Sunday After Awhile/ Tore Down/ Have
You Ever Been Mistreated/ Born Under A Bad
Sign/ Grown In The Blues/ The Crossroads Blues
R: Ex. Audience.   S: Benefit concert for the T.J.
Martell Foundation, Avery Fisher Hall, Lincoln
Center, New York City May 2 '94.   C: ECD. Dcc.
Booklet with information about the T.J. Martell
Foundation. Time 76:58.

CD - JEWEL BOX 2
HOME RECORDS HR-5942-5
Falstaff Beer (Cream radio spot '67) (1:00)/ I Want
To Know (Power House '66) (2:13)/ I Feel Free
('66 live version) (2:52)/ Strange Brew ('67 live
recording) (2:51)/ Sunshine Of Your Love
(Winterland '68) (5:53)/ Outside Woman Blues
(live) (3:13)/ Tales Of Brave Ulysses (live) (3:01)/
Born Under A Bad Sign (live) (3:04)/ Change Of
Address (unreleased Blind Faith instrumental)
(3:23)/ Little Wing (live Derek and Dominoes)
(6:20)/ Evil (Derek and Dominoes outtake) (4:25)/
Have You Ever Loved A Woman (Derek and
Dominoes outtake) (4:59)/ After Midnight ('70
version with horns) (3:17)/ I Shot The Sheriff (live
'74) (5:18)/ Cocaine (live '86) (4:12)/ Knockin' On
Heaven's Door (Clapton vocal) (2:03)/ Sugar
Sweet (with Freddie King) (2:51)/ Rockin' Daddy
(with Howlin' Wolf) (3:40)/ Why Does Got To Be
So Sad (with Buckwheat Zydeco) (4:43)
R: Vg-Ex.   S: Rare live and unreleased tracks.
C: ECD. Dcc. Pic CD. Time 71:28.

CD- JOURNEYMAN OUTTAKES
ARMS 02PR
Pretending/ Forever/ Don't Turn Your Back/
Breaking Point (instrumental)/ No Alibis/ Lead Me
On/ Hard Times/ Running On Faith/ Something

About You/ Murdoch's Men (instrumental)/ Higher
Power (instrumental)
R: Ex.   S: Outtakes and rough mixes. Power
Station Studios and Skyline Studios, New York
Mar.-Apr. '89.   C: Japanese CD.

CD - LAYLA
PALOMINO PAL-018-A
Tears In Heaven (4:32)/ Wonderful Tonight (4:37)/
Cocaine (7:09)/ Layla (6:07)/ Lay Down Sally
(4:26)/ Pretending (5:55)/ Running On Faith (6:43)/
I Shot The Sheriff (6:47)/ Let It Rain (5:23)/ Behind
The Sun (4:17)/ Tearing Us Apart (6:19)/ Blues
Power (4:31)
R: Exs. Soundboard.   C: Australian CD. Dcc.

CD - LEGEND COMES ALIVE
KEEP OUT KO-0001/2
CD1: Smile/ Let It Glow/ Can't Find My Way
Home/ Better Make It Through Today/ I Shot The
Sheriff/ Key To The High Way
CD2: Willie & The Hand Jive, Get Ready/ Badge/
Presence Of The Load/ Singin' The Blues
R: G.   S: Budokan, Japan Nov. 2 '74.
C: Japanese CD.

CD - LIVING ON BLUES POWER VOL. 2
EXR 21
I Shot The Sheriff (6:56)/ Crossroads (6:58)/
Crossroads (7:06)/ Crossroads (4:00)/
Instrumental (2:23)/ It's Hard To Find A Friend
(4:31)/ Til I See You Again (2:40)/ Instrumental
(6:21)/ Evil/ Nobody Knows You When You're
Down And Out (3:32)/ Instrumental (3:59)/ It's Too
Late To Be Sorry (2:18)/ It's Too Late To Be Sorry
(6:39)/ Instrumental (2:53)/ Instrumental (10:28)
R: Vg-Ex.   S: Criteria Studios, Miami '74.
C: ECD. Dcc.

CD - THE 100TH SHOW
LIVE STORM LSCD 52578
CD1: Intro - Terraplane (4:47)/ Come In My
Kitchen (2:56)/ Malted Milk (3:00)/ How Long
(3:16)/ Kidman (2:35)/ County Jail (3:23)/ 44
(4:14)/ Standin' Round Cryin' (4:26)/ Going Away
(3:42)/ Blues All Day Long (3:56)/ Hoochie
Coochie Man (3:46)/ Hurts Me Too (3:18)/ Blues
Before Sunrise (2:45)/ Someday After Awhile
(3:31)/ Tore Down (2:48)/ White Room (6:58)
CD2: Badges (5:58)/ Wonderful Tonight (7:12)/
Stone Free (4:52)/ Circus Left Town (4:28)/ Tears
In Heaven (4:24)/ Five Long Years (4:47)/ Tearin'
Us Apart (5:48)/ Crossroads (6:02)/ Groaning The
Blues (6:56)/ Layla (8:43)/ Ain't Nobody's
Business (5:02)
R: Ex. Audience.   S: Royal Albert Hall, London,
England Mon. Feb. 28 '94.   C: ECD.

CD - RAINBOW NIGHT
SLOWHAND MUSIC ECRNO 141/142
CD1: Malted Milk/ Terraplane Blues/ How Long/
32-20/ Kidman Blues/ Country Jail Blues/ Forty
Four/ Leave Me Alone/ Tell Me Mama/ White
Room/ Badge/ Wonderful Tonight/ Stone Free

CD2: Circus Left Town/ Tears In Heaven/ Crossroads/ Tearing Us Apart/ Groaning The Blues/ Cocaine/ Ain't Nobody Business/ Layla R: Vg.   S: Rainbow Hall, Nagoya Japan Oct. 14 '93.   C: Japanese CD.

CD - ROYAL ALBERT HALL 1990 & 1991
YELLOW CAT YC 025
Key To The Highway (6:51)/ Worried Life Blues (5:14)/ All Your Love (5:05)/ Have You Ever Loved A Woman (8:18)/ Johnnie's Boogie (3:22)/ Blues Medley: Standing Around Crying, Ramblin' On My Mind (10:05)/ Hideaway (5:54)/ Watch Yourself (5:05)/ Sweet Home Chicago (8:53)
R: Exs. Soundboard.   S: Royal Albert Hall, England '90 & '91.   C: ECD. Dcc. Track 6 with Buddy Guy. Track 8 with Buddy Guy, J. Vaughan, Robert Cray & Albert Collins.

CD - SAME OLD BLUES POWER
HALLMARK HM 028
Everybody Ought To Make A Change/ Motherless Children/ I Shot The Sheriff/ Same Old Blues/ Blues Power/ Tangle In Love/ Badge/ Behind The Sun/ Wonderful Tonight/ Let It Rain/ Have You Ever Love A Woman
S: USA '85.   C: ECD. Time 70:05.

CD - STARTING FROM THE ROOTS
EC IN PERSON 004
White Room/ Steppin' Out/ Wonderful Tonight/ She's Waiting/ She Loves You/ Badge, Let It Rain/ Double Trouble/ Cocaine/ Layla
R: Vgs.   S: Garden State Arts Center, Holmdel, NJ June 28 '85.   C: Japanese CD.

CD - TANGLED UP IN BLUES
EC IN PERSON 005
Tulsa Time/ Mother Children/ White Room/ She's Waiting/ Badge/ Let It Rain/ Double Trouble/ Cocaine/ Layla/ Further On Up The Road
R: Vgs.   S: Performing Arts Center, Saratoga Spring, NY June 25 '85.   C: Japanese CD.

CD - TEARS IN HEAVEN
GRAPEFRUIT GRA-011-A
Signe (3:47)/ Tears In Heaven (4:41)/ Circus Has Left Town (4:41)/ My Father's Eyes (6:25)/ Running On Faith (6:49)/ Walkin' Blues (7:28)/ San Francisco Bay Blues (4:43)/ Malted Milk Blues (4:43)/ Worried Life Blues (5:17)/ Old Love (8:25)/ My Father's Eyes (6:08)
R: Exs. Soundboard.   S: USA Jan. 16 '92.
C: Australian CD. Dcc.

CD - TELL THE BLUES
EC IN PERSON 011
Sign Language/ Hello Friend/ Further On Up The Road/ All Our Past Times/ Double Trouble/ Tell The Truth/ Can't Find My Way Home/ Knockin On Heaven's Door/ Badge/ Key To The Highway
R: G-Vg.   S: Jacksonville, FL July 11 '76.
C: Japanese CD.

CD - THIRD APPEARANCE
EC IN PERSON 005/006
CD1: The Core/ I Shot The Sheriff/ Untitled Blues, Stormy Monday/ Knockin' On Heaven's Door
CD2: One Night With You/ Nobody Knows You/ We're All The Way/ Sign Language/ Alberta Alberta/ Badge/ Key To The Highway/ Layla
R: G-Vg. Hiss.   S: Shi-Kokaido, Nagoya Japan Sept. 30 '77.   C: Japanese CD.

CD - THROUGH THE YEARS (VOL. 1)
BANANA BAN-005-A
I Shot The Sheriff (7:22)/ Lay Down Sally (4:30)/ Tulsa Time (3:27)/ Worried Life Blues (9:42)/ Let It Rain (6:24)/ Double Trouble (8:27)/ Sweet Eliza (3:57)/ Wonderful Tonight (5:42)/ Blues Power (5:55)/ Have You Ever Loved A Woman (12:01)/ Layla (8:23)
R: Ex. Soundboard.   S: Europe '83.
C: Australian CD. Dcc.

CD - THROUGH THE YEARS (VOL. 2)
BANANA BAN-005-B
Tulsa Time (3:28)/ Tangled In Love (4:21)/ Behind The Sun (4:17)/ Wonderful Tonight (4:47)/ I Shot The Sheriff (7:04)/ Same Old Blues (9:33)/ Blues Power (4:29)/ She's Waiting (5:33)/ Badge (3:52)/ Let It Rain (7:23)/ Layla (7:16)/ Forever Man (2:51)/ Introducing The Band (3:05)/ Further On Up The Road (5:15)
R: Ex. Soundboard.   S: USA '85.   C: Australian CD. Dcc.

CD - THROUGH THE YEARS (VOL. 3)
BANANA BAN-005-C
Crossroads (6:52)/ White Room (6:47)/ I Shot The Sheriff (7:22)/ Hung Up On Your Love (5:17)/ Wonderful Tonight (4:46)/ Miss You (5:51)/ Tearing Us Apart (6:43)/ Holy Mother (6:39)/ Badge (8:56)/ Let It Rain (4:59)/ Cocaine (7:14)
R: Ex. Soundboard.   S: Europe '87.
C: Australian CD. Dcc.

CD - THROUGH THE YEARS (VOL. 4)
BANANA BAN-005-CD
Layla (part 1 - 5:08)/ Layla (part 2 - 3:23)/ Money For Nothing (5:11)/ Sunshine Of Your Love (5:45)/ Pretending (6:00)/ Running On Faith (6:47)/ Bad Love (6:06)/ Lay Down Sally (8:07)/ Hideaway (5:37)/ All Your Love (8:01)/ Tears In Heaven (4:36)
R: Ex. Soundboard.   S: Europe '87, '90. USA '93.   C: Australian CD. Dcc.

CD - TOUR REHEARSALS
SILVER RARITIES SIRA 105/106
CD1: Motherless Children/ Motherless Children/ High/ High/ High/ Why Does Love Got To Be So Sad/ Bell Bottom Blues/ Keep On Growing/ Knockin' On Heaven's Door/ Knockin' On Heaven's Door/ Knockin' On Heaven's Door/ Knockin' On Heaven's Door/ Eyesight To The Blind/ Eyesight To The Blind/ Eyesight To The Blind/ Eyesight To The Blind

CD2: High/ Motherless Children/ Teach Me To Be Your Woman/ Knocking On Heavens Door/ Knocking On Heavens Door/ Layla/ Mainline Florida/ Eyesight To The Blind/ Knockin' On Heaven's Door/ It's Too Late/ Well Allright/ Keep On Growing/ Bell Bottom Blues
R: Vg-Exs. Soundboard.   S: Criteria Studios, Miami June 11 '75.   C: ECD. Dcc. Time CD1 73:45. CD2 72:43.

CD - TULIPS AND COCAINE
TAKE IT LEAVE IT T 9409/10
CD1: Intro - Pretending (7:54)/ No Alibis (6:26)/ Running On Faith (7:06)/ I Shot The Sheriff (9:00)/ White Room (5:44)/ Can't Find My Way Home (7:08)/ Bad Love (6:27)/ Hard Times (4:09)/ Before You Accuse Me (6:26)/ Old Love (10:21)
CD2: Tearin' Us Apart (7:38)/ Wonderful Tonight (8:58)/ Introducing The Band (5:07)/ Cocaine (6:51)/ Instrumental (4:39)/ Layla (8:00)/ Tulpen Uit Amsterdam (2:12)/ Sunshine Of Your Love (9:49)
R: G. Audience.   S: Statenhal, Holland Feb. 24 '90.   C: ECD. Dcc.

CD - TWENTY ONE AND THREE LIVE
ECD 93103/4
CD1: Malted Milk/ Tarraplane Blues/ How Long/ 32-20/ Kidman Blues/ County Jail/ Forty Four/ Blues Leave Me Alone/ Tell Me Mama/ White Room/ Badge/ Wonderful Tonight/ Stone Free/ Circus Left Town/ Tears In Heaven
CD2: Crossroads/ Tearin' Apart/ Groaning Blues/ Cocaine/ Ain't Nobody's Business/ Layla*/ It's My Life/ You've Got To Love Her With A Feeling/ Tore Down
R: Exs. Audience.   S: Budokan Hall, Tokyo, Japan Oct. 26 '93. *Royal Albert Hall Feb. 21 '93. C: Japanese CD.

CD - WELCOME BACK TO NEW YORK
EC IN PERSON 009/10
CD1: Easy Now/ Let It Grow/ Can't Find My Way Home/ Key To The Highway/ Badge/ Little Wing/ Mainline Florida
CD2: Tell The Truth/ Blues Power/ Have You Ever Loved A Woman/ Little Queenie, Wille & The Hand Jive, Get Ready, Crossroads/ Layla
R: G-Vg.   S: Nassau Coliseum, Uniondale, NY June 30 '74.   C: Japanese CD.

CLASH, THE

CD - JAMAICAN AFFAIR
DR. GIG DGCD 033
London Calling (3:06)/ Police On My Back (2:55)/ The Guns Of Brixton (3:47)/ Magnificent Seven (2:36)/ Armagideon Time (2:50)/ Magnificent Seven (1:53)/ Junco Partner (2:57)/ Spanish Bomb (3:00)/ One More Time (2:26)/ Train In Vain (3:52)/ Bank Robber (2:48)/ This Is Radio Clash (4:08)/ Clampdown (4:00)/ Should I Stay Or Should I Go (2:38)/ Rock The Casbah (3:08)/ Straight To Hell (7:12)/ I Fought The Law (2:22)

R: Exs. Soundboard.   S: Kingston, Jamaica '82. C: ECD. Dcc.

CLAWFINGER

CD - LIVE, DUMB, UNRELEASED
Intro (1:05)/ Get It (4:33)/ Rosegrove (4:05)/ Wonderful World (2:42)/ Profit Teacher (2:42)/ I Don't Care (3:17)/ Stars And Stripes (3:29)/ Catch Me (4:34)/ Warfair (3:59)/ I Need You (5:24)/ Sad To See You (5:48)/ Don't Get Me Wrong (2:59)/ Nigger (4:29)/ Love (4:35)/ The Truth (4:24)/ Get It (4:43)*/ Love (3:01)*/ Stars And Stripes (3:52)*/ Profit Teacher (2:12)*
R: Ex. Audience. *Exs. Soundboard.   S: Track 1-15 live. Tracks 16-19 previously unreleased studio demos. Tracks 2, 5, 7 and 17 previously unreleased.   C: ECD. Dcc.

COCKER, JOE

CD - UNCHAIN MY HEART
GRAPEFRUIT GRA-027-A
Dear Landlord (4:03)/ You Can Leave Your Hat On (4:16)/ Two Wrong Things (5:06)/ Feelin' Allright (4:21)/ I Stand In Wonder (4:21)/ You Are So Beautiful (2:59)/ Civilized Man (4:44)/ Shelter Me (5:13)/ Unchain My Heart (5:20)/ Woman Loves A Man (4:29)/ With A Little Help From My Friends (8:27)
R: Vg-Ex. Soundboard.   S: Baden Baden, Germany '89.   C: Australian CD. Dcc.

COHEN, LEONARD

CD - FOR THE LOVE OF CAIN PART 1
RARE RECORDING COLLECTION RRC 037
Dance Me To The End Of Love/ It Is Murder/ Ain't No Cure For Love/ Bird On The Wire/ Everybody Knows/ First We Take Manhattan/ Crumbs Of Love/ Chelsea Hotel/ Tower Of Song/ Democracy/ Waiting for The Miracle
R: Exs. Soundboard.   S: Zurich May 21 '93. C: ECD. Time 71:30.

CD - FOR THE LOVE OF CAIN PART 2
RARE RECORDING COLLECTION RRC 038
I'm Your Man/ Joan Of Arc/ Closing Time/ Take This Waltz/ Sisters Of Mercy/ Hallelujah/ Right Before Your Eyes/ So Long, Marianne
R: Exs. Soundboard.   S: Zurich May 21 '93. C: ECD. Time 59:00.

CD - LIVE IN MONTREUX JUNE 25, 1976
YELLOW CAT RECORDS YC 004
Bird On A Wire/ So Long Marianne/ Who By Fire?/ That's No Way To Say Goodbye/ Storeroom/ One Of Us Cannot Be Wrong/ Lady Midnight/ There Is A War/ I Tried To Leave You/ Diamonds In The Mine/ Chelsea Hotel/ The Stranger Song/ Lover Lover Lover/ Sisters Of Mercy/ Tonight Will Be Fine
R: Exs. Soundboard.   S: Montreux June 25 '76. C: ECD. Dcc.

COLLINS, ALBERT

CD - JAMMIN' WITH ALBERT
BLUES TUNE BT 008
Good Golly Miss Molly/ I Got A Cold Cold Feeling/
Goin' Down Slow Jam/ Whiskey And Woman Jam/
Boogie Jam/ Funk Jam
R: Ex.   S: Montreux July '79. Tracks 5-6 Nyon
July '83 with Rory Gallagher.   C: Time 75:47.

COLLINS, PHIL

CD - IN THE AIR TONIGHT (VOL. 1)
BANANA BAN-007-A
I Don't Care Anymore (7:00)/ I Cannot Believe It's
True (5:24)/ This Must Be Love (4:38)/ Thru'
These Walls (6:08)/ Medley: I Missed Again,
Behind These Lines (7:39)/ You Know What I
Mean (2:51)/ The Roof Is Leaking (3:28)/ Don't Let
Him Steal Your Heart Away (5:48)
R: Exs. Soundboard.   S: USA '83.
C: Australian CD. Dcc.

CD - IN THE AIR TONIGHT (VOL. 2)
BANANA BAN-007-B
The West Side (11:31)/ In The Air Tonight (5:57)/
Medley: Like China, Only You Know And I Know,
You Can't Hurry Love, It Don't Matter To Me
(13:30)/ Hand To Hand (10:08)/ In Soto F (6:59)/
People Get Ready (3:14)/ Doesn't Anybody Stay
Together Anymore (4:45)
R: Exs. Soundboard.   S: USA '83.
C: Australian CD. Dcc.

CD - IN THE AIR TONIGHT (VOL. 3)
BANANA BAN-007-C
I Don't Care Anymore (6:41)/ The Roof Is Leaking
(3:40)/ I Cannot Believe It's True (5:07)/ This Must
Be Love (4:34)/ You Know What I Mean (2:47)/
Thru' These Walls (5:35)/ The Westside (6:210/
Like China (5:35)/ You Can't Hurry Love (3:34)/ it
Don't Matter To Me (4:18)/ In Soto F (9:28)/ In The
Air Tonight (6:00)/ Hand In Hand (8:12)
R: Exs. Soundboard.   S: USA '83.
C: Australian CD. Dcc.

CD - THE LAST SHOW IN PARADISE
AMERICAN CONCERT SERIES ACS 061
Hand In Hand (9:08)/ Hang In Long Enough
(4:29)/ Against All Odds (Take A Look At Me Now
- 3:24)/ Don't Lose My Number (4:35)/ Inside Out
(5:21)/ Do You Remember? (5:30)/ Who Said I
Would (4:29)/ Another Day In Paradise (5:36)/
Separate Lives (5:26)/ Saturday Night And Sunday
Morning (1:54)/ The West Side (10:06)/ That's The
Way It Is (5:44)
R: Exs. Soundboard.   S: Live.   C: ECD. Dcc.

CD - WITH OR WITHOUT GENESIS
AMERICAN CONCERT SERIES ACS 062
Something Happened On The Way To Heaven
(4:48)/ One More Night (5:50)/ Colours (8:38)/
Drum Solo (2:38)/ In The Air Tonight (6:22)/
Introduction Of The Band (13:27)/ You Can't Hurry

Love (2:53)/ Two Hearts (3:02)/ Sussidio (6:57)/
Groovy Kind Of Love (3:32)/ Easy Lover (4:50)/
Always (4:40)/ Take Me Home (9:12)
R: Exs. Soundboard.   S: New York City '90.
C: ECD. Dcc.

CONCRETE BLONDE

CD - MEXICAN HEARTBEAT
ROCKS 92134
Bloodletting (The Vampire Song) (7:44)/ Ghost Of
A Texas Ladies' Man (3:52)/ When You Smile
(6:05)/ Long Time Again (2:43)/ Someday (3:30)/
Heal It Up (6:49)/ Jenny I Read (5:16)/ Days And
Days (9:59)/ Joey (5:09)/ Mexican Moon (11:56)/
Shout (5:05)/ Castles Made Of Sand (4:40)
R: Vg. Audience.   S: The Wiltern, LA Mar. 10
'93.   C: ECD.

COOPER, ALICE

CD - ALICE - LIVE AT ELECTRIC LADYLAND
LOBSTER RECORDS LOB 036
No More Mr. Nice Guy (2:23)/ Billion Dollar Babies
(2:52)/ Only Women Bleed (8:57)/ Sick Things
(3:04)/ Feed My Frankenstein (5:41)/ Cold Ethyl
(3:04)/ Love's Loaded Gun (4:05)/ I'm Eighteen
(4:26)/ Go To Hell (5:25)/ School's Out (4:24)/ Hey
Stoopid (4:20)
R: Exs.   S: Electric Ladyland Studios, NYC Sept.
13 '91.   C: ECD.

CD - NO MORE MR. NICE GUY
GRAPEFRUIT GRA-030-A
Cold Ethyl (3:13)/ No More Mr. Nice Guy (2:56)/
Clones (We're All) (2:50)/ Under My Wheels
(2:25)/ Billion Dollar Babies (5:27)/ Who Do You
Think We Are? (2:56)/ Guilty (4:18)/ Ooh Baby
(He's Out) (3:05)/ Grim Facts (3:02)/ I'm Eighteen
(3:51)/ It Is My Body (2:24)/ You And Me (2:17)/
Only Women Bleed (6:05)/ Unfinished Sweet
(4:41)/ Escape (3:01)/ I Love The Dead (2:36)/ Go
To Hell (4:04)/ I Never Cry (2:57)/ It's Hot Tonight
(3:09)/ School's Out (10:11)
R: Vg-Ex. Soundboard.   S: USA '78-'82.
C: Australian CD. Dcc.

CD - NOBODY LIKES ME
TRACE
Intro, Painting A Picture (2:08)/ Freak Out Song
(3:47)/ Nobody Likes Me (3:16)/ I've Written Home
To Mother (1:20)/ A.C. Instrumental (3:19)/
Science Fiction (6:39)/ Going To The River (2:07)/
Ain't That Just Like A Woman (2:32)
S: Toronto Rock 'N' Roll Festival '69.

COREA, CHICK MEETS JOE HENDERSON

CD - TINKLE-TINKLE
JAZZ FILE JF 1002
Blues Connotation (10:30)/ Piano Intro (4:36)/
Humpty Dumpty (8:02)/ Tinkle Tinkle (10:20)/ I've
Got You Under My Skin (18:03)/ Chim Chim
Cheree (10:26)

R: Exs. Soundboard.   S: Montreux July 15 '81.
C: ECD. Dcc.

COSTELLO, ELVIS

CD - BRUTAL YOUTH TOUR 1994
BLUE MOON RECORDS BMCD31
No Action/ The Beat/ Accidents Will Happen/
Beyond Belief/ Sulky Girl/ London's Brilliant
Parade/ Deep Dark Truthful Mirror/ Everyday I
Write The Book/ Hand In Hand/ Clown Strike/
Kinder Murder/ Less Than Zero/ Rocking Horse
Road/ Still Too Soon To Know/ You Tripped At
Every Step/ Shipbuilding/ Mystery Dance/
Watching The Detectives/ You Belong To Me/ 13
Steps Lead Down, Radio Radio
R: Exs. Soundboard.   S: Europe July '94.
C: ECD. Dcc. Time 78:27.

CD - LIVE AT GLASTONBURY, ENGLAND, JUNE 1994
FESTIVAL MUSIC FMCD 004/005
CD1: Intro - No Action/ The Beat/ Waiting For The
World/ Beyond Belief/ Sulky Girl/ London's Brilliant
Parade/ Deep Dark Truthful Mirror/ Olivers Army/
Less Than Zero/ Clown Strike/ Kinder Murder/
Clubland/ Rocking Horse Road
CD2: Man Out Of Time/ Watching The Detectives/
You Belong To Me/ 13 Steps Lead Down, Radio
Radio/ Lipstick Vogue, I Don't Want To Go To
Chelsea, Lipstick Vogue/ Alison/ Tracks Of My
Tears, Tears Of A Clown, Clown Time Is Over/
Accidents Will Happen/ All The Rage/ What's So
Funny About Peace, Love & Understanding/ Pump
It Up/ Band Introduction/ Sulky Girl/ Rocking Horse
Road/ All The Rage/ 13 Steps Lead Down, Radio
Radio
R: Vg-Ex. Audience.   C: ECD. Dcc. Pic CDs.

CD - UNPLUGGED & UNSHAVED
THE SMOKING CROCODILE SMOKE 11
Deep Dark Truthful Mirror/ Hurry Down Dooms
Day/ So Like Candy - I Want You/ Other Side Of
Summer/ Bama Laura Bama Lou/ God's Comic/
Let Him Dangle/ Baby Play Around/ Tramp The
Dirt Down/ Strange/ How To Be Dumb/ Alison/ My
Hidden Shame/ Watch Your Step/ Georgie And
Her Rival/ Home Is Anywhere You Hang Your
Head/ Suit Of Lights
R: Ex. Soundboard.   S: Tracks 1-5 MTV
Unplugged. Tracks 6-9 BBC Late Show. Tracks
10-17 LA Tour Rehearsals.   C: ECD. Dcc.
Time 73:23.

CD - YOUTHFUL ELVIS
HOME RECORDS - HR 5975 - 2
No Actions (1:52)/ The Beat (3:01)/ Deep Dark
Truthful Mirror (4:46)/ Every Day I Write The Book
(2:38)/ Hand In Hand (2:14)/ Clown Strike (5:53)/
Kinder Murder (3:11)/ Less Than Zero (3:02)/
Rocking Horse Road (5:42)/ Still Too Soon To
Know (3:58)/ You Tripped At Every Step (4:39)/
Shipbuilding (3:59)/ Mystery Dance (2:05)/
Watching The Detectives (4:28)/ You Belong To

Me (2:19)/ Thirteen Steps Lead Down (5:40)/
Favourite Hour (4:10)/ I Don't Want To Go
(Chelsea) (2:08)
R: G-Vg. Audience.   S: Foro Italico, Rome, Italy
July '94.   C: ECD. Dcc. Pic CD.

COUNTING CROWS

CD - ADAM THE UNTOUCHABLE
HOME RECORDS HR5992-4
White Stallions (unreleased) (4:47)/ Omaha (4:14)/
Anna Begins (5:20)/ Ghost Train (5:54)/ Mr. Jones
(4:51)/ Perfect Blue Buildings (5:49)/ Round Here
(6:09)/ Children (unreleased) (5:21)/ Rain King
(4:56)/ Margery (unreleased) (4:43)/ Time And
Time Again (4:50)/ Murder Of One (6:54)/ Sullivan
Street (5:24)/ Wiseblood (unreleased) (4:27)/
Omaha (4:10)
R: R: Vg-Ex. Audience. Seems to be a tape-speed
problem at beginning.   S: Koln, Germany Apr.
'94.   C: ECD. Dcc. Pic CD.

CD - AS FUNKY AS THEY CAN BE
ALLEY CAT AK 037
I Gotta Get Out/ Round Here/ Anna Begins/
Omaha/ Time And Time Again/ Mr. Jones/ Wise
Blood/ Elizabeth/ Margery/ A Murder Of One/
Sullivan Street/ Round Here/ Mr. Jones
R: Ex. Audience.   S: Club Soda, Montreal,
Canada '94.   C: ECD. Dcc. Pic CD. Time 67:41.

CD - CARVING OUT OUR NAMES
KISS THE STONE KTS 297
Round Here/ A Murder Of One/ Anna Begins/
Round Here/ Mr. Jones/ Rain King/ Anna Begins/
Sullivan Street/ Elizabeth/ Margery/ Four More
Reasons/ Ghost Train/ Wise Blood/ Time And
Time Again/ The Ghost In You
R: Tracks 1-9 Exs. Soundboard. Tracks 10-15 Ex.
Audience.   S: Tracks 1-3 London Aug. 7 '94.
Tracks 4-8 Roxy, Hollywood Mar. 17 '94. Track 9
Melkweg, Amsterdam Apr. 14 '94. Track 10 Roxy,
Hollywood Mar. 17 '94. Tracks 11-15 Roxy,
Hollywood Mar. 18 '94.   C: ECD. Dcc. Pic CD.
Time 77:51.

CD - CHILDREN IN BLOOM
KISS THE STONE KTS 337
Good Night Elizabeth/ Round Here/ Omaha/ Anna
Begins/ Ghost Train/ Children In Bloom/ Time And
Time Again/ Rain Kings/ Perfect Blue Buildings/
Mr. Jones/ Margery/ A Murder Of One/ Wise
Blood/ Sullivan Street
R: Exs. Soundboard.   S: Europe '94.   C: ECD.
Dcc. Pic CD. Time 73:41.

CD - HOTTEST TICKET IN BOSTON
HOME RECORDS HR 5922 7
Untitled (4:58)/ Round Here (5:17)/ Time And Time
Again (4:55)/ Mr. Jones (4:21)/ Anna Begins
(5:00)/ Wise Blood (4:14)/ Omaha (4:04)/ 40 Years
(unreleased song) (3:37)/ Rain King (6:27)/ Get
Inside (3:39)/ Margery (4:46)/ Perfect Blue
Building (6:21)/ Ghost Train (5:24)/ A Good Year

For The Roses (3:34)/ Sullivan Street (5:35)
R: Ex. Audience.   S: Pearl Street Nightclub,
Boston Jan. 24 '94.   C: ECD. Dcc.

CD - MAY AND NOTHING BEFORE
ROYAL SOUND MUSIC RSM 056
Round Here/ Mr. Jones/ Rain King/ Anna Begins/
Sullivan Street/ Round Here/ Time And Time
Again/ Wise Blood/ Omaha/ Margery
S: Tracks 1-5 Irvine Meadows, CA '94. Track 6
alternate version live New York '94. Tracks 7-10
Boston, MA '94.   C: ECD.

CD - SLEEPING IN A PERFECT BLUE
TEDDY BEAR RECORDS TB 45
Goodnight Elizabeth (6:16)/ Round Here (6:27)/
Omaha (3:52)/ Anna Begins (5:07)/ Ghost Train
(4:58)/ Children And Bloom (5:18)/ Time And Time
Again (4:34)/ Ranking (5:59)/ Perfect Blue Building
(5:49)/ Mr. Jones (4:44)/ Margery (4:39)/ A Murder
Of One (7:02)/ Wise Blood (5:16)/ Sullivan Street
(5:34)
R: Ex. Audience.   S: Teatro Palladio, Roma Apr.
28 '94.   C: ECD. Dcc. Pic CD.

CD - THIEVISH MAGPIES
FLASHBACK WORLD PRODUCTIONS
FLASHBACK.05.84.0231
Gotta Get Out (5:07)/ Round Here (5:22)/ Anna
Begins (4:53)/ Omaha (4:30)/ Time And Time
Again (4:44)/ Cannon Ball (4:15)/ Elizabeth (6:21)/
Marjori (4:24)/ The Murder Of One (7:17)/ Sullivan
Street (5:20)
R: Ex. Audience.   S: First Avenue Club, Minn.
Feb. 3 '94.   C: ECD. Time 56:41.

CD - TRUE HEART
OCTOPUS OCTO 035
Goodnight Elizabeth (6:16)/ Round Here (6:23)/
Omaha (3:52)/ Anna Begins (5:02)/ Ghost Train
(4:58)/ Children And Bloom (5:18)/ Time And Time
Again (4:34)/ Ranking (5:59)/ Perfect Blue Building
(5:49)/ Mr. Jones (4:44)/ Margery (4:34)/ A Murder
Of One (7:01)/ Wise Blood (5:19)/ Sullivan Street
R: Exs. Soundboard.   S: Italy Apr. '94.
C: ECD. Dcc. Pic CD.

COVERDALE - PAGE

CD - THE FIRST STAGE
CP-001/2
CD1: Opening Tape/ Absolution Blues/ Slide It In/
Rock And Roll/ Over Now/ Kashmir/ Pride And
Joy/ Take A Look At Yourself (acoustic)/ Take Me
For A Little While/ In My Time Of Dying
CD2: Here I Go Again/ White Summer, Black
Mountain Side/ Don't Leave Me This Way/ Shake
My Tree/ Still Of The Night/ Out On The Tiles
Intro, Black Dog/ The Ocean Intro, The Wanton
Song Intro, Feeling Hot
S: Nippon Budokan, Tokyo Japan Dec. 14 '93.

CD - FIRST AND LAST
BU01-02-NAGO1-02

CD1: Intro - Opening Tape (1:50)/ Absolute Blues
(4:25)/ Slide It In (2:40)/ Rock & Roll (4:09)/ Over
Now (5:30)/ Kashmir (7:50)/ Pride & Joy (1:58)/
Keyboard Solo (3:17)/ Drum Solo (:25)/ Take A
Look At Yourself (4:00)/ Take Me For A Little
While (6:54)/ In My Time Of Dying (9:52)
CD2: Here I Go Again (5:22)/ Guitar Solo (6:06)/
Don't Leave Me This Way (7:18)/ Drum Solo
(2:09)/ Shake My Tree (3:12)/ Theramin Solo
(3:21)/ Still Of The Night (6:18)/ Black Dog (6:00)/
The Ocean (1:03)/ Feeling Hot (4:40)
CD3: Absolution Blues (6:10)/ Slide It In (2:43)/
Rock & Roll (4:16)/ Over Now (5:32)/ Kashmir
(7:52)/ Pride & Joy (6:02)/ Take A Look At
Yourself (4:37)/ Take Me For A Little While (7:07)/
In My Time Of Dying (10:30)
CD4: Here I Go Again (5:07)/ Guitar Solo (8:13)/
Don"t Leave Me This Way (12:03)/ Shake My Tree
(4:11)/ Whole Lotta Love (4:00)/ Shake My Tree
(1:06)/ Still Of The Night (6:26)/ Out On The Tiles,
Feeling Hot (6:06)
R: G-Vg. Audience.   S: Tokyo Dec. 14 '93.
Nagoya Dec. 22 '93.   C: Japanese CD. Fold-
open digi-pack colour cover.

CD - FROM TOKYO TO KASHMIR
OFF BEAT XXCD 16 1/2
CD1: Intro - Absolution Blues (6:05)/ Slide It In
(2:48)/ Rock & Roll (4:10)/ Over Now (5:23)/
Kashmir (7:48)/ Pride & Joy (5:40)/ Take A Look
At Me Now (4:20)/ Take Me For A Little While
(7:00)/ In My Time Of Dying (9:45)
CD2: Here I Go Again (5:08)/ White Summer,
Black Mountain Side (7:48)/ Don't Leave Me This
Way (11:00)/ Shake My Tree (6:37)/ Still Of The
Night (6:24)/ Black Dog (7:30)/ The Ocean,
Feeling Hot (5:18)
R: G. Audience.   S: Tokyo Dec. 15 '93.
C: Japanese CD. Dcc.

CD - LIVE IN JAPAN
COCOMELOS CM 029/30
CD1: Intro - Absolution Blues (6:18)/ Slide It In
(2:42)/ Rock & Roll (4:13)/ Over Now (5:45)/
Kashmir (7:47)/ Pride And Joy (5:50)/ Take A Look
At Me Now (4:12)/ Take Me For A Little While
(7:00)/ In My Time Of Dying (9:45)
CD2: Here I Go Again (5:08)/ White Summer,
Black Mountain Side (7:48)/ Don't Leave Me This
Way (11:00)/ Shake My Tree (6:37)/ Still Of The
Night (6:24)/ Black Dog (7:30)/ The Ocean,
Feeling Hot (5:18)
R: G. Audience.   S: Tokyo Dec. 15 '93.
C: ECD. Dcc.

CD - ONE MORE CHECK
TARANTURA T1CD 001
Jam (1:30)/ For Your Life (4:45)/ Nobody's Fault
But Mine (4:55)/ Absolution Blues (1:38)/ Dazed &
Confused (3:50)/ In My Time Of Dying (5:08)/
Dancing Days (2:01)/ Bron-Y-Aur Stomp (8:21)/ In
My Time Of Dying (10:00)/ White Summer (1:59)/
Whole Lotta Love (5:05)/ Communication
Breakdown (3:28)/ Stairway To Heaven (2:50)/

Jam (4:21)/ Whole Lotta Love (6:02)/ Jam (1:21)
R: G-Vg. Audience.   S: Tracks 1-6 Tokyo Dec.
17 '93. Tracks 7-13 Osaka Dec. 20 '93. Tracks 14-
16 Nagoya Dec. 22 '93.   C: Japanese CD.
Gatefold sleeve. Used 'Pig' for key words of song
titles.

CD - OVER NOW
METAL CRASH MECD 2155/56
CD1: Intro - Absolution Blues (6:06)/ Slide It In
(2:49)/ Rock' N 'Roll (4:48)/ Over Now (5:23)/
Kashmir (9:04)/ Pride And Joy (6:36)/ Take A Look
At Yourself (4:48)/ Take Me For A Little While
(7:46)/ In My Time Of Dying (9:45)/
CD2: Here I Go Again (6:14)/ White Summer
(9:16)/ Don't Leave Me This Way (11:52)/ Shake
My Tree (6:54)/ Still Of The Night (7:49)/ Black
Dog (8:18)/ The Ocean, Feeling Hot (5:23)/ Rock'
N ' Roll (4:38)
R: G-Vg. Audience.   S: Yoyogi Olympic Pool,
Tokyo Dec. 18 '93.   C: ECD. Dcc.

CD - PRIDE AND JOY
CP-9315A/B
CD1: Absolution Blues/ Slide It In/ Rock 'N' Roll/
Over Now/ Kashmir/ Pride And Joy/ Take A Look
At Yourself (acoustic)/ Take Me for A Little While/
In My Time Of Dying
CD2: Here I Go Again/ White Summer, Black
Mountain Side/ Don't Leave Me This Way/ Shake
My Tree/ Still Of The Night/ Out On The Tiles,
Black Dog/ The Ocean, Feelin' Hot
S: Budokan Hall, Tokyo Dec. 15 '93.   C: Two
stickers included.

CD THE REHEARSALS 1993
EJ 011 AND EJ 012
CD1: Absolution Blues/ Slide It In/ Rock And Roll/
Over Now/ Kashmir/ Pride 'N' Joy/ Take A Look At
Yourself/ Take Me For A Little While/ In My Time
Of Dying
CD2: Here I Go Again/ Don't Leave This Way/
Feelin' Hot/ Still Of The Night/ Whisper A Prayer/
Black Dog/ Shake My Tree
R: Vg-Ex.   S: Rehearsals '93.   C: Dcc. Time
CD1 53:33. CD2 44:02.

CD - WESTERN DAZE
HARD KNOCKERS HSP-2621/ HSP-2624
CD1: Absolution Blues/ Slide It In/ Rock And Roll/
Over Now/ Kashmir/ Pride And Joy/ Take A Look
At Yourself/ Take Me For A Little While/ In My
Time Of Dying
CD2: Here I Go Again/ White Summer Black
Mountain Side, Kashmir Reprise/ Don't Leave Me
This Way/ Shake My Tree/ Still Of The Night/ Out
On The Hills, Black Dog/ The Ocean, Feelin' Hot
CD3: Absolution Blues/ Slide It In/ Rock And Roll/
Over Now/ Kashmir/ Pride And Joy/ Take A Look
At Yourself/ Take Me For A Little While/ In My
Time Of Dying
CD4: Here I Go Again/ White Summer Black
Mountain Side, Over The Hills And Faraway/ Don't
Leave Me This Way/ Still Of The Night/ Out On

The Hills, Black Dog/ The Ocean, Feelin' Hot
R: G. Audience.   S: Osaka Castle Hall, Osaka,
Japan Dec. 20 and 21 '93.   C: Japanese CD.
Dcc. CD1 57:01. CD2 56:10. CD3 58:16.
CD4 56:45.

CD - WHOLE LOTTA LOVE
VICTORY 22/12 9301/2
CD1: Opening Set/ Absolution/ Slide It In/ Rock
And Roll/ Over Now/ Kashmir/ Pride & Joy,
Keyboard Solo (Santa Claus Is Coming To Town)/
Take A Look At Yourself/ Take Me For A Little
While/ In My Time Of Dying
CD2: Here I Go Again/ White Summer, Black
Mountain Side, Kashmir (Reprise)/ Don't Leave
Me This Way, Drum Solo, Guitar Solo/ Shake My
Tree/ Whole Lotta Love/ Shake My Tree Encore/
Still Of The Night/ Out On The Tiles, Black Dog,
The Ocean, The Wanton Song, Feeling Hot
R: Audience recording.   S: Nagoya, Japan Dec.
22 '93.

CRACKER

CD - LIVE POTATOES
ROYAL SOUND MUSIC RSM 053
Take Me Down To The Infirmatory/ I See The
Light/ Mr. Wrong/ Low/ This Is Cracker Soul/ Teen
Angst/ Euro-Trash Girl/ Sweet Potatoes/ Teen
Angst #2/ Low #2/ I See The Light #2
S: The Coach House, San Juan Capistrano, CA
'93.   C: ECD.

CD - TEEN ANGST
KISS THE STONE KTS 296
Take Me Down To The Infirmary/ I See The Light/
Mr. Wrong/ Low/ This Is Cracker Soul/ Teen Angst
(What The World Needs Now)/ Euro-Trash Girl/
Sweet Potato/ Teen Angst (What The World
Needs Now)/ Low/ I See The Light
R: Exs.   S: USA '94.   C: ECD. Dcc. Pic CD.
Time 56:13.

CD - WORDS OF WISDOM
HOME RECORDS HR 5923 9
Someday (3:09)/ Happy Birthday To Me (4:47)/
This Is Cracker Soul (3:29)/ Mr. Wrong (4:36)/
Lonesome Johnny Blues (3:27)/ Teen Angst (What
The World Needs Now) (4:37)/ Euro Trash Girl
(8:58)/ Shut Us Down (1:40)/ (What's So Funny
About) Peace, Love & Understanding (2:35)/ Take
Me Down To The Infirmary (4:09)/ I See the Light
(5:08)/ Low (5:23)/ Sweet Potato (4:37)/ Teen
Angst (What The World Needs Now (4:31)/ Low
(4:49)/ I See The Light (5:12)
R: Exs.   S: USA '93. Tracks 14-16 acoustic.
C: ECD. Dcc.

CRANBERRIES

CD - STORIES TO BE TOLD
KISS THE STONE KTS 317
Ode To My Family (6:12)/ Linger (5:08)/ False
(2:59)/ Empty (3:39)/ Pretty (2:16)/ Sunday (3:32)/

I Still Do (3:31)/ Wanted (2:11)/ Ridiculous
Thoughts (4:33)/ Not Sorry (4:41)/ Linger (5:18)/
Dreams (4:15)/ Liar (2:56)/ How (2:59)
R: Exs. Soundboard.   S: Live in USA '94. Tracks
1-4 acoustic set. Tracks 5-14 electric set.
C: ECD. Dcc. Pic CD. Time 54:13.

CD - THOUGHTS THAT LINGER
HAWK 052
Ode To My Family (6:38)/ Sunday (3:46)/ Linger
(5:22)/ False (3:14)/ Empty (4:07)/ O' To My
Family (4:58)/ Sunday (3:43)/ Linger (5:31)/ False
(3:00)/ Empty (3:00)
R: Ex. Audience.   S: Los Angeles Dec. 11 and
12 '93.   C: ECD. Dcc. Pic CD.

CRASH TEST DUMMIES

CD - AHHH, AHHH, AHHH, AHHH
MONTANA MO 10030
C: This is a copy of 'Dummies At Home' (KTS 299)
with the songs switched around.

CD - DUMMIES AT HOME
KISS THE STONE KTS 299
Androgynous/ In The Days Of The Caveman/ The
Ghosts That Haunt Me/ I Think I'll Disappear Now/
How Does A Duck Know?/ MMM MMM MMM
MMM/ When I Go Out With Artists/ Swimming In
Your Ocean/ Superman Song/ Afternoons And
Coffeespoons/ Comin' Back Soon/ At My Funeral/
Afternoons And Coffeespoons
R: Ex. Soundboard.   S: Tracks 1-10 Walker
Theatre, Winnipeg, Canada Jan. '94. Tracks 11-12
Toronto, Canada '92. Track 13 New York '94.
C: ECD. Dcc. Pic CD.

CD - KAMIKAZE RIDE
HOME RECORDS HR5949-8
God Shuffled His Feet (4:24)/ In The Days Of The
Caveman (4:10)/ I Think I'll Disappear Now (5:20)/
How Does A Duck Know? (3:40)/ When I Go Out
With Artists (4:41)/ Swimming In Your Ocean
(3:37)/ If I Had My Way (4:49)/ Mmm Mmm Mmm
Mmm (4:19)/ Superman's Song (5:31)/ Afternoons
And Coffeespoons (7:26)
R: Ex. Audience.   S: Universal Amphitheatre, LA
May 13 '94.   C: ECD. Pic CD.

CREAM

CD - LONG TIME COMIN'
HAWK 048
Sunshine Of Your Love #1 (2:45)/ Sunshine Of
Your Love #2 (3:51)/ Sunshine Of Your Love #3
(4:11)/ Sunshine Of Your Love #4 (6:58)/
Sunshine Of Your Love #5 & 6 (2:45)/ Born Under
A Bad Sign (4:39)/ Crossroads #1 & 2 (5:32)/
Crossroads #3 (3:29)/ Sunshine Of Your Love
(6:27)/ Born Under A Bad Sign (6:05)/ Crossroads
(4:20)/ Sunshine Of Your Love (5:42)/ Born Under
A Bad Sign (3:41)/ Crossroads (4:23)
R: Ex.   S: Tracks 1-12 Power Plant Studios Jan.

11 '93. Tracks 13-15 Rock & Roll Hall Of Fame
Jan. 12 '93.   C: ECD. Dcc. Pic CD.

CD - REAL CREAM
DETROIT GOLD RC-01,02
CD1: Tales Of Brave Ulysses/ NSU/ Sitting On
Top Of The World/ Sweet Wine/ Rolling And
Tumbling/ Spoonful
CD2: Steppin Out/ Train Time/ Toad/ I'm So Glad/
NSU/ Sleepy Time Time/ Sunshine Of Your Love
R: G-Vg. Some static on CD2 tracks 5-7.
S: Detroit Grande Ballroom Oct. '67. CD2 tracks 5-
7 Winterland Mar. 8 '68.   C: ECD. Dcc. Time
CD1 67:42. CD2 69:52.

CD - THE RETURN OF A SUPERGROUP
ROCK CALENDER RECORDS RC 2111
Tales Of Brave Ulysses (4:21)/ White Room
(5:24)/ Sitting On Top Of The World (4:40)/ I'm So
Glad (8:49)/ Rollin' And Tumblin' (4:22)/ Sweet
Wine (14:36)/ Politician (6:21)/ Born Under A Bad
Sign (7:28)/ Sunshine Of Your Love (5:58)
R: Vg.   S: Tracks 1-6 Civic Auditorium, San Jose
May 25 '68. Jack Bruce Band - Track 7 Passaic,
Capitol Theatre '89. Tracks 8-9 Bottom Line NYC
'89.   C: ECD.

CROSBY, DAVID

CD - NAKED IN THE RAIN
KISS THE STONE KTS 330
In My Dreams (6:00)/ Naked In The Rain (3:40)/
Rusty And Blue (6:06)/ Hero (4:43)/ 'Till It Shines
On You (5:10)/ Thousand Roads (5:02)/ Cowboy
Movie (8:33)/ Motherless Children (8:35)/ Almost
Cut My Hair (5:26)**/ Deja Vu (9:57*)/ Long Time
Gone (5:31)*/ Wooden Ships (10:27)*
R: Exs. Soundboard.   S: Whiskey, LA, CA Dec.
'93.   C: ECD. Dcc. Pic CD. *With Graham Nash.
**With Chris Robinson.

CROSBY & NASH

CD - THE BEST TWO OUT OF THREE
TRIANGLE PYCD 091
Deja Vu (9:52)/ I Used To Be King (5:20)/
Laughing (7:42)/ Box Of Rain (5:30)/ Military
Madness (3:15)/ Melody (4:55)/ Drive My Car
(3:53)/ Word Less Song (3:52)/ Flying Man (3:49)/
King Of The Mountain (2:38)/ Song Of The
Samurai (5:26)/ Dancer (4:45)
R: Ex. Soundboard. Tracks 6-11 *Vg.   S: Tracks
1-5 Feb. '94 USA. Tracks 6-11 '80. Track 12 '76.
C: ECD. Dcc.

CROSBY, NASH & YOUNG

CM - PRISON BENEFIT
ZUMA 9302
Page 43/ And So It Goes/ Immigration Man/ Heart
Of Gold/ Needle And The Damage Done/ Wooden
Ships/ Harvest/ Only Love Can Break Your Heart/
South Bound Train/ Almost Cut My Hair/ Helpless/

Southern Man/ Suite: Judy Blue Eyes
R: Tracks 1-10 FM radio. Tracks 11-13 audience
recording.   S: Prison Benefit, Winterland June 26
'72. Tracks 11-13 Stills-Young Band Summer '76.

CROSBY, STILLS & NASH

CD - WOODSTOCK 1994
OCTOPUS RECORDS OCTO 044
Love The One You're With (5:55)/ Military
Madness (3:27)/ Helplessly Hoping (2:19)/ Deja
Vu (7:30)/ Only Waiting For You (4:28)/ Marrakesh
Express (3:25)/ It Won't Go Away (4:10)/ Unequal
Love (4:49)/ In My Life (2:20)/ Long Time Gone
(4:30)/ Street To Lean On (3:32)/ For What's It's
Worth (5:14)/ Pre Road Downs (2:45)/ Southern
Cross (4:04)/ Wooden Ships (8:59)/ Carry On
(6:18)/ Happy Birthday Woodstock (4:34)
R: Exs. Broadcast.   S: Woodstock Festival,
Saugerties, NY Aug. 13-14 '94.   C: ECD. Dcc.
Pic CD.

CROSBY, STILLS, NASH & YOUNG

CD - HELPLESS BELIEVERS
BLACK LEMON RECORDS BL-668
Teach Your Children/ Love The One Your With/
Long May You Run/ Long Time Gone/ Southern
Cross/ Only Love Can Break Your Heart/ Wooden
Ships/ Suite: Judy Blue Eyes/ You Don't
Have To Cry/ Blackbird/ Unknown Legend
R: G-Vg.   S: Tracks 1-11 Golden Gate Park, San
Francisco Nov. 3 '91 (in memory of Bill Graham).
Tracks 9-11 LA '82. Track 12 Oregon '92.

CROW, SHERYL

CD - RUN, BABY, RUN
KISS THE STONE KTS 348
Nobody Needs You When Your Down/ Can't Cry
Anymore/ Run Baby Run/ The Na-Na Song/
Strong Enough/ No One Said It Would Be Easy/
Leaving Las Vegas/ What Can I Do For You/ I
Shall Believe
R: Exs. Soundboard.   S: On tour '94.   C: ECD.
Dcc. Pic CD. Time 52:54.

CD - WEDNESDAY NIGHT STATE THEATER
HOME RECORDS HR5983-0
Can't Cry Anymore (4:20)/ All I Wanna Do (5:13)/
Leaving Las Vegas (6:07)/ Father Son (3:55)/
Solidity (5:20)/ The Na-Na Song, Everybody
(5:56)/ Strong Enough (3:04)/ Run Baby Run
(7:29)/ What I Can Do For You (7:18)/ I Shall
Believe (7:31)/ No One Said It Would Be Easy
(6:07)/ Happy (2:53)
R: Exs. Soundboard.   S: State Theater,
Nashville Dec. 15 '93.   C: ECD. Dcc. Pic CD.

CROWDED HOUSE

CD - ANOTHER TIME, ANOTHER PLACE
TEDDY BEAR RECORDS TB 50

Kari Kan (3:31)/ Its Own Natural Way (3:38)/
Distant Sun (5:13)/ Fall At Your Feet (4:22)/
Fingers Of Love (4:22)/ Into Temptation (6:11)/
Better Be Home Soon (5:06)/ Locked Out (4:18)/
In My Command (4:36)/ Weather With You (9:06)/
Don't Dream It's Over (5:12)/ Locked Out (3:53)*/
Private Universe (5:07)*/ In My Command (4:02)*/
Nails In My Feet (5:21)*
R: Exs. Soundboard.   S: Hammersmith Apollo,
London, England Nov. '93. *Acoustic session BBC
'93.   C: ECD. Dcc. Pic CD.

CD - FLEADH
KISS THE STONE KTS 322
When You Come (5:59)/ In My Command (4:14)/
Fall At Your Feet (5:06)/ Chocolate Cake (5:53)/
Distant Sun (5:26)/ Pineapple Head (4:10)/ Four
Seasons In One Day (5:01)/ There Goes God
(4:52)/ Been Locked Out (5:47)/ Weather With You
(5:23)/ Private Universe (7:19)/ Don't Dream It's
Over (4:50)/ Catherina Wheels (6:02)/ Aborigine
Chant (5:28)/ Goodnight And Joy Be With You All
(1:21)
R: Ex.   S: 'Fleadh', Finsbury Park, London,
England 11-06-'94.   C: ECD. Yellow/green
cover. Pic CD. Time 76:57.

CD - IT'S ONLY NATURAL
KISS THE STONE KTS 266
Kare Kare/ It's Only Natural/ Born On The Bayou/
Distant Sun/ Fall At Your Feet/ Chocolate Cake/
Into Temptation/ Better Be Home Soon/ Been
Locked Out/ In My Command/ Weather With You/
Don't Dream It's Over
R: Exs. Soundboard.   S: On tour '93.   C: ECD.
Dcc. Pic CD.

CD - LIVE IN LA
SOUNDS ALIVE CD 2400130
It's Only Natural/ Don't Dream It's Over/ When
You Come/ Weather With You/ Tall Trees/ Sister
Madley/ Medley: Smoke On The Water, Exodus/
Fall At Your Feet/ There Goes God/ Spellbound/
All I Ask/ Chocolate Cake/ Medley: Rock The
Casbah, You Sexy Thing/ Mean To Me/ Whispers
And Moans/ Six Months In A Leaky Boat/
Something So Strong/ World Where You Live
S: LA June. 10 '91.   C: ECD.

CD - STAGE TIME
THE SWINGIN' PIG RECORDS TSP-CD-175-2
CD1: Tall Trees/ Something So Strong/ Weather
With You/ Into Temptation/ There Goes God/
World Where You Live/ It's Only Natural/ All I Ask/
Don't Dream It's Over/ Mean To Me
CD2: When You Come/ Chocolate Cake/ Fall At
Your Feet/ The Same Language As Me/ Sister
Madley/ How I'm Gonna Sleep Without You/ I See
Red/ The Weeping Song/ Better Be Home Soon/
Throw Your Arms Around Me/ Four Seasons in
One Day
R: Exs. Soundboard.   S: Albani Musicclub,
Winterthur, Switzerland Oct. 28 '91.   C: ECD.

CULT, THE

CD - SANCTUARY
BANANA BAN-009-A
Love (5:19)/ Nirvana (4:54)/ Christian (4:19)/
Hollow Man (4:42)/ Rain (5:05)/ Dreamtime (3:05)/
She Sells Sanctuary (5:25)/ Go West (5:21)/ Horse
Nation (3:32)/ Phoenix (4:26)
R: Vg-Ex. Soundboard.   S: Europe '86.
C: Australian CD. Dcc.

THE CURE

CD - CURED (VOL. 1)
BANANA BAN-006-A
Shake Dog Shake (4:50)/ A Strange Day (4:09)/ A
Night Like This (5:01)/ Catch (2:43)/ Pictures Of
You (8:02)/ Fascination Street (4:55)/ Lullaby
(4:43)/ Dressing Up (3:08)/ The Same Deep Water
As You (10:28)/ Just Like Heaven (2:48)
R: Vg-Exs. Soundboard.   S: Europe '90.
C: Australian CD. Dcc.

CD - CURED (VOL. 2)
BANANA BAN-006-B
The Walk (4:07)/ Primary (3:37)/ In Between Days
(2:58)/ A Forest (10:47)/ Disintegration (7:19)/
Close To Me (4:08)/ Let's Go To Bed (3:31)/ Why
Can't I Be You (5:54)/ Never Enough (5:19)/ Boys
Don't Cry (3:06)
R: Ex. Audience.   S: Europe '90.   C: Australian
CD. Dcc.

CD - CURED (VOL. 3)
BANANA BAN-006-C
In Your House (3:11)/ M (3:04)/ Jumping Someone
Else's Train (5:42)/ A Forest (5:44)/ Play For
Today (4:23)/ Torture (4:18)/ All I Want (5:34)/ Hot
Hot Hot!!! (3:27)/ In Between Days (3:08) How
Beautiful You Are (5:24)/ Perfect Girl (2:29)/ Boys
Don't Cry (2:54)/ Why Can't I Be You (3:00)
R: Exs. Soundboard.   S: Europe '80. USA '87.
C: Australian CD. Dcc.

CYPRESS HILL

CD - LEGALIZED
SHINOLA SH 69013
Insane In The Brain (4:43)/ I Ain't Goin' Like That
(3:19)/ Real Estate (3:06)/ Stoned In The Way Of
The Walk (3:58)/ When The Shit Goes Down
(3:03)/ I Wonna Get High (2:39)/ Cock The
Hammer (3:48)/ Hits From The Bong (3:35)/ Real
Estate (2:54)/ How I Could Just Kill A Man (2:28)/
What Go Around Come Around Kid (1:27)/ Lock
Down (0:48)/ Hand On The Pump (4:16)/ I Ain't
Goin' Out Like That (2:10)/ The Bridge Is Over
(3:03)/ Cock The Hammer (2:30)/ Lick A Shot
(3:41)/ Insane In The Brain (3:34)
R: Ex. Audience.   S: USA '93.   C: ECD. Dcc.
Time 56:32.

D

DAVIS, MILES

CD - HUMAN NATURE
JAZZ FILE JF 1001
You're Under Arrest (10:04)/ Human Nature
(7:26)/ Medley: Mrs. Morrisine, You're Under
Arrest (23:27)/ Spring (15:12)/ Decoy (5:27)
R: Exs. Soundboard.   S: Montreux, July 14 '85.
C: ECD. Dcc.

DANZIG

CD - THE TOWER OF THE DARK SIDE
METAL CRUSH MECD 1176
How The Gods Kill (6:21)/ Mother (3:27)/ Am I
Demon (6:25)/ Twist Of Cain (3:29)/ Mother (3:12)/
Invocation (2:54)/ When Death Had No Name
(4:58)/ Not Of This World (3:38)/ Intro, Come To
Getcha (5:08)/ Snakes Of Christ (4:05)/ It's
Coming Down (3:10)/ Mother (3:17)/ How The
Gods Kill (6:08)/ Her Black Wings (4:23) Twist Of
Cain (3:50)/ Long Way Back From Hell (4:46)/
Dirty Black Summer (4:16)
R: Vg-Ex. Audience.   S: Tracks 1-2 USA '93.
Tracks 3-8 Los Angeles '89. Tracks 9-17 Buffalo
May 30 94.   C: ECD. Dcc. Pic CD.

DEAD CAN DANCE

CD - SINFUL GARDEN
KISS THE STONE KTS 370
Yulunga (6:34)/ Solo (2:39)/ Sinful Garden (6:05)/
The Song Of Sybil (4:42)/ Desert Sun (4:06)/
Mystical Rain (5:58)/ Woman (2:35)/ Watch Over
Me (4:36)/ Horn Solo (3:52)/ The Wind That
Shakes The Barley (2:54)/ I Am Stretched On
Your Grave (4:41)/ Morning (3:57)/ Sailing The
Seas (3:50)/ Remembrance (5:09)/ Cantara (5:59)
R: Exs. Audience.   S: Wiltern Theatre, San
Francisco Dec. 15 '93.   C: ECD. Pic CD.

DEEP PURPLE

CD - BERLIN 5.29.70
DP-009
Wring That Neck/ Mandrake Root/ Speed King
R: Poor.   S: Berlin, Germany May 29 '70.
C: Japanese CD. Time 56:00.

CD - BERLIN 1971
DPC-001
Child In Time/ Mandrake Root/ Strange Kind Of
Woman/ Into The Fire/ Paint It Black/ Black Night/
Lucille
R: G. Audience. Hiss.   S: Berlin, Germany May
22 '71.   C: Japanese CD. Dcc. Gillan asks
bootlegger about microphone. Time 76:05.

CD - BLACK NIGHT
GRAPEFRUIT GRA-022-A
Intro: Toccata (1:32)/ Highway Star (5:36)/ Strange

Kind Of Woman, Superstar (8:04)/ Perfect
Strangers (6:07)/ Lazy (3:21)/ Space Truckin'
(24:47)/ Speed King (9:00)/ Black Night (7:45)/
Smoke On The Water (7:45)
R: Ex. Soundboard.   S: Knebworth, England '85.
C: Australian CD. Dcc.

CD - CHICAGO 7.20.71
DP-001
Black Night/ Paint It Black/ Hard Road/ Highway
Star/ The Mule*/ Lazy/ Space Truckin'
R: G. Audience. Tracks 4-7 Poor. Audience.
S: Tracks 1-3 Chicago July 20 '71. Tracks 4-7
West Palm Beach, Florida '72.   C: Japanese CD.
Dbw. Yellow type. Time 74:53.

CD - GOTEBERG 2.72
DP-004
Strange Kind Of Woman/ Child In Time/ The Mule/
Lazy/ Space Truckin'/ Fireball/ Lucille
R: Poor. Audience. Distant.   S: Goteberg Feb.
'72.   C: Japanese CD. Dbw. Red Type.
Time 69:24.

CD - KOLN 4.4.70
DP-007 1-2
CD1: Speed King/ Mumblin' Thing Blues/ Wring
That Neck
CD2: Paint It Black/ Mandrake Root
R: Poor-G. Audience.   S: Koln Apr. 4 '70.
C: Japanese CD. Blue/black cover. Purple type.
Time CD1 41:06. CD2 40:18.

CD - THE LEGEND LIVES ON
OCTOPUS OCTO 062
Intro, Highway Star (5:33)/ Black Knight (4:53)/
Anyone's Daughter (3:41)/ Child In Time (9:13)/
Lazy (7:04)/ Space Truckin' (2:41)/ Woman From
Tokyo (2:22)/ Pain It Black (5:52)/ Smoke On The
Water (8:26)
R: Ex. Audience.   S: Europe during 'The Battle
Rages On ...' tour '93.   C: ECD. Pic CD.

CD - LONG BEACH 4.15.73
DP-012
Highway Star/ Smoke On The Water/ Strange
Kind Of Woman/ Mary Long/ Lazy/ Space Truckin'
R: G-Vg. Audience.   S: Long Beach, CA Apr. 15
'73.   C: Japanese CD. Purple/black cover. Blue
type. Time 70:42.

CD - MARK III
DPC-003-4
CD1: Burn/ Stormbringer/ The Gypsy/ Lady
Double Dealer/ Mistreated/ Smoke On The Water/
You Fool No One (1)
CD2: You Fool No One (2), The Mule/ Space
Truckin'/ Going Down/ Highway Star/ Highway
Star
R: G. Audience.   S: Paris, France Apr. '7 '75.
C: Japanese CD. Black/silver cover.
Time CD1 51:38. CD2 57:29.

CD - MUNCHEN 6.10.70
DP-008
Child In Time/ Wring That Neck/ Mandrake Root
R: G. Audience.   S: Munchen June 10 '70.
C: Japanese CD. Dcc. Time 57:24.

CD - MUNCHEN 12.70
DP-002
Yodel/ Speed King/ Into The Fire/ Child In Time/
Mandrake Root/ Black Night/ Lucille
R: Poor. Audience.   S: Munchen Dec. '70.
C: Japanese CD. Green/black cover. Orange type.
Time 72:28.

CD - NURUMBERG 1973
DPC-002
Highway Star/ Smoke On The Water/ Strange
Kind Of Woman/ Mary Long/ Lazy/ Space Truckin'
R: G. Audience. Some distortion.   S: Nurumberg,
Germany Jan. 19 '73.   C: Japanese CD. Dcc.
Time 75:31.

CD - SPIRIT OF FREEDOM
BANZAI BZCD 027/28
CD1: Highway Star/ Ram Shackle Man/ Leo/
Fireball/ Perfect Stranger/ Solitaire/ John Lord
Solo/ Knocking At Your Backdoor/ Devil's
Daughter
CD2: Anya/ The Battle Rages On/ Child In Time
(includes drum solo and guitar solo)/ Space
Truckin'/ Woman From Tokyo/ Speedking/ Smoke
On The Water
R: Poor-Good. Audience.   S: Palasport, Genova,
Italy June 21 '94.   C: ECD. Dcc. Pic CDs. Time
CD1 55:46. CD2 64:51.

CD - STUTTGART 2.16/17.72
DP-010
Highway Star/ No No No/ The Mule/ Speed King/
Mumblin' Thing Blues/ Space Truckin'/ Strange
Kind Of Woman*
R: Poor-G. Audience. *G-Vg. Audience.
S: Tracks 1-3 Stuttgart Feb. 16 '72. Tracks 4-6
Stuttgart Feb. 17 '72. Track 7 Speyer Sept. 5 '71.
C: Japanese CD. Green/Blue cover. Time 64:50.

CD - TORONTO 7.2.71
DP-003-1-2
CD1: Speed King/ Strange Kind Of Woman/ Paint
It Black/ Demon's Eye
CD2: Child In Time/ Mandrake Root/ Black Night
R: Poor-G. Low vocal level.   S: Toronto July 2
'71.   C: Japanese CD. Dbw. Red type. Time
CD1 38:27. CD2 52:14.

CD - WALVERHAMPTON 2.20.72
DP-005-1-2
CD1: Highway Star/ Strange Kind Of Woman/
Child In Time/ The Mule
CD2: Lazy/ Space Truckin'/ Fireball/ Lucille
R: G. Audience.   S: Walverhampton, England
Feb. 20 '72.   C: Japanese CD. Time CD1 50:24.
CD2 41:02.

CD - WELCOME JOE
ALL OF US AS 29/2
CD1: Intro/ Highway Star/ Ramshackle Man/
Maybe I'm A Leo/ Fireball/ Perfect Strangers/
Pictures Of Home/ Jon Lord Solo/ Knockin' At
Your Backdoor/ Anyone's Daughter/ Anya
CD2: The Battle Rages On/ When A Blind Man
Cries/ Lazy/ Satch Boogie/ Space Truckin'/
Woman From Tokyo/ Paint It Black/ Speed King/
Smoke On The Water
R: G. Audience.   S: Expo, Genova, Italy June 22
'94.   C: ECD. Dcc. Time CD1 68:07. CD2 53:40.

DEF LEPARD

CD - LET'S GET ROCKED
GRAPEFRUIT GRA-031-A
Let's Get Rocked (5:02)/ Tear It Down (3:58)/
Women (6:21)/ Another Hit And Run (6:46)/ Too
Late For Love (5:31)/ Histeria (7:00)/ Make Love
Like A Man (6:19)/ Foolin' (5:14)/ Animal (4:16)
R: Ex. Soundboard.   S: Los Angeles '93 part
one. See 'Rocket' (GRA-031-B) for part two.
C: Australian CD. Dcc.

CD - ONE STEP BEYOND
RAZOR'S EDGE RZCD 0057/58
CD1: Intro - Let's Get Rocked/ Tear It Down/
Women/ Too Late For Love/ Hysteria/ Make Love
Like A Man/ Guitar Solo/ Foolin'/ Animal
CD2: Guitar Solo/ Gods Of War/ Rocket? Tonight/
Have You Ever Needed Someone So Bad/
Armageddon It/ Pour Some Sugar On Me/ Rock
Of Ages/ Love Bites/ Can't Get Enough Of Your
Love (with Bryan Adams)
R: G. Audience.   S: 'Le Zenith' May 16 '93.
C: ECD. Dcc. Pic CDs. Time CD1 57:50.
CD2 67:03.

CD - ROCKET
GRAPEFRUIT GRA-031-B
Rocket (11:06)/ Two Steps Behind (5:11)/ Have
You Never Needed Someone So Bad (5:42)/
Medley: Black Betty, Armageddon It (6:52)/ Pour
Some Sugar On Me (5:27)/ Rock Of Ages (5:10)/
Love Bites (7:42)/ Photograph (5:22)
R: Ex. Soundboard.   S: Los Angeles '93 part
two. See 'Let's Get Rocked' (GRA-031-A) for part
one.   C: Australian CD. Dcc.

DEPECHE MODE

CD - DEVOTIONAL TOUR
X REKORDS 101-2
CD1: Higher Love/ Policy Of Truth/ World In My
Eyes/ Walking In My Shoes/ Behind The Wheel/
Halo/ Stripped/ Condemnation/ Judas/ Piano
Number
CD2: Mercy In You/ I Feel You/ Never Let Me
Down Again/ Rush/ In Your Room/ Personal
Jesus/ Enjoy The Silence
R: Vg-Ex. Audience.   S: Hallen Stadion, Zurich,
Switzerland May 21 '93.   C: ECD.

CD - I FEEL YOU
GRAPEFRUIT GRA-010-A
Higher Love (6:23)/ Policy Of Truth (4:58)/ Halo
(4:37)/ Stripped (5:05)/ Condemnation (3:47)/
Judas (5:06)/ I Feel You (7:10)/ Never Let Me
Down Again (4:51)/ Rush (4:40)/ In Your Room
(6:36)/ Personal Jesus (5:44)/ Enjoy The Silence
(6:37)/ Everything Counts (5:12)
R: Exs. Soundboard.   S: Chicago, USA '92.
C: Australian CD. Dcc.

CD - I FEEL YOU
MOGUL NIGHTMARE RECORDS MNR 015
Higher Love/ Policy Of Truth/ Walkin' In My Shoes/
Halo/ Stripped/ Condemnation/ Judas/ I Feel You/
Never Let Me Down Again/ Rush/ In Your Room/
Personal Jesus/ Enjoy The Silence/ Everything
Counts
R: Ex.   S: Europe '93.   C: ECD. Time 77:30.

CD - JONES BEACH
RED PHANTOM RPCD 2181-2182
CD1: Intro - Rush (6:57)/ Halo (4:46)/ Behind The
Wheel (5:19)/ Everything Counts (6:25)/ World In
My Eyes (6:25)/ Walking In My Shoes (6:31)/
Stripped (5:21)/ Condemnation (4:05)/ I Want You
Now (4:49)
CD2: In Your Room (6:49)/ Never Let Me Down
Again (5:00)/ I Feel You (7:18)/ Personal Jesus
(7:23)/ Somebody (4:17)/ Enjoy The Silence
(9:07)/ A Question Of Time (4:41)
R: G-Vg. Audience.   S: Wantagh Theater, Jones
Beach, NY June 16 '94.   C: ECD. Dcc. Pic CD.

DEREK & THE DOMINOS

CD - BLIND DOMINOS
KEEP ON KEEPING ON KOKO 003
Well Allright/ Sea Of Joy/ Sleeping In The Ground/
Under My Thumb/ It's Too Late/ Got To Get
Better/ Matchbox/ Matchbox/ Blues Power/ It's My
Life Baby/ Got To Get Better
R: Tracks 1-10 Vg-Ex. Tracks 11-12 Poor-G.
S: Tracks 1-4 (Blind Faith) Hyde Park, London
June 7 '69. Tracks 5-10 (Derek & The Domino's)
Johnny Cash TV Show Nov. 5 '70. Track 11
(Clapton, Buddy Guy & Jr. Wells) L'Olympia, Paris
Sept. 29 '70. Track 12 (Derek & The Domino's)
Kleinhan's Music Hall, Buffalo, NY Oct. 29 '70.
C: Japanese CD. Dcc. Time 72:13.

CD - GARAGE
ASTEROID AR-07-1/2
CD1: Got To Get Better In A Little While/ Roll
Over/ Blues Power/ Stormy Monday/ Chuck Berry
Medley: Hey Little Queenie, Sweet Little Rock'N
Roller
CD2: Why Does Love Got To Be So Sad/ Tell The
Truth/ Let It Rain/ Every Day I Have The Blues
R: G. Audience.   S: UK Oct. '70.

CD - LIVE AT TAMPA
RED LIGHT RL-1001/2
CD1: Layla/ Got To Get Better In A Little While/

Key To The Highway/ Why Does Love Got To Be
So Sad
CD2: Blues Power/ Have You Ever Loved A
Woman/ Bottle Of Red Wine/ Let It Rain
R: Poor.   S: Curtis Hickson Hall, Tampa, Florida
Dec. 1 '70.

DI MEOLA, AL

CD - CLASSIC AND ELECTRIC GUITARS
ALL OF US AS 17
Orient Blue, Passion Grace & Fire (7:35)/ Short
Tales Of The Black Forest (10:01)/ Electric
Rendezvous (8:37)/ Al Di's Theme (8:38)/ Theme
To The Mothership (8:12)/ Race With The Devil
On Spanish Highway (10:08)/ Advantage (2:15)
R: Ex. Audience.   S: Amsterdam, Rocktempel
May 5 '82.   C: ECD. Dcc.

DINOSAUR JR.

CD - FREAKIN' LIVE!
DEAD DOG RECORDS SE 436
Kieblin'/ Get Me/ Hickery Wind/ Budge/ Get Me/
Severed Lips/ Raisins/ Thumb/ Freakscene/
Water/ Keep The Flow/ The Lung/ The Wagon/
Tarpit/ I Live For That Look
R: Vg-Ex.   S: USA '92-93.   C: ECD. Dbw.
Green and yellow type. Time 67:03.

DR. JOHN

CD - THE RETURN OF THE MIGHTY NIGHT TRIPPER
KLONDYKE RECORDS DR 24
Iko Iko (6:30)/ Right Place Wrong Time (5:22)/
Walk On Gilded Splinters (13:13)/ Didn't He
Ramble (4:19)/ More Than You Know (5:57)/ Goin'
Back To New Orleans (10:24)/ Mardi Gras Medley
(16:38)/ Night Tripper Outro (1:34)
S: Europe '93.   C: ECD.

DOOBIE BROTHERS, THE

CD - AMERICAN TOUR '91
SOUNDS ALIVE SA 24005
Dangerous (6:00)/ Rockin' Down The Highway
(3:06)/ Jesus is Just Allright (4:48)/ The Doctor
(3:45)/ Need A Little Taste Of Love (3:41)/
Showdown (4:37)/ South Of The Border (5:04)/
Excited (5:20)/ South City Midnight Lady (5:47)/
Black Water (4:59)/ Something You Said (5:02)/
Take Me In Your Arms (3:39)/ Long Train Runnin'
(5:08)/ China Grove (3:08)/ Listen To The Music
(5:26)
R: Exs. Soundboard.   S: USA Tour '91.
C: ECD. Dbw. Blue type.

DOORS, THE

CD - APOCALYPSE NOW
KISS THE STONE KTS 267
Five To One/ Mack The Knife, Alabama Song/
Backdoor Man/ You're Lost Little Girl/ Love Me

Two Times/ When The Music's Over/ Wild Child/
Money/ Wake Up/ Light My Fire/ The End/
Unknown Soldier
R: Exs. Soundboard.   S: 'Waiting For The Sun'
tour '68.   C: ECD. Pic CD. Time 73:16.

CD - CENTRAL PARK NEW YORK AUG. 21 1972
BLACK DOG BD 004
Tightrope Ride (4:13)/ In The Eye Of The Sun
(5:14)/ The Mosquito (8:14)/ Love Me Two Times
(5:55)/ Jam (7:00)/ I'm Horny, I'm Stoned (5:57)/
Ships With Sails (8:25)/ Jam (3:32)/ Good Rockin'
Tonight (7:42)/ Light My Fire (11:40)/ Close To
You (5:54)
R: Poor-G.   S: Central Park, New York Aug. 21
'72.   C: ECD. Dcc.

CD - THE COMPLETE MATRIX CLUB TAPES
KISS THE STONE KTS 3013/3014/3016
CD1: Back Door Man (5:49)/ My Eyes Have Seen
You (3:01)/ Soul Kitchen (4:19)/ Get Off My Life
(4:25)/ When The Music's Over (13:09)/ Close To
You (3:08)/ Crawling King Snake (5:08)/ I Can't
See Your Face In My Mind (3:27)/ People Are
Strange (2:22)/ Who Do You Love? (3:57)/
Alabama Song (3:48)/ The Crystal Ship (3:16)
CD2: Twentieth Century Fox (2:58)/ Moonlight
Drive (6:41)/ Summer's Almost Gone (3:53)/
Unhappy Girl (4:12)/ Woman Is The Devil, Sittin'
Round Thinkin', Rock Me (8:36)/ Break On
Through (4:25)/ Light My Fire (8:36)/ The End
(14:29)
CD3: My Eyes Have Seen You (3:58)/ Soul
Kitchen (6:15)/ I Can't See Your Face In My Mind
(2:22)/ People Are Strange (3:23)/ When The
Music's Over (12:27)/ Money (3:31)/ Who Do You
Love? (4:50)/ Moonlight Drive (6:04)
CD4: Summer's Almost Gone (4:04)/ I'm A King
Bee (5:20)/ Gloria (6:04)/ Break On Through
(5:02)/ Summertime (9:42)/ Back Door Man (5:45)/
Alabama Song (3:30)/ The End (4:56)
R: Vg-Ex.   S: Matrix Club, San Francisco. CDs
1-2 Mar. 7 '67. CDs 3-4 Mar. 10 '67.   C: ECD.
Book-style digi-pack. Full color booklet. Pic CDs.

CD - FREEDOM MAN
BANZAI BZBX 036
CD1: Intro - Roadhouse Blues/ Ship Of Fools/
Break On Through/ Universal Mind/ Alabama
Song, Back Door Man, Five To One/ Moonlight
Drive/ Who Do You Love/ Money/ Light My Fire/
When The Music's Over
CD2: The Spy/ Break On Through/ Peace Frog/
Blue Sunday/ Light My Fire/ Soul Kitchen/ Love
Me Two Times/ Maggie McGill/ Roadhouse Blues/
Alabama Song, Back Door Man, Five To One,
Ship Of Fools
CD3: When The Music Is Over/ Back Door Man/
Break On Through/ When The Music's Over/ Ship
Of Fools/ Light My Fire/ The End
R: CD1 Vg. Audience. CD2 G. Audience. CD3 G.
Audience.   S: CD1 Felt Forum, New York Jan.
18 '70. CD2 and CD3 track 1 Long Beach Arena

Feb. 2 '70. CD3 tracks 2-7 Isle Of Wright Festival Aug. 29 '70.   C: ECD. Full colour cardboard slipcase. Pic CDs. Full color book. Time CD1 70:18. CD2 71:58. CD3 77:28.

CD - THE LIZARD KING (VOL. 1)
BANANA BAN-011-A
Alabama Song (1:36)/ Back Door Man (2:11)/ Five To One (3:11)/ I Can't See Your Face In My Mind (3:15)/ People Are Strange (2:17)/ Money (That's What I Want) (2:41)/ Who Do You Love? (4:37)/ Summer's Almost Gone (3:54)/ I'm A King Bee (3:53)/ Gloria (5:47)/ Summertime (8:52)/ Close To You (3:07)/ Rock Me Baby (8:31)/ The Hill Dwellers (2:45)/ Light My Fire (8:56)
R: Vg-Ex. Soundboard.   S: '67-'68.
C: Australian CD. Dcc. Gold disc.

CD - THE LIZARD KING (VOL. 2)
BANANA BAN-011-B
Moonlight Drive (5:50)/ Break On Through (4:01)/ Crystal Ship (2:53)/ 20th Century Fox (2:46)/ Unhappy Girl (3:59)/ Love Street (3:02)/ Love Me Two Times (3:17)/ Unknown Soldier (3:52)/ You're Lost Little Girl (3:15)/ Wild Child (2:34)/ Wake Up (1:53)/ Five To One (6:03)/ The End (16:24)/ Touch Me (3:03)/ Moonlight Drive (2:53)/ Light My Father (2:55)
R: G-Vg. Soundboard.   S: '67-'68.
C: Australian CD. Dcc. Gold disc.

CD - THE LIZARD KING (VOL. 3)
BANANA BAN-011-C
Roadhouse Blues (5:53)/ Back Door Man (2:34)/ Five To One (6:10)/ Money (That's What You Want) (2:59)/ Rock Me Baby (6:41)/ Little Red Rooster (6:33)/ Who Do You Love? (8:07)/ Medley: Light My Fire, Fever, Summertime, St. James Infirmary (17:53)/ The End (16:36)
R: G-Vg. Soundboard.   S: Canada '70.
C: Australian CD. Dcc. Gold disc.

CD - THE LIZARD KING (VOL. 4)
BANANA BAN-011-D
Back Door Man, Love Hides (7:10)/ Roadhouse Blues (5:30)/ When The Music's Over (19:53)/ People Get Ready (0:43)/ Train I Ride (3:41)/ Baby Please Don't Go (3:34)/ Train I Ride (13:49)/ Bullfrog Blues (3:12)/ Break On Through (5:17)/ Someday Soon (6:13)
R: G-Vg. Soundboard.   S: Canada '70.
C: Australian CD. Dcc. Gold disc.

12" - MIAMI 69
LIVING THEATRE RECORDS 1
S1: Back Door Man/ Five To One/ Touch Me Time (18:18)
S2: Love Me Two Times/ When The Music's Over Time (22:00)
R: Good mono.   S: Dinner Key Auditorium, Miami, FL Jan. 3 '69.   C: 500 numbered copies.

CD - MR. MOJO RISIN' AGAIN - THE LIVE PERFORMANCE '93 AND MORE
MONTANA MO 10015
Roadhouse Blues/ Break On Through/ Light My Fire/ Five To One/ Little Red Rooster/ Who Do You Love/ Go Insane/ The Hill Dwellers/ People Are Strange/ Love Street/ Love Me Two Times/ The Soft Parade/ Summer's Almost Gone/ Manish Boy
R: Vg.   S: '68-'93 USA.   C: ECD. Dcc. Time 71:14.

CD - SHATTERED
KISS THE STONE KTS 350
Roadhouse Blues (5:37)/ When The Music's Over (20:39)/ Mystery Train, Extended Jam (26:48)/ Break On Through (5:18)/ Someday Soon (3:53)/ Backdoor Man (7:02)/ Little Red Rooster (6:23)
R: Ex.   S: Original, unmixed and uncut soundboard tapes. Tracks 1-6 Seattle Center Coliseum, Seattle June 5 '70. Track 7 Pacific National Exhibition Coliseum, Vancouver, Canada June 6 '70.   C: ECD. Dcc. Pic CD.

CD - TOUCH ME
GRAPEFRUIT GRA-050-B
Moonlight Drive (5:50)/ Break On Through (4:01)/ Crystal Ship (2:53)/ 20th Century Fox (2:46)/ Unhappy Girl (3:59)/ Love Street (3:02)/ Love Me Two Times (3:17)/ Unknown Soldier (3:52)/ You're Lost Little Girl (3:15)/ Wild Child (2:34)/ Wake Up (1:53)/ Five To One (6:03)/ The End (16:24)/ Touch Me (3:03)/ Moonlight Drive (2:53)/ Light My Fire (2:55)
R: Ex.   S: San Francisco '67. Seattle '70. Sweden '68.   C: Australian CD. Dcc.

CD - WESTBURY MUSIC FAIR
OCTOPUS OCTO 003
Roadhouse Blues (7:20)/ Peace Frog (3:47)/ Alabama Song (2:00)/ Back Door Man (2:16)/ Five To One (9:38)/ Celebration Of The Lizard (16:03)/ Soul Kitchen (9:23)/ Light My Fire (11:00)/ Build Me A Woman (3:44)/ When The Music Is Over (12:01)
R: Vg-Ex. Audience.   S: Long Island, New York Apr. 19 '68.   C: ECD. Dcc. Pic CD.

CD - WHEN THE MUSIC'S OVER
ON STAGE CD 12029
Build Me A Woman (3:37)/ Universal Mind (4:52)/ Who Do You Love (6:09)/ Dead Cats, Dead Rats (1:54)/ Break On Through (4:43)/ Close To You (3:59)/ Alabama Song (Whiskey Bar) (1:58)/ Backdoor Man (2:22)/ Love Hides (1:49)/ Five To One (4:34)/ When The Music's Over (14:51)
R: Vg-Ex.   S: LA, New York, Boston, Philadelphia, Pittsburgh, Detroit, Copenhagen '68-'70.   C: ECD.

DRAKE, NICK

TANWORTH-IN-ARDEN 1967/68
ANTHOLOGY ANT. 15. 11

My Sugar So Sweet (1:43)/ Get Together (1:54)/
Don't Think Twice It's Allright (2:19)/ Believe Me
Pretty Mama (2:01)/ Don't Be Afraid To Lie (2:32)/
Down The Highway (3:03)/ Sunday Baby (2:21)/
Winter Is Gone (2:37)/ Here Comes The Blues
(3:44)/ All My Trying (1:50)/ She Could Sleep In
My Bed Once Again (3:15)/ Cocaine Blues (2:02)/
True Song (2:47)/ Summertime (1:33)/ Black Man
Blues (2:34)/ The Season Of The Rain (3:03)/ The
Reason Of The Seasons (2:45)/ To The Garden
(1:50)
R: Vg. Some hiss.   S: Tanworth-In Arden '67/'68.
C: ECD. Dbw. Purple text.

DREAM THEATER

CD - A KICK INTO A DREAM
METAL CRASH NCCD 2186/87
CD1: Intro - Pull Me Under (9:02)/ 6:00 (5:48)/
Take The Time (12:25)/ Caught In A Web (8:07)/
Lifting Shadows Off A Dream (6:05)/ The Ones
Who Help To Set The Sun (6:31)
CD2: The Mirror (6:44)/ Lies (67:24)/ Another Day
(4:46)/ Crotomania (6:42)/ Voices (9:54)/ The
Silent Man (5:58)/ Metropolis (10:47)
R: G. Audience.   S: Manhattan Center, NYC Oct.
28 '94.   C: ECD. Dcc. Pic CD.

CD - CLASSIC LIVE
REBORN CLASSICS RC 1045
Under The Glass Moon/ Only A Matter Of Time/
Surrounded/ Pull Me Under/ The Ytse Jam/
Another Day/ The Killing Hand/ Take The Time/
Vital Star
R: Gm. Audience.   S: Fort Lauderdale, USA
Dec. '92.

CD - DANCE OF ETERNITY
ROCKS 92111
Metropolis - Part 1 (10:11)/ Under A Glass Moon
(8:15)/ Status Seeker (5:26)/ Wait To Sleep (8:55)/
To Live Forever (11:15)/ Another Day (4:46)/ Pull
Me Under (8:41)/ Instrumental (5:21)/ Learning To
Live (13:37)
R: Ex. Audience.   S: Impax Club, Buffalo May 18
'93.   C: ECD. Dcc.

CD - THE DANCE OF ETERNITY
WHY NOT WOT 2014/2015
CD1: Metropolis Part 1/ A Fortune In Lies/ Under
A Glass Moon/ Surrounded/ The Ytse' Jam (also
drum solo)/ Forever/ Take The Time
CD2: Pull Me Under/ Another Day/ The Killing
Hand/ A Change Of Season/ Wait For Sleep/
Learning To Live
R: Ex.   S: Aug. '93.   C: ECD.

CD - DREAM OUT LOUD
KISS THE STONE KTS 243
Metropolis Part 1/ Under A Glass Moon/ Nothing Is
Sacred/ Medley/ Wait For Sleep/ Surrounded/
Take The Time/ Medley/ Forever/ Mike Portnoy
Drum Solo/ Another Day/ Pull Me Under/ Learning
To Live

R: Exs. Audience.   S: NYC May 18 '93.
C: ECD. Dcc. Pic CD.

CD - LIVE IN LONG ISLAND II
HARD LINER HCD 0293
Take The Time (12:01)/ Wait For Sleep (3:40)/
Learning To Live (12:59)/ Change Of Seasons
(20:18)/ Another Won (5:35)/ Your Majesty (3:51)/
Two Far (5:33)/ March Of The Tyrant (5:42)
R: G-Vgs. Audience.   S: Sparks Club, Long
Island Oct. 4 '92.   C: ECD.

CD - LORDS OF SOUND
KISS THE STONE KTS 282/83
CD1: Metropolis Part 1/ Under A Glass Moon/ A
Fortune In Lies/ Wait for Sleep, Surrounded/ Take
The Time
CD2: To Live Forever, Drum Solo/ Status Seeker/
Another Day/ Pull Me Under/ Instrumental Jam/
Learning To Live
R: Vg-Exs.   S: Milwaukee, WI June 29, '93.
C: ECD. Dcc. Pic CDs. Time CD1 44:53.
CD2 49:44.

CD - MAJESTIC HARMONIES
BACK STAGE BKCD 089
Metropolis Part 1 (9:35)/ Mission Impossible
(1:50)/ Afterlife (6:06)/ Under A Glass Moon (7:16)/
Wait For Sleep, Keyboard Solo (3:12)/ Surrounded
(5:55)/ Take The Time (10:56)/ Pull Me Under
(8:31)/ Vital Star (5:45)/ Another Won (5:36)/ Your
Majesty (3:52)/ A Vision (11:16)
R: Ex.   S: Track 1-8 Stockholm, Sweden Oct. 27
'93. Tracks 9-12 early studio sessions '86.
C: ECD. Dcc. Pic CD.

DURAN DURAN

CD - ACOUSTIC WORLD
KISS THE STONE KTS 269
Hungry Like The Wolf (6:33)/ Ordinary World
(5:26)/ Serious (4:21)/ Girls On Film (5:50)/ Rio
(6:20)/ Planet Earth (4:32)/ Come Undone (6:36)/
Too Much Information (5:29)
R: Exs. Soundboard.   S: USA '93.   C: ECD.
Dcc. Pic CD.

CD - ORDINARY WORLD
GRAPEFRUIT GRA-039-A
Planet Earth (4:47)/ Hungary Like The Wolf (6:36)/
Ordinary World (5:32)/ Come Undone (7:09)/ The
Chauffeur (7:47)/ Girls On Film (5:17)/ Notorious
(5:18)/ Too Much Information (4:59)/ Save A
Prayer (6:51)/ Rio (6:07)
R: Exs. Soundboard.   S: California '93.
C: Australian CD. Dcc.

CD - WORLD BROADCAST
HAWK 023
Planet Earth (5:45)/ Hungry Like A Wolf (6:42)/
Ordinary World (5:35)/ Come Undone (7:08)/ The
Chauffeur (8:02)/ Girls On Film (5:41)/ Notorious
(5:21)/ Too Much Information (5:03)/ Save A
Prayer (7:34)/ Rio (7:02)

DYLAN, BOB

R: Exs. Soundboard.   S: Tower Records,
Hollywood May 15 '93.   C: ECD. Pic CD.

DYLAN, BOB

CD - A DAY IN THE LIFE
GOLD STANDARD
Tell Me Mama/ I Don't Believe You/ Baby Let Me
Follow You Down/ Just Like Tom Thumb's Blues/
Leopard Skin Pillbox Hat/ One Too Many
Mornings/ Ballad Of A Thin Man/ Tell Me Mama/ I
Don't Believe You/ Baby Let Me Follow You Down/
Leopard Skin Pillbox Hat/ One Too Many
Mornings/ Ballad Of A Thin Man/ Like A Rolling
Stone
S: Tracks 1-6 Glasgow Odeon May 19 '66. Track 7
Birmingham Odeon May 12 '66. Tracks 8-10
Liverpool Odeon May 14 '66. Tracks 13-14
Manchester Free Trade Hall May 17 '66.
C: ECD. Dcc.

CD - A WEEK IN THE LIFE
GOLD STANDARD RAZO 14
Tell Me Mama/ I Don't Believe You/ Baby Let Me
Follow You Down/ Just Like Tom Thumb's Blues/
Leopard Skin Pillbox Hat/ One Too Many
Mornings/ Ballad Of A Thin Man/ Tell Me Mama/ I
Don't Believe You/ Baby Let Me Follow You Down/
Leopard Skin Pillbox Hat/ One Too Many
Mornings/ Ballad Of A Thin Man/ Like A Rolling
Stone
R: Ex. Soundboard.   S: Tracks 1-6, 13-14
Manchester Free Trade Hall May 17 '66. Track 7
Birmingham Odeon May 12 '66. Tracks 8-10
Liverpool Odeon May 14 '66. Tracks 11-12 May 16
'66.   C: ECD. Dcc. Time /5:23.

CD ALIAS VOL. 1
DIAMONDS IN YOUR EAR
Midnight Special/ Mean Old Railroad/ Acne/ I'll Fly
Away/ Swing And Turn Jubilee/ Come Back Babe/
Sittin' On Top Of The World/ Wichita/ Big Joe/
Dylan And Victoria/ It's Dangerous/ Glory Glory/
Overseas Stomp/ You Can Always Tell/ Xmas
Island/ Cocaine/ London Waltz/ Will The Circle Be
Unbroken/ Ye Playboys And Playgirls/ With God
On Our Side/ Only A Pawn In The Game/
Downtown Blues/ Nashville Skyline Rag/ Election
Year Rag/ Somebody Else's Troubles
S: Dylan as a sideman on other artists sessions.
C: ECD. Time 73:21.

CD - ALIAS VOL. 2
DIAMONDS IN YOUR EAR
Is Anybody Going To San Antone/ Wallflower/
Blues Stay Away From Me/ Me And Paul/ Faded
Love/ I'm So Restless/ The Cripples Crow/ Stormy
Weather Cowboy/ It's Not The Spotlight/ Silver
Moon/ Big City Woman/ Who Love/ Pretty Boy
Floyd/ Nuggets Of Rain/ Sold American/ Don't Go
Home With Your Hard-On/ Hazel/ Sign Language
S: Dylan as a sideman on other artists sessions.
C: ECD. Time 75:44.

CD - BEFORE THE FLOOD AND AFTER THE FIRE
LUNA LU 9318
Farewell (9:09)/ Hard Rain (18:57)/ Bob Dylan's
Dream (6:22)/ Boots Of Spanish Leather (11:00)/
John Brown (11:23)/ Who Killed Davey Moore
(5:54)/ Blowin' In The Wind (2:58)/ Make Me A
Pallet On Your Floor (only know performance -
3:33)/ Emmett Till (5:06)
R: G.   S: Tracks 1-7 Studs Terkel's War
Museum, WFMT, Chicago May '63.   C: ECD.
Dbw. Red type.

CD - BELGRAD '91
RED SKY RECORDS CD 1004
New Morning (2:58)/ Ballad Of A Thin Man (4:48)/
All Along The Watchtower (3:18)/ Shelter From
The Storm (4:53)/ Gotta Serve Somebody (7:04)/
It's All Over Now, Baby Blue (5:54)/ Gates Of
Eden (4:02)/ Don't Think Twice It's Allright (5:29)/
Girl From The North Country (4:05)/ Knockin' On
Heaven's Door (5:22)/ Just Like A Woman (5:12)/
Shooting Star (5:20)/ One More Cup Of Coffee
(3:50)/ Like A Rolling Stone (5:54)/ Blowin' In The
Wind (3:58)
R: G-Vg. Audience.   S: FK Zemun Stadium,
Belgrad, Yugoslavia June 11 '91.

CD - BLACKBUSHE
WANTED MAN MUSIC WMM 024/025/026
CD1: My Back Pages/ Love Here With A Feeling/
Baby Stop Crying/ Just Like Tom Thumb Blues/
Shelter From The Storm/ It's All Over Now Baby
Blue
CD2. A Change Is Gonna Come/ Mr. Tambourine
Man/ The Long And Winding Road/ Laissez-Faire/
Gates Of Eden/ True Love Tends To Forget
CD3: Just Like A Woman/ To Ramona/ Don't
Think Twice It's Allright/ All Along The
Watchtower/ All I Really Want To Do/ Band
Introductions/ It's Allright Ma
R: Vg.   S: Blackbushe, England July 15 '78.
C: ECD. Dcc.

CD - BLONDE ON BLONDE - HIGHWAY 61 - MONO MIXES
THE GOLD STANDARD 339/313
CD1: HIGHWAY 61: Like A Rolling Stone/
Tombstone Blues/ It Takes A Lot To Laugh, It
Takes A Train To Cry/ From A Buick 6/ Ballad Of
A Thin Man/ Queen Jane Approximately/ Highway
61 Revisited/ Just Like Tom Thumb's Blues/
Desolation Row/ Positively 4th St./ Can You
Please Crawl Out Your Window?
CD2: BLONDE ON BLONDE: Rainy Day Women
Nos. 12 & 36/ Pledging My Time/ Visions Of
Johanna/ One Of Us Must Know (Sooner Or
Later)/ I Want You/ Stuck Inside Of Mobile With
The Memphis Blues Again/ Leopard Skin Pillbox
Hat/ Just Like A Woman/ Most Likely You Go Your
Way And I'll Go Mine/ Temporary Like Achilles/
Absolutely Sweet Marie/ 4th Time Around/
Obviously 5 Believers/ Sad Eyed Lady Of The
Lowlands

R: Exm.   S: The cover says 'These mono mixes have been sourced from original releases. Some surface noise is evident but this is preferable to the effects of no noise de-clicking, the surface noise is not enough to interfere with the music.' C: ECD. Dcc. Time CD1 73:28. CD2 57:08

CD - BLOWIN' IN THE WIND
I MITI DEL ROCK
Knockin' On Heaven's Door/ Lay Lady Lay/ Just Like Tom Thumb's Blues/ Rainy Day Women/ It Ain't Me Babe/ Tell Me Mama/ I Don't Believe You/ Baby Let Me Follow You Down/ Leopard Skin Pill Box Hat/ Ballad Of A Thin Man
R: Poor.   S: Tracks 1-5 Madison Square Garden, NYC Jan. 31 '74. Tracks 6-10 Manchester, England May 17 '66.   C: ECD. Italian music magazine giveaway. Time 76:13.

CD - THE COMPLETE SUPPER CLUB RECORDINGS
ROCKS 92115/18
CD1: Absolutely Sweet Marie (4:48)/ Lay Lady Lay (5:16)/ Blood In My Eyes (4:14)/ Queen Jane Approximately (9:03)/ Has Anybody Seen My Love (8:00)/ Disease Of The Conceit (5:59)/ I Want You (6:14)/ Ring Them Bells (6:07)/ My Back Pages (6:24)/ Forever Young (6:47)
CD2: Ragged And Dirty (5:07)/ Lay Lady Lay (4:49)/ I'll Be Your Baby Tonight (5:02)/ Queen Jane Approximately (8:26)/ Jack-O-Roe (6:09)/ One Too Many Mornings (5:28)/ I Want You (6:13)/ Ring Them Bells (5:47)/ My Back Pages (6:09)/ Forever Young (7:01)
CD3: Ragged And Dirty (4:48)/ One More Cup Of Coffee (6:09)/ Blood In My Eyes (5:40)/ Queen Jane Approximately (8:22)/ I'll Be Your Baby Tonight (5:09)/ Disease Of Conceit (5:30)/ I Want You (6:05)/ Ring Them Bells (5:52)/ My Back Pages (6:07)/ Forever Young (7:13)
CD4: Ragged And Dirty (5:63)/ Lay Lady Lay (5:04)/ Has Anybody Seen My Love (7:03)/ Weeping Willow Blues (4:23)/ Delia (6:58)/ Jim Jones (5:35)/ Queen Jane Approximately (8:00)/ Ring Them Bells (4:32)/ Jack-O-Roe (5:57)/ Forever Young (7:04)/ I Shall Be Released (8:30)
R: G. Audience.   S: Supper Club, NY Nov. 17 '93.   C: ECD. Box set.

CD - CREATURES VOID OF FORM
THE RAZORS EDGE RAZ 001
Mr. Tambourine Man/ Love Minus Zero, No Limit/ Vincent Van Gogh/ Maggies Farm/ Isis*/ Railroad Boy/ I Pity The Poor Immigrant/ Shelter From The Storm**/ Romance In Durango**/ You're Gonna Make Me Lonesome*/ Rita May/ I Want You*/ Goin Going Gone*/ Knockin' On Heaven's Door/ Gotta Travel On
R: Vg-Ex.   S: The Warehouse, New Orleans, Louisiana May 3 '76. *State Fair Arena, Oklahoma City, Oklahoma May 18 '76. ** Municipal Auditorium, San Antonio, Texas May 11 '76. C: ECD. Dcc. Time 73:13.

CD - THE CRITICS CHOICE VOL. 1 & 2
WANTED MAN MUSIC WMM 052/053 2-CD
CD1: Watching The River Flow/ Just Like A Woman/ All Along The Watchtower/ Stuck Inside Of Mobile/ Leopard Skin Pill Box Hat/ Political World/ Has Anybody Seen My Love/ What Was It You Wanted/ Don't Think Twice It's Allright/ Gates Of Eden/ Hollis Brown/ It's All Over Now Baby Blue/ Hard Rain/ Song To Woody
CD2: Knockin' On Heaven's Door/ Everything Is Broken/ Tight Connection To My Heart/ Man In A Long Black Coat/ I Shall Be Released/ Like A Rolling Stone/ Dark As A Dungeon/ Highway 61/ You're A Big Girl Now/ What Was It You Wanted/ Love Minus Zero/ One More Cup Of Coffee/ My Back Pages/ Man Of Constant Sorrow/ It Takes A Lot To Laugh/ Lamb Chop And Co.
R: Vg-Ex. Audience.   S: Hammersmith Odeon, London. CD1 Tracks 1-10 Feb. 5 '90. Tracks 11-14 Feb. 6 '90. CD2 Tracks 1-8 Feb. 6 '90. Tracks 9-11 Feb. 3 '90. Tracks 12-15 Feb. 4 '90. Track 16 ?.   C: ECD. Dcc. Time CD1 69:43. CD2 69:27.

CD - THE CRITICS CHOICE VOL. 3
WANTED MAN MUSIC WMM 054 CD
My Back Pages/ Man Of Constant Sorrow/ I Dreamed I Saw St. Augustine/ Barbara Allen/ Gates Of Eden/ License To Kill/ One More Cup Of Coffee/ It's All Over Now Baby Blue/ Mama You Been On My Mind/ Eileen Aroon/ Just Like A Woman/ John Brown
R: Ex. Audience.   S: Various locations in the US in '88.   C: ECD. Dcc. Time 60:35.

CD - THE CRITICS CHOICE VOL. 4
WANTED MAN MUSIC WMM 055 CD
The Lakes Of Pontchartrain/ Nadine/ The Ballad Of Frankie Lee And Judas Priest/ Ballad Of Hollis Brown/ Silvio/ Clean Cut Kid/ Wild Mountain Thyme/ Watching The River Flow/ Two Soldiers/ Tomorrow Is A Long Time/ Give My Love To Rose/ San Francisco Bay Blues/ Just Like Tom Thumb's Blues/ Every Grain Of Sand
R: Ex. Audience.   S: Various locations in the US in '88.   C: ECD. Dcc. Time 60:43 .

CD - THE CRITICS CHOICE VOL. 5 & 6
WANTED MAN MUSIC WMM 056/057 2-CD
CD1: Like A Rolling Stone/ Maggies Farm/ Forever Young/ Seeing The Real You At Last/ Shelter From The Storm/ I Shall Be Released/ When The Night Comes From The Sky/ Emotionally Yours/ Deadman Deadman/ To Romana/ Tomorrow Is A Long Time/ Gotta Serve Somebody/ Chimes Of Freedom*/ Rainy Day Women Nos. 12 & 35**
CD2: I Want You/ Lenny Bruce/ Ballad Of Frankie Lee And Judas Priest/ Ballad Of A Thin Man/ I'll Remember You/ Senor/ Watching The River Flow/ John Brown/ The Lonesome Death Of Hattie Carroll/ I Dreamed I Saw St. Augustine/ Simple Twist Of Fate/ I'll Be Your Baby Tonight/ Man Of Peace/ Heart Of Mine/ Go Down Moses
R: Ex. Audience.   S: Wembley Arena, London.

CD1 Oct. 16 '87. CD2 Tracks 1-3 Oct.14 '87
Tracks 4-9 Oct. 15 '87. Tracks 10-15 Oct. 17 '87.
C: ECD. Dcc. *Roger McGuinn vocals and guitar.
**Roger McGuinn and Ron Wood guitars. Time
CD1 67:03. CD2 73:09.

CD - DARED TO BE FREE
ROCK CALENDAR
Stuck Inside Of Mobile/ You're A Big Girl Now/
Rita May/ Lay Lady Lay/ Idiot Wind/ Knockin' On
Heaven's Door/ Gotta Travel On/ Mr. Tambourine
Man/ Love Minus Zero/ No Limit/ Vincent Van
Gogh/ Maggie's Farm/ Mozambique/ Isis
R: G-Vg. Soundboard.   S: The Warehouse, New
Orleans May 3 '76.   C: ECD. Songs not in order
performed. Should be tracks 8-13 followed by 1-7.
Time 71:16.

CD - THE DEEDS OF MERCY
RAZOR'S EDGE RAZ 002
Shooting Star/ God Knows/ God Knows/ What
Good Am I?/ Most Of The Time/ Everything Is
Broken/ Political World/ Born In Time/ Dignity/
Shooting Star/ Disease Of Conceit/ Ring Them
Bells/ Most Of The Time/ What Was It You
Wanted/ Series Of Dreams/ Series Of Dreams/
Series Of Dreams
R: Ex.   S: Studio sessions Mar-Apr. '89.
C: ECD. Dcc. Time 76:10.

CD - DISCOVER BROKEN
OFF BEAT RECORDS XXCD 18
Maggies Farm/ Mozambeque/ Isis/ Shelter From
The Storm/ Romance In Durango/ You're Gonna
Make Me Lonesome When You Go/ Oh Sister/
Lay Lady Lay/ Going Going Gone/ You're A Big
Girl Now/ Idiot Wind/ Knockin' On Heaven's Door
R: Vg. Soundboard.   S: San Antonio 5/11/76.
C: Japanese CD. Dcc.

CD - THE DYLAN/CASH SESSIONS
SPANK RECORDS SP 106
One Too Many Mornings/ Mountain Dew/ I Still
Miss Someone/ Careless Love/ Matchbox/ That's
Allright Mama/ Big River/ Girl From The North
Country/ I Walk The Line/ You Are My Sunshine/
Ring Of Fire/ Guess Things Happen That Way/
Just A Closer Walk With Thee/ Blue Yodel/ Blue
Yodel No. 5/ I Threw It All Away/ Living The Blues/
Girl From The North Country/ Nashville Skyline
Rag/ I Threw It All Away/ Peggy Day/ Country Pie/
Tonight I'll Be Staying Here With You
R: Ex. Soundboard.   S: Tracks 1-15 studio
outtakes Columbia Studios, Nashville Feb. 17-18
'69. Tracks 16-18 'Johnny Cash Show' Ryman
Auditorium, Nashville May 1 '69. Tracks 19-23
'Nashville Skyline' quad mixes Columbia Studios,
Nashville Feb. 13-14 '69.   C: Japanese CD. Dcc.
Time 67:47

CD - FAREWELL BLOOMFIELD
CUTTLEFISH RECORDS CFR 004/05
CD1: Gotta Serve Somebody/ I Believe In You/
Like A Rolling Stone/ Man Gave Names To All The

Animals/ Simple Twist Of Fate/ Ain't Gonna Go To
Hell/ Girl From The North Country/ Slow Train/
Abraham Martin And John/ Let's Keep It Between
Us
CD2: Mary From The Wild Moor/ Covenant
Woman/ Solid Rock/ Just Like A Woman/ The
Groom's Still Waiting At The Altar/ When You
Gonna Wake Up/ In The Garden/ Blowin' In The
Wind/ City Of Gold
R: Ex. Soundboard.   S: Fox Warfield, USA Nov.
15 '80.   R: ECD. Dcc. Mike Bloomfield plays
guitar on CD1 track 3 and CD2 track 5.

CD - FIRST SUPPER
WANTED MAN MUSIC WMM 47/48
CD1: Absolutely Sweet Marie/ Lay Lady Lay/
Blood In My Eyes/ Queen Jane Approximately/
Tight Connection To My Heart/ Disease Of
Conceit/ I Want You/ Ring Them Bells/ My Back
Pages/ Forever Young
CD2: Ragged & Dirty/ Lay Lady Lay/ I'll Be Your
Baby Tonight/ Queen Jane Approximately/ Jack-A-
Roe/ One Too Many Mornings/ I Want You/ Ring
Them Bells/ My Back Pages/ Forever Young
R: Ex. Audience.   S: The Supper Club, New
York Nov. 16 '93.   C: ECD. Dcc

CD - FOOD FOR YOUR EARS
Song To Woody/ It's Allright Ma/ Positively 4th St./
Just Like A Woman/ Baby Blue/ Watchtower/ I'll
Be Your Baby Tonight/ Trail Of The Buffalo/ Mr.
Tambourine Man/ Rainy Day Women/ Simple
Twist Of Fate/ I'll Remember You/ Golden Vanity
R: Vg-Ex.   S: USA '91-'92.   C: Time 78:16.

CD - FREEWHEELIN' OUTTAKES
VIGOTONE VIGO 115
Baby Please Don't Go/ Corrina Corrina/ The Death
Of Emmett Till/ Mixed Up Confusion/ Lonesome
Whistle Blues/ Talkin John Birch Paranoid Blues/
Milkcow's Calf Blues/ That's Allright Mamma/
Rocks And Gravel/ Going To New Orleans/ Let Me
Die In My Footsteps/ The Ballad Of Hollis Brown/
Wichita/ Sally Gal/ What Ya Gonna Do/ Mixed Up
Confusion/ Corrina Corrina/ Milkcow's Calf Blues/
Wichita/ What Ya Gonna Do/ Baby I'm In The
Mood For You/ Sally Gal
R: Vg-Ex.   S: Columbia Studios Apr. - Nov. 62.
Time 72:41.

CD - FROM BROADWAY TO THE MILKWAY
LEA LIVE RL CD 17
If Not For You/ Union Sundown/ Just Like A
Woman/ Drifter's Escape/ Tangled Up In Blue/
Love Minus Zero, No Limit/ Little Moses/ Visions
Of Johana/ Don't Think Twice/ Idiot Wind/
Absolutely Sweet Marie/ The Lonesome Death
R: G. Audience.   S: Tracks 1-11 Greek Theatre,
Berkeley May 8 '92. Track 12 San Francisco May
4 '92.

CD - FROM THE COAST OF BARCELONA
BLACK COAT RECORDS BC-01/02 2-CD
CD1: Hard Times/ Stuck Inside Of Mobile With

The Memphis Blues Again/ All Along The Watchtower/ Just Like A Woman/ Tangled Up In Blue/ The Man In Me/ Watching The River Flow/ Little Moses/ Tomorrow Night/ It's All Over Now Baby Blue
CD2: Mr. Tambourine Man/ Cat's In The Well/ I And I/ Maggie's Farm/ Man In The Long Black Coat/ It Ain't Me Baby/ Boots Of Spanish Leather*/ Born In Time*
R: G-Vg. Audience.   S: Poble Espanyol de Montjuic, Barcelona, Spain July 2 '93. *Pabellon Araba, Vitoria, Spain July 2 '93.   C: ECD. Dcc. Time CD1 76:09. CD2 77:33.

CD - FROM THE COAST OF BARCELONA
RAZORS EDGE RAZ-009/10
CD1: Highway 61 Revisited/ Jokerman/ All Along The Watchtower/ Just Like A Woman/ Maggie's Farm/ I And I/ License To Kill/ A Hard Rain's Gonna Fall/ It Ain't Me Babe/ It's Allright Ma/ Simple Twist Of Fate/ Masters Of War/ Ballad Of A Thin Man
CD2: Enough Is Enough/ Every Grain Of Sand/ Lay Lady Lay/ Like A Rolling Stone/ Mr. Tambourine Man/ Don't Think Twice/ Girl From The North Country/ Knockin' On Heaven's Door/ Senor/ The Times They Are A'Changin'/ Tombstone Blues/ Blowin' In The Wind/ It's All Over Now Baby Blue/ Tupelo Honey/ Leopard Skin Pill-Box Hat
R: G-Vg. Audience. Tracks 13-15 Vg. Soundboard.   S: Miniestadio, Barcelona, Spain June 28 '84. CD2 tracks 13-15 Slane Castle, Slane, Ireland July 8 '84.   C: ECD. Time CD1 71:40. CD2 72:51.

CD - THE GENUINE BOOTLEG SERIES
SCORPIO 94-14-01,02,03
CD1: Black Cross, I Was Young When I Left Home (Bonnie Beecher's apartment, Minneapolis Dec. 22 '61)/ Ballad For A Friend (Leeds Music publisher's demo, New York Jan. '62)/ Hero Blues, Whatcha Gonna Do? (recorded for 'The Freewheelin' Bob Dylan' Columbia Studios, New York Dec. 6 '62)/ Tomorrow Is A Long Time (Witmark Music publisher's demo, New York probably Dec. '62)/ Milk Cow Blues (recorded for 'The Freewheelin' Bob Dylan' Columbia Studios, New York Apr. 24 '62)/ Rocks And Gravel (stereo cut - Columbia Studios, New York Nov. 13 '62)/ You've Been Hiding Too Long (New York Town Hall Apr. 12 '63)/ Farewell (Witmark Music publisher's demo, New York probably Dec. '63)/ Baby Let Me Follow You Down (Witmark Music publisher's demo, New York probably Jan. '64)/ That's All Right Mama, Sally Free And Easy, New Orleans Rag (recorded for 'Another Side Of Bob Dylan', Columbia Studios, New York June 9 '64)/ You Don't Have To Do That (recorded for 'Bringing It All Back Home', Columbia Studios, New York Jan. 13 '65)/ Can You Please Crawl Out Your Window? (this take was issued accidentally in place of 'Positively Fourth Street' on early copies of that 45. Recorded for 'Highway 61 Revisited',

Columbia Studios, New York June 16 '65)/ Desolation Row (Columbia Studios, New York July 30 '65 - this 'Electric' version was superceded by the original take)/ (Seems Like A) Freeze Out (Sunset Sound Studios, LA Nov. 30-Dec.1 '65)/ She's Your Lover Now (Columbia Studios, New York Jan. 21 '66)
CD2: The Painting By Van Gogh (Denver Hotel Room Mar. 12 '66)/ What Kind Of Friend Is This? (Glasgow Hotel Room May 18-19 '66)/ One Too Many Mornings (The Gaumont Theatre, Sheffield May 16 '66)/ Sign Of The Cross, All American Boy, Nothing Was Delivered (the basement of 'Big Pink', West Saugerties, New York summer '67)/ I Threw It All Away, Honey, Just Allow Me One More Chance (recorded for 'Self Portrait', Columbia Studios, Nashville June '69)/ Working On A Guru (recorded with George Harrison for 'New Morning' in Columbia Studios, New York May 1 '70)/ Down In The Flood (recorded at The New York Academy Of Music, for The Band's 'Rock Of Ages' album Jan. 1 '72)/ Goodbye Holly (recorded for the soundtrack to 'Pat Garrett And Billy The Kid', Columbia Disco Studios, Mexico City Jan. 20 '73)/ Rock Me Mama (recorded for the soundtrack to 'Pat Garrett And Billy The Kid', Burbank Studios, Burbank Feb. '73) Nobody 'Cept You (Recorder Studios, Santa Monica Nov. 2 '73)/ Idiot Wind (included on the original 'Blood On The Tracks' test pressing. Columbia A&R Studios, New York Dec. 17 '74)/ Hurricane (Columbia Studios, New York July 30 '75)/ Stop Now ('Street Legal' sessions, Rundown Studios, Santa Monica May 2 '78)/ (You Treat Me Like A) Stepchild (Civic Center, Augusta, Maine Sept. 15 '78)
CD3: Trouble In Mind (Muscle Shoals Studios, Alabama May 1-11 '79)/ Yonder Comes Sin, Caribbean Wind (Rundown Studios, Santa Monica Oct. '80)/ Don't Ever Take Yourself Away (Clovers Recorder Studio, Los Angeles Apr.-May '81)/ Thief On The Cross (Saenger Performing Arts Center, New Orleans Nov. 10 '81)/ Sweetheart Like You (Power Station Studios, New York mid Apr. '83)/ Someones Got A Hold Of My Heart, Tell Me (Power Station Studios, New York Apr.-May '83)/ Jokerman, Blind Willie McTell (scheduled for inclusion on original version of 'Infidels'. Power Station Studios, New York Apr.-May '83)/ New Danville Girl (Cherokee Studios, LA Dec. '84) Important Words (Sunset Sound Studios, LA Apr.-May '87) Dignity (New Orleans Mar.-Apr. '89)/ Like A Ship (recorded for 'Traveling Wilburys Volume Three', LA Apr. '90)/ Series Of Dreams (New Orleans Mar.-Apr. '89)
R: Ex.   C: ECD. Elaborate full-color fold-out cardboard sleeve. Excellent full-color book. Time CD1 73:50. CD2 74:28. CD3 76:43.

CD - HARD TIMES IN ALABAMA
REAL LIVE
CD1: Hard Times/ Stuck Inside Of Mobile/ All Along The Watchtower/ You're A Big Girl Now/ Tangled Up In Blue/ Born In Time/ Watching The River Flow/ Jim Jones/ Tomorrow Night/ Gates Of

Eden
CD2: Don't Think Twice/ Cats In The Well/ I And I/ Shelter From The Storm/ Everything Is Broken/ What Good Am I?/ Maggie's Farm/ It Ain't Me Babe/ Black Jack Davey, God Knows, Series Of Dreams (Wolftrap, VA Sept. 8 '93)/ Poncho And Lefty, Hard Times (Austin, Tx May 5 '93)
R: Vg-Ex. Audience. S: Huntsville, Alabama Apr. 19 '93. C: ECD. Time CD1 74:51. CD2 74:19.

CD - HIMSELF
TUFF BITES
CD1: I Can't Be Satisfied/ If Not For You/ All Along The Watchtower/ The Miners Song/ It Takes A Lot To Laugh/ I And I/ Silvio/ Mama You've Been On My Mind/ Boots Of Spanish Leather
CD2: Mr. Tambourine Man/ Gates Of Eden/ Unbelievable/ I've Been All Around This World/ The Times They Are A Changin'/ Maggie's Farm/ Shooting Star/ Rainy Day Women/ It Ain't Me Babe
R: Vg-Ex. Audience. S: Youngstown, Ohio Nov. 2 '92. C: ECD. Dcc. Fold-out digi-pack. Time CD1 53:57. CD2 57:01.

CD - HOLD THE FORT (LOCK UP THE WAREHOUSE)
WANTED MAN MUSIC WMM 40/41
CD1: Mr. Tambourine Man/ It Ain't Me Babe/ Vincent Van Gogh/ Maggie's Farm/ One Too Many Mornings/ Mozambique/ Isis/ Blowin' In The Wind/ Railroad Boy/ Deportees/ I Pity The Poor Immigrant/ Shelter From The Storm/ I Threw It All Away
CD2: Stuck Inside of Mobile/ You're A Big Girl Now/ Rita Mae/ Lay Lady Lay/ You're Gonna Make Me Lonesome/ I Want You/ Going Going Home/ Idiot Wind/ Knockin On Heaven's Door/ Gotta Travel On
R: Ex. S: Fort Worth May 16 '76. Warehouse, New Orleans May 3 '71. Oklahoma State Fair May 18 '76. C: ECD. Dcc.

CD - IF MY THOUGHTDREAMS COULD BE SEEN
ROCKS 92135
A Hard Rain's Gonna Fall (8:32), I Shall Be Released (3:59), Ring Them Bells (3:27) (Live '94)/ Forever Young (5:16) (David Letterman Show Nov. 18 '93)/ Poncho And Lefty (4:55), Hard Times (4:29) (Willie Nelson Tribute May 25 '93)/ Heartland (2:33) (with Willie Nelson Jan. 93)/ Chimes Of Freedom (3:22) (Bill Clinton Inaugural Jan. 18)/ Boots Of Spanish Leather, Across The Borderline (8:28), Answer Me (3:29) (Sevilla Oct. 17 '93)/ Soon (3:47) (Gershwin Celebration, NY Mar. 11 '87)/ License To Kill (2:44) (Amnesty International TV show, LA June. 6 '86)/ Don't Start Me Talking (3:03), License To Kill (5:07), Jokerman (5:27) (NYC Mar. 22 '84)/ Blowin' In The Wind (5:31) (Barcelona June. 28 '84)
R: Vg-Ex. C: ECD. Dcc.

CD - IF NOT FOR YOU
RED PHANTOM RPCD 2119/20
Just Like A Woman/ Mozambique/ One Too Many Mornings/ Isis-Harmonica/ Isis/ Positively/ Oh Sister/ One More Cup Of Coffee/ Sara/ Just Like A Woman/ Hurricane/ Lay Lady Lay/ Oh Sister/ You Ain't Goin' Nowhere
R: G-Vg. S: S.I.R. Rehearsal Studio, LA Jan. 23 '76. C: ECD.

CD - ISLE OF WIGHT
WANTED MAN MUSIC WMM 39
She Belongs To Me/ I Threw It All Away/ Maggie's Farm/ Wild Mountain Thyme/ It Ain't Me Babe/ To Ramona/ Mr. Tambourine Man/ I Dreamed I Saw St. Augustine/ Lay Lady Lay/ Highway 61/ One Too Many Mornings/ I Pity The Poor Immigrant/ Like A Rolling Stone/ I'll Be Your Baby Tonight/ Quinn The Eskimo/ Minstrel Boy/ Rainy Day Woman
R: Vg-Ex. S: Aug. 31 '69. C: ECD. Dbw. Purple text. Time 55:13.

CD - JAPAN 1994
CD1: Jokerman/ Shelter From The Storm/ Watchtower/ Just Like A Woman/ Tangled Up In Blue/ I'll Be Your Baby Tonight/ Tomorrow Night/ Mr. Tambourine/ Baby Blue/ Everything Is Broken*
CD2: God Knows/ I And I/ Maggies' Farm/ Man In The Long Black Coat/ It Ain't Me Babe/ Lay Lady Lay*/ Born In Time*/ Under The Red Sky*/ Times They Are A Changin'*
R: G. S: Fukuoka, Japan Feb. 14 '94. *Urawa, Japan Feb. 18 '94. C: Japanese CD. Double jewel case in a white cardboard sleeve. Time CD1 72:09. CD2 69:23.

CD - JOHN BIRCH SOCIETY BLUES
EXIT RECORDS
Talkin' John Birch Society Blues/ Corrina Corrina/ East Laredo/ In The Evening/ I'll Keep It With Mine/ Ramblin' Gamblin' Willie/ Mixed Up Confusion/ Who Killed Davey Moore/ Long John/ Percy's Song
R: G. Some surface noise. S: Minnesota Hotel Dec. 22 '61. Studio sessions Apr.-Dec. '62. Carnegie Hall Oct. 26 '63. Studio sessions Aug.- Oct. '63. Studio sessions June 9 '64. Studio sessions Jan. 65. C: ECD. Time 39:11.

CD - JOKERMAN
BOO! BOO 004
Jokerman (7:29)/ The Man In Me (5:21)/ All Along The Watchtower (5:25)/ I Don't Believe You (7:08)/ Tangled Up In Blue (8:44)/ I'll Be Your Baby Tonight (7:21)/ Love Minus Zero, No Limit (5:27)/ Masters Of War (5:52)/ Boots Of Spanish Leather (6:45)/ God Knows (5:36)/ I Believe In You (6:51)/ Maggie's Farm (7:06)
R: Ex. Audience. S: '94 World Tour, Eastern Europe summer '94. C: ECD. Dcc.

CD - JOKERMAN AND QUEEN MARY
ZIM'S FIRST EAT

CD1: Jokerman/ If You See Her, Say Hello/ All Along The Watchtower/ Simple Twist Of Fate/ Tangled Up In Blue/ Under The Red Sky/ Tomorrow Night/ It's All Over Now Baby Blue/ Mr. Tambourine Man/ Don't Think Twice It's Allright
CD2: God Knows/ In The Garden/ Maggie's Farm/ Ballad Of A Thin Man/ It Ain't Me, Babe
R: G-Vg. Audience.   S: Sendai, Japan '94.
C: Japanese CD. Dcc. Pic CD. Time CD1 74:12. CD2 40:16.

CD - LIKE A ROLLING STONE, THE HIDDEN TV-SHOWS
ANGRY DINO AD 1014
A Hard Rain's Gonna Fall (8:00)/ Blowin' In the Wind (3:48)*/ Railroad Boy (2:52)*/ Deportees (4:00)*/ I Pity The Poor Immigrant (4:23)*/ Mozambique (3:53)/ Mister Tambourine Man (4:12)/ The Times They Are A Changin' (4:30)/ I Dreamed I Saw St. Augustine (3:00)*/ Diamonds & Rust (5:04)*/ When I Paint My Masterpiece (5:28)**/ Like A Rolling Stone (7:10)/ Isis (5:43)/ Just Like A Woman (5:42)/ Knockin' On Heaven's Door (4:30)***/ Lay Lady Lay (4:50)
R: Vg. Soundboard.   S: Track 1-6 Hughes Stadium, Colorado State University, Fort Collins May 23 '76. Track 7-16 Bellevue Biltmore Hotel, Clearwater Apr. 22 '76.   C: ECD. Dcc. *With Joan Baez. **With Bobby Neuwirth. ***With Roger McGuinn.

CD - LIVE & ALIVE '92
IMTRAT
Pretty Peggy O/ Simple Twist Of Fate/It Takes A Lot To Laugh/ Silvio/ Little Moses/ Boots Of Spanish Leather/ Gates Of Eden/ Unbelievable/ Queen Jane Approximately/ Man In A Long Black Coat/ Maggie's Farm/ What Good Am I?/ Rainy Day Women/ It Ain't Me Babe
R: G.   S: Broome County, Binghampton Oct. 19 '92.   C: ECD. Time 60:01.

CD - LIVE AT THE PITSTOP 78 - GAZA STRIP
WANTED MAN MUSIC WMM 43/44
CD1: My Back Pages/ She's Love Crazy/ Mr. Tambourine Man/ Shelter From The Storm/ It's All Over Now Baby Blue/ Tangled Up In Blue/ Ballad Of A Thin Man/ Maggies Farm/ I Don't Believe You/ Like A Rolling Stone/ I Shall Be Released/ Senor
CD2: Rainy Day Women/ It Ain't Me Babe/ One More Cup Of Coffee/ Blowin' In The Wind/ Girl From The North Country/ Where Are You Tonight/ Masters Of War/ Just Like A Woman/ To Ramona/ All Along The Watchtower/ All I Want To Do/ Band Intro's/ It's Allright Ma/ Forever Young/ Changin' Of The Guards
R: Vg. Audience.   S: Seattle Nov. 10 '78.
C: ECD. Dcc.

CD - THE LIVE DYLAN
BLACK PANTHER
Visions Of Johanna/ Fourth Time Around/ It's All Over Now Baby Blue/ Desolation Row/ Just Like A

Woman/ Mr. Tambourine Man
R: G.   S: Dublin, Ireland May 5 '66.   C: ECD. Time 41:36.

CD - LIVE IN ILLINOIS 4/11/91
REAL LIVE RL CD 10
Man In The Long Black Coat (5:46)/ Watching The River Flow (4:55)/ Simple Twist Of Fate (7:47)/ I'll Be Your Baby Tonight (4:13)/ All Along The Watchtower (4:33)/ Gotta Serve Somebody (6:54)/ Golden Vanity (5:51)/ I'll Remember You (4:42)/ Ballad Of A Thin Man (8:01)/ What Good Am I (8:35)/ Highway 61 Revisited (5:58)
S: Illinois, Envanston Nov. 4 '91.   C: Japanese CD.

CD - THE LONESOME SPARROW SINGS
BLACK NITE CRASH 003
You Don't Have To Do That, It's All Over Now Baby Blue, If You Gotta Go, She Belong To Me, Love Minus Zero ('Back Home' outtakes Jan. 13-15 '65)/ Convention Message, If You Gotta Go (Miami Convention May 12 '65)/ Sitting On A Barbed Wire Fence, Crawl Out Your Window (2), From A Buick 6, Desolation Row, Can You Please Crawl Out Your Window, I Wanna Be Your Lover, Jet Pilot Eyes ('Highway' outtakes June 16 - July 30 '65)/ Visions Of Johanna, Medicine Sunday, Visions Of Johanna, She's Your Lover Now ('Blonde' outtakes Nov. '65 - Jan. '66)
R: Ex.   C: ECD. Time 74:52.

CD - LONESOME TOWN VOL. 2
FLAMINGO
Ballad Of A Thin Man/ Refugee/ Rainy Day Women/ Seeing The Real You At Last/ Across The Borderline/ I And I/ Like A Rolling Stone/ In The Garden/ Blowin' In The Wind/ Uranium Rock/ Knockin' On Heaven's Door
R: Vg-Ex. Audience.   S: Chicago June 29 '86.
C: ECD. Time 55:40.

CD - LUCKY 13
GOLD STANDARD
Jim Jones/ Tomorrow Night/ Hard Times/ You're Gonna Quit Me/ Blackjack Davey/ Poncho And Lefty/ I And I/ License To Kill/ Born In Time/ God Knows/ Emotionally Yours/ Series Of Dreams/ Under The Red Sky*
R: Ex. Audience. *Vg. Audience.   S: Tracks 1-2 New Orleans, Louisiana Apr. 23 '93. Tracks 3, 6 Willie Nelson Tribute Birthday Bash May '93. Track 4 Shoreline Amphitheatre, Mountain View, CA Oct. 9 '93. Tracks 5, 7, 13 London, England Feb. 7 '93. Track 8 Louisville, Kentucky Apr. 12 '93. Tracks 9, 12 Wolf Trap, Vienna, Virginia Sept. 8 '93. Track 10 Wolf Trap, Vienna, Virginia Sept. 9 '93. Track 11 Seattle, Washington Aug. 21 '93.
C: ECD. Dcc. Time 75:34.

CD - MASTERS OF WAR
CD1: Jokerman/ Shelter From The Storm/ All Along The Watchtower/ She Belongs To Me/ Tangled Up In Blue/ Watching The River Flow/

Tomorrow Night
CD2: Masters Of War/ Don't Think Twice/ Series
Of Dreams/ I And I/ Maggie's Farm/ Man In A
Long Black Coat/ It Ain't Me Babe
R: Vg.   S: Hiroshima, Japan Feb. 16 '94.
C: ECD. Time CD1 54:07. CD2 45:52.

CD - MASTER OF WOODSTOCK
V-15372-14
Jokerman/ Just Like A Woman/ All Along The
Watchtower/ It Takes A Lot To Laugh It Takes A
Train To Cry/ Don't Think Twice Its Allright/
Masters Of War (Slow Version)/ Its All Over Now
Baby Blue/ God Knows/ I Shall Be Released/
Highway 61/ Rainy Day Women Nos. 12 & 35/ It
Ain't Me Babe
R: Exs. Soundboard.   S: Woodstock Festival,
Saugerties, New York Aug. 14 '94.   C: ECD.
Dcc. Time 78:17.

CD - MEN OF PEACE
ART OF MUSIC AOM 40505
Tangled Up In Blue/ I'll Be Your Baby Tonight/
Man Of Peace/ The Ballad Of Frankie Lee And
Judas Priest/ John Brown/ Simple Twist Of Fate/
Ballad Of A Thin Man/ Stuck Inside Of Mobile With
The Memphis Blues Again/ Chimes Of Freedom/
Gotta Serve Somebody/ Joey/ All Along The
Watchtower/ Knockin' On Heaven's Door*/ Touch
Of Grey**
R: Ex. Soundboard.   S: JFK Stadium July 10 '87.
*Los Angeles '89. **Eugene, Oregon '87.
C: ECD. Dcc. With The Grateful Dead.
Time 77:39.

CD - MERAN' 92
7700-1/7700-2
CD1: 2x2/ Pretty Peggy - O/ Maggie's Farm/ Every
Grain Of Sand/ Seeing The Real You At Last/ I
Dreamed I Saw St. Augustine/ I'll Be Your Baby
Tonight/ To Ramona/ Girl Of The North Country/
Mr. Tambourine Man
CD2: Don't Think Twice, It's Allright/ Everything Is
Broken/ Shelter From The Storm/ The Times They
Are A-Changing/ Like A Rolling Stone/ What Good
Am I?/ Along The Watchtower/ Blowing In The
Wind
R: Ex.   S: Meran July 7 '92.   C: ECD. Dcc.
Time CD1 54:20. CD2 47:54.

CD - THE MINNESOTA TAPES
WANTED MAN MUSIC WMM 33/34/35
CD1: As I Go Ramblin' Round/ Death Don't Have
No Mercy/ It's Hard To Be Blind/ This Train Is
Bound For Glory/ Harmonica Solo/ Talking Fish
Blues/ Pastures For Plenty/ Railroad Bill/ Will The
Circle Be Unbroken/ Man Of Constant Sorrow/
Pretty Polly/ Railroad Boy/ James Alley Blues/
Why'd You Cut My Hair/ This Land Is Your Land/
Two Trains Running/ Wild Mountain Thyme
CD2: How Did O/ Car Car/ Don't You Push Me
Down/ Come See/ I Want It Now/ San Francisco
Bay Blues/ A Long Time Growing/ Devilish Mary/
Candy Man/ Baby Please Don't Go/ Hard Times In

New York Town/ Stealin'/ Poor Lazarus/ I Ain't Got
No Home/ It's Hard To Be Blind/ Dink's Song/ Man
Of Constant Sorrow/ The Story Of East Orange
N.J.
CD3: Naomi Wise/ Wade In The Water/ I Was
Young When I Left Home/ In The Evening/ Baby
Let Me Follow You Down/ Sally Girl/ Gospel
Plough/ Long John/ Cocaine/ VD Blues/ VD Waltz/
VD City/ VD Gunners Blues/ See That My Grave
Is Kept Clean/ Ramblin' Round/ Black Cross
R: Vg. Some hum.   S: CD1 May '61. CD2 Dec.
'61. CD3 Tracks 1-8 May '61. Tracks 9-18 Dec.
'61.   C: ECD. Dbw. Green type. Time CD1
60:22. CD2 51:08. CD3 50:10.

CD - MR. TAMBOURINE MAN (VOL. 1)
BANANA
The Times They Are A Changin'/ Spanish Harlem
Incident/ Talkin John Birch Society Paranoid
Blues/ To Ramona/ Gates Of Eden/ If You Gotta
Go Go Now/ It's Allright Ma/ I Don't Believe You/
Who Killed Davey Moore
R: Ex.   S: Philharmonic Hall, NYC Oct. 31 '64.
C: Australian CD. Dcc. Time 50:25.

CD - MR. TAMBOURINE MAN (VOL. 2)
BANANA
Mr. Tambourine Man/ A Hard Rain's Gonna Fall/
Talkin' World War 3 Blues/ Don't Think Twice/ The
Lonesome Death Of Hattie Carroll/ Mama You
Been On Mind/ With God On Our Side/ It Ain't Me
Babe/ All I Really Wanna Do
R: Ex.   S: Philharmonic Hall, NYC Oct. 31 '64.
C: Australian CD. Dcc. Time 50:29.

CD - MR. TAMBOURINE MAN (VOL. 3)
BANANA BAN-012-C
Tell Me, Momma (4:36)/ I Don't Believe You (She
Acts Like We Never Met) (6:03)/ Baby Let Me
Follow You Down (3:34)/ Just Like Tom Thumb's
Blues (6:45)/ Leopard Skin Pill Box Hat (4:57)/
One Too Many Mornings (3:44)/ Ballad Of A Thin
Man (7:44)/ Like A Rolling Stone (7:11)
R: Vg.   S: Manchester, England May 17 '66.
C: Australian CD. Time 44:43.

CD - MR. TAMBOURINE MAN (VOL. 4)
BANANA BAN-012-D
I Don't Believe You (She Acts Like We Never
Have Met) (3:58)/ Just Like Tom Thumb's Blues
(5:15)/ Ballad Of A Thin Man (5:01)/ Subterranean
Homesick Blues (3:36)/ Had A Dream About You
Baby (2:58)/ Simple Twist Of Fate (6:58)/ Highway
61 Revisited (4:40)/ Don't Think Twice (It's All
Right) (4:39)/ Knockin' On Heaven's Door (5:03)/
Silvio (3:56)/ I Shall Be Released (4:37)/ Like A
Rolling Stone (6:21)/ It Ain't Me Babe (5:45)/
Masters Of War (4:51)/ Maggie's Farm (3:31)
R: Poor.   S: Bristol, Conn. Aug. 4 '88.
C: Australian CD. Time 70:26.

CD - NASHVILLE 1969
YELLOW DOG YD 049
One Too Many Mornings #1 (3:25)/ One Too Many

Mornings #2 (4:06)/ Good Old Mountain Dew
(1:54)/ I Still Miss Someone (2:34)/ Careless Love
(7:15)/ Matchbox (3:13)/ That's Allright Mama
(2:50)/ Big River (2:04)/ Girl Of The North Country
(3:51)/ I Walk The Line (2:48)/ You Are My
Sunshine (3:28)/ Ring Of Fire (2:33)/ Guess
Things Happen That Way (1:51)/ Just A Closer
Walk With Thee (2:55)/ Blues Yodel #1 (3:11)/
Blues Yodel #5 (2:47)/ I Threw It All Away (2:25)/
Livin' The Blues (2:38)/ Girl Of The North Country
(3:25)
R: Ex.   S: Nashville '69.   C: ECD. Dcc. With
Johnny Cash.

CD - THE NEVER ENDING TOUR (FEATURING LIZ SIOUSSI)
TAKE IT OR LEAVE IT T 9417/18
CD1: Keep Movin' On (4:24)/ The Man In Me
(3:08)/ All Along The Watchtower (6:04)/ Tangled
Up In Blue (8:47)/ Watching The River Flow (4:52)/
Stuck In Mobile With The Memphis Blues Again
(6:42)/ Silvio (5:02)/ Tomorrow Night (5:07)/ Jim
Jones (6:17)/ Gates Of Eden (6:02)/ It's All Over
Now Baby Blue (5:57)
CD2: Cats In The Well (5:47)/ I And I (8:32)/ The
Times They Are A Changin' (5:23)/ Highway 61
Revisited (7:11)/ Ballad Of A Thin Man (9:18)/
Everything Is Broken (8:07)/ It Ain't Me Babe
(11:08)
R: Vg. Audience.   S: Musiccentre Frits Philips,
Eindhoven Feb. 17 '93.   C: ECD. Dcc. With Liz
Sioussi.

CD - NEW FOUND FAITH
WANTED MAN MUSIC WWM 058/59
CD1: Gotta Serve Somebody/ I Believe In You/
When You Gonna Wake Up?/ When He Returns/
Man Gave Names To All The Animals/ Precious
Angel/ Slow Train/ Covenant Woman
CD2: Gonna Change My Way Of Thinking/ Do
Right To Me Baby/ Solid Rock/ Saving Grace/
What Can I Do For You/ Saved/ In The Garden/
Blessed Be Thy Name/ Pressing On
R: Vg. Audience.   S: Fox Warfield Theatre, San
Francisco Nov. 1 '79.   C: ECD. Dcc. Time CD1
47:35. CD2 46:56.

CD - NEW YORK '74
RED SKY RECORDS CD 1001
Most Likely You Go Your Way And I'll Go Mine
(3:59)/ Lay Lady Lay (3:02)/ Just Like Tom
Thumb's Blues (5:43)/ Rainy Day Woman Nos. 12
& 35 (3:30)/ It Ain't Me Babe (3:21)/ Ballad Of A
Thin Man (4:05)/ All Along The Watchtower (2:15)/
Ballad Of Hollis Brown (4:14)/ Knockin' On
Heaven's Door (4:01)/ The Times They Are A-
Changin' (2:57)/ Don't Think Twice It's All Right
(3:52)/ Gates Of Eden (5:16)/ Just Like A Woman
(4:43)/ It's Allright Ma I'm Only Bleeding (5:26)
S: Madison Square Gardens, NYC Jan. 31 '74.

CD - NO PHOTOGRAPHS PLEASE
WANTED MAN MUSIC WMM 051 CD
Subterranean Homesick Blues/ Lonesome Town/

Highway 61 Revisited/ You're A Big Girl Now/
John Brown/ All Along The Watchtower/ Barbara
Allen/ Girl Of The North Country/ Mr. Tambourine
Man/ Silvio/ I Shall Be Released/ Like A Rolling
Stone/ Blowin' In The Wind/ One Too Many
Mornings/ Knockin' On Heaven's Door/
Congratulations/ Maggies Farm
R: G-Vg. Audience.   S: Birmingham NEC, UK
June 7 '89.   C: ECD. Dcc. Time 77:49.

CD - ODDS & ENDS (UNSURPASSED MAESTRO VOL. 1)
SICK CAT 006
What You Gonna Do/ Sally Gal/ Ramblin' Down
Thru' The World/ You Bin Hidin' Too Long/ Suzy
(instrumental)/ You Don't Have To Do That/ Jet
Pilot/ Working On A Guru/ Let Me See/ Lilly
Rosemary/ Nuggets Of Rain/ Hurricane/ Am I Not
Yours/ Seven Days/ Yonder Comes Sin/ Mystery
Train/ Watered Down/ Honey Wait/ That's Allright
Mama
R: G.   S: Various sources '60-'70.   C: Track 8
with George Harrison '70. Track 11 with Bette
Middler.   C: Japanese CD.

CD - OH MERCY OUTTAKES
WANTED MAN MUSIC
Shooting Star/ Go Knows (1)/ God Knows (2)/
What Good Am I/ Most Of The Time (1)/
Everything Is Broken/ Political World/ Born In
Time/ Dignity/ Shooting Star/ Disease Of Conceit/
Ring Them Bells Part (1)/ Ring Them Bells Part
(2)/ Most Of The Time (2)/ Series Of Dreams (1)/
What Was It You Wanted/ Series Of Dreams (2)
R: Vg. Soundboard.   C: ECD. Dcc. Time 70:42 .

CD - OUTSIDE THE EMPIRE
WANTED MAN MUSIC WMM 060 1-CD
Danville Girl/ Tight Connection/ Clean Cut Kid/ I'll
Remember You/ Seeing The Real You At Last/
Something's Burning/ Trust Yourself/ Emotionally
Yours/ When The Night Comes Fallin'.../ Never
Gonna Be The Same Again/ Waiting To Get Beat/
Straight As In Love/ The Very Thought Of You/
Drifting Too Far From Shore/ Who Loves You
More/ Go Away Little Boy
R: Exs. Soundboard.   S: Studio outtakes '85.
C: ECD. Dcc. Time 76:46.

CD - PECO'S BLUES
SPANK PRODUCTIONS SP-107
Billy (1)/ Billy (2)/ Turkey/ Turkey 2 or Tom Turkey/
Billy Surrenders/ And He's Killed Me Too/
Goodbye E Holly/ Peco's Blues (1)/ Peco's Blues
(2)/ Billy (3)/ Knockin' On Heaven's Door (1)/
Sweet Amarillo/ Knockin' On Heaven's Door (2)/
Knockin' On Heaven's Door (3)/ Final Theme (1)/
Final Theme (2)/ Rock Me Mama (1)/ Rock Me
Mama (2)/ Billy (4)/ Billy (5)/ Instrumental (1)/
Instrumental (2)/ Final Theme (3)/ Final Theme (4)
R: Ex. Soundboard.   S: 'Pat Garret And Billy The
Kid' outtakes. Tracks 1-9 CBS Discos Studios,
Mexico City Jan. 20 '73. Tracks 10-24 Burbank
Studios, Burbank Feb. '73.   C: Japanese CD.

Dcc. Time 70:19.

CD - THE PICNIC AT BLACKBUSHE
HOLLOW HORN RECORDS HH 15778
CD1: My Back Pages/ Love Her With A Feeling/
Baby Stop Crying/ Shelter From The Storm/ Girl
From The North Country/ Ballad Of A Thin Man/
Maggie's Farm/ Simple Twist Of Fate/ Like A
Rolling Stone/ I Shall Be Released/ Is Your Love
In Vain?/ Where Are You Tonight/ Gates Of Eden
CD2: True Love Tends To Forget/ One More Cup
Of Coffee/ Blowin' In The Wind/ I Want You/
Senor/ Master Of War/ Just Like A Woman/ To
Ramona/ Don't Think Twice It's Allright/ All I Really
Want To Do/ It's Allright Ma/ Forever Young/
Changing Of The Guards/ The Times They Are A
Changin'
R: Vg-Ex. Audience.   S: Blackbushe Aerodrome,
Camberley, Surrey, England July 15 '78. With Eric
Clapton.

CD - POSITIVERY 4TH NIGHT
BDJ-001-2
CD1: Joker Man/ Lay Lady Lay/ All Along The
Watchtower/ I Don't Believe You/ Tangled Up In
Blue/ Positively 4th Street/ Tomorrow Night/ Mr.
Tambourine Man/ It's All Over Now Baby Blue
CD2: Series Of Dreams/ I And I/ Maggie's Farm/
Man In The Long Black Coat/ It Ain't Me Babe/ It's
Allright Ma*/ I Forget More Than You'll Ever
Know*/ Like A Rolling Stone*/ Blowin' In The
Wind*
R: Vgs. Audience. *G. Audience.   S: Budokan,
Japan Feb. 9 '94. *Budokan, Japan Mar. 5 '86 with
Tom Petty & The Heartbreakers.   C: Japanese
CD. Dbw. Time CD1 64:08. CD2 51:38.

CD - POSSUM BELLY OVERALLS
GOLD STANDARD NASH 105
Ghost Riders In The Sky/ Cupid/ All I Have To Do
Is Dream/ Gates Of Eden/ I Threw It All Away/ I
Don't Believe You/ Matchbox/ True Love Your
Love/ Wonder When My Swamp's Gonna Catch
On Fire/ I'm Goin' Fishing/ Honey Just Allow Me
One More Chance/ Rainy Day Women/ Song To
Woody/ Mama You Been On My Mind/ Don't Think
Twice It's Allright (Instrumental)/ Yesterday/ Just
Like Tom Thumb Blues/ Da Doo Ron Ron/ One
Too Many Mornings/ Folsom Prison Blues*/ Ring
Of Fire*
R: Ex. Soundboard. *Vg. Soundboard.
S: Tracks 1-19 Columbia Studios, Nashville May
'70. Tracks 20-21 Columbia Studios, Nashville
May '69.   C: ECD. Dcc. Time 63:50.

CD - THE PROPHET AND THE CLOWN
BOD-CD 215
Group Announcement (0:34)/ Are You Ready For
The Country (3:07)/ Ain't That A Lot Of Love
(3:51)/ Looking For A Love (2:49)/ Loving You Is
Sweeter Than Ever (3:08)/ I Want You (2:52)/ The
Weight (3:59)/ Helpless (2:19)/ Knockin' On
Heaven's Door (4:48)/ Will The Circle Be
Unbroken (2:06)

R: G-Vg. Audience.   S: '75 Tour.   C: ECD.
Dbw. Red/green type.

CD - RISE AGAIN
WANTED MAN MUSIC WMM 36/37
CD1: Gotta Serve Somebody/ I Believe In You/
Like A Rolling Stone/ Man Gave Names To All The
Animals/ Just Like Tom Thumb Blues/ Fever/ All
Along The Watchtower/ Ain't Gonna Go To Hell/
Girl From The North Country/ Slow Train/ To
Ramona/ We Just Disagree/ Simple Twist Of Fate/
Saved/ Don't Think Twice
CD2: Abraham, Martin And John/ Rise Again/
Let's Keep It Between Us/ Mary From The Wild
Moor/ Solid Rock/ Just Like A Woman/ Senor/
What Can I Do For You/ When You Gonna Wake
Up/ In The Garden/ Blowin' In The Wind/ City Of
Gold/ It's All Over Now Baby Blue/ Hard Rain
R: Vg. Audience.   S: Seattle Nov. 30 '80.
C: ECD. Dbw. Yellow background. Purple type.
Time CD1 65:48. CD2 62:45.

CD - ROUGH CUTS
BLACK NITE CRASH BNC 001/2
C: ECD. Dcc. See 'Rough Cuts' (Gold Standard
57118XK1) for songs and source.

CD - ROUGH CUTS
GOLD STANDARD 57118XK1
CD1: Sweetheart Like You/ Someone's Got A
Hold Of My Heart/ Lord Protect My Child/ Angel
Flying Too Close To The Ground/ Foot Of Pride/ I
And I/ Tell Me/ Union Sundown/ Julius And Ethel/
Jokerman/ License To Kill/ Man Of Peace/ Don't
Fall Apart On Me Tonight/ Neighborhood Bully
CD2: Blind Willie McTell/ This Was My Love (take
1)/ This Was My Love (take 2)/ Angel Flying Too
Close To The Ground/ Dark Groove/ Don't Fly
Unless It's Safe/ Clean Cut Kid/ Death Is Not The
End/ Sweetheart Like You/ Union Sundown (take
2)/ The 'Sweetheart' Rehearsals
R: Exs. Soundboard.   S: 'Infidels' studio
sessions Apr. 11 - May 8 '83.   C: Japanese CD.
Dcc. Time CD1 76:23. CD2 68:03.

CD - SECOND SUPPER
WANTED MAN MUSIC WMM 49/50
CD1: Ragged & Dirty/ One More Cup Of Coffee/
Blood In My Eyes/ Queen Jane Approximately/ I'll
Be Your Baby Tonight/ Disease Of Conceit/ I Want
You/ Ring Them Bells/ My Back Pages/ Forever
Young
CD2: Ragged & Dirty/ Lay Lady Lay/ Tight
Connection To My Heart/ Weeping Willow/ Delia/
Jim Jones/ Queen Jane Approximately/ Ring
Them Bells/ Jack-A-Roe/ Forever Young/ I Shall
Be Released
R: Ex. Audience.   S: The Supper Club, New
York Nov. 17 '93.   C: ECD. Dcc.

CD - SENSEI
HOME RECORDS HR 5987-9
Jokerman (7:50)/ Shelter From The Storm (7:31)/
All Along The Watchtower (5:02)/ Tangled In Blue

(5:43)/ Watching The River Flow (4:54)/ Master Of
War (4:55)/ Don't Think Twice It's Alright (6:04)/
Series Of Dreams (6:26)/ I And I (6:45)/ Maggie's
Farm (4:47)/ Man In The Long White Coat (7:19)/
It Ain't Me Babe (7:42)
R: Ex. Audience.   S: Kosel Nenkin Kaikan,
Hiroshima, Japan Feb. 16 '94.   C: ECD. Dcc.
Pic CD.

CD - 7 YEARS OF BAD LUCK
SPANK RECORDS SP 102
Hero Blues (take 1)/ Whatcha Gonna Do (take 1)/
Oxford Town (take 1)/ / I Shall Be Free (take 1)/ I
Shall Be Free (take 2)/ I Shall Be Free (take 3)/ I
Shall Be Free (takes 4 and 5)/ Hero Blues (version
2)/ You've Been Hiding Too Long/ You Don't Have
To Do That/ Positively Van Gogh (version 1)/
Positively Van Gogh (version 2)/ Just Like A
Woman/ Gates Of Eden/ I Threw It All Away/ I
Don't Believe You/ Telephone Wire/ Honey Just
Allow Me One More Chance
R: Vg.   S: Columbia Studios, NYC Dec. 6 '62.
'Self Portrait' session '69.   C: Japanese CD.

CD - SHADOWS IN THE SOUND
ROTATION ROTA 02/3
CD1: Intro - I'm Movin' On (5:09)/ The Man In Me
(4:40)/ All Along The Watchtower (6:51)/ Tangled
Up In Blue (10:27)/ I'll Remember You (4:57)/
Stuck Inside Of Mobile With The Memphis Blues
Again (8:40)/ It Takes A Lot To Laugh It Takes A
Train To Cry (7:05)/ Tomorrow Night (5:19)/ Jim
Jones (7:04)/ Mr. Tambourine Man (7:09)/ Don't
Think Twice It's Allright (8:13)
CD2: Cats In The Well (6:37)/ I And I (7:54)/
Simple Twist Of Fate (8:16)/ Highway 61 Revisited
(6:27)/ What Good Am I (5:39)/ Rainy Day Woman
No. 12 & 35 (4:38)/ It Ain't Me Babe (9:24)/ Seeing
The Real You At Last (4:48)/ I And I (5:48)/ In The
Garden (6:43)/ Rock 'Em Dead (4:19)
R: Ex. Audience.   S: CD1 and CD2 tracks 1-7
Utrecht, Holland Feb. 16 '93. CD2 tracks 8-11
Morrison, Denver July 26 '86.   C: ECD. Dcc.

CD - SINGS FOR HIS SUPPER
GOLD STANDARD
Sally Gal/ Ragged And Dirty/ Lay Lady Lay/ Tight
Connection (Has Anybody Seen My Love)/
Weeping Willow/ Delia/ Jim Jones/ Queen Jane
Approximately/ Ring Them Bells/ Jack-A-Roe/
Forever Young/ I Shall Be Released/ The Girl I
Left Behind
R: G-Vg. Audience.   S: Tracks 1, 13 Folk Song
Festival, NYC Oct. 29 '61. Tracks 2-12 The
Supper Club, Late Show, NYC Nov. 17 '93.
C: ECD. Dcc. Time 73:47.

CD - SONGS FOR PATTY VALENTINE
WANTED MAN MUSIC WMM 38
Pretty Boy Floyd (Jack Elliot vocal)/ How Long/
Abandoned Love/ Hurricane/ Rita Mae/ Oh Sister/
Simple Twist Of Fate/ Hurricane/ People Get
Ready/ Never Let Me Go/ It Ain't Me Babe
R: *G. Audience. Rest Vg-Ex. Soundboard.

Audience.   S: Tracks 1-3 Other End, New York
July 3 '75. Tracks 4 (July 28) and 5 (July 30)
Columbia Studios, New York '75. Tracks 6-8
WTTN-TV Studios, Chicago Sept. 10 '75. Track 9
Sir Studios, New York Oct. '75. Track 10 Montreal
Dec. 4 '75. Track 11 Cambridge, Massachusetts
Nov. 20 '75.   C: ECD. Dcc. Time 54:12.

CD - STUMBLIN' ALONG
HAWK 058
You're Gonna Quit Me (3:49)/ Stuck Inside Of
Mobile With the Memphis Blues Again (8:38)/ All
Along The Watchtower (5:27)/ Born In Time (7:52)/
Silvo (4:24)/ I And I (7:32)/ Jim Jones (5:15)/
Gates Of Eden (9:33)/ Don't Think Twice It's All
Right (4:32)/ God Knows (5:13)/ Maggie's Farm
(7:19)
R: Vg-Ex. Audience.   S: Hollywood Bowl, Oct. 2
'93.   C: ECD. Dcc. Pic CD.

CD - THROUGH A BULLET OF LIGHT
GOLOM 774554
CD1: Long Ago Far Away/ Long Time Gone/ Ain't
Gonna Grieve/ Blowin' In The Wind/ Farewell/ Bob
Dylan's Blues/ Seven Curses/ Paths Of Victory/ All
Over You/ When The Ship Comes In/ The Times
They Are A-Changin'/ John Brown/ Talkin' John
Birch Paranoid Blues/ I Shall Be Free/ Hero Blues/
Tomorrow Is A Long Time/ Only A Hobo/ Whatcha
Gonna Do Gypsy Lou/ Baby Let Me Follow You
Down/ A Hard Rain's Gonna Fall/ Don't Think
Twice Its Allright
CD2: Oxford Town/ Masters Of War/ Walkin' Down
The Line/ The Death Of Emmett Till/ Bob Dylan's
Dream/ Quit Your Low-Down Ways/ Baby I'm In
The Mood For You/ Ballad Of Hollis Brown/ Girl
From The North Country/ Boots Of Spanish
Leather/ Let Me Die In My Footsteps/ Bound To
Lose Bound To Win/ I'd Hate To Be You/ Percy's
Song/ Guess I'm Doing Fine/ Eternal Circle/
Mamma You Been On My Mind/ Mr. Tambourine
Man/ I'll Keep It With Mine
R: Ex.   S: Witmark & Sons publisher's demos.
C: ECD. Dcc. Time CD1 73:40. CD2 68:43.

CD - THROUGH A GLASS DARKLY
RAZOR'S EDGE RAZ 005/006
CD1: Jokerman/ Shelter From The Storm/ All
Along The Watchtower/ She Belongs To Me/
Tangled Up In Blue/ Watching The River Flow/
Tomorrow Night/ Masters Of War/ Don't Think
Twice/ Series Of Dream
CD2: I & I/ Maggie's Farm/ Man In A Long Black
Coat/ It Ain't Me Babe/ If You See Her Say Hello/
Shooting Star/ Born In Time/ To Ramona/ God
Knows/ Blowin' In The Wind
R: Vg-Ex. Audience.   S: Hiroshima Feb. 16 '94.
C: Dcc. Pic CD. Time CD1 73:12.
CD2 74:15.

CD - TRIPLE NIGHT
BDJ 3-4
CD1: Jokerman/ You're A Big Girl Now/ All Along
The Watchtower/ Just Like A Woman/ Tangled Up

In Blue/ Knockin' On Heaven's Door/ Tomorrow Night/ A Hard Rain's Gonna Fall/ Don't Think Twice It's All Right/ Series Of Dreams
CD2: I And I/ Maggie's Farm/ What Good Am I/ Blowin' In The Wind/ Born In Time/ Gates Of Eden/ I'll Remember You/ The Lonesome Death Of Hattie Carroll/ I Shall Be Released
R: Vg-Ex. Audience.   S: CD1 live at NHK Hall, Tokyo, Japan Feb. 20 '94. CD2 tracks 5 & 6 Budokan, Tokyo, Japan Feb. 8 '94. CD2 tracks 7-9 Kouseinenkin Kaikan, Tokyo, Japan Feb. 15 '94. C: Japanese CD. Dcc. Pic CDs.Time CD1 73:58. CD2 72:29.

CD - TRUE STORIES
METEOR FRONT ROW FRONT FM 2107
Ballad Of A Thin Man/ In The Summertime/ Shot Of Love/ Walk Around Heaven All Day/ Times Are A Changing/ Let's Begin/ Lenny Bruce Is Dead/ Saved/ I Believe In You/ Like A Rolling Stone/ 'Til I Get It Right/ Man Gave Names To All Animals/ Maggie's Farm/ Girl From The North Country
R: Exs. Soundboard.   S: Palace Des Sports, Avignon, France July 25 '81.   C: ECD. Pic CD.

CD - THE WITMARK DEMOS
OFF BEAT RECORDS XXCD14
CD1: Baby I'm In The Mood For You/ Quit Your Lowdown Ways/ Long Time Gone/ Long Ago Far Away/ Ain't Gonna Grieve/ Seven Curses/ Let Me Die In My Footsteps/ Bob Dylan's Blues/ Talkin John Birch Paranoid Blues/ The Death Of Emmett Till/ Hero Blues/ Only A Hobo/ All Over You/ Bound To Lose Bound To Win/ Baby Let Me Follow You Down/ A Hard Rain's Gonna Fall/ Don't Think Twice It's Allright/ Oxford Town/ Masters Of War/ Girl From The North Country/ I Shall Be Free/ Tomorrow Is A Long Time
CD2: Boots Of Spanish Leather/ Bob Dylan's Dream/ Farewell/ Guess I'm Dancing Fine/ John Brown/ Whatcha Gonna Do/ Gypsy Lou/ Paths Of Victory/ Walking Down The Line/ Ballad Of Hollis Brown/ I'd Hate To Be You On That Dreadful Day/ Blowin' In The Wind/ When The Ship Comes In/ The Times They Are A-Changin'/ Mama You Been On My Mind/ Mr. Tambourine Man/ I'll Keep It With Mine
R: Vg-Ex.   S: Witmark Demos '62.
C: Japanese CD. Time CD1 69:44. CD2 65:15.

CD - WOODSTOCK REVISITED
DR. GIG DGCD 030
Jokerman (7:20)/ Just Like A Woman (7:24)/ All Along The Watchtower (5:20)/ If I Die (7:01)/ Don't Think Twice It's Alright (5:52)/ Masters Of War (4:57)/ It's All Over Now Baby Blue (7:35)/ God Knows (4:58)/ I Shall Be Released (6:02)/ Highway 61 Revisited (6:05)/ Rainy Day Woman #12 & 35 (5:26)
R: Exs. Soundboard.   S: Woodstock '94.
C: ECD. Dcc.

E

EAGLES, THE

CD - BACK TO THE FAST LANE
RED PHANTOM RPCD 2179/2180
CD1: Hotel California (6:51)/ Victim Of Love (4:16)/ New Kid In Town (5:05)/ Wasted Time (5:29)/ Pretty Maids All In A Row (4:16)/ Girl From Yesterday (3:26)/ I Can't Tell You Why (5:07)/ New York Minute (7:04)/ Ordinary Average Guy (4:21)/ Lyin' Eyes (6:41)/ One Of These Nights (4:30)/ Tequila Sunrise (3:00)/ Help Me Make It Thru The Night (4:36)/ Love Will Keep Us Alive (5:54)/ Forgiveness (8:08)
CD2: You Belong To The City (4:07)/ Boys Of Summer (5:03)/ Funky No. 49 (4:03)/ Smuggler's Blues (5:07)/ Life's Been Good (7:37)/ All She Wants To Do Is Dance (4:58)/ Heartache Tonight (5:24)/ Life In The Fast Lane (6:23)/ Get Over It (3:44)/ Rocky Mountain Way (7:35)/ Already Gone (5:12)/ Desperado (4:56)/ Take It Easy (4:31)
R: Vg. Audience.   S: Giants Stadium, East Rutherford, NJ Aug. 24 '94.   C: ECD. Dcc. Pic CDs.

CD - THE BOYS FROM YESTERDAY
COCOMELOS RECORDS CM 032/33
CD1: Hotel California/ Victim Of Love/ New Kid In Town/ Wasted Time/ Pretty Maids All In A Row/ The Girl From Yesterday/ I Can't Tell You Why/ New York Minute/ Ordinary Average Guy/ I yin' Eyes/ One Of These Nights/ Tequila Sunrise/ Help Me Through The Night/ The Heart Of The Matter/ Love Will Keep Us Alive
CD2: Learn To Be Still/ You Belong The City/ The Boys Of Summer/ Funk 49/ Dirty Laundry/ Smugglers Blues/ Life's Been Good/ All She Wants To Do Is Dance/ Heartache Tonight/ Life In The Fast Lane/ Get Over It/ Amazing Grace, Rocky Mountain Way/ Already Gone/ Desperado
R: Vg-Ex. Audience.   S: Irvine, CA May 29 '94.
C: ECD. Dcc. Pic CD. Total time 158:07.

CD - LIFE IN THE FAST LANE
GRAPEFRUIT GRA-021-A
Hotel California (6:25)/ Life In The Fast Lane (5:20)/ Life's Been Good (8:33)/ Take It Easy (4:41)/ Already Gone (4:52)/ Peaceful Easy (4:30)/ Good Day In Hell (4:46)/ Midnight Flyer (3:57)/ Twenty One (1:34)/) Ol' 55 (3:57)/ James Dean (3:41)/ Doolin' Dalton (8:44)/ Take It Easy (version #2) (7:03)
R: Vg-Ex. Soundboard.   C: USA '74-'80.
C: Australian CD. Dcc.

EMERSON, LAKE AND PALMER

CD - ESSENTIAL
ROCK CALENDAR RECORDS RC 2117
The Barbarian (5:27)/ Take A Pebble Part 1 (7:56)/ Take A Pebble Part II (11:57)/ Tarkus (25:54)/ Knife-Edge (6:20)/ Rondo ('69 - 16:55)

R: G. Audience. S: Auditorium Theater, Chicago Aug. 21 '71. C: ECD. Dbw.

CD - PAST AND PRESENT
BEST BEAT BB 892
Tarkus (17:01)/ Take A Pebble (11:04)/ C'est La Vie (4:09)/ Lucky Man (2:45)/ Pictures At An Exhibition (Excerpts) (14:06)/ Watching Over You (4:02)/ Tank (8:58)/ The Enemy God Dances With The Black Spirits (2:43)/ Nutrocker (3:32)
R: Vg. Audience. S: Live from USA tour '78.
C: ECD.

CD - RONDO
AMERICAN CONCERT SERIES ACS 002
Hoedown (4:11)/ Still You Turn Me On (3:01)/ Lucky Man (2:35)/ Karn Evil 9 (25:28)/ Rondo (18:55)
R: Exs. Soundboard. S: Long Beach, CA.
C: ECD. Dcc.

ENO, BRIAN / DAVID BYRNE

CD - GHOSTS
KLONDYKE RECORDS KR 21
Interview/ Mea Culpa/ Into The Spirit Womb/ Regiment/ The Friends Of Amos Tutuola/ America Is Waiting/ The Carrier/ Very Very Hungry/ On The Way To Zagora/ Les Hommes Ne Le Sauront Jamais/ A Secret Life/ Come With Us/ Mountain Of Needles
R: Vg-Ex. Soundboard. Some hiss. S: Studio versions. C: ECD. Dbw. Time 47:31.

ETHERIDGE, MELISSA

CD - ALL AMERICAN GIRL
NOT GUILTY NG 520894
CD1: Intro - Come To My Window/ No Souvenirs/ All American Girl/ Yes I Am/ If I Wanted To/ Don't You Need/ Similar Features/ Ain't It Heavy/ Occasionally/ You Can Sleep While I Drive/ Chrome Plated Heart/ Silent Legacy
CD2: Royal Station/ I'm The Only One/ 2001/ Must Be Crazy For Me/ Bring Me Some Water/ Maggie Mae/ Like The Way I Do/ The Angels (Chicago '93)/ Keep It Precious (Chicago '93).
R: Exs. Soundboard. S: Montreal '94.
C: ECD. Dcc. Pic CDs. Time CD1 61:42.
CD2 72:39.

CD - BONSOIR MONTREAL
WESTERN BEAT RSM 048 2
CD1: Come To My Window (4:09)/ No Souvenirs (4:36)/ All American Girl (6:45)/ Yes I Am (4:45)/ If I Wanted To (4:24)/ Don't You Need (5:12)/ Similar Features (5:59)/ Ain't It Heavy (4:30)/ Occasion Alley (4:18)/ You Can't Sleep While I Drive (4:15)/ Chrome Plated Heart (6:25)/ Silent Legacy (6:54)
CD2: Royal Station (11:26)/ I'm The Only One (6:01)/ 2001 (4:02)/ Must Be Crazy For Me (10:50)/ Bring Me Some Water (5:31)/ Maggie Mae (6:46)/ Like The Way I Do (14:06)/ Place Your Hand (3:26)/ The Angels (4:18)/ The Boy

Feels Strange (3:33)
S: Montreal, Canada '94. C: ECD. Ooops - the version we got had Jackson Brown 'Every Man's Alive' (RSM 047-2). I would think this would be an excellent quality CD considering other releases from this company.

CD - CHROME PLATED HEART
OHM 008
Chrome Plated Heart/ Don't You Need/ Similar Features/ Precious Pain/ I Want You/ Bring Me Some Water/ Like The Way I Do
R: Exs. Soundboard. C: ECD. Dcc. Time 38:36.

CD - V
LUNATIC LU 2002
Ain't It Heavy/ The Angels/ Similar Features/ No Souvenirs/ You Can Sleep When I Drive/ Keep It Precious/ I'm The Only One (show promo)/ Bring Me Some Water/ Meet Me In The Back/ Like The Way I Do/ 2001
R: Exs. Soundboard. S: Chicago Aug. '93.
C: ECD. Dcc. CD looks like a record. Time 69:08.

CD - GRATER LADY
RARE RECORDING COLLECTION RRC 014
Brave And Crazy/ Place Your Hand/ You Can Sleep While I Drive/ Occasionally/ Dance Without Sleeping/ Keep It Precious/ Must Be Crazy For Me/ Bring Me Some Water/ Meet Me In The Back/ Like The Way I Do/ 2001
R: Exs. Soundboard. S: Geneva Oct. 27 '92.
C: ECD. Dcc. Time 73:00.

CD - MOST WANTED
MO 10020
C: See 'V' (LU 2002) for songs and source.

CD - PASSION AND PROMISE
LIVE STORM LSCD 51535
Ain't It Heavy (5:11)/ The Angels (4:51)/ Similar Features (4:40)/ No Souvenirs (5:07)/ I Will Never Be The Same (Welcome Home Roxy Carmichael) (5:21)/ Brave & Crazy (4:42)/ Lay Your Hand (4:59)/ The Letting Go (4:13)/ Me And Bobby McGee (Los Angeles Aug. '92 solo acoustic) (4:51)/ I'm The Only One (Sullivan Stadium, Foxboro, MA Sept. 26 '93) (5:49)/ Come To My Window (Portland, OR Sept. 26 '93 solo acoustic) (3:33*)/ Talking To My Angel (Portland, OR Sept. 26 '93 solo acoustic) (3:05)*/ Yes I Am (Chicago, IL Dec. 15 '92) (4:40)*/ Piece Of My Heart (Portland, OR Sept. 26 '93 solo acoustic) (9:09)*/ Pink Cadillac (In The Ritz, Indianapolis Nov. 11 '90) (6:17)*
R: Exs. Soundboard. *Ex. Audience.S: Festhalle, Bremen, Germany Oct. 10 '92. C: ECD. Sepia-tone cover.

CD - SHAKIN' THE PEAKS
OHM 012 A/B
CD1: No Souvenirs (5:41)/ Brave And Crazy (4:36)/ Chrome Plated Heart (7:38)/ Place Your Hand (5:20)/ You Can Sleep While I Drive (5:32)/

Occasionally (3:16)/ Dance Without Sleeping (5:36)/ Let Me Go (7:14)/ Keep It Precious (9:04) CD2: Must Be Crazy For Me (7:42)/ Bring Me Some Water (5:20)/ Meet Me In The Back (8:22)/ Like The Way I Do (10:23)/ 2001 (8:26)
R: Exs. Soundboard.   S: Europe '92.   C: ECD. Dcc.

EURYTHMICS, THE

CD - LET'S GO
THAT'S LIFE TL 930002
Right By Your Side (6:29)/ Thorn In My Side (5:17)/ Sweet Dreams Are Made Of This (5:43)/ Would I Lie To You (5:12)/ Missionary Man (5:05)/ Sisters Are Doin' It For Them Selves (4:51)/ The Miracle Of Love (7:13)/ Sexcrime (4:06)
R: Exs. Soundboard.   S: Live.   C: ECD. Dcc.

CD - SEXCRIME
THAT'S LIFE TL 930001
Sexcrime (4:07)/ Let's Go (4:53)/ The Last Time (4:42)/ Here Comes The Rain Again (7:35)/ It's Alright Baby's Coming Back (6:03)/ When Tomorrow Comes (5:43)/ There Must Be An Angel (7:10)/ Who's That Girl (4:10)
R: Exs. Soundboard.   S: Live.   C: ECD. Dcc.

EXTREME

CD - CASTLE WARHEADS 1994
OCTOPUS RECORDS OCTO 021
It's A Monster (4:18)/ Warheads (4:26)/ Kid Ego (4:45)/ Do You Wanna Play? (2:06)/ Rest In Peace (5:01)/ Am I Ever Gonna Change (6:46)/ Drum Solo (2:26)/ Cupid's Dead (6:47)/ Midnight Express (instrumental) (4:39)/ More Than Words (4:16)/ Decadence Dance (7:01)/ Naked (5:21)/ Get The Funk Out (4:59)/ Mutha (8:57)*/ Play That Funky Music (5:15)*
R: Exs. Soundboard.   S: Castle Donnington, UK June 4 '94. *Los Angeles July '89.   C: ECD. Dcc. Pic CD.

CD - DREAMS COME TRUE
KISS THE STONE KTS 312
It's (A Monster) (4:28)/ Warheads (4:14)/ Kid Ego (4:44)/ Do You Wanna Play, Rest In Peace (7:08)/ Am I Ever Gonna Change (6:46)/ Drum Solo (2:28)/ Cupid's Dead (6:46)/ Acoustic Instrumental (4:39)/ More Than Words (4:18)/ Decadence Dance (7:01)// Naked (5:12)/ Get The Funk Out (5:07)
R: Exs. Soundboard.   S: Europe '94.   C: ECD. Dcc. Pic CD.

F

FAITH NO MORE

CD - EPIC (VOL. 1)
BANANA BAN-051-A
The Real Thing (7:54)/ As The Wurm Turns (2:58)/ We Care Alot (3:56)/ Surprise! You're Dead (2:31)/ Epic (4:51)/ War Pigs (8:21)/ Easy (2:49)/ From Out Of Nowhere (3:10)/ The Real Thing (6:47)/ Underwater Love (3:27)/ We Care A Lot (3:46)
R: Vg-Ex. Soundboard.   S: USA, Europe '90-'91.
C: Australian CD. Dcc.

CD - EPIC (VOL. 2)
BANANA BAN-051-B
Land Of Sunshine (3:39)/ Midlife Crisis (4:05)/ As The Wurm Turns (2:34)/ RV (3:56)/ We Care A Lot (4:03)/ Epic (4:36)/ Real Thing (7:44)/ Underwater Love (3:36)/ We Care A Lot (3:54)/ Epic (4:51)/ Woodpecker From Mars (5:46)
R: Vg-Ex. Soundboard.   S: USA '92.
C: Australian CD. Dcc.

CD - UNDRESSED
DEAD DOG RECORDS SE 426
Intro - Final Countdown/ Surprise Your Dead/ Be Aggressive/ The Crab Song/ Midlife Crisis/ RV/ Land Of Sunshine/ We Care A Lot/ Chinese Arithmetic/ A Small Victory/ Easy/ Introduce Yourself/ Caffeine/ Epic
R: Vg-Ex. Audience.   S: Werchter July 4 '93.
C: ECD.

FERRY, BRYAN

CD - 1994/95 WORLD TOUR
TOUR RECORDS TRCD-1994
Introduction (2:56)/ Spell On You (5:23)/ Slave To Love (4:29)/ Your Painted Smile (3:15)/ Wasteland, Windswept (7:21)/ New York City (4:42)/ Manouna (4:55)/ Can't Let Go (5:22)/ Carrick Fergus (3:41)/ Virginia Plain (2:49)/ Jealous Guy (6:26)/ In Every Dream Home (7:58)/ Edition Of You (3:54)/ Love Is The Drug (5:07)/ Avalon (4:57)/ Lets Stick Together (4:53)
R: Ex. Audience.   S: The Aston Villa Leisure Centre, Birmingham, England Oct. 26 '94.
C: ECD. Dcc. Pic CD.

FIRM, THE

CD - LIVE U.S.A. 1986
THE CONCERT SERIES TCS-CD-002
Fortune Hunter (4:49)/ Make Or Break (4:44)/ Prelude (1:55)/ Money Can't Buy (4:48)/ Satisfaction Guaranteed (4:17)/ Radioactive (3:20)/ All The King's Horses (3:16)/ Cadillac (6:13)/ You've Lost That Loving Feeling (5:05)/ Midnight Moonlight (11:08)/ Tear Down The Walls (4:55)
R: Exs. Soundboard.   S: Radio broadcast.
C: ECD.

FISH

CD - BAGPIPE - DISASTER
RARITIES SPECIAL RS 005
Vigil (9:25)/ Credo (9:11)/ Incubus (11:04)/
Shadowplay (7:44)/ Lucky (5:17)/ Heart Of Lothian
(5:19)/ Fugazy (11:33)/ Internal Exile (4:33)/
Market Square Heroes, The Laugh (6:17)
R: Ex. Audience.   S: Internal Exile Tour, Utrecht,
Holland, Vredenburg Dec. 17 '91.   C: ECD.

CD - TAKE A VIEW FROM THE HILL!
KLONDYKE RECORDS KR 013
Fearless (6:25)/ Boston Tea Party (4:03)/ Credo
(7:26)/ Family Business (6:40)/ View From The Hill
(4:37)/ She Chameleon (3:47)/ Kayleigh (4:05)/
The Company (4:34)/ Just Good Friends (6:08)/
Internal Exile (5:28)/ Cliche (7:19)/ The Last Straw
Happy Ending (5:47)/ Five Years (6:30)
R: Vg. Audience.   S: Europe '93.   C: ECD.
Dcc.

4 NON BLONDES

CD - LIVE IN USA
VAMPIRE VR 50004
Pleasantly Blue/ What's Up/ Spaceman/ Morphine
+ Chocolate/ Need It Bad/ In My Dreams
R: Poor-G. Audience.   S: New York, Sept. 4 '93.
C: ECD. Time 24:55.

FRANKIE GOES TO HOLLYWOOD

CD - SEX FROM MARS
GERMAN RECORDS GERMAN REC. 038
Relax/ Born To Run/ Two Tribes/ For Heaven's
Sake/ Kill The Pain/ The Power Of Love/
Maximum Joy/ Welcome To The Pleasure Dome/
Lunar Baby/ Rage Hard/ War/ Krisco Kisses/ The
Only Star In Heaven/ Watching The Wildlife/
Warriors Of The Wasteland
R: Vg-Ex.   S: Bruxelles '87.   C: ECD. Dcc.
Digi-pack. Time 71:05.

FRIPP, ROBERT

CD - ELEVEN IMPROVISATIONS
MOON CHILD 931112
Improvisations Numbers 1 To 11
R: Gs. Audience.   S: London, England Jan. 8
'87.   C: Japanese CD.

FRIPP, ROBERT & DAVID SYLVIAN

CD - A NEW DREAM
RED PHANTOM RPCD 2149/50
CD1: God's Monkey (6:21)/ Brightness Falls
(6:23)/ Every Colour You Are (5:46)/ Jean The
Birdman (3:57)/ Firepower (7:15)/ Damage (4:36)/
Exposure (5:33)/ Gone To Heart (2:23)/ 20th
Century Dreaming (8:43)
CD2: Wave (6:13)/ Riverman (5:13)/ Darshaw
(11:22)/ The First Day (5:21)/ Blinding Light Of
Heaven (4:09)

R: Exs. Soundboard.   S: Nakano Sun Plaza Hall,
Tokyo Oct. 26 '93.   C: ECD. Dcc.

CD - THE DAY BEFORE
ALL OF US ASO6
Introduction - First Day's Morning/ Fire Power/
Unreleased/ The First Day/ Jean The Birdman/
20th Century Dreaming/ Unreleased/ Unreleased/
Unreleased/ Bringing Down The Light/ Block
Head/ Asturias/ Ghost (acoustic)/ Sean The
Byrdman
R: Vgs. Audience.   S: Europe '92.

CD - THE FIRST DAY
9 20305 2
Soundscape/ Firepower/ Ascension/ Song/
Subterranean Burn/ First Day/ Jean The Birdman/
Splatology/ Mood #1/ Protopunk/ Blinding Light Of
Heaven/ Urban Landscape
R: Vg. Audience.   S: Mar. '92.   C: Japanese CD.

CD - KINGS
FLYING TIGERS FTCD 0018
Soundscape (9:22)/ Firepower (2:32)/ Bringing
Down The Light (10:46)/ She's Trouble To Me
(8:15)/ Jean The Birdman (4:15)/ 20th Century
Dreaming (2:42)/ Tallow Moon (8:33)/ Chromatic
Fantasy (2:54)/ She's Killing Me (4:54)/ Blockhead
(4:04)/ Asturias (3:32)/ God Saved My Life (4:39)/
She's Killing Me (4:56)/ Jean The Birdman (4:20)
R: Exs. Audience.   S: Italian tour.   C: ECD.
Dcc. Pic CD.

CD - KINGS - SECOND CHAPTER
FLYING TIGERS FTCD 0046
God's Monkey (6:17)/ Brightness Falls (6:40)/
Every Color You Are (5:49)/ Jean The Birdman
(4:02)/ Firepower (7:47)/ The Only One To Loved
(5:00)/ Tallow Moon (6:17)/ Darshan (12:35)/
Wave (6:25)/ 20th Century Dreaming (8:45)/ Gone
To The Earth (2:25)
R: Exs. Audience.   S: Italian tour.   C: ECD.
Dcc. Pic CD.

CD - THE ROAD TO GRACELAND 1993
DSRF 211, 212
CD1: God's Monkey/ Brightness Falls/ Every
Colour You Are/ Firepower/ Jean The Birdman/
Damage/ Exposure/ Gone To Earth/ 20th Century
Dreaming - A Shaman's Song/ Wave/ River Man/
Darshan, The Road To Graceland
CD2: The First Day/ Talking The Veil
R: Vg-Exs. Audience.   S: Complete show Oct.
21 '93.   C: Japanese CD.

CD - TOKYO 1993
LIVE STORM LSCD 52522
C: See 'A New Dream' (RPCD 2149/50) for songs
and source.

G

GABRIEL, PETER

CD - ALIVE & BUMPIN'
OCTOPUS RECORDS OCTO 016-017
CD1: Come Talk To Me (6:38)/ Quiet Steam -
Steam (7:47)/ Across The River, Slow Marimbas
(7:40)/ Shaking The Tree (7:27)/ Blood Of Eden
(6:47)/ San Jacinto (7:49)/ Kiss That Frog (5:53)/
Washing Of The Water (4:06)/ Solsbury Hill (4:31)
CD2: Digging In The Dirt (7:59)/ Sledgehammer
(5:28)/ Secret World (10:21)/ Don't Give Up (7:12)/
In Your Eyes (10:01)
R: Ex. Audience.   S: Modena, Italy Nov. 16 and
17 '93.   C: ECD. Dcc. Pic CD.

CD - DIGGING IN EUROPE '93
FUN FACTORY 003
Games Without Frontiers (5:05)/ Solsbury Hill
(5:13)/ Shock The Monkey (5:45)/ Come Talk To
Me (6:15)/ Steam (7:13)/ Blood Of Eden (5:56)/
Kiss The Frog (4:48)/ Digging In The Dirt (7:06)/
Sledgehammer (4:57)/ In Your Eyes (9:57)/ San
Jacinto (5:32)/ Secret World (6:13)
R: Vg-Ex. Soundboard.   S: Rotterdam, Apr.
27/28 '93 & USA '87.   C: ECD. Dcc.

CD - FOR YOUR EYES AND EARS
OHM 025-A/B
CD1: Come Talk To Me/ Steam/ Games Without
Frontiers/ Across The River/ Shaking The Tree/
Blood Of Eden/ San Jacinto/ Love Town
CD2: Kiss That Frog/ Washing Of The Water/
Solsbury Hill/ Diggin' In The Dirt/ Sledgehammer/
Secret World/ In Your Eyes/ Biko
R: Vg-Ex. Audience.   S: Europe '93.   C: ECD.
Dbw. Blue type. Time CD1: 61:30. CD2: 61:30.

CD - GLASTONBURY FESTIVAL 1994
FESTIVAL MUSIC FMCD-001/002
CD1: Introduction/ Come Talk To Me/ Steam/
Games Without Frontiers/ Across The River,
Shakin' The Tree/ Blood Of Eden/ Red Rain/ San
Jacinto Solisbury Hill/ Digging In The Dirt
CD2: Sledgehammer/ Secret World/ In Your Eyes/
Biko/ Band Introductions/ Love Town/ Shock The
Monkey/ Washing Of The Water/ Solisbury Hill/
Sledgehammer
R: Ex. Audience.   Glastonbury Festival, England
June '94. Tracks 6-10 National Exhibition Centre,
Birmingham, England May 25 '93.   C: ECD. Dcc.
Pic CDs. Time CD1 73:36. CD2 76:11.

CD - MUSIC WITHOUT FRONTIERS
COLLECTORS PLEASURE COP 009
San Jacinto (6:40)/ Shock The Monkey (5:59)/
Games Without Frontiers (5:09)/ No Self Control
(5:31)/ Mercy Street (8:23)/ Don't Give Up (7:24)/
Solsbury Hill (4:59)/ Lay Your Hands On Me
(7:52)/ Sledgehammer (4:47)/ In Your Eyes (11:41)
R: Vg-Ex.   S: Live in the USA during '88.
C: ECD. Dbw.

GARCIA, JERRY

CD - EMOTION
KLONDYKE RECORDS KR 011
I Second That Emotion (10:00)/ Tangled Up In
Blue (10:15)/ The Harder They Come (14:05)/
Mystery Train (9:02)/ Knockin' On Heaven's Door
(14:10)/ Tore Up Over You (10:18)/ Moonlight
Midnight (7:20)
R: G-Vg. Soundboard.   S: San Jose, CA July 3
'82.   C: ECD. Dcc.

CD - HOW SWEET IT IS
RARE RECORDING COLLECTION RRC 032
Sugaree/ Catfish John/ How Sweet It Is/ Sitting In
Limbo/ That's Alright Mama/ Deal
R: Vg. Soundboard.   S: Capitol Theater,
Passaic, NJ Jan. 3 '80.   C: ECD. Dbw. 60:30.

GENESIS

CD - BESIDE THE SILENT MIRROR
ARCHIVES ARC 012
Happy The Man (4:22)/ Stagnation (11:15)/ The
Light (11:40)/ Twilight Alehouse (10:55)/ The
Musical Box (15:18)/ The Knife (10:17)/ Going Out
To Get You (6:36)
R: Poor. Muffled. Audience.   S: 'La Ferme',
France Mar. 7 '71.   C: ECD. Dbw. Brown type.

CD - 18 MILLION DOLLARS TO DANCE
GERMAN RECORDS GEN CD 0.17
No Son Of Mine/ The Lamb Lies Down On
Broadway/ Jesus He Knows Me/ Invisible Touch/
Driving The Last Spike/ Tonight Tonight Tonight/ I
Can't Dance/ Land Of Confusion/ Hold On My
Heart/ Home By The Sea/ Second Home By The
Sea
R: Exs. Soundboard.   S: Live in USA '92 except
track 2 USA '77 and track 6 USA Forum '86.
C: ECD. Time 73:16.

CD - FIRST WE WERE FIVE
ROCK CALENDAR RECORDS RC 2113
Dancing With The Moonlight Knight (8:13)/ The
Cinema Show (10:28)/ I Know What I Like (5:17)/
Firth Of Fifth (6:52)/ The Musical Box (10:06)/ The
Battle Of Epping Forest (11:42)/ Supper's Ready
(21:16)
R: G. Audience.   S: Tuffs University, Medford,
MA Nov. 7 '73.   C: ECD.

CD - IN THE BEGINNING VOL. 3
EXTREMELY RARE EXR 13
Carpet Crawlers (demo take #1)/ Carpet Crawlers
(demo take #2)/ Carpet Crawlers (demo take #3)/
Carpet Crawlers (demo take #4)/ I Know What I
Like (intro)/ The Waiting Room (demo)/ The
Cinema Show (studio take #1)/ The Cinema Show
(studio take #2)/ The Waiting Room (sound
effects)/ Lillywhite Lilith (demo)/ The Waiting
Room (demo)/ Anyway (demo)/ The Supernatural
Anaesthetist (demo - Phil on vocals)/ The Lamia
(demo)/ Riding The Scree (demo)/ Silver Song

(demo - Phil on vocals)
R: Vg-Ex.   S: Studio.   C: ECD. Time 62:05.

CD - IN THE BEGINNING VOL. 4
EXTREMELY RARE EXR 014
Happy The Man (demo)/ Silver Song (demo - Phil
on vocals)/ Only Your Love (demo - Phil on
vocals)/ Studio Improvisation/ Studio
Improvisation/ The Battle Of Epping Forest/ The
Battle Of Epping Forest/ The Battle Of Epping
Forest/ The Battle Of Epping Forest/ The Battle Of
Epping Forest/ The Cinema Show/ The Cinema
Show/ Dancing With The Moonlit Knight/ The
Battle Of Epping Forest/ The Last Time/ You
Really Got Me/ The Battle Of Epping Forest/ The
Battle Of Epping Forest/ The Battle Of Epping
Forest/ The Battle Of Epping Forest/ I Know What
I Like/ I Know What I Like/ The Cinema Show
R: Vg-Ex.   S: Studio - various takes, demos and
instrumentals.   C: ECD. Time 76:46.

CD - IN THE BEGINNING VOL. 5
EXTREMELY RARE EXR 018
Drum Solo/ Firth Of Fifth (instrumental)/ Firth Of
Fifth (faster version)/ The Cinema Show
Rehearsal (rehearsal)/ After The Ordeal (fast
version)/ Dancing With The Moonlit Knight (piano
and vocal takes)/ Dancing With The Moonlit Knight
(vocals, organ, drums, bass)/ Dancing With The
Moonlit Knight (whole ensemble)/ The Battle Of
Epping Forest (5 instrumental rehearsals)/ The
Battle Of Epping Forest (instrumental rehearsal)/
The Cinema Show (rehearsal)
R: Vg.   S: Studio.   C: ECD. Time 66:10.

CD - THE LAMB LIES DOWN ON BROADWAY -
OUTTAKES
OUTTAKES COMPANY G 092110
The Lamb Lies Down On Broadway (4:31)/
Cuckoo Cocoon I (2:16)/ Cuckoo Cocoon II (2:21)/
In The Cage (7:24)/ The Grand Parade Of Lifeless
Packaging (2:45)/ Back In New York City I (5:44)/
Back In New York City II (5:52)/ Counting Out
Time (1:61)/ Anyway (3:13)/ The Lamia (7:05)/ In
The Rapids I (1:45)/ In The Rapids II (1:20)
R: Exs. Soundboard.   C: ECD.

CD - LIVE IN PAVIA
FU 203
Happy The Man (3:29)/ Fountain Of Salmacis
(10:04)/ Twilight Alehouse (8:56)/ Bye Bye Johnny
(10:16)/ Musical Box (11:35)/ The Return Of The
Giant Hogweed (9:36)/ The Knife (9:16)
R: Poor-G.   S: Palazzo Delle Eposizioni, Pavia
Apr. 15 '72.   C: ECD. Dcc. Pic CD.

CD - SOME OF YOU ARE GOING TO DIE
ALTERNATIVE RECORDING COMPANY ARC
004
Supper's Ready/ Watcher Of The Skies/ The
Musical Box/ Get 'Em Out By Friday/ The Return
Of The Giant Hogweed/ The Knife
R: Ex.   S: De Montford Hall, Leicester Jan. 28
'73. Free Trade Hall, Manchester Feb. 4 '73.

C: ECD. Made by fans for fans.

CD - ROMA 18 APRILLE 1972
TINTAGEL TICD 009
Happy The Man (4:35)/ Stagnation (9:23)/ The
Fountain Of Salmacis (8:44)/ Twilight Alehouse
(7:51)/ Improvisation (3:09)/ The Musical Box
(10:32)/ The Return Of Giant Hogweed (7:55)/ The
Knife (9:11)/ Going Out To Get You (3:40)
R: Ex. Audience.   S: Rome Apr. 18 '72.
C: ECD. Dbw. Yellow/blue type. Pic CD.

GERMS

7" - (GI)
CRASH 001
S1: Manimal (2:15)
S2: Strange Notes (1:37), Dragon Lady (1:48)
R: Exs.   S: 'Tooth And Nail' sessions '79.
C: Numbered. DBW pic sleeve.

GETZ, STAN

CD - POETRY IN JAZZ
JAZZ FILE JF 1003
Jet Lag (7:41)/ Plaza (7:52)/ After A Dream (7:56)/
Academy Of Love (9:00)/ Pretty City (14:42)/
Secret People (8:50) Cancau Do Sol (5:52)/
Utopia (5:54)
R: Exs. Soundboard.   S: Montreux July 20 '78.
C: ECD. Dcc.

GILL, VINCE

CD - A POCKET FULL OF LIVE SONGS
ROYAL SOUND MUSIC RSM 060 SQ CD
Oklahoma Borderline/ Cinderella/ Pocket Full Of
Gold/ Ridin' The Rodeo/ One More Last Chance/
Take Your Memory With You/ Tryin' To Get Over
You/ Rita Ballou/ Whenever You Come Around/
What The Cowgirls Do/ Don't Let Our Love Start
Slippin' Away/ Nothing Like A Woman/ South Side
Of Dixie/ When I Call Your Name/ Liza Jane/ I Still
Believe In You
S: 'When Love Finds You' US tour.   C: ECD.

GIN BLOSSOMS

CD - IN BLOOM
KISS THE STONE KTS 259
Hold Me Down (4:47)/ What (3;55)/ Idiot Summer
(4:31)/ Just South Of Nowhere (3:09)/ Soul Deep
(3:37)/ Cheatin' (3:59)/ Allison Road (3:27)/ Mrs.
Rita (4:17)/ Hey Jealousy (4:10)/ 29 (3:53)/ Until I
Fall Away (3:19)/ It's Not Too Much (4:06)/ Just
South Of Nowhere (3:17)/ Cheatin' (3:48)/ Mrs.
Rita (4:35)/ Wasting My Time (3:20)/ Standing In
The Wheat (5:54)
R: Exs. Soundboard.   S: Tracks 1-9 Belly Up,
Solana Beach, CA '93. Tracks 10-17 Cabaret
Metro, Chicago '93.   C: ECD. Dcc. Pic CD.

CD - SMALL CLUB
HOME RECORDS HR 5913-9

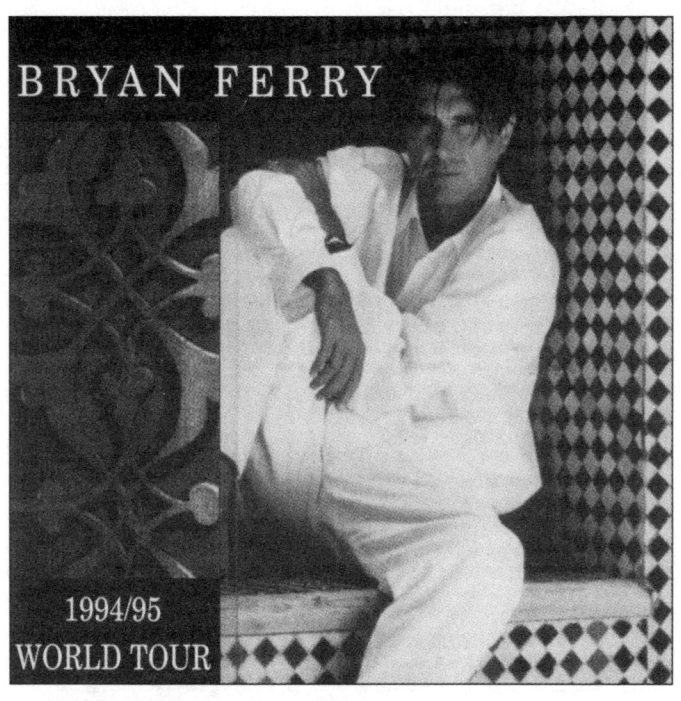

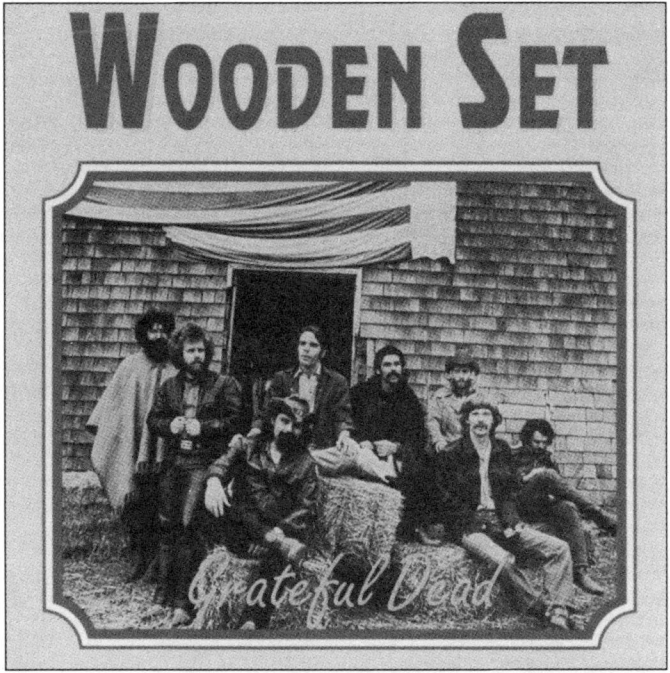

Hold Me Down (5:09)/ What (3:43)/ Indian
Summer (4:41)/ South Of Nowhere (3:18)/ Soul
Deep (3:03)/ Cheatin' (4:36)/ Allison Road (3:27)/
Mrs. Rita (4:12)/ Hey Jealousy (4:00)/ Folsom
Prison Blues (3:01)/ Weeds (6:09)/ Allison Road
(3:58)*/ Hold Me Down (4:29)*/ Mrs. Rita (4:06)*
R: Exs. Soundboard. *Audience.   S: Belly Up,
Solana Beach, CA '93. Tracks 12-14 USA '93.
C: ECD. Dcc.

GRATEFUL DEAD, THE

CD - A DIFFERENT SHOW IN THE SAME STADIUM
VIVID SOUND PRODUCTIONS VSP 51018/19
CD1: Jack Straw (8:06)/ Bertha (7:17)/ Little Red
Rooster (8:38)/ Althea (7:27)/ When I Paint My
Masterpiece (5:16)/ Tennessee Jed (7:49)/ The
Music Never Stopped (8:19)/ Help On The Way
(10:06)/ Franklin's Tower (10:36)
CD2: Samson & Delilah (6:20)/ Ship Of Fools
(7:25)/ Corrina Corrina (8:55)/ Drums (20:06)/
Space (11:13)/ The Wheel (6:25)/ I Need A
Miracle (4:08)/ The Days Between (10:45)/ Not
Fade Away (2:25)
R: Exs. Soundboard.   S: Autzen Stadium,
Eugene Aug. 22 '93.   C: ECD. Dcc.

CD - ABSOLUTELY
VIVID SOUND PRODUCTIONS VSP 51022/23
CD1: Shakedown Street (16:28)/ T For Texas
(8:02)/ Peggy-O (6:51)/ Jack Straw (5:01)/ Bird
Song (11:40)/ Hell In Bucket (6:05)/ Don't Ease
Me In (3:13)/ Beat It On Down The Line (3:02)/
Loser (6:36)
CD2: Picasso Moon (6:50)/ Sugaree (11:08)/ New
Minglewood Blues (7:26)/ Ramble On Rose (7:50)/
When I Paint My Masterpiece (5:10)/ Rubin And
Cherrie (7:13)/ Let It Grow (11:43)/ Turn On Your
Lovelight (7:22)/ Baba O'Riley (3:26)/ Tomorrow
Never Knows (2:34)
R: Vg-Ex.   S: CD1 Tracks 1-7 Civic Center
Auditorium, San Francisco Dec. 31 '84. Tracks 8-9
Berkeley Community Theatre Aug. 25 '72. CD2
tracks 1-8 Buckeye Lake, Ohio June. 9 '91. Tracks
1-8 Buckeye Lake, Ohio July 1 '92.   C: ECD.
Dcc.

CD - AIN'T SUPERSTITIOUS
SILVER RARITIES SIRA 141/142 2-CD
CD1: Cold Rain & Snow/ Promised Land/ Ramble
On Rose/ Ain't Superstitious/ Down In The Bottom/
Bird Song/ Comes A Time/ Deal/ The Music Never
Stopped/ Just Like Tom Thumb's Blues
CD2: Estimated Prophet/ Terrapin Station/ Drums/
Space/ I Need A Miracle/ Morning Dew/ Throwing
Stones/ Not Fade Away/ Keep Your Day Job
R: Exs. Soundboard.   S: Hershey Park '85.
C: ECD. Dcc. Time CD1 60:24. CD2 74:49.

CD - ANOTHER DAY IN THE SUNSHINE
KISS THE STONE KTS 341/42
CD1: Touch Of Grey (6:01)/ Greatest Story Ever
Told (5:13)/ So Many Roads (7:02)/ New

Minglewood Blues (7:32)/ Lazy River Road (8:03)/
Mexicali Blues (5:40)/ Big River (6:00)/ Friend Of
The Devil (9:36)/ Eternity (9:11)/ Liberty (6:21)/
China Cat Sunflower (5:51)
CD 2: I Know You Rider (5:32)/ Women Are
Smarter (8:33)/ Wave To The Wind (8:18)/
Terrapin Station (16:34)/ Drums - Space (4:00)/
Long Way To Go Home (6:29)/ The Other One
(8:09)/ Morning Dew (13:42)/ The Weight (5:56)
R: Exs. Soundboard.   S: Dean E. Smith Center,
Chapel Hill, NC Mar. 25 '93.   C: ECD. Pic CDs.

CD - BACK TO FANTASY
AMERICAN CONCERT SERIES 056
Truckin' (7:46)/ Crazy Fingers (8:13)/ Playing In
The Band (9:19)/ Uncle John's Band (10:43)/
Drums (8:20)/ Space (6:35)/ I Need A Miracle
(3:39)/ Dear Mr. Fantasy (7:03)/ Goin' Down The
Road Feelin' Bad (6:37)/ Around And Around
(6:48)
R: Exs. Soundboard.   S: Dominquez.   C: ECD.
Dcc. See 'New American Dreams' for part 1.

CD - BACK TO THE STARS
CD1: Intro - Touch Of Gray/ Wang Dang Doodle/
Althea/ Me And My Uncle/ Mexicali Blues/ Lazy
River Road/ Eternity/ Lucy In The Sky With
Diamonds
CD2: Box Of Rain/ Aiko Aiko/ Playin In The Band/
Uncle John's Band/ Drums/ Space/ The Wheel/ All
Along The Watch Tower/ Morning Dew/ Rain
R: Poor- G. Audience.   S: Rosemont Horizon,
Chicago Mar. 17 '94.   C: ECD. Dcc. Pic CD.
Time CD1 55:27. CD2 79:54.

CD - THE BILL GRAHAM BENEFIT CONCERT
HM 010 CD
CD1: Introduction By David Graham (2:55)/ Hell In
A Bucket (6:53)/ China Cat Sunflower, I Know
Your Rider (12:59)/ Wang Dang Doodle (8:46)/
Born On The Bayou (3:56)/ Bad Moon Rising
(2:54)/ Proud Mary (3:34)
CD2: Trucking, The Other One, Wharf Rat (24:27)/
Sunshine Dream (5:23)/ Forever Young (6:38)/
Touch Of Grey (8:35)/ Amazing Grace (Joan
Baez, Graham Nash, Kris Kristofferson on vocals)
(5:06)
R: Exs. Soundboard.   S: Golden Gate Park, San
Francisco Nov. 3 '91.   C: ECD. CD1 tracks 5-8
John Fogerty on vocals & guitar.

CD - THE BILL GRAHAM BENEFIT CONCERT
LIVE STORM LSCD 52513
C: See 'The Bill Graham Benefit Concert' (HM 010
CD) for songs and source.

CD - BLUES FOR ALLAH
TRIANGLE PYCD 097
Help On The Way (7:15)/ Franklin's Tower (8:07)/
Help On The Way (8:07)/ Lazy Lightning (4:53)/
The Music Never Stopped (6:04)/ Staccato Jam
(6:37)/ Franklin's Tower (4:48)/ Blues For Allah
(8:23)/ Drums (3:18)/ Blues For Allah (11:23)
R: Exs. Soundboard. Tracks 9-11 Ex. Audience.

S: Recorded in '75. Tracks 9-11 Winterland June 17.   C: ECD. Dcc.

CD - CELESTIAL SYNAPSE
TEDDY BEAR RECORDS TB 40
Dire Wolf (3:10)/ Dark Hollow (3:43)/ Rosalie McFall (2:45)/ Cassidy (5:39)/ Deep Elem Blues (4:59)/ Monkey & Engineer (2:20)/ Oh Babe It Ain't No Lie (6:13)/ Ripple (4:33)/ On The Road Again (2:36)/ It Must Have Been The Roses (5:34)/ Jack-A-Roe (??)/ To Lay Me Down (8:35)/ Heaven Help The Fool (6:01)/ Bird Song (7:53)/ Ripple (4:43)/ We Bid You Goodnight (3:30)
R: Exs. Soundboard.   S: Warfield Theatre, San Francisco Oct. 10 & 11 '80. Track 15 Fillmore East, NYC Apr. 28 '71. Track 16 Fillmore East, NYC Apr. 29 '71.   C: ECD. Dcc. Pic CD.

CD - DAWN OF THE DEAD
KISS THE STONE KTS 227/28
CD1: Here Comes Sunshine/ Walkin' Blues/ Lazy River Road/ Queen Jane Approximately/ Bird Song/ Promised Land/ China Cat Sunflower, I Know You Rider/ Way To Go Home
CD2: Truckin', Good Morning Little Schoolgirl, Smokestack Lightnin'/ Drums/ Space/ The Last Time/ Standing On The Moon/ One More Saturday Night/ I Fought The Law
R: Exs. Soundboard.   S: Eugene, Oregon Aug. 21 '93.   C: ECD. Pic CDs.

CD - DAYBREAK ON THE LAND
VIGOTONE VT-126/7
CD1: Intro - Casey Jones/ Me And My Uncle/ Hard To Handle/ Bertha/ Playin' In The Band/ Birdsong/ Big Boss Man/ Medley: Cryptical, Drum, Other One, Wharf Rat/ Sugar Magnolia
CD2: Truckin'/ Loser/ Next Time You See Me/ The Greatest Story Ever Told/ Johnny B. Goode/ Ripple/ Medley: Not Fade Away, Going Down The Road Feelin' Bad/ Turn On Your Love Light
R: Exs. Soundboard.   S: Capitol Theater, Port Chester, NY Feb. 200 '71.   C: ECD. Dcc.

CD - DEAD AGAIN
KISS THE STONE KTS 251/52
CD1: Hell In A Bucket/ Peggy-O/ Same Thing/ Loose Lucy/ Mexicali Blues/ Maggie's Farm/ Tennessee Jed/ Picasso Moon/ Rock'N'Roll Ride On Me
CD2: Corrina/ Crazy Fingers/ Playing In The Band/ Uncle John's Band, Drums, Space/ I Need A Miracle, Wharf Rat, The Weight/ Not Fade Away
R: Vg-Ex. Soundboard.   S: Soldier Field, Chicago June 26 '93.   C: ECD. Dcc. Pic CDs.
Total time: 2:17:11.

CD - DEAD EASY
CT 50005
Dire Wolf (3:10)/ Dark Hollow (3:42)/ Rosalie McFall (2:42)/ Cassidy (5:34)/ Deep Elem Blues (4:57)/ Monkey & The Engineer (2:19)/ Oh Babe It Ain't No Lie (6:11)/ Ripple (4:27)/ On The Road Again (2:35)/ It Must Have Been The Roses

(5:33)/ Jack-A-Roe (4:04)/ To Lay Me Down (8:33)/ Heaven Help Us All (6:00)/ Bird Song (7:55)
R: Exs. Soundboard.   S: Warfield Theatre, San Francisco Oct. 11 '80.   C: ECD. Dcc.

CD - DEAD MEN CAN'T DIE
FLASHBACK 12 93 0222
CD1: Shake Down Street (13:44)/ Medley: C.C. Ryder, It Takes A Lot To Laugh, It Takes A Train To Cry (10:46)/ Black Throated Wind (6:38)/ High Time (7:46)/ Cassidy (7:17)/ Deal (9:43)/ It's All Over Now Baby Blue (6:49)
CD2: Medley: Franklins Tower, Estimated Prophet, Dark Star, Drums, Space (50:14)/ I Need A Miracle (4:43)/ Standing On The Moon (9:12)/ Turn On Your Lovelight (6:53)
R: Exs. Soundboard.   S: Madison Square Garden, NYC Sept. 20 '91.   C: ECD. Dcc.

CD - DEADLY JAWS
TUFF BITES T.B. 94.1002
Jack Straw (6:40)/ Cold Rain And Snow (9:07)/ Wang Dang Doodle (9:40)/ Candyman (10:09)/ Mexicali Blues (5:42)/ Picasso Moon (7:11)/ Box Of Rain (4:56)
R: Exs. Soundboard.   S: Boston Sept. 26 '91.
C: ECD. Dcc. Digi-pack.

CD - D.O.A.
BC-1002-1
CD1: I Know You Rider, Hurts Me Too, Dancing In The Street (20:55)/ Midnight Hour (18:35)
CD2: Good Morning Little Schoolgirl (11:10)/ Lindy (2.53)/ Stealin' (2:59)/ The Same Thing (12:05)
R: G-Vg. Soundboard.   S: Avalon Ballroom, San Francisco '66.   C: ECD. Dcc.

CD - ELEKTRIK ALMANAK
GOLD STANDARD ELE-973
Cosmic Charley/ Casey Jones/ Good Lovin'/ Cold Rain & Snow/ It's A Man's Man's World/ Dancin' In The Street/ Morning Dew
R: Vg-Ex. Soundboard.   S: Harpur College, Binghampton, New York May 4 '70.   C: ECD. Dcc. Time 72:50.

CD - GOOD LOVIN' GONE BAD
VIVID SOUND PRODUCTIONS 51004/5
CD1: Bertha (6:27)/ Greatest Story Ever Told (3:35)/ West LA Fadeaway (7:27)/ Me And My Uncle (3:01)/ Big River (5:06)/ Ramble On Rose (7:09)/ When I Paint My Masterpiece (5:10)/ Brown-Eyed Woman (5:45)/ The Music Never Stopped (9:49)/ Gloria (7:33)/ Corrina Corrina (7:53)
CD2: Crazy Fingers (8:47)/ Playing In The Band (7:32)/ Uncle John's Band (8:40)/ Drums (11:57)/ Space (6:40)/ I Need A Miracle (5:15)/ Wharf Rat (10:27)/ Throwing Stones (8:01)/ Not Fade Away (6:45)
R: Exs. Soundboard.   S: Soldier Field, Chicago June 26 '92.   C: ECD. Dcc.

CD - JAM BOYD SILVER BOWL
ALL OF US AS 12/2
CD1: Intro - Touch Of Grey/ Walkin Blues/ Althea/
When I Paint My Masterpiece/ Row Jimmy/
Cassidy/ Samson And Delilah/ Help On The Way/
Slipknot/ Franklin's Tower
CD2: Looks Like Rain/ Terrapin Station/ Drumz/
Space/ Other One/ Wharf Rat/ Throwing Stones/
Love Light/ E. Brokedown Palace
R: Exs. Soundboard.   S: Las Vegas, Nevada
May 16 '93.   C: ECD. Dcc. Time CD1 78:09.
CD2 77:51.

CD - JAZZ FOR ALLAH
THE SMOKING CROCODILE SMOKE 1
Help On The Way, Slipknot, Franklin's Tower/
Stronger Than Dirt/ Slipknot, Franklin's Tower/
Crazy Fingers/ Help On The Way, Slipknot/ Lazy
Lightning
R: Exs. Soundboard.   S: Outtakes.   C: ECD.
Dcc. Time 76:50.

CD - LAZY LIGHTNINGS
RARE RECORDING COLLECTION RRC 042
Tennessee Jed/ Cassidy/ Pretty Peggy-O/ Mama
Tried/ Mission In The Rain/ Brown Eyed Women/
Lazy Lightning, Supplication/ Row Jimmy Row/
Music Never Stopped/ Might As Well
R: Exs. Soundboard.   S: Auditorium Theatre,
Chicago June 29 '76.   C: ECD. Dcc. Time 73:20.

CD - LEFT IN THE VAULTS VOL. 1
FLASHBACK 08.94.0233
CD1: Intro - Tennessee Jed (8:17)/ Cassidy (4:36)/
Pretty Peggy (8:28)/ Mama Tried (3:02)/ Mission In
The Rain (6:58)/ Looks Like Rain (8:07)/ Brown
Eyed Woman (5:10)/ Lazy Lightning (2:53)/
Supplication (5:14)/ Row Jimmy Row (9:34)/ Music
Never Stopped (5:52)/ Might As Well (6:11)
CD2: Samson And Delilah (6:33)/ Candyman
(7:43)/ Medley: Playing In The Band, The Wheel,
Playing In The Band (reprise) (28:27)/ St. Stephan
(4:44)/ Not Fade Away (15:18)/ St. Stephan
(reprise) (1:01)/ One More Saturday Night (4:59)
R: Exs. Soundboard.   S: Auditorium Theater,
Chicago June 29 '76.   C: ECD. Dcc. Digi-pack.

CD - NEW MEXICAN DREAMS
AMERICAN CONCERT SERIES 055
Let The Good Times Roll (3:50)/ The Race Is On
(3:10)/ Help Is On The Way (8:10)/ Franklin's
Tower (10:25)/ Queen Jane Approximately (6:01)/
Loser (7:23)/ Me And My Uncle (3:00)/ Mexicali
Blues (5:02)/ One More Saturday Night (5:42)/
Touch Of Grey (6:48)
R: Exs. Soundboard.   S: Dominquez.   C: ECD.
Dcc. See 'Back To Fantasy' for part 2.

CD - NOT FAR AWAY ACROSS THE BAY
RARE RECORDING COLLECTION RRC 013
Franklin's Tower (13:12)/ Minglewood Blues
(6:31)/ Tennessee Jed (8:42)/ Looks Like Rain
(7:32)/ Don't Ease Me In (3:56)/ Playing In The
Band (10:14)/ Jam (5:30)/ Not Fade Away (9:29)/

Sugar Magnolia (8:02)
R: G-Vg.   S: Oakland '80.   C: ECD. Dcc.
Time 75:30.

**CD - ON THE BUS (ARTIFACTS FOR THE MIND
AND BODY)**
TEDDY BEAR RECORDS TB 31/2
CD1: The Other One (2:17)/ Cryptical
Envelopment (9:50)/ The Other One (Reprise)
(8:20)/ New Potato Caboose (11:11)/ Doin' That
Rag (5:51)/ Cosmic Charlie (5:48)/ Mountains Of
The Moon (4:46)
CD2: Dark Star (22:35)/ St. Stephens (6:33)/ The
Eleven (7:07)/ Turn On Your Lovelight (17:23)/
Hey Jude (7:27)
R: Vg-Ex. Soundboard.   C: ECD. Dcc. Pic CDs.

CD - PAIN IN MY HEART
OIL WELL RSC 034 CD
High Heel Sneakers/ Pain In My Heart/ Cold Rain
And Snow/ Beat It On Down The Line/ Cream Puff
War/ The Same Thing He Was/ A Friend Of Mine/
Smokestack Lightning/ I'm A King Bee/ Midnight
Hour
R: Vg-Ex. Soundboard.   S: Sausalito Dec. 13
'66.   C: ECD. Dcc. Time 69:02.

CD - RAINFOREST BENEFIT
NOT GUILTY RELEASE NG 44 03 94 2
CD1: Aiko Aiko (6:44)/ Feel Like A Stranger (7:10)/
West LA Fadeaway (7:54)/ Little Red Rooster
(9:30)/ Box Of Rain (5:16)/ Ramble On Rose
(6:53)/ When I Paint My Masterpiece (6:37)/ Don't
Ease Me In (7:46)/ Chinese Bones (6:28)/
Neighborhood Girls (3:56)
CD2: Supplication (8:02)/ Man Smart Woman
Smarter (7:00)/ Every Time You Go Away (6:30)/
What's Going On (6:03)/ Rainforest Space,
Drums, The Wheel (18:03)/ Throwing Away
Stones, Not Fade Away (19:00)
R: Exs. Soundboard.   S: Rainforest Benefit,
Madison Square Garden Sept. 24 '88.   C: ECD.
Dcc. Pic CD.

CD - RENEGADES
VIVID SOUND PRODUCTIONS 51026/27
CD1: Let The Good Times Roll (3:50)/ The Race
Is On (3:10)/ Help On The Way (8:10)/ Franklin'
Tower (10:25)/ Queen Jane Approximately (6:01)/
Loser (7:23)/ Me And My Uncle (3:00)/ Mexicali
Blues (5:02)/ One More Saturday Night (5:42)/
Touch Of Grey (6:48)
CD2: Truckin' (7:46)/ Crazy Fingers (8:13)/ Playing
In The Band (9:19)/ Uncle John's Band (10:43)/
Drums (8:20)/ Space (6:35)/ I Need A Miracle
(3:39)/ Dear Mr. Fantasy (7:03)/ Goin' Down the
Road Feelin' Bad (6:37)/ Around And Around
(6:48)
R: Vg-Ex. Soundboard.   S: Dominguez Hills, CA
May 5 '90.   C: ECD. Dcc.

CD - ROSE GARLAND
TEDDY BEAR RECORDS TB 32
Dire Wolf (4:32)/ Hard To Handle (5:18)/ Mason's

Children (4:49)/ Black Peter (8:06)/ Good Lovin'
(9:46)/ Cold Rain And Snow (5:22)/ China Cat
Sunflower (4:42)/ I Know You Rider (5:57)/ Me &
My Uncle (3:26)/ St. Stephen (5:48)/ Not Fade
Away (2:38)/ Going Down The Road Feeling Bad
(7:00)/ Not Fade Away (Reprise) (3:13)
R: Ex. Soundboard.   S: Tracks 1-9 Golden
Concourse, San Diego, CA Jan. 10 '70. Tracks 10-
13 GYM. S.U.N.Y., Stony Brook, NY Oct. 30th '70
(second show).   C: ECD. Dcc. Pic CD.

CD - SCARLET FIRE
HAWK 039/40
CD1: Cold Rain & Snow (6:21)/ Wang Dance
Doodle (6:25)/ Lazy River Road (7:03)/ Queen
Jane Approximately (6:18)/ Ramble On Rose
(9:32)/ Black-Throated Wind (7:29)/ Liberty (6:43)/
Scarlet Begonias (8:22)/ Fire On The Mountain
(11:49)
CD1: Way To Go Home (9:29)/ Corinna (9:46)/
Uncle John's Band (10:22)/ I Need A Miracle
(4:44)/ Standing On The Moon (9:03)/ Sugar
Magnolia (11:27)/ I Fought The Law (3:43)
R: G-Vg. Audience.   S: Silver Bowl, Las Vegas
May 14 '93.   C: ECD. Dcc. Pic CD.

CD - SOLDIER FIELD I
INTERNATIONAL BROADCAST RECORDINGS
IBR 2305
Bertha (6:27)/ Greatest Story Ever Told (3:35)/
West L.A. Fadeaway (7:27)/ Me And My Uncle
(3:01)/ Big River (5:06)/ Ramble On Rose (7:09)/
When I Paint My Masterpiece (5:10)/ Brown-Eyed
Woman (5:45)/ The Music Never Stopped (9:49)/
Gloria (7:33)/ Corrina Corrina (7:53)
R: Exs, Soundboard.   S: Soldier Field, Chicago
June 26 '92.   C: ECD. Dcc.

CD - SOLDIER FIELD II
INTERNATIONAL BROADCAST RECORDINGS
IBR 2315
Crazy Fingers (8:47)/ Playing In The Band (7:32)/
Uncle John's Band (8:40)/ Drums (11:57)/ Space
(6:40)/ I Need A Miracle (5:15)/ Wharf Rat (10:27)/
Throwing Stones (8:01)/ Not Fade Away (6:45)
R: Exs. Soundboard.   S: Soldier Field, Chicago
June 26 '92.   C: ECD. Dcc.

CD - SPRING BREAK
HAWK 059
Days Between (3:49)/ Peggy-O (8:38)/ Mama
Tried (5:27)/ Big River (7:52)/ Me And My Uncle
(4:24)/ Maggies Farm (7:32)/ El Paso (5:15)/ Black
Throated Wind (9:33)
R: Exs. Soundboard.   S: Track 1 and 6 Omni
Apr. 1 '94. Track 2 Ohio Mar. 21 '94. Track 3-4
Ohio Mar. 20 '94. Track 5-6 Nassau Mar. 24 '94.
Track 7 Omni Mar. 30 '94.   C: ECD. Dcc.
Pic CD.

CD - SUNDANCER
GOLD STANDARD SUN-911
Stealin'/ Wham!/ Hey Little One/ I'm A Hog For
You Baby/ You Don't Have To Ask/ Cold Rain And

Snow/ Next Time You See Me/ Viola Lee Blues/
Big Boss Man/ Sitting On Top Of The World/
Dancing In The Streets/ I Know You Rider/ He
Was A Friend Of Mine/ Next Time You See Me/
Good Morning Little Schoolgirl
R: Vg-Ex. Soundboard.   S: Tracks 1-7 Troupers
Hall, LA Mar. 2 '66. Tracks 8-14 Fillmore
Auditorium, San Francisco July 3 '66. Track 15
Matrix Club, San Francisco Jan. '66.   C: ECD.
Dcc. Time 71:54.

CD - TAKE A TRIP ON THE GOLDEN ROAD
WITH THE GRATEFUL DEAD
GOLD STANDARD 94-14-04
Me And My Uncle/ Lied Cheated/ He Was A
Friend Of Mine/ Smokestack Lightning/ Morning
Dew/ It Hurts Me Too/ Beat It On Down The Line/
Dancin' In The Streets/ The Golden Road (To
Unlimited Devotion)/ Cream Puff War/ Gold Rain
And Snow/ Viola Lee Blues/ Death Don't Have No
Mercy
R: Vg-Ex. Soundboard.   S: Winterland Ballroom,
San Francisco Mar. 18 '67.   C: ECD. Dcc.
Time 72:06.

GREEN DAY

CD - ENDLESS HEADTRIP
ALLEY KAT AK 048
Welcome To Paradise/ One Of My Lies/ Chump/
Longview/ Burn Out/ Only Of You/ Christie Road/
2,000 Light Years Away/ Knowledge/ Going To
Pasalacqua/ F.O.D./ Paper Lanterns/ Dominated
Love Slave/ Road To Acceptance
R. G. Audience.   S: First Avenue Club
Minneapolis Mar. 29 '94.   C: ECD. Dcc. Pic CD.

CD - GREEN
SHINOLA SH 69034
Welcome To Paradise/ One Of My Lies/ Chump/
Long View/ Basket Case/ When I Come Around/
Burn Out/ F.O.D./ Knowledge/ Paper Lanterns/
Dominated Love Slave/ One Of My Lies/ Road To
Acceptance/ Only Of You/ Chump/ Long View/
Burn Out/ 2000 Light Years Away
R: Exs. Soundboard.   S: Woodstock '94.
C: ECD. Time 60:48.

CD - HAVING A BLAST
COCOMELOS RECORDS CM036
Welcome To Paradise/ One Of My Lies/ Chump/
Long View/ Basket Case/ When I Come Around/
Burnout/ F.O.D./ Welcome To Paradise/ Only Of
You/ Chump/ Long View/ Burnout/ Burnout/ 2,000
Light Years Away/ Christie Road/ F.O.D./ Going
To Pasalacqua/ F.O.D./ Knowledge/ Paper
Lanterns/ Dominated Love Slave/ One Of My Lies/
Road To Acceptance
R: Tracks 1-8 Exs. Soundboard. Tracks 9-22 G.
Audience.   S: Tracks 1-8 Woodstock '94. Tracks
9-22 California '94.   C: ECD. Dcc. Pic CD. 77:31.

CD - SPITTING
KISS THE STONE KTS 394

Going To Pasalacqua/ Chump/ Longview/ Burnout/ Coming Clean/ When I Come Around/ Welcome to Paradise/ 2,000 Light Years Away/ Basket Case/ All By Myself/ Dominated Love Slave/ F.O.D./ Paper Lanterns/ Christie Road/ She/ One Of My Lies/ Only Of You/ Road To Acceptance
R: Ex.   S: Aragon Ballroom, Chicago Nov. 10 '94.   C: ECD. Dcc. Pic CD. Time 55:23.

CD - WOODSTOCK 1994 & MUCH MORE
OCTOPUS OCTO 051
Welcome To Paradise (3:58)/ What Are My Lies (2:08)/ Chump (3:28)/ Longview (3:18)/ Basket Case (3:00)/ When I Come Around (2:46)/ Burnout (2:23)/ F.O.D. (2:36)/ Paper Lanterns (3:15)/ Welcome To Paradise (4:10)/ What Are You Lies (2:35)/ Chump (2:46)/ Longview (3:31)/ Burnout (2:18)/ Only Of You (3:50)/ Christy Road (4:03)/ Going To Passalacqua (Infatuation) (4:08)/ Knowledge (2:28)/ 2,000 Light Years Away (1:56)/ F.O.D. (2:46)/ Paper Lanterns (includes bits & pieces of several crazy covers) (10:56)/ Dominated Love Slave (2:30)
R: Exs. Soundboard.   S: Tracks 1-9 Woodstock Festival Saugerties, NY Aug. 13 '94. Tracks 10-22 Tempe, Florida Mar. '94.   C: ECD. Dcc. Pic CD.

GUNS N' ROSES

CD - GET IN THE RING
UZI SUICIDE GNR 30151
CD1: Intro/ MC/ It's So Easy/ Welcome To The Jungle/ Mr. Brownstone/ Live And Let Die/ Nightrain/ So Fine/ Attitude/ Double Talkin' Jive/ Slash Solo/ Voodoo Chile/ Civil War/ Wild Horses/ Patience/ It's All Right/ November Rain
CD2: Horn Section Intro/ Bad Obsession/ Band Intro/ Matt Sorum Solo/ You Could Be Mine/ Slash Solo/ The Godfather/ All I Ever Needed/ Sweet Child O' Mine/ Only Woman Bleed/ Knockin' On Heaven's Door/ Don't Cry/ The Wall/ Paradise City/ Outro
R: Poor-G. Audience.   S: 'Get In The Ring Mother Fucker' world tour, The Dome Jan. 15 '93.   C: ECD. Dcc. Time CD1 74:07. CD2 64:28.

CD - GET IN THE RING MOTHER F**KER ROUND II
R11 MUSIC CD 01/02
CD1: Night Train (5:06)/ Mr. Brownstone (4:39)/ Live & Let Die (3:44)/ Welcome To The Jungle (5:32)/ Attitude (1:56)/ It's So Easy (3:25)/ Double Talking Jive (10:53)/ Ain't The First (2:52)/ You're Crazy (4:54)/ Used To Love Her (3:18)/ Patience Includes Imagine (8:43)/ Knockin' On Heaven's Door (11:24)/ November Rain (9:43)
CD2: Dead Horse (6:44)/ Band Introductions (includes drum solo) (4:18)/ You Could Be Mine (includes Slash solo & guitar - piano duet) (14:09)/ Sweet Child 'O' Mine (7:34)/ Paradise City (9:48)/ Dead Flowers (4:39)/ Knockin' On Heavens Door (Mike Monroe on harmonica - 12:28)/ Honky Tonk Woman (with Ron Wood & Mike Monroe - 4:54)/

Paradise City (10:18)
R: G. Audience.   S: Milton Keynes, England May 29 '93. CD2 tracks 4-9 Milton Keynes May 30 '93.
C: ECD. Dcc.

CD - HEAVEN WAR
CLASSICAL CL 007
It's So Easy/ Shadow Of Your Love/ Move To The City/ Knockin' On Heaven's Door/ Whole Lotta Rosie/ Patience/ Salt Of The Earth/ Civil War/ Down On The Farm/ Patience/ Mr. Brownstone/ Knockin' On heaven's Door
R: Vg-Ex.   S: Tracks 1, 5 The Marquee, London June 28 '87. Tracks 2-4 The Roxy, LA Mar. 29 '87. Track 6 American Music Awards, LA Shrine Auditorium Jan. 30 '89. Track 7 Rolling Stones Tour, Atlantic City Convention Center Dec. 19 '89. Tracks 8-9 Farm Aid II, Indianapolis Hooters Dome, Apr. 7 '90. Track 10-12 Rock In Rio II, Maracana Stadium Jan. 20 '91.   C: ECD. Dcc. Time 68:53.

CD - LIVE IN ARGENTINA
BIG MUSIC BIG 086/87
CD1: It's So Easy/ Mr. Brownstone/ Live And Let Die/ Welcome To The Jungle/ Attitude/ Double Talkin' Jive/ Dead Flowers/ You Ain't The First/ You're Crazy/ Used To Love Her/ Patience/ Imagine/ Knockin' On Heaven's Door
CD2: November Rain/ Dead Horse/ Matt Sorum Drum Solo/ You Could Be Mine/ Slash Solo/ Godfather's Theme/ Sweet Child O'Mine/ Don't Cry Mother/ Paradise City
R: Exs. Soundboard.   S: Estadio River Plate July 16 '93.   C: ECD. Dcc. Pic CD. Total time 117:08.

CD - LIVE IN ARGENTINA
PING PONG PPR 001-02
C: See ' Live In Argentina' (Big Music 086/87).

CD - NICE FELLAS
HAPPY SKULL SK-04/05
CD1: Welcome To The Jungle/ Mr. Brownstone/ Live & Let Die/ Attitude/ Nice Boy/ So Fine/ Double Talkin' Jive/ Goodnight Irene/ You Don't Want Me/ I Used To Love Her/ Patience
CD2: Knockin' On Heaven's Door/ November Rain/ Everybody Needs Somebody/ I Keep Smiling/ Slash Solo/ Sweet Child O'Mine/ Don't Cry/ Paradise City
R: G-Vg. Audience.   S: Hartford, Conn. Mar. 9 '93.   C: ECD. Dcc. Time CD1 64:30. CD2 56:47.

CD - NOVEMBER RAIN (VOL. 4)
BANANA BAN-015-D
Intro (0:59)/ Live And Let Die (15:14)/ Theme From 'The Godfather' (4:11)/ Sweet Child O' Mine (7:38)/ Welcome To The Jungle (6:48)/ Only Women Bleed (1:21)/ Knockin' On Heaven's Door (3:49)/ Mama Kin (4:30)/ Train Kept A-Rollin' (4:31)/ Don't Cry (7:11)/ Paradise City (6:59)
R: Ex. Soundboard.   S: Europe '92.
C: Australian CD. Dcc.

CD - SWEET CHILD O'MINE (VOL. 2)
BANANA BAN-014-B
Pretty Tied Up (The Perils Of Rock And Roll
Decadence) (5:23)/ Mr. Brownstone (4:00)/
Patience (6:16)/ Theme From 'The Godfather'
(1:40)/ Double Talkin' Jive (4:21)/ Welcome To
The Jungle (4:240/ Only Women Bleed (0:57)/
Knockin' On Heaven's Door (11:32)/ You Could Be
Mine (8:58)/ Civil War (7:13)/ I Keep Smiling (5:15)
R: G. Soundboard.   S: America '91.
C: Australian CD. Dcc. Gold disc.

CD - 20 LTD
MINOTAURO RECORDS 20a/20b
CD1: Introduction (3:53)/ Welcome To The Jungle
(5:50)/ Mr. Brownstone (4:56)/ Live And Let Die
(4:00)/ Attitude (3:00)/ Instrumental Blues (9:10)/
Yesterday (3:22)/ Double Talkin' Jive (8:00)/
Instrumental Voodoo Chile (2:20)/ Civil War (8:23)
CD2: It's Alright (7:40)/ November Rain (10:10)/
Solo Matt Sorum (6:10)/ You Could Be Mine
(9:16)/ Instrumental Slash (3:40)/ The Godfather
(3:30)/ Sweet Child O'Mine (6:45)/ Knockin' On
Heaven's Door (9:04)/ Don't Cry (6:30)/ Paradise
City
R: Vg.   S: Buenos Aires, Argentina Dec. 5 '92.
C: ECD.

CD - YOU COULD BE MINE (VOL. 1)
BANANA BAN-013-A
Wild Horses (3:52)/ Live And Let Die (3:31)/ Don't
Cry (4:32)/ Bad Obsession (6:56)/ Medley: Double
Talkin' Jive, Voodoo Chile (Slight Return) (8:46)/
Civil War (8:10)/ November Rain (9:57)/ Knockin'
On Heaven's Door (10:13)/ Pretty Tied Up (The
Perils Of Rock 'N' Roll Decadence) (5:12)/ You
Could Be Mine (6:03)
R: Exs. Soundboard.   S: USA '93.
C: Australian CD. Dcc.

H

HACKETT, STEVE

CD - FULL MOON AND EMPTY SKIES
ALTERNATIVE RECORD COMPANY ARC 009-
10
CD1: Medley: Myopia, Los Endos, Ace Of Wands,
Hackett To Bits/ Camino Royale/ Vampire With A
Healthy Appetite/ Sierra Quemada/ Take These
Pearls/ In The Heart Of The City/ Walking Away
From Rainbows/ There Are Many Sides To The
Night/ Dark As The Grave/ Death Charge/ Always
Somewhere Else/ Lost In Your Eyes
CD2: Every Day/ Medley: Spectral Mornings, Firth
Of Fifth, Clocks/ Medley: Black Light, Blood On
The Rooftops, Horizons/ Nuovo Cinema Paradiso/
...In The Quiet Earth/ The Air-Conditioned
Nightmare/ Racing In A (1)/ Slogans (2)/ Time To
Get Out (2)/ The Steppes (2)/ Kim (3)/ Medley:
The Show, I Know What I Like (3)/ Overnight
Sleeper (4)
R: Vg. Audience. Some G.   S: Frascati, Villa

Torlonia July 5 '93. (1) Bremen, Musikladen
Oct.17 '79. (2) Chicago, Park West Oct. 10 '80. (3)
Mestre, Paslasport Nov. 28 '80. (4) Reading Rock
Festival June 28 '81.   C: ECD. Dcc. Limited
edition of 1000 copies. Time CD1 67:53.
CD2 75:50.

HARRY, DEBORAH

CD - THE ULTIMATE BLOND
LIVE STORM LSCD 51529
Union City Blue (5:32)/ Dreaming (3:52)/ I Want
That Man (4:04)/ Heart Of Glass (4:23)/ Rapture
(6:23)/ (I'm Always) Touched By Your Presence
Dear (3:05)/ Hanging Around On The Telephone
(2:35)/ Standing In My Way (2:48)/ The Bright Side
(5:30)/ French Kissin' In The U.S.A. (4:43)/ Call
Me (3:22)/ Atomic (5:11)/ The Hunter (3:53)/ Love
Light (3:53)/ Get Your Way (5:11)/ Kiss It Better
(3:52)/ Detroit 442 (2:27)/ Bike Boy (2:31)
R: Vg-Ex. Audience.   S: 'Summer XS' Wembley
Stadium July 7 '91. Tracks 13-18 Town And
Country Club, London Nov. '89.

HAWKWIND

CD - KINGS OF SPEED, LORDS OF LIGHT
GOLDEN VOID PRODUCTION
Needle Gun (5:50)/ Ejection, Time We Left This
World Today (9:00)/ Blue Shift, The Right Stuff
(12:35)/ Snake Dance, Night Of The Hawks (9:00)/
Levitation (13:00)/ Masters Of The Universe
(6:00)/ The Golden Void (7:00)/ Paranoia Part 2,
Hassanisahba (7:05)/ LSD (9:50)
H: G-Vg. Audience.   S: Latin Quarter, Detroit
May 18 '91.   C: ECD. Dcc. Pic CD.

HEART

CD - DESIRE ROCKS ON UNPLUGGED AND
ELECTRIC
ROYAL SOUND MUSIC RSM 052 SQ
Battle Of Evermore/ Rage/ Love Hurts/ Black On
Black/ Ring Them Bells/ Back To Avalon/ Dog And
Butterfly/ Cherry Blossom Road/ Will You Be
There (In The Morning)/ The Woman In Me/ Alone/
These Dreams/ Barracuda/ Nothin' At All/ What
About Love/ Who Will You Run To
S: Seattle '88, Hollywood '93 and Canada '94.
C: ECD.

CD - HEART 'N' ZEPPELIN
ALL OF US AS 26
Rock And Roll (4:14)/ Heartless (4:47)/ The Battle
Of Evermore (4:48)/ White Lightning & Wine
(5:26)/ The Rover (5:03)/ Devil Delight (4:50)/
Magic Man (9:28)/ Crazy On You (4:31)/
Barracuda (3:53)
R: Exs. Soundboard.   S: Chicago '76.   C: ECD.
Dcc.

CD - UNPLUGGED
KISS THE STONE KTS 291
Back To Avalon (4:41)/ Dog And Butterfly (6:39)/

Cherry Blossom Road (5:02)/ These Dreams (4:53)/ Will You Be There (4:41)/ The Woman In Me (5:29)/ Alone (4:25)/ Love Hurts (4:09)/ Crazy On You (not 'Dream Boat Annie' as on cover - 5:03)/ Ring Them Bells (4:16)
R: Exs. Soundboard. S: Whistler, Canada Mar. 18 '94. C: ECD. Dcc. Pic CD.

HELMET

CD - EARTH TONES
HAWK 004
Sinatra/ Your Head/ Distracted/ Better/ Turned Out/ Iron Head/ He Feels Bad/ Give It/ Black Top/ Role Model/ In The Meantime/ Unsung
R: G-Vg. Audience. S: LA '92. C: ECD. Dcc. Pic CD. Time 52:122.

HENDRIX, JIMI

CD - CALLING LONG DISTANCE
DYNAMITE STUDIO DS930055
The Burning Of The Midnight Lamp/ Little Miss Lover/ Foxy Lady/ Catfish Blues/ Oh Man Is This Me Or What?/ Purple Haze/ Fire/ Getting My Heart Back/ Spanish Castle Magic/ Slow Walkin' Talk/ Hendrix, Cox Jam/ Hey Baby/ Red House
S: Track 1 Stockholm Sept. 11 '67. Track 2 studio outtake Oct. '67. Track 3-4 Holland Nov. 10 '67. Track 5 Tony Hall interview Dec. 15 '67. Track 6 Canada Mar. 19 '68 second show. Tracks 7-8 Miami Pop May 18 '68. Track 9 second show, Winterland, San Francisco Oct. 11 '68. Track 10 Robert Wyatt outtake Oct. '68. Track 11 Electric Lady Studios '70. Track 12-13 Copenhagen Sept. 11 '70. C: Japanese CD.

CD - DE LANE LEA DEMOS AND OLYMPIC OUTS
GOLD STANDARD
Purple Haze (De Lane Lea Studios Feb. 7 '67 or Olympic Studios Feb. 3 '67)/ Red House (takes 1-4 De Lane Lea Studios Dec. 12 '66 or Mar. 29 '67)/ Ma-Pouppee-Qui-Fait-No (De Lane Lea Studios winter '66-'67)/ I Don't Live Today (takes 1-4 De Lane Lea Studios Feb. 20 '67)/ The Wind Cries Mary (De Lane Lea Studios Jan. 11, 17 Feb. 7 '67)/ Takin' Care Of No Business (Olympic Studios May 4 '67)/ Gypsy Blood (Olympic Studios Feb. 26 '69)/ Lover Man (Olympic Studios Feb. '69)/ Little One (Olympic Studios Jan. 26 '68)/ Room Full Of Mirrors (Olympic Studios Feb. 14-16 '69)/ Mr. Bad Luck (May 4 '67)/ Sunshine Of Your Love (Feb. '69)/ Shame Shame Shame (Feb. '69)/ Cat Talkin' To Me (Olympic Studios Jan. '68 or Feb. '69)
R: Exs. Soundboard. C: ECD. Dcc. Time 70:36.

CD - DON'T MISS HIM THIS TIME (THE COMPLETE SHOW)
TRIANGLE PYCD 096
Let Me Stand Next To Your Fire (3:37)/ Hey Joe (4:54)/ Spanish Castle Magic, Drum Solo (9:06)/ Sunshine Of Your Love, Spanish Castle Magic

(2:54)/ Red House (14:13)/ I Don't Live Today (7:28)/ Foxy Lady (6:09)/ Purple Haze (5:49)/ Voodoo Child (10:36)
R: Ex. Soundboard. S: International Sport Arena, San Diego '69. C: ECD. Dcc.

CD - EVERY WAY TO PARADISE
TINTAGEL TIBX 0021/22/23/24
CD1: Earth Blue (instrumental - Record Plant Jan. '70) (4:23)/ Look Over Yonder (rough mix - T.T.G. Studios, Hollywood Oct. '68) (3:04)/ Room Full Of Mirrors (rough mix - Record Plant Apr. '69) (3:05)/ Electric Indians (Electric Ladyland Studios Aug. 9-12 '69) (8:56)/ Voodoo Blues (Electric Ladyland Studios Aug. 9-12 '66) (4:51)/ Cactus (Record Plant, New York May 22 '69) (3:22)/ Driving South Jam (instrumental jam unknown location) (45:26)
CD2: America The Beautiful (studio recording '68/'69) (4:50)/ Cherokee Mist (Record Plant, New York May 2 '68) (6:42)/ Valleys Of Neptune (Record Plant May 2 '68) (31:16)/ Martin Luther King (Record Plant, Late '69) (5:49)/ Home Acoustic Jam (Jim's house, Sept. 69) (14:33)/ Gypsy Sunset (unreleased studio outtake location unknown) (2:59)/ Valleys Of Neptune (Record Plant May 2/5 '68) (5:44)
CD3: Where Some (instrumental, Electric Ladyland Studio late '68/'69) (4:16)/ Seven Dollars In My Pocket (Record Plant Studios Jan. 23 '70) (14:24)/ Instrumental Jam (Electric Ladyland Studio Late '68/'69) (5:04)/ Calling All Devil's Children (T.T.G. Studios, Hollywood Oct. 21 '68) (7:37)/ Easy Blues (Record Plant Studios, New York '69/'70) (7:45)/ Little Drummer Boy - Silent Night (location unknown, David Onorah, Harry Simeone & Katherine Devis vocals) (2:27)/ Danny Boy (location unknown, instrumental) (5:08)/ Tomorrow Never Knows (Cafe Au Go Go, New York June 17 '68) (21:57)
CD4: The Things I Used To Do (Record Plant Studios '69) (6:51)/ Untitled Jam (Record Plant Studios May 15 '69) (3:43)/ Ain't Too Proud To Beg (BBC Studios Oct. 6 '67) (4:53)/ Shame, Shame, Shame (location unknown late '68) (1:56)/ Jungle Jam (Hit Studios Sept. '69) (4:39)/ Jazz Jimi Jazz (Record Plant Studios '69) (6:16)/ Little One (take 2)(Olympia Studio Jan. 26 '68) (6:00)/ Little One (take 2) (Olympic Studios Jan. 26 '68) (7:07)/ Demo Outtake (with Robert Wyatt) (T.T.G. Studios, Hollywood Oct. 30 '68) (4:14)/ Gloomy Monday (with Curtis Knight) (takes 1 & 2) (PPX Studios, New York July '67) (3:18)
R: Vg-Ex. Some G. C: ECD. Box set. Dcc. Each case has Dcc. Pic CDs. 24 page book.

CD - THE FILLMORE CONCERTS
WHOOPY CAT WKP-0006/7
CD1: Power Of Soul/ Lover Man/ Hear My Train A Comin'/ Them Changes/ Machine Gun/ Auld Lang Syne/ Who Knows/ Steppin' Stone/ Burning Desire/ Fire/ Ezy Ryder
CD2: Machine Gun/ Power Of Soul/ Stone Free/ Them Changes/ Message To Love/ Stop
R: Vg. Soundboard. S: Fillmore East, NYC Dec.

31 '69.   C: Japanese CD.

CD - FLAMING GUITAR
ROCK CALENDAR RECORDS RC 2108
Hear My Train A' Comin'/ Fire/ Spanish Castle
Magic/ Red House/ I Don't Live Today/ Foxy Lady/
Purple Haze/ Voodoo Chile/ Room Full Of Mirrors/
Sunshine Of Your Love
R: G. Audience.   S: San Jose Pop Festival May
25 '69.   C: ECD.

CD - FREAK OUT BLUES
GH 001
Intro By Jimi (0:03) (US Army broadcast '67)/
Midnight Lightning (4:02) (Olympic Studio Feb. 14
'69)/ Voodoo Chile (8:57) (Record Plant May 2
'68)/ Rainy Day Try Out (1:33) (Record Plant May
10 '68)/ Red House (6:55) (TTG Studios Oct. 21
'68)/ Bleeding Heart (3:39) (Record Plant May
'70)/ Blue Window Jam (8:23) (Mercury Studio
Mar. 15 '69)/ Villanova Junction Blues (3:55)
(Record Plant Nov. 14 '69)/ Funky Blues Jam
(1:46) (unknown)/ Once I Had A Woman (5:17)*/
Police Blues (11:13)*/ Country Blues (6:40)*/
Freedom Jam (8:27)*/ Acoustic Medley (3:23)
R: G-Vg.   S: Record Plant Jan. 23 '70. *Jimi's
NYC apartment early '70.   C: ECD. Dbw.

CD - GONE BUT NOT FORGOTTEN
TEDDY BEAR RECORDS TB 21
Tax Free (9:51)/ Killin' Floor (5:17)/ Fire (2:51)/
Red House (9:41)/ Foxy Lady (4:50)/ Hey Joe
(5:28)/ Spanish Castle Magic (4:05)/ Purple Haze
(6:38)
R. G-Vg.   S: Second show, Capitol Theatre,
Ottawa, Canada Mar. 19 '68.   C: ECD. Pic CD.

CD - GYPSY HAZE
LORDS OF ARCHIVE RECORDS L.A.R. 6
Message Of Love/ Ezy Rider, Paper Airplanes
(false start)/ Paper Airplanes/ Earth Blues/ Them
Changes (take 1)/ Them Changes (take 2)/ Lover
Man (take 1)/ Lover Man (take 2)/ Paper
Airplanes*/ Lover Man*/ Hear My Train*/ Them
Changes*/ Little Drummer Boy**
R: Ex. Soundboard. **Vg. Some hiss.   S: Record
Plant, NYC late '69. *First show, Fillmore East,
NYC Dec. 31 '69. **Late '69 Band Of Gypsys
promo for radio airplay Dec. '69.   C: ECD. Dcc.
Time 63:23.

CD - IT'S ONLY A PAPERMOON
LUNA RECORDS 9420
Here Comes Your Lover Man (4:08)/ Let Me Stand
Next To Your Fire (3:19)/ Foxy Lady (5:06)/ Red
House (15:12)/ Hey Jude (7:05)/ Sunshine Of Your
Love, Getting My Heart Back Together Again
(9:19)/ Can You Please Crawl Out Your Window
(5:28)/ Purple Haze (6:10)/ Are You Experienced
(8:52)/ I Don't Live Today (7:05
R: G-Vg.   S: Tracks 1-8 Fillmore East, NYC Mar.
10 '68. Track 9 Col Ballroom, Davenport Aug. 11
'68. Track 10 San Jose Pop Festival, Santa Clara,
CA May 25 '69.   C: ECD. Dcc.

CD - 1968 A.D. PART TWO
WHOOPY CAT WKP-0013
1983... (A Merman I Should Turn To Be)/ Angel/
Cherokee Mist/ Hear My Train A Comin'/ Voodoo
Chile/ Cherokee Mist (Reprise)/ Gypsy Eyes/ Long
Hot Summer Night/ Have You Ever Been (To
Electric Ladyland)/ All Along The Watchtower/
Voodoo Chile/ Rainy Day Dream Away/ 1983... (A
Merman I Should Turn To Be)/ Have You Ever
Been (To Electric Ladyland)/ Little Miss Strange/
Somewhere/ 1983... (A Merman I Should Turn To
Be)
R: Ex. Soundboard. Tracks 11-14 Vg.   S: Tracks
1-8 home demos early '68. Tracks 9-17 studio
outtakes.   C: Japanese CD. Dcc. Time 74:59.

CD - NOT JUST A VOODOO CHILE
PILOT RECORDS HJCD071
Beyond The Valleys Of Neptune/ Martin Luther
King/ Come On/ Home Acoustic Jam
R: G.   S: Tracks 1 and 3 Record Plant May 2
'68. Track 2 Record Plant late '69. Track 4 Jimi's
House Sept. '69.

CD - THE OFFICIAL BOOTLEG ALBUM
YELLOW DOG YD 051
Drivin' South (3:21)/ Catfish Blues (5:29)/ Wait Till
Tomorrow (2:57)/ Burning Of The Midnight Lamp
(3:58)/ Sgt. Pepper's Lonely Hearts Club Band
(1:41)/ Hound Dog (2:43)/ Electric Church, Red
House (7:25)/ Are You Experienced? (6:18)/ Look
Over Yonder (2:30)/ Earth Blues (4:13)/ The Wind
Cries Mary (4:17)/ Little Wing (3:34)/ 1983... (A
Merman I Should Turn To Be) (7:39)/ Angel (3:20)/
God Save The Queen (5:06)/ Cherokee Mist
(7:08)
R: Vg-Ex.   C: ECD. Dcc.

CD - PARIS 66/67
WHOOPY CAT WKP-0012
Killing Floor (1:11)/ Hey Joe (2:50)/ Foxy Lady
(3:54)/ The Wind Cries Mary (3:23)/ Rock Me
Baby (3:41)/ Red House (6:01)/ Purple Hazed
(5:11)/ Wild Thing (5:37)/ Have Mercy (3:15)/ EXP
(2:14)/ Up From The Skies (4:37)/ Little Wing
(4:06)/ I Don't Live Today (8:19)/ Can You Please
Crawl Out Your Window? (3:11)
R: G-Vg.   S: Tracks 1-2 L'Olympia, Paris Oct. 18
'66. Tracks 3-8 L'Olympia, Paris Oct. 9 '67. Track
9 Flamingo Club, London Feb. 4 '67. Tracks 10-13
Konsethuset, Stockholm, Sweden Jan. 8 '68.
Track 14 Fillmore East, NYC May 10 '68.
C: Japanese CD. Dcc. Talk over first two tracks.
Time 68:26.

CD - PURPLE HAZE IN WOODSTOCK
ITM 960004
Announcement (0:33)/ Hear My Train A Coming
(9:29)/ Spanish Castle Magic (8:47)/ Lover Man
(4:47)/ Fire (3:14)/ Voodoo Chile (14:55)/ Star
Spangled Banner (3:53)/ Purple Haze (5:14)/ Hey
Joe (4:53)
R: Exs. Soundboard.   S: Woodstock, New York

Aug. 8 '69.   C: ECD. Dbw. Red type. Disc reads 'Albert Collins - Alive And Cool' (ITM 960003) but it's Hendrix.

CD - SOTHEBY'S PRIVATE REELS
JHR OO3/004
CD1: Castles Made Of Sand #1 (2:48)/ Spanish Castle Magic #1 (2:50)/ Jam #1 (4:48)/ Electric Ladyland #1 (5:04)/ Wait Until Tomorrow #1 (3:24)/ Ain't No Telling #1 (1:54)/ Instrumental #1 (3:35)/ Instrumental #2 (3:36)/ All Along The Watchtower (3:48)/ One Rainy Wish #1 (3:52)/ She's So Fine (2:37)/ Axis Bold As Love (3:31)/ EXP (1:55)/ Up From The Skies (2:55)/ Calling All Devil's Children (12:52)/ Electric Ladyland #2 (6:17)
CD2: Jam #2 (4:30)/ Electric Ladyland #3 (4:37)/ Wait Until Tomorrow #2 (3:15)/ Ain't No Telling #2 (1:46)/ Instrumental #3 (3:23)/ Instrumental #4 (3:25)/ Castles Made Of Sand #2 (2:40)/ Spanish Castle Magic #2 (2:40)/ Jam #3 (12:26)/ Electric Ladyland #4 (5:28)/ One Rainy Wish #2 (3:40)/ May This Be Love (3:16)/ Fire (2:50)/ Are You Experienced? (4:22)/ Foxy Lady (3:27)/ I Don't Live Today (4:02)/ Radio One Jingle (1:07)
R: Vg. Soundboard.   S: Studio.   C: ECD. Dbw.

CD - STUDIO EXPERIENCE
SODIUM HAZE MUSIC SH 009
Jam 1/ Jam 2/ Look Over Yonder*/ Send My Love To You*/ Drifting (demo)/ Belly Button Window (demo)/ Freedom*/ Valley Of Neptune*/ Long Hot Summer Night (acoustic)/ 1983 (acoustic demo)/ Angel (acoustic demo)/ Voodoo Chile*/ Come On*/ Gypsy Eyes (demo)
R: G.   S: Home tape '69. *Unreleased take.

CD - STUDIO RECORDINGS 1967-68
KISS THE SKY 00016
Purple Haze (experimental mix)/ Red House (four takes)/ Ma Pouppee Qui Fait No (cover version)/ I Don't Live Today (four takes)/ Fire (instrumental)/ The Wind Cries Mary (instrumental)/ Takin' Care Of Business (complete with horns)/ Cryin' Blue Rain (slow blues)/ Lover Man (alternative version)/ There Ain't Nothing Wrong (Noel Redding vocal)/ Room Full Of Mirrors (alternative version)/ Look Over Yonder (alternative version)/ Sunshine Of Your Love (studio version)/ Shame Shame Shame (alternative version)/ Cat Talkin' To Me (Mitch Mitchell vocals)
R: Ex. Soundboard.   S: Tracks 1-6 '67. Tracks 7-15 '68.   C: ECD. Dcc. Time 70:36.

CD - THANK'S OTTAWA FOR THE MEMORIES
LUNA RECORDS LU 9319
Intro, Killin' Floor/ Tax Free/ Fire/ Red House/ Foxy Lady/ Hey Joe/ Spanish Castle Magic/ Purple Haze/ Hound Dog (acoustic)/ Hey Joe/ Purple Haze/ Hear My Train A Comin' (acoustic)
S: Ottawa, Canada Mar. 19 '68. *Marquee Club. **Outtakes.   C: ECD.

CD - THIS GUITAR ON FIRE
BLACK SUN MUSIC BSM 001
Hear My Train A Comin' (9:30)/ Fire (6:12)/ Spanish Castle Magic (5:20)/ Red House (11:39)/ I Don't Live Today (6:43)/ Foxy Lady (3:23)/ Purple Haze (3:43)/ Voodoo Chile (15:30)/ Room Full Of Mirrors (2:24)/ Sunshine Of Your Love (4:33)
R: G. Audience.   S: San Jose Pop Festival Mar. 15 '69.   C: ECD. Dcc.

CD - TTG STUDIOS???
WHO AM I? WAI 015
I'm A Man/ Help Me In My Weakness/ Instrumental/ Lover Man (instrumental)/ Freedom/ Drifting/ Instrumental/ I See Fingers.../ Calling All Devil Children (Party)/ Organ Jazz Solo/ Let The Sun Take A Holiday/ Rainy Day Rain All Day/ Gypsy Eyes/ Three Little Bears/ Tax Free/ Instrumental/ Instrumental/ Instrumental/ Valley Of Neptune (take 1)/ Valley Of Neptune (take 2)
R: Poor-G.   S: Studio outtakes '68 - '70.

CD - THE ULTIMATE BBC COLLECTION 1967
CLASSICAL CL 006
Hey Joe (4:01)/ Foxy Lady (2:45)/ Stone Free (3:26)/ Love Or Confusion (2:55)/ Purple Hazed (3:04)/ Killing Floor (2:27)/ Fire (2:33)/ The Wind Cries Mary (3:05)/ Wild Thing (1:51)/ Burning Of The Midnight Lamp (3:41)/ Jam #1 (3:20)/ Jam #2 (5:02)/ Little Miss Lover (2:55)/ Drivin' South (4:48)/ Experiencing The Blues (5:27)/ Hound Dog (2:43)/ All Along The Watchtower (3:57)/ Can You Please Crawl Out Your Window (3:25)/ Spanish Castle Magic (3:12)/ Day Tripper (3:14)/ Getting My Heart Back Together (4:57)/ Wait Until Tomorrow (3:04)
R: Ex. Soundboard.   S: BBC '67.   C: ECD. Dcc.

CD - UNSURPASSED STUDIO TAKES
YELLOW DOG YD 050
Hey Joe (unreleased reference vocal) (3:06)/ Lover Man (3:11)/ All Along The Watchtower (unreleased different mix) (3:59)/ Three Little Bears (12:37)/ Indian Song (also known as 'Cherokee Mist') (7:09)/ Trying To Be (In Love) (7:21)/ Crosstown Traffic (2:28)/ Message To Love (7:43)/ Crash Landing (4:25)/ Somewhere (Over The Rainbow) (3:23)/ Double Guitars (3:23)/ Astro Man Jam (11:26)
R: Exs. Soundboard.   S: Unreleased studio takes.   C: ECD. Dcc.

CD - WINTERLAND VOL. 1
WHOOPY CAT
CD1: First Show/ Are You Experienced/ Voodoo Child (Slight Return)/ Red House/ Foxy Lady/ Like A Rolling Stone/ This Is America/ Purple Haze
CD2: Second Show/ Tax Free/ Lover Man/ Sunshine Of Your Love/ Killing Floor/ Hey Joe/ This Is America/ Purple Haze.
S: Winterland, San Francisco.   C: Japanese CD.

CD - WINTERLAND VOL. 3
WHOOPY CAT
CD1: Fire/ Lover Man/ Like A Rolling Stone/ Foxy
Lady/ Jam/ Tax Free/ Hey Joe/ Purple Haze/ Wild
Thing
CD2: Foxy Lady/ Manic Depression/ Sunshine Of
Your Love/ Little Wing/ Spanish Castle Magic/ Red
House/ Voodoo Child (Slight Return)/ This Is
America/ Purple Haze
S: Winterland, San Francisco.   C: Japanese CD.

CD - WOKE UP THIS MORNING AND FOUND
MYSELF DEAD
RL CD 0068
Red House/ Wake Up This Morning And You Find
Yourself Dead/ Bleeding Heart/ Morrison's
Lament/ Tomorrow Never Knows/ Uranus Rock/
Outside Woman Blues/ Sunshine Of Your Love
R: G. Audience.   S: NYC Mar. 13 '68.

HENLEY, DON

CD - CALIFORNIA DESPERADOS
WESTERN BEAT RSM 40 SQ
Boys Of Summer/ End Of Innocence/ One Of
These Nights/ Well Well Well/ Margaritaville*/
Volcano*/ Hotel California/ Life In The Fast Lane/
The Heart Of The Matter/ Sunset Grill/ Dirty
Laundry/ All She Wants To Do Is Dance/
Desperado
R: Exs. Soundboard.   S: Labour Day Benefit
Concert, Fox Bowl Stadium, Boston '93.
C: ECD. Dcc. *With Jimmy Buffett. Time 71:58.

HERSH, KRISTIN

CD - SPARKLE
KISS THE STONE KTS 310
Sundrops (4:10)/ Houdini Blues (4:51)/ Me And My
Charms (4:45)/ Your Ghost (3:12)/ Firepile (2:22)/
Pearl (4:08)/ Delicate Cutters (4:12)/ Soap And
Water (2:29)/ Uncle June & Aunt Kiyoti (2:23)/
Cottonmouth (2:47)/ Your Ghost (2) (3:15)/ Me
And My Charms (2) (4:28)/ Houdini Blues (2)
(4:31)/ Sundrops (2) (3:54)/ A Loon (4:54)/ Me And
My Charms (3) (4:43)/ Your Ghost (3) (3:12)
R: Exs. Soundboard.   S: 'Hips And Makers'
promotional tour '94.   C: ECD. Dcc. Pic CD.
Time 64:21.

HIATT, JOHN

CD - LIGHTNING ROD GUITARS
ROCKS 92128
It's Come To You (4:23)/ Drive South (5:41)/
Paper Thin (4:41)/ Hold My Baby Tight (6:57)/
Child Of The Wild Blue Yonder (7:50)/ Straight Out
Of Time (5:44)/ A Thing Called Love (7:32)/ Cross
My Fingers (3:59)/ Feels Like Rain (6:04)/ Have A
Little Faith In Me (5:10)/ Perfectly Good Guitar
(4:55)
R: Ex. Audience.   S: Grant Park, Chicago June
26 '93.   C: ECD.

CD - A THING CALLED LIVE
ROYAL SOUND MUSIC RSM 043 SQ
Icy Blue Heart (4:44)/ Drive South (6:02)/ Cross
My Fingers (4:44)/ Paper Thin (5:22)/ Like Ya Dad
Did (6:32)/ Thing Called Love (7:20)/ Slow Turning
(10:09)/ Seven Little Indians (5:05)/ Is Anybody
There (5:56)/ Bring Back Your Love To Me (4:20)/
Child Of The Wild Blue Yonder (5:42)/ Rock Back
Billy (5:43)
R: Exs. Soundboard.   S: 'Perfectly Good Guitar'
tour California '93. Track 8-12 'Stolen Moments'
tour USA '90.   C: ECD. Dcc.

HITCHCOCK, ROBYN & THE EGYPTIANS

CD - STAND BACK, DENNIS!
FEG 001
I Often Dream Of Trains/ I Wish I Was A Pretty
Girl/ The Cars She Used To Drive/ Acid Bird/
Bass/ Tropical Flesh Mandala/ Element Of Light/
I'm Only You/ Birdshead/ Flesh No. 1/ Balloon
Man/ The Man With The Lightbulb Head/ Heaven/
Uncorrected Personality Traits/ Listening To The
Higsons/ The Queen Of Eyes/ A Globe Of Frogs/
Sad Eyed Lady Of The Lowlands/ The Crystal
Ship
R: Exs. Audience.   S: Tracks 1-17 Athens,
Georgia Mar. 2 '88. Track 18 KCRW-FM, Santa
Monica, CA Apr. 24 '89. Track 19 KROQ-FM, Los
Angeles Apr. 24 '89.   C: ECD. Dbw. Yellow type.
Time 74:00.

HOLE

CD - COURTNEY LOVE & HOLE
SHINOLA SH 69012
Pretty On The Inside (4:12)/ Violet (2:51)/ Garbage
Man (2:54)/ Berry (5:44)/ Dicknail (5:48)/ Mrs.
Jones (3:26)/ Doll Parts (8:15)/ Starbelly (4:11)/
Teenage Whore (1:45)/ Babydoll (5:10)
R: G-Vg. Audience.   S: Seattle '93.   C: ECD.
Dcc.

CD - KISS AWAY THE DARKEST DAY
KISS THE STONE KTS 347
Credit In The Straight World (2:39)/ Beautiful Son
(2:44)/ Miss World (3:07)/ Gutless (2:39)/ Softer
Softest (3:50)/ Doll Parts (3:46)/ Beautiful Son
(2:21)/ Credit In The Straight World (2:36)/
Teenage Whore (2:27)/ Do It Clean, Pennyroyal
Tea (6:57)/ Plump (2:38)/ Never Go Away (1:07)/
Jennifer's Body (4:22)/ Asking For It (5:03)/
Gutless (2:29)/ I Think That I Would Die (3:42)/
Credit In The Straight World (2:39)/ Doll Parts
(3:50)/ Violet (3:49)
R: Exs. Soundboard.   S: Tracks 1 to 6 & 12 to 21
Europe '94. Tracks 7 to 11 Europe '93.   C: ECD.
Dcc. Pic CD. Time 65:30.

CD - LIVE AMSTERDAM 92
HOLE CD93
Doll Parts/ Pretty On The Inside/ Garbage Man/
Violet/ Teenage Whore/ Berry/ Mrs. Jones/
Babydoll/ Dicknail/ Starbelly

R: G. Audience.   C: ECD. Red/white cover.

CD - PRETTY PLEASE
HAWK 006
Pretty On The Inside/ Garbage Man/ Burn Black/
Dick/ Teenage Whore/ Drown Soda/ Berry/
Shinner/ Baby Doll
R: Ex. Audience.   S: California Dec. 12 '91.
C: ECD. Dcc. Pic CD. Time 37:08.

CD - SEATTLE 1993
LIVE STORM LSCD 51617
C: See 'Courtney Love & Hole' (SH 69012) for
songs and source.

HOOKER, JOHN LEE

CD - THE MONTREUX ALBUM
THE SWINGIN' PIG TSP-CD-167
I'm So Lonely/ Mable/ I'm In The Mood/ Crawlin'
Kingsnake/ Baby Lee/ It Serves Me Right To
Suffer/ Boom Boom/ Boogie Chillun I/ The Healer/
Boogie Chillun II
R: Exs. Soundboard.   S: Montreux, Switzerland
July 11 '90.   C: ECD. Time 59:43.

CD - TWICE AS BLUES
CLASSICAL SHOTS - ROBESPIERRE
RECORDS CSCD 003
Ride Johnny Ride (with John Hammond) (4:12)/
Crawlin' King Snake (with Ry Cooder) (6:25)/ I'm
In A Mood For Love (with Bonnie Raitt) (6:40)/ You
Gimme So Much Trouble (with Johnny Johnson)
(4:22)/ Born For Good Luck (Bad Luck Do Me No
Harm) (with Robert Cray) (6:36)/ Higher And
Higher Session (with Robert Cray, Bonnie Raitt,
John Hammond, Johnny Johnson, Ry Cooder,
Albert Collins, Charlie Mussel White) (13:28)/
Boogie Chillun (with Eric Clapton) (5:30)/ Red
House (with Randy California and Booker T.
Jones) (5:30)
R: Exs. Soundboard.   S: Sweetwater, Mill Valley,
CA Mar. 9 '92.   C: ECD. Dcc.

HOT TUNA

CD - TUNA FISHING IN AMERICA
TEDDY BEAR RECORDS TB 37
Keep Your Lamp Trimmed And Burning (6:44)/ Hit
Single #1 (6:40)/ Bowlegged Woman, Knock-
Kneed Man (7:05)/ Easy Now (7:26)/ Song From
The Stainless Cymbal (4:41)/ Invitation (16:54)/ I
Wish You (7:24)
R: Exs. Soundboard. Some hiss.   S: Loews
Theatre, Syracuse, NY Sept. 8 '76.   C: ECD.
Dcc. Pic CD.

HOUSTON, WHITNEY

CD - I WILL ALWAYS LOVE YOU
PALOMINO PAL-014-A
I Will Always Love You (5:07)/ I Have Nothing
(5:41)/ Saving All My Love For You / I Wanna
Dance With Somebody (5:53)/ How Will I Know?

(7:15)/ I'm Your Baby Tonight (4:26)/ Mercy
Mercy, What's Going On? (6:10)/ Revelation Is
Here (3:33)/ So Emotional (4:10)/ My Name Is Not
Susan (4:18)/ He's Alright (1:37)/ Who Do You
Love (5:30)/ I Wanna Dance With Somebody
(6:10)/ Saving All My Love for You (3:58)
R: Exs. Soundboard.   C: Australian CD. Dcc.

CD - OUT OF AFRICA
KISS THE STONE KTS 384/85
CD1: Intro - Love's In Need Of Love Today/ So
Emotional/ Saving All My Love For You/ I Wanna
Dance With Somebody/ How Will I Know/ All At
Once/ Where You Are/ Lover For Life/ My Name Is
Not Susan/ Queen Of The Night/ African Beat/ I
Have Nothing
CD2: Touch The World/ Love Is/ Amazing Grace/
Master Blaster/ I Will Always Love You/ I'm Every
Woman/ The Greatest Love Of All/ Back Home/
I'm Every Woman (Reprise)
R: Exs. Soundboard.   S: Johannesburg, South
Africa '94.   C: ECD. Dcc. Pic CDs.

HUSKER DU

CD - SUPERNOVA
KISS THE STONE KTS 309
These Important Years/ Charity Chastity Prudence
And Hope/ Standing In The Rain/ Back From
Somewhere/ Ice Cold Ice/ You're A Soldier/ Could
You Be The One/ Too Much Spice/ Everytime,
Bed Of Nails/ Tell You Why Tomorrow/ What's
Going On/ Chartered Trips/ Green Eyes/
Celebrated Summer/ She's A Woman (And Is Now
A Man)/ Never Talking To You Again/ Gotta Lotta/
Hare Krishna
R: Exs. Soundboard.   S: Live in 1987.
C: ECD. Dcc. Pic CD. Time 66:28.

I

IDOL, BILLY

CD - RE-GENERATED
KISS THE STONE KTS 232
White Wedding/ Shock To The System/ Eyes
Without A Face/ Pumping On Steel/ Adam In
Chains/ Heroin/ Rebel Yell/ Mony Mony/ Come On
Come On/ Eyes Without A Face/ White Wedding/
Flesh For Fantasy/ Hot In The City/ Dead On
Arrival/ Dancing With Myself
R: Exs. Soundboard.   S: Tracks 1-8 '93. Tracks
9-15 USA '86.   C: ECD. Dcc. Pic CD.
Time 78:21.

INXS

CD - DIRTY HEARTS IN SANTA MONICA
ROYAL SOUND MUSIC RSM 039
Communication/ The Gift/ Taste It/ Need You
Tonight/ Mediate/ Got That Need/ Suicide Blonde/
Send A Message/ All Around/ What You Need/
New Sensation/ Kick/ Devil Inside/ Heaven Sent/

It's Only Time/ Messenger/ Bitter Tears/ Mystify/ Don't Change
S: California '93.   C: ECD.

CD - 10:15 PM
MONTANA MO 10011
Need You Tonight/ Suicide Blonde/ This Time/ Listen Like Thieves/ Mystify/ Bitter Tears/ Taste It/ What You Need/ Kick/ All Around/ Devil Inside/ Kiss The Dirt/ I Send A Message/ Shine Like It Does/ Guns In The Sky/ New Sensation// By My Side/ Don't Change/ The Swing/ Never Tear Us Apart
R: Ex.   S: Sydney, LA.   C: ECD. Dcc. 70:59.

IRON MAIDEN

CD - ANOTHER LIFE
METAL MEMORY MM 90008
Wrathchild (2:50)/ Purgator (3:13)/ Sanctuary (4:02)/ Remember Tomorrow (5:25)/ Another Life (6:23)/ Twilight Zone (2:31)/ Strange World (5:19)/ Murders In The Rue Morgue (3:57)/ Iron Maiden (3:51)/ Transylvania (5:47)/ Drifter (8:10)
S: Kosei Nenkin Hall, Nagoya, Japan May 23 '81.
C: ECD. Dcc.

CD - BACK IN THE VILLAGE
MELTDOWN ML 91606
CD1: Aces High/ 2 Minutes To Midnight/ The Trooper/ Revelations/ Murders In The Rue Morgue/ Phantom Of The Opera/ Flight Of The Icarus/ Rhyme Of The Ancient Mariner/ Losfer Words
CD2: Powerslave/ Guitar Solo/ Number Of The Beast/ Hallowed Be Thy Name/ 22 Acacia Avenue/ Iron Maiden/ Run To The Hills/ Running Free/ Sanctuary
S: Hammersmith Oct. 12 '84.   C: ECD. Dcc.

CD - BYE BYE BRUCE
LIVE STORM LSCD 51509
Be Quick Or Be Dead (3:21)/ The Trooper (4:07)/ Instrumental (2:59)/ The Evil (That Men Do) (4:13)/ Hallowed By Thy Name (7:17)/ Wrathchild (2:51)/ From Here To Eternity (5:13)
S: Pinewood Studios, London Aug. 28 '93.
C: ECD. Dcc. Bruce's last gig with Iron Maiden.
Part of the 'Raising Hell' show.

CD - CHILDREN OF THE DEVIL
LEOPARD LCD 125-2
CD1: Caught Somewhere In Time (3:15)/ 2 Minutes To Midnight (5:48)/ Sea Of Madness (5:50)/ Children Of The Damned (4:10)/ Stranger In A Strange Land (5:58)/ Wasted Years (4:47)/ Rhyme Of The Ancient Mariner (17:26)
CD2: Heaven Can Wait (6:50)/ Phantom Of The Opera (6:54)/ Hallowed By Thy Name (6:48)/ Iron Maiden (4:26)/ Number Of The Beast (4:36)/ Run To The Hills (3:45)/ Running Free (6:17)/ Sanctuary (4:47)
S: Theatro Tenda, Milano Dec. 16 '86.   C: ECD. Dcc. Booklet.

CD - CONCERT OF THE BEAST
MAIN EVENT RECORDS ME-CD-006
CD1: Murders In The Rue Morgue (4:12)/ Wrathchild (3:04)/ Run To The Hills (4:08)/ Children Of The Damned (4:45)/ The Number Of The Beast (4:49)
CD2: The Prisoner (5:48)/ Hallowed Be Thy Name (7:20)/ Phantom Of The Opera (7:19)/ Iron Maiden (4:29)
S: New York Palladium June 29 '82.   C: ECD Dcc.

CD - CROSS-EYED MARY
ALTERNATIVE RECORD COMPANY ARC 011
Phantoms Of The Opera/ Innocent Exile/ Drifter/ Sanctuary/ Prowler/ Running Free/ Remember Tomorrow/ I've Got The Fire/ Cross-Eyed Mary/ The Trooper/ Revelations/ Flight Of Icarus/ 22 Acacia Ave./ The Number Of The Beast
R: Vg-Ex.   S: Saarbrucken, HM Festival Apr. 20 '81 and Dortmund, Westfalenhalle Dec. 18 '83.
C: ECD. Time 65:48.

CD - FEAR OF LIVE
METEOR BANG 1-002
Be Quick Or Be Dead/ The Number Of The Beast/ From Here To Eternity/ Wasting Love/ Killers/ The Evil That Men Can Do/ Afraid To Shoot Strangers/ Fear Of The Dark/ Seven Can Wait/ Run To The Hills/ Two Minute To Midnight
R: Vg.   S: The Ritz, New York June 8 '92.
C: Japanese CD.

CD - MONSTER OF ROCK
SPIDER GLASS SGCD 014/2
The Number Of The Beast (4:35)/ Wrathchild (2:54)/ From Here To Eternity (4:09)/ Can I Play With Madness (3:53)/ Wasting Love (6:30)/ Tall Gunner (4:04)/ The Evil That Men Do (4:19)/ Afraid To Shoot Strangers (7:56)/ Fear Of The Dark (7:23)/ Let Her Go (5:55)
R: Exs. Soundboard.   S: Italy '92.   C: ECD. Dcc.

J

JACKSON, JANET

CD - SEX IS HAPPINESS
TEDDY BEAR TB 19/2
CD1: Intro (1:26)/ If (6:00)/ Medley: What Have You Done For Me (2:45), Nasty (7:38)/ Medley: Let's Wait Awhile (4:26), Come Back To Me (4:25)/ Throb (4:58)/ Medley: When I Think Of You (3:11), Escapade (2:33), Miss You Much (3:57)/ Love Will Never Do Without You (4:55)/ Any Time Any Place (6:15)
CD2: Again (8:05)/ Allright (4:59)/ What'll I Do (6:27)/ Black Cat (6:39)/ Rythm Nation (8:56)/ This Time (9:15)/ That's The Way Love Goes (5:20)/ Because (8:45)
R: Vg. Audience.   S: Target Center, Minneapolis Dec. 7 '93.   C: ECD. Dcc.

CD - THROB
GRAPEFRUIT GRA-041-A
What Have You Done For Me Lately? (3:08)/
Nasty (4:24)/ Let's Wait Awhile (4:06)/ Come Back
To Me (4:23)/ When I Think Of You (3:27)/
Escapade (2:24)/ Miss You Much (3:40)/ Love Will
Never Do (Without You) (4:26)/ Alright (4:06)/
Black Cat (10:35)/ Rhythm Nation (4:54)/ That's
The Way Love Goes (7:58)/ Because Of Love
(5:23)/ Again (3:20)/ Throb (4:38)
R: Ex. Audience.   S: Minneapolis, USA '93.
C: Australian CD. Dcc.

JACKSON, MICHAEL

CD - THE KING OF POP (VOL. 1)
BANANA BAN-016-A
Wanna Be Startin' Something (4:58)/ Human
Nature (5:26)/ Heartbreak Hotel (4:19)/ I Want You
Back (1:04)/ Rock With You (3:46)/ Lovely One
(5:58)/ Working Day And Night (7:14)/ Beat It
(6:26)/ Billie Jean (6:12)/ Shake Your Body (Down
To The Ground) (6:10)/ Thriller (4:130/ I Just Can't
Stop Loving You (5:49)/ Bad (6:32)
R: Exs. Soundboard.   S: World tour '87.
C: Australian CD. Dcc.

THE KING OF POP (VOL. 2)
BANANA BAN-016-B
Jam (6:38)/ Wanna Be Startin' Something (6:00)/
Human Nature (5:03)/ Smooth Criminal (4:34)/ I
Just Can't Stop Loving You (6:53)/ She's Out Of
My Life (3:43)/ I Want You Back (1:06)/ The Love
You Save (1:03)/ I'll Be There (3:59)/ Thriller
(6:11)
R: Exs. Soundboard.   S: Europe '92.
C: Australian CD. Dcc.

CD - THE KING OF POP (VOL. 3)
BANANA BAN-016-C
Billie Jean (6:44)/ Working Day And Night (8:56)/
Beat It (7:27)/ Will You Be There (9:07)/ Black Or
White (4:34)/ Heal The World (8:11)/ Man In The
Mirror (11:53)
R: Exs. Soundboard.   S: Europe '92.
C: Australian CD. Dcc.

JAGGER, MICK

CD - FROM FAR EAST TO DOWN UNDER
THE SWINGIN' PIG TSP-CD-130-1, 130-2
CD1: Just Another Night/ Honky Tonk Woman/
Throwaway/ Tumbling Dice/ Miss You/ Harlem
Shuffle/ Radio Control/ Ruby Tuesday/ Lonely At
The Top/ It's Only Rock 'N' Roll/ War Baby
CD2: You Can't Always Get What You Want/ Foxy
Lady/ Party Doll/ Wild Colonial Boy/ Gimme
Shelter/ Start Me Up/ Jumping Jack Flash/
Sympathy For The Devil/ (I Can't Get No)
Satisfaction/ Brown Sugar (with Tina Turner)/ It's
Only Rock 'N' Roll (with Tina Turner)
R: Exs. Soundboard.   S: Japan & Australia '88.
C: ECD.

CD - STATE OF SHOCK
HOT SHOT HS 29 101
Gimme Shelter (5:47)/ Start Me Up (3:40)/ Brown
Sugar (3:32)/ Jumping Jack Flash (4:18)/ (I Can't
Get No) Satisfaction (5:17)/ Stomp (2:56)/
Impromptu Jam (0:44)/ Lonely At The Top (3:14)/
Miss You (5:39)/ State Of Shock (with Tina Turner
- 2:33)/ It's Only Rock 'n' Roll (with Tina Turner)/
Just Another Night (4:25)/ Honky Tonk Woman
(3:26)/ You Can't Always Get What You Want
(7:08)/ Foxy Lady (3:34)
R: Poor.   S: Sydney, Australia Nov. 15 '88.
C: Japanese CD.

JAMES

CD - A STRANGE DAY
KISS THE STONE KTS 334
Out To Get You/ Next Lover/ Sit Down/ Low Low
Low/ Laid/ Come Home/ P.S./ Five-O/ Say
Something/ Lullaby/ Born Of Frustration/
Sometimes/ Low Low Low/ Say Something/
Sometimes/ Laid/ Five-O/ Tomorrow
R: Exs. Soundboard.   S: Europe Nov. '93.
C: ECD. Dcc. Pic CD. Time 73:21.

CD - SOUNDS & MOODS
OCTOPUS OCTO 17
Born Of Frustration (6:23)/ Sound (7:12)/ Laid
(2:25)/ The Knuckle To Far (4:16)/ Understand
(working title) (4:21)/ Out To Get You (4:40)/ Low
Low Low (2:16)/ Skin Diving (6:59)/ P.S. (4:56)/
Lullaby (3:57)/ Sometimes (5:21)/ Johny Yen
(6:12)/ Sometimes (4:43)
R: Ex. Audience.   S: Tracks 1-11 Brixton
Academy, London Dec. '93. Tracks 12-13
Woodstock '94.   C: ECD. Dcc. Pic CD.

JANES ADDICTION

CD - AT ATLANTA'S COTTON CLUB
LORDS OF ARCHIVE RECORDS L.A.R. 7
Up The Beach/ Whores/ 1%/ Idiots Rule/
Ted...Just Admit It/ Standing In The Shower/
Thank You Boys/ Trip Away/ Summertime Rolls/
Ocean Size/ Mountain Song/ Pigs In Zen/ Jane
Says
R: G-Vg.   S: Atlanta's Cotton Club Feb. 8 '89.
C: ECD. Dcc. Full color booklet with photos taken
a few weeks before this gig. Time 64:18.

CD - IDIOTS RULE (VOL. 1)
BANANA BAN-024-A
My Time (3:39)/ Whores (3:56)/ Pigs In Zen (5:16)/
Ain't No Right (2:44)/ I Would For You (3:08)/
Idiots Rule (3:02)/ Trip Away (3:25)/ Mountain
Songs (4:25)/ Up The Beach (2;47)/ Mountain
Song (3:54)/ 1% (3:25)/ Idiots Rule (Version #2 -
3:09)/ Ain't No Right (Version #2 - 3:28)/ Ted...
Just Admit It (8:51)/ Had A Dad (4:08)/ Chip Away
(3:04)
R: Ex.   S: USA '87, '91.   C: Australian CD.
Dcc.

CD - IDIOTS RULE (VOL. 2)
BANANA BAN-024-B
Up The Beach (3:08)/ Whores (3:57)/ No One's
Leaving (3:07)/ Ain't No Right (2:37)/ Idiots Rule
(2:50)/ Three Days (10:57)/ Been Caught Stealing
(4:15)/ Summertime Rolls (7:07)/ Mountain Song
(4:09)/ Stop (4:12)/ Then She Did, Obvious (8:17)/
Ocean Size (5:06)/ Jane Says (6:01)
R: Ex. Audience. S: USA '91. C: Australian
CD. Dcc.

CD - TRIP AWAY
ALLEY CAT AK043
Kettle Whistle/ Obvious/ Romeo/ Idiots Rule/
Bobhaus/ Ted Just Admit It/ Standing In The
Shower/ Had A Dad/ I Would For You/ Ocean
Size/ Trip Away/ Mountain Song/ Chip Away/ Had
A Dad (demo)/ Pigs In Zen (demo)
R: Ex. Audience. S: Cabaret Metro Chicago
Nov. 29 '88. C: ECD. Dcc. Time 73:00.

JAPAN

CD - EUROPEAN SON
935-2
Don't Rain On My Parade/ Obscure Alternatives/
Love Is Infectious/ Deviation/ European Son/
Suburban Love/ Suburban Berlin/ Adolescent Sex/
The Unconventional/ Automatic Gun/ Sometimes I
Feel So Low/ European Son/ I Second That
Emotion/ Quiet Life
R: Vg-Ex. Soundboard. S: Tracks 1-10 Mar. 5
'79. Tracks 11-12 Mar. 12 '79. Tracks 13-14 Mar.
17 '80. C: ECD. Dcc. Pic CD. Time 63:20.

CD - ORIENTAL PERFORMANCE 1980
INSECT RECORDS IST 25
Swing (5:47)/ Gentlemen Take Polaroids (5:47)/
Alien (5:06)/ Rhodesia (5:20)/ Quiet Life (4:46)/
Obscure Alternatives (6:32)/ Taking Islands In
Africa (4:46)/ Methods Of Dance (6:06)/ Ain't That
Peculiar (4:28)/ Sometimes I Feel So Low (3:35)/
Halloween (3:50)/ European Son (3:36)/ Life In
Tokyo (6:29)/ Adolescent Sex (6:08)/ Automatic
Gun (4:02)
R: Vg. C: ECD. Dcc.

JEFFERSON AIRPLANE

CD - THE SAGA OF SIDNEY SPACEPIG
YELLOW DOG YD 042
This Is My Life (And I Like It) (alternate version
'66)/ Pretty As You Feel (extended version Hot
Tuna Jam '71)/ Saga Of Sidney Spacepig
(instrumental part 1 '69)/ Saga Of Sidney
Spacepig (unreleased vocal part 2 '69)/ Saga Of
Sidney Spacepig (instrumental part 3 '69)/ Feel So
Good (extended version '71)/ Song For All
Seasons (alternate vocals and mix '69)/ She Has
Funny Cars/ This Is My Life (And I Like It)/ Get
Together/ High Flying Bird
R: Ex. Soundboard. S: Outtakes from the boxed
set and live '66. C: ECD. Dcc. Time 66:44.

JELLYFISH

CD - CALIFORNIA DREAMING
HOME RECORDS HR 5916 2
That Is Why (4:09)/ New Mistake (4:32)/ Joining A
Fan Club (4:49)/ I Wanna Stay Home (4:21)/ The
Ghost At Number One (5:33)/ The Man I Used To
Be (4:47)/ Baby's Coming Back (2:45)/ The King Is
Half Undressed (3:51)/ No Matter What (3:03)/
Now She Knows She Is Wrong (2:42)/ Jet (3:38)/
No Matter What (2:53)/ Let Em In (4:55)/ The King
Is Half Undressed (3:56)
R: Exs. Soundboard. Tracks 10-14 Audience.
S: Coach House, San Juan Capistrano '93. Tracks
10-14 live in US '90 and '91. C: ECD. Dcc.

JETHRO TULL

CD - A SACKFUL OF TROUSER SNAKES
OMBS 098 (DISC ONE)
CD1: Wond'ring Aloud (2:00)/ Skating Away On
The Thin Ice Of A New Day (3:25)/ Jack-In-The-
Green (2:33)/ Thick As A Brick (12:32)/
Introduction (1:01)/ Velvet Green (6:08)/ Hunting
Girl (5:09)/ Too Old To Rock And Roll Too Young
To Die (3:51)
CD2: Excerpts Of Beethoven's 9th Symphony
(3:14)/ Minstrel In The Gallery (5:27)/ Cross-Eyed
Mary (3:28)/ Aqualung (7:57)/ Wind-Up (8:10)/
Back-Door Angels (7:01)/ Locomotive Breath
(9:26)
R: Vg. Audience. Some surface noise.
S: Anaheim Convention Center Apr. 6 '77.
C: ECD. Dcc.

JOEL, BILLY

CD - AFTER THE FLOOD
KISS THE STONE KTS 326-27
CD1: No Man's Land/ Pressure/ Ballad Of Billy
The Kid/ Leningrad/ Prelude - Angry Young Man/
Allen Town/ Scenes From An Italian Restaurant/
Honesty/ My Life/ I Go To Extremes/ An Innocent
Man
CD2: Shades Of Grey/ River Of Dreams/ We
Would All Go Down Together/ We Didn't Start The
Fire/ A Hard Day's Night/ It's Still Rock And Roll
To Me/ You May Be Right/ Only The Good Die
Young/ Big Shot/ Piano Man
R: Exs. Soundboard. S: Europe '94. C: ECD.
Dcc. Pic CD. Time CD1 68:18. CD2 54:56.

CD - IT'S STILL ROCK & ROLL TO ME (VOL. 1)
BANANA BAN-018-A
Piano Man (5:29)/ Somewhere Along The Line
(2:53)/ You're My Home (3:54)/ Travelin' Prayer
(3:37)/ The Entertainer (8:18)/ Everybody Loves
You Now (3:00)/ Captain Jack (7:00)
R: Vg-Ex. S: USA '74. C: Australian CD. Dcc.

CD - IT'S STILL ROCK & ROLL TO ME (VOL. 2)
BANANA BAN-018-B
Stormfront (6:25)/ Allentown (4:01)/ Angry Young
Man (7:30)/ Scenes From An Italian Restaurant

(7:30)/ The Downeaster Alexa (3:25)/ Goodnight Saigon (7:10)/ I Go To Extremes (4:55)/ Pressure (6:05)/ Leningrad (5:14)/ My Life (6:28)/ Innocent Man (5:30)/ Shameless (5:59)
R: Exs. Soundboard.   S: Europe '92.
C: Australian CD. Dcc.

CD - IT'S STILL ROCK & ROLL TO ME (VOL. 3)
BANANA BAN-018-C
We Didn't Start The Fire (5:39)/ Shout (5:46)/ Uptown Girl (2:25)/ It's Still Rock & Roll To Me (4:51)/ You May Be Right (5:05)/ Only The Good Die Young (6:22)/ Matter Of Trust (5:36)/ Big Shot (7:31)/ That's Not Her Style (7:55)/ Piano Man (6:04)
R: Exs. Soundboard.   S: Europe '92.
C: Australian CD. Dcc.

CD - MY LIFE
GRAPEFRUIT GRA-045-A
Stormfront (6:25)/ Allentown (4:01)/ Scenes From An Italian Restaurant (7:30)/ The Downeaster 'Alexa' (3:25)/ Goodnight Saigon (7:01)/ I Go To Extremes (4:55)/ Pressure (6:05)/ Leningrad (5:14)/ My Life (6:28)/ Innocent Man (5:30)/ Shameless (5:59)
R: Exs. Soundboard.   C: London, England '90 part one. See ' We Didn't Start The Fire' (GRA-045-B) for part two.   C: Australian CD. Dcc.

CD - TEMPTATION
BIG MUSIC BIG 090
No Man's Land/ Blonde Over Blue/ Shades Of Grey/ River Of Dreams/ No Man's Land/ Shameless/ Only The Good Die Young/ River Of Dreams/ All About Soul/ You Got Me Hummin'/ I'll Cry Instead
R: Exs. Soundboard.   S: Track 1 New York Aug. '93. Track 2 Long Island May '93. Tracks 3-7 Boston Sept. '93. Tracks 8-9 New York Oct. '93. Tracks 10-11 New York '81.   C: ECD. Purple/black cover. Pic CD. Time 45:35.

CD - UP THE SINNERS
OCTOPUS RECORDS OCTO 029-30
CD1: Intro - No Man's Land (7:24)/ Pressure (5:05)/ Billy The Kid (5:51)/ Leningrad (4:42)/ Prelude - Angry Young Man (6:25)/ Allentown (4:14)/ Scenes From An Italian Restaurant (7:43)/ Honesty (4:08)/ My Life (6:19)/ I Go To Extremes (4:57)/ An Innocent Man (6:13)
CD2: Shades Of Grey (4:43)/ River Of Dreams (5:22)/ We Would All Go Down Together (7:37)/ We Didn't Start The Fire (5:14)/ A Hard Day's Night (2:30)/ It's Still Rock 'N' Roll To Me (5:00)/ You May Be Right (4:55)/ Only The Good Die Young (4:27)/ Big Shot (4:56)/ Piano Man (6:01)
R: Ex. Audience.   S: 'River Of Dreams' world tour, Festhalle, Frankfurt, Germany June 18 '94.
C: ECD. Dcc. Pic CD

CD - WE DIDN'T START THE FIRE
GRAPEFRUIT GRA-045-B
We Didn't Start The Fire (5:39)/ Shout (5:46)/

Uptown Girl (2:25)/ It's Still Rock & Roll To Me (4:51)/ You May Be Right (5:05)/ Only The Good Die Young (6:22)/ Matter Of Trust (5:36)/ Big Shot (7:31)/ That's Not Her Style (7:55)/ Piano Man (6:04)
R: Exs. Soundboard.   C: London, England '90 part two. See ' My Life' (GRA-045-A) for part one.
C: Australian CD. Dcc.

JOHN, ELTON

CD - A SINGLE MAN IN MOSCOW
OCTOPUS RECORDS OCTO 013/14
CD1: Your Song (4:13)/ 60 Years On (5:22)/ Daniel (3:55)/ Skyline Pigeon (4:05)/ Take Me To The Pilot (6:56)/ Rocket Man (7:46)/ Don't Let The Sun Go Down On Me (5:25)/ Good Bye Yellow Brick Road (3:32)/ Roy Rogers (3:25)/ Candle In The Wind (3:26)/ Ego (4:12)/ Where To Now St. Peter (3:59)/ He'll Have To Go (3:31)/ I Heard It Through The Grapevine (11:55)
CD2: Funeral For A Friend (3:05)/ Tonight (7:28)/ Better Off Dead (2:59)/ Idol (3:54)/ I Think I'm Gonna Kill Myself (3:41)/ I Feel Like A Bullet (3:44)/ Bennie And The Jets (12:05)/ Sorry Seems To Be The Hardest Word (3:36)/ Part-Time Love (3:07)/ Crazy Water (6:57)/ Song For Guy (7:11)/ Saturday Nights, Pinball Wizard (9:53)/ Crocodile Rock, Get Back, Back In The U.S.S.R. (3:28)
R: Exs. Soundboard.   S: Rossya Hotel Hall, Moscow May 18 '79.   C: ECD. Dcc.

CD - DANIEL
OIL WELL RSC 022 CD
Funeral For A Friend/ Love Lies Bleeding/ Rocket Man/ Benny & The Jets/ Daniel/ Honky Cat/ Candle In The Wind/ Hercules/ Goodbye Yellow Brick Road/ Elderberry Wine/ Your Song/ Saturday Night's Alright
R: Exs. Soundboard.   S: Newcastle May 6 '73.
C: ECD. Dcc. Time 69:00.

CD - FINE CHINA
BIG MUSIC BIG 092
I Heard It Through The Grapevine/ Daniel/ Island Girl/ Candle In The Wind/ Rocket Man/ Sorry Seems To Be The Hardest Word/ Philadelphia Freedom/ Funeral For A Friend (Love Lies Bleeding)/ Your Song
R: Exs. Soundboard.   S: Europe Mar. 11 '77.
C: ECD. Pic CD. Time 49:37.

CD - GREEN AS A SPROUT
TBUCDA 102
Funeral For A Friend/ Love Lies Bleeding/ Ball & Chain/ Empty Garden/ Song For A Guy/ Nobody Wins/ Elton's Song/ Chloe/ Where To Know St. Peter/ Rocket-Man/ Benny And The Jets/ Just Like Belgium/ Daniel/ Crocodile Rock
R: Ex. Audience.   S: Vorste, Nationale Centre, Brussels 9-5-82.   C: ECD. Dcc. Time 76:30.

CD - ROCKET MAN (VOL. 2)
BANANA BAN-019-B

I Need You To Turn To (2:54)/ Your Song (4:31)/ Country Comfort (5:43)/ Border Song (3:32)/ Indian Sunset (6:45)/ Amoreena (5:01)/ My Father's Gun (4:54)/ Sorry Seems To Be The Hardest Word (4:31)/ Island Girl (4:43)/ Medley: He's Got The Whole World In His Hands, Your Song, Daniel (1:39)/ Your Song Version #2 (4:10)/ R: Ex. Soundboard.   S: USA '70. Europe '76. C: Australian CD. Dcc.

CD - ROCKET MAN (VOL. 3)
BANANA BAN-019-C
The Bitch Is Back (3:38)/ Pinball Wizard (4:51)/ Blue Eyes (3:01)/ Bennie And The Jets (9:20)/ Rocket Man (1:48)/ All Quiet On The Western Front (5:120/ Your Song (3:31)/ Saturday Night's Alright For Fighting (7:11)/ Daniel (4:01)/ Crocodile Rock (4:22)/ Don't Go Breaking My Heart (3:37)/ Whole Lotta Shakin' Goin' On (0:56)/ Jingle Bells (0:17)/ I Saw Her Standing There (1:34)/ Twist And Shout (3:36)
R: G-Vg.   S: Europe '82.   C: Australian CD. Dcc.

CD - SACRIFICE
GRAPEFRUIT GRA-013-A
The Bitch Is Back (4:15)/ Philadelphia Freedom (5:54)/ Levon (5:29)/ Simple Life (5:40)/ The One (6:03)/ The Last Song (3:36)/ I Don't Wanna Go On With You Like That (5:05)/ Take Me To The Pilot (5:16)/ Don't Let The Sun Go Down On Me (6:45)/ Pinball Wizard (4:22)/ Sacrifice (4:54)/ Sad Songs (Say So Much) (5:25)
R: Exs. Soundboard.   S: Foxboro, Massachusetts '93.   C: Australian CD. Dcc.

CD - SATURDAY SUN SESSIONS
EJCD348
Saturday Sun (3:48)/ Sweet Honesty (3:10)/ Stormbringer (3:45)/ Way To Blue (2:55)/ Go Out And Get It (3:23)/ The Day Is Done (2:18)/ Time Has Told Me (3:20)/ You Get Brighter (3:27)/ This Moment (2:35)/ I Don't Mind (2:33)/ Pied Piper (2:14)/ I Heard It Through The Grapevine (7:22)/ I Feel Like A Bullet (3:33)/ Bennie And The Jets (9:19)/ Tonight (2:54)/ Better Off Dead (4:20)/ I Think I'm Gonna Kill Myself (3:17)
R: Tracks 1-11 Ex. Tracks 12-18 G. Audience. S: Tracks 1-11 Sound Techniques, Chelsea July '70. Tracks 12-18 Universal Ampitheatre, Los Angeles Sept. 26 '79.   C: ECD. Dcc.

CD - THE UNSURPASSED DICK JAMES DEMOS VOL. 3
YELLOW DOG YD 043
Scarecrow (2:29)/ Velvet Fountain (2:41)/ Annabella (3:22)/ Reminds Me Of You (2:50)/ I Love You & That's All That Matters (2:53)/ Last To Arrive (2:40)/ There Is Still A Little Love (2:19)/ There's Still Time For Me (2:35)/ Sarah's Coming Back (2:11)/ Lady What's Tomorrow (4:06)/ I Need You To Turn To (2:55)/ Son Of Your Father (3:02)/ The Tide Will Turn For Rebecca (3:02)/ Rock And Roll Madonna (3:08)/ Gray Seal (3:05)/ The Cage

(4:27)/ Rock Me When He's Gone (2:06)/ Holiday Inn (1:38)/ I Get A Little Bit Lonely (1:08) R: Ex. Soundboard. Some surface noise. C: ECD. Dcc.

CD - WORLD CLASS
KISS THE STONE KTS 270/271
CD1: Take Me To The Pilot/ Empty Garden/ Simple Life/ The One/ Come Down In Town/ Sorry Seems To Be The Hardest Word/ Captain Fantastic And The Brown Dirt Cowboy/ The Last Song/ Funeral For A Friend, Love Lies Bleeding/ Rocket Man
CD2: Benny And The Jets/ Sad Songs Say So Much/ The Show Must Go On/ Saturday Night's Alright For Fightin'/ Don't Let The Sun Go Down On Me/ Jumpin' Jack Flash/ Your Song/ Sacrifice/ Candle In The Wind
R: Exs.   S: Live '93.   C: Ecd. Dcc. Pic CD.

JONES, RICKIE LEE

CD - STAGE PIRATES
RARE RECORDING COLLECTION RRC 0035
Something Cool/ We Belong Together/ Pirates (So Long Lonely Avenue)/ Instrumental/ Easy Money/ Chuck E's In Love/ Danny's All-Star Joint/ Montreux Jammin', I Heard It Through The Grapevine/ Long Distance Love/ Coolsville/ Traces Of The Western Slopes/ Deep Space/ Texas Girl At The Funeral Of Her Father
R: Exs. Soundboard.   S: Montreux July 16 '82. C: ECD. Dcc. Time 73:40.

JUNK YARD

CD - LIVE CAD CLUB
NOT GUILTY NG-61091
Killing Time (5:10)/ Back On The Streets (4:38)/ Give The Devil His Due (3:50)/ Clean The Dirt (4:12)/ Hollywood (4:08)/ Misery Loves Company (2:48)/ Throw It All Away (3:14)/ Lost In The City (3:06)/ Hands Off (6:37) Texas (8:17)/ Should I Stay Or Should I Go (2:36)
R: G-Vg. Audience.   S: Cat Club, New York Aug. 7 '91.   C: ECD.

K

KENTUCKY HEADHUNTERS, THE

CD - DIRTY PICKIN'
ROYAL SOUND MUSIC RSM 026 SQ
The Ghost Of Hank Williams/ Just Ask Fo' Lucy/ Honky Tonk Walkin'/ Walk Softly (On This Heart O Mine)/ Dixiefried/ Little Red Rooster/ Freedom Stomp/ Spirit In The Sky/ Dumas Walker
S: New York '93.   C: ECD.

KILLING JOKE

CD - JOKING APART
FESTIVAL MUSIC FM CD008

Communion (8:08)/ Wardance (4:06)/
Pandemonium (5:08)/ Change (5:10)/ Exorcism
(8:14)/ Requiem (3:52)/ Love Like Blood (7:08)/
Mathematics Of Chaos (7:11)/ Psyche (5:42)/ Age
Of Greed (7:50)/ King & Queens (4:11)/ The Wait
(3:48)/ We Have Joy (3:08)/ Empire Song (2:46)
R: Ex. Audience.   S: The Phoenix Festival,
Stratford Upon Avon, England July '94. Tracks 10-
14 Brixton Academy, London, England.   C: ECD.
Dcc. Pic CD.

KING CRIMSON

CD - A DAY AT THE EDGE OF THE WORLD
GOLD STANDARD
Larks Tongue In Aspic Part One/ Dr. Diamond
Intro/ Dr. Diamond/ Improvisation/ Exiles/ Easy
Money/ Book Of Saturday/ Talking Drum/ Larks
Tongue #2/ Larks Tongue Continued (fades in)/
21st. Century Schizoid Man
S: Agora, Cleveland, Ohio Mar. '73.   C: ECD.

CD - A WEIRD PERSON'S GUIDE TO KING CRIMSON
INVASION UNLIMITED IU 9412 1
Trio A Strange One/ Night Watch/ Groon/ Train To
Hell/ Lark's Tongues In Aspic Pt. III/ As Far As We
Think It's Unknown/ I Wonder/ Three Of A Perfect
Pair/ Man With An Open Heart/ Thursday Morning/
Kick The Donkey/ Nightmares In Red/ No. 1 Mr.
Wonderful/ Starless
R: Vg-Ex.   S: Tracks 1-2 rehearsals, TV Studios,
Paris '74. Track 3 Summit Studio, Denver Jan. '72.
Track 4 Richard's Club, Atlanta '73. Track 5-9
Studio '83. Track 10 Deram 7" '68. Track 11-12
Parlophone 7" May '67. Track 13 Marquee '71.
Track 14 rehearsal, TV Studios, Paris '74.
C: ECD. Dcc. Time 74:13.

CD - CELEBRATION OF THE LIZARD
GOLD STANDARD KC-21-94-05
Introduction/ Pictures Of A City/ Formentara Lady/
The Devils Triangle/ Cirkus/ Pandaemonia/ 21st.
Century Schizoid Man/ Celebration Of The Lizard/
Cadence And Cascade
S: Orpheum Theatre, Boston Mar. 27 '72.
C: ECD.

CD - FORMENTERA MEMORIES
ALL OF US AS 33
Presentation/ Pictures Of City/ Formentara Lady,
Sailor's Tale/ Circus/ Groon/ 21st Century
Schizoyd Man/ Earthbound/ Cadence And
Cascade
R: G-Vg. Audience. Static.   S: Orpheum Theater,
Boston Mar. 27 '72.   C: ECD. Dbw. Pic CD.
Time 66:24.

CD - GET THY BEARINGS
SCORPIO SC 102
CD1: 21st Century Schizoid Man/ Why Didn't You
Just Drop In/ Epitaph/ Get They Bearings/ Talk To
The Wind/ Court Of The Crimson King

CD2: War/ Get Thy Bearings/ 21st Century
Schizoid Man
R: G.   S: CD1 and CD2 track 1 Chesterfield Park
Sept. 7 '69. CD2 track 2 'Top Gear' BBC. CD2
track 3 audience recording.   C: ECD.

CD - LIVE AT ORPHIUM THEATRE
MOON CHILD MC 910102
Larks' Tongues In Aspic Part 1 (10:49)/ Easy
Money (6:39)/ The Night Watch (4:43)/ Fracture
(15:07)/ The Talking Rhythm Box (13:44)/ Larks'
Tongues In Aspic Part 2 (6:33)/ 21st Century
Schizoid Man (8:01)
R: Vgm. Audience.   S: Boston May 4 '73.
C: Japanese CD.

CD - LIVE LARKS
MOON CHILD 930809
Opening - Dr. Diamond/ Larks' Tongues In Aspic
Part 1/ Easy Money/ Improvisation (Trio)/ Exiles/
Improvisation/ The Talking Drum/ Larks' Tongues
In Aspic Part 2
R: Vg. Audience.   S: Palace Theater, Waterbury
May 6 '73.   C: Japanese CD.

CD - NO PUSSYFOOTING
BRINX BL 13101972
CD1: Lark's Tongues In Aspic Part 1/ Book Of
Saturday/ Instrumental #1/ Doctor D/ Instrumental
#2/ Instrumental #3 Part 1
CD2: Instrumental #3 part 2/ Easy Money/ Fallen
Angel/ Instrumental #4/ Exiles/ Talking Drum/
Lark's Tongues In Aspic Part 2
S: Zoom Club, Frankfurt Oct. 13 '72.
C: Japanese CD.

CD - THE SHELTERING SKY
OFF BEAT RECORDS XXCD 5
CD1: Intro...Discipline/ Thela Hun Ginjeet/ Red/ M-
Atte Kudasai/ The Sheltering Sky/ Frame By
Frame
CD2: Neal And Jack And Me/ Neurotica/ Elephant
Talk/ Larks Tongues In Aspic Part2
R: Ex. Audience.   S: Nagoya, Japan Dec. 10 '81.
C: Japanese CD.

CD - SONGS FOR EUROPE
N.D.A.L. NDAL10001
Easy Money/ Lament/ Book Of Saturday/ Exiles/
The Mincer/ The Talking Drum/ Lark's Tongues In
Aspic Part 2/ 21st Century Schizoid Man/ Epitaph/
The Court Of The Crimson King
S: Track 1-8 Concertgebouw, Amsterdam Nov. 23
'73. Tracks 9-10 BBC Top Gear Session, London
May 6 '69.

CD - STRANGE TALES OF THE SAILORS
DYNAMITE 911802
Pictures Of The City (9:03)/ Cadence And
Cascade (4:55)/ Groon (13:40)/ 21st Century
Schizoid Man (9:33)/ Intro (1:17)/ Earthbound
(9:23)/ King Crimson Experiment (1:36)/ The
Sailors Tales (6:29)/ Here Comes The Flood

R: G-Vgs.   S: KLF Studios, Denver Mar. 13 '72. C: Japanese CD.

CD - TALK SEX WITH A TOTAL STRANGER
AMERICAN CONCERT SERIES 041
Lark's Tongues In Aspic Part One (10:56)/ Easy Money (7:06)/ Train To Health (3:44)/ Lark's Tongues In Aspic Part Two (6:37)/ The Great Deceiver (3:01)/ Lament (4:05)/ The Night Watch (4:19)/ Starless And Bible Black (11:34)
R: Ex.   S: Atlanta and Pittsburgh.   C: ECD. Dcc.

CD - THE TALKING RHYTHM BOX
CAT FOOD CAT 1
Larks Tongues In Aspic Part 1 (short version)/ Easy Money/ The Night Watch/ Fracture (incomplete)/ Book Of Saturday/ Lament/ Improvisation (Talking Rhythm Box)/ Exiles/ Dr. Diamond/ Larks Tongues In Aspic Part 1 (long version)/ Larks Tongues In Aspic Part 2 (incomplete)/ 21th Century Schizoid Man
S: Tracks 1-8 Hamburg, Germany Nov. 2 '73. Tracks 9-12 West Palm Beach June. 20 '73. C: Japanese CD.

KINKS, THE

CD - ON THE ROAD AGAIN
OFF BEAT RECORDS XXCD 21-1/2
CD1: Intro - Sweet Lady Geneviere/ A Well Respected Man/ Do It Again/ Till The End Of Day/ Destroyer/ Low Budget/ Phobia/ Looney Barron/ Drift Away/ Did Ya/ Ape Man/ Celluloid Heroes/ Over The Edge/ Only A Dream/ Come Dancing/ Aggravation, New World/ I'm Not Like Everyone Else
CD2: Welcome To Sleazy Town/ All Day And All Of The Night/ Encore: Lola/ You Really Got Me/ Bonus Trax: Wall Of Fire*/ Where Have All The Good Time Gone*/ Waterloo Sunset*/ Hatred*/ David*/ Twist & Shout*
R: Vg-Exs. Soundboard.   S: Kose Nenkin-Hall, Osaka Oct. 3 '93. *Nenkin-Hall, Tokyo Oct. 4 '93 and Kani Hoken-Hall, Tokyo Oct. 5 '93.
C: Japanese CD. Dcc. Time 70:04. CD2 42:37.

KISS

CD - COLD GIN
PIPELINE PPL 526
Detroit Rock City (5:15)/ Cold Gin (4:48)/ Strutter (3:17)/ Fits Like A Glove (4:47)/ Heaven's On Fire (4:04)/ Guitar Solo (4:08)/ Exciter (4:11)/ War Machine (4:10)/ Drum Solo (5:17)/ Young And Wasted (4:41)
R: Ex. Audience.   S: Atlanta Sept. 6 '92 part 1. C: ECD. Dcc. See 'Love Gun' (PPL 527) for part 2.

CD - DEATH KISS
BABY CAPONE BC 010/2
CD1: Intro (1:58)/ Detroit Rock City (4:54)/ Cold Gin (4:56)/ Creatures Of The Night (5:14)/ Fits Like A Glove (4:37)/ Heaven's On Fire (4:08)/

Thrills In The Night (4:26)/ Guitar Solo (4:16)/ Under The Gun (4:07)/ War Machine (4:31)/ Eric Carr Song (4:42)/ Young And Wasted (4:24)/ I Love It Loud (6:02)
CD2: I Still Love You (9:32)/ Love Gun (3:52)/ Lick It Up (4:16)/ Black Diamond (6:28)/ Rock And Roll All Night (7:14)/ Deuce (3:38)/ Strutter (3:14)/ Beth (1:58)/ I Stole Your Love (3:32)/ Ladies Room (2:12)
R: Vg-Ex.   S: Cover says Denver Jan. 12 '85 however announcer says 'Allright Detroit'.
C: ECD. Dcc.

CD - DIAMOND KISSES
BLACK ROSE BRR 0494
Detroit Rock City (4:07)/ Cold Gin (4:15)/ Strutter (3:03)/ Fits Like A Glove (4:13)/ Heaven's On Fire (3:52)/ Creatures Of The Night (3:40)/ I Love It Loud (3:00)/ I Still Love You (5:33)/ I Had Enough (Into The Fire) (3:45)/ Love Gun (3:18)/ Rock N' Roll All Nite (5:54)/ La Bamba (1:50)/ Lick It Up (4:06)/ Oh Susanna (1:52)/ Black Diamond (5:31)
R: G. Audience. Speed off a bit.   S: Zwolle, Ijsselhall Apr. '84.   C: ECD. Dcc.

CD - FLAMING YEARS
BACKSTAGE BKCD 088
C: See 'Rock And Roll All Nite' (BIG 093) for songs and source. BIG version sounds better.

CD - FLAMING YOUTH
ANGRY DINO AD 1010
Deuce (3:26)/ Strutter (3:21)/ Flaming Youth (3:56)/ Hotter Than Hell (2.44)/ Firehouse (3:18)/ Shout It Out Loud (3:45)/ 100,000 Years (10:00)/ Black Diamond (7:02)/ Detroit Rock City (3:40)/ Let Me Go Rock'n'Roll (3:05)/ Makin' Love (3:52)/ Cold Gin (8;07)/ Nothin' To Loose (3:06)/ Rock'N'Roll All Night (3:51)/ I Stole Your Love (3:19)/ Take Me (3:10)/ Ladies Room (2:40)/ Love Gun (1:58)/ Calling Dr. Love (3:09)
R: Vg. Tracks 11-19 G-Vg.   S: Various US tours '76-'77.   C: ECD. Dcc.

CD - KISS ARMY
CAPRICORN RECORDS CR 2002
Detroit Rock City/ Let It Go Rock And Roll/ Firehouse/ Makin' Love/ Cold Gin/ Nothing To Lose/ God Of Thunder/ Rock And Roll All Night/ Black Diamond
R: Poor-Good. Soundboard.   S: Budokan Hall, Tokyo '77.   C: Australian CD. Dcc. Time 49:42.

CD - KISS KOLLEKTION VOL. 1
KISS KOLLEKTION KK 1 CD
Deuce, She, Black Diamond ('Midnight Special' TV show)/ Deuce/ Strutter/ She/ Firehouse/ Love Theme From Kiss/ You're Much Too Young/ Let Me Know/ Black Diamond/ Let Me Go Rock 'n Roll/ Shock Me/ Rip It Up/ Rocket Ride/ New York Groove
S: Tracks 4-13 Washington '74. Tracks 14-17 Ace Frehley's 'Just For Fun' tour, Long Beach '93.
C: ECD.

CD - KISS KOLLEKTION VOL. 2
KISS KOLLECKTION KK 2 CD
Deuce/ Strutter/ C'mon And Love Me/ Hotter Than
Hell/ Firehouse/ She/ Ladies In Waiting/ Nothin' To
Lose/ 100,000 Years/ Black Diamond/ Detroit
Rock City/ Deuce/ Breakout/ Parasite/ Shot Full Of
Rock/ Rock Soldiers/ Interview
S: Tracks 1-10 Detroit, Michigan '76. Tracks 11-12
Arsenio Hall TV show '93. Tracks 13-16 Ace
Frehley's 'Just For Fun' tour, Long Beach '93.
C: ECD.

CD - KISS KOLLEKTION VOL. 3
KISS KOLLEKTION KK 3 CD
Detroit Rock City/ Take Me/ Let Me Go Rock 'n
Roll/ Ladies Room/ Firehouse/ Makin' Love/ I
Want You/ Cold Gin, Ace's Guitar Solo/ Do You
Love Me/ Nothin' To Lose/ God Of Thunder, Drum
Solo/ Rock 'n Roll All Nite/ Shout It Out Loud/
Beth/ Black Diamond/ SKID ROW: Cold Gin/
ANTHRAX: Parasite
S: Tokyo, Japan Apr. 4 '77.   C: ECD.

CD - KISS KOLLEKTION VOL. 4
KISS KOLLEKTION KK 4 CD
Detroit Rock City/ Cold Gin/ Strutter/ Calling Dr.
Love/ Is That You/ Firehouse/ Talk To Me/ You're
All What I Want/ 2,000 Men/ I Was Made For
Loving You/ New York Groove/ Lovegun/ Rock 'n
Roll All Nite/ Shout It Out Loud/ King Of The Night
Time World/ Black Diamond
S: London, England '80.   C: ECD.

CD - KISS KOLLEKTION VOL. 5
KISS KOLLEKTION KK 5 CD
Introduction - Nothing To Lose (Detroit '76)/ Let
Me Go Rock 'n Roll (NY '77)/ 100,000 Years
(Detroit '76)/ Hotter Than Hell (Detroit '76)/ Strutter
(Detroit '76)/ Detroit Rock City/ Fits Like A Glove/
Exciter/ War Machine/ Gimme More & Guitar Solo/
I Love It Loud/ I Still Love You/ Up All Night/ Won't
Get Fooled Again
S: Miami, Florida '83 except where noted.
C: ECD.

CD - KISSIN' TIME IN SAN FRANCISCO
BLACK DIAMOND RECORDS BDR 73981 A
Deuce/ Strutter/ You Got To Choose/ Hotter Than
Hell/ Firehouse/ Watching You/ Guitar Solo/
Nothing To Loose/ Parasite/ 100,000 Years/ Black
Diamond/ Cold Gin/ Let Me Rock'N' Roll/ A World
Without Heroes (instrumental demo '81)/ The
Difference Between Men & Boys (instrumental
demo '81)/ Young & Waysted (demo '71)/ Shout It
Out Loud (demo '71)
R: G-Vg. Soundboard. Tracks 14-16 G.   S: San
Francisco '74.   C: ECD. Dcc. Pic CD. 75:00.

CD - LOVE GUN
PIPELINE PPL 527
I Have Had Enough (4:05)/ Bass Solo (3:47)/ I
Love It Loud (3:09)/ I Still Love You (6:24)/
Creatures Of The Night (6:05)/ Love Gun (3:46)/
Rock And Roll Night (10:26)/ Lick It Up (5:54)/

Country Man (:35)/ Winchester Cathedral (1:53)/
Black Diamond (6:05)
R: Ex. Audience.   S: Atlanta Sept. 6 '92 part 1.
C: ECD. Dcc. See 'Cold Gin' (PPL 526) for part 1.

CD - ROCK AND ROLL ALL NITE
BIG MUSIC BIG 093
Detroit Rock City (3:51)/ King Of The Nightime
World (3:27)/ Let Me Go Rock'N'Roll (3:13)/
Strutter (3:45)/ Hotter Than Hell, Nothin' To Lose
(7:30)/ Cold Gin, Ace's Guitar Solo (7:56)/ Shout It
Out Loud (2:47)/ Do You Love Me (3:42)/ Bass
Solo, Gods Of Thunder, Drum Solo (7:45)/
Rock'N'Roll All Nite, Deuce (5:13)/ Fire House
(4:47)/ Black Diamond (6:16)
R: Vg-Ex. Soundboard.   S: 'Destroyer World
Tour', Toronto, Canada Sept. 6 '76.   C: ECD.
Dcc. Pic CD.

CD - ROCK CITY
NR 02/2
CD1: Introduction/ Love Gun/ Deuce/ Parasite/
Unholy/ 100,000/ Cold Gin/ Watching You/
Firehouse/ I Want You/ I Was Made For Loving
You/ Calling Doctor Love/ Makin' Love/ Domino/
Tears Are Falling/ War Machine
CD2: Lick It Up/ Forever/ Creature Of The Night/ I
Love It Loud/ Detroit Rock City/ Strutter/ She/ Soy
Kissero/ La Bamba/ Black Diamond/ Heavens On
Fire/ Rock And Roll All Night
R: Vg. Audience.   S: Buenos Aires '94.
C: ECD. Black cover. Red type. Time CD1 66:59.
CD2 56:35.

CD - THEY'RE ALIVE
DEAD DOG RECORDS SE 442
Detroit Rock City/ Cold Gin/ Strutter/ Shandie/
Calling Dr. Love/ Firehouse/ Talk To Me/ Is That
You/ 2000 Man/ I Was Made For Lovin' You/ New
York Groove/ Love Gun/ Rock'N Roll All Nite/
Shout It Out Loud/ King Of The Night Time World/
Black Diamond
R: G-Vg. Soundboard.   S: Live USA '80.
C: ECD. Pic CD. Time 71:52.

KRAFTWERK

CD - KRAFTWERK
GERMANOFON 941001
Ruckzuck (7:47)/ Stratovarius (12:10)/ Megaherz
(9:30)/ Vom Himmel Hoch (10:12)
R: Exs. Soundboard.   C: ECD. Pic CD.

CD - KRAFTWERK 2
GERMANOFON 94002
Klingklang (17:36)/ Atem (2:57)/ Strom (3:52)/
Spule 4 (5:20)/ Wellenlange (9:40)/ Harmonika
(3:17)
R: Exs. Soundboard.   C: ECD. Pic CD.

KRAVITZ, LENNY

CD - ACOUSTIC
KISS THE STONE KTS 332

Are You Gonna Go My Way (6:26)/ Believe (5:13)/ Rosemary (5:36)/ Just Be A Woman (4:06)/ Sister (7:15)/ Always On The Run (3:57)/ My Precious Love (5:54)/ Let Love Rule (6:43)/ Are You Gonna Go My Way (3:26)/ Always On The Run (5:57)
R: Tracks 1-8 Exs. Soundboard. Tracks 9-10 G-Vg. Audience.   S: Tracks 1-8 USA '94. Tracks 9-10 Daytona Beach May '93.   C: ECD. Dcc. Pic CD.

CD - ALWAYS ON THE RUN (VOL. 1)
BANANA BAN-023-A
Flower Child (4:00)/ Mr. Cabdriver (4:12)/ Freedom Train (4:33)/ Be (4:48)/ My Precious Love (6:24)/ Cold Turkey (6:14)/ If Six Were Nine (5:27)/ Fear (12:53)/ Let Love Rule (10:06)/ Always On The Run (4:56)/ Are You Gonna Go My Way? (3:25)/ Fields Of Joy (6:52)
R: Ex. Soundboard.   S: Europe, USA '90, '92, '93.   C: Australian CD. Dcc. Gold disc.

CD - ALWAYS ON THE RUN (VOL. 2)
BANANA BAN-023-B
Mr. Cabdriver (4:02)/ Be (4:19)/ My Precious Love (5:56)/ If Six Were Nine (6:35)/ Does Anybody Out There Even Care? (4:55)/ Let Me Be (3:32)/ Blues For Sister Someone (5:25)/ Let Love Rule (8:43)/ Freedom Train (8:12)/ Are You Gonna Go My Way? (3:39)/ Always On The Run (4:04)
R: Ex.   S: Europe, USA '91, '92, '93.
C: Australian CD. Dcc.

L

L7

CD - WHEN THE STINK HITS THE FAN
KISS THE STONE KTS 358
Everglade (3:04)/ Death Wish (4:46)/ Stuck Here Again (3:26)/ Pretend We're Dead (2:54)/ Fast And Frightening (3:15)/ Questioning My Sanity (3:31)/ Scrap (3:58)/ Enter Sandman, We Care A Lot, Slide (3:55)/ Diet Pill (3:12)/ Shove (2:55)/ Monster (2:34)/ Shitlist (3:02)/ Right On Thru (Diet Pill) (3:42)
R: Exs. Soundboard.   S: Tracks 1-6 Glastonbury Festival June 24 '94. Tracks 7-11 Europe Dec. 17 '92 Tracks 12-14 USA June 6 '92.   C: ECD. Dcc. Pic CD.

LANG, k.d.

CD - BLUE SKY ABOVE WIDE PLAINS
FLASHBACK 09 93 0219
Angel With A Lariat (2:52)/ Johnny Get Angry (4:33)/ Honky Tonk All Night (3:44)/ Look Stop And Teardrops (4:08)/ Sugar Moon (2:52)/ Broken Hearted (2:52)/ Three Cigarettes In An Ashtray (3:20)/ I'm Down To My Last Cigarette (3:06)/ Tune Into My Wave (3:43)/ Seven Lonely Days (3:10)/ Crying (4:13)/ Turn Me Around (3:40)/ If You Need Me (4:52)/ Hanky Panky (2:05)/ Miss Chatalain (6:01)/ Trail Of A Broken Heart (3:56)/

Constant Craving (4:25)/ Big Big Love (3:07)/ Crying (4:19)
R: Exs. Soundboard.   S: Tracks 1-4 Cabaret Metro, Chicago July 3 '88. Tracks 15-19 NY May '93.   C: ECD. Dcc.

CD - CONSTANT CRAVING
GRAPEFRUIT GRA-008-A
Save Me (4:38)/ The Mind Of Love (3:35)/ Still Thrives This Love (3:26)/ Don't Let The Stars Get In Your Eyes (2:52)/ Luck In My Eyes (5:21)/ Outside Myself (5:51)/ Wash Me Clean (4:03)/ Miss Chatelaine (4:41)/ Ridin' The Rails (2:58)/ Big Big Love (3:15)/ Pullin' Back The Reins (5:29)/ Constant Craving (4:40)/ Big Boned Gal (5:06)/ Trail Of Broken Hearts (3:25)/ Constant Craving (#2) (3:01)/ Big Big Love (#2) (3:01)/ Crying (4:11)
R: Exs. Soundboard.   S: Toronto, Canada '93.
C: Australian CD. Dcc.

CD - LOVE SO SWEET
HAWK 062
Don't Let The Stars Get In Your Eyes (8:49)/ Luck In My Eyes (5:08)/ Outside My Self (6:08)/ Wash Me Clean (5:10)/ Memphis (t:27)/ Horse Back (1:48)/ Miss Chatelaine (7:53)/ Ridin' The Rails (4:53)/ Big Big Love (3:46)/ Pullin' Back The Reins (5:24)/ Constant Craving (4:50)
R: G-Vg. Audience.   S: Tupperware Theatre Sept. 6 '92.   C: ECD. Dcc. Pic CD.

CD - MY PRIVATE IDAHO
MONTANA MO 10010
Save Me/ The Mind Of Love/ So It Shall Be/ Miss Chatelaine/ Season Of Hollow Soul/ Black Coffee/ Wash Me Clean/ Constant Craving/ Crying/ Barefoot
R: Exs. Soundboard.   S: Quebec, Canada '93.
C: ECD. Dcc. Time 45:55.

CD - STRINGS 'N' THINGS
KISS THE STONE KTS 328
I Save Me (4:11)/ The Mind Of Love (3:35)/ So It Shall Be (5:27)/ Miss Chatelaine (4:38)/ Season Of Hollow Soul (4:29)/ Black Coffee (4:10)/ Wash Me Clean (4:02)/ Constant Craving (4:23)/ Crying (5:03)/ Barefoot (3:59)
R: Exs. Soundboard.   S: USA '94.   C: ECD. Dcc. Pic CD.

LED ZEPPELIN
(see pages 204 and 205)

CD - A FIGHTING FINISH
SILVER RARITIES SIRA 122/123
CD1: The Song Remains The Same/ Sick Again/ Nobody's Fault But Mine/ Over The Hills/ Since I've Been Loving You/ No Quarter/ Ten Years Gone/ The Battle Of Evermore/ Going To California
CD2: Mystery Train/ Black Country Woman/ Bron-Y-Aur Stomp/ Trampled Underfoot/ White Summer, Black Mountain Side/ Kashmir/ Guitar Solo/ Achilles' Last Stand/ Stairway To Heaven/

Whole Lotta Love/ Rock And Roll
R: Gm. Audience.   S: Oakland July 24 '77.
C: ECD. Dcc. Time 75:30. CD2 63:59.

CD - A NIGHT AT THE HEARTBREAK HOTEL
MISSING LINK ML 011/012/013
CD1: Immigrant Song (5:17)/ Heartbreaker (8:07)/
Over The Hills And Far Away (5:11)/ Black Dog
(5:39)/ Since I've Been Loving You (7:51)/
Stairway To Heaven (9:28)/ Going To California
(4:17)/ That's The Way (6:00)/ Tangerine (3:04)/
Bron-Y-Aur Stomp (4:42)
CD2: Dazed & Confused, The Crunge (27:21)/
What Is And What Should Never Be (4:26)/
Dancing Days (3:31)/ Moby Dick (19:36)
CD3: Whole Lotta Love Medley: Boogie Chillen,
Let's Have A Party, Mary Lou, Heartbreak Hotel,
Going Down Slow (24:50)/ Rock & Roll (3:58)/ The
Ocean (4:12)/ Louie Louie (4:16)/ Thank You
(6:46)/ Communication Breakdown (3:33)/ Bring It
On Home (9:23)/ Weekend (2:37)*
R: Gm. Audience. *Very poor.   S: Forum,
Inglewood June 25 '72.   C: Japanese CD. Dcc.

CD - A WEEK FOR BADGE HOLDERS L.A. 6 DAYS 1977
TARANTURA T19CD-BOX
CD1: Intro - The Song Remains The Same (6:15)/
The Rover Intro, Sick Again (6:01)/ Nobody's Fault
But Mine (6:42)/ Over The Hills And Far Away
(6:02)/ Since I've Been Loving You (7:55)/ No
Quarter (26:43)
CD2: Ten Years Gone (8:44)/ Battle Of Evermore
(5:21)/ Going To California (4:43)/ Black Country
Woman (1:41)/ Bron-Y-Aur Stomp (6:43)/ White
Summer (7:33)/ Black Mountain Side (2:12)/
Kashmir (9:11)
CD3: Out On The Tiles, Moby Dick (17:23)/
Heartbreaker (8:33)/ Guitar Solo (includes Star
Spangled Banner, Dixie) (16:12)/ Achilles Last
Stand (8:55)/ Stairway To Heaven (11:23)/ Whole
Lotta Love (1:24)/ Rock And Roll (3:57)
CD4: The Song Remains The Same (6:17)/ The
Rover Intro, Sick Again (6:02)/ Nobody's Fault But
Mine (6:44)/ Over The Hills And Far Away (6:02)/
Since I've Been Loving You (8:01)/ No Quarter
(includes Sakura) (26:55)/ Ten Years Gone (8:06)
CD5: The Battle Of Evermore (5:22)/ Going To
California (4:44)/ Black Country Woman (1:40)/
Bron-Y-Aur Stomp (6:55)/ White Summer (7:39)/
Black Mountain Side (2:07)/ Kashmir (9:11)
CD6: Out On The Tiles Intro, Moby Dick (17:44)/
Over The Hills And Far Away (6:03)/ Guitar Solo
(includes Star Spangled Banner) (14:33)/ Achilles
Last Stand (8:55)/ Stairway To Heaven (11:02)/
Whole Lotta Love (1:17)/ Rock And Roll (3:55)
CD7: The Song Remains The Same (6:18)/ The
Rover Intro, Sick Again (6:11)/ Nobody's Fault But
Mine (6:44)/ Over The Hill And Far Away (6:03)/
Since I've Been Loving You (7:56)/ No Quarter
(26:44)
CD8: Ten Years Gone (9:12)/ Battle Of Evermore
(5:23)/ Going To California (4:48)/ Black Country
Woman (1:39)/ Bron-Y-Aur Stomp (6:50)/ White

Summer (7:28)/ Black Mountain Side (2:07)/
Kashmir (9:14)
CD9: Trampled Underfoot (8:44)/ Out On The
Tiles Intro, Moby Dick (17:43)/ Guitar Solo
Includes Star Spangled Banner (15:56)/ Achilles
Last Stand (8:55)/ Stairway To Heaven (11:23)/
Whole Lotta Love (1:25)/ Rock And Roll (4:01)
CD10: The Song Remains The Same (6:16)/ The
Rover Intro, Sick Again (6:03)/ Nobody's Fault But
Mine (6:45)/ In My Time Of Dying, Rip It Up
(10:55)/ Since I've Been Loving You (7:56)/ No
Quarter (27:55)
CD11: Ten Years Gone (9:02)/ The Battle Of
Evermore (5:33)/ Going To California (5:21)/ Black
Country Woman (2:21)/ Bron-Y-Aur Stomp (6:55)/
White Summer (7:35)/ Black Mountain Side (2:23)/
Kashmir (9:25)/ Trampled Underfoot (7:42)
CD12: Out On The Tiles Intro, Moby Dick (26:33)/
Guitar Solo (includes Dixie, Star Spangled
Banner) (14:35)/ Achilles Last Stand (8:35)/
Stairway To Heaven (11:25)/ Whole Lotta Love
(2:27)/ Communication Breakdown (3:23)
CD13: The Song Remains The Same (1:15 Cut)/
The Rover Intro, Sick Again (5:59)/ Nobody's Fault
But Mine (6:45)/ Over The Hills And Far Away
(6:02)/ Since I've Been Loving You (8:05)/ No
Quarter (26:55)
CD14: Ten Years Gone (9:12) The Battle Of
Evermore (5:24)/ Going To California (4:48)/
That's Alright (1:44)/ Black Country Woman (1:44)/
Bron-Y-Aur Stomp (6:55)/ White Summer (7:55)/
Black Mountain Side (2:40)/ Kashmir (9:14)
CD15: Out On The Tiles Intro, Moby Dick (4:44
Cut)/ Guitar Solo (includes Star Spangled Banner)
(21:23)/ Achilles Last Stand (8:44)/ Stairway To
Heaven (11:23)/ It'll Be Me (2:54)
CD16: The Song Remains The Same (6:15)/ The
Rover Intro, Sick Again (5:58)/ Nobody's Fault But
Mine (6:45)/ Over The Hills And Far Away (6:05)/
Since I've Been Loving You (8:02)
CD17: No Quarter (27:44)/ Ten Years Gone (9:02)
CD18: The Battle Of Evermore (5:26)/ Going To
California (4:46)/ Going Down South (1:02)/ Black
Country Woman (1:45)/ Bron-Y-Aur Stomp (6:55)/
Dancing Days (3:45)/ White Summer (7:25)/ Black
Mountain Side (2:32)/ Kashmir (9:03)/ Trampled
Underfoot (7:44)
CD19: Out On The Tiles Intro, Moby Dick (16:02)/
Guitar Solo (includes Star Spangled Banner)
(24:55)/ Achilles Last Stand (8:55 cut)/ Stairway
To Heaven (11:12)/ Whole Lotta Love (1:45)/ Rock
And Roll (3:55)
R: Vg-Ex. Audience.   S: The Forum, Inglewood,
California '77. CD1-3 June 21. CD5-6 June 22.
CD7-9 June 23. CD10-12 June 25. CD13-15 June
26. CD 16-19 June 27. CD4 June 14 Madison
Square Garden, NYC June 14 '77.   C: Japanese
CD. Each show comes in its own gatefold slip
case. The first 10 sets contained 2 posters. The
rest of the limited edition of 150 only had one
poster (B&w). All of this comes in a black box with
a B&w picture and gold lettering. Another excellent
package from Tarantura. Very rare.

CD - A WEEK FOR BADGE HOLDERS L.A. 6 DAYS 1977
(TARANTURA T19CD-BOX)

<- OUT ON THE TILES
CD1-3 June 21.

OVER THE HILLS AND
FAR AWAY ->
CD4 June 14 Madison
Square Garden, NYC
June 14 '77.
CD5-6 June 22.

<- GOOD NIGHT,
MOONLIGHT
CD7-9 June 23.

BADGE HOLDERS
ANNUAL MEETING ->
CD10-12 June 25.

<- THAT'S ALRIGHT
CD13-15 June 26.

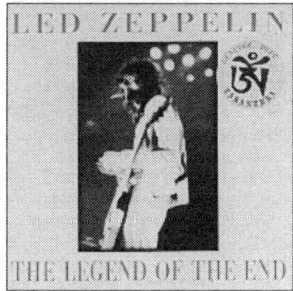

THE LEGEND OF
THE END ->
CD 16-19 June 27.

CD - AFTERNOON DAZE
MUD DOGS RECORDS MUD DOGS-013-15
CD1: Immigrant Song (4:56)/ Heartbreaker (6:56)/ Since I've Been Loving You (8:19)/ Black Dog (6:16)/ Dazed And Confused (23:56)/ Stairway To Heaven (9:45)
CD2: Celebration Day (6:00)/ That's The Way (6:40)/ Going To California (7:52)/ Tangerine (3:30)/ What Is And What Should Never Be (5:15)/ Moby Dick (19:25)
CD3: Whole Lotta Love Medley: Boogie Woogie, Cocaine, Rave On, Your Time Is Gonna Come, I'm A Man, The Hunter, Mary Lou, Pretty Woman, How Many More Times (28:37)/ Organ Solo (4:06)/ Thank You (7:18)/ Communication Breakdown (5:32)
R: Poor-Gm. Audience.   S: Budokan, Tokyo, Japan Sept. 24 '71.   C: Japanese CD. Dcc.

CD - AIR RAIDS OVER GERMANY
TECUMSEH TRC 005
Dazed & Confused (17:52)*/ Bring It On Home (9:50)*/ Whole Lotta Love Medley: Everybody Needs Somebody To Love, Boogie Children, Baby I Don't Care, Let's Have A Party, I Can't Quit You, The Lemon Song (22:21)**/ Train Kept A Rollin' (2:21)***/ Nobody's Fault But Mine (5:24)***/ Black Dog (5:07)***
R: Tracks 1-2 Poor-Gm. Audience. Tracks 3-6 Gm. Soundboard.   S: Tracks 1-2 Berlin, Germany. *July 12 '70. **Mar. 19 '73. ***Nuremberg, Germany June 27 '80.
C: Japanese CD. Red & white slick around cardboard sleeve.

CD - AND IT MAKES ME WONDER
AMERICAN CONCERT SERIES 046
Rock And Roll (3:45)/ Celebration Day (3:33)/ Black Dog (5:46)/ Over The Hills And Far Away (6:07)/ Misty Mountain Hip (4:43)/ Since I've Been Loving You (8:13)/ No Quarter (12:30)/ The Song Remains The Same (5:17)/ The Rain Song (7:48)/ Stairway To Heaven (9:52)
R: Vgs. Soundboard.   S: Buffalo, New York July 15 '73.   C: ECD. Dcc.

CD - ANOTHER TRIP
BIG MUSIC BIG BX 007 -
4023/4024/4025/4026/4027
CD1 - 1967-69: Gotta Find My Baby (Demo '67) (3:50)/ You Shook Me (Olympic Studios Sept. 27 '68) (7:31)/ Communication Breakdown (BBC 'Top Gear' Radio Show Mar. 3 '69) (2:58)/ Dazed And Confused (Staines, England Mar. 25 '69)/ Train Kept A Rollin' (2:54), I Can't Quit You Baby (5:58), How Many More Times (19:23), Babe I'm Gonna Leave You (7:30), Sittin' And Thinkin' (7:00) (Fillmore West, San Francisco Apr. 27 '69)/ The Girl I Love She Got Long Black Hair (2:59), Something Else (2:06) (Aeolian Hall Studio 2 June 16 '69)/ What Is And What Should Never Be (Maida Vale Studio 4 June 24 '69) (4:24)
CD2 - 1970-72: White Summer-Black Mountain Side (Julie Felix TV Show Apr. 28 '70) (5:04)/ John

Paul Jones Organ Improvisation (6:00), Out On The Tiles (4:07), Blueberry Hill (3:17), Bring It On Home (9:47), Whole Lotta Love Medley: Includes Let That Boy Boogie, Movin' On, I've Got A Girl, Some Other Guy, Think It Over, The Lemon Song (17:13) (The Forum, Inglewood Sept. 4 '70)*/ Moby Dick (15:34) (Maple Leaf Gardens, Toronto, Canada Sept. 4 '71)/ Friends (5:21) (Koseinenkin Kaikan, Osaka, Japan Sept. 29 '71)*/ The Rover (1:03) (Rolling Stones Mobile Studio, Stargroves, UK May '72)/ No Quarter (7:27) (Electric Ladyland Studios, New York June '72)
CD3 - 1973: Schooldays (2:42), Nadine (1:02), Round And Round (3:03), Move On Down The Line (2:06), Shakin' All Over (2:31) (Chicago Auditorium, Chicago July 6 '73)/ Rock And Roll (4:02), Celebration Day (3:26), Black Dog (6:43), Over The Hills And Far Away (6:56), Misty Mountain Hop (4:56), Since I've Been Loving You (8:46), No Quarter (13:38), The Song Remains The Same (5:29), The Rain Song (8:49) (Madison Square Garden, New York July 29 '73)
CD4 - 1975-77: Sick Again (5:35), Kashmir (9:44), Trampled Underfoot (8:11) (Memorial Auditorium, Dallas Mar. 4 '75)/ Tangerine (6:26), That's The Way (8:47), Ten Years Gone (6:13) (Earl's Court, London May 24 '75)/ Battle Of Evermore (USA '77) (6:00)/ Black Country Woman (2:35), Bron Y Aur Stomp (5:00), Jimmy Page Guitar Experimentation (9:51), Achilles Last Stand (9:37) (Cleveland Apr. 27 '77)
CD5 - 1979-80: Hot Dog (Knebworth Festival, Hertfordshire, England Aug. '79) (3:11)/ All My Love (Rotterdam, Holland June 21 '80) (5:39)/ Nobody's Fault But Mine (6:21), Black Dog (6:35) (Messhalle, Nuremberg, Germany June 27 '80)/ In The Evening (10:46), Stairway To Heaven (11:47), Heartbreaker (9:59) (Hallenstadion, Zurich, Switzerland June 29 '80)/ Money (Festhalle, Frankfurt, Germany June 30 '80) (5:19)/ Whole Lotta Love (Eissporthalle, Berlin, Germany July 7 '80) (18:59)
R: Ex. Some Vg-Ex. Soundboard. *Vg-Ex. Audience.   C: ECD. Dcc. Box set. Pic CDs. Color book. Follow up to Big Records' 'Through The Years' (Big 002).

CD - BABE I'M GONNA LEAVE YOU
DYNAMITE STUDIOS DS92J031
Moby Dick (27:48)/ Heartbreaker Medley: Whole Lotta Love, Boogie Children (23:22)/ Untitled Instrumental Take #1 (0:48)/ Untitled Instrumental Take #2 (1:06)/ Untitled Instrumental Take #3 (1:58)/ Untitled Instrumental Take #4 (2:55)/ Untitled Instrumental Take #5 (4:20)/ Untitled Instrumental Take #6 (4:55)/ Untitled Instrumental Take #7 (4:59)
R: Exs. Soundboard.   S: Detroit, Michigan July 13 '73 and studio '68.   C: Japanese CD. Dcc.

CD - BACK ON THE WEST COAST
MAD DOGS O31/032
CD1: Immigrant Song (4:16)/ Heartbreaker (6:29)/ Since I've Been Loving You (6:37)/ Black Dog

(4:45)/ Dazed & Confused (19:35)/ Stairway To
Heaven (8:01)/ Celebration Day (3:41)
CD2: That's The Way (6:46)/ Going To California
(4:07)/ What Is & What Should Never Be (3:50)/
Moby Dick (10:49)/ Whole Lotta Love Medley:
Boogie Children, Mary Lou, Mess Of Blues, You
Shook Me (20:06)/ Communication Breakdown
(5:23)
R: Poor. Mono. Audience.   S: Berkeley
Community Center, CA Sept. 13 '71.
C: Japanese CD. Dcc.

CD - BADGE HOLDERS BEST LIVE IN CONCERT 1969
DOUBLE TIME DTD 006 1-2
CD1: I Can't Quit You (5:05)/ I Gotta Move (2:43)/
Dazed & Confused (9:45)/ How Many More Times
(1:53)/ You Shook Me (5:23)/ Communication
Breakdown (3:03)/ I Can't Quit You (4:31)/ Dazed
& Confused (6:48)/ What Is & What Should Never
Be (4:25)/ Communication Breakdown (2:46)/
Travelling Riverside Blues (5:20)/ Whole Lotta
Love (6:12)
CD2: Communication Breakdown (3:21)/ I Can't
Quit You (6:13)/ You Shook Me (10:10)/ White
Summer (8:17)/ Dazed & Confused (16:13)/ How
Many More Times (11:09)
R: G-Vgm. Soundboard.   S: CD1 tracks 1-4 in
Stockholm Mar. 14 '69. Tracks 5-8 London Mar. 3
'69. Tracks 9-12 London June 24 '69. CD2 London
June 27 '69.   C: ECD. Dcc.

CD - BALTIMORE 1972
IMMIGRANT IM-026-28
CD1: Immigrant Song/ Heartbreaker/ Black Dog/
Since I've Been Loving You/ Stairway To Heaven/
Going To California/ That's The Way
CD2: Tangerine/ Bron-Y-Aur Stomp/ Dazed And
Confused/ What Is And What Should Never Be/
Moby Dick
CD3: Whole Lotta Love/ Rock And Roll/
Communication Breakdown
R: G-Vg. Audience.   S: Civic Center, Baltimore
June 11 '72.   C: Japanese CD. Dcc. Time CD1
56:03. CD2 68:35. CD3 36:44.

CD - BATH 1970
LE-MON RECORDING CO. LZ 1&2
CD1: Immigrant Song (3:24)/ Heartbreaker (6:00)/
Dazed And Confused (14:50)/ Bring It On Home
(9:07)/ Since I've Been Loving You (9:07)/ Organ
Solo - Thank You (13:32)/ The Boy Next Door
(That's The Way) (5:05)/ What Is And What
Should Never Be (4:24)
CD2: Moby Dick (14:35)/ How Many More Times
Medley: The Hunter, Gotta Keep Moving, Boogie
Children, Honey Bee, That's Alright, Long
Distance Call Blues, The Lemon Song (26:58)/
Whole Lotta Love (6:06)/ Communication
Breakdown (4:26)/ Long Tall Sally Medley: Johnny
Be Goode, Say Mama, That's Alright (9:46)
R: Poor-Gm. Audience.   S: Bath, England June
28 '70.   C: ECD.

CD - BBC ZEP
ANTRABATA REFERENCE MASTER ARM 25371
CD1: Introduction (1:13)/ Immigrant Song (3:10)/
Heartbreaker (5:39)/ Since I've Been Loving You
(7:23)/ Black Dog (6:07)/ Dazed And Confused
(20:44)/ Stairway To Heaven (8:46)
CD2: Going To California (6:02)/ That's The Way
(6:56)/ What Is And What Should Never Be (5:46)/
Whole Lotta Love Medley (22:07)/ Thank You
(6:33)/ Communication Breakdown (6:03
R: Exs. Soundboard.   S: Radio Broadcast, Paris
Theatre, London Apr. 1 '71.   C: Japanese CD.
Cardboard sleeve with reproduction of William
Stout cover from the vinyl release of the same
name over double jewel case. Limited numbered
edition of 325.

CD - BBC ZEP ORIGINAL MASTER
TARANTURA T2CD-7-1,2
CD1: Immigrant Song (3:25)/ Heartbreaker (5:25)/
Since I've Been Loving You (7:20)/ Black Dog
(5:02)/ Dazed And Confused (19:35)/ Stairway To
Heaven (8:21)
CD2: Going To California (4:23)/ That's The Way
(6:12)/ What Is And What Should Never Be (4:12)/
Whole Lotta Love Medley: Boogie Woogie,
Truckin', Little Mama, Fixin' To Die, That's Alright,
For What's It's Worth, Mess O' Blues, Honey Bee,
Lemon Song (21:35)/ Thank You (7:23)/
Communication Breakdown (5:30)/ End by John
Peel
R: Ex. Soundboard.   S: BBC, Paris Studios,
London. Recorded Apr. 1 '71, broadcast Apr. 4
'71.   C: Japanese CD. Reproduction of William
Stout sketch from the record of the same name.

CD - BLACK DOG VOL. 1
BANANA BAN 054A
Heartbreaker (6:31)/ Thank You (8:05)/ What Is &
What Should Never Be (4:17)/ Communication
Breakdown (4:52)/ We're Gonna Groove (3:46)/
Since I've Been Loving You (7:01)/ Whole Lotta
Love (2:43)/ Communication Breakdown (2:21)/
Dazed & Confused (8:42)/ Babe I'm Gonna Leave
You (6:41)/ How Many More Times (12:21)
R: Vg-Exm. Soundboard.   S: Vancouver Mar. 21
'70. Tracks 8-11 Copenhagen Mar. 13 '69.
C: Australian CD. Dcc. Time 67:51.

CD - BLACK DOG (VOL. 2)
BANANA BAN-054-B
Stairway To Heaven (9:32)/ Celebration Day
(5:15)/ That's The Way (7:370/ Going To California
(4:19)/ What Is And What Should Never Be (4:54)/
Moby Dick (3:00)/ Immigrant Song (3:16)/
Heartbreaker (5:41)/ Black Dog (5:55)/ Dazed And
Confused (19:12)
R: Vg. Soundboard.   S: Toronto Sept. 4 '71.
Tracks 7-10 London Apr. 1 '71.   C: Australian
CD. Dcc. Time 68:30.

CD - BLACK DOG (VOL. 3)
BANANA BAN-054-C
Stairway To Heaven (9:04)/ Since I've Been

Loving You (7:56)/ Going To California (4:26)/ That's The Way (6:19)/ What Is And What Should Never Be (false start - 0:26)/ What Is And What Should Never Be (5:05)/ Whole Lotta Love (9:30/ That's All Right Mama (1:50)/ For What It's Worth (1:51)/ Mess Of Blues (4:57)/ The Lemon Song (1:49)/ Whole Lotta Love (2:40)/ Thank You (7:13)/ Communication Breakdown (5:37)
R: Vg-Exm. Soundboard.   S: London Apr. 1 '71.
C: Australian CD. Dcc. Time 68:13.

CD - BLACK DOG (VOL. 4)
BANANA BAN-054-D
Dazed And Confused (26:06)/ No Quarter (21:04)/ Tangerine (3:33)/ That's The Way (7:10)/ Bron-Y-Aur Stomp (6:08)/ Trampled Underfoot (9:03)
R: Vgm. Soundboard.   S: London May 24 '75 not the 25th as the cover claims.   C: Australian CD. Dcc. Time 73:07.

CD - BLITZKRIEG OVER EUROPE
TARANTURA T3CD-5
CD1: The Train Kept A Rollin'/ Nobody's Fault But Mine/ Black Dog/ In The Evening
CD2: Achilles Last Stand/ White Summer/ Black Mountain Side/ Kashmir/ Stairway To Heaven
CD3: The Train Kept A Rollin'/ Nobody's Fault But Mine/ Black Dog/ Stairway To Heaven
R: Vg-Exs. Soundboard. Runs a bit slow.
S: CD1-2 Festhalle, Frankfurt June 30 '80. CD3 tracks 1-3 Messehalle, Nuremberg June 27 '80. Tracks 4-6 Mannheim July 2 '80 not Vienna June 26 '80 as claimed by cover. Tracks 7-8 Sporthalle, Cologne June 18 '80.   C: Japanese CD. Dcc. Embossed gatefold sleeve. Time: CD1 - 63:12/ CD2 66:44/ CD3 55:22.

CD - THE BONHAM SESSIONS
HAMMERJACK HJ 013
Wailing Sounds (2:37)/ Cause I Love You (2:45)/ Flashing Lights (3:11)/ Keep Your Hands On The Wheel (4:20)/ Jim's Blues (3:41)/ George Wallace Is Rollin' In This (2:22)/ Thumping Beat (3:07)/ Union Jack Car (3:00)/ So Glad To See You Here (3:33)/ Baby Come Back (2:33)/ Rockestra Theme (4:23)/ Immigration Song (2:42)/ Out On The Tiles (3:38)/ Custard Pie (4:47)/ The Rover 2:05)/ In My Time Of Dying (7:12)/ Trampled Underfoot (3:52)/ In The Light (5:22)/ The Want One Song (3:32)/ Sick Again (3:38)/ Hots For Nowhere (4:08)/ Going To California (3:48)
R: G-Vg.   C: ECD. Dcc.

CD - BONZO'S BIRTHDAY PARTY
MUD DOGS 018-019
CD1: Rock And Roll (3:59)/ Celebration Day (3:25)/ Black Dog (6:48)/ Over The Hills And Far Away (6:22)/ Misty Mountain Hop (4:43)/ Since I've Been Loving You (7:55)/ No Quarter (13:12)/ The Song Remains The Same (5:35)/ The Rain Song (8:36)/ Stairway To Heaven (9:25)
CD2: Dazed & Confused (28:35)/ Moby Dick (16:14)/ Happy Birthday (0:35)/ Heartbreaker (6:25)/ Whole Lotta Love (11:27)/ The Ocean

(4:16)
R: Poor-Gm. Audience.   S: The Forum, Inglewood May 31 '73.   C: Japanese CD. Dcc.

CD - BONZO'S BIRTHDAY PARTY
TARANTURA TMQ TCD72007
CD1: Rock And Roll/ Celebration Day/ Black Dog/ Over The Hills And Far Away/ Misty Mountain Hop/ Since I've Been Loving You/ No Quarter/ The Song Remains The Same/ The Rain Song
CD2: Dazed And Confused/ Stairway To Heaven/ Moby Dick/ Happy Birthday Bonzo!
CD3: Heartbreaker/ Whole Lotta Love/ The Ocean
R: Gm. Audience.   S: The Forum, Inglewood May 31 '73.   C: Japanese CD. Dcc. Embossed fold-out sleeve. Pic CDs. Time CD1 62:04. CD2 58:50. CD3 23:49.

CD - BUFFALO SIXTY NINE
NEW PLASTIC RECORDS NP 55002
Communication Breakdown (3:28)/ I Can't Quit You Baby (6:09)/ Heartbreaker (4:35)/ Dazed And Confused (14:55)/ White Summer, Black Mountain Side (10:06)/ How Many More Times (11:32)
R: Poor Mono. Audience.   S: Kleinhans Music Hall, Buffalo, NY Oct. 30 '69.   C: ECD. Dcc.

CD - BURN LIKE A CANDLE
SMOKING PIG LZCA-01/2/3
CD1: Introduction (1:41)/ Immigrant Song (3:36)/ Heartbreaker (8:07)/ Over The Hills And Far Away (5:11)/ Black Dog (5:39)/ Since I've Been Loving You (7:51)/ Stairway To Heaven (9:28)/ Going To California (4:17)/ That's The Way (6:00)/ Tangerine (3:04)
CD2: Bron-Y-Aur Stomp (4:42)/ Dazed & Confused, The Crunge (27:21)/ What Is And What Should Never Be (4:26)/ Dancing Days (3:31)/ Moby Dick (19:36)
CD3: Whole Lotta Love Medley: Boogie Children, Let's Have A Party, Mary Lou, Heartbreak Hotel, Going Down Slow (24:50)/ Rock And Roll (3:58)/ The Ocean (4:12)/ Louie Louie (4:16)/ Thank You (6:46)/ Communication Breakdown (3:33)/ Bring It On Home (9:23)/ Weekend (2:37)*
R: G-Vgm. Audience. *Very poor.   S: LA June 25 '72.   C: Japanese CD. Dcc. Artwork by William Stout. Includes a poster.

CD - THE BUTTERQUEEN
UNBELIEVABLE MUSIC UM 026/27/28
CD1: Rock And Roll (4:14)/ Celebration Day (3:43)/ Bron-Y-Aur Stomp (:18)/ Black Dog (5:54)/ Over The Hills And Far Away (6:40)/ Since I've Been Loving You (8:17)/ No Quarter (10:54)/ Dazed And Confused (29:15)
CD2: The Song Remains The Same (5:45)/ The Rain Song (7:44)/ Rock And Roll (3:52)/ Celebration Day (3:33)/ Black Dog (4:00)/ Since I've Been Loving You (8:56)/ No Quarter (11:35)/ The Song Remains The Same (5:34)/ The Rain Song (8:31)/ Stairway to Heaven (11:08)
CD3: Dazed And Confused (29:30)/ Whole Lotta Love (14:25)/ Heartbreaker, Whole Lotta Love

(20:25)*/ Communication Breakdown (4:22)*/ The Ocean (4:42)*
R: Vgs. Soundboard. *Gm. Audience.   S: CD1 and CD2 tracks 1-3 Forth Worth, Texas May 19 '73. CD2 tracks 3-10 and CD3 tracks 1-2 Madison Square Gardens, NYC July 27 '73. CD3 tracks 3-5 Kezar Stadium, San Francisco June 2 '73.
C: ECD. Dcc.

CD - CHIEN NOIR
ANTRABATA REFERENCE MASTER ARM 200680/230680
CD1: The Train Kept A Rollin'/ Nobody's Fault But Mine/ Black Dog/ In The Evening/ The Rain Song/ Hot Dog/ All My Love/ Trampled Underfoot/ Since I've Been Loving You
CD2: Achilles Last Stand/ White Summer, Black Mountain Side/ Kashmir/ Stairway To Heaven/ Rock And Roll/ Whole Lotta Love
CD3: The Train Kept A Rollin'/ Nobody's Fault But Mine/ Black Dog/ In The Evening/ The Rain Song/ Hot Dog/ All My Love/ Trampled Underfoot/ Since I've Been Loving You
CD4: Achilles Last Stand/ White Summer, Black Mountain Side/ Kashmir/ Stairway To Heaven/ Rock And Roll/ Communication Breakdown
R: Exs. Soundboard.   S: CD1 Brussels June 20 '80. CD2 Brussels June 20 '80. CD3 Bremen June 23 '80. CD4 Bremen June 23 '80.   C: Japanese CD. Full color cardboard slipcover over jewel case with Dcc. Includes a certificate of authenticity. Limited edition of 325. Time CD1 60:27. CD2 58:46. CD3 55:56. CD4 44:06.

CD - COMPLETE BERLIN
SILVER RARITIES SIRA 111/112
CD1: Train Kept A Rollin'/ Nobody's Fault But Mine/ Black Dog/ In The Evening/ The Rain Song/ Hot Dog/ All My Love/ Trampled Underfoot/ Since I've Been Loving You
CD2: White Summer, Black Mountainside/ Kashmir/ Stairway To Heaven/ Rock And Roll/ Whole Lotta Love
R: Exs. Soundboard.   S: Berlin July 7 '80.
C: ECD. Dcc.

CD - COMPLETE BOSTON TEA PARTY
ARMS 07/08 PR
CD1: Train Kept A' Rollin' (3:01)/ Plant Talks (3:10)/ I Can't Quit You (5:40)/ As Long As I Have You (12:51)/ Dazed & Confused (12:32)/ You Shook Me (9:05)/ As Long As I Have You (15:07)/ I Can't Quit You (6:15)
CD2: Dazed & Confused (14:10)/ You Shook Me (9:26)/ Pat's Delight (11:47)/ Babe I'm Gonna Leave You (7:19)/ How Many More Times Medley: For Your Love, The Hunter (21:54)/ Communication Breakdown (6:00)
R: Gm. Audience.   S: Boston Jan. 23 '69 and Jan. ? '69.   C: Japanese CD. Dcc.

CD - COMPLETE EARL'S COURT ARENA 75
CD1: Rock & Roll (4:11)/ Sick Again (5:18)/ Over The Hills & Far Away (8:04)/ In My Time Of Dying

(12:23)/ The Song Remains The Same (6:10)/ The Rain Song (7:57)/ Kashmir (10:10)
CD2: No Quarter (21:36)/ Tangerine (4:11)/ Going To California (6:45)/ That's The Way (7:12)/ Bron-Y-Aur (7:01)/ Trampled Underfoot (10:20)
CD3: Moby Dick (cut) (21:20)/ Dazed & Confused, Woodstock (32:24)/ Stairway To Heaven (10:20)/ Whole Lotta Love Medley, The Crunge (5:18)/ Black Dog (5:29)
R: G-Vgs. Audience.   S: London May 18 '75.
C: Japanese CD. Dcc.

CD - THE COMPLETE GEISHA TAPE
TARANTURA TS-3
CD1: Immigrant Song/ Heartbreaker/ Since I've Been Loving You/ Black Dog/ Dazed And Confused (also Pennies From Heaven)/ Stairway To Heaven/ Celebration Day
CD2: Guitar Changes/ That's The Way/ Going To California/ Tangerine/ Friends
CD3: Whole Lotta Love (also Boogie Woogie, Tossin' & Turnin', Twist & Shout, Fortune Teller, Good Times Bad Times, You Shook Me)/ Communication Breakdown
R: Vgs. Soundboard.   S: Koseinenkin Kaikan, Osaka, Japan Sept. 29 '71.   C: Japanese CD. Dcc. Gatefold sleeve. Time CD1 73:48. CD2 47:17. CD3 53:39.

CD - THE COMPLETE TAPES VOL. 1 (1968/69)
TINTAGEL 0032/0033/0034
CD1: I Can't Quit You (6:29), I Gotta Move (3:04), Dazed And Confused (10:42), How Many More Times (2:00) (Tivoli Gardens, Stockholm Sept. 20 '68)/ For Your Love (Fillmore West, San Francisco, CA Jan. 10 '69)/ As Long As I Have You Medley (12:06)/ You Shook Me (7:44)/ Communication Breakdown (4:52) (Teen Club, Gladsaxe, Copenhagen, Denmark Mar. 13 '69)
CD2: Train Kept A Rollin' (2:58), How Many More Times Medley (19:21), Killing Floor (7:36), Babe I'm Gonna Leave You (7:30), Sitting And Thinking (6:56), Pat's Delight (7:19) (Fillmore West, San Francisco, CA Apr. 27 '69)
CD3: The Girl I Love (3:14), Something Else (2:15), What Is And What Should Never Be (4:29), Travelling Riverside Blues (3:16) (John Peel Session, London June 23 '69)/ Good Times, Bad Times (2:57), Heartbreaker (5:02) (Lyceum Ballroom, London Oct. 12 '69)/ Jenning's Farm Blues (takes 1 to 10) (16:48), Jenning's Farm Blues (take 11) (6:19) (Olympia Studios, London Nov. 69)
R: Vg-Ex. Audience/Soundboard.   C: ECD. Box set. Booklet with B&w pictures. Pic CDs.

CD - THE COMPLETE TAPES VOL. 2 (1970/71)
TINTAGEL TIBX 000043/000044/000045
CD1: We're Gonna Groove, Dazed And Confused, Heartbreaker, How Many More Times (Jazz Festival, Montreaux Mar. 14 '70)/ Bring It On Home (Dorten Auditorium, Raleigh, North Carolina Apr. 7 '70)/ I Wanna Be Her Man, Down By The

Seaside, That's The Way, Friends, Poor Tom, Hey Hey What Can I Do (Bron-Y-Aur Cottage, Wales May '70)
CD2: Immigrant Song, What Is And What Should Never Be, Moby Dick, Communication Breakdown Medley, That's The Way, Whole Lotta Love Medley, Bron-Y-Aur Stomp (Forum, Inglewood, CA Sept. 4 '70)
CD3: Since I've Been Loving You, Black Dog, Stairway To Heaven, Going To California, Thank You (BBC Paris Studio, London Mar. 25 '71)/ Four Sticks, Gallows Pole, Misty Mountain Hop, Rock And Roll Music (KB Hallen, Copenhagen, Denmark June 3 '71)/ Celebration Day (Budokan Hall, Tokyo, Japan Sept. 23 '71)
R: Vg-Ex. Some G. Audience/Soundboard.
C: ECD. Box set. Booklet with B&w and color pictures. Pic CDs.

CD - COPENHAGEN WARM-UPS
TARANTURA T4CD-2
CD1: Opening (2:09)/ The Song Remains The Same (5:39)/ Celebration Day (3:12)/ Black Dog (5:55)/ Nobody's Fault But Mine (6:12)/ Over The Hills And Far Away (6:12)/ Misty Mountain Hop (4:25)/ Since I've Been Loving You (8:26)/ No Quarter (14:11)/ Hot Dog (3:15)
CD2: The Rain Song (8:50)/ White Summer, Black Mountain Side (4:51)/ Kashmir (8:50)/ Trampled Underfoot (5:48)/ Achilles Last Stand (8:35)/ Guitar Solo (5:31)/ In The Evening (6:33)/ Stairway To Heaven (8:54)/ Rock And Roll (3:28)
CD3: The Song Remains The Same (5:34)/ Celebration Day (3:09)/ Black Dog (5:62)/ Nobody's Fault But Mine (6:05)/ Over The Hills And Far Away (6:16)/ Misty Mountain Hop (4:24)/ Since I've Been Loving You (8:08)/ No Quarter (13:55)/ Ten Years Gone (7:04)/ Hot Dog (3:14)
CD4: The Rain Song (7:28)/ White Summer, Black Mountain Side (4:48)/ Kashmir (8:53)/ Trampled Underfoot (5:42)/ Sick Again (4:42)/ Achilles Last Stand (8:43)/ Guitar Solo (5:25)/ In The Evening (6:22)/ Stairway To Heaven (8:15)/ Whole Lotta Love (6:36)
R: Vgs. Audience. S: Falkoner Theater, Copenhagen, Denmark. CD1-2 July 23 '79. CD3-4 July 24 '79. C: Japanese CD. Gatefold slipcase. Multicolored ZOSO stamped on cover.

CD - THE DARK TOWER
TARANTURA T70CD-3/4
CD1: We're Gonna Groove (4:16)/ I Can't Quit You (6:20)/ White Summer (4:53)/ Black Mountain Side (6:33)/ Dazed & Confused (16:43)/ Heartbreaker (7:08)
CD2: Since I've Been Loving You (6:39)/ Organ Solo (2:21)/ Thank You (6:27)/ What Is & What Should Never Be (4:54)/ Moby Dick (16:00)/ How Many More Times (7:20)
R: Gm. Audience. S: Montreux Mar. 14 '70.
C: Japanese CD. Dcc. Gatefold sleeve. Pic CDs.

CD - DAZED & CONFUSED
MAD DOG MDR LZ001-2

CD1: Rock & Roll (3:51)/ Sick Again (5:30)/ Over The Hills & Far Away (6:34)/ In My Time Of Dying (10:39)/ The Song Remains The Same (5:13)/ The Rain Song (7:22)/ Kashmir (8:30)/ Since I've Been Loving You (7:28)*/ Trampled Underfoot (8:54)
CD2: Dazed & Confused (38:30)/ Stairway To Heaven (10:54)/ Whole Lotta Love (8:36)/ Black Dog (5:28)/ Heartbreaker (7:55)
R: G-Vgm. Audience. S: Los Angeles, California Mar. 25 '75. *Mar. 27 '25. CD2 tracks 2-5 Mar. 24 '75. C: Japanese CD. Dcc. Cover lists date as Mar. 28.

CD - DENMARK '69
DEEP MIK 028
Train Kept A Rollin' (2:48)/ I Can't Quit You (5:37)/ Dazed & Confused (10:56)/ You Shook Me (8:55)/ Communication Breakdown (2:29)/ Dazed & Confused (8:59)/ Babe I'm Gonna Leave You (6:43)/ How Many More Times (12:25)
R: Tracks 1-4 Gm. Audience. Tracks 5-9 G-Vgm. Soundboard. S: Copenhagen tracks 1-4 Brondby Pop Club Mar. 15 '69. Tracks 5-9 pro-shot video Mar. 13 '69. C: ECD. Dcc.

CD - THE DESTROYER
SMILIN' EARS SECD 77-301-2
CD1: The Song Remains The Same (6:12)/ Sick Again (6:00)/ Nobody's Fault But Mine (6:14)/ In My Time Of Dying (9:39)/ Surrender (:10)/ Since I've Been Loving You (8:30)/ No Quarter (21:05)/ Ten Years Gone (8:33)/ Battle Of Evermore (5:29)/ Going To California (4:26)
CD2: Black Country Woman (2:15)/ Bron-Y-Aur Stomp (5:00)/ White Summer (5:45)/ Moby Dick (17:15)/ Guitar Solo (9:31)/ Achilles Last Stand (9:26)/ Rock & Roll (4:00)/ Trampled Underfoot (6:30)
R: Gm. Audience. S: Cleveland Apr. 28 '77.
C: Japanese CD. Dcc.

CD - THE DESTROYER III
TARANTURA T3CD-8
CD1: The Song Remains The Same (6:33)/ The Rover (Introduction), Sick Again (6:23)/ Nobody's Fault But Mine (7:16)/ In My Time Of Dying (11:05)/ Since I've Been Loving You (7:35)/ No Quarter (19:44)
CD2: Ten Years Gone (8:18)/ The Battle Of Evermore (6:24)/ Going To California (4:35)/ Black Country Woman (2:33)/ Bron-Y-Aur Stomp (5:54)/ White Summer (5:17)/ Black Mountain Side (1:44)/ Kashmir (8:34)
CD3: Out On The Tiles, Moby Dick (fade out) (14:43 Cut)/ Guitar Solo With Star Spangled Banner (11:12)/ Achilles Last Stand (9:45)/ Stairway To Heaven (10:44)/ Whole Lotta Love/ Rock And Roll (4:32)
R: Vg-Ex. Audience. S: Capitol Centre, Landover, Maryland May 30 '77. C: Japanese CD. Full color slip case. Includes a 10" X 10" color poster of Page.

CD - THE DESTROYERS

TARANTURA T6CD-1/2

CD1: The Song Remains The Same/ The Rover,
Sick Again/ Nobody's Fault But Mine/ In My Time
Of Dying/ Since I've Been Loving You/ No Quarter
CD2: Ten Years Gone/ The Battle Of Evermore/
Going To California/ Black Country Woman/ Bron-
Yr-Aur Stomp/ White Summer/ Black
Mountainside/ Kashmir
CD3: Out On The Tiles, Moby Dick/ Jimmy's Bow
(with Star Spangled Banner)/ Achilles Last Stand/
Stairway To Heaven/ Rock And Roll/ Trampled
Underfoot
CD4: The Song Remains The Same/ The Rover,
Sick Again/ Nobody's Fault But Mine/ In My Time
Of Dying/ Surrender, Since I've Been Loving You/
No Quarter (also Nutcracker Suite)
CD5: Ten Years Gone/ The Battle Of Evermore/
Going To California/ Black Country Woman/ Bron-
Yr-Aur Stomp/ White Summer/ Black Mountain
Side/ Kashmir
CD6: Out On The Tiles/ Moby Dick/ Jimmy's bow
(also Star Spangled Banner)/ Achilles Last Stand/
Stairway To Heaven/ Rock And Roll/ Trampled
Underfoot
R: CD1-3 Exs. Soundboard. CD4-6 Vgs.
Audience.   S: Richfield Coliseum, Cleveland
CD1-3 Apr. 27 '77. CD4-6 Apr. 28 '77.
C: Japanese CD. Dcc. Two triple gatefold sleeves.
Poster. Calendar. 600 numbered copies. Time
CD1 55:23. CD2 41:31. CD3 56:25. CD4 53:25.
CD5 39:19. CD6 55:42.

CD - DISCOVER AMERICA

TARANTURA T3CD-10

CD1: Intro, Rock And Roll (3:44)/ Celebration Day
(3:26)/ Bring On Home Intro (:17)/ Black Dog
(5:02)/ Over The Hills And Far Away (6:23)/ Misty
Mountain Hop (4:55)/ Since I've Been Loving You
(7:12)/ No Quarter (14:34)
CD2: The Song Remains The Same (5:38)/ The
Rain Song (7:54)/ Dazed And Confused (27:23)/
Stairway To Heaven (10:45)
CD3: Moby Dick (26:34)*/ Heartbreaker (7:23)*/
Whole Lotta Love (13:55)*/ The Ocean (4:23)**
R: Ex. Soundboard.   S: Memorial Auditorium,
Dallas, Texas May 18 '73. Madison Square
Garden, NYC July 27* and 28** '73.
C: Japanese CD. The pic CDs come inside full
color pic sleeves. These are housed in a three
color box with an altered American flag - Tarantura
logo replaces stars.

CD - DIXIE

ANTRABATA REFERENCE MASTER ARM
180577

CD1: The Song Remains The Same/ The Rover
Intro - Sick Again/ Nobody's Fault But Mine/ In My
Time Of Dying/ Since I've Been Loving You/ No
Quarter
CD2: Ten Years Gone/ The Battle Of Evermore/
Going To California/ Black Country Woman/ Bron-
Y-Aur Stomp/ White Summer - Black Mountain
Side/ Kashmir/ Out On The Tiles

CD3: Moby Dick/ Guitar Solo, Dixie, Guitar Solo/
Achilles Last Stand/ Stairway To Heaven/ Rock
And Roll
R: Poor-G. Audience.   S: Jefferson Coliseum,
Birmingham, Alabama May 18 '77.   C: Japanese
CD. Full color cardboard slipcover over jewel case
with Dcc. Includes a certificate of authenticity.
Limited edition of 325. Time CD1 63:18. CD2
67:35. CD3 45:57.

CD - D'YA FEEL ALRIGHT?

MAD DOGS 029/30

CD1: We're Gonna Groove/ Dazed And Confused
(incomplete)/ Heartbreaker/ Bring It On Home/
White Summer, Black Mountain Side/ Since I've
Been Loving You/ Organ Solo, Thank You
CD2: What Is And What Should Never Be/ Moby
Dick/ How Many More Times/ Whole Lotta Love/
Communication Breakdown
R: Poor mono. Audience. Speed fluctuations. Hiss.
S: Forum, Inglewood Mar. 27 '70.   C: Japanese
CD. Dcc. Time CD1 63:31. CD2 69:19.

CD - EARL'S COURT 1975

MUD DOGS 024/025/026

CD1: Rock And Roll/ Sick Again/ Over The Hills
And Far Away/ In My Time Of Dying/ The Song
Remains The Same/ The Rain Song/ No Quarter
CD2: Kashmir/ Tangerine/ Going To California/
That's The Way/ Bron-Yr-Aur Stomp/ Trampled
Underfoot/ Moby Dick
CD3: Dazed And Confused/ Stairway To Heaven/
Whole Lotta Love/ Black Dog/ Heartbreaker/
Communication Breakdown
R: Poor. Audience.   S: Earl's Court, London May
25 '75.   C: Japanese CD.

CD - EARLY DAYS, LATTER DAYS

ED 30569/24773/19477/09477

CD1: Train Kept A Rollin'/ I Can't Quit You Babe/
Dazed & Confused/ You Shook Me/ White
Summer, Black Mountain Side/ How Many More
Times Medley/ Communication Breakdown
CD2: Rock And Roll/ Celebration Day/ Black Dog/
Misty Mountain Hop/ Since I've Been Loving You/
Heartbreaker/ Whole Lotta Love/ The Ocean
CD3: The Song Remains The Same/ Sick Again/
Nobody's Fault But Mine/ Since I've Been Loving
You/ No Quarter/ Ten Years Gone/ Robert Plant
Announcement/ Rich Cole Announcement
CD4: The Song Remains The Same/ Sick Again/
Nobody's Fault But Mine/ Since I've Been Loving
You/ No Quarter/ Ten Years Gone
R: CD1 Poor-G. Audience. CD2 G. Audience. CD3
Poor-G. Audience. CD4 Poor. Audience.
S: CD1 Fillmore East, NYC May 30 '69. CD2
Three Rivers Stadium, Pittsburgh July 24 '73. CD3
Chicago Stadium, Chicago Apr. 9 '77. CD4
Riverfront Coliseum, Cincinnati Apr. 19 '77.
C: ECD. Full color fold-out cardboard sleeve.
Rivals some Tarantura packaging. Each disc
comes in a black envelope with one of the
symbols. CD1 65:36. CD2 55:07. CD3 62:42.
CD4 60:01.

CD - ELECTRIC MAGIC
SCORPIO LZ-91-03-03
Rock & Roll (3:52)/ Celebration Day (3:36)/ Black Dog (5:39)/ Over The Hills & Far Away (6:00)/ Misty Mountain Hop (4:54)/ Since I've Been Loving You (8:04)/ No Quarter (9:51)/ The Song Remains The Same (5:38)/ The Rain Song (7:59)
R: Exs. Soundboard.   S: New York July 28 '73.
C: ECD. Dcc. This is the 28th not the 29th as stated on the cover.

CD - THE ELECTRIC MAGIC SHOW
MAD DOGS 033/34
CD1: Heartbreaker/ Black Dog/ Since I've Been Loving You/ Rock And Roll
CD2: Stairway To Heaven/ Going To California/ That's The Way/ Tangerine/ Dazed And Confused/ What Is And What Should Never Be/ Celebration Day/ Moby Dick
R: Poor mono. Audience.   S: Empire Pool, Wembley, London Nov. 20 '71.   C: Japanese CD. Dcc. Time CD1 51:13. CD2 51:09.

CD - EYE THANK YEW
TARANTURA T4CD-4
CD1: Train Kept A Rollin' (3:58)/ Nobody's Fault But Mine (5:20)/ Black Dog (5:38)/ In The Evening (9:13)/ The Rain Song (9:07)/ Hot Dog (4:03)/ All My Love (5:47)/ Trampled Underfoot (8:57)/ Since I've Been Loving You (9:00)
CD2: Achilles Last Stand (10:04)/ White Summer (6:51)/ Black Mountain Side (1:41)/ Kashmir (9:14)/ Stairway To Heaven (10:58)/ Communication Breakdown (2:48)/ Rock & Roll (3:30)
CD3: Train Kept A Rollin' (3:52)/ Nobody's Fault But Mine (5:17)/ Black Dog (5:48)/ In The Evening (8:53)/ The Rain Song (8:15)/ Hot Dog (4:12)/ All My Love (5:35)/ Trampled Underfoot (8:44)/ Since I've Been Loving You (10:33)
CD4: Achilles Last Stand (10:50)/ White Summer (7:42)/ Black Mountain Side (2:08)/ Kashmir (5:24)/ Rock And Roll (3:23)/ Whole Lotta Love (13:43)*
R: Vgm. Soundboard. *Gs. Audience.
S: Mannheim. CD1-2 July 3 '80. CD3-4 July 2 '80.
C: Japanese CD. Dcc. Gatefold sleeve. Pic CDs.

CD - THE FINAL EVER IN THE STATES
MISSING LINK 014/015
CD1: The Song Remains The Same (5:45)/ The Rover Intro - Sick Again (6:21)/ Nobody's Fault But Mine (6:05)/ Over The Hills And Far Away (5:28)/ Since I've Been Loving You (8:44)/ No Quarter (22:53)
CD2: Ten Years Gone (9:57)/ The Battle Of Evermore (5:06)/ Going To California (5:06)/ Mystery Train (1:13)/ Black Country Woman (1:52)/ Bron-Y-Aur Stomp (6:03)/ Trampled Underfoot (6:51)
CD3: White Summer, Black Mountain Side (8:04)/ Kashmir (9:42)/ Guitar Solo (includes Star Spangled Banner) (7:24)/ Achilles Last Stand (9:11)/ Stairway To Heaven (10:41)/ Whole Lotta

Love (1:17)/ Rock And Roll (3:52)
R: Gm. Audience.   S: Oakland-Alameda County Coliseum, Oakland, CA July 24 '77.
C: Japanese CD. Dcc.

CD - FIRST DAY
ARMS 03-04 PR
CD1: Rock & Roll (5:05)/ Celebration Day (3:28)/ Black Dog (5:10)/ Over The Hills & Far Away (5:30)/ Misty Mountain Hop (5:49)/ Since I've Been Loving You (8:03)/ No Quarter (9:10)/ The Song Remains The Same (4:36)/ The Rain Song (7:55)
CD2: Dazed & Confused (26:51)/ Stairway To Heaven (10:14)/ Moby Dick (11:00)/ Heartbreaker Medley: Whole Lotta Love, Boogie Children (14:52)/ The Ocean (4:21)/ Communication Breakdown (3:16)
R: Gm. Audience.   S: Tampa, Florida May 5 '73.
C: Japanese CD. Dcc.

CD - FIXING TO DIE
GOLD STANDARD FIX-1/2
CD1: We're Gonna Groove (3:11)/ I Can't Quit You (6:17)/ Dazed & Confused (16:42)/ Heartbreaker (5:21)/ White Summer, Black Mountain Side (10:10)/ Since I've Been Loving You (6:30)/ Organ Solo (0:46)/ Thank You (5:48)
CD2: Moby Dick (13:45)/ How Many More Times Medley: The Hunter, Boogie Children, Move On Down The Line, Fixing To Die, Down By The River Side, The Lemon Song, Be Bop A Lula/ Whole Lotta Love (6:51)
R: Poor mono. Audience.   S: Helsinki, Finland Feb. 23 '70.   C: Japanese CD. Dcc.

CD - FOR BADGE HOLDERS ONLY
ROCKWROK RW 3301-2-3
CD1: The Song Remains The Same (5:15)/ Sick Again (6:04)/ Nobody's Fault But Mine (6:49)/ Over The Hills And Far Away (6:10)/ Since I've Been Loving You (8:15)/ No Quarter Part 1 (12:49)/ No Quarter Part 2 (15:28)
CD2: Ten Years Gone (8:57)/ The Battle Of Evermore (5:25)/ Going To California (4:58)/ Black Country Woman (4:07)/ Bron-Y-Aur Stomp (1:54)/ White Summer, Black Mountain Side (4:57)/ Kashmir (9:02)/ Trampled Under Foot (6:46)
CD3: Moby Dick (11:11)/ Star Spangled Banner, Guitar Solo (14:57)/ Achilles Last Stand (8:58)/ Stairway To Heaven (11:03)/ Whole Lotta Love (1:35)/ Rock And Roll (4:01)
R: Gs. Audience.   S: Los Angeles June 21 '77.
C: Japanese CD. Dcc sleeve over three jewel cases. Poster.

CD - FOR YOUR LOVE
SILVER RARITIES SIRA 134/135 2-CD
CD1: The Train Kept A Rollin' (3:00)/ I Can't Quit You Babe (6:04)/ As Long As I Have You (10:50)/ Dazed And Confused (11:09)/ How Many More Times (14:33)
CD2: White Summer (7:15)/ Killing Floor (4:39)/ You Shook Me (8:35)/ Pat's Delight (10:10)/ Babe I'm Gonna Leave You (6:04)/ Communication

Breakdown (5:06)/ For Your Love (8:02)
R: G-Vg. Audience.   S: Fillmore West Jan. 10
'69.   C: ECD. Dbw. Gold type.

CD - FRAME BY FRAME
AMERICAN CONCERT SERIES 027
Heartbreaker (6:13)/ Thank You (8:00)/ That's The
Way (6:32)*/ What Is And What Should Never Be
(4:14)/ Communication Breakdown (5:00)/ We're
Gonna Groove (3:48)/ Since I've Been Loving You
(6:57)/ Whole Lotta Love (2:44)/ Stairway To
Heaven (8:59)*
R: Vgm. Soundboard.   S: Vancouver Mar. 21
'70. *Toronto Sept. 4 '71.   C: ECD. Dcc.

CD - GET BACK TO L.A.
TARANTURA T9CD-1
CD1: Rock & Roll (2:51)/ Sick Again (4:59)/ Over
The Hills & Far Away (7:53)/ In My Time Of Dying
(11:33)/ The Song Remains The Same (6:18)/ The
Rain Song (7:31)/ Kashmir (9:06)
CD2: No Quarter (26:01)/ Trampled Underfoot
(7:38)/ Moby Dick (21:22)
CD3: Dazed & Confused (34:33)/ Stairway To
Heaven (12:00)/ Whole Lotta Love (9:06)/ Black
Dog (5:58)/ Heartbreaker (8:24)
CD4: Rock & Roll (3:01)/ Sick Again (4:56)/ Over
The Hills & Far Away (7:58)/ In My Time Of Dying
(11:41)/ The Song Remains The Same (6:54)/ The
Rain Song (6:51)/ Kashmir (10:09)/ Since I've
Been Loving You (8:31)
CD 5: No Quarter (27:16)/ Trampled Underfoot
(9:52)/ Moby Dick (24:35)
CD6: Dazed & Confused (40:55)/ Stairway To
Heaven (11:30)/ Whole Lotta Love (8:36)/ Black
Dog (5:33)
CD7: Rock & Roll (4:03)/ Sick Again (5:34)/ Over
The Hills & Far Away (9:38)/ In My Time Of Dying
(14:07)/ The Song Remains The Same (6:54)/ The
Rain Song (6:51)/ Kashmir (10:09)/ Since I've
Been Loving You (8:31)
CD8: No Quarter (29:02)/ Trampled Underfoot
(12:22)/ Moby Dick (27:30)
CD9: Dazed & Confused (43:20)/ Stairway To
Heaven (13:28)/ Whole Lotta Love (9:15)/ Black
Dog (4:50)
R: G-Vg. Audience.   S: Los Angeles. CD1-3 Mar.
24 '75. CD4-6 Mar. 25 '75. CD7-9 Mar. 27 '75.
C: Japanese CD. Dcc sleeve with 9 CDs in
individual sleeves. Plastic dust cover over outer
sleeve. Excellent packaging.

CD - GOING DOWN TO DETROIT
ZEPPELIN LIVE ARCHIVES ZLA 9312/3
CD1: Intro - Rock & Roll (Cut) (1:02)/ Celebration
Day (3:34)/ Black Dog (5:31)/ Over The Hills & Far
Away (6:14)/ Misty Mountain Hop (5:05)/ Since
I've Been Loving You (9:02)/ No Quarter (Cut)
(12:15)/ The Song Remains The Same (5:36)/ The
Rain Song (8:27)/ The Ocean (2:36)
CD2: Dazed & Confused (30:52)/ Stairway To
Heaven (11:45)/ Heartbreaker (7:38)/ Whole Lotta
Love Medley (16:06) Incl. I'm Going Down -

Boogie Chillen/ Communication Breakdown - The
Crunge (4:54)
R: Poor-G. Audience.   S: Detroit July 12 '73.
C: Japanese CD. Dcc.

CD - THE GRANDE BALL
MISSING LINK ML-010
Train Kept A Rollin'/ I Can't Quit You/ Dazed And
Confused/ You Shook Me/ How Many More
Times/ Train Kept A Rollin'/ You Shook Me/
Communication Breakdown/ As Long As I Have
You
R: Gm. Tracks 5-9 Poor mono.   S: Tracks 1-4
NYC Jan. 31 '69. Tracks 5-9 San Francisco Apr.
25 '69.   C: Japanese CD. Dcc. Not Detroit and
Chicago as cover claims. Time 59:56.

CD - HEADLEY GRANGE
IMMIGRANT IM-008
The Rover/ In My Time Of Dying/ Trampled
Underfoot/ In The Morning (take 1)/ The Wanton
Song (take 1)/ Sick Again/ Hots On For Nowhere/
The Wanton Song (take 2)/ Take Me Home/ In
The Morning (take 2)/ Trampled Underfoot (takes
1 to 6)/ The Rover (takes 1 to 3)
R: Vg.   S: Headley Grange Studio, Hampshire
'73 to '74 during 'Physical Graffiti' sessions.
C: Japanese CD. Dbw. Gold type. Time 67:24.

CD - IDENTIFICATION REQUIRED
MEN AT WORK WORK 5534-2
CD1: Immigrant Song (3:25)/ Heartbreaker (5:34)/
Black Dog (5:46)/ Going To California (4:25)/
That's The Way (5:51)/ What Is & What Should
Never Be (4:35)/ Communication Breakdown
(5:33)/ Stairway To Heaven (9:09)/ Whole Lotta
Love Medley (10:56)
R: Exs. Soundboard.   S: London, England Apr. 1
'71.   C: ECD. Dcc. Pic CD.

CD - IN A DAZE
KEEP OUT KO 93103/04
CD1: Immigrant Song/ Heartbreaker/ Since I've
Been Loving You/ Black Dog/ Dazed And
Confused/ Stairway To Heaven/ Celebration Day
CD2: Going To California/ What Is & What Should
Never Be/ Moby Dick/ Whole Lotta Love/ Medley:
Boogie Woogie, My Baby Left Me, Mess Of Blues,
You Shook Me/ Communication Breakdown
R: G. Audience. Some hiss.   S: Toronto, Ontario,
Canada Sept. 4 '71.   C: Japanese CD. Dcc.
Songs fade-in. 500 numbered copies. Time CD1
57:46. CD2 57:49.

CD - IN THE EVENING
ON STAGE CD 12005
Nobody's Fault But Mine (5:30)/ Train Kept A
Rollin' (3:22)/ Black Dog (5:15)/ Since I've Been
Loving You (9:20)/ In The Evening (7:55)/ All My
Love (5:49)/ Trampled Underfoot (7:56)/ The Rain
Song (6:31)/ Kashmir (8:14)
R: Exm. Soundboard.   S: Brussels, Belgium
June 20 '80.   C: ECD. Dcc.

CD - IN THROUGH THE OUTTAKES
MUSICHIEN MCH 1975
Darlene (5:13)/ Fool In The Rain (6:15)/
Carouselambra (8:22)/ In The Evening (6:07)/
Southbound Suarez (4:15)/ The Wanton Song
(4:22)/ Custard Pie (5:18)/ In The Light (6:02)/
Trampled Underfoot
R: Gm. Soundboard.   S: Polar Studios Nov.-Dec.
'78. Tracks 6-9 Headley Grange Dec. '73 - June
'74.   C: ECD. Dcc.

CD - IN THROUGH THE OUTTAKES PART 1
WIDGET 7800-WW101
Darlene (5:13)/ Fool In The Rain (6:05)/
Carouselambra (6:32)/ Fool In The Rain 2 (6:04)/
Hot Dog (3:13)/ In The Evening (6:21)/
Southbound Suarez (4:16)/ In The Light (5:18)
R: Vg. Soundboard. Crackles.   S: Polar Studios
Nov.-Dec. '78.   C: Japanese CD. One of the first
bootleg CDs.

CD - IN THROUGH THE OUTTAKES PART 2
WIDGET 7800-WW102
The Wanton Song (4:14)/ Custard Pie (5:23)/ In
The Light (5:58)/ Trampled Underfoot (10:35)/
Trampled Underfoot (3:40)/ Sick Again (3:42)/ The
Rover (1:02)/ Hots On For Nowhere (instrumental)
(3:04)/ In My Time Of Dying (3:03)/ In The Light 2
(5:18)
R: Vg. Soundboard. Crackles.   S: Headley
Grange Dec. '73 - June '74.   C: Japanese CD.
One of the first bootleg CDs.

CD - JAPANESE WARM-UPS VOL. 2
CA-022-1A-2A
CD1: Rock And Roll (4:19)/ Black Dog (4:56)/
Misty Mountain Hop (4:36)/ Since I've Been Loving
You (7:09)/ The Song Remains The Same (6:25)/
The Rain Song (7:33)/ Dazed And Confused
(18:37)
CD2: Stairway To Heaven (3:43)/ Over The Hills
And Far Away (5:19)/ Whole Lotta Love Medley:
Everybody Needs Someone To Love, Boogie
Chillen, That's Alright, Lights Out, Going Down
Slow (20:51)/ Immigrant Song (3:12)/ Whole Lotta
Love Medley (cut): Everybody Needs Somebody
To Love, We Say Yeah, Leave My Woman Alone,
All Shook Up, Lawdy Miss Clawdy, Heartbreak
Hotel, Naturally, Going Down Slow (24:40)*
R: Poor mono. Audience. *G.   S: Kyoto Oct. 10
'72. *Osaka Oct. 9 '72.   C: Japanese CD. Dcc.

CD - THE JUMPLEG
TARANTURA T3CD-7
CD1: Rock And Roll (3:33)/ Sick Again (4:57)/
Over The Hills And Far Away (7:44)/ In My Time
Of Dying (10:23)/ The Song Remains The Same
(6:28)/ The Rain Song (7:42)/ Kashmir (8:12)
CD2: No Quarter (19:12)/ Trampled Underfoot
(8:15)/ Moby Dick (19:12)
CD3: Dazed And Confused (29:33)/ Stairway To
Heaven (10:44)/ Whole Lotta Love (1:48)/ Black
Dog (5:43)/ Heartbreaker (6:55)

R: Vg-Ex. Audience.   S: Madison Square
Garden, NYC Feb. 12 '75.   C: Japanese CD.
Cardboard fold-out case.

CD - KINGDOM OF ZEPPELIN
SILVER RARITIES SIRA 131/132/133 3-CD
CD1: The Song Remains The Same/ Sick Again/
Nobody's Fault But Mine/ Over The Hills & Far
Away/ Since I've Been Loving You/ No Quarter
CD2: Ten Years Gone/ Battle Of Evermore/ Going
To California/ Black Country Woman/ Bron-Y-Aur
Stomp/ White Summer, Black Mountain Side/
Kashmir
CD3: Moby Dick/ Page Solo/ Achilles Last Stand/
Stairway To Heaven/ Whole Lotta Love/ Rock &
Roll
R: Poor-G. Audience.   S: Kingdome, Seattle July
17 '77.   C: ECD. Time CD1 71:27. CD2 64:48.
CD3 71:17.

CD - THE LAST
IMMIGRANT IM-010-11
CD1: The Train Kept A Rollin' (3:08)/ Nobody's
Fault But Mine (5:59)/ Black Dog (5:37)/ In The
Evening (8:32)/ The Rain Song (7:37)/ Hot Dog
(3:24)/ All My Love (5:50)/ Trampled Underfoot
(12:25)/ Since I've Been Loving You (9:25)
CD2: White Summer, Black Mountain Side
(18:32)/ Kashmir (8:43)/ Stairway To Heaven
(15:08)/ Rock And Roll (4:20)/ Whole Lotta Love
(16:43)
R: Exs. Soundboard.   S: Berlin July 7 '80.
C: Japanese CD. Dcc.

CD - THE LAST REHEARSAL
MISSING LINK ML 002
White Summer (take 1) (2:28)/ White Summer,
Black Mountain Side (5:35)/ Achilles Last Stand
(part 1) (6:26)/ Achilles Last Stand (part 2) (3:34)/
Stairway To Heaven (10:27)/ Stairway To Heaven
(9:46)*/ Black Dog (6:05)*
R: Vg. Soundboard. *G. Audience.   S: Rainbow
Theatre, London May '80 not Windsor Sept. 80 as
claimed by cover. *Copenhagen May '71.
C: Japanese CD. Dcc.

CD - LAST STAND (VOL. 1)
BANANA BAN-028-JA
Sick Again (6:11)/ Nobody's Fault But Mine (6:32)/
In My Time Of Dying (10:54)/ Since I've Been
Loving You (8:23)/ No Quarter (20:35)/ Ten Years
Gone (8:32)/ The Song Remains The Same (cut -
3:40)/ Out On The Tiles, Moby Dick (cut - 8:26)
R: Exs. Soundboard.   S: Cleveland Apr. 27 '77.
C: Australian CD. Dcc.

CD - LAST STAND (VOL. 2)
BANANA BAN-028-B
The Battle Of Evermore (6:38)/ Going To
California (5:01)/ Black Country Woman (5:44)/
Bron-Y-Aur Stomp (1:08)/ White Summer (4:01)/
Kashmir (18:29)/ Achille's Last Stand (9:41)/
Stairway To Heaven (10:09)/ Rock And Roll
(3:58)/ Trampled Underfoot (6:52)

R: Exs. Soundboard.   S: Cleveland Apr. 27 '77.
C: Australian CD. Dcc.

CD - LAST STAND (VOL. 3)
BANANA BAN-028-C
Train Kept A Rollin' (3:18)/ Nobody's Fault But
Mine (5:55)/ Black Dog (5:44)/ In The Evening
(8:25)/ Rain Song (8:17)/ Hot Dog (3:46)/ All My
Love (6:12)
R: Exs. Soundboard.   S: Zurich June 29 '80.
C: Australian CD. Dcc.

CD - LAST STAND (VOL. 4)
BANANA BAN-028-D
Trampled Underfoot (8:55)/ Since I've Been
Loving You (10:04)/ Achilles Last Stand (9:33)/
White Summer, Black Mountainside (9:35)/
Kashmire (6:20)
R: Exs. Soundboard.   S: Zurich June 29 '80.
C: Australian CD. Dcc.

CD - LED ZEPPELIN
MAD DOGS DX I-X
CD1: Immigrant Song/ Heartbreaker/ Dazed And
Confused/ Bring It On Home/ That's The Way/
Since I've Been Loving You
CD2: Organ Solo, Thank You/ What Is And What
Should Never Be/ Moby Dick/ Whole Lotta Love/
Communication Breakdown
CD3: Immigrant Song/ Heartbreaker/ Since I've
Been Loving You/ Black Dog/ Dazed And
Confused/ Stairway To Heaven/ That's The Way/
Going To California
CD4: What Is And What Should Never Be/ Whole
Lotta Love/ Weekend/ Rock And Roll/
Communication Breakdown/ Organ Solo, Thank
You
CD5: Rock And Roll/ Sick Again/ Over The Hills
And Far Away/ In My Time of Dying/ The Song
Remains The Same/ The Rain Song/ Kashmir
CD6: No Quarter/ Trampled Underfoot/ Moby Dick
CD7: Dazed And Confused (includes
'Woodstock')/ Stairway To Heaven/ Whole Lotta
Love/ Black Dog
CD8: The Song Remains The Same/ The Rover
Intro, Sick Again/ Nobody's Fault But Mine/ In My
Time of Dying/ Since I've Been Loving You
CD9: No Quarter (includes 'Nutcracker Suite')/
Ten Years Gone/ The Battler Of Evermore/ Going
To California/ Low Hide/ Black Country Woman/
Bron-Yr-Aur Stomp/ White Summer, Black
Mountain Side/ Kashmir
CD10: Out On The Tiles/ Moby Dick/ Guitar Solo
(includes 'Star Spangled Banner')/ Achilles Last
Stand/ Stairway To Heaven/ Whole Lotta Love/
Rock And Roll
S: CD1-2 San Diego Sports Arena, San Diego
Sept. 3 '70. CD3-4 Forum, Inglewood Aug. 21 '71.
CD5-7 Louisiana State University, Baton Rouge
Feb. 28 '75. CD8-10 Madison Square Garden,
NYC June 7 '77.   C: Japanese CD. Box set with
red velvet cover. Comes with a '69 tour pamphlet.
Pic CDs.

CD - LED ZEPPELIN III
TARANTURA TARANTIC CD 19128
Friends (3:25)/ Immigrant Song (2:41)/ Out On
The Tiles (3:34)/ Bron-Y-Aur (1:39)/ Poor Tom #1
(0:39)/ Poor Tom #2 (2:42)/ Hey Hey What Can I
Do (1:49)/ The Rover Instrumental (2:27)/ That's
The Way #1 (2:42)/ That's The Way #2 (1:35)/
That's The Way #3 (0:22)/ That's The Way #4
(0:45)/ That's The Way #5 (3:32)/ Friends #2
(1:17)/ Bron-Y-Aur #2 (2:28)/ Bron-Y-Aur #3
(1:01)/ Bron-Y-Aur #4 (5:05)/ Instrumental (0:34)/
Instrumental (1:24)/ Since I've Been Loving You
(0:35)/ Since I've Been Loving You (0:28)/ Since
I've Been Loving You (0:24)/ Since I've Been
Loving You (0:26)/ I Wanna Be Her Man (1:40)/
Down By The Seaside (1:02)/ Down By The
Seaside (0:47)/ Down By The Seaside (0:44)/
Down By The Seaside (1:14)/ Down By The
Seaside (0:34)/ Down By The Seaside (0:33)/
Down By The Seaside (2:27)/ Down By The
Seaside (2:25)/ Gallows Pole (2:05)/ Gallows Pole
(0:30)/ Instrumental (0:37)/ Instrumental (0:49)/
Instrumental (3:56)
R: Vg.   S: Bron-Y-Aur, Headley Grange May '70.
C: Japanese CD. Gatefold sleeve with rotating
wheel. Exact copy of original 'III' record sleeve
except for the TARANTURA logo that appears as
wheel is rotated. Pic CD.

CD - LET'S HAVE A PARTY
ARMS 15PR
Whole Lotta Love Medley: Everybody Needs
Somebody To Love, Boogie Chillen, Baby I Don't
Care, Let's Have A Party, I Can't Quit You, The
Lemon Song (22:10)
R: Exs. Soundboard.   S: Berlin, Germany Mar.
19 '73.   C: Japanese CD. Dcc.

LIGHTER THAT AIR
TEDDY BEAR TB 51
Blues Mama (includes 'That's Allright Mama')
(6:33)/ That's The Way (5:34)/ The Battle Of
Evermore (7:10)/ Going To California (4:24)/ Black
Country Woman (5:44)/ Bron-Y-Aur Stomp (5:11)/
Hey Hey What Can I Do (3:56)/ Lighter Than Air
(3:58)/ I Wanna Be Her Man (2:06)/ Down By The
Seaside (5:14)/ Friends (3:13)*/ Poor Tom (2:55)*/
Stairway To Heaven (3:46)
R: G-Vg. *G.   S: Various locations '70 and '72.
C: ECD. Dcc. Pic CD.

CD - LIVE VOL. 1
JOKER JOK-008-A
Rock & Roll/ Celebration Day/ Bring It On Home/
Black Dog/ Over The Hills And Far Away/ Misty
Mountain Hop/ Since I've Been Loving You/ No
Quarter
R: Vgm. Soundboard.   S: NYC July 28 '73.
C: Australian CD. Time 47:13.

CD - LIVE VOL. 2
JOKER JOK-008-B
Heart Breaker (6:32)/ Thank You (8:10)/ What Is
And What Should Never Be (4:21)/

Communication Breakdown (4:56)/ We're Gonna Groove (3:45)/ Since I've Been Loving You (7:01)/ Whole Lotta Love (2:44)/ We're Gonna Groove (3:45)/ Operator (4:13)*
R: Vgm. *Vgs.   S: Vancouver Mar. 21 '70. *'68.
C: Australian CD.

CD - LIVE VOL. 3
JOKER JOK-008-C
You Shook Me/ Communication/ I Can't Quit You Baby/ Dazed And Confused/ What Is And What Should Never be/ Communication Breakdown/ Whole Lotta Love
R: Vgm. Soundboard.   S: London Mar. 3 '69 and June 24 '69.   C: Australian CD. Time 31:57.

CD - LIVE VOL. 4
JOKER JOK-008-D
Train Kept A Rollin' (3:20)/ Nobody's Fault But Mine (5:20)/ Black Dog (5:00)/ In The Evening (8:49)/ Rain Song (8:25)/ Hot Dog (3:56)/ All My Love (6:13)
R: Exs. Soundboard.   S: Zurich June 29 '80.
C: Australian CD.

CD - LIVE - JAPAN WARM UPS
TARANTURA ITLFF LIVE 1-2
CD1: Rock & Roll (4:01)/ Black Dog (5:28)/ Over The Hills & Far Away (5:50)/ Misty Mountain Hop (5:12)/ Since I've Been Loving You (7:34)/ Dancing Days (4:02)/ The Song Remains The Same (5:50)/ The Rain Song (7:29)/ Dazed & Confused (includes The Crunge) (26:42)
CD2: Stairway To Heaven (10:52)/ Moby Dick (16:10)/ Whole Lotta Love Medley: Everybody Needs Someone To Love, Leave My Woman Alone, All Shook Up, Lawdy Miss Clawdy, Heartbreak Hotel, Going Down Slow (28:30)/ Stand By Me (6:13)/ Immigrant Song (3:35)
R: G-Vg. Audience.   S: Osaka Oct. 9 '72.
C: Japanese CD. Gatefold.

CD - LIVE ON THE LEVEE
SILVER RARITIES SIRA 113/114
CD1: Rock And Roll/ Sick Again/ Over The Hills And Far Away/ When The Levee Breaks/ In My Time Of Dying/ The Song Remains The Same/ The Rain Song/ Kashmir/ The Wanton Song
CD2: No Quarter/ Trampled Underfoot/ Moby Dick/ How Many More Times/ Stairway To Heaven/ Whole Lotta Love/ Black Dog
R: G. Audience.   S: Chicago Jan. 21 '75.
C: ECD. Dcc. CD1 63:37. CD2 61:49.

CD - LOOVE
TARANTURA T2CD-9
CD1: Immigrant Song (3:51)/ Heartbreaker (5:27)/ Since I've Been Loving You (7:59)/ Dazed & Confused (18:58)/ Black Dog (6:15)/ Stairway To Heaven (9:58)/ Going To California (4:18)/ That's The Way (6:28)/ What Is And What Should Never Be (5:24)
CD2: Four Sticks (6:41)/ Gallow's Pole (5:18)/ Whole Lotta Love Medley: Boogie Chillen,

Trucking Little Mama, Mess Of Blues, The Lemon Song (20:32)/ Communication Breakdown, Celebration Day (8:05)/ Misty Mountain Hop (4:25)/ Rock And Roll (4:01)
R: G. Audience.   S: Copenhagen, Denmark May 3 '71.   C: Japanese CD. Dcc. Gatefold sleeve.

CD - MAGICAL MYSTERY TAPE
TARAMOPHONE COMPANY TMMT-1
Sugar Baby (take 1) (2:56)/ Sugar Baby (take 2) (1:36)/ Wanton Song (exercise 1-2) (2:10)/ Exercise (4:29)/ The Rover (take 1) (:45)/ The Rover (take 2) (1:53)/ Night Flight (take 1) (2:02)/ Night Flight (take 2) (3:37)/ Night Flight (take 3) (:59)/ Night Flight (take 4) (:24)/ Night Flight (take 5) (1:05)/ Night Flight (take 6) (2:38)/ School Days (3:33)/ Nadine (:55)/ Round And Round (3:14)/ Move On Down The Line (2:31)/ Love Me Like A Hurricane (2:46)/ C'mon Pretty Baby/ Dynamite (1:05)/ Shakin' On All Over (2:38)/ Exercise (:27)/ Hungry For Love (1:29)/ I'll Never Get Over You (2:24)/ Reelin' And Rockin' (1:42)/ Surrender (:28)/ Drum Exercise (Rock And Roll) (:23)/ Keyboard Exercise (Thank You) (:45)
R: Exs. Soundboard.   S: Chicago Auditorium, Chicago July 6 '73.   C: Japanese CD. Full color gatefold sleeve. take off of Beatles' 'Magical Mystery Tour' cover. Comes with a poster the same as the cover. Pic CD.

CD - MAJESTIC HOLIES
IMMIGRANT IM015-16
CD1: Rock And Roll (4:40)/ Over The Hills And Far Away (6:00)/ Black Dog (6:21)/ Misty Mountain Hop (5:40)/ Since I've Been Loving You (8:13)/ Dancing Days (4:56)/ Bron-Y-Aur Stomp (6:38)/ The Song Remains The Same (6:20)/ The Rain Song (7:57)
CD2: Dazed And Confused Medley (cut): San Francisco, Superstition (29:20)/ Stairway To Heaven (10:21)/ Whole Lotta Love Medley: Everybody Needs Somebody To Love, Boogie Woogie, Baby I Don't Care, Let's Have A Party, I Can't Quit You Baby, Lemon Song (26:30)
R: Gm. Audience.   S: Berlin Mar. 19 '73.
C: Japanese CD. Dcc.

CD - MEMPHIS
NEPTUNE
CD1: Bootlegger's Intro/ We're Gonna Grove/ Dazed And Confused/ Heartbreaker/ Bring It On Home/ White Summer, Black Mountain Side/ Since I've Been Loving You/ Organ Solo/ Thank You
CD2: What Is And What Should Never Be/ Moby Dick/ How Many More Times/ Whole Lotta Love/ Announcement
R: Poor-G.   S: Midsouth Coliseum, Memphis Apr. 17 '70.   C: Japanese CD. Cardboard gatefold sleeve. Pic CD. CD1 71:02. C2 65:45.

CD - MEMPHIS 1970
ZOSO 003/004
CD1: M.C. - We're Gonna Groove/ Dazed And

Confused/ Heartbreaker/ Bring It On Home/ White Summer, Black Mountain Side/ Since I've Been Loving You/ Organ Solo, Thank You/ What Is And What Should Never Be

CD2: Moby Dick/ Introducing Members, How Many More Times Medley: Going Down, Ravel's Bolero, The Hunter, Boogie Woogie, Trucking Little Mama, Memphis Tennessee, It's Alright Mama, How Many More Times/ Whole Lotta Love

R: Poor-G. A bit better sound than 'Memphis' (Neptune).   S: Midsouth Coliseum, Memphis Apr. 17 '70.   C: Japanese CD. Dcc. Time CD1 77:54. CD2 59:45.

CD - MONSTERS OF ROCK
TARANTURA T3CD-9

CD1: Intro - Rock And Roll (4:05)/ Celebration Day (3:43)/ Bring It On Home Intro, Black Dog (5:54)/ Over The Hills And Far Away (6:45)/ Misty Mountain Hop (5:29)/ Since I've Been Loving You (7:56)/ No Quarter (13:54)/ The Song Remains The Same (6:04)/ The Rain Song (8:03)

CD2: Dazed And Confused (34:15)/ Stairway To Heaven (10:54)

CD3: Moby Dick (24:35)/ Heartbreaker (7:34)/ Whole Lotta Love (15:12)/ Dancing Days (1:16 Cut)

R: Ex. Soundboard.   S: Seattle Center Colosseum, Seattle July 17 '73. CD3 Cobo Hall, Detroit July 13 '73.   C: Japanese CD. Each CD in a B&w cardboard picture sleeve. These are housed in a full color Shuffle Pak.

CD - MOTOR CITY DAZE
ANTRABATA REFERENCE MASTER ARM 120773 (3 CDs)

CD1: Rock and Roll (fades in)/ Celebration Day/ Black Dog/ Over The Hills And Far Away/ Misty Mountain Hop/ Since I've Been Loving You/ No Quarter

CD2: The Song Remains The Same, Rain Song/ Dazed And Confused

CD3: Stairway To Heaven/ Moby Dick (edit)/ Heartbreaker/ Whole Lotta Love/ Communication Breakdown/ The Ocean/ Sunshine Woman*

R: G-Vg. Audience. *Poor-G.   S: Cobo Hall, Detroit, MI July 12 '73. *World Service Rhythm & Blues recorded Mar. 19 '69, broadcast Apr. 14 '69. Japanese CD. Full color cardboard slipcover over jewel case with Dcc. Includes a certificate of authenticity. Limited edition of 325. Time CD1 46:47. CD2 46:38. CD3 54:18.

CD - NO QUARTER
H-BOMB MUSIC HBM93020104-7

CD1: Rock And Roll (3:58)/ Sick Again (5:14)/ Over The Hills And Far Away (7:11)/ In My Time Of Dying (11:04)/ The Song Remains The Same (5:15)/ The Rain Song (7:40)

CD2: Kashmir (8:53)/ No Quarter (24:26)/ Since I've Been Loving You (7:40)/ Trampled Underfoot (8:57)

CD3: Moby Dick (28:04)/ Dazed And Confused (39:06)

CD4: Stairway To Heaven (13:35)/ Whole Lotta Love (10:10)/ Black Dog (4:44) Communication Breakdown (2:42)/ Heartbreaker (8:36)

R: Vgm. Audience.   S: Seattle Mar. 21 '75.   C: Japanese CD. Dcc. 500 numbered copies.

CD - NO USE GRECO
TARANTURA GRECO 1

CD1: Rock & Roll (3:57)/ Over The Hills & Far Away (5:09)/ Black Dog (5:22)/ Misty Mountain Hop (5:05)/ Since I've Been Loving You (7:12)/ Dancing Days (4:02)/ Bron-Y-Aur Stomp (5:40)/ The Song Remains The Same (5:30)/ The Rain Song (7:11)

CD2: Dazed & Confused (21:11)/ Stairway To Heaven (9:21)/ Whole Lotta Love Medley: Everybody Needs Somebody To Love, Boogie Chillen, Got A Lot Of Living To Do, Let's Have A Party, You Shook Me, The Lemon Song (21:43)/ Heartbreaker (6:12)/ Immigrant Song (3:54)/ Communication Breakdown (4:20)

R: Vg-Exs. Audience.   S: Osaka Oct. 2 '72.   C: Japanese CD. Dcc. Vinyl gatefold case. Pic CDs.

CD - THE NOBS
TARANTURA T70CD-12

CD1: Dazed And Confused (16:28)/ Heartbreaker (6:24)/ White Summer (4:21)/ Black Mountain Side (7:58)/ Since I've Been Loving You (8:57)/ Organ Solo (1:26)/ Thank You (6:11)/ Moby Dick (16:57)

CD2: How Many More Times Medley: The Hunter, Move On Down The Line, Trucking Little Mama (21:35)/ Whole Lotta Love (6:46)/ Communication Breakdown (5:05)/ Come On Everybody (3:24)/ Something Else (2:06)/ Bring It On Home (8:15)/ Long Tall Sally (5:56)

R: Gm. Audience.   S: Copenhagen, Denmark Feb. 28 '70.   C: Japanese CD. Gatefold cardboard sleeve.

CD - OLYMPIAHALLE 1973
IMMIGRANT IM-022-23

CD1: Rock And Roll/ Over The Hills And Far Away/ Black Dog/ Misty Mountain Hop/ Since I've Been Loving You/ Dancing Days/ Bron-Y-Aur Stomp/ The Song Remains The Same/ The Rain Song

CD2: Dazed And Confused/ Stairway To Heaven/ Whole Lotta Love/ Heartbreaker

R: Poor-G.   S: Olympiahalle, Munich, Germany Mar. 17 '73.   C: Japanese CD. Dcc. Time CD1 57:32. CD2 74:03.

CD - ONE MORE FOR THE ROAD
RED HOT RH-012/013

CD1: Rock 'N' Roll/ Celebration Day/ Black Dog/ Over The Hills And Far Away/ Misty Mountain Hop/ Since I've Been Loving You/ No Quarter/ The Song Remains The Same/ Rain Song

CD2: Dazed And Confused/ Stairway To Heaven/ Moby Dick

R: G. Audience.   S: The Arena, Milwaukee, Wisconsin July 10 '73.   C: Japanese CD. Dcc.

Time CD1 64:05. CD2 52:01.

CD - ONE MORE MAGIC
IMMIGRANT IM-019-21
CD1: Intro - Rock And Roll/ Celebration Day/ Bring It On Home/ Intro, Black Dog/ Over The Hills And Far Away/ Misty Mountain Hop/ Since I've Been Loving You/ No Quarter
CD2: The Song Remains The Same/ The Rain Song/ Dazed And Confused
CD3: Stairway To Heaven/ Moby Dick/ Heartbreaker/ Whole Lotta Love/ The Ocean
R: Exs. Soundboard.   S: Madison Square Garden, New York July 28 '73.   C: Japanese CD. Dcc. CD1 50:10. CD2 45:40. CD3 70:25.

CD - PLEEEASE
SILVER RARITIES SIRA 126/127/128 3-CD
CD1: Rock And Roll/ Sick Again/ Over The Hills And Far Away/ In My Time Of Dying/ The Song Remains The Same/ The Rain Song/ Kashmir
CD2: No Quarter/ Trampled Underfoot/ Moby Dick
CD3: Dazed And Confused/ Stairway To Heaven/ Whole Lotta Love/ Heartbreaker
R: Poor-G. Audience.   S: Vancouver, Canada Mar. 19 (not 20 as cover says) '75.   C: ECD.
Time CD1 52:29. CD2 50:04. CD3 68:55.

CD - PRIME CUTS
DYNAMITE STUDIO DS 92S041-2
CD1: No Quarter (21:39)/ Tangerine (4:34)/ That's The Way (7:04)/ Bron-Y-Aur Stomp (8:11)/ Trampled Underfoot (9:22)
CD2: Dazed And Confused, Woodstock (33:02)/ Stairway To Heaven (12:47)/ Whole Lotta Love Medley: The Crunge, Black Dog (12:50)
R: Vgm. Soundboard.   S: Earl's Court, London May 24 '75.   C: Japanese CD. 12" by 12" box with color cover. Reproduction of concert programme.

CD - PSYCHEDELIC RAW BLUES
IMMIGRANT IM 017-018
CD1: Train Kept A Rollin' (2:58)/ I Can't Quit You (4:53)/ Dazed & Confused (9:09)/ Pat's Delight (7:38)/ How Many More Times Medley: (includes 'The Hunter') (10:11)/ You Shook Me (7:32)/ How Many More Times Medley: The Hunter, Boogie Chillen, Truckin' Mama, Lemon Song (20:38)
CD2: As Long As I Have You Medley: Fresh Garbage, Shake, Suzie Q (18:07)/ Killing Floor (6:58)/ White Summer, Black Mountain Side (11:07)/ Babe I'm Gonna Leave You (6:18)/ Pat's Delight (11:04)
R: G-Vgm. Audience.   S: CD1 tracks 1-6 New York Jan. 31 '69. Track 7 Dusseldorf, Germany Mar. 11 '70. CD2 San Francisco Apr. 24 '69.
C: Japanese CD.

CD - PUNK
TARANTURA T2CD-8
CD1: Good Times Bad Times (0:32)/ Communication Breakdown (3:11)/ I Can't Quit You (6:41)/ Heartbreaker (5:52)/ Dazed &

Confused (17:46)/ White Summer, Black Mountain Side (13:03)
CD2: What Is And What Should Never Be (4:57)/ Moby Dick (12:11)/ How Many More Times Medley: The Hunter, Boogie Chillen, Move On Down The Line, The Lemon Song (21:06)/ Come On Everybody (3:16)/ Something Else (2:18)
R: Vgs. Audience.   S: San Francisco Nov. 6 '69.
C: Japanese CD. Dcc. Gatefold cardboard sleeve. Picture CDs.

CD - ROCK AND ROLL HALL OF FAME
KISS THE STONE KTS 404
Bring It Home/ Long Distance Call Blues/ Baby Please Don't Go/ Medley: When The Levee Breaks, For What It's Worth/ Wonderful One/ When the Levee Breaks/ 29 Palms/ What is And What Should Never Be/ Ship Of Fools/ Whole Lotta Love
S: Tracks 1-4 Led Zeppelin Rock And Roll Hall Of Fame induction ceremony, Grand Ballroom, Waldorf Astoria Hotel, New York City Jan. 12 '95. Tracks 5-6 Page And Plant London Studios Nov. 1 '94. Tracks 7-10 Robert Plant Parkpop Fest, Denhaag, Holland June 26 '93.   C: ECD. Pic CD.

CD - ROUTE 66
TARANTURA T4CD-3
CD1: Immigrant Song/ Heartbreaker/ Black Dog/ Since I've Been Loving You/ Stairway To Heaven
CD2: Dazed And Confused/ What Is And What Should Never Be/ Moby Dick/ Whole Lotta Love/ Rock And Roll
CD3: Immigrant Song/ Heartbreaker/ Over The Hills And Far Away/ Black Dog/ Since I've Been Loving You
CD4: Dazed And Confused/ Moby Dick
R: Gm. Audience.   S: CD1-2 The Auditorium, San Bernardino June 22 '72. CD3-4 The Forum, Inglewood June 25 '72.   C: Japanese CDs. Gatefold cardboard sleeve. Time CD1 59:07. CD2 72:56. CD3 73:57. CD4 73:13.

CD- ROYAL ALBERT PRESENTATION
IMMIGRANT IM-001
C'mon Everybody (2:30)/ Whole Lotta Love (6:01)/ Communication Breakdown (4:03)/ Something Else (2:01)/ Bring It On Home (7:11)/ How Many More Times Medley: Oh Rosie, Be On My Side, The Hunter, Boogie Chillun, Move On Down The Live, Bottle Up And Go, Leave My Woman Alone (16:11)/ Whole Lotta Love (6:32)*
R: Poor mono. Soundboard. *Gm.   S: Royal Albert Hall, London Jan. 9 '70.   C: Japanese CD. Dcc.

CD - RUNNING BEAR
ORIGINAL CLASSIC RECORDS NETHERLANDS - THE GOLD STANDARD LZRB-01/02
CD1: Immigrant Song (3:38)/ Heartbreaker (6:45)/ Black Dog (5:05)/ Since I've Been Loving You (7:32)/ Celebration Day (4:08)/ Stairway To Heaven (7:16)/ Bron-Y-Aur Stomp (4:03)/ Dazed & Confused (23:36)

CD2: What Is And What Should Never Be (4:51)/ Moby Dick (11:36)/ Whole Lotta Love Medley: Boogie Chillen, Mary Lou, Running Bear, That's Alright Mama, Hoochie Coochie Man, Shape I'm In, Going Down Slow (22:10)/ Rock And Roll (3:51)/ Communication Breakdown (3:37) R: Poor mono. Audience.   S: Amsterdam, Holland May 27 '72.   C: ECD. Dcc. Time CD1 70:49. CD2 51:46.

CD - SAN FRANCISCO '69
AULICA A137
As Long As I Have You (18:52)/ Killing Floor (6:50)/ White Summer (9:38)/ Babe I'm Gonna Leave You (6:44)
R: Ex. Soundboard. Some surface noise.
S: Fillmore West Apr. 24 '69 not Jan. 9 '69 as claimed on cover.   C: ECD. Dbw. Pic CD.

CD - SEATTLE SUPERSONIC
207.19-214
CD1: Rock & Roll (3:58)/ Sick Again (5:14)/ Over The Hills & Far Away (7:11)/ In My Time Of Dying (11:04)/ The Song Remains The Same (5:15)/ The Rain Song (7:40)/ Kashmir (8:53)/ No Quarter (part 1) (18:20)
CD2: No Quarter (part 2) (6:06)/ Since I've Been Loving You (7:40)/ Trampled Underfoot (8:57)/ Dazed & Confused (39:06)/ Stairway To Heaven (2:35)
R: Vgm. Audience.   S: Seattle, Washington Mar. 21 '75.   C: Japanese CD. Dcc. 'Moby Dick' listed on cover but not on CD.

CD - SECOND DAZE
MUD DOGS 011-012
CD1: Rock And Roll (3:30)/ Black Dog (5:01)/ Over The Hills And Far Away (5:40)/ Misty Mountain Hop (4:24)/ Since I've Been Loving You (7:42)/ Dancing Days (4:18)/ Bron-Y-Aur Stomp (4:52)/ The Song Remains The Same (5:04)/ The Rain Song (7:14)
CD2: Dazed & Confused (23:48)/ Stairway To Heaven (8:50)/ Whole Lotta Love Medley: Everybody Needs Someone To Love, Boogie Chillen, Got A Lot Of Livin' To Do, Let's Have A Party, You Shook Me, The Lemon Song (21:18)
R: Poor-Gm. Audience.   S: Tokyo, Japan Oct. 3 '72.   C: Japanese CD. Dcc.

CD - 2ND NIGHT IN A JUDO ARENA
TARANTURA T2CD-6
CD1: MC Goro Itoi/ Rock And Roll (3:30)/ Black Dog (5:21) Over The Hills And Far Away (5:59)/ Misty Mountain Hop (5:30)/ Since I've Been Loving You (7:55)/ Dancing Days (4:06)/ Bron-Yr-Aur Stomp (7:31)/ The Song Remains The Same (5:54)/ The Rain Song (7:49)
CD2: Dazed And Confused (27:25)/ Stairway To Heaven (9:27)/ Whole Lotta Love (22:49) / Immigrant Song (4:37)/ The Ocean (4:24)
R: Gm. Audience.   S: Budokan Hall, Tokyo Oct. 3 '72.   C: Japanese CD. Dcc. Gatefold cardboard sleeve.

CD - SEVENTH HEAVEN
IMMIGRANT IM 006-007
CD1: The Song Remains The Same (5:14)/ Sick Again (6:10)/ Nobody's Fault But Mine (6:20)/ Over The Hills And Far Away (5:15)/ Since I've Been Loving You (8:30)/ No Quarter (22:06)/ Ten Years Gone (9:18)/ The Battle Of Evermore (5:11)/ Going To California (5:41)
CD2: Mystery Train (0:42)/ Black Country Woman (1:40)/ Bron-Y-Aur Stomp (6:00)/ White Summer, Black Mountain Side (7:20)/ Kashmir (9:27)/ Trampled Underfoot (7:07)/ Guitar Solo, Achilles Last Stand (14:58)/ Stairway To Heaven (10:17)/ Whole Lotta Love (1:06)/ Rock And Roll (3:45)
R: G-Vgm. Audience.   S: Oakland, CA July 24 '77.   C: Japanese CD. Dcc. Starts cut off most songs.

CD - SHAKE FOR ME BABY
MISSING LINK ML 017
Kashmir (9:42)/ No Quarter (24:00)/ Tangerine (2:50)/ Stairway To Heaven (11:51)/ Whole Lotta Love (1:19)/ Rock & Roll (3:58)
R: G-Vgm. Soundboard.   S: Tracks 1-3 Earl's Court, London May 25 '75. Tracks 4-6 in Seattle July 17 '77.   C: Japanese CD. Dcc.

CD - SPARE PARTS 1980
POT #003
Stairway To Heaven (11:09)/ Rock & Roll (3:19)/ Whole Lotta Love (14:17)/ Rock And Roll (3:22)/ Whole Lotta Love (12:40)/ Rock And Roll (4:17)/ Whole Lotta Love (16:35)
R: Vgs. Soundboard. Tracks 4-5 Poor-G. Audience.   S: Tracks 1-3 Mannheim July 2 '80 not Vienna June 26 '80 as claimed on cover. Tracks 4-5 Munich July 5 '80. Tracks 6-7 Berlin July 7 '80.   C: Japanese CD. Dcc.

CD - STAIRWAY TO HEAVEN (VOL. 1)
BANANA BAN-050-A
Rock And Roll (3:13)/ Celebration Day (3:43)/ Ramble On (0:20)/ Black Dog (5:55)/ Over The Hills And Far Away (6:43)/ Misty Mountain Hop (4:39)/ Since I've Been Loving You (8:16)/ No Quarter (10:43)/ The Song Remains The Same (5:13)/ Rain Song (8:22)
R: Exs. Soundboard.   S: Fort Worth, Texas May 19 '73.   C: Australian CD. Dcc.

CD - STAIRWAY TO HEAVEN (VOL. 2)
BANANA BAN-050-B
Stairway To Heaven (10:47)/ Medley: Dazed And Confused (5:45), San Francisco (Be Sure To Wear Flowers In Your Hair) (2:45), Dazed And Confused (20:25)/ *Medley: Whole Lotta Love (cut - 2:33), Everybody Needs Somebody To Love (2:06), Whole Lotta Love (4:35), You're So Square (Baby I Don't Care) (1:48), Let's Have A Party (2:17), I Can't Quit You Baby (5:33), The Lemon Song (1:28), Whole Lotta Love (2:18)
R: Exs. Soundboard.   S: Tracks 1-2 Fort Worth, Texas May 19 '73. *Essen Mar. 22 '73.
C: Australian CD. Dcc.

CD - STAIRWAY TO HEAVEN (VOL. 3)
BANANA BAN-050-C
Rock And Roll (4:17)/ Sick Again (6:27)/ Over The
Hills And Far Away (8:14)/ In My Time Of Dying
(13:00)/ The Song Remains The Same (5:26)/ The
Rain Song (8:17)/ Kashmir (10:06)/ No Quarter
(8:52)/ Trampled Underfoot (8:09)/ Moby Dick
(1:07)
R: Exs. Soundboard.   S: Dallas, Texas Mar. 4
'75.   C: Australian CD. Dcc.

CD - STAIRWAY TO HEAVEN (VOL. 4)
BANANA BAN 050D
Stairway To Heaven (10:06)/ San Francisco,
Dazed & Confused (21:04)/ Whole Lotta Love
Medley: Boogie Chillen, Baby I Don't Care, Let's
Have A Party, I Can't Quit You Baby, The Lemon
Song (15:42)/ Heartbreaker Medley: Bouree, 59th
Street Bridge Song (7:21)
R: Exs. Soundboard.   S: Vienna Mar. 16 '73.
C: Australian CD. Dcc.

CD - STAND BY ME
APOLLONIA LZ91010-11
CD1: Rock & Roll (3:39)/ Black Dog (5:09)/ Over
The Hills & Far Away (5:23)/ Misty Mountain Hop
(4:53)/ Since I've Been Loving You (7:11)/
Dancing Days (4:01)/ Bron-Y-Aur Stomp (4:43)/
The Song Remains The Same (5:19)/ The Rain
Song (7:11)/ Moby Dick (16:00)
CD2: Dazed & Confused (27:01)/ Stairway To
Heaven (9:06)/ Whole Lotta Love Medley (22:21)/
Stand By Me (6:15)/ Immigrant Song (3:36)
R: G-Vgs. Audience.   S: Osaka Oct. 4 '72. CD1
tracks 1, 10, and CD2 tracks 1, 4, 5 Osaka Oct. 9
'72.   C: Japanese CD. Dcc.

CD - STEPMOTHERS CLUB
MAD DOGS 027/8
CD1: Immigrant Song/ Heartbreaker/ Dazed And
Confused (includes The Crunge)/ Stairway To
Heaven
CD2: Organ Improvisation, Thank You/ Whole
Lotta Love/ Since I've Been Loving You*/ Black
Dog*
R: Poor-G. Audience.   S: Rearranged Newcastle
City Hall show from Nov. 30 '72 not Stepmothers
Club, Birmingham, UK Mar. 20 '71 as claimed on
cover. *Vigorelli Stadium, Milan, Italy July 14 '71.
C: Japanese CD.

CD - STEPMOTHERS RETURN TO THE CLUB
TOUR 1971
ZEPPELIN LIVE ARCHIVES ZLA-9314/5
CD1: Immigrant Song/ Heartbreaker/ Dazed And
Confused/ Stairway To Heaven/ Thank You
CD2: Whole Lotta Love/ I Can't Quit You Baby/
White Summer, Black Mountain Side/ How Many
More Times
R: Poor-G. Audience.   S: CD1 and CD2 track 1
Rearranged Newcastle City Hall show from Nov.
30 '72 not Stepmothers Club, Birmingham, UK
Mar. 20 '71 as claimed on cover. CD2 tracks 2-4
Wien, Austria Mar. 9 '70.   C: Japanese CD. Dcc.

CD1 52:28. CD2 63:34.

CD - THE STORM OF FANATICS
MUD DOGS 016/017
CD1: Immigrant Song/ Heartbreaker/ Since I've
Been Loving You/ Black Dog/ Dazed And
Confused/ Stairway To Heaven/ Celebration Day
CD2: Bron-Yr-Aur Stomp/ That's The Way/ Going
To California/ What Is And What Should Never Be/
Moby Dick/ Whole Lotta Love/ Communication
Breakdown
R: Vg. Audience.   S: Budokan, Tokyo, Japan
Sept. 23 '71.   C: Japanese CD.

CD - THUNDERSTORM
TARANTURA T4CD-5
CD1: Intro - Opening (1:25)/ Rock And Roll (3:55)/
Sick Again (6:03)/ Over The Hills And Far Away
(7:34)/ In My Time Of Dying (13:22)/ The Song
Remains The Same (6:23)/ The Rain Song (9:35)
CD2: Kashmir (9:12)/ No Quarter (28:12)/
Tangerine (5:02)/ Going To California (5:34)/
That's The Way (7:43)/ Bron-Y-Aur Stomp (7:30)
CD3: Trampled Underfoot (6:30)/ Moby Dick
(23:45)
CD4: Dazed And Confused (31:12)/ Stairway To
Heaven (11:37)/ Whole Lotta Love, The Crunge,
Black Dog (13:02)
R: Ex. Audience.   S: Earl's Court Arena, London
May 23 '75.   C: Japanese CD. Each Pic CD is in
a slip-case with photos from the concert. These
come in a full color Shuffle Pak.

CD - TOTALLY TANGIBLE
BLIMP BL 001
The Wanton Song (3:31)/ The Wanton Song
(6:41)/ In The Morning (In The Light) (6:12)/
Trampled Underfoot (19:16)/ In The Morning (In
The Light) (5:36)/ Sick Again (4:04)/ The Rover
(acoustic) (1:00)/ Hots On For Nowhere (demo
instrumental) (3:49)/ In My Time Of Dying (12:29)
R: Vg-Ex.   S: Headley Grange, England Nov. '73
- May '74.   C: ECD. Dcc.

CD - TOUR DE FORCE
TARANTURA TCD MSG 123
CD1: Rock & Roll (3:57)/ Celebration Day (3:27)/
Black Dog (5:45)/ Over The Hills & Far Away
(6:13)/ Misty Mountain Hop (4:56)/ Since I've
Loving You (8:17)/ No Quarter (12:43)/ The Song
Remains The Same (5:43)/ The Rain Song (7:59)
CD2: Dazed & Confused (29:11)/ Stairway To
Heaven (11:28)/ Moby Dick (28:10)
CD3: Heartbreaker Medley: Whole Lotta Love,
Boogie Chillen (20:38)/ The Ocean (4:30)
R: Exs. Soundboard.   S: MSG, NYC July 28 '73.
C: Japanese CD. Dcc. Gatefold cardboard sleeve.
Pic CDs.

CD - TROUBLE IN VANCOUVER
GOLD STANDARD LZP 388
Immigrant Song (5:35)/ Heartbreaker (7:55)/ Black
Dog (5:05)/ Since I've Been Loving You (7:51)/
Stairway To Heaven (9:19)/ Going To California

(5:40)
R: Gm. Audience.   S: Seattle June 18 '72.
C: ECD. Dcc.

CD - TULSA HILLBILLY
TARANTURA T2CD10
CD1: Immigrant Song (5:02)/ Heartbreaker (8:10)/
Dazed And Confused (19:31)/ Bring It On Home
(11:09)/ That's The Way (6:58)/ Bron-Y-Aur Stomp
(5:32)/ Since I've Been Loving You (8:13)
CD2: Organ Solo, Thank You (13:13)/ What Is And
What Should Never Be (4:18)/ Moby Dick (19:04)/
Whole Lotta Love Medley: Baby Please Don't Go,
That's Alright, My Baby Left Me, Boogie Chillen
(19:27)/ Communication Breakdown (5:48)
R: Poor-Gm. Audience.   S: Tulsa, Oklahoma
Aug. 21 '70.   C: Japanese CD. Dcc. Gatefold
cardboard sleeve.

CD - TWINIGHT
IMMIGRANT IM-002-3
CD1: Train Kept A Rollin' (2:56)/ I Can't Quit You
(5:59)/ As Long As I Have You Medley: Fresh
Garbage, The Lemon Song, Cat's Squirrel, I'm A
Man, Cadillac No Money Down, Hush Little Baby
(19:37)/ You Shook Me (9:38)/ How Many More
Times Medley: Oh Rosie, The Hunter, Mulberry
Bush (19:19)
CD2: Train Kept A Rollin' (4:42)*/ Killing Floor
(7:31)/ Sweet Jelly Roll/ Baby, I'm Gonna Leave
You (7:00)/ White Summer, Black Mountain Side
(9:35)*/ Sittin' And Thinkin' (7:33)/ Moby Dick
(7:17)/ Dazed & Confused (12:19)/
Communication Breakdown (4:10)
R. Vgs. Soundboard. *Gm. Audience.
S: Fillmore West - Apr. 27 '69 except *Jan. 9 '69.
C: Japanese CD. Silver/black cover. Runs slow.

CD - TWO DAYS BEFORE
SILVER RARITIES SIRA 129/130 2-CD
CD1: Immigrant Song/ Heartbreaker/ Dazed &
Confused/ Bring It On Home/ That's The Way/
Bron-Y-Aur Stomp/ Since I've Been Loving You/
Thank You
CD2: What Is What Should Never Be/ Moby Dick/
Whole Lotta Love Medley/ Communication
Breakdown/ Train Kept A Rollin'/ Blueberry Hill/
Long Tall Sally
R: G-Vg. Audience.   S: Oakland, CA Sept. 2 '70.
C: ECD. Dcc. Time CD1 71:07. CD2 72:38.

CD - THE ULTIMATE BBC COLLECTION (1969-1971)
CLASSICAL CL 005
Communication Breakdown (3:18)/ I Can't Quit
You (6:15)/ You Shook Me (10:07)/ Immigrant
Song (3:13)/ Heartbreaker (5:04)/ Dazed And
Confused (16:09)/ Going To California (3:49)/
Stairway To Heaven (8:40)/ Black Dog (5:09)/
Whole Lotta Love (4:18)
R: Ex. Soundboard.   S: Tracks 1-3 London May
27 '69. Tracks 4-10 London Apr. 1 '71.   C: ECD.
Dcc.

CD - ULTRA RARE TRACKS
MISSING LINK ML 001
Stairway To Heaven #1 (3:48)/ Stairway To
Heaven #2 (4:03)/ Acoustic Demo #1 (1:26)/
Acoustic Demo #2 (0:26)/ Black Dog (6:54)/ No
Quarter (4:05)/ Stairway To Heaven #3 (6:59)/
Untitled Instrumental (1:03)/ Stairway To Heaven
#4 (6:10)/ Stairway To Heaven #5 (8:16)/ I Wanna
Be Her Man (1:39)/ Acoustic Demo #3 (1:52)/
Acoustic Demo #4 (2:58)/ Acoustic Demo #5
(4:56)/ Acoustic Demo #6 (3:55)/ Acoustic Demo
#7 (3:55)
R: Ex. Soundboard.   S: Headly Grange Jan. '71.
Tracks 11-16 Bron-Y-Aur May '70.   C: Japanese
CD. Dcc.

CD - WALK DON'T RUN (L.A. 2 DAYS)
TARANTURA T4CD-1
CD1: Walk, Don't Run (2:17)/ Immigrant Song
(4:03)/ Heartbreaker (6:23)/ Since I've Been
Loving You (7:11)/ Black Dog (5:32)/ Dazed And
Confused (20:13)/ Stairway To Heaven (9:05)/
Celebration Day (3:36) That's The Way (6:44)/
What Is And What Should Never Be (4:16)
CD2: Moby Dick (17:52)/ Whole Lotta Love
(23:42)/ Communication Breakdown (7:37)/ Organ
Solo (13:52)
CD3: Immigrant Song (4:05)/ Heartbreaker (6:56)/
Since I've Been Loving You (7:20)/ Black Dog
(5:59)/ Dazed And Confused (21:17)/ Stairway To
Heaven (9:10)/ That's The Way (6:44)/ Going To
California (4:04)
CD4: What Is And What Should Never Be (4:33)/
Whole Lotta Love Medley: Boogie Woogie, I'm
Movin On, That's Alright, Mess O' Blues, Got A Lot
Of Livin' To Do, Honey Bee (25:35)/ Weekend
(3:59)/ Rock And Roll (3:55)/ Communication
Breakdown (6:44)
R: G-Vg. Audience.   S: CD1-2 LA Forum Aug.
22 '71. CD3-4 LA Forum Aug. 21 '71.
C: Japanese CD. Gatefold slipcase. CD sleeves
have TMOQ logo.

CD - WHEN THE LEVEE BREAKS
TNT STUDIO TNT 920122-24
CD1: Rock & Roll (4:05)/ Sick Again (5:50)/ Over
The Hills & Far Away (7:38)/ In My Time Of Dying
(10:08)/ The Song Remains The Same (5:23)/ The
Rain Song (7:50)/ Kashmir (9:45)/ No Quarter
(19:16)
CD2: Trampled Underfoot (8:36)/ Moby Dick
(23:40)/ Dazed & Confused (25:28)
CD3: Stairway To Heaven (12:22)/ Whole Lotta
Love (2:01)/ Black Dog (8:13)/ Heartbreaker
(6:45)/ When The Levee Breaks (8:24)/ The
Wanton Song (4:09)/ How Many More Times
(12:30)
S: CD1-2 and CD3 tracks 1-4 Montreal Feb. 6 '75.
CD3 tracks 5-7 Chicago Jan. 20 '75.
C: Japanese CD. Dcc.

CD - WHO'S BIRTHDAY
TARANTURA T2CD-15
CD1: Intro - Bring It On Home (2:42 cut)/ White

Summer (5:44)/ Black Mountain Side (6:34)/ Since I've Been Loving You (7:12)/ Organ Solo (3:34)/ Thank You (5:45)/ What Is And What Should Never Be (1:44 cut)/ Moby Dick (18:12)/ CD2: How Many More Times Medley: Ravel's Bolero, The Hunter, Boogie Woogie, Trucking Little Mama, Mess O' Blues, My Baby Don't Law, Lemon Song (22:18)/ Whole Lotta Love (7:44)
R: Vg. Audience.   S: Curtis Hickson Hall, Tampa, Florida Apr. 9 '70.   C: Japanese CD. Cardboard gatefold sleeve. Pic CDs.

CD - WHOLE LOTTA LOVE (VOL. 1)
BANANA BAN-008-A
I Can't Quit You Baby (5:20)/ Medley: As Long As I Have You, I'm A Man (18:10)/ You Shook Me (9:47)/ Introductions (0:40)/ How Many More Times (19:36)/ Dazed & Confused (11:18)
R: Vgs. Soundboard.   S: San Francisco Apr. 27 '69.   C: Australian CD. Dcc.

CD - WHOLE LOTTA LOVE (VOL. 2)
BANANA BAN-008-B
You Shook Me (5:13)/ I Can't Quit You Baby (4:26)/ Communication Breakdown (3:01)/ Dazed & Confused (6:41)/ What Is And What Should Never Be (4:21)/ Communication Breakdown (version #2 - 2:39)/ Whole Lotta Love (6:07)/ The Lemon Song (5:47)/ Babe I'm Gonna Leave You (6:30)/ Sittin' And Thinkin' (6:51)/ I Can't Quit You Baby (version #2 - 5:08)/ I Gotta Move (3:02)/ Dazed & Confused (version #2 - 9:46)/ How Many More Times (1:41)
R: G-Vgs. Soundboard.   S: Tracks 1-7 London Mar. 3 '69. Tracks 8-10 San Francisco Apr. 27 '69. Tracks 11-14 Stockholm Mar. 14 '69.
C: Australian CD. Dcc.

CD - WHOLE LOTTA LOVE (VOL. 3)
BANANA BAN-008-C
Communication Breakdown (3:22)/ I Can't Quit You Baby (6:18)/ You Shook Me (10:12)/ White Summer (8:25)/ Dazed & Confused (10:55)/ Medley: How Many More Times, The Lemon Song (11:44)
R: Exm. Soundboard.   S: London June 27 '69.
C: Australian CD. Dcc.

CD - WHOLE LOTTA LOVE (VOL. 4)
BANANA BAN 008D
Train Kept A Rollin' (2:55)/ I Can't Quit You Baby (5:53)/ Dazed & Confused (14:01)/ You Shook Me (10:17)/ How Many More Times Medley: The Hunter, Suzie Q, The Lemon Song, Eyesight To The Blind, Boogie Chillen (instrumental) (20:53)
R: Exs. Soundboard.   S: Dallas Aug. 31 '69.
C: Australian CD. Dcc.

CD - YELLOW ZEPPELIN
TARANTURA T2CD-011-1,2
CD1: The Train Kept A Rollin' (3:12)/ I Can't Quit You (5:29)/ Dazed And Confused (11:05)/ Killing Floor, The Lemon Song, Needle Blues (5:58)/ Babe I'm Gonna Leave You (6:44)/ How Many

More Times (11:05)
CD2: White Summer, Black Mountain Side (9:44)/ As Long As I Have You Medley: Fresh Garbage, Shake, Hush (13:24)/ You Shook Me (8:54)/ Pat's Delight t (13:12)
R: G-Vg. Audience.   S: Full show. Image Club, Miami Jan. 17 '69.   C: Japanese CD. Yellow box with clear window contains CDs in a full color cardboard gatefold sleeve and a T-shirt. Pic CDs. Artwork is a take-off on Beatles' 'Yellow Submarine' artwork.

CD - YOU SHOCK ME
THE ENTERTAINERS CD 0292
Rock & Roll (4:21)/ Sick Again (5:12)/ Over The Hills & Far Away (8:07)/ In My Time Of Dying (12:41)/ The Song Remains The Same (7:07)/ What Is And What Should Never Be (4:33)/ Stairway To Heaven (8:43)/ You Shook Me (10:09)/ Whole Lotta Love Medley: Boogie Chillen, Mess Of Blues (10:17)/ Immigrant Song (3:36)
R: Ex. Soundboard.   S: Tracks 1-5 in Dallas Mar 4 '75. Tracks 6, 7, 9, 10 London Apr. 1 '71. Track 8 London June 27 '69.   C: ECD. Dcc.

CD - ZIG ZAG ZEP
TARANTURA T3CD-013
CD1: Intro - Rock And Roll (3:22)/ Over The Hills And Far Away (6:33)/ Black Dog (5:56)/ Misty Mountain Hop (4:33)/ Since I've Been Loving You (7:21)/ Dancing Days (4:45)/ Bron-Y-Aur Stomp (5:32)
CD2: The Song Remains The Same (2:07 cut)/ Dazed And Confused (21:33)/ Stairway To Heaven (10:33)/ Whole Lotta Love Medley: Boogie Woogie, Baby I Don't Care, Let's Have A Party, I Can't Quite You, Lemon Song (15:23)
R: Vg. Soundboard. First two tracks distorted and unbalanced.   S: Stadthalle, Vienna, Austria Mar. 16 '73.   C: Japanese CD. Three color cardboard gatefold sleeve. Pic CDs.

LEMONHEADS, THE

CD - NEW YORK NEW YORK
MONTANA MO 10006
It's A Shame About Ray/ Alison's Starting To Happen/ Stove/ Big Part/ Mallo Cup/ Rudderless/ Shaky Ground/ Gold Plated Door/ Ride With Me/ It's About Time/ Hannah And Gabi/ Rockin' Stroll/ Being Around/ Confetti/ Dawn Can't Decide/ Hate Your Friend/ Luka/ Mrs. Robinson/ My Drug Buddy/ Kitchen/ I Forget You Forget/ Glad Don't Know/ Frank Mills/ Left For Dead/ I Give Up/ Will You Still Love Me Tomorrow/ Down About It/ Rest Assured/ Big Gay Heart/ Into Your Arms
R: Ex. Audience.   S: New York '92-'93.
C: ECD. Dcc. Time 77:14.

CD - THE SECRET LIFE OF EVAN DANDO
HAWK 017
Being Around (1:54)/ Confetti (2:16)/ Alison's Starting To Happen (2:16) It's A Shame About Ray (2:46)/ Burning Blue (2:22)/ Ride With Me (3:40)/

Stove (2:39)/ Frank Mills (2:07)/ It's About Time (2:56)/ My Drug Buddy (3:03)/ Big Gay Heart (3:49)/ Down About it (2:45)/ In Your Eyes (3:06)/ Divan (2:06)/ The Great Big No (3:22)/ Hanni & Gabi (2:59)/ Mallo Cup (2:41)/ $1000 Wedding (3:22)/ Barstool Blues (2:20)/ Different Drum (3:09) R: Ex. Audience.   S: McCabes Guitar Shop, LA CA May '93.   C: ECD. Dcc. Pic CD.

CD - WITH REAL LEMON JUICE
HOME RECORDS HR 5914-7
Stove (3:22)/ Confetti (2:33)/ Mallocup (2:04)/ Glad I Don't Know (1:33)/ Rudderless (3:04)/ It's A Shame About Ray (2:52)/ Drug Buddy (2:55)/ Ride With Me (3:34)/ Kitchen (2:14)/ Making It Known (2:52)/ Hanna And Gabi (2:33)/ Inside You (2:16)/ Being Around (2:13)/ Will You Love Me Tomorrow (2:12)/ Shaky Ground (2:00)/ In My Solitude (1:57)/ Into Your Arms (2:02)/ Dawn Can't Decide (2:14)/ Hate Your Friend (2:22)/ Luka (4:05)/ Gold Plated Door (1:38)/ It's About Time (2:49)/ Mrs. Robinson (3:24)/ Down About It (2:19)/ Rest Assured (2:23)/ Big Gay Heart (4:13)/ Rockin' Stroll (1:53)/ Allison's Starting To Happen (1:46)/ Different Drum (2:32)
R: G-Vg.   S: '92-'93.   C: ECD. Dcc.

LENNON, JOHN

CD - CHRISTMAS PRESENT
WHITE FLY WF 001/3
CD1: Mother (5:04)/ Imagine (3:31)/ Come Together (4:15)/ Give Peace A Chance (7:37)/ Cold Turkey (3:31)/ Too Much Monkey Business (1:58)/ Brown Eyed Handsome Man (2:44)/ Rock Island Line (2:35)/ Chords Of Fame (4:08)/ Rock Island Line No. 2 (electric version - 2:53)/ Jealous Guy (4:18)/ Mirror, Mirror (On The Wall) (take 1 - 2:28)/ Mirror, Mirror (On The Wall) (take 5 - 2:38)/ Dear Prudence (White Album demo '68 - 4:39)/ Cold Turkey (electric rehearsal - 4:14)/ New York City (live show - 3:00)/ Watching The Wheels (demo '80 - 3:54)/ Dear Yoko (3:46)/ My Life (version 1 - 2:21)/ (Just Like) Starting Over (rough mix Aug. '80 - 4:56)
CD2: I Found Out (acoustic - 4:05)/ God (2:47)/ The Worst Is Over Now (take 1 - 2:16)/ Beautiful Boy (composing sequence - 5:53)/ When A Boy Meets A Girl (take 1, John's Birthdays '69-'70 - 2:11)/ I'm So Tired (with Mike Love - 3:02)/ Sexy Sadie (2:20)/ The Maharishi Song (with Yoko - 3:16)/ Revolution (mid '68 - 3:56)/ God (late '70s - 2:20)/ How (late '70s - 4:32)/ Beautiful Boy, Memories (Howling At The Moon) (1:59)/ The Dakota Rap, Across The River (3:33)/ I'm The Greatest (4th pass with Ringo '73 - 3:56)/ How Do You Sleep (7:39)/ Oh My Love (2:10)/ Untitled Jam (1:51)/ Imagine (piano solo - 2:58)/ Woman Is The Nigger Of The World (John & Yoko '72 - 1:56)/ Real Life (piano demo - 4:16)/ I'm Steppin' Out (take 1 - 5:04)/ I Don't Want To Face It (1:54)/ I Watch Your Face (2:07)/ My Life (take 1 - 3:12)
CD3: Woman Is The Nigger Of The World (5:53)/ Well, Well, Well (rehearsal Aug. 22 '72 - 5:23)/

Come Together (rehearsal - Aug. 18 '72 - 5:33)/ Hound Dog, Long Tall Sally (jam Aug. 21 '72 - 5:21)/ Don't Let Me Down (2:03)/ Yer Blues (with Keith Richards, Eric Clapton & Mitch Mitchell 4:04)/ Rock & Roll People (3:02)/ Mind Games (2:14)/ Jealous Guy (4:17)/ Imagine (Mike Douglas Show - 3:36)/ Give Me Some Truth (3:36)/ Power To The People (4:16)/ John Sinclair (2:50)/ Instant Karma (3:00)/ Ain't That A Shame (2:25)/ On The Caribbean (3:06)/ Intuition (2:51)/ Stand By Me (partial mix - 1:52)/ Oh, Yoko (4:00)/ I Saw Her Standing There (with Elton John - 2:49)/ I'm Loosing You (3:51)
R: As with any set having so many sources, sound quality varies. Generally G-Vg. Some excellent. S: CD1 tracks 1-4 Madison Square Garden, NY '72. CD1 tracks 5-8, CD2 track 1 acoustic demos. CD1 track 11, CD3 tracks 7, 11 alternate takes. CD1 tracks 12-13 Tokyo, Japan '77. CD1 tracks 15-16 New York '72. CD1 tracks 18-19, CD3 track 21 Bermuda Tapes '80. CD2 tracks 2, 22-24, CD3 track 1 demos. CD2 tracks 6-8 spring '68. CD2 tracks 12-13 Dakota late '70s. CD2 tracks 15-18 with Nicky Hopkins and Plastic Ono Band, Imagine Sessions. CD2 tracks 20-21 Thanksgiving '79. CD3 track 5 rehearsal. CD3 track 8 unreleased promo. CD3 tracks 9, 17, 19 rough mixes. CD3 track 12 early studio take. CD3 tracks 13-14 Chrysler Arena Dec. 12 '71. CD3 tracks 15-16 Mar. '72.   C: ECD. Box set. Booklet with listings lifted (without permission) out of HOT WACKS... how imaginative. Next time send royalties or at least free CDs to the address in the front of this book.

CD - THE COMPLETE MAY PANG TAPES
ORANGE FIFTEEN
Slippin' & Slidin'/ Rip It Up/ Bring It On Home To Me, Send Me Some Loving #1/ Bring It On Home To Me/ Send Me Some Loving #2/ Peggy Sue #1/ Ain't That A Shame #1/ Ain't That A Shame #2/ Be Bop A Lula #1/ Ya Ya #1/ Do You Want To Dance #1/ Stand By Me #1/ Bring It On Home To Me, Send Me Some Loving #3/ Ya Ya #2/ That'll Be The Day/ Do You Want To Dance #2/ Stand By Me #2/ Peggy Sue #2/ Be Bop A Lula #2/ Slippin' & Sliddin' #2/ Whole Lotta Love/ Thirty Days
S: Studio Oct. '74.   C: ECD.

CD - THE LOST LENNON TAPES VOLUMES 30/31/32
BAG 5102/3/4A/B
CD1: Intro - It's Not Too Bad (embryonic version of 'Strawberry Fields' - 3:29)/ She Can Talk To Me (early piano demo of 'Hey Bulldog' - 00:46)/ Cry Baby Cry (early demo fragments - 3:23)/ Two Virgins Outtake (May '68 - 1:47)/ Plastic Ono Band Jam (1:39)/ Look At Me (alternate vocals - 2:52)/ I'm The Greatest (piano demo - :37)/ How?, Child Of Nature, Oh Yoko! (piano demos - 4:25)/ Oh Yoko (3:23)/ Sally And Billy (2:03)/ Come Together (Aug. '72 'One To One' rehearsal - 1:47)/ Happy Girl (1:10)/ I'll Make You Happy (3:56)/ How Do You Sleep? (rehearsal '71 - 3:45)/ It's So Hard

(run through - 4:44)/ I Don't Wanna Be A Soldier I Don't Wanna Die (run through - 4:34)/ Intuition (take 4 of piano demos - 3:04)/ I Know (take 2 of guitar demos - 3:00)/ I Know (alternate of finished version - 3:43)/ Aisumasen (I'm Sorry) (near final mix - 4:00)/ Steel And Glass (piano version - 1:44)/ Walls And Bridges Rundown (1:56)/ Mirror Mirror On The Wall (take 2 of piano demos '77 - 4:34) CD2: Tennessee (home demo '76 - 3:04)/ Memories (home demo '76 - 6:03)/ Sally And Billy (home demo '76 - 3:28)/ She Is A Friend Of Dorothy's (home demo '77 - 3:55)/ The Boat Song (demo - 2:08)/ Pedro The Fisherman (demo - 1:04)/ Many Rivers To Cross Pt. 2 (demo), My Girl (2:24)/ Instrumental 1979 (1:02)/ I'm Stepping Out (incomplete take - 1:29)/ Dear Yoko (incomplete take - 5:04)/ Woman (rehearsal - 4:26)/ Woman (vocal track - 1:54)/ Woman (finishing touches - 2:13)/ Clean Up Time (rehearsal - 6:01)/ Nobody Told Me (different take - 3:51)/ I Am The Walrus (parody), Watching The Wheels (rehearsal take - 4:01)/ Woman (instrumental - 2:26)/ Woman (alternate take - 3:39)/ Living On Borrowed Time (early take - 4:20)/ I'm Losing You (alternate take - 3:54)
R: Vg- Ex.   C: Australian CD. Dcc.

CD - 'ONE TO ONE' REHEARSALS VOL. 1
ORANGE SIXTEEN
Come Together/ Tequila/ New York City/ It's So Hard/ Move On Fast, Back Off Boogaloo/ Woman Is The Nigger Of The World/ Sisters O Sisters/ Give Peace A Chance/ Instrumental Jam/ Unchained Melody/ Well Well Well/ Born In A Prison/ Instant Karma
S: Live in the studio.   C: ECD.

CD - 'ONE TO ONE' REHEARSALS VOL. 2
ORANGE SEVENTEEN
Mother/ We're All Water/ Come Together/ Open Your Box/ Cold Turkey, Don't Worry/ Jam #1/ Jam #2/ We're All Water #2/ Roll Over Beethoven/ Give Peace A Chance/ Tequila #2/ Jam #3
S: Live in the studio.   C: ECD.

CD - PILL
MISSING IN ACTION - NEVER END
Imagine (acoustic solo NYC '71) (2:47)/ Child Of Nature (London '68) (2:33)/ Let's Twist Again (with Bowie NYC '75) (3:03)/ One Of The Boys (unreleased NYC '75) (3:05)/ Mind Games (NYC '73) (3:44)/ Yer Blues (instrumental '68) (1:20)/ Out Of Blue (no choir NYC '73) (4:12)/ She Was A Friend Of Dorothy (unreleased NYC '75) (2:36)/ Girls & Boys (NYC '79) (2:19)/ Mucho Mungo (solo LA '73) (2:04)/ Cold Turkey (NYC '69) (4:46)/ I Found Out (uncensored solo version NYC '70) (3:19)/ #9 Dream (solo NYC '73) (1:21)/ Instant Karma (London '70) (3:06)/ Dear Yoko (Bermuda '79) (3:31)/ I'm Stepping Out (Bermuda '79) (4:23)/ Pill (NYC '72) (1:39)/ Real Love (first version of 'Girl & Boys') (3:50)
R: G-Vg. Some Ex.   C: ECD. Sepia-tone picture of Lennon. Gold disc.

CD - PRECIOUS & RARE (VOL. 1)
BANANA BAN-020-A
Watching The Wheels (acoustic - 3:01)/ Corrina, Corrina (electric - 1:14)/ Beautiful Boy (acoustic and congas - 2:43)/ Dear Yoko (#1 acoustic - 1:00)/ Dear Yoko (#2 acoustic - 4:23)/ Borrowed Time (acoustic - 5:01)/ Move Over Ms. L (#1 acoustic - 1:34)/ Move Over Ms. L (#2 acoustic - 1:54)/ Here We Go Again (acoustic - 3:01)/ Maybe Baby (acoustic - 1:55)/ Rave On (acoustic - 1:16)/ Whatever Gets You Thru The Night (acoustic - 5:30)/ Woman (acoustic and rhythm box - 2:47)/ God Save Us (acoustic and congas - 1:58)/ I Know (I Know) (acoustic - 3:16)/ (Just Like) Starting Over (acoustic and rhythm box - 4:18)
R: G-Vg. Some Ex.   S: USA '70's - '80.
C: Australian CD. Dcc.

CD - PRECIOUS & RARE (VOL. 3)
BANANA BAN-020-C
Cookin' (In The Kitchen Of Love) (piano - 2:29)/ Nobody Told Me (piano - 2:19)/ Woman Is The Nigger Of The World (acoustic - 2:14)/ I'm Stepping Out (acoustic with rhythm box - 4:33)/ New York City (acoustic - 2:13)/ Woman (acoustic with rhythm box - 3:31)/ Beautiful Boy (acoustic - 4:05)/ Mind Games (piano - 3:32)/ I Found Out (acoustic - 4:05)/ Watching The Wheels (piano - 3:21)/ Woman (acoustic take 9 - 3:58)/ Nobody Told Me (acoustic - 3:19)/ Rock And Roll People (piano - 3:32)/ Oh! Yoko (acoustic with Yoko - 4:40)
R: Vg-Ex. Some G.   S: USA '70-'80.
C: Australian CD. Dcc.

CD - PRECIOUS & RARE (VOL. 4)
BANANA BAN-020-D
People Get Ready (piano), How (3:02)/ God (acoustic, take 2 - 3:45)/ Borrowed Time (acoustic - 3:54)/ She Said, She Said #1 (excerpts - 1:06)/ She Said, She Said #2 (acoustic - 0:59)/ She Said, She Said #3 (acoustic - 1:00)/ (Just Like) Starting Over (acoustic and rhythm box - 2:18)/ Cookin' (In The Kitchen Of Love) (piano - 2:42)/ Only The Lonely (acoustic - 1:02)/ Mucho Mungo (acoustic, take 2 - 3:03)/ #9 Dream (acoustic, take 2 - 3:11)/ I'm Stepping Out (piano - 3:30)/ Well, Well, Well (acoustic - 1:15)/ Watching The Wheels (acoustic - 3:02)/ San Francisco Bay Blues (acoustic - 0:45)/ Look At Me ('68 acoustic - 3:06)/ Cold Turkey (acoustic - 3:44)/ Maggie Mae (acoustic - 0:28)/ Julia (instrumental, acoustic - 2:54)
R: Vg. Some Ex. Some poor.   S: '70s - '80.
C: Australian CD. Dcc.

LEVELLERS, THE

CD - BACK TO NATURE
KISS THE STONE KTS 248
Warning (6:27)/ 100 Years Of Solitude (3:57)/ Sell Out (4:45)/ This Garden (5:19)/ One Way (6:00)/ Belaruse (3:42)/ Battle Of The Beanfield (3:34)/ Is This Art? (3:00)/ Another Man Cause (4:55)/ The Riverflow (3:30)/ Julie (3:26)/ Julie (reprise - 2:23)/

Liberty (4:42)/ Subvert (3:08)
R: Ex.   S: '93.   C: ECD. Dcc. Pic CD.

LIGHTFOOT, GORDON

CD - READ MY MIND
RARE RECORDING COLLECTION RRC 034
Race Among The Ruins/ The Wreck Of The
Edmund Fitzgerald/ Summertime Dream/ I'd Do It
Again/ Never Too Close/ The Last Time I Saw
Her/ If You Could Read My Mind/ Cobwebs And
Dust/ High And Dry/ Sundown/ Garden Rag/ All
The Lovely Ladies/ Christian Island/ Old Dan's
Records/ I'm Not Supposed To Care/ Canadian
Railroad Trilogy/ Beautiful/ Early Morning Rain/
Spanish Moss
R: Exs. Soundboard.   S: Montreux '77.
C: ECD. Dcc. Time 73:45.

LITTLE STEVEN

CD - NATIVE AMERICAN
WINGED WHEEL WW9414
Freedom/ Sanctuary/ Los Desaparecidos, The
Disappeared Ones/ Bitter Fruit/ Checkpoint
Charlie/ Vote, That Mutha Out/ No More Party's/
Undefeated, Everybody Goes Home/ Native
American/ Sun City
R: Exs. Audience.   S: Ritz, NY Oct. 14 '87.
C: ECD. Full-color gatefold cardboard sleeve.
Tracks 9-10 Springsteen on vocals. CD looks like
a record. Time 73:08.

LIVE

CD - I ALIVE
KISS THE STONE KTS 383
The Dam At Otter Creek (5:38)/ Beauty Of Grey
(5:06)/ Lightning Crashes (6:04)/ I Alone (4:22)/
Selling The Drama (3:43)/ Operation Spirit (5:05)/
Iris (4:12)/ Pain Lies On The Riverside (5:11)/
Selling The Drama (3:14)
R: Exs. Soundboard.   S: USA '94.   C: ECD.
Pic CD.

LIVING COLOUR

CD - 4 NEVER SATISFIED FRIENDS
BACKSTAGE BKCD072
Never Satisfied/ Leave It Alone/ Bi/ Love Rears Its
Ugly Head/ Open Letter (To A Landlord)/
Nothingness/ Leave It Alone/ Auslander/ Love
Rears Its Ugly Head/ Cult Of Personality/
Nothingness/ Elvis Is Dead
R: Exs. Soundboard.   S: Tracks 1-6 VPRO
Studio Sessions, Hilversum, Holland Feb. 14 '93.
Tracks 7-11 Sun City Festival, Sheffield, UK Aug.
'93. Tracks 12-13 Spring Break Festival, Daytona
Beach Mar. 20 '93.   C: ECD. Dcc. Time 70:00.

LOS LOBOS

CD - EAST LOS ANGELENOS
ROYAL SOUND MUSIC RSM 030

Evangeline 'Gonna Rock'/ Come On Let's Go/ Will
The Wolf Survive/ Is This All There Is/ I Got To Let
You Know/ Our Last Night/ One Time One Night/
My Baby's Gone/ A Matter Of Time/ The Hardest
Time/ All I Wanted To Do Is Dance/ Why Do You
Do/ Let's Say Goodnight/ I Got Loaded/ Shakin'
Shakes/ Set Me Free/ Don't Worry Baby/ Walking
Song/ Buzz Buzz Buzz/ My Baby's Gone #2/ La
Bamba
S: USA '87.   C: ECD.

LYNOTT, PHIL & JOHN SYKES

CD - 'THE THREE MUSKETEERS'
TAURUS TAU 118
Yellow Pearl (3:41)/ Old Town (3:56)/ A Night In
The Life Of A Blues Singer (5:28)/ Sarah (3:17)/
No More (4:34)/ Parisienne Walkways (4:48)/ Solo
In Soho (6:0 2)/ King's Call (4:50)/ Cold Sweat
(2:49)/ Baby Drives Me Crazy (9:58)/ The Boys
Are Back In Town (4:17)/ Dancing With The
Moonlight (4:05)
R: G. Audience.   S: Goteborg '83.   C: ECD.
Black/silver cover. Red type.

M

MADONNA

CD - BAD, BAD GIRL
EROS 01
CD1: Intro/ Erotica/ Fever/ Vogue/ Rain/ Express
Yourself/ Deeper And Deeper/ Why It's So Hard/
In This Life
CD2: Like A Virgin/ Bye Bye Baby/ I'm Going
Bananas/ La Isla Bonita/ Holiday/ Justify My Love/
Everybody/ Outro
R: Exs. Soundboard.   S: Sydney Nov. 19 '93.
C: ECD. Dcc.

CD - EROTICA BLUES
BEST BUY RECORDS BBR CD 006
Intro (0:42)/ Erotica (5:57)/ Holiday (6:03)/ Papa
Don't Preach (5:54)/ Material Girl (4:54)/ Cherish
(4:42)/ Vogue (5:14)/ Justify My Love (8:10)/ Like
A Virgin (4:31)/ Why Is It So Hard? (5:08)/ Express
Yourself (5:14)/ Open Your Heart (7:20)/ Rain
(9:57)
R: Exs. Soundboard.   S: USA '93.   C: ECD.
Dbw. Red type.

CD - EXOTICA
BACK STAGE BK 061/62
CD1: Erotica (6:46)/ Fever (4:55)/ Vogue (5:31)/
Rain (9:57)/ Express Yourself (5:21)/ Deeper &
Deeper (7:20)/ Why It's So Hard (6:30)/ In This
Life (6:47)/ The Beast Within Remix (6:05)
CD2: Like A Virgin (6:18)/ Bye Bye Baby (4:26)/
I'm Going Bananas (2:42)/ La Isla Bonita (7:15)/
Holiday (12:47)/ Justify My Love (8:16)/ Everybody
(11:50)
R: Exs. Soundboard.   S: Sydney Cricket Sports

Ground Nov. 19 '93.   C: ECD. Dcc. Fold-open digi-pack.

CD - THE GIRLIE SHOW
GS CD 001/002
CD1: Introduction (0:39)/ Erotica (6:01)/ Fever (4:50)/ Vogue (5:27)/ Rain, Just My Imagination (9:20)/ Express Yourself (5:00)/ Deeper & Deeper (6:30)/ Why It's So Hard (6:24)/ In This Life (7:08)/ The Beast Within (6:05)/ Like A Virgin, Falling In Love Again (5:54)/ Bye Bye Baby (4:33)/ Going Bananas (2:15)/ La Isla Bonita (4:50)
CD2: Dialogue, Marching Orders (2:18)/ Holiday (11:18)/ Justify My Love (8:44)/ Everybody (includes band introductions & solos - 9:41)/ Finale (1:07)/ The Erotic Supreme (mega mix - 30:03)/ Like A Prayer (unreleased promo - 8:50)/ Keep It Together (major ultimix - 7:11)
R: Vg-Ex.   S: Wembley Stadium, London, England Sept. '93. CD2 tracks 6-8 different source.   C: ECD. Dbw. Blue/gold type. Pic CD.

CD - GIRLIE SHOW EXPERIENCE
KISS THE STONE KTS 255/56
CD1: Rain/ Express Yourself/ Deeper And Deeper/ Why It's So Hard/ In This Life/ The Beast Within Remix/ Like A Virgin
CD2: Bye Bye Baby/ I'm Going Bananas/ La Isla Bonita/ Holiday/ Justify My Love/ Everybody
R: Exs. Soundboard.   S: Live '93.   C: ECD. Dcc. Pic CDs. Total time 90:34.

CD - MATERIAL GIRL (VOL. 2)
BANANA BAN-026-B
Holiday (5:58)/ Material Girl (4:47)/ Cherish (7:15)/ Into The Groove (5:47)/ Vogue (5:32)/ Keep It Together (11:04)/ Holiday (6:08)/ Into The Groove (6:13)/ Love Me, The World Go 'Round (5:14)
R: Exs. Soundboard.   S: USA '93.
C: Australian CD. Dcc.

CD - MATERIAL GIRL (VOL. 4)
BANANA BAN-026-D
Sooner Or Later (I Always Get My Man) (3:59)/ Hanky Panky (3:35)/ Material Girl (4:06)/ Cherish (5:36)/ Into The Groove (5:27)/ Vogue (5:110/ Holiday (5:56)/ Family Affair, Keep It Together (9:49)/ Happy Birthday To You (3:15)/ Fever (5:25)/ Bad Girl (5:21)
R: Exs. Soundboard.   S: Europe '90. USA '86.
C: Australian CD. Dcc. Gold disc.

CD - MATERIAL GIRL
PIPELINE PPL 534
Express Yourself (6:00)/ Open Your Heart (4:37)/ Causing A Commotion (4:54)/ Like A Virgin (5:10)/ Like A Prayer (7:44)/ Live To Tell (5:53)/ Papa Don't Preach (5:51)/ Material Girl (4:33)/ Cherish (5:37)/ Into The Groove (5:30)/ Vogue (5:17)/ Holiday (6:01)/ Keep It Together (10:30)
R: Exs. Soundboard.   S: European Tour '92 part 1.   C: ECD. Dcc. See 'Star Light' (PPL 535) for part 2.

CD - STAR LIGHT
PIPELINE PPL 535
Star Light (4:55)/ True Blue (4:55)/ White Heat (5:47)/ Dress You Up (2:16)/ Material Girl (3:49)/ Where's The Party (5:13)/ Into The Groove (8:13)/ La Isla Bonita (6:08)/ Who's That Girl (7:58)
R: Exs. Soundboard.   S: European Tour '92 part 1.   C: ECD. Dcc. See 'Material Girl' (PPL 534) for part 1.

CD - VOGUE
GRAPEFRUIT GRA-005-A
Erotica (6:39)/ Vogue (5:28)/ Rain, Just My Imagination (Running Away With Me) (9:33)/ Express Yourself (5:03)/ Deeper And Deeper (6:35)/ Like A Virgin/Falling In Love Again (6:00)/ Bye Bye Baby (4:38)/ I'm Going Bananas (2:16)/ La Isla Bonita (4:47)/ Holiday (9:50)/ Everybody Is A Star, Everybody (11:03)
R: Exs. Soundboard.   S: London '93.
C: Australian CD. Dcc.

MANOWAR

CD - THE KINGS OF METAL
BANZAI BZCD 007
Manowar (4:24)/ Fighting The World (3:45)/ Drum Solo (2:37)/ Metal Warriors (7:38)/ Kings Of Metal (3:58)/ Herz Aus Stahl (13:57)/ Ride The Dragon (4:29)/ Hail And Kill (4:12)/ The Glory Of Achilles (3:31)/ Black Wind, Fire And Steel (10:34)/ Battle Hymn (11:30)/ Outtro (3:20)
R: Vg. Audience.   C: ECD. Dcc. Pic CD.

MARILLION

CD - IN SESSION TONIGHT
TAKE IT OR LEAVE IT T 9411
Forgotten Sons (7:31)/ Three Boats Down From The Candy (4:10)/ The Web (8:12)/ He Knows You Know (3:36)/ Garden Party (7:06)/ Charting The Single (4:40)/ Grendel (18:18)/ Market Square Heroes (3:37)/ Three Boats Down From The Candy (4:21)
R: Exs. Soundboard.   S: Tracks 1-3 Friday Rock Show session, Maidavalle Studio 6 Jan. 29 '82. Tracks 4-6 Roxon demo, Roxon Studio, Oxfordshire July 18 and 19 '81. Tracks 7-9 EMI demo, Fair Deal Studio, London Sept. 6 '82.
C: ECD. Dcc.

CD - THE LAST FISH
AMERICAN CONCERT SERIES ACS 016
Hotel Hobbies (4:06)/ Warm Wet Circles/ That Time Of The Night (The Short Straw) (10:18)/ Kayleigh (4:25)/ Lavender (2:49)/ Bitter Suite (8:03)/ Heart Of Lothian (4:04)/ The Last Straw (5:47)/ Incommunicado (4:59)/ Garden Party (6:43)/ Market Square Heroes Part 1 (4:31)/ Let's Twist Again (2:53)/ Market Square Heroes Part 2 (2:33)
R: Vg-Ex. Soundboard.   S: Milwaukee.
C: ECD. Dcc.

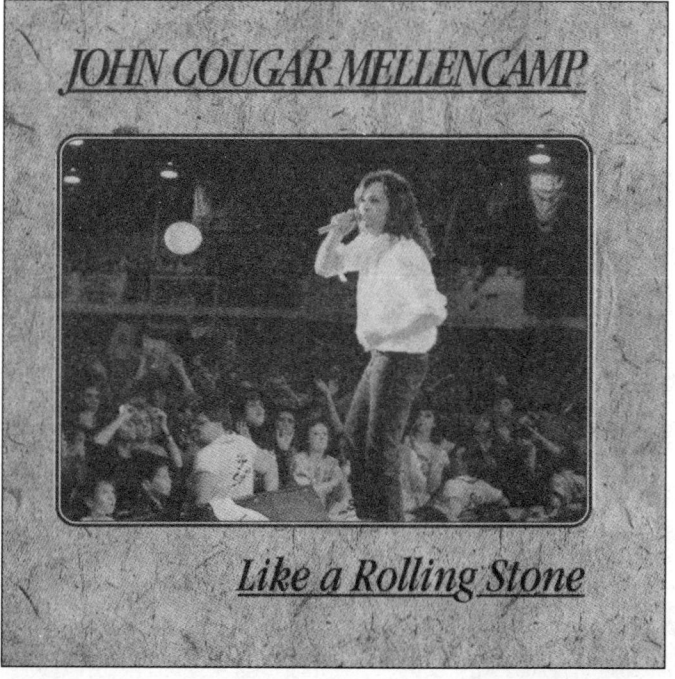

MARLEY, BOB

CD - CHARMING HAZE
OCTOPUS OCTO 059
Trenchtown Rock (5:20)/ Them Belly Full (3:21)/ Rebel Music (5:19)/ I Shot The Sheriff (4:31)/ Crazy Baldhead (5:13)/ Want More (5:51)/ No Woman No Cry (5:17)/ Lively Up Yourself (6:00)/ Kinky Reggae (6:56)/ Positive Vibrations (4:44)/ Medley: Rat Race, War, No More Trouble, Get Up, Stand Up (26:13)
R: Ex. Soundboard.   S: Europe '76 World Tour.
C: ECD. Dcc. Pic CD.

CD - DOWNTOWN TRENCHMAN
KISS THE STONE KTS 308
Catch A Fire (4:25)/ Trenchtown Rock (5:58)/ Concrete Jungle (6:04)/ Midnight Ravers (6:38)/ Talkin' Blues (6:08)/ Rebel Music (3 O'clock Roadblock) (7:34)/ I Shot The Sheriff (12:24)/ Natty Dread (8:15)
R: Exs. Soundboard.   S: Quiet Knight Club, Chicago 6/10/75.   C: ECD. Dcc. Pic CD. 57:29.

CD - IS THIS LOVE
GRAPEFRUIT GRA-012-A
Positive Vibration (5:08)/ Them Belly Full (But We Hungry) (3:37)/ Rebel Music (4:56)/ War, No More Trouble (6:17)/ Running Away, Crazy Baldhead (9:19)/ I Shot The Sheriff (4:29)/ No Woman, No Cry (6:41)/ Is This Love (5:57)/ Jamming (7:36)/ Easy Skanking (4:46)/ Get Up, Stand Up (4:55)/ Exodus (10:42)
R: Exs. Soundboard.   S: Ahoy, Rotterdam, Holland '78.   C: Australian CD. Dcc.

CD - REDEMPTION
KISS THE STONE KTS 340
Concrete Jungle (alternate studio) (3:57)/ Get Up, Stand Up ('73 studio demo) (3:47)/ Talkin' Blues ('74 studio demo) (4:33)/ Amadu ('74 alternate studio) (3:20)/ Jah Live (2:38)/ Smile Jamaica Dub ('76 alternate studio) (2:22)/ Turn Your Lights Down Low ('77 studio demo) (3:49)/ Exodus ('77 studio demo) (8:01)/ Running Away ('78 studio demo) (4:31)/ Who Colt The Game ('78 studio demo) (3:15)/ I Know A Place ('78 studio demo) (4:00)/ Ride Natty Ride ('Tuff Gong' rehearsal '79 (11:07)/ Give Thanks And Praises ('80 studio demo) (3:38)/ Chant Down Babylon ('80 studio demo) (4:48)/ Babylon Feel Dis One ('80 studio demo) (2:15)/ Zion Train ('Tuff Gong' rehearsal '0) (3:56)/ Shot The Sheriff ('Tuff Gong' rehearsal '80) (2:56)/ Redemption Song ('80 Essex House Hotel, New York) (2:29)
R: Ex. Soundboard.   C: ECD. Pic CD.

CD - REVOLUTION
KISS THE STONE KTS 3001/01
CD1: Melody (5:07)/ Slavery (4:08)/ Steppin' Out Of Babylon (4:44)/ That's The Way (4:39)/ Intro, Natural Mystic (6:17)/ Positive Vibration (5:01)/ Revolution (4:54)/ I Shot The Sheriff (4:42)/ War, No More Trouble (5:18)/ Zimbabwe (3:34)/

Jamming (5:16)
CD2: No Woman No Cry (6:37)/ Zion Train (4:11)/ Exodus (6:50)/ Redemption Song (4:01)/ Could You Be Loved (4:20)/ Work (4:32)/ Notty Bread (4:29)/ Is This Love? (3:38)/ Get Up, Stand Up (3:06)/ Coming In From The Cold (4:26)/ Lively Up Yourself (6:41)
R: Exs. Soundboard.   S: Dortmund June 26 '80.
C: ECD. Dcc. Pic CD.

MARSHALL TUCKER BAND, THE

CD - SILVERADO
ROYAL SOUND MUSIC RSM 030
Heard It In A Love Song/ Take The Highway/ Cattle Drive/ See You One More Time/ Sing My Blues/ Fire On The Mountain/ I'm On My Way/ This Ol' Cowboy/ Can't You See/ It Takes Time/ Tell The Blues To Take Off Tonight/ I'll Be Loving You/ Silverado/ Searching For A Rainbow
S: Live USA '87.   C: ECD.

MATTEA, KATHY

CD - ASKING US TO DANCE
ROYAL SOUND MUSIC RSM 059SQ CD
The Streets Of Your Town/ Time Passes By/ Standing Knee Deep In A River (Dying Of Thirst)/ Maybe She's Human/ Untold Stories/ Nobody's Gonna Rain On Our Parade/ Clown In Your Rodeo/ Love At The Five And Dime/ Asking Us To Dance/ Where've You Been/ Walking Away A Winner/ Train Of Memories/ Eighteen Wheels And A Dozen Roses/ Life As We Knew It
S: Live in USA '94.   C: ECD.

MAY, BRIAN

CD – BACK TO THE LIGHT TOUR
B.T.T.L. MUSIC CD 148/149
CD1: The Dark (taped intro) (1:46)/ Back To The Light (5:42)/ Tie Your Mother Down (6:41)/ Love Token (8:45)/ Headlong (9:18)/ Love Of My Life (6:11)/ '39 (vocal intro)/ Let Your Heart Rule Your Head (6:35)/ To Much Love Will Kill You (4:46)/ Keyboard Solo (4:33)/ Since You've Been Gone (3:37)
CD2: Now I'm Here (with guitar solo) (12:10)/ Resurrection (with drum solo) (11:11)/ Band Introduction (4:36)/ Last Horizon (3:37)/ We Will Rock You (7:36)/ Teo Torriatte (4:56)/ Hammer To Fall (6:31) (Birmingham Dec. 3 '93)/ Driven By You (4:44)*/ Tie Your Mother Down (5:19)*/ The Dream Is Over (5:27)*/ Hammer To Fall (6:29)*
R: Exs. Audience.   S: Aston Villa Leisure Center, Birmingham Dec. 5 '93. *Brixton Academy, London June 15 '93.   C: ECD. Dcc. Pic CDs.

CD – LONG LIVE THE QUEEN
SUGARCANE RECORDS SC 52014
Intro: The Dark (taped)/ Back To The Light/ Driven By You/ Tie Your Mother Down/ Love Token/ Headlong/ Love Of My Life/ '39 (vocal intro)/ Let Your Heart Rule Your Head/ Too Much Love Will

Kill You/ Now I'm Here (with instrumental solo)/ Resurrection/ Last Horizon/ Hammer To Fall/ We Will Rock You
R: Vgs. Audience.   S: Beacon Theater, New York City Mar. 14 '93.   C: ECD. Dcc. Time 74:20

CD – WE WILL ROCK THE PALACE
BMY 021
Driven By You/ Tie Your Mother Down/ Love Of My Life/ Too Much Love Will Kill You/ Resurrection (with instrumental solo)/ Last Horizon/ Hammer To Fall/ We Will Rock You/ One Vision*/ A Kind Of Magic*/ Under Pressure*/ Another One Bites The Dust*/ Bohemian Rhapsody*/ Crazy Little Thing Called Love*
R: Exs. Radio Broadcast.   S: The Palace, LA Apr. 6 '93. *Queen Wembley, London July '86.
C: ECD. Dcc. Time 75:26

McBRIDE, MARTINA

CD – GREETINGS FROM THE WILD WILD WEST
ROYAL SOUND MUSIC RSM 054 SQ
The Time Has Come/ True Love Never Dies (previously unreleased)/ A Woman Knows/ Your Cheatin' Heart (previously unreleased)/ Goin' To Work/ That's Me/ She Ain't Seen Nothing Yet/ Independence Day/ I Hear You Knockin' (previously unreleased)/ True Blue Fool/ Strangers/ Cheap Whiskey/ Life #9/ My Baby Loves Me
S: Crazy Horse, Santa Ana, CA '94.   C: ECD.

McCARTNEY, PAUL

CD – THE ALTERNATE 'PRESS TO PLAY'
ORANGE THIRTEEN
Move Over Busker/ Good Times Coming, Feel The Sun/ It's Not True/ Press/ However Absurd/ Stranglehold/ Footprints/ Yvonne/ Write Away/ Tough On A Tightrope/ Pretty Little Head/ Spies Like Us #1/ Spies Like Us #2/ Only Love Remains (live)/ Talk More Talk #1/ Talk More Talk #2
S: Studio '86.   C: ECD.

CD – BACK IN THE U.S.A. (VOL. 1)
BANANA BAN-029-A
Got To Get You Into My Life (3:13)/ We Got Married (7:06)/ The Long And Winding Road (3:50)/ Sgt. Pepper's Lonely Hearts Club Band (6:08)/ Can't Buy Me Love (2:21)/ Put It There (2:47)/ Things We Said Today (4:51)/ Eleanor Rigby (2:58)/ Back In The USSR (3:03)/ I Saw Her Standing There (3:19)/ Coming Up (5:06)/ Let It Be (3:47)/ Hey Jude (7:33)/ Get Back (3:45)/ Medley: Golden Slumbers (1:37)/ Carry That Weight (1:40)/ The End (4:05)
R: Exs. Soundboard.   S: Europe '90.
C: Australian CD. Dcc.

CD – GOOD TIMES COMIN'
VIGOTONE VT 121
Rock Show (intro)/ Suicide (complete demo)/

Improvisation 1/ Improvisation 2/ Blackpool (proposed B side early '80s)/ Twenty Flight Rock/ Peggy Sue/ I'm Gonna Love You Too/ Sweet Little Sixteen/ Loving You/ We're Gonna Move/ Matchbox/ Cut Across Shorty/ Blue Moon Of Kentucky/ Sally G. / Country Dreamer/ On The Wings Of A Nightingale/ Hanglide/ Press/ Yvonne/ Good Time Comin', Feel The Sun/ Rock Show (outro)
R: Vg-Ex.   S: Tracks 6-14 'One Hand Clapping' sessions. Tracks 15-17 outtakes and demos. Tracks 18-21 'Press To Play' sessions.
C: Japanese CD.

CD – HEY TOKYO!
KISS THE STONE KTS 250
Matchbox/ Just Because/ Good Rockin' Tonight/ Be Bop A Lula/ Midnight Special/ C Moon/ The Long And Winding Road/ Linda Lu/ Twenty Flight Rock/ Let Me Roll It/ We Can Work It Out/ Lady Madonna/ Magical Mystery Tour/ Live And Let Die/ Paperback Writer/ Back In The U.S.S.R./ Hey Jude
R: Exs. Soundboard.   S: Tokyo, Japan Nov. '93.
C: ECD. Dcc. Pic CD.

CD – HOME DEMOS
ORANGE FOURTEEN
Super Big Heatwave/ Don't You Wanna Dance/ Hello, How Do You Like The Lyrics/ Waterspout/ Backwards Traveller/ After You've Gone/ Boil Crisis/ No No Not To Norfolk/ Unknown Instrumental/ Cage, Instrumental Version/ Cage (with vocals)/ Instant Decisions/ Jam #1/ Jam #2/ Jam #3/ Mull Of Kintyre (instrumental version)/ Mull Of Kintyre (with vocals)/ Jam #4
S: Recorded at his farm in Scotland '77.
C: ECD.

CD – OVER SEATTLE
OFF BEAT RECORDS XXCD 15
Venus And Mars, Rock Show, Jet/ Let Me Roll It/ Spirits Of Ancient Egypt/ Medicine Jar/ Maybe I'm Amazed/ Call Me Back Again/ Live And Let Die/ Picasso's Last Words/ Richard Cory/ Blue Bird/ You Give Me The Answer/ Listen To What The Man Said/ Let' Em In
R: Vg. Soundboard.   S: Seattle Kingdome '76.
C: Japanese CD. Dcc. Time 60:58.

CD – SAYONARA MR. PAUL
LIVE STORM LSCD51550
C: ECD. Dcc. See 'Hey Tokyo' (KTS 250) for songs and source.

CD – STUDIO TRACKS VOL. 1
CHAPTER ONE CO 25132
Blue Sway/ Waterspout/ Keep Under Cover/ Rain Clouds/ On The Wings Of Nightingale/ Treat Her Gentry/ Lonely Old People/ You Gave Me The Answer/ Ebony And Ivory/ Same Time Next Year/ Twice In A Lifetime/ Country Dreamer/ Daytime, Nighttime Suffering/ Back On My Feet/ Summertime/ Bogey Wobble

S: Tracks 1, 3, 5-8, 11, 15 home demos. Others studio outtakes. C: ECD.

CD - STUDIO TRACKS VOL. 2
CHAPTER ONE CO 25142
Rupert Song (version 1)/ Tippi Tippi Tone/ Flying Horses/ When The Wind Is Blowing/ The Castle Of The King Of The Birds/ Sunshine Sometime/ Sea-Cornish Wafer/ Sea Melody/ Rupert Song (version 2)/ Yvonne/ Wanderlust/ Did We Meet Somewhere Before
S: Home demos '90. C: ECD.

CD - STUDIO TRACKS VOL. 3
CHAPTER ONE CO 0057
Robbers Ball/ My Carnival/ Cage/ Hey Diddle/ Tragedy/ Love For You/ Mama's Little Girl/ Night Out/ Wild Prairie/ Tomorrow (instrumental)/ Proud Mum/ Oriental Nightfish/ Lunchbox-Odd Sox
S: Studio outtakes '72-'79. C: ECD.

McGUINN, ROGER

CD - THE DAY OF THE EAGLE
LOBSTER RECORDS LOB 037
Someone To Love (4:29)/ Car Phone (4:57)/ You Bowed Me (3:56)/ Tiffany Queen II (3:43)/ Trees Are Gone (4:44)/ Love That Never Dies (3:52)/ If We Never Meet Again (4:39)/ King Of The Hill (5:42)/ Mr. Tambourine Man (2:21)/ Turn Turn Turn (3:35)/ Eight Miles High (4:15)/ Dream Land (4:57)/ Across The USA (3:09)/ Mr. Spaceman (2:39)/ So You Want To Be A Rock 'N Roll Star (2:47)/ Back Stage Pass (4:32)/ Don't You Write Her Off (3:14)/ It Doesn't Matter (4:09)/ Chestnut Mare (5:46)
R: Exs. Soundboard. S: Tracks 1-11 Electric Ladyland Studios, NYC June 7 '91. Tracks 12-14 Bottom Line, NYC Sept. 18 '91. Tracks 15-19 McGuinn, Clark and Hillman, Roxy, LA '80.
C: ECD. Dcc.

McKEE, MARIA

CD - BREATHE
KISS THE STONE KTS 238
East Of Eden/ I Can't Make It Alone/ My Lonely Sad Eyes/ Goodbye/ I Forgive You/ My Girl Hood Among The Outlaws/ This Property Is Condemned/ Breathe/ Nobody's Child/ The Way Young Lover's Do/ Why Wasn't I More Grateful (When Life Was Sweet)/ You Gotta Sin To Get Saved/ You Are The Light
R: Vg. Audience. S: Live '93. C: ECD. Dbw. Pic CD. Time 56:45.

MEATLOAF

CD - ANYTHING FOR LOVE
GRAPEFRUIT GRA-023-A
I'd Do Anything For Love (But I Don't Do That) (12:15)/ You Took The Word Right Out Of My Mouth (9:48)/ All Revved Up With No Place To Go (7:45)/ Rock And Roll Dreams Come Through

(10:46)/ Two Out Of Three Ain't Bad (8:58)/ Out Of The Frying Pan (And Into The Fire) (11:15)/ Life Is A Lemon And I Want My Money Back (11:33)
R: Vg -Ex. Soundboard. S: London '93 part one. See 'Heaven Can Wait' (GRA-023-B) for part two.
C: Australian CD. Dcc.

CD - BACK LIVE FROM HELL!!
MANIC MONSTER MUSIC MMM 010
I'd Do Anything For Love (But I Won't Do That) (12:16)/ You Took The Words Right Out Of My Mouth (Hot Summer Night) (8:56)/ Two Out Of Three Ain't Bad (8:40)/ Life Is A Lemon And I Want My Money Back (10:02)/ Objects In The Rear View Mirror May Appear Closer Than They Are (12:20)/ Bat Out Of Hell (11:22)/ Paradise By The Dashboard Light, Paradise, Let Me Sleep On It, Praying For The End Of Time (15:34)
R: Exs. Soundboard. S: Houston Theatre, Broadway, NYC during the 'Back To Hell' tour Sept. 18 '93. C: ECD. Dcc. Pic CD.

CD - BAT MEAT
ALL ABOUT FAME AAF 026
I'd Do Anything For Love (But I Won't Do That)/ You Took The Words Right Out Of My Mouth/ Out Of The Frying Pan (And Into The Fire)/ Life Is A Lemon And I Want My Money/ Paradise By The Dashboard Light/ Wasted Youth
R: Ex. Audience. S: On tour '93. C: ECD. Dcc. Time 77:30.

CD - HEAVEN AND HELL
MONTANA MO 10007
Bat Out Of Hell/ You Took The Words Right Out Of My Mouth/ All Revved Up With No Place To Go (Hot Summer Night)/ Paradise By The Dashboard Light/ Let Me Sleep On It/ Johnny Be Good/ River Deep Mountain High
R: Exs. Soundboard. S: LA '77. C: ECD. Time 61:45.

CD - HEAVEN AND HELL II
MONTANA MO 10016
I'd Do Anything For Love (12:10)/ You Took The Words Right Out Of My Mouth (8:10)/ Two Out Of Three Ain't Bad (8:40)/ Life's A Lemon And I Want My Money Back (10:02)/ Objects In Rear View Mirror May Appear Closer Than They Are (11:54)/ Bat Out Of Hell (11:21)/ Paradise By The Dashboard Light (15:37)
R: Exs. Soundboard. S: USA '94. C: ECD. Dcc. Pic CD.

CD - HEAVEN CAN WAIT
GRAPEFRUIT GRA-023-B
Heaven Can Wait (11:02)/ Objects In The Rear View Mirror May Appear Closer Than They Are (11:10)/ Bat Out Of Hell (14:37)/ Paradise By The Dashboard Light, Let Me Sleep On It, Praying For The End Of Time (18:34)/ Wasted Youth, Everything Louder Than Everything Else (4:49)/ Dead Ringer For Love (6:48)
R: Vg -Ex. Soundboard. S: London '93 part two.

See 'Anything For Love' (GRA-023-A) for part one.
C: Australian CD. Dcc.

CD - LIVE AT NAUSSAU COLISEUM 9-1-1978 WITH SPECIAL GUEST TODD RUNDGREN
YELLOW CAT YC 024
Intro, Bolero (3:58)/ Bat Out Of Hell (11:04)/ Hot Summer Night (6:17)/ All Revved Up With No Place To Go (12:42)/ Heaven Can Wait (7:10)/ Paradise By The Dashboard Light, Master Edit (18:52)/ More Than You Deserve (4:18)/ Just One Victory (4:44)/ Two Out Of Three Ain't Bad (8:33)
R: Exs. Soundboard.   S: Nassau Coliseum 9/1/'78.   C: ECD. Dcc.

CD - TO HELL AND BACK
KISS THE STONE KTS 244-45
CD1: I'd Do Anything For Love (But I Won't Do That) (13:39)/ You Took The Words Right Out Of My Mouth (9:49)/ All Revved Up With No Place To Go (7:45)/ Rock & Roll Dreams Come Through (10:52)/ Medley: Two Out Of Three Ain't Bad, Out Of The Frying Pan (And Into The Fire) (24:22)/ Life Is A Lemon And I Want My Money Back (9:45)
CD2: Heaven Can Wait (11:03)/ Objects In The Rear View Mirror May Appear Closer Than They Are (11:50)/ Bat Out Of Hell (11:56)/ Band Introduction (2:46)/ Medley: Paradise In The Dashboard Light, Let Me Sleep On It (18:44)/ Medley: Everything Louder Than Everything Else, Wasted Youth (4:50)/ Dead Ringer For Love (6:48)
R: Ex. Audience.   S: On tour '93.   C: ECD. Dcc. Pic CD.

MEGADEATH

CD - BLACK SHADOWS
HOME RECORDS HR 5935-3
Holy Wars (6:53)/ Sweating Bullets (4:48)/ In My Darkest Hour (6:05)/ Symphony Of Destruction (3:54)/ Peace Sells (4:07)/ Anarchy In The UK (4:58)/ Ashes In Your Mouth (6:04)/ Countdown (4:11)/ Skin O' My Teeth (4:00)
R: Exs. Soundboard.   S: Oakland, CA '94.
C: ECD. Dcc. Pic CD.

CD - MEGADEATH LIVE IN SAN FRANCISCO
TAURUS RECORDS TAU 117
Holywar - Punishment Due (8:53)/ Skin O' My Teeth (3:48)/ Lucretia (3:46)/ Hook In Mouth (5:05)/ Devils Island (4:59)/ Countdown To Extinction (5:23)/ Sweating Bullets (5:23)/ In My Darkest Hour (6:36)/ The Conjuring (4:40)/ Ashes In Your Mouth (6:02)/ Symphony Of Destruction (4:08)/ Good Morning - Black Friday (3:25)/ Peace Sells (3:06)/ Anarchy In The U.K. (3:18)
R: Exs. Soundboard.   S: San Francisco, CA '92.
C: ECD. Dcc.

CD - SUICIDE SOLUTION
RAZOR'S EDGE RZCD 0008
Holy Wars (3:12)/ The Punishment Due (4:09)/ Skin O' My Teeth (3:03)/ Wake Up Dead (3:59)/ Countdown To Extinction (4:41)/ Sweating Bullets

(5:39)/ In My Darkest Hours (6:22)/ The Conjuring (5:28)/ Ashes In Your Mouth (5:58)/ Symphony Of Destruction (3:46)/ Peace Sells (5:56)/ Anarchy In The UK (3:54)
R: Poor-G. Audience.   C: ECD. Pic CD.

MELLENCAMP, JOHN

CD - JUNIOR
ROYAL SOUND MUSIC RSM 045
CD1: When Jesus Left Birmingham/ Junior/ Human Wheels/ Beige To Beige/ Sweet Evening Breeze/ To The River/ French Shoes/ What If I Came Knocking/ Love And Happiness/ Martha Say/ The Real Life/ Get A Leg Up/ Again Tonight/ Authority Song/ Small Town/ Pink Houses
S: Chicago '93.   C: ECD.

CD - LIKE A ROLLING STONE
WINGED WHEEL WW9411/12
CD1: Intro - Paper In Fire/ Jack & Diane/ Hard Times For A Honest Man/ Lonely Ol' Night/ Check It Out/ Rain On the Scarecrow/ Down And Out In Paradise/ The Real Life/ Empty Hands/ Rumbleseat/ Medley: Hand To Hold On To, Chain Gang/ Small Town/ Minutes To Memories
CD2: Hotdogs And Hamburgers/ Thundering Hearts/ Crumblin' Down/ R.O.C.K. In The U.S.A./ Medley: Play Guitar, Gloria, The Wild Thing/ Hurts So Good/ Authority Song/ Pink Houses/ Like a Rolling Stone/ Cheery Bomb
R: G-Vgs. Audience.   S: Halle Des Fetes, Lausanne, Switzerland Jan. 22 '88.   C: ECD.
Full-color gatefold cardboard sleeve. CD looks like a record. Time CD1 60:57. CD2 56:53.

CD - WHEELS ARE TURNING
KISS THE STONE KTS 234
When Jesus Left Birmingham (5:05)/ Junior (4:11)/ Human Wheels (5:29)/ Beige To Beige (4:35)/ Sweet Evening Breeze (4:48)/ To The River (3:59)/ French Shoes (3:49)/ What If I Came Knockin' (5:09)/ What If I Came Knockin' (4:39)*/ Do Re Mi (2:47)**/ This Land Is Your Land (3:10)**
S: Gallery 37, Chicago Sept. 11 '93. *David Letterman Late Show, New York City Sept. 1 '93.
**New York '88.   C: ECD. Pic CD.

METALLICA

CD - BEYOND THE WALL OF SOUND
OCTOPUS OCTO 060
Master Of Puppets (8:31)/ For Whom The Bell Tolls (4:09)/ Welcome Home, Sanitarium (6:18)/ Ride The Lightning (6:55)/ Bass Solo (4:51)/ Whiplash (4:13)/ The Thing That Should Not Be (5:39)/ Peanuts, Four Horsemen (7:01)/ Am I Evil? (3:50)/ Damage Inc. (6:05)/ Blitzkrieg (4:02)
R: Exs. Soundboard.   S: Aardshok Festiva, Zwolle, 'Ijsellhall', Holland Feb. 8 '87.   C: ECD. Dcc. Gold disc.

CD - DESTROYER
TWOLIPS PRODUCTIONS CD3M93TLP

CD1: Creeping Death/ Harvester Of Sorrow/ Sanitarium/ Of Wolf And Man/ Wherever I May Roam/ The Thing That Should Not Be/ The Unforgiven/ Disposable Heroes
CD2: Jason Rap, Bass Solo/ Orion/ To Live Is To Die, The Call Of Ktulu/ Four Horsemen/ For Whom The Bell Tolls/ Fade To Black/ Master Of Puppets/ Seek And Destroy
CD3: Battery/ Nothing Else Matters/ Sad But True/ Last Caress/ One/ Enter Sandman/ So What
R: Exs. Soundboard.   C: ECD. Dcc.

CD - EARTHQUAKE HITS BUFFALO
METAL CRASH MECD 2174-2175
CD1: Intro - Breadfan (5:58)/ Master Of Puppets (3:42)/ Wherever I May Roam (7:15)/ Harvester Of Sorrow (6:46)/ Welcome Home (Sanitarium) (6:56)/ The God That Failed (6:45)/ The Killer Medley: Ride The Lightning, No Remorse, Phantom Lord, Fight Fire With Fire (7:34)/ For Whom The Bell Tolls (6:15)/ Disposable Heroes (8:38)/ Seek And Destroy (8:59)
CD2: Intro - Nothing Else Matters (7:36)/ Creeping Death (7:31)/ Fade To Black (8:13)/ Whiplash (5:51)/ Sad But True (7:34)/ One (9:06)/ Enter Sandman (6:08)/ So 'Fucking' What (3:02)
R: Exs. Soundboard.   S: Buffalo - first date of the 'Shit Hits The Sheds' tour May 30 '94.   C: ECD. Dcc. Pic CDs.

CD - ENTER MUDMAN
KISS THE STONE KTS 344/45
C: See 'Woodstock '94' (OCTO 042/043) for songs and source.

CD - ENTER THE STUDIO
WHO AM I? MET 23
Enter Sandman/ Unforgiven/ Nothing Else Matters/ Wherever I May Roam/ Sad But True/ Holier Than Thou/ Nothing Else Matters/ Disposable Heroes/ Battery/ Welcome Home/ Master Of Puppets
R: Vg-Ex. Soundboard.   S: Tracks 1-7 demos for 'Metallica'. Tracks 8-11 demos for 'Master Of Puppets'.   C: ECD. Dcc. Time 59:41.

CD - FADE TO BLACK
GRAPEFRUIT GRA-007-B
The Star Spangled Banner (6:25)/ Orion (2:19)/ To Live Is To Die, The Call Of Ktula (6:20)/ Four Horsemen (4:59)/ For Whom The Bell Tolls (5:38)/ Fade To Black (7:02)/ Master Of Puppets (3:31)/ Seek And Destroy (17:32)
R: Exs. Soundboard.   S: Europe '93 part two. See 'Nothing Else Matters' and 'Wherever I May Roam'.   C: Australian CD. Dcc.

CD - GARAGE DAYS AND MORE
CDMT 620
Helpless/ The Small Hours/ The Wait/ Crash Course In Brain Surgery/ Last Caress, Green Hell/ Stone Cold Crazy/ Killing Time/ Enter Sandman (demo)/ The Unforgiven (demo)/ Nothing Else Matters (demo)/ Wherever I May Roam (demo)/ Sad But True (demo)/ One (demo)/ Nothing Else

Matters (Elevator version)/ So What
R: Exs. Soundboard.   C: ECD. Dcc. Time 73:50.

CD - NO LIMITS NO LAWS
KISS THE STONE KTS 306
Of Wolf And Man (4:36)/ Disposable Heroes (9:29)/ The Four Horsemen (5:04)/ Fade To Black (7:53)/ Master Of Puppets (4:09)/ Battery (5:15)/ Sad But True (5:51)/ So What (2:51)
R: Exs. Soundboard.   S: Gentofte Stadium, Copenhagen, Denmark May 28 '93.   C: ECD. Dcc. Pic CD.

CD - NOTHING ELSE MATTERS
GRAPEFRUIT GRA-007-C
Battery (5:40)/ Nothing Else Matters (5:27)/ Sad But True (5:46)/ Last Caress (1:16)/ One (8:08)/ Enter Sandman (6:21)/ So What (3:02)
R: Exs. Soundboard.   S: Europe '93 part three. See 'Fade To Black' and 'Wherever I May Roam'.
C: Australian CD. Dcc.

CD - WELCOME TO THE FUN PALACE
ROCKS 92085/86
CD1: Intro - Blackened (6:05)/ For Whom The Bells Toll (4:37)/ Welcome Home, Sanitarium (6:17)/ The Four Horsemen (5:01)/ Harvester Of Sorrow (4:55)/ Eye Of The Beholder (6:55)/ Jason's Bass Solo (5:09)/ To Live Is To Die (2:00)/ Master Of Puppets (7:23)/ One (7:52)/ Seek And Destroy (6:54)
CD2: ...And Justice For All (10:18)/ How Many More Times (4:37)/ Creeping Death (6:44)/ Fade To Black (7:22)/ Kirk's Guitar Solo (3:04)/ Little Wing (3:18)/ Battery (4:37)/ Symptom Of The Universe (1:24)/ The Prowler (1:17)/ Run To The Hills (:18)/ The Frayed Ends Of Sanity (:58)/ The Wait (3:10)/ Last Caress (1:18)/ Am I Evil? (4:04)/ Whiplash (4:29)/ Breadfan (4:10)
R: Exs. Soundboard.   S: Osaka May 17 '89.
C: ECD. Uninspired art on an unneeded box. Should've been in a double jewel case.

CD - WELCOME TO THE SNAKEPIT
HAMMERJACK HJ 001/2
CD1: Intro - Enter Sandman/ Creeping Death/ Harvester Of Sorrow/ Welcome Home, Sanitarium/ Sad But True/ Wherever I May Roam/ Of Wolf And Man, Guitar Solo/ The Unforgiven/ And Justice For All Medley: Eye Of The Beholder, Blackened, Frayed Ends Of Sanity, And Justice For All, Blackened/ Bass, Guitar Solo/ Through The Never
CD2: For Whom The Bell Tolls/ Fade To Black/ Master Of Puppets/ Seek And Destroy/ Whiplash/ Nothing Else Matters/ Am I Evil/ Last Caress/ One/ Damage Inc./ Motorbreath
R: Ex. Audience.   S: Brabanthallen Den Bosch, Holland Dec. 7 '92.   C: ECD. Box set with full color cover and full color poster.

CD - WHEREVER I MAY ROAM
GRAPEFRUIT GRA-007-A
Creeping Death (7:10)/ Harvester Of Sorrow

(6:17)/ Welcome Home (Sanitarium) (6:20)/ Of Wolf & Man (4:02)/ Wherever I May Roam (6:27)/ The Thing That Should Not Be (6:42)/ Disposable Heroes (8:48)
R: Exs. Soundboard.   S: Europe '93 part one. See 'Fade To Black' and 'Nothing Else Matters'.
C: Australian CD. Dcc.

CD - WOODSTOCK '94
OCTOPUS OCTO 042/043
CD1: Intro - Breadfan (5:50)/ Master Of Puppets (3:17)/ Wherever I May Roam (7:30)/ Harvester Of Sorrow (6:50)/ Fade To Black (8:31)/ For Whom The Bell Tolls (7:53)/ Seek & Destroy (10:37)
CD2: Nothing Else Matters (8:40)/ Creeping Death (7:05)/ Whiplash (4:41)/ Sad But True (8:26)/ One (7:00)/ Enter Sandman (6:43)/ So What (3:22)
R: Exs. Soundboard.   S: Woodstock Festival, Saugerties, New York Aug. 13-14 '94.   C: ECD. Dcc.

MIDNIGHT OIL

CD - BLUE SKY RED EARTH
BIG MUSIC BIG 084
Feeding Frenzy (6:26)/ Dead Heart (6:44)/ My Country (4:50)/ Blue Sky Mine (5:19)/ Sell My Soul (5:44)/ Truganini (5:18)/ Warakurna (4:42)/ Short Memory (5:22)/ Beds Are Burning (4:50)/ Earth And Sun And Moon (4:37)/ My Country (4:54)/ Blue Sky Mine (4:24)/ In The Valley (3:38)/ Dead Heart (6:14)/ Warakurna (4:32)
R: Exs. Soundboard.   S: Tracks 1-10 Europe July '93. Tracks 11-15 acoustic set Toronto, Canada '93.   C: ECD. Blue and black cover. Purple type. Pic CD.

MILLER, STEVE

CD - LIVE AT THE BEACON THEATRE
SOUNDS ALIVE CD 2400150
Fly Like An Eagle/ Wild Mountain Honey/ Come On In My Kitchen/ Going To The Country/ Nothing Lasts/ Going To Mexico/ The Joker/ Take The Money And Run/ Gangster Of Love/ Your Cash Ain't Nothing But Trash/ Shu Ba Da Du Ma Ma Ma
S: Beacon Theatre, NY '77.   C: ECD.

MINISTRY

CD - HOUSE OF BONES
RTW 008
Flashback/ Missing/ Deity/ Stigmata/ No Bunny (Pailhead)/ Golden Dawn/ No Devotion (Revolting Cocks)/ The Light Pours Out Of Me (Magazine)/ Smothered Hope (Skinny Puppy)
R: Exs. Soundboard.   C: ECD. Dcc. Time: 54:41.

MITCHELL, JONI

CD - JUST ICE
KISS THE STONE KTS 360
Sex Kills/ Moon At The Window/ Magdalene Laundry/ Hejira/ Cherokee Louise - A Song For

Mary/ Nightflight Home/ Loves Cry/ Poem - The Fish Bowl/ Just Like This Train/ Happiness Is The Best Facelift
R: Exs. Soundboard.   S: Toronto, Canada Sept. 23 '94.   C: ECD. Dcc. Pic CD. Time 47:00.

MONSTER MAGNET

CD - SONGS OF CALIGULA
HAWK 020
Superjudge (6:29)/ Snake Dance (2:56)/ Medicine (4:28)/ Nod Scene (6:00)/ Twin Earth (3:59)/ Cage Around The Sun (7:42)/ Face Down (4:12)/ Evil (Is Going On) (3:06)/ Spine Of God (11:41)/ Black Mastermind (8:54)
R: Ex. Audience.   S: Whiskey A Go Go, LA Aug. 26 '93.   C: ECD. Orange/black cover. Pic CD.

MORRISON, VAN

CD - GLORIA
GRAPEFRUIT GRA-015-A
Baby Please Don't Go (1:22)/ Gloria (1:07)/ Here Comes The Night (1:20)/ Brown Eyed Girl (2:22)/ Jackie Wilson Said (2:43)/ Glad Tidings (3:37)/ Sweet Thing (4:27)/ I've Been Working (3:30)/ Into The Mystic (2:08)/ Moondance (2:38)/ Wavelength (3:29)/ Dweller On The Threshold (4:12)/ Cleaning Windows (4:22)/ Where Did You Stay (3:30)/ Domino (4:29)/ You're My Woman (5:57)/ Blue Money (4:00)/ Tupelo Honey (6:22)/ Wild Night (4:30)/ Que Sera Sera, Hound Dog (2:45)/ Send In The Clowns (3:47)
R: Vg-Ex. Soundboard.   S: Europe/USA '68-'85.
C: Australian CD. Dcc.

CD - LAUGHING IN THE WIND
GOLD STANDARD RAL-515
Ballerina/ Domino/ If I Ever Need Someone/ These Dreams Of You/ And It Stoned Me/ Come Running/ Bit By Bit/ Hey Where Are You/ Lorna/ I Need Your Kind Of Loving/ Rock & Roll Band/ Funny Face/ I Shall Sing/ Laughing In The Wind/ Street Theory/ Foggy Mountain Top/ There There Child/ It Hurts To Want It So Bad/ Feedback On Highway 101
R: Ex. Soundboard.   S: Tracks 1-12 studio demos '69-'70. Tracks 13-19 studio recordings '74-'75.   C: ECD. Dcc. Time 73:57.

CD - LIVE IN EDINBURGH AT THE PLAYHOUSE (FEATURING BONO AND BOB DYLAN)
YELLOW CAT YC 015
Celtic Swing (2:45)/ Solid Ground (3:04)/ Vanlose Stairway (4:24)/ Got My Eyes On You (5:50)/ It's All In The Game (5:12)/ Foreign Windows (4:36)/ Cleaning Windows (3:43)/ Dweller On The Threshold (3:46)/ A Sense Of Wonder (4:23)/ The Healing Has Begun (6:24)/ This Love Will Shurely Last Forever (3:11)/ In The Garden (5:21)/ Gloria, Shaking All Over (with Bono) (13:09)/ It's All Over Now Baby Blue (with Dylan, Bono, Chrissie Hynde, Elvis Costello, Kris Kristofferson & Stevie

Windwood) (10:08)
R: Exs. Soundboard.   S: The Playhouse,
Edinburgh, Scotland and The Point, Dublin,
Ireland Feb. 6 '93.   C: ECD. Dcc.

CD - MOONLIGHT SERENADE
TEDDY BEAR TB22
Moondance (4:40)/ Glad Tidings (3:40)/ Crazy
Love (2:58)/ Come Running (6:20)/ The Way
Young Lovers Do (3:22)/ Everyone (3:03)/ Brown-
Eyed Girl (2:12)/ And It Stoned Me, These Dreams
Of You (7:45)/ Caravan (6:43)/ Cyprus Avenue
(12:02)/ Into The Mystic (5:25)
R: Vg-Ex. Soundboard.   S: Fillmore West, San
Francisco Apr. 26 '70.   C: ECD. Dcc. Pic CD.

CD - MOONSHINE WHISKEY
OIL WELL RSC 024 CD
Dead Or Alive/ Moonshine Whiskey/ You're My
Woman/ These Dreams Of You/ Domino/ Call Me
Up In Dreamland/ Blue Money/ Buona Sera/ Into
The Mystic/ I've Been Working/ Friday's Child/
Hound Dog/ Just Like A Woman
R: Exs. Soundboard.   S: Sacramento Sept. 9
'71.   C: ECD. Dcc. Time 68:21

CD - MY NAME IS RAINCHECK
SMOKIN' CROCODILE SMOKE IV/V
CD1: Did Ye Get Healed/ Tore Down A La
Rimbaud/ Vanlose Stairway/ Wonderful Remark/
Crazy Love/ My Name Is Raincheck/ See Me
Through/ Ain't That Lovin' You Baby?/ Don't Cry
No More/ Stormy Monday/ Help Me/ Good
Morning Little Schoolgirl/ Moondance
CD2: I'll Take Care Of You/ Tupelo Honey/ You
Don't Know Me/ Lonely Avenue/ In The Garden/
Have I Told You Lately/ Shakin' All Over/ It's All
Over Now Baby Blue/ Foreign Window/ Buona
Sera
R: Ex. Audience.   S: Manchester Apollo,
England Mar. 4 '94. Track 9 Apollo Feb. 25 '94.
Track 10 Playhouse, Edinburgh, Scotland June 7
'94.   C: ECD. Dcc. Time CD1 72:24. CD2 72:38.

CD - NAKED IN THE JUNGLE
GOLD STANDARD ANA-728, MOR-768
Wild Night/ Brand New Day/ When The Evening
Sun Goes Down/ Nobody Really Knows/ Caravan/
The Way Young Lovers Do/ Spare Me A Little
(with Jackie DeShannon)/ You've Got The Power/
Try For Sleep/ Naked In The Jungle/ And The
Streets Only Knew Her Name/ Grits Ain't
Groceries/ Don't Change On Me/ Down To Earth/
Mechanical Bliss/ Real Real Gone/ Foreign
Window (with Bob Dylan)
R: Exs. Soundboard.   S: Tracks 1-6 studio
demos '69-'71. Track 7-16 studio recordings '74-
'76. Track 17 live with Dylan late '80s.   C: ECD.
Dcc. Gold disc.

CD - THIS IS VAN MORRISON
TRADITIONAL LINES TL 1318
Dead Or Alive (5:18)/ Moonshine Whiskey (7:48)/
You're My Woman (5:59)/ These Dreams (Of You)

(3:26)/ Domino (6:13)/ Call Me Up In Dreamland
(3:36)/ Blue Money (4:11)/ Buona Sera (3:41)/ Into
The Mystic (5:43)/ I've Been Working (6:13)/
Friday's Child (5:42)/ Hound Dog (2:47)/ Just Like
A Woman (7:37)
R: Ex. Soundboard.   S: CA Sept. 19 '71.
C: ECD. Dcc.

CD - WILD NIGHT
SILVER RARITIES SIRA 115/116
CD1: I'm Not Feeling It Anymore/ Why Must I
Always Explain/ See Me Through/ Domino/
Cleaning Windows/ Vanlose Stairway/ Moon
Dance/ Haunts Of Ancient Peace/ So Quiet In
Here/ That's Where It's At/ Wild Night/ Route 66,
Shake Rattle & Roll/ Shot Of Rhythm And Blues/
Irish Heartbeat
CD2: Wavelength/ Tore Down A La Rimbaud/
Youth Of 1000 Summers/ A Town Called
Paradise/ Did Ye Get Healed/ Its All In The Game/
Lonely Avenue/ In The Garden, Daring Night, Real
Real Gone/ Solid Ground, When Heart Is Open/
Brown Eyed Girl/ Star of The Country Down/
What'd I Say/ Gloria, Shakin All Over/ Its All Over
Now Baby Blue
R: Vg. Audience.   S: Hammersmith Apollo,
London Mar. 22 '75.   C: ECD. Dcc.

MORRISSEY

CD - FAMOUS WHEN DEAD
CHELSEA RECORDS CFC 005
I Know It's Gonna Happen Someday/ You're
Gonna Need Someone On Your Side/ Tomorrow/
Glamorous Glue/ Suedehead/ He Knows I'd Love
To See Him/ We'll Let You Know/ You're The One
For Me, Fatty/ Certain People I Know/
Sister I'm A Poet/ Alsatian Cousin/ Such A Little
Thing Makes Such A Big Difference/ The Girl
Least Likely To/ Jack The Ripper/ Seasick Yet Still
Docked/ We Hate It When Our Friends Become
Successful/ November Spawned A Monster
R: Poor-G. Audience.   S: Arco Arena,
Sacramento, CA Oct. 14 '92.   C: ECD. Dcc.
Time 74:12.

CD - NEW YORK, NEW YORK
HOME RECORDS HR 5926 2
The Loop (4:03)/ The National Front Disco (7:10)/
November Spawned A Monster (4:52)/ We Hate It
When Our Friends Become Successful (2:32)/
Your Are The One For Me, Fatty (2:57)/
Suedehead (3:57)/ Glamorous Glue (4:17)/ We'll
Let You Know (4:24)/ Such A Little Thing Makes
Such A Big Difference (5:48)/ Alsatian Cousin
(2:18)/ Certain People I Know (3:08)/ The Last Of
The Famous International Playboys (3:27)/ Let
The Right One In (2:45)/ Jack The Ripper (4:23)/
He Knows I'd Love To See Him (3:27)/ Girls Least
Likely To (4:38)
R: Vg. Audience.   S: Tracks 1-13 Roseland Nov.
25 '92. Tracks 14-16 Orlando '92.   C: ECD. Dbw.
Yellow background. Pink type. Pic CD.

MOTLEY CRUE

CD - SECRETS OF TONE
HOME RECORDS HR 5938-1
Take Me To The Top (4:04)/ Look That Kill (5:14)/
Red Hot (4:04)/ Starry Eyes (5:28)/ Piece Of The
Action (4:54)/ Merry Go Round (3:45)/ Shout At
The Devil (3:55)/ Hotter Than Hell (3:44)/ Live
Wire (5:23)/ Knock Em Dead (5:48)/ Live Wire
(3:33)/ Kickstart My Heart (4:48)
R: G.   S: Tracks 1-18 Pasadena show, tracks
11-12 Dallas show.   C: ECD. Dbw. Red Type.

MOULD, BOB

CD - THE CALM BEFORE THE STORM
KISS THE STONE KTS 272
Wishing Well (4:58)/ Out Of Your Life (3:46)/ Hear
Me Calling (4:05)/ See A Little Light (3:22)/ Stand
Guard (4:42)/ Celebrated Summer (4:28)/ Hanging
Tree (5:13)/ The Act We Act (5:03)/ Can't Fight It
(3:32)/ Walls In Time (6:12)/ Poison Years (4:31)/
Stop Your Crying (4:35)/ Could You Be The One
(3:01)/ It's Too Late (3:59)/ Lonely Afternoon
(3:59)/ Sinners And Their Repentance (4:10)/
Hardly Getting Over It (5:16)/ Makes No Sense At
All (3:05)
R: Exs. Soundboard.   S: McCabe's Guitar Shop,
Santa Monica, CA May 17 '91.   C: ECD. Dcc.
Pic CD.

MOTHER LOVE BONE

CD - HELLO HOMETOWN
ROCKS 92060
This Is Shangrila (3:40)/ Capricorn Sister (3:06)/
Half Ass Monkeyboy (4:17)/ Bone China (3:26)/
Heartshine (4:02)/ Mr. Danny Boy (6:06)/ Come
Bite The Apple (5:32)/ Thru Fade Away (3:25)/
Star Dog Champion (4:25)/ Holy Roller (6:33)/
Hold Your Head Up (5:18)/ I'm In Love With My
Car (3:17)
R: Exs. Soundboard.   S: The Vogue, Seattle
Jan. 3 '90.   C: ECD. Dcc.

CD - RHAPSODY IN CHARTREUSE
PITCHFORK RECORDS PF400
Country Shad And The Fist (2:16)/ Stardog
Champion (5:22)/ Sub Wah Fare Slide #2 (4:06)/
Show Down (7:14)/ Chole Dancer (2:10)/ Dream
Come True (3:04)/ Gentle Groove (2:32)/ Greasy
(2:38)/ Heartshine (4:42)/ Ever Kissed A Lady
(8:15)/ Greasy (2:04)/ These Are No Blues (4:06)/
Sub Wah Fare Slide #1 (3:58)/ Thru Fade Away
(3:26)/ Rhapsody In Chartreuse (4:10)/ Hold Your
Head Up (5:25)
R: Exs. Soundboard.   S: Studio sessions '88-89.
C: ECD. Dbw.

CD - THERE WAS LIFE BEFORE PEARL JAM
NEW PLASTIC RECORDS NP 55001
This Is Shangrila (6:53)/ Come Bite The Apple
(5:45)/ Bone China (3:53)/ Heartshine (4:50)/
Capricorn Sister (3:53)/ Gentle Groove (4:07)/

Thru Fadeaway (3:44)/ Mr. Danny Boy (4:49)/ LA
Woman (3:42)
R: Poor-G. Audience.   S: Bumbershoot Festival,
Seattle Sept. '89.   C: ECD.

MOTORHEAD

CD - BURN IN BLOODY HELL
HOME RECORDS - HR 5939-4
Dr. Rock (3:48)/ Sister (2:45)/ No Voices (5:04)/
Just Cause You've Got (7:19)/ Going To Brazil
(3:23)/ Singing The Blues (3:24)/ Killed By Death
(5:54)/ Aces Of Spades (4:03)/ Eat The Rich
(4:37)/ Built For Speed (4:53)/ Death Forever
(3:58)
R: Exs. Soundboard.   S: USA '93.   C: ECD.
Dcc. Pic CD.

N

NELSON, WILLIE

CD - HOME ON THE ROAD
ROYAL SOUND MUSIC RSM 025 SQ
Whiskey River (the intro)/ Night Life/ Across The
Borderline/ Heartland/ Don't Give Up/ The Most
Original Sin/ Still Is Still Movin' To Me/ Midnight
Rodeo (with Lyle Lovett)/ Blue Eyes Cryin' In The
Rain/ On The Road Again/ Whiskey River (the
outro)
S: The Roxy, LA summer '93.   C: ECD.

NICKS, STEVIE

CD - LIVESPACE
ROYAL SOUND MUSIC RSM 038
Outside The Rain/ Dreams/ Talk To Me/ Stand
Back/ Whole Lotta Trouble/ Love's A Hard Game
To Play/ Stop Draggin' My Heart Around/ Edge Of
Seventeen/ Landslide/ Rooms On Fire/ Gold Dust
Woman/ Alice/ No Spoken Word
S: Austin, Texas and Hollywood, CA '93.
C: ECD.

NINE INCH NAILS

CD - COMING DOWN FAST
KISS THE STONE KTS 303
Terrible Lies (5:16)/ Sin (4:13)/ March Of The Pigs
(3:45)/ Something I Can Never Have (6:19)/
Closer (6:29)/ Reptile (6:04)/ Wish (3:38)/ Such
(4:22)/ The Only Time (5:14)/ Get Down Make
Love (3:26)/ Down In It (4:23)/ Big Man With A
Gun (2:23)/ Head Like A Hole (7:13)/ Dead Souls
(7:04)/ Help Me I Am In Hell (2:45)/ Happiness In
Slavery (6:35)
R: Ex. Audience.   S: Atlanta, Georgia '94.
C: ECD. Dcc. Pic CD.

CD - DEMOS & REMIXES
BLUE MOON RECORDS BMCD 13
Down In It (4:35)/ Sanctified (5:44)/ Kinda I Want
To (4:43)/ Twist (4:47)/ Down In It (big whole mix)

(4:08)/ Suck (live) (5:25)/ Supernaut (original) (6:29)/ Down In It (demo) (4:01)/ Head (version) Flood Mix (5:50)/ Sin (DJ edit) (3:33)/ Head Like A Hole (Go-Go mix) (5:24)/ Wish (DJ edit) (3:59)/ Suck (demo) (3:49)/ Down In It (Skin mix) (3:55) R: Exs. Soundboard.   S: Tracks 1-5 studio demos from 1988. Track 6 is live. Track 7 is original version with Trent Razor on vocals. Tracks 8-14 various promotional mixes.   C: ECD. Dcc. Pic CD.

CD - HAMMERING IT HOME 94
Terrible Lie/ Sin/ March Of The Pigs/ Something I Can Never Have/ Closer/ Reptile/ Wish/ Suck/ The Only Time/ Get Down Make Love/ Down In It/ Big Man With A Gun/ Head Like A Hole/ Dead Souls/ Help I'm In Hell/ Happiness In Slavery R: Vg-Exs. Soundboard.   S: London '94. C: ECD. Dbw. Blue and yellow type. Time 78:32.

CD - HOLE IN YOUR HEAD
HOME RECORDS HR 5918 4
Terrible Lie (4:16)/ Sin (4:16)/ March Of Pigs (2:50)/ Something I Can Never Have (6:04)/ Closer (5:23)/ Reptile (6:30)/ Wish (3:39)/ Suck (3:39)/ The Only Time (5:15)/ Get Down Make Love (3:23)/ Down In It (6:37)/ Big Man With Gun (7:25)/ Head Like A Hole (6:25)/ Keep Calling Me (2:43)/ Pinion (3:07)/ Happiness In Slavery (3:13) R: G-Vg. Audience.   S: Hollywood Palace Apr. 27 '94.   C: ECD. Dcc.

CD - KILLER INSTINCT
TEDDY BEAR RECORDS TB 46
Sin (3:42)/ Sanctified (5:42)/ That's What I Get (4:28)/ Get Down Make Love (4:05)/ The Only Time (5:38)/ Down In It (4:31)/ Head Like A Hole (6:38)/ Now I'm Nothing, Terrible Life (6:13)/ Physical (4:43)/ The Only Time (5:34)/ Suck (5:14)/ That's What I Get (4:25)/ Something (4:10) R: G-Vg. Audience.   S: Various locations USA '90-'91.   C: ECD. Dcc. Pic CD.

CD - MARCH OF THE PIGS
TEDDY BEAR TB 54
Terrible Lie (4:16)/ Sin (4:16)/ March Of The Pigs (2:50)/ Something I Can Never Have (6:04)/ Closer (5:23)/ Reptile (6:30)/ Wish (3:39)/ Suck (4:10)/ The Only Time (5:15)/ Get Down Make Love (3.23)/ Down In It (6:37)/ Big Man With A Gun (7:25)/ Head Like A Hole (6:25)/ Keep Calling Me (2:43)/ Pinion (3:07)/ Happiness Is Slavery (3:13) R: G-Vg. Audience.   S: California '94.   C: ECD. Dcc. Pic CD.

CD - NOTHING IS NEXT
FRONT ROW / METEOR FM 1105 CD
C: See 'When The Whip Comes Down' (KTS 343) for songs and source.

CD - PUREST FEELING
HAWK HAWK 026
Intro (2:23)/ Sanctified (5:39)/ Maybe Just Once

(5:10)/ The Only Time (5:12)/ Kinda I Want To (5:02)/ That's What I Get (4:19)/ Purest Feeling (2:59)/ Ringfinger (5:54)/ Down In It (6:17) R: Vg-Ex. Soundboard.   S: Cleveland, Ohio Nov. '88.   C: ECD. Dcc. Pic CD.

CD - SELF DESTRUCTION MEN
METAL CRASH MECD 1167
Terrible Lies (5:04)/ Sin (4:13)/ March Of Pigs (3:54)/ Something I Could Never Have (6:21)/ Closer (5:45)/ Reptile (5:58)/ Wish (3:42)/ Suck (4:22)/ The Only Time (5:14)/ Get Down Make Love (3:35)/ Down In It (4:13)/ Big Man With A Gun (2:15)/ Head Like A Hole (7:16)/ They Keep Calling Me (6:21)/ Help Me In Hell (2:41)/ Happiness In Slavery (6:23) R: Ex. Audience.   S: International Ballroom, Houston, Texas May 4 '94.   C: ECD. Dcc. Pic CD.

CD - SLAUGHTER IN THE AIR
KISS THE STONE KTS 391/92
CD1: Intro - Mr. Self Destruct/ Sin/ March Of The Pigs/ Piggy/ Reptile/ Gave Up/ Happiness In Slavery/ Eraser/ Hurt/ The Downward Spiral/ Wish/ Suck/ Ruiner/ Down In It/ Head Like A Hole CD2: Closer/ Dead Souls/ I Do Not Want This/ Something I Can Never Have/ Intro/ Sanctified/ Maybe Just Once/ The Only Time/ Kinda I Want To/ That's What I Get/ Purest Feeling/ Ringfinger/ Down In It R: Ex. Audience. CD2 Tracks 5-13 Exs. Soundboard.   S: Universal Amphitheater, Los Angeles Nov. 10 '94. CD2 Tracks 5-13 outtakes from Right Track, Cleveland Nov. '88.   C: ECD. Pic CD. Time CD 1 73:55. CD2 69:45.

CD - SLAVES
HAWK 003
Terrible Lie/ Sin/ Physical/ The Only Time/ Suck/ That's What I Get/ Wish/ Get Down Make Love/ Ringfinger/ Down In It/ Head Like A Hole R: G-Vg. Audience.   S: New Orleans, LA July 12 '91.   C: ECD. Orange/black cover. Time 51:55.

CD - TIME TO SUCK
Sin/ Sanctified/ That's What I Get/ Get Down Make Love/ The Only Time/ Down In It/ Head Like A Hole/ Now I Am Nothing, Terrible Lie/ Physical/ The Only Time/ Suck/ That's What I Get/ Something R: G. Audience.   S: Tracks 1-7 USA '90, 8-13 '91.   C: ECD. Time 64:57.

CD - WHEN THE WHIP COMES DOWN
KISS THE STONE KTS 343
Terrible Lies (7:15)/ Sin (5:38)/ March Of Pigs (2:28)/ Something I Could Never Have (6:37)/ Closer (6:05)/ Reptile (3:59)/ Wish (3:40)/ Suck (4:30)/ Burn (5:18)/ The Only Time (5:18)/ Down In It (5:03)/ Keep On Calling Me (6:00)/ Help Me In Hell (2:40)/ Happiness In Slavery (5:34)/ Head Like A Hole (5:14) R: Exs. Soundboard   S: Woodstock Festival,

Saugerties, New York Aug. 13 '94.   C: ECD.
Dcc. Pic CD. Time 75:45.

CD - WOODSTOCK '94
OCTOPUS OCTO 039
C: See 'When The Whip Comes Down' (KTS 343)
for songs and source.

CD - WOODSTOCK 1994
SHINOLA SH 69026
Terrible Lie/ Sin/ March Of The Pigs/ Something I
Can Never Have/ Closer/ Reptile/ Wish/ Suck/
Burn/ The Only Time/ Down In It/ Dead Souls/
Help Me I Am In Hell
R: Exs. Soundboard.   S: Woodstock '94.
C: ECD. Time 70:19.

NIRVANA

CD - ALL ACOUSTICALLY
KISS THE STONE KTS 253
About A Girl/ Come As You Are/ Jesus Wants Me
For A Sunbeam/ Dumb/ The Man Who Sold The
World/ Pennyroyal Tea/ Polly/ On A Plain/ Plateau/
Lake Of Fire/ All Apologies/ Where Did You Sleep
Last Night/ Radio Friendly Unit Shifter/ Drain You/
Breed/ Serve The Servants/ Rape Me/ Heart-
Shaped Box/ Pennyroyal Tea/ Scentless
Apprentice/ Lithium/ Guitar Demolition
R: Exs. Soundboard.   S: Tracks 1-12 acoustic
USA '93. Tracks 13-22 Pier 48, Seattle Dec. '93.
C: ECD. Dcc. Pic CD.

CD - AQUA SEAFOAM SHAME
ROCKS 92114
Radio Friendly Unit Shifter (4:32)/ Drain You
(3:45)/ Breed (3:04)/ Serve The Servants (3:11)/
Rape Me (2:52)/ Heart-Shaped Box (4:32)/
Pennyroyal Tea (3:42)/ Scentless Apprentice
(3:32)/ Lithium (4:29)/ Gallons Of Rubbing Alcohol
Flow Through The Strip (6:19)/ School (2:40)/
Smells Like Teen Spirit (4:40)/ Territorial Pissings
(3:27)
R: Ex.   S: Tracks 1-10 Seattle Dec. '93. Tracks
11-14 Seattle Nov. '92.   C: ECD.

CD - BLEW
GRAPEFRUIT GRA-004-C
School (2:38)/ Scoff (3:58)/ Love Buzz (3:21)/
Floyd The Barber (2:08)/ Dive (3:42)/ Polly (2:38)/
Big Cheese (3:33)/ Spank Thru (3:08)/ About A
Girl (3:14)/ Negative Creep (2:19)/ Blew (3:03)/
Love Buzz (3:25)/ Son Of A Gun (2:48)/
Turnaround (2:21)/ D7 (3:47)/ Molly's Lips (1:50)/
In Bloom (4:28)/ Stay Away (3:26)
R: Vg-Ex. Audience.   S: Leeds, UK '89. USA '89
& '92.   C: Australian CD. Dcc.

CD - COME AS YOU ARE
AULICA A 164
Breed (2:48)/ Serve The Servants (3:06)/ Come
As You Are (3:14)/ Smells Like A Teen Spirit
(4:23)/ Sliver (1:51)/ Dumb (2:53)/ In Bloom (4:00)/

About A Girl (2:32)/ Lithium (3:52)/ Pennyroyal
Tea (3:29)/ School (2:16)/ Polly (2:40)/ Very Ape
(1:47)/ Lounge Act (2:22)/ Rape Me (2:25)/
Territorial Pissings (2:30)/ All Apologies (3:30)/ On
A Plain (2:50)/ Scentless Apprentice (3:14)/ Heart-
Shaped Box (3:57)
R: Poor-G. Audience.   S: Palasport, Modena '94.
C: ECD. Dcc.

CD - COME AS YOU ARE
GRAPEFRUIT GRA-004-A
About A Girl (3:12)/ Come As You Are (4:03)/
Dumb (2:51)/ Man Who Sold The World (3:41)/
Polly (3:15)/ On A Plain (3:30)/ Plateau (3:20)/
Lake Of Fire (2:53)/ All Apologies (3:34)/ Where
Did You Sleep Last Night (4:44)/ Radio Friendly
Unit Shifter (4:28)/ Drain You (3:29)/ Breed (3:06)/
Serve The Servants (3:24)/ Rape Me (2:36)/
Heart-Shaped Box (4:31)/ Pennyroyal Tea (3:41)/
Scentless Apprentice (3:27)/ Lithium (5:32)/
Smells Like Teen Spirit (4:59)
R: Exs. Soundboard.   S: Pier 48, Seattle Dec.
'93.   C: Australian CD. Dcc.

CD - THE COMPLETE RADIO SESSIONS
BLUE MOON RECORDS BMCD18
Love Buzz/ About A Girl/ Polly/ Spanks Thru/ Son
Of A Gun/ Molly's Lips/ D-7/ Turnaround/ Dumb/
Drain You/ Endless-Nameless/ Been A Son/ Punk
Rock Polly/ Aneurysm/ Something In The Way/
Here She Comes Now/ Where Did You Sleep Last
Night/ Drain You/ Polly/ Territorial Pissing/ Lithium
R: Exs. Soundboard.   S: Tracks 1-4 Maida Vale
Studios, London Nov. 26 '89. Tracks 5-8, Maida
Vale Studios, London Nov. 21 '89. Tracks 9-11
Maida Vale Studios, London Sept. 3 '91. Tracks
12-15 Maida Vale Studios, London Nov. 5 '91.
Tracks 16-17 Hilversum Studios, Holland Nov. 24
'91. Tracks 18-20 MTV Studios, New York Jan. 10
'92. Tracks 18-21 MTV Awards, Los Angeles Sept.
10 '92.   C: ECD. Time 72:27.

CD - THE ETERNAL LEGACY
KISS THE STONE KTS 336
Love Buzz/ About A Girl/ Polly/ Spank Through/
Son Of A Gun/ Molly's Lips/ D-7/ Turnaround/
Dumb/ Drain You/ Endless-Nameless/ Drain You/
Aneurysm/ School/ Floyd The Barber/ Smells Like
Teen Spirit/ About A Girl/ Polly/ Sliver/ Breed/
Come As You Are/ Lithium/ Territorial Pissings
R: Exs. Soundboard.   S: Tracks 1-11 studio
sessions Europe 89-91. Tracks 12-23 Christmas
party California '91.
C: ECD. Pic CD.

CD - EUROPE '94
LIVE STORM LSCD 51312
C: ECD. Dcc. See 'Roma' (KTS 284) for songs
and source.

CD - THE FINAL FIX
CHELSEA RECORDS CFC 016
Radio Friendly Unit Shifter (4:08)/ 2 Drain You
(3:34)/ Breed (3:13)/ Serve The Servants (3:15)/

Come As You Are (3:35)/ Smell Like Teen Spirit (4:38)/ Sliver (1:54)/ Dumb (3:01)/ In Bloom (4:10)/ About A Girl (2:43)/ Lithium (4:01)/ Pennyroyal Tea (3:26)/ School (2:36)/ Polly (3:22)/ Very Ape (2:15)/ Lounge Act (2:41)/ Rape Me (2:48)/ Territorial Pissing (2:20)/ All Apologies (3:21)/ On A Plain (3:18)/ Scentless Apprentice (3:28)/ Heart-Shaped Box (4:37)/ Improvisation, Drum Solo (3:19)/ The Man Who Sold The World (3:23)
R: Exs. Soundboard.   S: Roma, Palaghiaccio Feb. 22 '94.   C: ECD. Dcc.

CD - HEART SHAPED BOX
GRAPEFRUIT GRA-004-B
Serve The Servants (3:48)/ Scentless Apprentice (3:42)/ School (2:59)/ Breed (3:04)/ Lithium (4:37)/ Come As You Are (3:47)/ Milk It (4:29)/ Drain You (3:48)/ Tourette's (2:20)/ Very Ape (2:20)/ Heart-Shaped Box (5:03)/ Rape Me (2:39)/ All Apologies (4:18)/ Polly (2:55)/ Dumb (2:43)/ Something In The Way (3:53)/ Where Did You Sleep Last Night (3:18)/ Smells Like Teen Spirit (4:51)/ Endless Nameless (9:04)
R: Vg-Ex. Audience.   S: Roseland Club, NYC '93.   C: Australian CD. Dcc.

CD - IN THE BLOOM
LOVE & MONEY LM01
Intro (2:00)/ School (2:05)/ Jam (5:17)/ Scoff (4:38)/ Love Buzz (3:45)/ Floyd The Barber (2:18)/ Dive (4:39)/ Another Rule (3:19)/ Big Cheese (4:29)/ Freedom Of Choice (3:15)/ About A Girl (2:48)/ Breed (3:49)/ Paper Cuts (4:43)/ Been A Son (2:06)/ Negative Creep (3:26)/ Blew (3:55)
R: Exs. Soundboard.   S: 'In The Bloom' tour '90. C: ECD. Purple/black cardboard slipcover with yellow text over jewel case. Pic CD.

CD - INTO THE BLACK
TRIBUTE 101/02/03/04/05/06
CD1: If You Must/ Downer/ Floyd The Barber/ Paper Cuts/ Spank Thru/ Beeswax/ Pen Cap Chew/ Beans/ Disco Goddess/ Lithium/ Happy/ New Wave (Polly) (acoustic)/ Son Of A Gun/ Dive/ About A Girl/ Opinion/ New Wave (Polly) - Speed Mix/ Aneurysm/ Something In The Way/ Been A Son/ Polly/ Smells Like Teen Spirit/ Territorial Pissings
S: Ultra Rare Demos And Sessions - Tracks 1-8 Ted Ed and Fred demos '86. Tracks 9-15 'Bleach' rough mixes. Track 16 Kurt Cobain - solo acoustic Olympic,WA Sept. '90. Tracks 17-19 Mark Goodier studio session London, England Nov. '90. Tracks 21-23 MTV Studios New York '90.
CD2: Aero Zeppelin/ Buzz Cut/ Beeswax/ Mexican Seafood/ Pen Cap Chew/ Mr. Moustache/ Blandest/ Downer/ Floyd The Barber/ Paper Cuts/ Spank Thru/ Sifting/ In Bloom/ Immodium/ Aneurysm/ Polly (acoustic)/ Dive/ Lithium (take 6)/ Sappy
S: Tracks 1-12 Master Demo Recordings, Reciprocal Studios Seattle Dec. 24 '88. Tracks 13-19 Smart Studios, Madison, WI Apr. '90.

CD3: Jesus Wants Me For A Sunbeam/ Aneurysm/ Drain You/ Floyd The Barber/ Smells Like A Teen Spirit/ About A Girl/ Polly/ Breed/ Sliver/ Love Buzz/ Lithium/ Been A Son/ Negative Creep/ On A Plane/ Blew/ Rape Me/ Territorial Pissings/ Secret
S: Paramount Theatre, Seattle Oct. 31 '91.
CD4: Breed/ Drain You/ Aneurysm/ School/ Sliver/ In Bloom/ Come As You Are/ Lithium/ Smells Like A Teen Spirit/ On A Plane/ Negative Creep/ Been A Son/ All Apologies/ Dumb/ Stay Away/ Territorial Pissings/ Smells Like A Teen Spirit/ Territorial Pissings
S: Tracks 1-16 Reading Festival, London, England Aug. '92 from BBC master tapes. Tracks 17-18 Saturday Night Live '92.
CD5: Radio Friendly Shifter/ Drain You/ Breed/ Serve The Servants/ Come As You Are/ Smells Like A Teen Spirit/ Sliver/ Dumb/ In Bloom/ About A Girl/ Lithium/ Pennyroyal Tea/ School/ Polly/ Francis Farmer Will Have Her Revenge On Seattle/ Milk It/ Rape Me/ Territorial Pissings/ Jesus Wants Me For A Sunbeam
S: Last American show part 1 - Seattle Centre Coliseum Jan. 8 '94.
CD6: The Man Who Sold The World/ All Apologies/ Scentless Apprentice/ On A Plane/ Heart Shaped Box/ Blew/ Love Buzz/ About A Girl/ Polly/ Spank Thru/ Turn Around/ Molly's Lips/ Dementia 7/ Pretty Scary/ Dumb/ Drain You/ Here I Am/ Meltdown/ Courtney Love's Complete Eulogy For Kurt Cobain
CD6 Tracks 1-6 Last American show part 2. Tracks 7-18 John Peel Sessions '90-'91 from BBC master tapes. Track 19 Remembrance, Seattle Center Flag Pavilion Apr. 10 '94.
R: Ex. Some Vg. Soundboard and Audience.
C: ECD. Box set with full color front. Full color book. Pic CDs.

CD - KURT'S HOME GUITAR REHEARSALS
HERMES 02
Serve The Servants (3:24)/ Heart Shaped Box (4:36)/ Rape Me (2:38)/ Francis Farmer Will Have Her Revenge On Seattle (4:18)/ Pennyroyal Tea (2:58)/ Blew (1:03)/ All Apologies (2:07)/ Smells Like A Teen Spirit (5:33)/ In Bloom (4:25)/ Radio Friendly Unit Shifter (3:37)/ Come As You Are (3:15)/ Lithium (4:01)/ Lounge Art (2:27)/ Drain You (3:02)/ Polly (2:36)/ Something In The Way (4:11)/ About A Girl (2:33)/ I Hate Myself And I Want To Die (3:10)
R: Ex.   C: ECD. Dcc. Kurt solo.

CD - THE LAST AMERICAN CONCERT
DEAD DOG RECORDS SE 445
Radio Friendly Unit Shifter/ Drain You/ Stay Away/ Serve The Servant/ Rape Me/ Heart Shaped Box/ Pennyroyal Tea/ Scentless Apprentice/ Lithium/ Aneurysm/ School/ Floyd The Barber/ About A Girl/ Polly/ In Bloom// Negative Creep/ Blew/ Love Buzz/ Smells Like Teen Spirit/ Dive/ Another Rule
R: Exs. Soundboard.   S: Live USA '94.
C: ECD. Pic CD. Time 75:57.

CD - THE LAST CRY
BANZAI BZCD 014
Radio Friendly Unit Shifter (4:12)/ Drain You
(3:34)/ Breed (3:10)/ Serve The Servants (3:18)/
Come As You Are (3:34)/ Smells Like Teen Spirit
(4:38)/ Sliver (2:15)/ Dumb (3:01)/ In Bloom (4:01)/
About A Girl (2:46)/ Lithium (3:59)/ Pennyroyal
Tea (3:26)/ School (2:45)/ Polly (2:53)/ Very Ape
(2:18)/ Lounge Act (2:38)/ Rape Me (2:27)/
Territorial Pissings (2:36)/ All Apologies (3:22)/ On
A Plain (3:18)/ Scentless Apprentice (3:45)/ Heart-
Shaped Box (7:50)
R: Exs. Soundboard.   C: ECD. Dcc. Pic CD.

CD - LIVE IN SEATTLE '93
THE SWINGIN' PIG RECORDS TSP CD 172
Radio Friendly Unit Shifter/ Drain You/ Breed/
Serve The Servants/ Rape Me/ Heart-Shaped
Box/ Pennyroyal Tea/ Scentless Apprentice/
Lithium/ Destroy Jam/ Heart-Shaped Box*/ Rape
Me*/ Smells Like Teen Spirit**/ Come As You
Are**
R: Exs. Soundboard.   S: Seattle '93. (*)
'Saturday Night Live' TV show, NYC '93. (**) Del
Mar, CA Dec. 28 '91.   C: ECD. Time 54:14.

CD - LIVE 1994
BACKSTAGE BKCD074
About A Girl (3:24)/ Come As You Are (4:06)/
Jesus Wants Me For A Sunbeam (4:29)/
Pennyroyal Tea (3:45)/ Polly (3:11)/ On A Plain
(4:07)/ Plateau (3:19)/ Lake Of Fire (2:53)/ All
Apologies (3:40)/ Where Did You Sleep Last Night
(4:58)/ Drain You (3:45)/ Breed (2:58)/ Serve The
Servants (3:23)/ Rape Me (2:35)/ Heart-Shaped
Box (4:31)/ Pennyroyal Tea (3:41)/ Scentless
Apprentice (3:23)/ Lithium (4:13)/ End Of The
Show (6:21)
R: Exs. Soundboard.   S: Tracks 1-10 Unplugged
Session '94. Tracks 11-19 USA.   C: ECD.
Time 73:00.

CD - THE LOST CONCERT
AMERICAN FLY AF 003
Love Buzz (3:53)/ Floyd The Barber (3:02)/ Scoff
(4:17)/ Dive (3:49)/ About A Girl (2:36)/ Spank
Through (3:44)/ Breed (3:31)/ In Bloom (4:24)/
School (3:22)/ Been A Son (1:51)/ Negative Creep
(3:06)/ Blew (2:53)/ Soundcheck: In Bloom (4:07)/
Floyd The Barber (2:42)/ Aneurysm (3:21)/ Draw
To You (3:37)/ Smells Like Teen Spirit (4:48)/
Polly (2:56)/ Sliver (2:11)/ Come As You Are
(3:42)/ Lithium (4:17)/ It's Closing Soon
(unreleased) (2:39)*
R: Exs. Soundboard. *Poor.   S: Hollywood
Palladium, Aug. '90. Tracks 16-21 USA '91. Track
22 by Kurt Cobain and Courtney Love in Rio De
Janeiro, Brazil.   C: ECD. Dcc.

CD - MORE LIVE TITS
TEDDY BEAR RECORDS TB 25
T.V. Personalities (3:26)/ Aneurysm (4:38)/ Drain
You (3:46)/ School (2:28)/ Floyd The Barber

(2:26)/ About A Girl (2:56)/ Polly (2:54)/ Breed
(3:06)/ Sliver (2:09)/ Lithium (4:09)/ Love Buzz
(3:53)/ Come As You Are (3:42)/ Been A Son
(2:15)/ Negative Creep (2:27)/ On A Plain (3:08)/
Blew (4:50)/ Dumb (2:40)/ Pennyroyal Tea (3:45)/
Endless Nameless (6:19)
R: G-Vg. Audience.   S: London, Astoria Theatre,
May 5 '91.   C: ECD. Dcc. Pic CD.

CD - MORITURI SALUTANT
SHALOM SH 69001
Radio Friendly Unit Shifter (4:19)/ Drain You
(3:46)/ Breed (3:09)/ Serve The Servants (3:09)/
Rape Me (2:49)/ Heart-Shaped Box (4:27)/ Penny
Royal Tea (3:39)/ Scentless Apprentice (3:28)/
Lithium (4:08)/ Destroy Jam (4:55)/ Come As You
Are (3:43)/ Lithium (3:23)/ Smells Like A Teen
Spirit (5:20)/ On A Plain (3:38)/ Stay Away (3:49)/
Territorial Pissings (3:07)/ Aneurysm (4:45)/
School (2:27)
R: Exs. Soundboard.   S: US Tour '94. Tracks 11-
18 USA '91.   C: ECD.

CD - ON STAGE IN EUROPE
SOUNDS ALIVE SA 24 004
Smells Like Teen Spirit (4:34)/ Drain You (3:39)/
Aneurysm (4:24)/ School (2:33)/ Floyd The Barber
(2:22)/ About A Girl (2:57)/ Polly (2:37)/ Lithium
(4:14)/ Silver (2:05)/ Breed (2:51)/ Been A Son
(2:06)/ Negative Creep (2:39)/ On A Plain (3:03)/
Blew (3:05)/ Love Buzz (3:17)/ Come As You Are
(3:45)/ Territorial Pissings (3:38)
R: Exs. Soundboard.   S: Paradiso, Amsterdam
Nov. 25 '91. Track 16-17 O'Brian Pavilion, Del
Mar, CA Dec. 28 '91.   C: ECD.

CD - OUT OF THE BLUE
OCTOPUS OCTO 036
Scoff (4:33)/ Love Buzz (4:20)/ Floyd The Barber
(2:33)/ Dive (7:23)/ About A Girl (2:43)/ Spank
Thru (3:16)/ Big Cheese (4:11)/ Another Rule
(3:18)/ Breed (5:02)/ Been A Son (3:34)/ Negative
Creep (10:54)/ Help Me (3:20)
R: Exs. Soundboard.   S: Seattle University,
Seattle '89.   C: ECD. Dcc. Pic CD.

CD - OUTCESTICIDE - IN MEMORY OF KURT COBAIN
BLUE MOON BMCD 14
If You Must/ Downer/ Floyd The Barber/ Paper
Cuts/ Spank Thru/ Beeswax/ Pen Cap Chew (Jan
1 '88)/ Blandest (June 11 '88)/ Polly (acoustic)
(Jan. '89)/ Misery Loves Company (Jan. '89)/
Sappy (acoustic) (Jan. '89)/ Do You Love Me
(June '89)/ Been A Son (Aug. '89)/ Junkyard (Nov.
'89)/ Opinion (Feb. '90)/ D.7 (Mar. '90)/ Imodium/
Pay To Play/ Sappy/ Here She Comes Now (Nov.
'91)/ Where Did You Sleep Last Night? (Nov. '91)/
Return Of The Rat (Nov. '91)/ Talk To Me (Dec.
'91)
R: Vg-Ex.   S: Tracks 1-7 first demo tape,
Reciprocal Recording Seattle Jan. 23 '88. Tracks
17-19 unreleased Sub Pop mini album, Smart

Studios, Madison, WI Apr. '90. All other tracks are studio outtakes, demos and rehearsals.
C: ECD. Dcc.

CD - PAIN
BEST BUY RECORDS BBR CD 008
Rape Me (2:50)/ Heart-Shaped Box (4:31)/ Smells Like Teen Spirit (4:28)/ Come As You Are (3:45)/ Lithium (3:54)/ All Apologies (3:58)/ Serve The Servants (3:13)/ Drain You (3:31)/ Aneurysm (4:22)/ The Man Who Sold The World (3:51)/ Dumb (2:46)/ On A Plain (2:45)/ Pennyroyal Tea (3:44)/ Scentless Apprentice (3:29)/ Lake Of Fire (2:35)/ Polly (2:33)/ In Bloom (4:20)/ Blue (3:02)
R: Exs. Soundboard.   C: ECD.

CD - ROMA
KISS THE STONE KTS 284
Radio Friendly Unit Shifter/ Drain You/ Breed/ Serve The Servants/ Come As You Are/ Smells Like Teen Spirit/ Sliver/ Dumb/ In Bloom/ About A Girl/ Lithium/ Pennyroyal Tea/ School/ Polly/ Very Ape/ Lounge Act/ Rape Me/ Territorial Pissings/ All Apologies/ On A Plain/ Scentless/ Apprentice/ Heart Shaped Box/ Demolition
R: Exs. Soundboard.   S: Palaghiaccio, Marino, Rome Feb. 22 '94.   C: ECD. Dbw. Yellow type. Pic CD. Time 75:34.

CD - SLIVER AND DUMB
FLYING TIGER FTCD 0050
Sliver (1:13)/ Dumb (2:40)/ In Bloom (4:09)/ About A Girl (2:52)/ Lithium (4:43)/ Pennyroyal Tea (3:43)/ School (3:14)/ Polly (3:18)/ Very Ape (1:57)/ Lounge Act (2:29)/ Rape Me (2:30)/ Territorial Pissing (2:40)/ All Apologies (4:55)/ On A Plain (3:53)/ Blew (3:12)/ Heart Shaped Box (5:00)
R: Ex. Audience.   S: Milan, Italy Nov. '91.
C: ECD. Pic CD.

CD - TRIBUTE TO CURT COBAIN SERIES VOL. 1 MEMORIAL LIVE IN JAPAN 1992
TTKKS 001
Negative Creep/ Been A Son/ On A Plain/ Something In The Way/ Blew/ Come As You Are/ Lithium/ Breed/ Territorial Pissings/ Grandma Take Me Home/ About A Girl/ School/ Aneurysm/ Love Buzz/ Polly/ Lounge Act/ Drain You/ Smells Like Teen Spirit
R: Vg.   S: Club Citta, Japan Feb. 17 '92.   CD: Japanese CD. Dcc.

CD - TRIBUTE TO KURT COBAIN SERIES VOL. 4 SOUNDBOARD RECORDING LIVE 1991
TTKKS 002
School/ Floyd The Barber/ Love Buzz/ Dive/ Spank Thru/ Breed/ Scoff/ About A Girl/ Molly's Lips/ Been A Soon/ Stain/ Negative Creep/ Blew
R: Vg-Exs. Soundboard.   S: Raji, Los Angeles Jan. 15 '90.   CD: Japanese CD. Dcc.

CD - TRIBUTE TO KURT COBAIN SERIES VOL. 5 SOUNDBOARD RECORDING LIVE 1990
TTKKS 005
Drain You/ Aneurysm/ School/ Smells Like Teen Spirit/ About A Girl/ Polly/ Sliver/ Breed/ Come As You Are/ Lithium/ Get Together/ Territorial Pissing
R: Vg-Exs. Soundboard.   S: Delmar, San Diego Dec. '91.   CD: Japanese CD. Dcc.

CD - TRICK OR TREAT
KISS THE STONE KTS 395
Jesus Wants Me For A Sunbeam/ Aneurysm/ Drain You/ School/ Floyd The Barber/ Smells Like Teen Spirit/ About A Girl/ Polly/ Breed/ Silver/ Love Buzz/ Lithium/ Been A Son/ Negative Creep/ On A Plain/ Blew/ Rape Me/ Territorial Pissings/ Endless-Nameless
R: Exs. Soundboard.   S: Paramount Theatre, Seattle Oct. 31 '91.   C: ECD. Dcc. Pic CD. Time 70:32.

CD - UNRELEASED TRACKS
VAR 01
Return Of The Rat (3:45)/ Aneurysm (4:50)/ Even In His Youth (3:08)/ Marygold (2:34)/ D-7 (3:48)/ Curmudgeon (2:59)/ Gallons Of Rubbing Alcohol Flow Through The Strip (7:33)/ I Hate Myself And I Want To Die (2:52)/ Here She Comes Now (5:00)/ Oh The Guilt (3:15)/ Do You Love Me? (3:33)/ M V (2:43)/ Happy Hour (3:24)/ Spank Thru (3:23)/ Pay To Play (3:28)/ Endless Nameless (6:40)
R: Ex.   C: ECD. Dcc.

CD - WHAT
PIPELINE PPL540
About A Girl (3:22)/ Come As You Are (4:06)/ Jesus Wants Me For A Sunbeam (4:29)/ Pennyroyal Tea #1 (3:45)/ Polly (3:11)/ On A Plain (4:07)/ Plateau (3:19) Lake Of Fire (2:53)/ All Apologies (3:46)/ Where Did You Sleep Last Night (4:58)/ Drain You (3:53)/ Breed (2:59)/ Serve The Servants (3:23)/ Rape Me (2:35)/ Heart-Shaped Box (4:31)/ Pennyroyal Tea #2 (3:41)/ Scentless Apprentice (3:23)/ Lithium (4:12)/ End Of The Show (6:20)
R: Exs. Soundboard.   S: Tracks 1-10 New York City '94. Tracks 11-19 Los Angeles '94.   C: ECD. Dcc.

CD - WIRED
CD02
Scoff/ Love Buzz/ Floyd The Barber/ Dive/ Polly/ Big Cheese/ Spank Thru/ About A Girl/ Junkyard/ Mr. Moustache/ Negative Creep/ Blew/ Dive/ Big Cheese/ Polly/ Spank Thru/ About A Girl/ Imodium/ Molly's Lips/ Sappy/ Blew
R: Tracks 1-12 Vg. Audience. Tracks 13-21 G. Audience.   S: Tracks: 1-12 Edwards, Birmingham, UK Oct. 29 '89. Tracks 13-21 Astoria, London, UK Dec.3 '89.   C: ECD. Time 72:25.

CD - XXII II MCMXCIV
OCTOPUS OCTO 001
Radio Friendly Unit Shifter (4:08)/ Drain You

(3:34)/ Breed (3:13)/ Serve The Servants (3:15)/
Come As You Are (3:35)/ Smells Like Teen Spirit
(4:38)/ Sliver (4:38)/ Dumb (3:01)/ In Bloom (4:10)/
About A Girl (2:43)/ Lithium (4:01)/ Pennyroyal
Tea (3:26)/ School (2:36)/ Very Ape (2:15)/
Lounge Act (2:41)/ Rape Me (2:41)/ Territorial
Pissing (2:20)/ All Apologies (3:21)/ On A Plain
(3:18)/ Scentless Apprentice (3:28)/ Heart-Shaped
Box (4:37)/ Improvisation (3:19)/ The Man Who
Sold The World (3:23)
R: Exs. Soundboard.   S: Palaghiaccio, Rome
Feb. 22 '94.   C: ECD. Pic CD.

CD - VA TE FAIRE ENCULER
BUGSY RECORDS BGS 033/2
CD1: Intro - Radio Friendly Unit Shifter (4:03)/ My
Sharona (1:37)/ Drain You (3:57)/ Breed (3:38)/
Serve The Servants (3:32)/ Come As You Are
(4:07)/ Smells Like A Teen Spirit (4:36)/ Sliver
(3:14)/ Dumb (2:59)/ In Bloom (4:22)/ About The
Girl (2:59)/ Lithium (4:51)/ Penny Royal Tea
(3:45)/ School (3:15)/ Polly (3:23)/ Very Ape
(1:55)/ Lounge Act (2:57)/ Rape Me (2:33)/
Territorial Pissing (3:51)/ The Man Who Sold The
World (4:32)
CD2: Francis Farmer Will Have A Revenge On
Seattle (4:05)/ Make You Happy (4:09)/ All
Apologies (3:37)/ On A Plain (3:12)/ Scentless
Apprentice (4:01)/ Heart-Shaped Box (4:38)/
Aneurism (4:56)/ Been A Son (3:24)/ All Apologies
(3:37)/ Blew (3:16)/ Star Away (3:34)/ Floyd The
Barber (2:19)/ Negative Creep (2:27)/ Love Buzz
(3:17)
R: Vg. Audience.   S: Rennes, France Feb. 16
'94.   C: ECD. Dcc. Pic CD.

NOFX

CD - BACK IN THE GARAGE
KISS THE STONE KTS 351
Please Play This Song On The Radio (3:36)/
Moron Brothers (3:11)/ The Longest Line (2:28)/
Showerdays (3:15)/ Linoleum (2:16)/ Leave It
Alone (2:10)/ Bob (2:49)/ Together On The Sand,
Nowhere (3:33)/ Punk Guy (1:09)/ Life Of Riley
(2:33)/ Stickin' In My Eyes (2:55)/ Straight Edge
(2:35)/ Lisa And Louise (3:17)/ A Perfect
Government (3:29)/ Kill All The Whiteman (3:25)/
Don't Call Me White (2:56)/ The Malachi Crunch
(3:22)/ The Brews (4:15)/ Johnny Appleseed
(2:41)/ She's Gone (3:04)/ Buggley Eyes (2:47)/
Lori Meyers (2:40)/ Soul Doubt (2:54)
R: Ex. Audience.   S: Tour '94.   C: ECD.
Pic CD.

NUMAN, GARY

CD - THE SACRIFICE TOUR '94
NEW MAN MUSIC CD NMM 94
Introduction, Pray (1:46)/ Question Of Faith (5:14)/
I Dream Of Wires (5:11)/ Noise Noise (4:16)/
Listen To The Sirens (3:15)/ Everyday I Die (4:36)/
Desire (4:12)/ Friends (3:25)/ Scar (3:33)/ Magic
(5:06)/ Me (5:00)/ Replicas (5:05)/ Stormtrooper In

Prag. (5:09)/ Deadliner (5:07)/ Bleed (6:22)/ Love
& Napalm (5:40)/ I'm An Agent (4:56)
R: Vg. Audience.   S: Birmingham Town Hall,
England Nov. 6 '94.   C: ECD. Dbw.

OASIS

CD - CRASHLANDING IN L.A.
HOME RECORDS HR 5997-2
Rock And Roll Star (7:20)/ Columbia (4:55)/ Fade
Away (4:14)/ Digsy's Dinner (2:48)/ Shakermaker
(5:38)/ Live Forever (5:04)/ Bring It On Down
(4:28)/ Up In The Sky (4:44)/ Slide Away (6:45)/
Cigarettes And Alcohol (4:30)/ Married With
Children (3:44)/ Supersonic (5:07)/ I Am The
Walrus (9:34)
R: Vg. Audience.   S: Whiskey A Go Go,
Hollywood Sept. 29 '94.   C: ECD. Dcc. Pic CD.

CD - SLIDE AWAY
KISS THE STONE KTS 381
Columbia (4:48)/ Shakermaker (4:47)/ Fade Away
(4:29)/ Digsy's Dinner (2:55)/ Live Forever (4:10)/
Bring It On Down (4:54)/ Up In The Sky (4:47)/
Slide Away (6:16)/ Cigarettes And Alcohol (4:28)/
Supersonic (5:11)/ I Am A Walrus (8:17)/
Shakermaker (5:01)/ Digsy's Dinner (2:50)/ Live
Forever (4:36)/ Cigarettes And Alcohol (4:37)/
Supersonic (2:59)/ Married With Children (2:51)
R: Ex. Tracks 12-17 Vg.   S: Tracks 1-11
Hultsfred Festival, Sweden Aug. 8 94. Tracks 12-
17 tour '94.   C: ECD. Dcc. Pic CD.

CD - SUPERSONIC POP REACTION
WALRUS MUSIC WMCD001
Columbia/ Fade Away/ Digsy's Dinner/ Shaker
Maker/ Live Forever/ Bring It On Down/ Up In The
Sky/ Slide Away/ Cigarettes And Alcohol/ I Am A
Walrus/ Supersonic/ Digsy's Dinner/ Married With
Children/ Live Forever/ Shaker Maker
R: Ex. Audience. Tracks 12-16 Ex. Soundboard.
S: Tracks 1-11, Astoria Theatre, London, England
Aug. 18 '94. Tracks 12-14 radio sessions May '94.
Tracks 15-16 Royal Albert Hall, London, England
at The Creation 'Undrugged' Show June 6 '94.
C: ECD. Dcc. Pic CD. Time 72:14.

OFFSPRING

CD - NITRO
METAL CRASH MECD 1190
Bad Habit (3:42)/ We Are One (3:48)/ Killboy
Powerhead (2:07)/ Burn It Up (3:37)/ Genocide
(3:38)/ Gotta Get Away (3:36)/ So Alone (1:59)/
Kick Him When He's Down (4:50)/ What
Happened To You (4:45)/ Come Out And Play
(3:39)/ Smash (2:57)/ LAPD (3:28)/ Nitro (4:22)/
Self Esteem (4:33)/
R: G-Vg. Audience.   S: New Daisy Theatre,
Memphis Nov. 4 '94.   C: ECD. Dcc. Pic CD.

CD - THE YEAR THAT PUNK BROKE
KISS THE STONE KTS 359
Bad Habit/ Get It Right/ Kill Boy Powerhead/ Burn
It Up/ Genocide/ Gotta Get Away - So Alone/ What
Are We Heading For/ What Happened To You/
Come Out And Play/ It'll Be A Long Time/ Self
Esteem/ We Are One/ Session
R: Exs. Soundboard.   S: Last night of 'Smash'
'94 world tour.   C: ECD. Dcc. Pic CD.

ORB

CD - DIPPING INTO THE CYBERWORLD
PSYCHO 01
Outlands (5:25)/ Mudslickers (2:41)/ Valley (8:34)/
Towers Of Dub (13:06)/ Uf. Orb (4:20)/ Little Fluffy
Clouds (8:10)/ Blue Room (10:50)/ Earth, Gaia
(1:23)/ Close Encounters (9:50)/ A Huge Ever
Growing Brain In The Center Of The Earth Loving
You (7:45)
R: Exs. Soundboard.   S: Tracks 1-9 Woodstock
Festival Aug. '94. Track 10 Radio FM England '94.
C: ECD. Dcc.

CD - EUROPE 1992
LIVE STORM LSCD 51548
Departure (4:17)/ Spanish Castles In Space
(13:18)/ Little Fluffy Clouds (8:03)/ The Blue Room
(11:25)/ Towers Of Dub (8:51)/ Star 6 & 7 8 9
(4:11)/ Earth (Gaia) (14:00)/ Close Encounters
(10:48)
R: Ex. Audience.   S: Europe '92.   C: ECD.

CD - THE PULSATING SOUND OF ORB
COLLECTORS PLEASURE COP 013
The Opera Introduction (3:40)/ Little Fluffy Clouds
(7:42)/ Towers Of Dub (5:55)/ Perpetual Dawn
(10:14)/ Star 6 & 7 & 9 (10:34)/ Outlands (7:22)/
Strung (1:01)/ A Huge Ever Growing Pulsating
Brain That Rules The Center Of The Ultraworld,
Loving U (18:12)/ A Huge Ever Growing Pulsating
Brain That Rules From The Center Of The
Ultraworld - Orbital Dance 'Loving You' Mix (7:59)
R: Ex. Audience.   C: ECD. Dcc.

P

PAGE, JIMMY

CD - MIDNIGHT MOONLIGHT
SWINGIN' PIG TSP CD113
Who's To Blame (4:08)/ Prelude (2:07)/ Over The
Hill & Far Away (5:25)/ Writes Of Winter (3:25)/
Tear Down The Walls (4:30)/ Emerald Eyes (3:35)/
Midnight Moonlight (10:35)/ In My Time Of Dying
(10:05)/ Prison Blues (6:38)/ Wasting My Time
(4:15)/ Custard Pie, Black Dog (3:37)/ Train Kept
A Rollin' (3:34)/ Stairway To Heaven (9:10)
R: Exs. Soundboard.   S: New York Oct. 22 '88.
C: ECD. Dcc.

PAGE - COVERDALE
See listings under 'COVERDALE - PAGE'

PAGE - PLANT
See listing under 'PLANT, ROBERT AND JIMMY
PAGE'

PALMER, ROBERT

CD - SHE MAKES MY DAY
GRAPEFRUIT GRA-035-A
Some Like It Hot (3:21)/ Every Kind Of People
(3:44)/ I Didn't Mean To Turn On You (3:47)/
Change His Ways (2:22)/ Sister Don't You Rough
It All Up (2:41)/ Woke Up Laughing (5:04)/ I'll Be
Your Baby Tonight (3:19)/ Sneakin' Sally Through
The Alley (2:58)/ Johnny And Mary (4:00)/ She
Makes My Day (4:50)/ Looking For Clues (3:25)/
Mother Should Have Told You (3:31)/ Simply
Irresistible (4:58)/ Mercy Mercy Me, I Want You
(4:29)/ Addicted To Love (5:18)
R: Exs. Soundboard.   S: Town & Country Club,
London '91.   C: Australian CD. Dcc.

PANTERA

CD - DOMINATION
GRAPEFRUIT GRA-036-A
New Level (4:03)/ Walk (5:35)/ The Art Of
Shredding (4:44)/ Domination (8:02)/ This Love
(1:21)/ Rise (5:53)/ By Demons Be Driven (5:14)/
Mouth Of War (4:00)/ Primal Concrete Sledge
(3:08)/ Cowboys From Hell (4:46)
R: G-Vg. Audience.   S: Switzerland '93.
C: Australian CD. Dcc.

CD - NO COMPROMISE NO SELL OUT
KISS THE STONE KTS 311
Guilty (4:07)/ Walk (5:18)/ Strength Beyond
Strength (3:57)/ Domination, Slaughter (7:46)/
Fuckin' Hostile (2:49)/ This Love (7:20)/ Mouth For
War (4:00)/ Cowboys From Hell (5:04)
R: Vg-Ex. Audience.   S: Europe 04-06-94.
C: ECD. Dcc. Pic CD.

CD - POWER GROOVE
HOME RECORDS HR5968/69
CD1: Intro - Use My Third Arm (5:14)/ A New
Level (4:08)/ Walk (7:23)/ Strength Beyond
Strength (5:54)/ Slaughtered (5:16)/ Domination,
Hollow (8:53)/ I'm Broken (6:01)/ Becoming (4:10)/
5 Minutes Alone (5:20)/ Exodus Song (8:39)/
Fucking Hostile (3:06)
CD2: This Love (8:25)/ Mouth For War (6:02)/
Primal Concrete Sledge (3:32)/ Stairway To
Heaven (5:18)/ Instrumental Jam (6:08)/ Blast
(4:39)/ Rise (5:57)*/ Cowboys From Hell (4:48)*/
Art Of Shredding (4:52)*/ By The Demons Be
Driven (4:59)*
R: G. Audience.   S: Complete show Santa
Monica Civic Centre, CA May 2 '94. *Europe Feb.
4 '93.   C: ECD. Pic CD.

CD - SUPPORT THE MADMEN
METAL CRASH MECD 1185
A New Level (4:06)/ Use My Third Arm (5:39)/
Walk (6:53)/ Strength Beyond Strength (3:38)/

Slaughtered (5:25)/ Domination, Hollow (9:57)/
Becoming (3:57)/ Five Minutes Alone (5:38)/
Fucking Hostile (2:56)/ This Love (6:28)/ Mouth
For War (6:49)/ Refuse Resist (2:00)/ Primal
Concrete Sledge (4:48)/ Planet Caravan (4:54)/
Cowboys From Hell (5:47)
R: Poor-G. Audience.   S: Nassau Coliseum,
Uniondale, NY Aug. 18 '94.   C: ECD. Dcc.

PANTERA/SHOK PARIS

CD - METAL MAGIC
REBORN CLASSICS RC 1025
PANTERA: Ride My Rocket/ I'll Be Alright/ Tell Me
If You Want It/ Latest Lover/ Biggest Part Of Me/
Metal Magic/ Widowmaker/ Nothin' On But The
Radio/ Sad Lover/ Rock Out/ SHOK PARIS:
Marsielles De Sade/ Battle Cry/ Burn It Down/ On
A Wing And A Prayer/ Chosen Ones/ Caged Tiger/
Never Say Why/ Go For The Throat/ Can't Fight
The Evil/ Run But Don't Hide
R: Exs. Soundboard.   C: ECD. Dcc. Time 78:03.

PAVEMENT

CD - GREEN AROUND THE GILLS
HOME RECORDS HR-5976
Grounded (4:41)/ Silent Kid (3:40)/ 5-4= Unity
(3:05)/ Big Gay Heart (2:29)/ Two States (2:28)/
Cut Your Hair (3:53)/ In The Mouth A Desert
(3:50)/ Down, Fight This Generation (7:55)/
Elevate Me Later (3:36)/ Newark Springs
Orchestra Song (4:55)/ Holly Springs Orchestra
Song (2:56)/ Forklift (3:01)/ Timekeeper (3:11)/ Hit
The Plane Down (3:51)/ Unfair (3:36)/ Summer
Babe (3:56)/ Conduit For Sale (4:07)/ Gold
Soundz (3:33)/ Debris Slide (2:18)
R: Vg. Audience.   S: Atlanta, Georgia Mar. '94.
C: ECD. Dcc.

CD - SUMMER BABE
HAWK 002
Loretta's Scars/ No Life Singed Here/ Trigger Cut/
Baptis Blacktick/ Debris Slide/ Zurich Is Stained/
Forklift/ Lions/ Box Elder/ Homer/ Perfume-V/ Two
States/ Summer Babe
R: Exs. Soundboard.   S: Sacramento, CA May
19 '92.   C: ECD. Time 39:07. Pic CD.

PEARL JAM

CD - ABDUCTED IN THE LAND OF DELI TRAY
STRANGLED STR 001
Release (5:30)/ Animal (3:22)/ Jeremy (5:35)/
Rearview Mirror (6:23)/ Go (3:32)/ Dissident
(3:30)/ Daughter (5:51)/ Black (5:27)/ Hold Me
(4:06)/ Porch (7:12)/ Elderly Woman Behind The
Counter (4:37)/ The Whipping (4:13)/ Glorified G
(4:29)/ Sonic Reducer (5:37)/ Baba O'Riley (6:11)/
Indifference (4:35)
R: G. Audience.   S: San Deigo, CA Nov. 2 '93.
C: ECD. Dcc.

CD - ACOUSTIC SONG BOOK
TEDDY BEAR RECORDS TB 18
State Of Love And Trust (3:50)/ Alive (5:22)/ Black
(5:30)/ Jeremy (5:20)/ Porch (4:25)/ Oceans
(5:33)/ Even Flow (5:12)/ Daughter (4:15)/
Glorified G. (2:24)/ Footsteps (3:55)
R: Ex.   S: Various locations '92 and '93.
C: ECD. Dcc. Pic CD.

CD - AGAINST
KISS THE STONE KTS 221
Release (4:30)/ Why Go (3:36)/ Deep (4:21)/
Jeremy (5:00)/ Medley: Daughter, W.M.A. (4:47)/
Garden (5:38)/ Even Flow (4:55)/ Go (2:34)/ Alive
(4:54)/ Black (5:16)/ Fuckin' Up (4:10)/ Leash
(2:49)/ Sonic Reducer (3:50)/ State Of Love &
Trust (3:41)/ Baba O'Riley (3:55)/ Animal (3:09)/
Rockin' In The Free World (6:48)
R: Exs. Soundboard.   S: USA '93.   C: ECD.
Dcc. Pic CD.

CD - ALIVE
GRAPEFRUIT GRA-003-B
State Of Love And Trust (4:09)/ Black (5:36)/ Alive
(6:02)/ Blood (3:56)/ W.M.A. (7:04)/ Better Man
(6:02)/ Elderly Woman Behind The Counter In A
Small Town (4:18)/ Rats, Ben (4:25)/ Already In
Love (4:30)/ Once (5:40)/ Sonic Reducer (4:00)/
Indifference (4:57)
R: Exs. Soundboard.   S: Atlanta Mar. 3 '94 part
two. See 'Daughter' (GRA-003-A) for part one.
C: Australian CD. Dcc.

CD - ALIVE AGAINST ONE
TARANTULA TNT 003
Blood/ Animal/ Rear View Mirror/ Beast Of Burden,
Alive/ Go/ Daughter/ Blues Jam, State Of Love
And Trust/ Dissident/ Glorified G/ Rats/ Whippin'/
Jeremy/ Black/ Drop The Leash/ Fuckin' Up/ Sonic
Reducer/ Indifference
R: Ex. Audience.   C: Japanese CD. Dcc.
Time 72:23.

CD - ALL NIGHT THING
METAL CRASH MECD 1086
Black (7:27)/ Still Running And Trust (4:20)/ Once
(3:41)/ Porch (8:00)/ Oceans (2:59)/ Even Flow
(5:58)/ Why Go (3:50)/ Jeremy (6:03)/ Deep
(4:44)/ Alive (5:48)
R: Vg. Audience.   C: ECD. Dcc. Pic CD.

CD - AND THE PEARLS SWEEP
HOME RECORDS - HR 5932/33
CD1: Intro - Release (4:44)/ Rearviewmirror
(5:56)/ Whipping (3:54)/ Go (2:02)/ Animal (2:57)/
Dissident (3:48)/ State Of Love And Trust (3:46)/
Breath (6:43)/ Blood (4:33)/ Daughter/ Hey Hey
My My (6:44)/ Why Go (3:44)/ Hold On/ Jeremy
(7:26)/ Even Flow (5:42)/ Black (5:43)/ Alive (5:11)
CD2: Porch (9:49)/ Rats (4:32)/ Immortality (6:23)/
Don't Want (unreleased) (4:53)/ Garden (6:52)/
Leash (4:03)/ Keep On Rockin' In The Free World
(8:52)/ Happy Trails (1:47)/ Indifference (4:52)/ Not
For You (unreleased) (5:42)/ Rearviewmirror

(5:01)/ Daughter, Hey Hey My My (5:02)/ Won't
Back Down (2:20)/ Elderly Woman Behind The
Counter In A Small Town (3:30)
R: Ex.   S: CD1 and CD2 tracks 1-9 Boston
Gardens Apr. '94. CD2 tracks 10-12 Saturday
Night Live Apr. '94. CD2 tracks 13-14 Pensacola
Apr. '94.   C: ECD. Dcc. Pic CD.

CD - ANIMAL
GRAPEFRUIT GRA-003-C
Release (4:25)/ Why Go (3:38)/ Deep (4:18)/
Jeremy (4:59)/ Daughter (4:46)/ Garden (5:35)/
Even Flow (4:54)/ Go (2:34)/ Alive (4:53)/ Black
(5:14)/ *ucking Up (4:09)/ Leash (2:49)/ Sonic
Reducer (3:49)/ State Of Love And Trust (3:40)/
Baba O'Riley (3:55)/ Animal (3:08)/ Rockin' In The
Free World (6:44)
R: Exs. Soundboard.   S: Los Angeles '93.
C: Australian CD. Dcc.

CD - ANIMAL BLOOD
BANZAI BZCD 005/006
CD1: Intro - Once (3:28)/ Even Flow (6:46)/ Alive
(5:09)/ Why Go (3:41)/ Black (5:25)/ Jeremy
(5:12)/ Oceans (3:23)/ Porch (8:34)/ Garden
(8:14)/ Deep (4:22)/ Release (4:38)/ Wash (4:07)/
Dirty Frank (5:46)
CD2: Go (2:40)/ Animal (2:43)/ Daughter (4:55)/
Glorified G (3:15)/ Dissident (3:30)/ Blood (2:58)/
Rearviewmirror (4:49)/ Elderly Woman Behind The
Counter In A Small Town (3:47)/ Leash (3:05)/
Indifference (4:08)/ State Of Love And Trust
(3:59)/ Fuckin' Up (4:30)/ Sonic Reducer (4:10)/
Hold Me (4:04)/ The Wipping (2:39)
R: Vg-Ex.   S: Various.   C: ECD. Pic CD.

CD - ATLANTA
KISS THE STONE KTS 287/88
CD1: Release/ Rearviewmirror/ Would Be/ Even
Flow/ Dissident/ Why Go/ Deep/ Jeremy/ Glorified
G/ Daughter/ Go/ Animal/ Garden
CD2: State Of Love And Trust/ Black/ Alive/ Blood/
W.M.A./ Better Man/ Elderly Woman Behind The
Counter In A Small Town/ Rats/ Already In Love/
Once/ Sonic Reducer/ Porch/ Indifference
R: Exs. Soundboard.   S: Fox Theater, Atlanta,
Georgia Apr. 3 '94.   C: ECD. Pic CDs. Time CD1
59:13. CD2 75:22.

CD - ATLANTA THE DAY BEFORE
KISS THE STONE KTS 379/80
CD1: Intro - Release (5:13)/ Go (3:02)/ Animal
(3:01)/ Dissident (3:37)/ Even Flow (5:20)/ Why Go
(3:36)/ Deep (4:18)/ Jeremy (5:16)/ Glorified G
(3:28)/ Daughter, W.M.A. (9:14)/ Blood (6:29)/
Footsteps (4:19)/ Once (3:12)/ Alive (5:06)
CD2: Black (6:50)/ State Of Love And Trust (4:15)/
Leash (5:27)/ The Kids Are Alright (2:18)/
Rearviewmirror (5:44)/ Not For You (6:30)/ Elderly
Woman Behind The Counter In A Small Town
(3:25)/ Out Of My Mind (5:04)/ Alone (3:41)/ Porch
(8:58)
R: Vg-Ex. Audience.   S: Fox Theater, Atlanta,
Georgia Apr. 2 '94.   C: ECD. Dcc. Pic CDs.

CD - ATTENZIONE
OCTOPUS OCTO 028
Even Flow (5:59)/ Once (3:36)/ State Of Love And
Trust (3:45)/ Alive (5:11)/ Why Go (3:40)/ Porch
(5:22)/ Attenzione, Jeremy (6:48)/ I've Got A
Feeling (5:05)/ Hunger Strike, Leash (4:06)
R: Vg-Ex. Audience.   S: Italy during the '10
European Tour' Feb. '92.   C: ECD. Dcc. Pic CD.

CD - BLACK
GRAPEFRUIT GRA-003-G
Oceans (3:06)/ Even Flow (4:58)/ Why Go (3:20)/
Jeremy (5:49)/ Deep (4:14)/ Alive (5:29)/ Black
(5:35)/ State Of Love And Trust (4:06)/ Porch
(7:30)
R: Exs. Soundboard.   S: London, England '92.
C: Australian CD. Dcc.

CD - BLOOD
GRAPEFRUIT GRA-003-E
Blood (5:02)/ Rats (4:58)/ Once (4:52)/ Porch
(11:45)/ Sonic Reducer (5:18)/ Even Flow (8:30)/
Indifference (4:31)
R: Exs. Soundboard.   S: USA Nov. 5 '93 part
two. See 'Jeremy' (GRA-003-D) for part one.
C: Australian CD. Dcc.

CD - DAUGHTER
GRAPEFRUIT GRA-003-A
Release (5:22)/ Rearview Mirror (5:13)/ Whippin'
(2:55)/ Even Flow (5:05)/ Dissident (3:25)/ Why Go
(3:42)/ Deep (4:26)/ Jeremy (6:47)
R: Exs. Soundboard.   S: Atlanta Mar. 3 '94 part
one. See 'Alive' (GRA-003-B) for part two.
C: Australian CD. Dcc.

CD - DEEP THROUGH THE YEARS
THE FLYING TIGERS FTBX 0051/52/53
CD1: Intro - Let Me Sleep (studio outtake '90)/
Even Flow, Once, Footsteps, Alive,Yellow
Ledbetter, Breath, State Of Love And Trust,
Release, Girl, Alone, Hold Up Your Head, Mystery
(studio outtakes '91)/ Wash, Black, Alive, Porch
(acoustic - Tower Record, Rockville Nov. 9 '91)
CD2: Sonic Reducer (studio outtake '92)/ Baba
O'Riley ('Singles' film premiere party '92)/ Wash
(Virgin Megastore, Paris Feb. 10 '92)/ Saying No!,
Drop The Leaves, I've Got A Feeling (Board Von
De Troge, Dee Haag '92)/ Jeremy (acoustic MTV
Studios, Unplugged session Mar. '92)/
Meaningless, Footsteps (Volkshaus, Zurich June 8
'92)/ Masters Of War (Madison Square Garden,
NYC Oct. 16 '92)/ Going Down (with the Xpensive
Winos) ('92)/ Steal Lie Trust (Europe '92)/ Porch,
Rockin' In The Free World (Pukkelpop Festival
Aug. '92)/ Footsteps, By Your Sides (acoustic -
Moutainview, CA Nov. 1 '92)
CD3: Roadhouse Blues (Hall Of Fame Jan. '93)/
Rockin' In The Free World (MTV Awards Sept.
'93)/ Don't Need, Hard To Imagine, Rearview
Mirror (studio outtake '93)/ Beast Of Burden
(Europe '93)/ The Kids Are Alright (Wichita,
Kansas Nov. 24 '93)/ Don't Need, Dissident, Why
Go, Glorified G, Go, Animal, Blood, W.M.A.,

Betterman, Elderly Woman Behind The Counter In A Small Town, Rats, Already In Love (Fox Theatre, Atlanta Apr. 3 '94)
R: Ex. Some Vg.   C: ECD. Box set with 24 page full-color book in English and Italian. Time CD1 78:43. CD2 77:17. CD3 75:14.

CD - DIFFERENT FACES
INTERNATIONAL BROADCAST RECORDINGS IBR 2425
Wash (3:55)/ Why Go (3:28)/ Jeremy (5:07)/ Deep (4:12)/ Alive (5:13)/ Black (6:17)/ State Of Love And Trust (3:55)/ Even Flow (4:55)/ Rockin' In The Free World (4:30)/ Release (4:17)/ Even Flow (5:53)/ Once (3:07)/ Porch (6:41)/ Garden (5:28)/ Leash (3:09)
R: Vg-Ex.   S: Tracks 1-9 World Music Theatre, Tinley Park Aug. 4 '92. Tracks 10-14 Cabaret Metro, Chicago, Mar. 28 '92. Track 15 LA Apr. '92.
C: ECD. Dcc.

CD - EUROPE '93
POST SCRIPT PSCD 1291
Animal (3:13)/ Go (2:52)/ Once (3;32)/ Blood (3:20)/ Even Flow (5:11)/ Jeremy (5:57)/ Glorified G (3:40)/ Daughter (4:30)/ Alive (6:43)/ Why Go (4:04)/ Leash (3:31)/ Porch (8:21)
R: Vg. Audience.   S: Finsbury, England July 7 '93.   C: ECD. Dcc.

CD - EUROPE '93
THE SWINGIN' PIG 164
Release/ Why Go/ Deep/ Jeremy/ Daughter/ Garden/ Even Flow/ Go/ Alive/ Black/ Fucking Up/ Leash/ Sonic Reducer
R: Exs. Soundboard.   S: The Ahoy, Rotterdam, The Netherlands July 16 '93.   C: ECD.
Time 56:04.

CD - FIVE ALIVE
MAGIC MUSHROOMS RECORDS 9207
Oceans (3:47)/ Love You Hate You (1:59)/ Black (5:40)/ Once (4:23)/ Pictures Of My Heart (4:11)/ Deep (4:37)/ Get Out Of (3:50)/ Meaning This (4:49)/ Porch (8:42)/ Improvisation (1:50)/ Garden (1:50)/ Rockin' In A Free World (5:30)/ Wash My Love (3:31)/ Even Flow (5:16)/ Jeremy (4:00)
R: Ex. Audience.   S: Tracks 1-13 June. 18 '92. Tracks LA 14-16 Apr. '92.   C: ECD. Dcc.

CD - THE 5 MUSKETEERS
BACKSTAGE 069
Wash (3:34)/ Dirty Frank (5:39)/ Oceans (2:45)/ Footsteps (3:56)/ Yellow Ledbetter (5:05)/ Breath (5:21)/ State Of Love And Trust (3:47)/ Release (5:10)/ Girl (4:56)/ Alive (5:48)/ Alone (3:24)/ Hold Your Head Up (5:00)/ Mistery (4:32)/ Roadhouse Blues (5:45)/ Break On Through (3:30)/ Light My Fire (8:11)
R: Tracks 1-13 Vg-Ex. Soundboard. Tracks 14-16 G. Audience.   S: Tracks 1-13 studio sessions. Tracks 14-16 with the Doors at the Rock And Roll Hall of Fame.   C: ECD. Dcc. Pic CD.

CD - FLASHPOINT
BIG MUSIC BIG 081
Wash (4:13)/ Why Go (3:27)/ Jeremy (5:18)/ Deep (4:32)/ Alive (5:25)/ Black (5:25)/ State Of Love & Trust (3:42)/ Even Flow (5:09)/ Roadhouse Blues (5:52), Break On Through (3:44), Light My Fire (8:11) (Eddie with The Doors)/ State Of Love & Trust (3:38)/ Baba O'Riley (4:01)
R: Exs. Soundboard.   S: LA and various other dates.   C: ECD. Dcc. Pic CD. Time 62:41.

CD - FREE WORLD
ALL OF US 01
Animal (3:06)/ Rockin' In The Free World (7:08)/ Footsteps (4:37)/ Alive (5:26)/ Daughter (4:06)/ Glorified G (2:26)/ Baba O'Riley (4:08)/ W.M.A. (6:03)/ Dissidence (3:26)/ Blood (2:53)/ Indifference (5:45)/ Rearview Mirror (4:22)/ Breath (3:48)/ Release (4:26)/ Dirty Frank (6:34)/ Sonic Producer (4:05)
R: Vg-Ex.   S: Tracks 1-2 MTV Awards Sept. 2 '93. Tracks 3-6 acoustic jam Nov. 4 '92. Tracks 7-16 secret surprise gig Mar. 13 '93.   C: ECD. Dcc.

CD - FROM THEN 'TIL NOW
PITCHFORK RECORDS PF 100
What? (3:25)/ 7 Up (3:41)/ Alive (5:47)/ Dollar Short (4:33)/ Answer (3:01)/ Release (5:07)/ The Wreck Of Edmunds Fitzgerald (4:11)/ A Breath And A Scream (5:48)/ 'E' Ballad (4:48)/ Weird 'A' (4:33)/ Richard's 'E' (3:47)/ The King (4:01)/ Believe You Me (3:21)/ Just A Girl (4:54)
R: Ex. Soundboard. Some static.   S. Unknown studio sessions late '90.   C: ECD. Dbw.

CD - HALLUCINOGENIC RECIPE
CD1: Thru Fade Away/ Savoy Fare Slide/ Waitin For You/ Stardog Champion/ Chloe Champion/ Half Ass Monkey/ Dream Come True/ Gentle Groove/ Greasy (She's So) Heartshine/ Untitled/ Ever Kiss A Lady/ Holly Roller/ These R No Blues/ Playground/ Savoy Fare Slide/ Country Shmoe & The Fist/ Rhapsody In Chartreuse
R: CD1 ?.   S: CD1 Mother Love Bone - studio master demos.
CD2: New God/ Tunnel Of Love/ Untitled/ Leech/ New God/ Richard E./ E Ballad (Black)/ Wreck/ Twist/ Fear/ Baby, Help Me.../ 33 RPS/ Wierd A (Animal)/ Pushing Forward Back/ The King (Evenflow)
R: Vg-Ex.   S: Tracks 1-8 Green River - 1st demos. Tracks 9-15 Stone Gossard - demos.
CD3: Just Wanted You To Know/ What Do You Want/ Believe/ Live/ Stand By/ It's Just A Book/ Just Wanted You To Know (2nd version)/ What The Fuck Is Up/ I'm Alive, How's That/ Broken Down/ What The Fuck Is Up (2nd version)/ Believe (2nd Version)/ I Don't Know/ Roadhouse Blues/ Break On Through/ Light My Fire/ Master Of War
R: Tracks 1-14 G. Tracks 15-18 Vg-Ex.
S: Tracks 1-14 Eddie Vedder - solo home demos. Tracks 15-17 Eddie with the remaining Doors at The Rock N Roll Hall Of Fame. Track 18 Eddie with Mike at the Bob Dylan tribute.

CD4: Let Me Sleep/ Ramblings 1/ Wash (Re-Mix)/ Dirty Frank/ Oceans (1st mix)/Footsteps/ Yellow Ledbetter/ Release/ Alive/ Breath/ State Of Love And Trust/ The Whipping/ Don't Need/ Hard To Imagine/ Girl/ Alone/ Mystery
CD4 G-Vg.   S: Tracks 1-2 Pearl Jam - It's Christmas Time '91. Tracks 3-11 Pearl Jam - 'Ten' outtakes. Tracks 12-17 Pearl Jam - 'VS.' outtakes.
CD5: Animal/ Why Go/ Jeremy/ Glorified G/ Daughter/ Evenflow/ Garden/ Blood/ State Of Love And Trust/ Porch/ Rearview Mirror/ Alone/ Rockin In A Free World (With Urge Overkill & Mudhoney)/ Indifference/ Leash (San Francisco Oct. 28 '93)/ Crazy Mary (with Victoria Williams - New Orleans, LA Nov. 17 '93).
R: G-Vg. Audience.   S: Tracks 1-14 Pearl Jam - live in Las Vegas at The Aladdin Dec. 1 '93.
C: ECD. Box set with full-color cover. Full color book with Pearl Jam family tree, history and pictures. OOOOPS - Someone forgot to put CD1 in the box we got.

CD - HOME
PLUTO RECORDS PLR CD 9409
CD1: Intro/ Releases/ Evenflow/ Dissident/ Intro/ Go/ Animal/ Jeremy/ Deep/ Why Go/ Daughter/ W.M.A./ Glorified/ Alive/ Once/ Footsteps Porch
CD2: Last Exit/ Big Wave/ Blood/ State Of Love And Trust/ I've Got A Feeling/ Rockin' In The Free World/ Intro/ Whippin/ Leash/ Black/ Crazy Mary/ Indifference
R: Vg-Ex. Audience.   S: Seattle Center Arena Aug. 12 '93. CD1 tracks 10-12 June 9 '93 Portland Meadows, Racetrack. CD1 track 1 Portland Meadows Racetrack July 12 '93. CD2 Tracks 8,9,13 Seattle Center Arena Aug. 12 '93.
C: ECD. Dcc. Fold-out digi-pack. Time CD1 64:65. CD2 71:14.

CD - IN ROCK WE TRUST
RED PHANTOM RPCD 1183
Walking The Cow (3:34)/ Elderly Woman (3:28)/ Corduroy (5:04)/ Daughter (Ramblings: Hey Hey My My, American Pie) (5:01)/ Black (5:44)/ Footsteps (4:10)/ Yellow Ledbetter (6:14)/ Let Me Sleep (It's Xmas Time) (2:19)/ Wash (4:50)/ Not For You (4:44)/ Immortality (5:32)/ Elderly Woman (3:40)/ Daughter (4:38)/ Black (6:59)/ Bee Girl (2:19)
R: Ex. Audience.   S: Bridge Benefit Concert, San Francisco Oct. 1 (tracks 1-8) and 2 (tracks 9-15) '94.   C: ECD. Dcc. Pic CD.

CD - INDIAN SUMMER
HAWK 044/45
CD1: Intro - Release (6:31)/ Animal (2:47)/ Why Go (3:45)/ Jeremy (5:37)/ Rearviewmirror (5:50)/ Go (3:08)/ Daughter (5:57)/ Even Flow (5:57)/ Dissident (3:38)/ Alive (4:58)/ Once (4:48)
CD2: Black (5:48)/ Hold Me (4:56)/ Porch (7:37)/ Elderly Woman Behind The Counter (4:39)/ The Whipping (4:12)/ Glorified G (4:20)/ Sonic Reducer (4:21)/ Baba O'Riley (5:57)/ Indifference (6:06)
R: G-Vg. Audience.   S: San Diego Civic Theatre,

San Diego Nov.'93.   C: ECD. Dcc.

CD - JEREMY
GRAPEFRUIT GRA-003-D
Release (6:19)/ Go (3:05)/ Animal (3:12)/ Why Go (4:08)/ Deep (5:01)/ Jeremy (6:01)/ Glorified G (3:15)/ Daughter (6:25)/ Alive (6:03)/ Rearview Mirror (6:40)
R: Exs. Soundboard.   S: USA Nov. 5 '93 part one. See 'Blood' (GRA-003-E) for part two
C: Australian CD. Dcc.

CD - JEWEL BOX 5
HOME RECORDS HR 5980-5
Not For You (5:32)/ Yellow Ledbetter (5:00)/ Whipping (2:30)/ Girl (4:52)/ Mystery (4:23)/ Alone (3:19)/ Footsteps (4:11)/ Meaningless (4:39)/ Hungerstrike (1:23)/ My Generation (:59)/ Baba O'Riley (3:49)/ I've Got A Feeling (4:01)/ Say No (4:13)/ Be Careful With Your Brother (1:23)/ Obedient (1:46)/ Love You Want You Hate You (1:57)/ Immortality (6:25)/ Corduroy (4:45)/ Hard To Imagine (4:16)/ Angel (2:23)/ Patriots (2:44)/ Happy Trails (1:46)
R: Ex. Soundboard/Audience.   S: Rare live and unreleased.   C: ECD. Dcc. Pic CD.

CD - KEEP ON ROCKIN' IN A FREE WORLD
MIND THE MAGIC MTM 012
State Of Love And Trust/ Alive/ Black/ Jeremy/ Proch/ Oceans/ I Love You Hate You/ Once/ Pictures Of My Heart/ Deep/ Get Out Of/ Meaning This/ Rockin' In A Free World
R: Exs. Soundboard.   S: Acoustic set LA '92.
C: ECD.

CD - THE KIDS ARE ALRIGHT
COCOMELOS RECORDS CM 024
Release/ Go/ Animal/ Why Go/ Deep/ Jeremy/ Dissident/ Even Flow/ Glorified G/ Daughter/ Blood/ Alive/ State Of Love & Trust/ Porch/ The Kids Are Alright/ Rearviewmirror/ Sonic Reducer/ Indifference
R: Vg. Audience.   S: Lake Front Arena, New Orleans Nov. 16 '93.   C: ECD. Pic CD.
Time 78:18.

CD - LIVE IN CHICAGO
SOUNDS ALIVE SA 24 003
Release (4:37)/ Even Flow (6:05)/ Once (3:22)/ State Of Love & Trust (3:58)/ Alive (5:30)/ Black (5:06)/ Deep (4:19)/ Jeremy (5:12)/ Why Go (3:12)/ Porch (6:37)/ Garden (5:49)/ Wash My Love (3:34)/ Rockin' In The Free World (5:26)/ Dirty Frank (5:39)
R: Exs. Soundboard.   S: Tracks 1-11 Cabaret Metro, Chicago Mar. 28 '92. Tracks 12-14 LA '92.
C: ECD.

CD - LIVE IN USA '93
AMT PRODUCTION
Release (4:30)/ Why Go (3:36)/ Deep (4:21)/ Jeremy (5:00)/ Garden (5:38)/ Even Flow (4:55)/ Go (2:34)/ Alive (4:54)/ Black (5:16)/ Fuckin' Up

(4:10)/ Leash (2:49)/ Sonic Reducer (3:50)/ Road
House Blues (5:54)/ Break On Through (3:35)/
Light My Fire (8:32)
R: Exs. Soundboard.　　S: USA '93.　　C: ECD.
Dcc.

CD - MANIFESTING MORRISON
HAWK HAWK 032/33
CD1: Release (6:12)/ Go (3:10)/ Animal (3:15)/
Why Go (4:09)/ Deep (5:02)/ Jeremy (5:57)/
Glorified G (3:31)/ Daughter (6:13)/ Alive (6:00)/
Rearviewmirror (6:52)
CD2: Blood (5:09)/ Rats (5:08)/ Once (4:42)/
Porch (11:44)/ Sonic Reducer (5:21)/ Even Flow
(8:30)/ Indifference (4:32)
R: Ex. Soundboard.　　C: ECD. Dcc. Pic CD.

CD - MESMERIZE
TEDDY BEAR RECORDS TB 41
Oceans (3:41)/ Love You Hate You (1:52)/
Release (5:34)/ Alive (5:57)/ Once (4:19)/
Footsteps (4:18)/ Deep (4:15)/ Drop The Leaves
(3:42)/ Meaningless (4:37)/ Porch (8:24)/
Improvisation (1:50)/ Masters Of War (6:15)/
Rockin' In The Free World (5:13)/ Not For You
(5:43)*/ Rearview Mirror (4:59)*/ Daughter, Hey
Hey My My (5:51)
R: Exs. Soundboard.　　S: Zurich, Switzerland
June 18 '92. *Saturday Night Live Apr. '94.
C: ECD. Dcc. Pic CD.

CD - NO ONE HERE GETS OUT ALIVE
SOFT PARADE 001
Jeremy/ Rearview Mirror/ Elderly Woman Behind
The Counter/ In A Small Town/ Even Flow/
Glorified G Daughter/ Garden Go/ Animal Alive/
Porch/ Fuckin' Up/ Leash/ Sonic Reducer/ Rockin'
In A Free World/ State Of Lust And Trust
R: G-Vg. Audience.　　S: Washington Oct. '93.
C: ECD. No cover. B&w sticker on a jewel case.

CD - ON TOUR
ROCKS 92108
Release (4:26)/ Why Go (3:37)/ Deep (4:24)/
Jeremy (5:12)/ Daughter (4:49)/ Garden (5:43)/
Evenflow (4:54)/ Go (2:33)/ Alive (4:52)/ Black
(5:14)/ Fucking Up (4:03)/ Leash (2:54)/ Sonic
Reducer (3:46)/ Wash (4:08)/ Alive (5:15)/ State
Of Love And Trust (3:39)/ Evenflow (5:01)
R: Exs. Soundboard.　　S: Live broadcast '93.
C: ECD.

CD - ONCE
GRAPEFRUIT GRA-003-F
Even Flow (4:59)/ Once (3:16)/ Alive (5:32)/
Jeremy (5:07)/ Porch (4:27)/ I've Got A Feeling
(8:05)/ Hunger Strike (1:25)/ My Generation (1:00)/
Rockin' In The Free World (5:10)
R: Exs. Soundboard.　　S: Hollywood Palladium,
LA '92.　　C: Australian CD. Dcc.

CD - PRIVATE RADIO
FTAG 34942
CD1: Release/ Rearview Mirror/ Don't Give In/

Evenflow/ Dissident/ Why Go?/ Deep/ Jeremy/
Glorified G/ Daughter/ Go/ Animal/ Garden
CD2: State Of Love And Trust/ Black/ Alive/ Blood/
W.M.A./ A Better Man/ Elderly Woman Behind The
Counter In A Small Town/ Rats/ Already In Love/
Once
R: Exs. Soundboard.　　S: Fox Theatre, Atlanta,
Georgia Apr. 3 '94.　　C: ECD. Dcc.

CD - PROUD
ROCKS 92107
Alive (5:21)/ Evenflow (5:09)/ Black (5:18)/ Why
Go (3:55)/ Jeremy (5:06)/ Deep (4:31)/ Alive
(5:19)/ Black (5:43)/ Leash (3:27)/ Rockin' In The
Free World (6:43)/ Roadhouse Blues (5:44)/ Break
On Through (3:11)/ Light My Fire (7:59)
R: Exs. Soundboard.　　S: Tracks 1-3 Utrecht '92.
Tracks 4-10 Pinkpop '92. Tracks 11-12 LA '93.
C: ECD. Dcc.

CD - RARE TRACKS II
MONTANA MO 10025
Going Down (4:25)/ Beast Of Burden, Rats (6:24)/
Yellow Ledbetter (5:08)/ Masters Of War (4:41)/
Whippin' (2:33)/ Girl (4:54)/ Mystery (4:27)/
Rockin' In A Free World (5:15)/ Breath (5:14)/
Alone (3:22)/ Don't Need (2:37)/ Hold Your Head
Up (4:59)/ Hard To Imagine (4:22)/ By Your Side
(2:34)/ Patriots (2:50)
R: Vg-Ex.　　S: Live in the USA 92-94.　　C: ECD.
Dbw. Blue type.

CD - RARITIES II
LUNATIC LU 2010
Going Down (4:25)/ Beast Of Burden, Rats (6:24)/
Yellow Ledbetter (5:08)/ Masters Of War (4:41)/
Whippin' (2:33)/ Girl (4:54)/ Mystery (4:27)/
Rocking In A Free World (5:15)/ Breath (5:14)/
Alone (3:22)/ Don't Need (2:37)/ Hold Your Head
Up (4:59)/ Hard To Imagine (4:22)/ By Your Side
(2:34)/ Patriots (2:50)
R: Vg-Ex.　　S: Live USA 92-94.　　C: ECD. Dcc.
Pic CD looks like a record - nice touch.

CD - SHELL IN THE DESERT
BEST BUY RECORDS BBR CD 009
Daughter (4:48)/ Alive (5:23)/ Jeremy (5:08)/
Animal (with Neil Young) (3:04)/ Even Flow (4:41)/
State Of Love And Trust (3:57)/ Master Of War
(4:56)/ Why Go (3:14)/ Release (4:30)/ Sonic
Reducer (3:50)/ Fuckin' Up (4:10)/ Black (5:16)/
Go (2:34)/ Leash (2:49)/ Dirty Frank (5:38)/
Rockin' In A Free World (with Neil Young) (6:18)
R: Vg-Ex.　　S: USA '94 except 4 and 16.
C: ECD.

CD - STAGE OF LOVE AND TRUST
DEAD DOG RECORDS SE 432
Wash/ Once/ Even Flow/ Alive/ Why Go/ Jeremy/
Oceans/ Porch/ Dirty Frank/ Master Of War/ State
Of Love And Trust/ Rear View Mirror/ Elderly
Woman Behind The Counter In A Small Town/
Dissident/ Daughter/ Go/ Blood/ Leash
R: Vg-Ex.　　S: '92-93.　　C: ECD. Dbw. 75:52.

CD - SURFER EDDIE'S SUNSHINE STATE
FLASHBACK 12 93 0221
Oceans (2:55)/ Why Go (3:48)/ Jeremy (5:04)/
State Of Love And Trust (4:36)/ Even Flow (5:07)/
Glorified G (3:17)/ Daughter (5:07)/ Go (2:48)/
Animal (2:45)/ Footsteps (4:14)/ Alive (5:12)/ Rats
(4:20)/ Blood (4:15)/ Crazy (5:35)*/ Indifference
(4:43)/ Leash (3:14)/ Three Days (3:32)
R: Ex. S: CA Oct. '93. C: ECD. *With Victoria
Williams.

CD - TWO TRACK DEMOS
COLLECTORS PLEASURE COP 003
Animal (2:50)/ Don't Need (2:35)/ Daughter (3:55)/
Go (2:40)/ W.M.A. (5:46)/ Blood (2:45)/ Glorified
G. (3:38)/ Rats (4:05)/ Leash (2:55)/ Hard To
Imagine (4:20)/ Alone (3:35)/ Indifference (4:55)/
Rearview Mirror (4:42)/ Elderly Woman Behind
The Counter In A Small Town (3:14)
R: Vg-Ex. Soundboard. C: ECD. Dcc. Pic CD.

CD - ULTRA RARE TRAX
MONTANA MO 10013
Footsteps/ Meaningless/ Hungerstrike/ My
Generation/ Baba O'Riley/ Roadhouse Blues/
Break On Through/ Light My Fire/ I've Got A
Feeling/ Untitled I/ Untitled II/ Untitled III/ Untitled
IV/ Leash/ Dirty Frank/ Animal/ Breathe
R: Vg-Ex. S: '92-'93 USA. C: ECD. Dcc. Time
69:05.

CD - UNCOVERED
CHELSEA RECORDS CFC 001
Roadhouse Blues/ Break On Through/ Light My
Fire/ Brass In Pocket/ Baba O'Riley/ Rockin' In
The Free World/ Sonic Reducer/ Hold Your Head
Up/ My Generation/ I've Got A Feeling/ Going
Down/ Masters Of War/ Fuckin' Up/ Beast of
Burden
R: G-Vg. S: Covers from various locations.
C: ECD. Dcc. Time 69:35.

CD - VERSUS THE WORLD
BACKSTAGE BKCD082
Footsteps (5:05)/ Daughter (3:58)/ Untitled (2:26)/
Alive (5:36)/ Black (5:30)/ Jeremy (5:50)/ Porch
(5:41)/ State Of Love & Trust (3:44)/ Even Flow
(5:18)/ Master Of War (4:47)/ Christmas Time
(2:52)/ Don't Need (2:34)/ Hard To Imagine (4:22)/
Hold Me (4:05)/ Fuckin' Up (4:05)/ Sonic Reducer
(3:35)/ The Park Where I Play The Pope (1:35)/
Improvisation 1 (1:51)/ Improvisation 2 (1:59)/
Footsteps (4:17)
R: Vg-Ex. S: Tracks 1-3 Mountainview, CA Nov.
1 '92. Tracks 4-9 MTV Unplugged Sessions. Track
10 Madison Square Garden, NYC Oct. 16 '93.
Tracks 1,16 studio outtakes. Tracks 12, 13, 17-20
USA '93. Track 14 Civic Theatre, San Diego Nov.
2 '93. Track 15 Rotterdam July 16 '93. C: ECD.
Dcc. Pic CD.

CD - VORTICAL
KISS THE STONE KTS 368/69
CD1: Rearviewmirror/ Glorified G/ Not For You/

Daughter/ Go/ Black/ Blood/ Animal/ Deep/
Jeremy/ Better Man/ Dissident/ Alive/ Once
CD2: Why Go/ Tell Me/ Even Flow/ Immortal/
Release, Elderly Woman Behind The Counter In A
Small Town/ Yellow Ledbetter/ Indifference/ Would
Be/ Three Days/ Satan's Bed/ Bee Girl/ Hold Me
R: Exs. Soundboard. S: Claims to be Boston
Gardens, Boston Apr. 10 '94 but it's really a
rearranged Atlanta Apr. 3 '94 plus some live B-
sides. C: ECD. Pic CD. CD1 60:28. CD2 45:20.

CD - WORLD JAM
WHY NOT? WOT 2024/25
CD1: Go (3:38)/ Animal (2:59)/ Even Flow (5:40)/
Glorified G (3:36)/ Daughter (6:21)/ Jeremy (5:10)/
Deep (4:40)/ Oceans (3:13)/ State Of Love And
Trust (4:11)/ Dissident (4:09)/ Alive (5:40)/ Porch
(6:32)
CD2: The Kids Are Allright (3:29)/ Rearview Mirror
(5:44)/ Black (8:18)/ Rockin' In The Free World
(6:12)/ Indifference (4:50)/ Sonic Reducer (4:45)/
Rats (4:24)/ Daughter, W.M.A. (5:55)/ Blood
(soundcheck) (2:26)/ Black (5:02) (acoustic)/
Daughter (3:20) (acoustic)
R: Vg-Ex. Audience. S: CD1, CD2 tracks 1-5
Wichita, Kansas Nov. 24 '93. Tracks 6, 8-9 New
Orleans Sept. '93. Tracks 7, 10-11 USA '93.
C: ECD. Dcc. Pic CD.

CD - WORLDWIDE
PEARL 001
Wash/ Dirty Frank/ Oceans (remix)/ Footsteps/
Yellow Ledbetter/ Breath/ State Of Love And
Trust/ Wash/ Once/ Even Flow/ Alive/ Jeremy/
Why Go?/ Porch
R: Exs. Soundboard. S: Tracks 1-7 studio.
Tracks 8-14 live in Hollywood '92. C: ECD. Dcc.
Pic CD. Time 61:05.

PETTY, TOM

CD - THE HOMECOMING CONCERT
ROCKS 9124/25
CD1: Love Is A Long Road (4:37)/ Into The Great
Wide Open (4:40)/ Listen To Her Heart (3:31)/ I
Won't Back Down (4:04)/ Free Fallin' (6:26)/
Psychotic Reactions (5:41)/ Death Ray Boogie
(5:16)/ Don't Come Round Here No More (8:47)/
Something In The Air (4:48)/ Mary Jane's Last
Dance (8:51)/ King's Highway (3:48)/ A Face In
The Crowd (4:47)
CD2: Ballad Of Easy Rider (4:14)/ Take Out Some
Insurance (5:38)/ Thirteen Days (4:44)/ Southern
Accents (5:43)/ Yer So Bad (3:04)/ Driving Down
To Georgia (6:52)/ Lost Without You (6:42)/
Refugee (4:39)/ Runnin' Down A Dream (4:55)/
Learning To Fly (5:03)/ Rainy Day Woman #35
(4:38)/ American Girl (4:24)/ Goodnight (3:07)
R: Exs. Soundboard. S: Gainesville, Florida Apr.
11 '93. C: ECD. Dcc.

CD - I WON'T BACK DOWN
GRAPEFRUIT GRA-025-A
Refugee (3:38)/ Don't Come Around Here No

More (5:47)/ Listen To Her Heart (3:15)/ Kings Road (3:35)/ Too Good To Be True (4:05)/ Here Comes My Girl (4:49)/ Built To Last (5:20)/ Kings Highway (3:09)/ Learning To Fly (4:03)/ Yer So Bad (3:01)/ Into The Great Wide Open (3:42)/ Psychotic Reaction (4:02)/ Something Else (1:42)/ Don't Bring Me Down (3:35)/ I Fought The Law (2:12)/ For What It's Worth (4:21)/ Ballad Of Easy Rider (3:15)/ Anyway You Want It (2:54)/ Don't Do Me Like That (2:57)/ I Won't Back Down (2:59)
R: Exs. Soundboard.   S: Birmingham, England '91.   C: Australian CD. Dcc.

CD - SHOUT
WINGED WHEEL WW-9413
Surrender (3:08)/ Jaguar And Thunderbirds (3:12)/ American Girl (5:04)/ Fooled Again, I Don't Like It (5:52)/ Luna (3:59)/ Listen To Her Heart (3:18)/ I Need To Know (3:04)/ Strangered In The Night (4:15)/ Dog On The Run (9:38)/ Route 66 (3:50)/ American Girl (4:16)/ Fooled Again, I Don't Like It (5:51)/ Breakdown (4:30)/ Strangered In The Night (4:05)/ Anything That's Rock & Roll (4:03)/ Shout! (5:05)
R: Exs. Audience.   S: Tracks 1-10 Chicago Apr. '77. Tracks 11-16 San Francisco June '77.
C: ECD. Full-color gatefold cardboard sleeve. CD looks like a record.

CD - SOUTHERN GENTLEMAN
KISS THE STONE KTS 273/74
CD1: Love Is A Long Road (5:05)/ Into The Great Wide Open (5:05)/ Listen To Her Heart (4:36)/ I Won't Back Down (4:01)/ Free Falling (6:07)/ Psychotic Reaction (6:54)/ Death Ray Boogie (6:17)/ Don't Come Around Here No More (8:09)/ Something In The Air (4:19)/ Mary Jane's Last Dance (9:04)
CD2: King's Highway (3:43)/ A Face in The Crowd (5:11)/ Ballad Of Easy Rider (3:22)/ Take Out Some Insurance (6:12)/ 13 Days (5:09)/ Southern Accents (6:01)/ Learning To Fly (5:03)/ Rainy Day Woman (4:22)/ American Girl (5:03)/ All Right For Now (2:12)
R: Exs. Soundboard.   S: Gainesville, Florida Apr. 11 '93.   C: ECD. Pic CDs.

PHISH

CD - CRUMBS OF KNOWLEDGE
TEDDY BEAR TB 57/2
CD1: Intro - Golgi Apparatus (4:26)/ It's Ice (5:00)/ Lizards (13:07)/ Tela (8:37)/ Wilson (5:41)/ AC/DC Bag (7:29)/ Colonel Forbin's Ace (7:10)/ Mockingbird (5:52)/ Sloth (4:43)
CD2: McGrupp (18:04)/ Mike's Tune (10:42)/ Runaway Jim (5:48)*/ Foam (7:59)*/ Horn (4:00)*/ Reba (11:55)*/ Llama (4:55)*
R: Exs. Soundboard.   S: CD1 Crest Theatre, Sacramento, CA Mar. 22 '93. *The Marquee, NYC Dec. 28 '90.   C: ECD. Pic CD.

CD - DINNER AND A MOVIE
TRIANGLE PYCD 098
Dinner And A Movie (3:41)/ Bouncing Around The Room (4:03)/ The Sloth (3:50)/ The Landlady (5:11)/ Reba (12:25)/ Living In The Street (3:37)/ Tweezer (9:54)/ Magilla (6:14)/ Run Like Antelope (11:06)/ Ya Mar (7:26)
R: Exs. Soundboard.   S: Wesleyan University, Middletown, CT '90.   C: ECD.

CD - FOLLOW ME TO GAMEHENGE
KISS THE STONE KTS 304/05
CD1: Buried Alive (2:22)/ Possum (10:44)/ It's Ice (3:29)/ Bouncing Around The Room (3:47)/ Split Open And Melt (8:23)/ Rift (7:42)/ Fee, Maze (10:46)/ Colonel Forbin's Ascent, Icculus, The Famous Mocking Bird (18:47)/ Run Like An Antelope(7:58)
CD2: Sanity (5:53)/ Llama (3:58)/ The Lizards, Mike's Song (9:33)/ I'm Hydrogen, Weekapawgroove (19:37)/ Horn (3:45)/ Poor Heart (2:38)/ Hairs On End, Vacuum Solo (9:51)/ Carolina In The Morning, Memories, Sweet Adeline (3:36)/ Suzie Greenberg (6:07)/ Sleeping Monkey (3:44)
R: Exs. Soundboard.   S: Santa Barbara, CA Apr. 4 '92.   C: ECD. Dcc. Pic CD.

CD - HOLIDAY RECORDING HOLIDAY SNAP
INSECT IST 72/73
CD2: Intro - Kung Chant/ Llama/ The Lizard/ Tela/ Wilson/ AC/DC Bag/ Colonel Forbin's Ascent/ The Famous Mocking Bird/ Sloth/ McGrupp And The Watchful Hosemasters/ Divided Sky
CD2: Julius/ Down With Disease/ If I Could/ Axilla Part II/ Lifeboy/ Sample In A Jar/ Wolfman's Brother/ Scent Of A Mule/ Dog Face Boy/ Plow/ Amazing Grace/ Tube
R: G. Audience.   S: Charleston, West Virginia June 26 '94.   C: ECD. Time CD1 78:29. CD2 78:31.

CD - JAMMIN' SANTANA
HQ 11
Runaway Jim/ Foam/ Sparkle/ Stash/ Rift/ You Enjoy Myself/ Llama/ Santana's Jam #1/ Santana's Jam #2/ David Bowie/ Catapjlt
R: Exs. Soundboard.   S: Stowe, VT July 25 '92.
C: ECD. Digi-pack. Time 77:41.

CD - A PHISHY STORY
TEDDY BEAR RECORDS TB 28
Intro - The Landlady (8:10)/ Rift (4:28)/ Language Instructions, Fire (4:28)/ You Enjoy Myself (16:17)/ Wilson... Brother (13:54)/ The Lizzards... Horn (13:58)/ Possum (14:58)
R: Exs. Soundboard.   S: Tracks 1-5 Providence, RI Mar. 13 '92. Track 6 Stowe, VT July 25 '92.
C: ECD. Dcc. Pic CD.

CD - PHISH ON PHISHIN' ON
TEDDY BEAR RECORDS TB 39
Curtain (6:21)/ Split Open & Melt (8:10)/ My Poor Heart (3:04)/ Guelah Papyrus (5:34)/ Maze (8:14)/

Moud (6:52)/ Fluffhead (15:02)/ Run Like An Antelope, Blues Jam, Big Black Fuzzy Creatures From Mars, Hawaii Vocal Jam, Lullaby Jam, Big Black Fuzzy Creatures From Mars, Antelope (18:19)
R: Exs. Soundboard.   S: Providence, RI Mar. 13 '92.   C: ECD. Dcc. Pic CD.

CD - ROCK EKLEKTIZISMEN
FLASHBACK 08.94.0236
CD1: Intro - Golgi Apparatus (4:48)/ No Goodbye (8:00)/ Divided Sky (11:52)/ I Didn't Know, Vacuum Solo (acapella) (4:39)/ You Enjoy Myself (15:48)/ Possum (7:34)/ The Lizards, Mike's Song (9:15)
CD2: Foam (8:31)/ I'm Hydrogen (8:19)/ Weekapawgroove (5:57)/ Carolina In The Morning (1:47)/ Stay (7:07)/ My Only Desire (4:41)/ Glide, Chalk Dust Torture (10:07)/ Bass And Drum Solo, Instrumental
R: Exs. Soundboard.   S: New Haven Mar. 1 '93.   C: ECD.

CD - SLOTH
HAWK 025
Suzie Greenberg (5:25)/ My Friend (6:35)/ Poor Heart (2:58)/ The Landlady (3:27)/ Nicu (5:37)/ Sloth (3:42)/ Divided Sky (13:12)/ Guelah Papyrus (1:14)/ It's Ice (10:08)/ Horn (3:41)/ I Don't Know (3:23)/ Possum (12:20)
R: Exs. Soundboard.   S: USA May 5 '92.   C: ECD. Pic CD.

PINK FLOYD

CD - A CD FULL OF SECRETS
PHANTOM RECORDS AYCD69
Candy And A Currant Bun (Mar. 11 '67) (2:43)/ See Emily Play (June 16 '67) (2:50)/ Flaming (single version Aug. 5 '67) (2:46)/ Apples And Oranges (Nov. 18 '67) (3:01)/ Paintbox (Nov. 18 '67) (3:28)/ It Would Be So Nice (Apr. 12 '68) (3:39)/ Julia Dream (Apr. 12 '68) (2:34)/ Point Me At The Sky (Dec. 17 '68) (3:34)/ Heartbeat Pigmeat (Jan. '70) (3:08)/ Crumbling Land (Jan '70) (4:13)/ Come In Number 51, Your Time Is Up (Jan. '70) (4:58)/ Biding My Time (May '71) (5:14)/ Money ('81 dance version Nov. 23 '81) (6:44)/ When The Tigers Broke Free (July 26 '82) (2:52)/ Not Now John ('Obscured' version Apr. '83) (4:24)/ Terminal Frost (Sept. 7 '87) (5:58)/ Run Like Hell (live version) Nov. 5 '87) (7:10)
R: Vg-Ex.   S: Alternate versions.   C: ECD. Dbw. Orange type.

CD - AFTERGLOW
OHM 026
Shine On You Crazy Diamond/ Brain Damage/ Wish You Were Here/ Lost Paradise/ Money/ Comfortably Numb/ Another Brick In The Wall Pt. 2
R: Ex. Audience.   S: Europe '90.   C: ECD. Dcc. Time 68:00.

CD - AND THE BELLS TOLLS
HOME RECORDS HR 5950/51
CD1: Intro - Astronomy Domine (3:39)/ Learning To Fly (5:05)/ What Do You Want From Me (4:50)/ On The Turning Away (6:14)/ Take It Back (6:13)/ Coming Back To Life (6:23)/ Sorrow (10:26)/ Keep Talking (7:08)/ One Of These Days (7:02)/ Shine On You Crazy Diamond (9:47)/ Breath In The Air (2:52)/ Time (6:50)
CD2: High Hopes (7:56)/ The Great Gig In The Sky (5:42)/ Wish You Were Here (5:43)/ Us And Them (6:35)/ Money (8:17)/ Another Brick In The Wall (7:11)/ Comfortably Numb (9:45)/ Hey You (5:08)/ Run Like Hell (8:25)
R: Poor-G. Audience.   S: Complete show, Louisiana May '94.   C: ECD. Dcc. Pic CD.

CD - THE BELL GETS LOUDER
KISS THE STONE KTS 339/40
CD1: Astronomy Domine/ Learning To Fly/ What Do You Want From Me/ On The Turning Away/ Take It Back/ Coming Back To Life/ Sorrow/ Keep Talking/ One Of These Days/ Shine On You Crazy Diamond/ Breath In The Air
CD2: Time/ High Hopes/ The Great Gig In The Sky/ Wish You Were Here/ Us And Them/ Money/ Another Brick In The Wall/ Comfortably Numb/ Hey You/ Run Like Hell/ Eclipse
R: Vg. Audience.   S: Yankee Stadium, NY June 11 '94. CD2 track 11 Giants Stadium, Meadowlands, NJ July 18 '94.   C: ECD. Dcc. Pic CD. Time CD1 75:07. CD2 79:03.

CD - BELLE DE COLOGNE
PF 020894
CD1: Intro - Astronomy Domine (4:30)/ Learning To Fly (5:39)/ What Do You Want From Me (4:44)/ Take It Back (5:34)/ A Great Day For Freedom (5:39)/ Sorrow (10:42)/ Keep Talking (7:06)/ One Of These Days (7:16)/ Shine On You Crazy Diamond (11:40)/ Breathe (2:37)/ Time (6:56)
CD2: High Hopes (8:00)/ The Great Gig In The Sky (5:23)/ Wish You Were Here (5:36)/ Us And Them (6:20)/ Money (9:08)/ Another Brick In The Wall (7:30)/ Comfortably Numb (10:22)/ Hey You (5:40)/ Run Like Hell (8:50)/ Keep Talking (5:28)*
R: Vg. Audience.   S: Mungersdorf Stadioon, Cologne, Germany Aug. 8 '94. *MTV's Pink Floyd weekend.   C: ECD. Dcc. Pic CD.

CD - DESK TAPE DARKSIDE II
HBO 2
Pigs On A Wing (1)/ Pigs On A Wing (2)/ Wish You Were Here/ Shine On You Crazy Diamond (parts 5-9)/ Brain Damage/ Eclipse
R: G-Vg.   S: Vienna & Berlin '77.   C: ECD. Dcc.

CD - THE DIVISION BELL TOUR 1994
CD1: Astronomy Domine/ Learning To Fly/ What Do You Want From Me/ Take It Back/ Lost For Words/ Sorrow/ Great Day For Freedom/ Keep Talking/ One Of These Days/ Shine On You Crazy Diamond/ Breathe

CD2: Time/ High Hopes/ Wish You Were Here/ Another Brick In The Wall/ The Great Gig In The Sky/ Us And Them/ Money/ Comfortably Numb/ Hey You/ Run Like Hell
R: Ex. Audience.   S: USA '94.   C: ECD. Dcc. Time CD1 70:22. CD2 68:09.

CD - EARL'S COURT 94
SYD001/SYD002
CD1: Intro - Shine On You Crazy Diamond/ Learning To Fly/ High Hopes/ Take It Back/ Coming Back To Life/ Sorrow/ Keep Talking/ Another Brick Wall/ One Of These Days
CD2: Speak To Me/ Breathe/ On The Run/ Time/ Breathe Reprise/ Great Gig In The Sky/ Money/ Us And Them/ Any Colour You Like/ Brain Damage/ Eclipse/ Wish You Were/ Comfortably Numb/ Run Like Hell
R: Ex. Audience.   S: Earl's Court Oct. 15 '94. C: ECD. Time CD1 72:52. CD2 72:49.

CD - EARL'S COURT OCTOBER 20TH 1994
LORDS OF ARCHIVE L.A.R. 4
CD1: Intro - Shine On You Crazy Diamond/ Learning To Fly/ High Hopes/ Take It Back/ Coming Back To Life/ Sorrow/ Keep Talking/ Another Brick Wall/ One Of These Days
CD2: Speak To Me/ Breathe/ On The Run/ Time/ The Great Gig In The Sky/ Money/ Us And Them/ Any Colour You Like/ Brain Damage/ Eclipse/ Wish You Were Here/ Comfortably Numb/ Run Like Hell
R: Ex. Audience.   S: Earl's Court Oct. 20 '94. C: ECD. Dcc. Booklet with color pictures from gig. Time CD1 73:14. CD2 71:16.

CD - FLOYD IN EUROPE
ALL OF US AS 36/2
CD1: Intro - Yet Another Movie/ Round And Round/ Sorrow/ The Dogs Of War/ Comfortably Numb/ Run Like Hell/ One Of These Days
CD2: Take It Back/ Wish You Were Here/ Us And Them/ Money/ Another Brick In The Wall/ High Hopes/ Time
R: Vg-Ex. Audience.   S: Lausanne Sept. 25 94. C: ECD. Dcc. Pic CD. CD1 49:40. CD2 45:30.

CD - FOR WHOM THE BELLS TOOL
PLUTO RECORDS PLR CD 9413/AB
CD1: Intro - Astronomy Domine (4:50)/ Learning To Fly (5:12)/ What Do You Want From Me? (4:30)/ A Great Day For Freedom (4:54)/ Sorrow (9:48)/ Take It Back (6:05)/ On The Turning Way (7:08) Keep Talking (6:50)/ One Of These Days (6:00)/ Shine On You Crazy Diamond (10:40)/ Breathe (2:55)/ Time (5:40)/ Breathe (1:10)
CD2: High Hopes (8:08)/ Wish You Were Here (5:45)/ Another Brick In The Wall (Part 2) (6:15)/ The Great Gig In The Sky (5:00)/ Us And Them (7:40)/ Money (8:05)/ Comfortably Numb (8:43)/ Hey You (4:25)/ Run Like Hell (7:32)
R: Exs. Audience.   S: Jack Murphy Stadium, San Diego Apr. 14 '94.   C: ECD. Pink/black/yellow cover. Booklet.

CD - THE GIANTS AT THE GIANTS
OCTOPUS OCTO 033-034
CD1: Shine On You Crazy Diamond (Part 1) (11:55)/ Learning To Fly (6:05)/ High Hopes (8:07)/ Take It Back (6:40)/ Coming Back To Life (6:11)/ Sorrow (10:16)/ Keep Talking (7:21)/ Another Brick In The Wall (Part 2) (7:05)/ One Of These Days (6:56)
CD2: Breathe, On The Run (9:28)/ Time (6:48)/ The Great Gig In The Sky (5:11)/ Money (8:17)/ Us And Them, Any Colour You Like (10:05)/ Brain Damage, Eclipse (6:33)/ Wish You Were Here (6:14)/ Comfortably Numb (10:06)/ Run Like Hell (8:47)
R: Vg-Ex. Audience.   S: Giants Stadium, East Rutherford, NJ July 17 '94.   C: ECD. Dcc.

CD - THE GREAT GIG ON THE MOON
TEDDY BEAR RECORDS TB 35
Eclipse Suite Medley: Speak To Me (2:04), Breathe (5:13), On The Run (3:30), Time (9:06), The Great Gig In The Sky (3:25), Money (6:25), Us And Them (3:00), Any Colour You Like (3:05), Brain Damage (4:03), Eclipse (7:12)/ One Of These Days (10:27)/ Careful With That Axe, Eugene (12:35)
R: Vg-Ex. Audience.   S: Sapporo, Japan Mar. 12 72.   C: ECD. Pic CD.

CD - JURASSIC SPARKS
RED PHANTOM RPCD 2165/66
CD1: Astronomy Domine (4:59)/ Learning To Fly (5:51)/ What Do You Want From Me (4:43)/ A Great Day For Freedom (4:23)/ A New Machine Part 2 (9:59)/ Take It Back (6:02)/ On The Turning Away (7:39)/ Keep Talking (7:09)/ One Of These Days (5:53)/ Shine On You Crazy Diamonds Part 1 (11:23)/ Breathe (2:51)/ Time (7:01)
CD2: High Hopes (8:41)/ Wish You Were Here (5:29)/ Another Brick In The Wall Part 2 (6:26)/ The Great Gig In The Sky (4:53)/ Us And Them (7:41)/ Money (8:48)/ Comfortably Numb (9:36)/ Hey You (4:48)/ Run Like Hell (8:35)
R: Ex. Audience.   S: Rose Bowl, Pasadena, CA Apr. 17 '94.   C: ECD. Dcc. Pic CD.

CD - JUST WARMIN' UP (THE REHEARSAL IN TAMPA)
OCTOPUS OCTO 055
Shine On You Crazy Diamond (12:36)/ High Hopes (10:14)/ Breathe In The Air (2:14)/ Time (6:12)/ The Great Gig In The Sky (5:31)/ Lost For Words (8:09)/ Wish You Were Here (5:01)/ Money (4:27)/ Us And Them (8:11)
R: A few cliches but still Ex.
S: Soundcheck/rehearsals, Tampa Stadium, Tampa '94.   C: ECD. Dcc. Gold disc.

CD - THE LIVE BELL
KISS THE STONE KTS 294/95
CD1: Intro - Astronomy Domine/ Learning To Fly/ What Do You Want From Me/ Take It Back/ Lost For Words/ Sorrow/ A Great Day For Freedom/ Keep Talking/ One Of These Days/ Shine On You

Crazy Diamond/ Breath In The Air/ Time
CD2: High Hopes/ Wish You Were Here/ Another
Brick In The Wall/ The Great Gig In The Sky/ Us
And Them/ Money/ Comfortably Numb/ Hey You/
Run Like Hell/ Astronomy Domine I*/ Astronomy
Domine II*
R: Vg-Ex. Audience.   S: Joe Robbie Stadium,
Miami, Florida, Mar. 30 '94. *Soundcheck.
C: ECD. Pic CDs.

CD - THE MAN & THE JOURNEY
GREAT DANE RECORDS GDR CD 9207
'The Man' Suite: Daybreak/ Work, Afternoon/
Doing It/ Sleep, Intro/ Sleep/ Nightmare/ Daybreak
Part Two/ 'The Journey': The Beginning/ Beset By
The Creatures Of The Deep/ The Narrow Way,
Part Three/ The Pink Jungle/ The Labyrinths Of
Auximenes/ Behold The Temple Of Light/ The End
Of The Beginning
R: Vg.   S: Concertgebow, Amsterdam Sept. 17
'69 from a Dutch radio broadcast.   C: ECD. Dcc.
Time 57:26.

CD - MONEY
PALOMINO PAL-016-A
Another Brick In The Wall (5:30)/ Speak To Me
(2:23)/ Breathe (3:02)/ Money (8:02)/ Wish You
Were Here (4:34)/ Time (6:38)/ Shine On You
Crazy Diamond (2:47)/ Learning To Fly (5:16)/ On
The Turning Away (7:33)/ One Of These Days
(6:08)/ Dogs Of War (8:00)/ The Great Gig In The
Sky (4.51)/ Brain Damage (4:07)
R: Ex.   C: Australian CD. Dcc.

CD - MUTINAE
VOX 1001/02
CD1: Intro - Shine On You Crazy Diamond (Part 1)
(5:44)/ Learning To Fly (5:44)/ High Hopes (8:03)/
Take It Back (5:38)/ Coming Back To Life (7:17)/
Sorrow (11:40)/ Keep On Talking (7:41)/ Another
Brick In The Wall (Part 2) (6:54)/ One Of These
Days (8:33)
CD2: Speak To Me (2:19)/ Breathe In The Air
(2:41)/ On The Run (4:25)/ Time (6:47)/ The Great
Gig In The Sky (5:07)/ Money (8:44)/ Us And
Them (7:16)/ Any Colour You Like (3:32)/ Brain
Damage (3:45)/ Eclipse (2:14)/ Wish You Were
Here (5:48)/ Comfortably Numb (10:44)/ Run Like
Hell (8:08)
R: Ex. Audience.   S: Moena, Italy Sept. 17 '94.
C: ECD. Dcc. Pic CD.

CD - MY UNCLE IS SICK BECAUSE THE
HIGHWAY IS GREEN
OIL WELL RSC 048 CD
Introduction/ Julia Dream/ Let There Be More
Light/ Murderistic Women/ Rain In The Country/ A
Saucerful Of Secrets/ If/ Interstellar Overdrive
R: Ex. Some surface noise.   S: Recorded for
BBC Radio Wolverhampton, England Mar. 18 '67.
C: ECD. Dcc. Time 40:53.

CD - THE 1994 WEST COAST TRIP
INSECT IST 39/40

CD1: Intro - Astronomy Domine/ Learning To Fly/
What Do You Want From Me/ Take It Back/ Lost
For Words/ Sorrow/ A Great Day For Freedom/
Keep Talking/ One Of These Days/ Shine On You
Crazy Diamonds/ Breathe In The Air/ Time
CD2: High Hopes/ Wish You Were Here/ Another
Brick In The Wall (Part 2)/ The Great Gig In The
Sky/ Us And Them/ Money? Comfortably Numb/
Hey You/ Run Like Hell
R: G-Vg. Audience.   S: Oakland Apr. 20 '94.
C: ECD. DCC. Time CD1 74:47. CD2 68:22.

CD - THE NIGHTS OF WONDER
ALTERNATIVE RECORDING COMPANY ARC
013-14
CD1: Astronomy Domine/ Learning To Fly/ What
Do You Want From Me/ On The Turning Away/
Take It Back/ A Great Day For Freedom/ Sorrow/
Keep Talking/ One Of These Days/ Shine On You
Crazy Diamond/ Another Brick In The Wall Pt. 2
CD2: High Hopes/ Wish You Were Here/ Speak
To Me/ Breathe/ On The Run/ Time/ A Great Gig
In The Sky/ Money/ Us And Them/ Any Colour
You Like/ Brain Damage/ Eclipse/ Comfortably
Numb/ Run Like Hell
R: Exs. Audience.   S: Cinecitta, Rome, Italy
Sept. 21 '94 and Sept. 19 '94.   C: ECD. Dcc.
Limited edition of 1000 copies for each of two
covers. Time CD1 77:39 and CD2 76:49.

CD - OBSCURITY
SUGARCANE RECORDS SC 52005/6
CD1: The Embryo (26:26)/ Fat Old Sun (12:45)/
Set The Controls For The Heart Of The Sun
(14:47)/ Atom Heart Mother (19:21)
CD2: Careful With That Axe Eugene (11:45)/
Cymbaline (11:30)/ Echoes (16:07)/ Obscured By
Clouds (4:35)/ When You're In (6:35)/ One Of
These Days (8:17)
R: Poor-G.   S: Case Western Reserve
University, Cleveland Nov. 6 '70. CD2 Tracks 4-6
Palace Theater, Waterbury Mar. 18 '73.
C: ECD.

CD - ON THE TURNING AWAY
SPIDER GLASS SGCD 011/2
Shine On You Crazy Diamond (12:24)/ Signs Of
Life (3:54)/ Learning To Fly (5:41)/ Yet Another
Movie (7:35)/ A New Machine (Part 1) (2:02)/
Terminal Frost (6:39)/ A New Machine (Part 2)
(9:57)/ Dogs Of War (8:15)/ On The Turning Away
(8:52)
R: Vg-Ex. Audience.   S: Chicago Sept. '87.
C: ECD. Dcc.

CD - OUT OF THIS WORLD
KISS THE STONE KTS 374/75
CD1: Shine On You Crazy Diamond/ Learning To
Fly/ High Hopes/ Take It Back/ Coming Back To
Life/ Sorrow/ Keep Talking/ Another Brick In The
Wall/ One Of These Days
CD2: Speak To Me - Breathe/ On The Run/ Time/
The Great Gig In The Sky/ Money/ Us And Them/
Any Colour You Like/ Brain Damage/ Eclipse/

Wish You Were Here/ Comfortably Numb/ Run
Like Hell
R: Exs. Soundboard.   S: Earl's Court, London
Oct. 20 '94.   C: ECD. Dbw. Orange type. Pic CD.

CD - PIGS OVER BEANTOWN
ALLEY KAT AK 049/50
CD1: Intro - Astronomy Domini/ Learning To Fly/
What Do You Want From Me/ On The Turning
Away/ Take It Back/ Poles Apart/ Keep Talking/
One Of These Days/ Shine On You Crazy
Diamond/ Breath
CD2: Time/ High Hopes/ The Great Gig In The
Sky/ Wish You Where Here/ Us And Them/
Money/ Another Brick In The Wall Part 2/
Comfortably Numb/ Hey You/ Run Like Hell
R: Vg-Ex. Audience.   S: Foxboro Stadium,
Foxboro, MA May 15 '94.   C: ECD. Dcc. Pic CD.

CD - THE PINK FLOYD EARLY SINGLES
0777 7 80572 2 2
Arnold Layne/ Candy And A Currant Bun/ See
Emily Play/ Scarecrow/ Apples And Oranges/
Paint Box/ It Would Be So Nice/ Julia Dream/
Point Me At The Sky/ Careful With That Axe
Eugene
R: Ex. Soundboard.   S: Studio tracks. Tracks 1-6
'67. Tracks 7-10 '68.   C: ECD. Dcc. Pic CD.
Time 33:39.

CD - PSYCHEDELICAMANIA
TEDDY BEAR RECORDS TB 34
Grantchester Meadows (6:38)/ Astronomy Domine
(8:33)/ Atom Heart Mother (18:40)/ Embryo
(10:47)/ Green Is The Colour (3:55)/ Careful With
That Axe Eugene (10:26)
R: Vg-Ex. Soundboard.   S: Fillmore West May
'70.   C: ECD. Dcc. Pic CD.

CD - RETURN OF THE SONS OF NOTHING
GOLD STANDARD RAL- 515 NAV-537
CD1: Embryo/ Fat Old Sun/ Set The Controls For
The Heart Of The Sun/ Atom Heart Mother/ One
Of These Days
CD2: Careful With That Axe Eugene/ Cymbaline/
Looking Through The Knothole In Granny's
Wooden Leg AKA Echoes
R: Vg-Ex. Audience.   S: Lisner Auditorium,
Washington Nov. 16 '71.   C: ECD. Dcc. Gold
discs. Time CD1 57:36. CD2 59:47.

CD - SERIOUS INTERMISSION
SERIOUS RECORDS 012 094
CD1: Intro - Shine On You Crazy Diamond/
Learning To Fly/ High Hopes/ Take It Back/
Coming Back To Life/ Sorrow/ Keep Talking/
Another Brick In The Wall/ One Of These Days
CD2: Speak To Me/ Breathe/ On The Run/ Time/
Breathe Reprise/ The Great Gig In The Sky/
Money/ Us & Them/ Any Colour You Like/ Brain
Damage/ Eclipse/ Wish You Were Here/
Comfortably Numb/ Run Like Hell
R: Ex. Audience.   C: ECD. Fold-open digi-pack.

CD - SOFTLY SPOKEN MAGIC SPELLS
CD1: Intro - Shine On You Crazy Diamond/
Learning To Fly/ Take It Back/ Sorrow/ Keep
Talking/ Wish You Were Here/ Another Brick Wall
Pt. 2/ One Of These Days/ High Hopes
CD2: Speak To Me/ Breathe/ On The Run/ Time/
Breathe Reprise/ Great Gig In The Sky/ Money/
Us And Them/ Any Colour You Like/ Brain
Damage/ Eclipse/ Comfortably Numb/ Run Like
Hell
R: Vgs. Audience.   S: Feyenoord Stadium,
Rotterdam 4/9/ '94.   C: ECD. Dcc. Pic CDs.
Time CD1 71:29. CD2 69:38.

CD - TAKE IT BACK
GRAPEFRUIT GRA-034-A
Astronomy Domine (5:58)/ Learning To Fly (5:52)/
What Do You Want From Me (4:26)/ Poles Apart
(4:26)/ Sorrow (10:01)/ Take It Back (6:04)/ On
The Turning Away (7:16)/ Keep Talking (7:11)/
One Of These Days (6:22)/ Shine On You Crazy
Diamond (11:36)
R: Ex. Audience.   S: USA '94.   C: Australian
CD. Dcc.

PLANT, ROBERT

CD - FATE OF THE WORLD
KLONDYKE RECORDS KR 015
Tall Cool One (4:57)/ Ramble On (5:20)/ 29 Palms
(6:08)/ Going To California (4:40)/ Promised Land
(7:29)/ What Is And What Should Never Be (6:52)/
Ship Of Fools (7:57)/ Whole Lotta Love (8:02)
R: Vg. Audience.   S: Europe '93.   C: ECD.
Dbw. Blue type.

CD - SLOW DANCER
CHAPTER ONE CO 25156
Other Arms (7:09)/ Horizontal Departure (4:13)/
Slow Dancer (10:04)/ Like I've Never Been Gone
(7:15)/ Big Log (6:34)/ Burning Down One Side
(5:03)
R: Exs. Soundboard.   S: Dallas '83.   C: ECD.
Dcc.

CD - 29 PALMS AND 1 PLANT
HAMMERJACK HJ 014
Interview/ 29 Palms/ Thank You/ That's Why I'm In
The Mood/ Whole Lotta Love/ Hurting Kind/ Ship
Of Fools/ If I Were A Carpenter/ Going To
California/ I Believe
R: Exs. Soundboard.   S: Amsterdam, Paradiso
Dec. 13 '93.   C: ECD. Dcc. Time 78:15.

CD - TWO DAYS IN THE COUNTRY
SILVER RARITIES SIRA 104
North Country/ Babe I'm Gonna Leave You/ In The
Evening/ Ramble On/ Misty Mountain/ Thank You/
29 Palms/ If I Were A Carpenter/ North Country/
Jesus On The Mainline/ Babe I'm Gonna Leave
You/ Whole Lotta Love
R: Ex. Audience.   S: Tracks 1-4 Cropredy Aug.
14 '92. Tracks 5-12 Cropredy Aug. 14 '92.
C: ECD. Dcc. Time 73:01.

PLANT, ROBERT AND JIMMY PAGE

CD - TOGETHER AGAIN
0P94PPB
Baby Please Don't Go (4:09)/ I Can't Quit You
(6:02)/ I've Been Down So Long (2:57)/ That's
Why I Love You (2:45)/ Train Kept A Rollin' (4:01)/
Ramble On (4:55)*/ Going To California (4:08)*/
What Is & What Should Never Be (6:20)**/ You
Shook Me (10:38)**/ Custard Pie, Black Dog
(3:53)***/ Train Kept A Rollin' (3:42)***/ Stairway
To Heaven (9:12)***
R: G-Vg. Audience.   S: Buxton May 17 '94.
*Cologne June 4 '93. **Brixton July 16 '93.
***Birmingham Nov. 21 '88.   C: ECD. Dcc.

POP, IGGY

CD - OUT ON THE STREETS AGAIN
KISS THE STONE KTS 236
Wild America (6:00)/ Louie-Louie (4:01)/ Highway
(3:32)/ Out On The Street Again (1:46)/ Social Life
(4:02)/ I'm Making This Up (1:55)/ Boogie Boy
(3:20)/ Raw Power (4:10)/ Caesar (4:08)/ I Wanna
Be Your Dog (4:32)/ No Fun (4:40)/ The
Passenger (6:00)/ Fuckin' Alone (4:35)/ Lust for
Life (5:19)/ Wild America (4:34)
R: Exs. Soundboard.   S: Tracks 1-9 Toronto,
Canada Oct. '94. Tracks 10-15 Lowland Paradise
Fest, Dronten, Holland '93.   C: ECD. Dcc.
Pic CD.

CD - ROCK HARD
KISS THE STONE KTS 399
Raw Power/ TV Eye/ I Wanna Be Your Dog/ The
Passenger/ Search And Destroy/ Lust For Life/
Home/ No Fun/ Cold Metal/ Louie-Louie/ Rip It Up/
Instinct/ Kill City/ 1969/ Penetration/ Power And
Freedom/ Your Pretty Face Is Going To Hell/ High
On You
R: Exs. Soundboard.   S: Tracks 1-11 Phoenix
July 17 '94. Tracks 12-18 New York July 20 '88.
C: ECD. Dcc. Pic CD. Time 77:21.

CD - TOUGH GUYS DO DANCE
TEDDY BEAR RECORDS TB 29
Down On The Street (3:13)/ Raw Power (3:53)/
T.V. Eye (5:45)/ Hate (7:36)/ Real Wild Child
(3:09)/ Loose (3:09)/ I Wanna Be Your Dog (4:20)/
The Passenger (6:15)/ Fuckin' Alone (5:13)/ Lust
For Life (5:21)/ Wild America (3:59)/ Home (3:49)/
Sickness (2:35)/ Louie Louie (7:54)/ I Wanna Be
Your Dog (acoustic version) (3:22)
R: Exs. Soundboard.   S: Tracks 1-14 Milano,
Italy Oct. 27 '93. Track 15 FM broadcast '93.
C: ECD. Pic CD.

PORNO FOR PYROS

CD - PORN AGAIN
HAWK 015
Orgasm (2:42)/ Sadness (2:27)/ Meija (3:31)/ Bad
Shit (3:530/ Tonight (3:30)/ Cursed Female (3:38)/
Cursed Male (4:53)/ Pets (3:32)/ Dominate Her

(2:43)/ Blood Rag (4:07)/ Packin' 25 (5:30)/ Black
Girlfriend (5:22)/ Porno For Pyros (4:30)
R: Ex. Audience.   S: Roskild Festival '93.
C: ECD. Dcc. Pic CD.

CD - WOODSTOCK 1994
OCTOPUS OCTO 049
Where You Coming From (6:25)/ Sadness (2:27)/
Meija (3:29)/ Bad Shit (4:49)/ Give Away (4:21)/
Swear I'd Kill Ya (4:25)/ Tahitian Sea (5:21)/
Cursed Female (3:51/ Pets (5:23)/ They Fell In
Love (2:48)/ Blow Away (3:50)/ Earth (2:15)/ Porno
For Pyros (3:49)/ Tonight (3:38)/ Cursed Male
(4:54)/ Dominate Her (2:42)/ Blood Rag (4:05)/
Packin' 25 (5:32)/ Black Girlfriend (4:58)
R: Exs. Soundboard.   S: Tracks 1-13 Woodstock
'94 Festival, Saugerties, NY. Tracks 14-19
Roskilde Festival '93.   C: ECD. Dcc. Pic CD.

PREMIATA FORNERIA MARCONI

CD - ANYTIME, ANYWHERE
TNT STUDIO TNT-930133/4
CD1: Celebration/ Four Holes In The Ground/
Paper Charms/ Dove...Quando/ Franco Mussida
Solo/ Out Of The Roundabout
CD2: Mr. Nine 'Till Five/ Chocolate Kings/
Harleguin/ Celebration
R: Vg.   S: Nakano Sunplaza, Tokyo, Japan Nov.
25 '75.   C: Japanese CD. Track listing incorrect.

PRESLEY, ELVIS

CD - ALL SHOOK UP
GRAPEFRUIT GRA-016-B
CC Rider (3:40)/ I Got A Woman (5:53)/ Love Me
(3:13)/ Tryin' To Get You (2:11)/ And I Love You
So (3:34)/ All Shook Up (1:01)/ Teddy Bear (Let
Me Be Your) (:50)/ Don't Be Cruel (2:13)/ You
Gave Me A Mountain (3:32)/ Help Me Make It
Through The Night (2:40)/ Polk Salad Annie
(7:04)/ Johnny Be Good (4:07), School Days (Ring
Ring Goes The Bell) (4:08)/ Just Pretend (3:56)/
How Great Thou Art (4:42)/ Burning Love (3:32)/
Hound Dog (1:21)/ Welcome To My World (1:40)/
Softly, As I Leave You (1:55)/ American Trilogy
(2:36)/ It's Now Or Never (2:27)/ O Sole Mio
(1:08)/ Little Darlin' (2:04)/ Little Sister (2:49)/
Can't Help Falling In Love (1:52)
R: Ex. Soundboard.   S: Springfield, Missouri '75.
C: Australian CD. Dcc.

CD - BLUE RAINBOW
ELVIS PRESLEY LIVE EPL 009-2CD
CD1: C.C. Rider/ I Got A Woman/ Amen/ I Got A
Woman/ Love Me/ Fairytale/ You Gave Me A
Mountain/ Jailhouse Rock/ Help Me/ All Shook Up/
Medley: Teddy Bear, Don't Be Cruel/ Trying To
Get To You/ Fever/ America The Beautiful/ Band
Introduction/ Early Morning Rain/ What'd I Say/
Johnny B. Goode
CD2: Love Letters/ Hail Hail Rock And Roll/ Hurt/
Hound Dog/ How Great Thou Art/ Funny How
Time Slips Away/ Blue Christmas/ Medley: Mistery

Train, Tiger Man/ Danny Boy*/ Gospel*/ Gospel**/
Burning Love/ Can't Help Falling In Love
R: Poor. Audience.   S: Memorial Coliseum, Fort
Wayne, Indiana Oct. 25 '76.   C: ECD. Dcc.
*Sung by S. Nielson. **sung by K. Westmoreland
Time CD1 44:50, CD2 33:18.

COMPLETE ON TOUR SESSIONS VOL. 1
VICKY CD 0211
Johnny B. Goode*/ Separate Ways*/ You Gave
Me A Mountain, You Gave Me A Molehill**/ I'll
Remember You, Polk Salad Annie, Polk Salad
Annie**/ Release Me**/ Proud Mary**/ Until It's
Time For You To Go/ Cattle Call, For The Good
Times, Over The Rainbow/ Separate Ways*/
Always On My Mind*/ I Can't Stop Loving You/
Funny How Time Slips Away**/ Burning Love**/
American Trilogy/ A Big Hunk Of Love**/ For The
Good Times**/ See See Rider**/ El Paso,
Dressing Room Conversation/ It's Over/ Film Title
Revelation, Little Rock Concert Promoter Interview
R: Vg-Ex.   S: Apr. '72. *Mar. 30 '72. **Mar. 31
'72.   R: ECD. Dcc.

CD - CRYING TIME IN VEGAS
Intro - Also Sprach Zarathustra/ See See Rider/ I
Got A Woman, Amen/ Love Me/ Steamroller
Blues/ You Gave Me A Mountain/ Trouble/ Blue
Suede Shoes/ R'n'R Medley/ Love Me Tender/
Fever/ Bridge Over Troubled Water/ Crying Time/
Suspicious Minds/ My Boy/ I Can't Stop Loving
You/ American Trilogy/ Mystery Train, Tiger Man/
Release Me/ Help Me Make It Through The Night/
Heartbreak Hotel/ What Now My Love/ Can't Help
Falling In Love
R: G. Audience.   S: Dec. 8 '73.   C: ECD. Dcc.
Time 58:01.

CD - DRUG STORY
ELVIS PRESLEY LIVE EPL 017-2CD
CD1: Intro/ C.C. Rider/ I Got A Woman/ Amen/
Until It's Time For You To Go/ If You Love Me Let
Me Know/ It's Midnight/ Big Boss Man/ You Gave
Me A Mountain/ Softly As I Leave You/ Hound
Dog/ American Trilogy
CD2: It's Now Or Never/ Band Introduction/
Medley: I Couldn't Live Without You, Bring It Back,
Aubrey/ It's Now Or Never/ Let Me Be There/ If
You Talk In Your Sleep/ Drug Story (Elvis talks
about the drug story)/ Hawaiian Wedding Song/
Can't Help Falling In Love
R: Poor. Audience.   S: Closing show, Hilton
Hotel, Las Vegas, Nevada Sept. 2 '74.   C: ECD.
Dcc. Time CD1 46:08. CD2 46:20.

CD - THE LAST SHOW
PREMIER MUSIC PM CD001
2001 Theme (1:13)/ CC Rider (4:07)/ I Got A
Woman, Amen (9:25)/ Love Me (3:04)/ Fairy Tale/
You Gave Me A Mountain (3:41)/ Jailhouse Rock
(2:34)/ It's Now Or Never (4:41)/ Little Sister
(1:52)/ Teddy Bear (:52)/ Don't Be Cruel (1:41)/
Please Please Me (3:26)/ I Can't Stop Loving You
(2:48)/ Bridge Over Troubled Water (4:58)/ Band

Introductions/ Early Morning Rain (1:55)/ Tell Me
What To Say (:43)/ Johnny B Goode (1:13)/ Band
Introductions, Solos (9:43)/ Hurt (2:10)/ Hound
Dog (5:05)/ Can't Help Falling In Love (1:45)/
Closing Theme (:25)
R: Poor-G.   S: Market Square Arena,
Indianapolis June 26 '77.   C: ECD. Dcc.

CD - SUSPICIOUS MINDS
GRAPEFRUIT GRA-016-A
CC Rider (3:08)/ Until It's Time For You To Go
(2:11)/ Polk Salad Annie (3:11)/ Love Me (1:33)/
All Shook Up (1:04)/ Teddy Bear (Let Me Be Your)
(1:06)/ Don't Be Cruel (1:07)/ Are You Lonesome
Tonight (2:38)/ I Can't Stop Loving You (2:28)/
Hound Dog (1:28)/ Bridge Over Troubled Waters
(4:09)/ Suspicious Minds (5:14)/ For The Good
Times (3:09)/ Band Instructions (1:30)/ American
Trilogy (4:58)/ Love Me Tender (2:38)/ A Big Hunk
Of Love (2:38)/ How Great Thou Art (3:02)/ Sweet
Sweet Spirit (2:34)/ Lawdy Miss Clawdy (2:10)/
Can't Help Falling In Love (1:51)
R: Ex. Soundboard.   S: USA '72.   C: Australian
CD. Dcc.

PRETENDERS, THE

CD - FIFTEEN HARD-ONS A DAY
TEDDY BEAR TB58
Night In My Veins (4:16)/ Talk Of The Town (3:00)/
Hollywood Perfume (4:11)/ My City Has Gone
(5:22)/ Don't Get Me Wrong (4:35)/ Revolution
(5:13)/ 977 (4:01)/ Money Talk (4:16)/ Kid (4:10)/
Message Of Love (3:45)/ Middle Of The Road
(4:25)/ Roomful Of Mirrors (4:15)/ I'll Stand By You
(4:30)/ Precious (3:29)/ Stop Your Sobbing (4:04)/
Fifteen Hard-Ons A Day (4:05)/ Brass In Pocket
(3:20)
R: Exs. Soundboard.   S: Rosemont Horizon,
Rosemont, IL Nov. 3 '94.   C: ED. Pic CD.

CD - NOW & THEN
KISS THE STONE KTS 324
Talk Of The Town (3:31)/ Hollywood Perfume
(3:58)/ Money Talk (4:05)/ Don't Get Me Wrong
(3:54)/ My City Was Gone (5:17)/ Kid (3:48)/ I'll
Stand By You (3:31)/ Back On The Chain Gang
(4:20)/ Night In My Veins (3:52)/ Middle Of The
Road (4:00)/ Mystery Achievement (5:49)/
Precious (4:27)/ The Wait (3:16)/ The Adulteress
(4:03)/ Message Of Love (3:28)/ Louie Louie
(3:44)/ Day After Day (5:13)/ Bad Boys Get
Spanked (3:30)/ Up The Neck (4:52)
R: Ex. Audience. Tracks 12-19 Exs. Soundboard.
S: Tracks 1-11 Europe '94. Tracks 12-19 Europe
winter '81.   C: ECD. Sepia-tone picture. Pic CD.

PRIMAL SCREAM

CD - CREAM DE LA SCREAM
HOME RECORDS HR 5934-6
Rocks (3:18)/ Movin' On Up (4:59)/ Don't Fight It,
Feel It (5:44)/ I'm Losing More Than I'll Ever Have
(5:11)/ Damaged, Stoned In Love With You (7:05)/

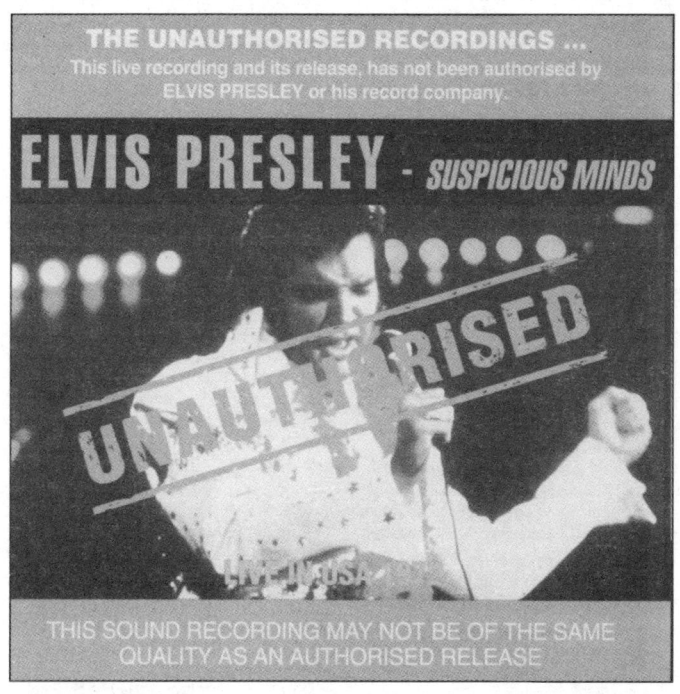

Funky Jam (4:34)/ Call On Me (3:42)/ I'm Gonna Cry Myself Blind (5:10)/ Give Out But Don't Give Up (9:53)/ Higher Than The Sun, Our Love Secret, Soul Train (9:16)/ Loaded (7:20)
R: Ex. Audience.   S: Rolling Stone, Milan, Italy May 1 '94.   C: ECD. Dcc. Pic CD.

PURPLE CHAIN
INSECT IST 36
Strutting/ Rocks/ Moving On Up/ Don't Fight It Feel It/ I'm Losing More Than I'll Ever Have/ Everybody/ Cry Myself Blind/ Give Out But Don't Give Up/ Higher Than The Sun/ Loaded
R: G-Vg. Audience.   S: Glasgow Barrowlands, Scotland Apr. 2 '94.   C: ECD. Dcc. Time 59:24.

PRIMUS

CD - YOU CAN'T PARTY WITHOUT ME!
HOME RECORDS HR 5915-8
Spaghetti Western (6:30)/ Those Damned Blue Collar Tweekers (7:21)/ Bob (4:29)/ My Name Is Mud (5:42)/ Jerry Was A Race Car Driver (2:13)/ The Old Diamondback Sturgeon (6:16)/ The Toys Go Winding Down (2:50)/ Pudding Time, Thieves (5:50)/ Sailing Seas Of Cheese (1:27)/ Pork Soda (2:24)/ Mr. Krinkle (5:01)/ John The Fisherman (1:30)/ Here Come The Bastards (3:44)/ Master Of Puppets (1:12)
R: Poor-G. Audience.   S: Fiddler's Green, Denver, Colorado June 26 '93.   C: ECD. Dcc.

PRINCE

CD - A BLACK ALBUM IN A DIRTY MIND
TCR 013
Le Grind/ Cindy C./ Dead On It/ When 2 R In Love/ Bob George/ Superfunky Califragisexy/ 2 Nigs United A W. Compton/ Rockhard In A Funky Place/ Vibrator Talk/ Vibrator/ Climax/ Lisa/ Billy's Sunglasses
R: Exs. Soundboard.   S: Studio.   C: ECD. Red/yellow cover. Time 73:04.

CD - BLUE
PLAY WITH ME PWM 008
Housequake/ Girls & Boys/ Slow Love/ Hot Thing/ Instrumental/ Strange Relationship/ Forever In My Life/ Kiss/ Beautiful Night
R: Vg. Soundboard.   S: Minneapolis '87.
C: ECD. Dcc. Pic CD. Time 60:57.

CD - CHERRY
PLAY WITH ME PWM 003
Raspberry Beret/ Girls & Boys/ Life Can Be So Nice/ All Day, All Night/ Controversy/ Mutiny/ Holly Rock/ Kiss/ Love Or Money/ Instrumental Warm Up/ Controversy/ Mutiny
R: Vg. Audience.   C: ECD. Blue cover. Red type. Pic CD. Time 52:31.

CD - FUNKY PARTY 2 NITE
KISS THE STONE KTS 246
Around The World In A Day (2:23)/ Christopher

Tracy's Parade (3:07)/ New Position (2:11)/ I Wonder U (3:25)/ Raspberry Beret (1:59)/ Delirious (1:50)/ Controversy (2:07)/ A Love Bizarre (5:56)/ Medley: Do Me Baby, How Much Is That Dog In The Window (6:52)/ Automatic (2:21)/ Medley: D.M.S.R., When Doves Cry (6:31)/ Under The Cherry Moon (3:44)/ Another (6:06)/ 17 Days (4:56)/ Head (10:07)/ Pop Life (4:27)/ Girls & Boys (6:08)/ Life Can Be So Nice (2:01)/ 1999 (3:09)
R: Exs. Soundboard.   S: Le Zenith, Paris Aug. 25 '86.   C: ECD. Dcc. Pic CD.

CD - IN ROCK 1977-1993
KISS THE STONE 3005/09
CD1 - 1977-'82: Just Another Sucker/ She's Just a Baby/ Lisa/ Turn It Up/ Medley: Feel U Up, Irresistible Bitch/ Possessed/ U Call Me/ Piano Jam Improvisation #1/ Piano Jam Improvisation #2/ Uptown/ I Wanna Be Your Lover/ Annie/ Christian/ Controversy/ When You Were Mine
CD2 - 1983-'85: A Better Place 2 Die/ Chocolate/ Old Friend For Sale/ D.M.S.R./ Free/ Gotta Shake This Feeling Baby/ When We're Dancing Close And Slow/ When The Saints Go Marchin' In/ Purple Rain/ A Case Of You
CD3 - 1986-'88: She Wants A Place In Heaven/ Big Tall Wall/ Alphabet Street Blues/ Medley: Girls And Boys, Holly Rock/ The Cross/ 80's Medley/ It's Gonna Be A Beautiful Night/ Housequake/ Blues In C/ Forever In My Life/ Wasn't My Faith/ Just My Imagination
CD4 - 1989-'91: Your Love Is So Hard/ Love...Thy Will Be Done/ Get Blue/ Bat Dance/ Sex/ Bambi/ Medley: Question Of U, Electric Man/ Medley: Party Man, What Have You Done For Me Lately/ Do Me Baby/ Nothing Compares 2 U/ Horny Pony/ Shake
CD5 - 1992-'93: I Hear Your Voice/ Hold Me/ Allegiance/ Thunder/ Daddy Pop/ Diamonds And Pearls/ Morning Paper/ Blue Light/ Medley: 1999, Baby I'm A Star, America, D.M.S.R., Johnny, It's Gonna Be A Beautiful Night/ Peach/ Race/ U Got Time Baby
R: Ex. Soundboard.   C: ECD. Box set. Booklet.

CD - INTERMISSION
CLINTON CL 790819
CD1: Intro/ Get Your House In Order/ The Undertaker/ Black Motherfucker/ Race/ Blue Light/ Delirious/ Drum Solo/ The Ride/ Bamby/ Jail House Rock/ Poure Goo
CD2: Come/ Endorphin Machine/ Peach/ Pope/ America/ Get Off/ Johnny/ N.P.G. In The M.F. House/ Deuce And Quarter/ Oilcan/ Six/ Jam One/ Get Your House In Order/ Jam Two
R: Vg-Ex. Audience.   S: Aftershow USA '93.
C: ECD. Dcc. Time CD1 67:53. CD2 72:11.

CD - LET THE GAMES BEGIN
ACORN MUSIC PRODUCTION AMCD 04
I've Got The Ride/ Blues Song 2/ Honky Tonk Woman/ Bambi/ Jailhouse Rock/ The Undertaker/ I'll Take You There/ Calling You, Well Done/ Heart In My Hand/ Deuce/ Call The Law/ Johnny/ House

In Order/ Come/ Endorphinemachine/ Peach
Extended
R: Vg.   S: Acon Studios, Kings Cross, London,
England Sept. 8 '93.

CD - LIVE AT THE SUMMIT
ROCKS 92113
Controversy/ Let's Work/ Do Me Baby/ DMSR/
How Come You Don't Call Me Anymore?/ How
Come You Don't Call Me Anymore?/ Lady Cab
Driver/ Automatic
R: G.   S: The Summit Houston Dec. 29 '82.
C: ECD. Dcc. Time 49:15.

CD - PEACH
GRAPEFRUIT GRA-040-A
Diamonds And Pearls, Let's Go Crazy (2:22)/ Kiss
(4:46)/ Cream (4:00)/ Purple Rain (4:11)/ Daddy
Pop (6:20)/ Raspberry Beret Medley: Raspberry
Beret, Delirious, Controversy (9:18)/ Get Off
(6:35)/ Sexy M.F. (3:30)/ Damn You (3:20)/ My
Name Is Prince (4:05)/ 1999 Medley: 1999, Baby
I'm A Star, America, D.M.S.R. (7:48)/ Pope (5:30)/
Peach (5:27)/ Sex Machine (6:20)
R: Vg. Audience.   S: USA '91. Paris & London
'93.   C: Australian CD. Dcc.

CD - PURPLE
PLAY WITH ME PWM 002
Positivity/ Wade In The Water/ The Ballad Of
Dorothy Parker/ Just My Imagination/ Jack U Off/
I'll Take You There/ Down Home Blues/ Cold
Sweat
R: Vg. Audience.   S: Roseland, New York Feb.
10 '88.   C: ECD. Dcc. Pic CD. Time 53:51

CD - RED
PLAY WITH ME PWM 009
Red House/ Charlie Parker/ Just My Imagination/
Wasn't My Faith/ Mutiny/ Sex Machine/
Housequake
R: Vg. Audience.   S: New Morning Club, Paris
June 14 '87.   C: ECD. Dbw. Red type. Pic CD.
Time 53:50

CD - 'SEVEN'
BAMBI 003/4
CD1: Intro/ Guess Who's Knockin/ Gold Nigger/
Levis's Solo/ Black MF In The House/ 2gether/
Intermission/ Call The Law/ Johnny/ My Name Is
Prince/ Sexy MF/ The Beautiful Ones/ Let's Go
Crazy/ Kiss/ Irresistible/ She's Alway's In My Hair/
Raspberry Beret/ The Cross/ Sign 'O' Times
CD2: Purple Rain/ Thunder/ Nothing Compares 2
U/ And Gold Created Woman/ Diamonds & Pearls/
I Love U In Me/ Little Red Corvette/ Strollin'/
Scandalous/ Girls & Boys/ Mayte's Dance/ Girls &
Mayte's Talking/ 1999/ Baby I'm A Star/ Rock The
House/ America/ DMSR/ Peach
R: Exs. Audience.   S: Mainz 5/9/'93.
C: Japanese. CD. Dcc. Time CD1 68:23.
CD2 57:51.

CD - WELCOME 2 THE BEAUTIFUL EXPERIENCE
KISS THE STONE KTS 285
Interactive/ Days Of Wild/ Now/ The Ride/ The
Jam/ I Believe In U/ Shhh/ What'd I Say/ Peak The
Technique/ Martial Law/ None Of Your Business
R: Exs. Soundboard.   S: Minneapolis Feb. 13
'94.   C: ECD. Dcc. Pic CD. Time 51:40.

CD - WHAT AM I DOING AFTERSHOW?
MAD 5
Oilcan/ Drum Solo/ Levi Talks/ Gold Nigger/ Call
The Law/ 2 Gether/ House/ Intermission/ Johnny/
Peach/ Race/ 1999/ Baby I'm A Star/ Rock The
House/ America/ D.M.S.R./ The Pope/ Peach
R: Poor.   S: After gig club party Brussels,
Belgium '93.

PULP

CD - FICTION ROMANCE
KISS THE STONE KTS 371
She's A Lady/ Lip Gloss/ Razzamatazz/
Underwear/ His 'N' Hers/ Common People/
Joyriders/ Do You Remember The First Time/
Babies
R: Exs. Soundboard.   S: Tour '94.   C: ECD.
Dcc. Pic CD. Time 46:41.

QUEEN

CD – A NIGHT AT THE COURT
TARANTULA TNT 007/8
CD1: Intro - Procession (taped)/ Tie Your Mother
Down/ Ogre Battle/ White Queen/ Somebody To
Love/ Medley: Killer Queen, Good Old Fashioned
Lover Boy, The Millionaire Waltz, You're My Best
Friend/ Bring Back That Leroy Brown/ Death On
Two Legs/ Brighton Rock/ '39/ You Take My
Breath Away/ White Man/ The Prophet's Song
CD2: Bohemian Rhapsody/ Stone Cold Crazy/ In
The Lap Of The Gods (revisited)/ Now I'm Here/
Liar/ Medley: Lucille, Jailhouse Rock, Stupid
Cupid, Be Bop A Lula/ God Save The Queen
(London June 6 '77)/ Procession/ Father To Son/
Son And Daughter/ Ogre Battle/ Hangman/ Keep
Yourself Alive (cut)
R: Vg-Ex.   S: Earls Court, London, England June
6 '77. Last 6 tracks on CD2 are from Town Hall,
Birmingham, England Nov. 21 '73.   C: ECD.
Dcc. Time CD1 73:29. CD2 59:53.

CD - BOHEMIAN RHAPSODY (VOL. 2)
BANANA BAN-038-B
One Vision (4:27)/ Tie Your Mother Down (3:55)/
In The Lap Of The Gods (2:16)/ Seven Seas Of
Rhye (1:42)/ Tear It Up (1:54)/ A Kind Of Magic
(5:55)/ Under Pressure (3:35)/ Another One Bites
The Dust (5:06)/ Who Wants To Live Forever?
(4:14)/ I Want To Break Free (3:26)/ Impromptu
(3:00)/ Gimme Some Lovin' (1:57)/ Brighton Rock

(8:04)/ Now I'm Here (5:20)
R: Vg-Ex. Soundboard. S: Europe '86.
C: Australian CD. Dcc.

CD - BOHEMIAN RHAPSODY (VOL. 3)
BANANA BAN-038-C
Love Of My Life (3:49)/ Is This The World We
Created? (2:36)/ You're So Square (Baby I Don't
Care) (1:28)/ Hello, Mary Lou (Goodbye Heart)
(1:24)/ Tutti Frutti (3:13)/ Bohemian Rhapsody
(4:30)/ Hammer To Fall (4:41)/ Crazy Little Thing
Called You (4:54)/ Radio Ga-Ga (5:58)/ We Will
Rock You (2:56)/ Friends Will Be Friends (2:00)/
We Are The Champions (3:32)
R: Vg-Ex. Soundboard. S: Europe '86.
C: Australian CD. Dcc.

CD – THE CARRIAGE OF MYSTERY
REX DISCS TSD VISION 686
One Vision/ Tie Your Mother Down/ In The Lap Of
The Gods (revisited)/ Seven Seas Of Rhye/ Under
Pressure/ Another One Bites The Dust/ Who
Wants To Live Forever/ Love Of My Life/
Bohemian Rhapsody/ Crazy Little Thing Called
Love/ We Will Rock You/ Friends Will Be Friends/
We Are The Champions/ Tear It Up/ A Kind Of
Magic/ I Want To Break Free/ Hammer To Fall/
God Save The Queen
R: Exs. FM–Broadcast. S: Mannheim, Germany
June 21 '86. C: ECD. Dcc. Pic CD. Wrong info
on cover. Time 69:13

CD – DOMO ARIGATO
AULICA A 2157
CD1: Intro: Flash's Theme (4:04) (taped)/ We Will
Rock You (3:21)/ Action This Day (5:08)/
Somebody To Love (7:52)/ Calling All Girls (4:24)/
Medley: Now I'm Here, Put Out The Fire, Dragon
Attack, Now I'm Here (12:30)/ Love Of My Life
(4:05)/ Save Me (6:02)
CD2: Get Down Make Love (5:02)/ Guitar Solo
(9:04)/ Body Language (3:09)/ Under Pressure
(4:28)/ Fat Bottomed Girls (5:28)/ Crazy Little
Thing Called Love (5:31)/ Spread Your Wings
(1:10) (short improvisation)/ Saturday Night's
Alright For Fighting (1:40)/ Bohemian Rhapsody
(5:43)/ Tie Your Mother Down (3:56)/ Another One
Bites The Dust (2:56)/ Jailhouse Rock (4:45)/ We
Are The Champions (3:50)/ God Save The Queen
(1:57)
R: Exs. Audience. S: Osaka, Japan October 24
'82. C: ECD. Dcc. Taken from "Get Down" 2-LP
vinyl.

CD – LIVE IN JAPAN 1982.10.29
BGS 1992–1
Intro: Flash's Theme (taped), Rock It/ We Will
Rock You/ Action This Day/ Play The Game/
Calling All Girls/ Medley: Now I'm Here, Put Out
The Fire, Dragon Attack, Now I'm Here/ Teo
Torriatte/ Guitar Solo/ Fat Bottomed Girls/ Crazy
Little Thing Called Love/ Bohemian Rhapsody/
Another One Bites The Dust/ We Will Rock You/
We Are The Champions/ God Save The Queen

R: Exs. Audience. S: Hokkaidoritso Sangyo
Kyoshinakaijo, Sapporo, Japan Oct. 29 '82.
C: Asia CD. Dcc. Time 73:43

LP - MAKE ME FEEL LIKE A MILLIONAIRE
S1: Tie Your Mother Down (3:45)/ Orge Battle
(4:55)/ White Queen (6:38)/ Somebody To Love
(6:13)/ Killer Queen (2:34)/ Good Old Fashion
Lover Boy (3:30)/ Millionaire Waltz (2:30)
S2: You're My Best Friend (2:00)/ Bring Back That
Leroy Brown (1:20)/ Death On Two Legs (4:50)/
Doing All Right (6:00)/ Brighton Rock (13:30)/
Guitar Solo
S3: '39 (4:00)/ You Take My Breath Away (3:45)/
White Man (11:50)/ Vocal Solo, Prophets Song,
Bohemian Rhapsody (5:10)/ Keep Yourself Alive
(4:50)/ Drum Solo
S4: Stone Cold Crazy (2:08)/ In The Lap Of The
Gods (3:50)/ Now I'm Here (4:30)/ Liar (8:20)/
Lucille (2:18)/ Jailhouse Rock (5:27)/ Stupid Cupid
(1:20)/ God Save The Queen (1:25)
R: Exs. Soundtrack for unused concert film.
S: Earl's Court, London June 7 '77. C: Eb. Silk
screened gatefold cover. Inside has B&w pictures
from show. Photocopy booklet with pictures from
show. One black record, one white. DL. Very
limited edition of 50 numbered copies - numbered
on back cover and records' paper sleeves.

CD - THE MERCURY IS RISING
ARC 003
Procession, Father To Son (6:50)/ Ogre Battle
(5:10)/ Son And Daughter (7:30)/ Keep Yourself
Alive (4:00)/ The Seven Seas Of Rhye (3:15)/
Modern Times Rock 'N' Roll (2:45)/ Liar (7:50)/
Flick Of The Wrist (*) (3:40)/ Medley (*): Killer
Queen, The March Of The Black Queen, Bring
Back Leroy Brown (4:10)/ Stone Cold Crazy(*)
(2:20)/ Somebody To Love (*) (5:00)/ 39 (**) You
Take My Breath Away (**) (2:55)/ Bohemian
Rhapsody (**) (5:10)/ Medley (**): Hey Big
Spender, Jailhouse Rock, Saturday Night, Be Bop
A Lula (10:45)
R: G-Vg. Some surface noise. S: Cleveland
Arena June 14 '74. (*) Santa Monica, Civic
Auditorium Mar. 22 '75. (**) Seattle Arena, Seattle
Mar. 13 '77. C: ECD. Dcc.

CD – REINA DE IPANEMA
BABY CAPONE BC 008
Intro: Machines (taped) – Tie Your Mother Down
(4:56)/ Seven Seas Of Rhye (3:13)/ Keep Yourself
Alive (2:47)/ Liar (1:54)/ It's A Hard Life (4:22)/
Now I'm Here (5:42)/ Is This The World We
Created...? (3:03)/ Love Of My Life (4:25)/
Brighton Rock (3:08)/ Hammer To Fall (4:56)/
Bohemian Rhapsody (5:16)/ Radio Ga Ga (6:12)/ I
Want To Break Free (3:23)/ We Will Rock You
(2:29)/ We Are The Champions (4:07)/ God Save
The Queen (1:57)
R: Exs. Video sound. S: Rio De Janero, Brazil
Jan. 19 '85. C: ECD. Dcc. From the official
video 'Live In Rio' (EMI–'85). Time 59:26.

LP – REMEMBER FREDDIE
ON STAGE RECORDS ON PD 2240
S1: We Will Rock You (slow/fast) (4:32)/ It's Late
(6:41)/ My Melancholy Blues (3:12)/ Spread Your
Wings (5:24)
S2: Now I'm Here (4:42)/ Ogre Battle (5:41)/ White
Queen (5:27)/ Medley: Bohemian Rhapsody, Killer
Queen, The March Of The Black Queen,
Bohemian Rhapsody (6:55)/ Bring Back That
Leroy Brown (1:48)
R: Exs. FM–Broadcast.   S: S1 BBC session '77
with audience overdubs (K.B.F.H. '78). S2 Live
Hammersmith Odeon Dec. 24 '75.   C: Italian LP.
Picture Disc.

CD - WE ARE THE CHAMPIONS
PALOMINO PAL-017-A
We Are The Champions (3:52)/ We Will Rock You
(2:56)/ Bohemian Rhapsody (3:59)/ Radio Ga Ga
(5:44)/ Love Of My Life (3:55)/ Mustapha (:20)/ Tie
Your Mother Down (3:29)/ Tear It Up (1:48)/ Killer
Queen (2:08)/ Now I'm Here (5:47)/ Crazy Little
Thing Called Love (5:00)/ Another One Bites The
Dust (3:47)/ Flash (3:22)/ Under Pressure (3:32)/
A Kind Of Magic (5:54)/ One Vision (4:25)/ Friends
Will Be Friends (1:56)/ I Want To Break Free
(3:25)
R: Vg. Soundboard.   C: Australian CD. Dcc.

CD – WE STILL ROCK YOU
ROLA 009
Now I'm Here/ Love Of My Life/ Is This The World
We Created?/ You're So Square/ Hello Mary Lou/
Tutti Frutti/ Bohemian Rhapsody/ Hammer To Fall/
Crazy Little Thing Called Love/ Radio Ga Ga/
Under Pressure/ Another One Bites The Dust/
Who Wants To Live Forever/ I Want To Break
Free/ Instrumental Jam/ We Will Rock You/
Friends Will Be Friends/ We Are The Champions/
God Save The Queen
R: Exs. FM–Broadcast.   S: Maimarktgelande,
Mannheim Germany June 21 '86.   C: ECD. Dcc.
Again a release from the '86 FM broadcast. Not
complete show. 'Friends Will Be Friends' not listed
on cover. Time 73:52

CD - ..WE WILL ROCK YOU (VOL. 3)
BANANA BAN-037-C
Love Of My Life (4:06)/ Another One Bites The
Dust (3:47)/ Mustapha (0:27)/ Hammer To Fall
(5:10)/ Crazy Little Thing Called Love (5:36)/
Bohemian Rhapsody (3:59)/ Radio Ga Ga (5:37)/ I
Want To Break Free (3:19)/ Jailhouse Rock (2:42)/
We Will Rock You (3:00)/ We Are The Champions
(4:13)
R: Exs. Soundboard.   S: World tour '85.
C: Australian CD. Dcc.

CD - YOU'RE MY BEST FRIEND
ON STAGE CD 12030
Sheer Heart Attack (3:36)/ I'm In Love With My
Car (2:02)/ Get Down Make Love (4:32)/ Let Me
Entertain You (3:14)/ Death On Two Legs (3:26)/
Killer Queen (1:58)/ Bicycle Race (1:35)/ You're

My Best Friend (2:09)/ Dreamer's Ball (3:46)/ '39
(3:26)/ Ogre Battle (4:59)/ White Queen (5:21)/
See What A Fool I've Been (4:22)/ Seven Seas Of
Rhye (3:07)/ Liar (8:35)/ In The Lap Of The Gods
(3:53)
R: Ex.   S: Europe '75-'79.   C: ECD. Dcc.

QUICKSILVER MESSENGER SERVICE

CD - SUMMER OF '68
BLUE KNIGHT RECORDS BKR 33
Light Your Windows (2:09)/ Dino's Song (3:37)/
The Fool (13:25)/ Who Do You Love (12:48)/
Mona (11:49)/ Smokestack Lightning (10:48)/
Codine (6:01)/ Back Door Man (4:30)/ Acapulco
Gold And Silver (12:01)
R: Vg-Ex. Some surface noise.   S: USA '68.
C: ECD.

R

RADIOHEAD

CD - CREEPSHOW
KISS THE STONE KTS 260
You (4:08)/ The Benz (3:56)/ Vegetable (3:40)/
Creep (4:09)/ Ripcord (3:10)/ Stop Whispering
(5:10)/ Pop Is Dead (2:13)/ Thinking About You
(3:21)/ Faithless The Wonder Boy (4:15)/ Blow Out
(5:48)
R: Ex. Audience.   C: The Whiskey, Hollywood
'93.   C: ECD. Dcc. Pic CD.

RAGE AGAINST THE MACHINE

CD - BULLETPROOF
KISS THE STONE KTS 319
Reaction 105 (1:38)/ Tire Me (3:18)/ Killing In The
Name (5:54)/ Know Your Enemy (5:48)/ Producer,
Fall From Grace Of The People (6:53)/ Township
Rebellion (5:10)/ Freedom (6:45)/ Fistfull Of Steel
(5:34)
R: Ex. Audience?.   S: Pinkpop Festival,
Londgraaf, Holland May 23 '94.   C: ECD. Dcc.
Pic CD.

CD - BURN YOURSELF ALIVE
MIND THE MAGIC MTM 039
Playing On The Jukebox/ Bombtrack/ Know Your
Enemy/ For The People/ Bullet In The Head/
Darkness/ Killing In The Name/ Township
Rebellion/ Playing On The Jukebox/ Know Your
Enemy (with Tool)/ Bullet In The Head/
Bombtrack/ For The People/ Playing On The
Jukebox
R: Exs. Soundboard.   S: Europe '93.   C: ECD.
Dcc. Time 72:00

CD - FUCK THE ADMINISTRATION
HOME RECORDS HR 5921 4
Know Your Enemy (6:16)/ People Of The Sun
(2:05)/ Take The Power Back (6:18)/ Fistfull Of
Steel (6:05)/ Killing In The Name Of (6:58) Bullet

In Your Head (5:39)/ Freedom Message (9:40)/
American Headline (8:05)/ Bombtrack (4:04)/
Township Rebellion (5:04)
R: Exs. Soundboard.   S: Shoreline June. 22 '93.
C: ECD. Dcc.

CD - THE KILLING ZONE
KISS THE STONE KTS 290
Bombtrack (4:25)/ Take The Power Back (6:48)/
Bullet In The Head (5:56)/ Know Our Enemy
(5:07)/ Wake Up (8:17)/ Settle For Nothing (5:17)/
Fistfull Of Steel (6:04)/ Killing In The Name (6:11)/
Freedom (6:01)/ Darkness Of Greed (3:44)*/
J.F.K. (15:30)*
R: Exs. Soundboard. *Audience.   S: Tracks 1-10
Melody, Stockholm, Sweden Feb. 2 '93. Tracks
10-11 St. Louis, USA '93.   C: ECD. Dcc. Pic CD.

CD - U.S.A. 1993
LIVE STORM LSCD 51511
Killing In The Name (5:38)/ Bullet In The Head
(5:21)/ Fistfull Of Steel (5:24)/ Wake Up (6:07)/
Settle For Nothing (5:15)/ Take The Power Back
(6:58)/ Bombtrack (4:06)/ Township Rebellion
(5:32)/ American Headlines (8:28)/ Know Your
Enemy (5:53)/ The People Of The Sun (1:52)/
Bullet In The Head (5:27)/ Freedom (4:00)
R: Exs. Soundboard.   S: USA '93.   C: ECD.

CD - WHO'S ON FIRST?
HAWK 028
Bombtrack (4:49)/ The Darkness Of Greed (4:09)/
Bullet In The Head (6:20)/ Killing In The Name
(6:09)/ How To Be Played On A Jukebox (9:19)/
Wake Up (6:29)/ Freedom (6:11)/ Take The Power
Back (6:04)
R: Vg-Ex. Soundboard.   S: USA '93.   C: ECD.
Dcc. Pic CD.

RAMONES, THE

CD - LET'S DANCE
FLASHBACK 06 91 0149
Blitzkrieg Bob (2:21)/ Remember You (2:22)/
Gimme Gimme Shock Treatment (1:45)/ I Wanna
Be Your Boyfriend (2:22)/ 53rd And 3rd (2:14)/
Havana Affair (1:56)/ California Sun (1:54)/ Judy Is
A Punk (1:25)/ I Don't Wanna Walk Around With
You (1:36)/ Today Your Love Tomorrow The
World (2:01)/ Beat On The Brat (2:33)/ Now I
Wanna Sniff Some Glue (1:34)/ Swallow My Pride
(2:08)/ Glad To See You Go (2:06)/ Chainsaw
(1:45)/ Listen To My Heart (1:53)/ Baby Sitter
(2:40)/ Baby Sitter (2:40)/ Oh Oh I Love Her So
(2:06)/ Commando (1:56)/ Let's Dance (2:05)/
Here Today Gone Tomorrow (3:08)/ I Can't Give
You Anything (1:50)/ Let's Dance (2:01)
R: Exs. Soundboard.   S: The Club, Cambridge,
Mass. May 12 '76.   C: ECD. Dcc.

R.E.M.

CD - COVERING 'EM
BACK STAGE BKCD057

California Dreamin' (2:27)/ Eight Miles Eight
(1:59)/ Roadrunner (1:52)/ Pale Blue Eyes (2:49)/
So You Want To Be A Rock'n' Roll Star (2:00)/
Femme Fatale (3:08)/ See No Exit (2:52)/ There
She Goes Again (3:18)/ Paint It Black (3:49)/
Radar Love (3:46)/ Pills (1:52)/ Have You Ever
Seen The Rain (2:27)/ In The Year 2525 (3:10)/
Smoking In The Boys Room (2:23)/ Toys In the
Attic (2:39)/ Love Is All Around (3:20)/ Funtime
(2:27)/ You Ain't Goin' Nowhere (5:37)/ One
(4:20)/ Mrs. Robinson (4:01)/ Sweet Jane (3:00)/
Afterhours (0:58)
R: Ex.   S: Various locations.   C: ECD. Dcc.
Pic CD.

CD - HITTING THE NOTE
BACK STAGE BKCD 076
Half A World Away (3:34)/ Disturbance At The
Heron House (4:00)/ Radio Song (4:31)/ Low
(5:01)/ Don't Give Up (4:16)/ Fall On Me (3:36)/
Belong (4:30)/ Love Is All Around (3:43)/ It's The
End Of The World As We Know It (4:55)/ Losing
My Religion (4:53)/ Should We Talk About The
Weather (3:18)/ Summertime (4:51)/ Moon River
(2:28)/ Dark Globe (2:20)/ One (4:24)
R: Ex.   S: Tracks 1-11 Unplugged Sessions Apr.
'91. Tracks 12,13 Borderline, London Mar. 15 '91.
Track 14 Milano, Italy May 15 '89. Track 15
Washington Jan. 20 '93.   C: ECD. Dcc. Pic CD.

**CD - IT'S R.E.M. JIM... BUT NOT AS WE KNOW
THEM**
TARANTULA TNT 006
Where's Captain Kirk/ Parade Of The Tin Soldiers/
See No Evil/ Good King Wenceslas/ Academy
Fight Song/ Spooky/ Dallas/ Half A World Away
Out Of Time/ Texarkana/ It's A Free World Baby/
Low/ Radio Song/ Country Feedback/ Losing My
Religion/ Near Wild Heaven/ Shiny Happy People/
Radio Song/ Me In Honey/ Everybody Hurts/ Drive
R: Vg-Ex.   S: Various.   C: ECD. Dcc.
Time 74:34.

CD - ...LOSING MY RELIGION (VOL. 2)
BANANA BAN-042-B
Oddfellows Local 151 (5:26)/ Little America (2:49)/
It's The End of The World As We Know It (And I
Feel Fine) (4:03)/ Begin The Begin (4:30)/ Strange
(2:59)/ Disturbance At The Heron House (3:25)/
Funtime (7:21)/ Moral Kiosk (4:41)/ Life And How
To Live It (4:36)/ Time After Time, Red Rain
(3:05)/ South Central Rain (I'm Sorry) (5:31)
R: Vg-Ex.   S: Europe '87.   C: Australian CD.
Dcc. Gold disc.

CD - ...LOSING MY RELIGION (VOL. 3)
BANANA BAN-042-C
Pop Song 89 (3:08)/ Exhuming McCarthy (3:25)/
Welcome To The Occupation (2:43)/ Disturbance
At The Heron House (3:24)/ Turn You Inside Out
(4:13)/ Orange Crush (3:59)/ Feeling Gravity's Pull
(5:27)/ Swan-Swan H (3:16)/ Begin The Begin
(3:37)/ Pretty Persuasion (4:01)/ I Believe (4:38)/
King Of Birds (4:58)/ Crazy (3:12)/ Finest

Worksong (3:53)/ You Are Everything (4:22)/ Academy Fight Song (4:01)/ Stand (3:03)/ Get Up (2:43)/ It's The End Of the World As We Know It (And I Feel Fine) (4:27)
R: Vg-Ex.   S: USA '89.   C: Australian CD. Dcc.

CD - ...LOSING MY RELIGION (VOL. 4)
BANANA BAN-042-D
World Leader Pretend (4:20)/ Half A World Away (3:16)/ Disturbance At The Heron House (3:28)/ Radio Song (4:30)/ Low (4:44)/ Love Is All Around (3:06)/ Tusk (1:14)/ Losing My Religion (4:25)/ Bandwagon (0:36)/ Endgame (3:12)/ Jackson (0:40)/ Swan-Swan H (2:33)/ Spooky (2:43)/ Radio Ethiopia (0:36)/ Fall On Me (2:52)/ Losing My Religion (Version #2) (4:29)/ Shiny Happy People (4:06)
R: Ex. Soundboard.   S: USA '91.   C: Australian CD. Dcc.

CD - RED RAIN
SILVER RARITIES SIRA 115/116
CD1: Finest Worksong/ These Days/ Lightning Hopkins/ Welcome To The Occupation/ Driver 8/ Feeling Gravity's Pull/ I Believe/ The One I Love/ Exhuming McCarthy/ Wolves Lower/ Fall On Me/ Superman/ Just A Touch
CD2: Odd Fellows Local 151/ Little America/ Its The End Of The World/ Begin The Begin/ Strange/ Disturbance At The Heron House/ Funtime/ Madhouse/ Moral Kaos/ Live And How To Live It/ Time After Time/ Rod Rain/ So Central Rain
R: Exs. Soundboard.   S: Utrecht, Holland Sept. 14 '87.   C: ECD. Black cover. Red Type. Time 49:40. CD2 48:18.

CD - REVOLUTION ON THE RADIO
MOUNTAIN STAGE MS 326
Dallas/ Radio Song/ Disturbance At The Heron House/ Low/ Swan Swan H/ Wild Train/ If You Go Away/ Birds Head/ My Youngest Son/ Hello In There/ Pop Song/ Get Up
R: Exs. Soundboard.   S: Capitol Plaza Theatre, Charleston, West Virginia Apr. 28 '91.   C: ECD. Dcc. Time 55:24.

CD - WOOD GREEN
TEDDY BEAR TB 61
World Leader Pretend (5:16)/ Radio Song (4:47)/ Fall On Me (3:23)/ It's The End Of The World As We Know It And I Feel Fine (5:34)/ Half A World Away (4:18)/ Belong (4:58)/ Love Is All Around (3:32)/ Losing My Religion (5:07)/ The One I Love (3:55)/ Welcome To The Occupation (2:23)/ Disturbance At The Heron House (3:20)/ Finest Worksong (3:18)/ Maps And Legends (3:50)/ Leaving On A Jet Plane, Sunday Morning (3:53)
R: Exs. Soundboard.   S: Tracks 1-8 '91 Radio Tours. Tracks 9-14 McCabes Guitar Shop, Santa Monica CA May 24 '87.   C: ECD. Pic CD.

CD - ALWAYS BLUE
DEAD DOG RECORDS SE-455
Suck My Kiss/ Always Blue/ Stone Cold Bush/ If You Have To Ask/ Hollywood/ Higher Ground/ Under The Bridge/ Me And My Friends/ Give It Away/ The Power Of Equality/ Funky Crime/ Nobody Weird Like Me/ Yellow Plane/ Blood Sugar Sex Magic/ So Fuckin' What
R: Exs. Soundboard.   S: Puckelpop Festival, Belgium Aug. 28 '94.   C: ECD. Time 72:21.

CD - FUNK FEST
BLUE MOON BMCD26
Give It Away/ Suck My Kiss/ Wet Weather Song/ Stone Cold Bush/ Funky Crime/ Backwoods/ Take Me Back/ In My Aeroplane/ Blood Sugar Sex Magik/ So Fuckin' What/ Higher Ground/ My Lovely Man/ Under The Bridge/ Me & My Friends/ Subterranean Homesick Blues/ Foxy Lady
R: Ex. Audience.   S: Tracks 1-14 Reading Festival 94. Tracks 15-16 unreleased demos. C: ECD. Dcc. Time 74:39.

CD - GIVE IT AWAY (VOL. 3)
BANANA BAN-039-C
Funky Crime (3:03)/ Nobody Weird Like Me (5:02)/ If You Have To Ask (4:26)/ Stone Cold Bush (3:56)/ Blood Sugar Sex Magik (4:28)/ Me And My Friends (2:54)/ Nobody Weird Like Me (4:53)/ Tiny Dancer (1:10)/ Special Secret Song Inside (4:53)/ Higher Ground (3:45)/ Mommy Where's Daddy (4:16)/ Knock Me Down (4:05)/ Higher Ground (version #2 - 4:50)/ Nobody Weird Like Me (version #2 - 4:03)/ Anarchy In The U.K. (1:12)/ Hollywood (Africa) (8:25)/ Knock Me Down (3:58)
R: Ex.   S: USA '91.   C: Australian CD. Dcc. Gold disc.

CD - PUSH TO FLUSH
TEDDY BEAR RECORDS TB 47
Out In L.A. (1:59)/ Organic Anti-Beat Box Band (3:32)/ Heartbreaker, Me And My Friends (4:07)/ Fight Like A Brave (3:55)/ Black-Eyed (4:00)/ Love Trilogy (4:00)/ Hollywood (Africa) (5:46)/ Police Helicopter (2:19)/ Special Secret Song Inside (3:39)/ Back In Black, Black Woods (4:32)/ Subterranean Homesick Blues (3:02)/ Anarchy In The UK (3:09)/ No Chump Love Sucker (2:36)/ Mommy Where's Daddy (??)/ Get Up And Jump (2:32)/ Magic Johnson (4:23)/ Never Mind (1:50)/ Bottle Ship Sex Rap, Freaky Styley (10:55)/ Fire (2:11)
R: G-Vg. Audience.   S: The Uplift Mofo Party Plan Tour, Bruxelles '88.   C: ECD. Dcc.

CD - READING
KISS THE STONE KTS 367
Give It Away (7:39)/ Suck My Kiss (4:20)/ Gone Away (6:47)/ Stone Cold Bush (4:02)/ Funky Crime (5:35)/ Backwoods (4:15)/ Take Me Back (1:51)/ In My Aeroplane (4:22)/ Blood Sugar Sex Magic (5:12)/ So Fuckin' What (2:27)/ Higher

Ground (5:22)/ My Lovely Man (5:16)/ Under The Bridge (4:56)/ Me And My Friend (3:08)
R: Ex. Audience.   S: Europe '94.   C: ECD. Dcc. Pic CD.

CD - SHARP N' NASTY
CANYON CANYON 96001
Soul To Squeeze (5:01)/ Nevermind (3:20)/ Blood Sugar Sex Magic (4:33)/ Suck My Kiss (4:20)/ Crosstown Traffic (3:00)/ Funky Crime (3:12)/ Me And My Friends (2:55)/ Magic Johnson (1:58)/ Subway To Venus (4:44)/ Higher Ground (3:45)/ Knock Me Down (4:00)/ Stone Cold Brush (3:50)/ Pussy You Sure Look Good To Me (4:50)/ Bullet Proofs (1:37)/ If You Have To Ask (4:13)/ Nobody Weird Like Me (5:03)/ Mummy Where Is Daddy? (4:24)/ Under The Bridge (4:41)
R: Exs. Soundboard.   S: San Francisco, CA '93. C: ECD. Dcc.

CD - WOODSTOCK 1994
OCTOPUS RECORDS OCTO 038
Give It Away (8:53)/ Suck My Kiss (6:00)/ Blown Away (Working Title) (4:34)/ Stone Cold Bush (4:53)/ If You Have To Ask (4:52)/ Organic Anti-Beat Box Band (5:12)/ My Other Faith (Working Title) (4:50)/ Blood Sugar Sex Magic (5:11)/ So What (InFUCKisation) (2:14)/ My Lovely Man (4:39)/ Higher Ground (5:53)/ Under The Bridge (4:49)/ Me & My Friends (5:42)/ The Power Of Equality (4:44)
R: Exs. Soundboard.   S: Woodstock Festival, Saugerties, NY August 13-14 '94.   C: ECD. Dcc. Pic CD.

REPLACEMENTS, THE

CD - HANGING IT UP
HAWK 054
I Will Dare (4:24)/ Bent Out Of Shape (3:16)/ Achin' To Be (3:56)/ Merry Go Round (4:04)/ Happy Town (3:05)/ Swinging Party (4:02)/ One Week At A Time (3:14)/ Waitress In The Sky (2:14)/ When It Began (3:20)/ Someone Take The Wheel (4:03)/ Talent Show, Send In The Clowns (5:01)/ Nobody (3:13) / Another Girl Another Planet (2:31)/ Hey Good Looking (3:15)/ I'll Be You (3:38)/ I Don't Know (2:20)/ Within Your Reach (3:57)/ Can't Hardly Wait (3:47)/ Hootenanny (3:49)
R: Exs. Soundboard.   S: Maddison, Wisconsin '92.   C: ECD. Dbw. Pic CD.

CD - SHIT, SHOWER & SHAVE
KISS THE STONE KTS 315
Talent Show/ 'Round And 'Round/ The Ledge/ Can't Hardly Wait/ September Girls/ Another Girl Another Planet/ Within Your Reach/ Left Of The Dial/ Alex Chilton/ Nightclub Jitters/ I'll Be You/ Bastards Of Young/ Talent Show/ Answering Machine/ Anywhere's Better Than Here/ Another Girl Another Planet/ Here Comes A Regular/ Achin' To Be/ Waitress In The Sky/ Don't Ask Why/ Satisfied/ I'll Be You/ I Will Dare

R: Exs. Soundboard.   S: Tracks 1-12 Lake Compounce, Bristol Connecticut Aug. 31 '89. Tracks 13-17 University of Wisconsin, Milwaukee, Wisconsin June '89. Tracks 18-23 Great Woods, Mansfield, Massachusetts Aug. 28 '89.   C: ECD. Dcc. Pic CD. Time 73:21.

ROLLING STONES, THE

CD - AT THE MARQUEE CLUB
THE SWINGIN' PIG TSP-CDS-RSAMC
Live With Me/ Dead Flowers/ I Got The Blues/ Let It Rock/ Midnight Rambler/ Satisfaction/ Bitch/ Brown Sugar/ Bitch
R: Vg-Ex. Soundboard.   S: Mar. 26 '71. C: ECD. Dbw.

CD - BLACK BOX
YELLOW DOG 046/047/048 - BLACK BOX CD1, CD2, CD3
CD1: Heart Of Stone (Oct. '64)/ Not Fade Away (Jan. 10 '64)/ And Mr. Spector And Mr. Pitney Came Too, Andrew's Blues (Feb. 4 '64)/ Don't Lie To Me, Hi Heel Sneakers, Stewed And Keefed, Look What You've Done, Tell Me Baby How Many Times, Down In The Bottom (June 10 '64)/ We're Wasting Time, Hear It, Sleepy City, Try A Little Harder, Somethings Just Stick In Your Mind (July - Sept. '64)/ As Time Goes By (July 11 '64)/ Blue Turns To Grey (Jan. 11 '65)/ Satisfaction (May 12 '65)/ Looking Tired (Sept. 5 '65)/ Paint It Black, Lady Jane (Mar. 3 '66)/ Get Yourself Together (Aug. 3 '66)/ Have You Seen Your Mother Baby Standing In The Shadows (Aug. 66)/ Have You Seen Your Mother Baby Standing In The Shadows (probably Aug.)/ Let's Spend The Night Together (Jan. 13 '67)
CD2: Get Yourself Together, Let's Spend The Night Together, All Sold Out, Yesterday's Papers, Ruby Tuesday, Complicated, Please, Go Home, My Obsession (Nov. 10 '66)/ Cosmic Christmas (Aug./Sept.)/ Family, Downtown Lucy, Hamburger To Go, I'm A Country Boy, Memo From Turner #1, Memo From Tuner #2, Sister Morphine, Still A Fool, You Got The Silver (Mar./May '68)/ Highway Child (June/July '68)
CD3: Sympathy For The Devil (June '68)/ Country Honk (May/June '69)/ Gimme Shelter, Lovin' Cup, Jiving Sister Fanny, Honky Tonk Woman (May/June' 69)/ All Down The Line (acoustic version), I Don't Know The Reason Why, I'm Going Down (Oct. '69)/ You Gotta Move, Brown Sugar #1 (Dec. '69)/ Brown Sugar #2, Bitch (May 9 '70)/ Good Time Woman, Sway (Oct. '70)/ Schoolboy Blues (May '70)
R: Ex. Soundboard.   S: Studio.   C: ECD. Box set with full color box. Each CD has a Dcc. A few more details would be good but otherwise another excellent item from the Yellow Dog.

CD - BRING IT BACK ALIVER
GOLD STANDARD 94-14-05
Jumpin' Jack Flash/ Prodigal Son/ You Gotta Move/ Carol/ Sympathy For The Devil/ Stray Cat

Blues/ Love In Vain/ I'm Free/ Under My Thumb/ Midnight Rambler/ Live With Me/ Little Queenie/ Satisfaction/ Street Fighting Man/ Honky Tonk Woman
R: G. Audience.   S: Early show, Oakland Coliseum Nov. 9 '69.   C: ECD. Dcc. Time 73:08.

CD - DEFINITIVE DEMOS 1963-1966
S6366-28
Diddley Daddy/ Road Runner/ Bright Lights Big City/ Baby What's Wrong/ I Want To Be Loved/ Snap Crackle Pop/ I'd Much Rather Be With The Boys/ And Mr. Spector And Mr. Pitney Came Too/ Andrew's Blues/ Hi-Heel Sneakers/ Stewed And Keefed/ Tell Me Baby (How Many More Times)/ Down In The Bottom/ Don't Lie To Me/ As Time Goes By/ Some Things Just Stick In Your Mind/ Each And Every Day Of The Year/ Heart Of Stone/ (Walkin' Thru The) Sleepy City/ We're Wastin' Time/ Try A Little Harder/ Everybody Needs Somebody To Love/ When Blue Turns To Grey/ I've Been Loving You Too Long/ Looking Tired/ Out Of Time/ Can't Believe/ If You Let Me
R: Ex. Some Vg-Ex. Soundboard. Some surface noise.   S: Tracks 1-5 IBC Studios, London Jan. '63. Tracks 6 & 7 Kingsway Studios, London Nov. '63. Tracks 8 & 9 Regent Sound Studios, London Feb. '64. Tracks 10-14 Chess Studios, Chicago June '64. Track 15 Kingsway Studios, London July '64. Tracks 16-21 Greenford Studios, London July '64. Track 22 RCA Studios, Hollywood Oct. '64. Track 23 RCA Studios, Hollywood Jan. '65. Track 24 RCA Studios, Hollywood May '65. Track 25 RCA Studios, Hollywood Sept. '65. Track 26 RCA Studios, Hollywood Mar. '66. Tracks 27 & 28 Olympic Studios, London Nov. 1966. Tracks 8 & 9 with guests Gene Pitney, Phil Spector and Graham Nash. Tracks 16-21 with guests Jimmy Page on bass and John McLaughlin.   C: ECD. Dcc. Time 75:38.

CD - FIRST NIGHT STAND / WASHINGTON '94 VOLUME 1
THE SWINGIN' PIG TSP-CD-180-1
Not Fade Away (5:11)/ Undercover Of The Night (4:40)/ Tumbling Dice (5:04)/ Live With Me (4:34)/ You Got Me Rocking (3:51)/ Rocks Off (5:28)/ Sparks Will Fly (4:49)/ Shattered (4:14)/ (I Can't Get No) Satisfaction (5:53)/ Beast Of Burden (5:17)/ Memory Motel (7:12)/ Out Of Tears (5:30)/ All Down The Line (4:49)/ Hot Stuff (5:26)
R: Ex. Audience.   S: RFK Stadium, Washington, DC Aug. 1 '94.   C: ECD.

CD - FIRST NIGHT STAND / WASHINGTON VOLUME 2
THE SWINGIN' PIG TSP-CD-180-2
I Can't Get Next To You (9:26)/ Brand New Car (5:43)/ Honky Tonk Women (5:45)/ Before They Make Me Run (4:10)/ The Worst (3:31)/ Love Is Strong (5:21)/ Monkey Man (5:48)/ I Go Wild (5:55)/ Start Me Up (2:51)/ It's Only Rock And Roll (5:19)/ Street Fighting Man (4:56)/ Brown Sugar (5:46)/ Jumpin' Jack Flash (5:49)

R: Ex. Audience.   S: RFK Stadium, Washington, DC Aug. 1 '94.   C: ECD.

HONKY TONK MOTEL
TEDDY BEAR TB 56
Not Fade Away (3:10)/ Tumbling Dice (4:39)/ You Got Me Rocking (4:14)/ Shattered (4:34)/ I Can't Get No Satisfaction (6:09)/ Beast Of Burden (4:46)/ Wild Horses (5:10)/ Heartbreaker (3:58)/ The Worst (2:54)/ Street Drivin' Man (4:41)/ Tumbling Dice (5:47)/ Start Me Up (4:26)/ It's Only Rock 'N' Roll (3:19)/ Brown Sugar (6:38)/ Jumping Jack Flash (6:30)
R: Vg-Ex. Audience.   S: Philadelphia Sept. 23 '94.   C: ECD. Dcc. Pic CD.

CD - I CAN'T GET NEXT TO YOU
COCOMELOS RECORDS CM034/35
CD1: Not Fade Away (5:11)/ Undercover Of The Night (4:40)/ Tumbling Dice (5:04)/ Live With Me (4:34)/ You Got Me Rocking (3:51)/ Rocks Off (5:28)/ Sparks Will Fly (4:49)/ Shattered (4:14)/ (I Can't Get No) Satisfaction (5:53)/ Beast Of Burden (5:17)/ Memory Motel (7:12)/ Out Of Tears (5:30)/ All Down The Line (4:49)/ Hot Stuff (5:26)
CD2: I Can't Get Next To You (9:26)/ Brand New Car (5:43)/ Honky Tonk Women (5:45)/ Before They Make Me Run (4:10)/ The Worst (3:31)/ Love Is Strong (5:21)/ Monkey Man (5:48)/ I Go Wild (5:55)/ Start Me Up (2:51)/ It's Only Rock And Roll (5:19)/ Street Fighting Man (4:56)/ Brown Sugar (5:46)/ Jumpin' Jack Flash (5:49)
R: G-Vg. Audience.   S: RFK Stadium, Washington Aug. 1 '94 - first night of the 'Voodoo Lounge' tour.   C: ECD. Dcc. Pic CD.

CD - IMPERIAL HEARTBREAKERS
DR. GIG DGCD 034-2
CD1: Intro - Not Fade Away/ Tumbling Dice/ You Got Me Rocking/ Shattered/ Rocks Off/ Sparks Will Fly/ I Can't Get No Satisfaction/ Beast Of Burden/ Out Of Tears/ Doo Doo Doo Doo Doo Heartbreaker/ I Go Wild
CD2: It's All Over Now/ Miss You/ Honky Tonk Women/ Before They Make Me Run/ The Worst/ Love Is Strong/ Monkey Man/ Street Fighting Man/ Start Me Up/ It's Only Rock 'N Roll/ Brown Sugar/ Jumping Jack Flash
R: Vg-Exs. Soundboard.   S: New Orleans Oct. 10 '94.   C: ECD. Dcc. Limited edition gold plated disc. Rime CD1 55:26. CD2 63:20.

CD - LES INROCKUPTIBLES
THE GOLD STANDARD LES-828
Honky Tonk Women/ If You Can't Rock Me Get Off My Cloud/ Hand Of Fate/ Ain't Too Proud To Beg/ Fool To Cry/ Starfucker/ Angie/ You Gotta Move/ You Can't Always Get What You Want/ Happy/ Tumbling Dice/ Midnight Rambler/ It's Only Rock And Roll/ Brown Sugar
R: G-Vg. Soundboard.   S: Alsace, France '76. C: ECD. Dcc. Time 72:37.

CD - LIVE IN BIRMINGHAM 1994
Not Fade Away/ Tumbling Dice/ You Got Me
Rocking/ Rocks Off/ Sparks Will Fly/ Satisfaction/
Beast Of Burden/ Out Of Tears/ Wild Horses/
Can't Get Next To You/ I Go Wild/ The Worst/
Love Is Strong/ Monkey Man
R: Vg. Audience.   S: Birmingham June 8 '94.
C: ECD. Dcc. Time 67:51.

CD - LIVE VOL. 1
JOKER JOK-053-A
Satisfaction (I Can't Get No)/ Ain't Too Proud To
Beg/ If You Can't Rock Me/ Get Off My Cloud/
Hand Of Fate/ Around And Around/ Little Red
Rooster/ Hey Negrita/ Hot Stuff/ Fool To Cry/ Star
Star/ Let's Spend the Night Together/ You Can't
Always Get What You Want
R: G.   S: Knebworth, UK '76.   C: Australian
CD.

CD - LIVE AT THE SUPERDOME NEW
ORLEANS '94
THE SWINGIN' PIG TSP CD 181-2
C: ECD. See 'Off With Our Heads' (IST 65/66) for
songs and source.

CD - LIVE FROM DETROIT 1969
MINOTAURO RECORDS CA 1111
Jumpin' Jack Flash (4:15)/ Carol (3:56)/ Sympathy
For A Devil (7:06)/ Stray Cat Blues (3:45)/ Love In
Vain (5:26)/ Prodigal Son (3:41)/ You Got To Move
(2:22)/ Under My Thumb (3:31)/ Midnight Rambler
(10:16)/ Live With Me (3:08)/ Queenie (4:06)/
Satisfaction (6:28)/ Honky Tonk Woman (4:08)/
Street Fighting Man (0:54)
R: Poor-G. Audience.   S: Detroit '69.   C: ECD.
Dbw. Red type. Pic CD.

CD - LIVE IN NEW ORLEANS
1094.1
C: ECD. Dbw. See 'Off With Our Heads' (IST
65/66) for songs and source.

CD - LIVE LOUNGE
FRONT ROW / METEOR FM 2111/12 2-CD
C: ECD. Dbw. See 'The Show Must Roll On'
(OCTO 053-054) for songs and source.

CD - MIAMI DICE
KISS THE STONE KTS 388/89
CD1: Intro - Intro, Note Fade Away/ Tumblin' Dice/
You Got Me Rocking/ Rocks Off/ Sparks Will Fly/
Live With Me/ Satisfaction's Beast Of Burden/
Angie/ Dead Flowers/ Sweet Virginia/
Heartbreaker/ It's All Over Now/ Stop Breaking
Down/ Who Do You Love
CD2: I Go Wild/ Miss You/ Honky Tonk Woman/
Before They Make Me Run/ The Worst/ Sympathy
For The Devil/ Monkey Man's Street Fighting Man/
Start Me Up/ It's Only Rock And Roll/ Brown
Sugar/ Jumping Jack Flash
R: Exs. Soundboard.   S: Miami, Florida Nov. 25
'94.   C: ECD. Dcc. Pic CDs. Time CD1 73:42.
CD2 72:38.

CD - NEW VOODOO IN NEW ORLEANS
AS 39/2
C: ECD. Dbw. See 'The Show Must Roll On'
(OCTO 053-054) for songs and source.

CD - OFF WITH OUR HEADS
INSECT IST 65/66
CD1: Intro, Not Fade Away (4:31)/ Tumbling Dice
(4:44)/ You Got Me Rocking (3:44)/ Shattered
(4:53)/ Rocks Off (4:48)/ Sparks Will Fly (4:22)/
Satisfaction (6:46)/ Beast Of Burden (5:24)/ Out Of
Tears (5:05)/ Heartbreaker (4:24)/ I Go Wild
(6:39)/ It's All Over Now (4:22)
CD2: Miss You (9:08)/ Honky Tonk Woman (5:10)/
Big Enough (4:13)/ The Worst (2:43)/ Love Is
Strong (5:30)/ Money Man (4:40)/ Street Fighting
Man (5:56)/ Start Me Up (4:21)/ It's Only Rock 'N'
Roll (4:59)/ Brown Sugar (5:48)/ Jumpin' Jack
Flash (6:20)
R: Vg-Exs. Soundboard.   S: New Orleans
Superdome Oct. 10 '94.   C: ECD. Dcc.

CD - ONE DOWN 55 TO GO!
SCORPIO
Start Me Up/ Bitch/ Tumbling Dice/ Sad Sad Sad/
Miss You/ Little Red Rooster/ Honky Tonk
Woman/ Mixed Emotions/ It's Only Rock And Roll/
Brown Sugar/ Jumping Jack Flash
R: Ex. Audience.   S: Toad's Place, New Haven,
Conn. Aug. 21 '89.   C: ECD. Dcc. Time 52:09.

CD - OUT FOR BLOOD
BANZAI BZBX 032/33
CD1: Not Fade Away (3.31)/ Tumbling Dice (4:41)/
You Got Me Rocking (3:59)/ Shattered (4:35)/
Rocks Off (5:24)/ Sparks Will Fly (4:57)/
Satisfaction (6:06)/ Beast Of Burden (4:55)/ Out Of
Tears (5:49)/ Wild Horses (5:30)/ All Down The
Line (4:38)/ Miss You (8:29)
CD2: Sad Sad Sad (4:24)/ I Go Wild (8:27)/ Honky
Tonk Women (5:14)/ Before They Make Me Run
(4:06)/ The Worst (2:43)/ Love Is Strong (5:55)/
Monkey Man (4:30)/ Start Me Up (4:17)/ Street
Fighting Man (5:31)/ It's Only Rock & Roll (4:48)/
Brown Sugar (4:34)/ Jumping Jack Flash (5:57)
R: G-Vg. Audience. CD2 track 7 skips.
S: Exhibition Stadium, Toronto, Canada on Aug.
19 '94.   C: ECD. Tall vinyl folder with pic CDs in
pockets.

CD - SECRET GIG, TORONTO 1994
TURTLE TR109
You Got Me/ Tumbling Dice/ Shattered/ Rocks Off/
Sparks Will Fly/ Monkey Man/ No Expectation/
Love Is Strong/ Brand New Car/ Honky Tonk
Woman/ I Go Wild/ Start Me Up/ Street Fighting
Man/ Brown Sugar/ Can't Get Next To You
R: G. Audience.   S: RPM Club, Toronto, Ontario,
Canada July '94.   C: ECD. Dcc. Pic CD.
Time 75:00.

CD - THE SHOW MUST ROLL ON
OCTOPUS OCTO 053-054
CD1: Intro, Not Fade Away (4:31)/ Tumbling Dice

(4:44)/ You Got Me Rocking (3:44)/ Shattered (4:53)/ Rocks Off (4:48)/ Sparks Will Fly (4:22)/ Satisfaction (6:46)/ Beast Of Burden (5:24)/ Out Of Tears (5:05)/ Heartbreaker (4:24)/ I Go Wild (6:39)/ It's All Over Now (4:22)/ Miss You (9:08) CD2: Honky Town Woman (5:10)/ Big Enough (4:13)/ The Worst (2:43)/ Love Is Strong (5:30)/ Money Man (4:40)/ Street Fighting Man (5:56)/ Start Me Up (4:21)/ It's Only Rock 'N' Roll (4:59)/ Brown Sugar (5:48)/ Jumpin' Jack Flash (6:20) R: Vg-Exs. Soundboard. S: New Orleans Superdome Oct. 10 '94. C: ECD. Dcc. Pic CDs.

CD - SPARKS WILL FLY
KISS THE STONE KTS 377
Not Fade Away/ Tumblin' Dice/ You Got Me Rocking/ Shattered/ Rocks Off/ Sparks Will Fly/ I Can't Get No, Satisfaction/ Out Of Tears/ Miss You/ Honky Tonk Woman/ The Worst/ Monkey Man/ Start Me Up/ It's Only Rock And Roll/ Street Fighting Man/ Brown Sugar/ Jumping Jack Flash R: Exs. Soundboard. S: Giants Stadium, New Jersey Aug. 14 '94. C: ECD. Dcc. Pic CD. Time 78:46.

CD - STILL ROLLING
FLASHBACK 08.94. 0238
C: ECD. Dcc. Embossed fold-open digi-pack. Nice package. See 'The Show Must Roll On' (OCTO 053-054) for songs and source.

CD - STONEAGED - SAN DIEGO SIXTY-NINE
TRADE MARK OF QUALITY TMOQ 71078
Jumpin' Jack Flash/ Carol/ Sympathy For The Devil/ Stray Cat Blues/ Prodigal Son/ You Gotta Move/ Love In Vain/ I'm Free/ Under My Thumb/ Midnight Rambler/ Live With Me/ Little Queenie/ (I Can't Get No) Satisfaction/ Honky Tonk Women/ Street Fighting Man R: G-Vg. Audience. S: Sports Arena, San Diego, CA Nov. 10 '69. C: Japanese CD. Cover is a repro of the original slick used for the vinyl boot. Time 68:10.

CD - SYRACUSE '94
SWINGIN' PIG HBR 002
CD1: Intro - Intro/ Not Fade Away/ Tumbling Dice/ You Got Me Rocking/ Shattered/ Rocks Off/ Sparks Will Fly/ I Can't Get No, Satisfaction/ Beast Of Burden/ Memory Motel/ Doo Doo Doo Doo Doo, Heartbreaker/ Love Is Strong/ It's All Over Now/ I Go Wild CD2: Miss You/ Introduction Of The Band/ Honky Tonk Women/ Before They Make Me Run/ The Worst/ Sympathy For The Devil/ Monkey Man/ Start Me Up/ It's Only Rock 'N' Roll/ Brown Sugar/ Jumping Jack Flash S: Carrier Dome, Syracuse Dec. 8 '94. C: ECD.

CD - TOOTH AND NAIL
OCTOPUS OCTO 064/65
CD1: Intro - Not Fade Away (4:06)/ Tumbling Dice (4:49)/ You Got Me Rocking (3:55)/ Rocks Off (5:16)/ Sparks Will Fly (4:49)/ Live With Me (4:29)/

I Can't Get No Satisfaction (6:44)/ Angie (4:14)/ Dead Flowers (4:26)/ Sweet Virginia (5:41)/ Heartbreaker (3:40)/ It's All Over Now (4:38)/ Stop Breaking Down (5:32)/ Who Do You Love? (4:16)/ I Go Wild (6:23) CD2: Miss You (14:30)/ Honky Tonk Women (5:27)/ Big Enough (4:08)/ The Worst (3:30)/ Sympathy For The Devil (6:21)/ Monkey Man (4:16)/ Street Fighting Man (5:20)/ Start Me Up (4:16)/ It's Only Rock 'N' Roll (5:19)/ Brown Sugar (6:30)/ Jumping Jack Flash (5:54) R: Vg. Audience. S: Joe Robbie Stadium, Miami Nov. 25 '94. C: ECD. Sepia tone picture. Pic CD.

CD - VANCOUVER FIRST NIGHT
OFF BEAT RECORDS XXCD20
CD1: Brown Sugar/ Bitch/ Rocks Off/ Gimmie Shelter/ Happy/ Loving Cup/ Ventilator Blues/ Torn & Frayed/ Sweet Virginia CD2: You Can't Always Get What You Want/ All Down The Line/ Midnight Rumbler/ Bye Bye Johnny/ Rip This Joint/ Jumpin' Jack Flash/ Street Fighting Man/ Honky Tonk Women/ Midnight Rumbler/ Love In Vain R: Poor-G. Audience. S: Vancouver June 3 '72 - first night of '72 US tour. C: Japanese CD. Dbw. Time CD1 39:45. CD2 57:12.

CD - THE VOODOO KISS
KISS THE STONE KTS 356/57
CD1: Not Fade Away/ Tumblin' Dice/ You Got Me Me Rockin'/ Shattered/ Rocks Off/ Sparks Will Fly/ (I Can't Get No) Satisfaction/ Beast Of Burden/ Out Of Tears/ Doo Doo Doo Doo Doo (Heartbreaker)/ I Go Wild/ It's All Over Now CD2: Miss You/ Honky Tonk Woman/ Walk Before They Make Me Run/ The Worst/ Love Is Strong/ Monkey Man/ Street Fighting Man/ Start Me Up/ It's Only Rock 'N' Roll/ Brown Sugar/ Jumpin' Jack Flash/ Love Is Strong*/ Start Me Up* R: Vg-Exs. Soundboard. S: Superdome, New Orleans Oct. 10 '94. *MTV's '94 Video Music Awards, Radio City Music Hall, NYC 08/09/94. C: ECD. Pic CD.

CD - VOODOO LIVE
FRONT ROW FM 2109/10
CD1: Intro - Not Fade Away (3:31)/ Tumbling Dice (4:37)/ You Got Me Rocking (4:02)/ Shattered (4:40)/ Rocks Off (5:18)/ Sparks Will Fly (5:04)/ (I Can't Get No) Satisfaction (6:06)/ Beast Of Burden (5:05)/ Out Of Tears (6:31)/ Memory Motel (6:46)/ All Down The Line (5:03)/ Miss You (8:57)/ Brand New Car (5:23) CD2: I Go Wild (9:08)/ Honky Tonk Woman (5:00)/ Before The Make Me Run (4:18)/ The Worst (2:47)/ Love Is Strong (5:04)/ Monkey Man (4:52)/ Start Me Up (4:20)/ It's Only Rock 'N' Roll (5:10)/ Street Fighting Man (5:09)/ Brown Sugar (4:53)/ Jumpin' Jack Flash (4:59) R: Ex. Audience. S: Giant Stadium, New York Aug. '94. C: ECD. Pic CD. Red/White cover. Yellow text. Pic CD.

CD - VOODOO LOUNGE WORLD TOUR '94
VICTORY 2-11894 & 2-21894 SBM
CD1: Not Fade Away/ Undercover Of The Night/
Tumbling Dice/ Live With Me/ You Got Me Rockin'/
Rocks Off/ Sparks Will Fly/ Shattered/ Satisfaction/
Beast Of Burden/ Memory Motel/ Out Of Tears/ All
Down The Line/ Hot Stuff
CD2: I Can't Get Next To You/ Introduction/ Brand
New Car/ Honky Tonk Women/ Before They Make
Me Run/ The Worst/ Love Is Strong/ Monkey Man/
I Go Wild/ Start Me Up/ It's Only Rock And Roll/
Street Fighting Man/ Brown Sugar/ Jumpin' Jack
Flash
R: G-Vg. Audience. S: RFK Stadium,
Washington Aug. 1 '94. CD: Japanese CD. Dcc.
Pic CDs. First boot from the tour. Time CD1 72:39.
CD2 73:44.

ROLLINS BAND, THE

CD - ALIEN BLUEPRINT
KISS THE STONE KTS 346
Step Back (2:24)/ Wrong Man (4:29)/ Right Here,
Too Much (6:31)/ Alien Blueprint (5:15)/ Civilised
(5:16)/ Fool (6:10)/ Disconnect (5:01)/ Volume 4
(5:07)/ Divine Object Of Hatred (4:22)/ Civilised
(4:42)/ Icon (3:46)/ Liar (8:07)
R: Exs. Soundboard. S: Tracks 1-7 Woodstock
'94. Tracks 8-13 Europe '94. C: ECD. Dcc.
Pic CD.

RONSTADT, LINDA

CD - IN CONCERT
DR. GIG DGCD 025
Lose Again/ That'll Be The Day/ Blue Bayou/ It
Doesn't Matter Any More/ Willin'/ Alison/ All That
You Dream/ Love Me Tender/ Just One Look/
Desperado/ Mohammed's Radio/ It's So Easy/
Band Introduction/ My Blue Tears, Poor Poor
Pitiful Me/ Tumbling Dice/ You're No Good/ Back
In The USA/ Someone To Lay Down Beside Me
R: Exs. Soundboard. S: Budokan, Tokyo Feb.
'79. C: ECD. Dcc. Time 73:05.

ROXETTE

CD - IT MUST HAVE BEEN LOVE
GRAPEFRUIT GRA-026-A
Hotblooded (4:06)/ Dangerous (4:57)/ Fading Like
A Flower (Every Time You Leave) (3:57)/ Church
Of Your Heart (3:22)/ Sleeping Single (4:16)/
Spending My Time (6:33)/ Watercolors In The
Rain (4:38)/ Paint (3:58)/ Knockin' On Every Door
(4:28)/ Dance Away (3:45)/ Big L (5:28)/ Things
Will Never Be The Same (3:26)/ It Must Have
Been Love (7:34)
R: Exs. Soundboard. S: Zurich, Switzerland '91
part one. See 'The Look' (GRA-026-B) for part
two. C: Australian CD. Dcc.

CD - THE LOOK
GRAPEFRUIT GRA-026-B
Dressed For Success (5:19)/ Soul Deep (12:21)/
The Look (8:21)/ Excited? (Do You Get) (4:28)/
Joyride (5:32)/ Listen To Your Heart (7:19)/
Perfect Day (5:21)
R: Exs. Soundboard. S: Zurich, Switzerland '91
part two. See 'It Must Have Been Love' (GRA-026-
A) for part one. C: Australian CD. Dcc.

ROXY MUSIC

CD - FIRST KISS
SCORPIO
CD1: If There Is Something/ The Bob (medley)/
Would You Believe/ Sea Breezes/ Remake,
Remodel/ Virginia Plain/ Chance Meeting/ 2 H.B./
Bitter End/ Ladytron/ Virginia Plain/ If There Is
Something
CD2: Ladytron/ The Bob (medley)/ Bogus Man
(Part 2)/ Sea Breezes/ Virginia Plain/ Chance
Meeting/ Remake, Remodel/ Do The Strand/
Pyjamarama/ Editions Of You/ Do The Strand
R: Ex. Soundboard. S: CD1 Tracks 1-5 Jan. 4
'72. Tracks 6-10 May 23 '72. Tracks 11-12 July
18 '72. CD2 Track 1 OGWT '72. Tracks 2-7 'In
Concert' '72. Tracks 8-10 Mar. 5 '73. Track 11
OGWT '73. C: ECD. Dcc. Time CD1 66:01.
CD2 63:44.

RUNRIG

CD - LIVE COLOGNE 11.06.1994
Medley: Every River, Edge Of The World/ Hearts
Of Olden Glory/ Dust/ Flower Of The West/
Medley: Only The Brave, Cnoc Na Feille/ Skye/
Siol Ghoraidh/ Medley: Tuireadh Iain Ruaidh,
Instrumental, Pride Of Summer/ Alba/ Pog Aon
Oidhche Earraich/ Loch Lomond
R: Ex. Audience. S: Tanzbrunnen, Cologne
Nov. 6 '94. C: ECD. Dcc. Time 70:35.

CD - LIVE
MALT 194
Protect And Survive/ Every River/ Edge Of The
World/ I'll Keep Coming Home/ Tear Down These
Walls/ Hearthammer/ Flower Of The West/ Alba/
Cearcal A Chuain/ Skye/ Loch Lomont/ Healer In
Your Heart/ The Cutter/ Eirinn/ Siol Ghoraidh
R: Ex. Audience. S: Tracks 1-11 Castle
Easplanade, Edinburgh, Scotland Aug. 31 '91.
Tracks 12-15 Hammersmith Odeon, London June
26 '91. C: ECD. Dcc. Time 76:22.

RUSH

CD - FLORIDA 1994
LIVE STORM LSCD 52605
CD1: Intro - Dream Line (5:06)/ The Spirit Of
Radio (4:59)/ The Analog Kid (6:02)/ Cold Fire
(4:29)/ Time Stands Still (5:54)/ Nobody's Hero
(5:13)/ Roll The Bones (6:09)/ Animate (7:31)/
Stick It Out (4:44)/ Double Agent (4:55)/ Limelight
(4:32)/ Mystic Rhythms (5:57)/ Closer To The
Heart (5:30)/ Show Don't Tell (5:18)
CD2: Leave The Thing Alone (10:08)/ Medley: The
Trees, Xanadu, Hemispheres, Tom Sawyer

(21:40)/ Force Ten (4:39)/ YYZ (5:01)/ Marathon
(7:04)*/ Red Barchetta (7:04)*/ The Pass (5:25)*/
War Paint (5:53)*/ Mission (5:58)*
R: G-Vg. Audience.   S: Thunderdome, St.
Petersburg, FL '94. *Bayfront Auditorium St.
Petersburg, FL '90.   C: ECD. Dcc.

CD - GANGSTER OF THE BOATS
INSECT RECORDS IST 21/22
CD1: Intro - Also Spracht Zarathustra/ Dreamline/
Spirit Of The Radio/ Analog Kid/ Cold fire/ Time
Stands Still/ Nobody's Hero/ Roll The Bones/
Animate/ Stick It Out/ Double Agent/ Lime Lite/
Mystic Rhythm/ Closer To The Heart/ Show Don't
Tell
CD2: Leave The Thing Alone/ The Rhythm
Method/ The Trees/ Xanadu/ Tom Swayer/ Force
Ten/ YYZ/ Subdivisions*/ Marathon/ Manhattan
Project*/ Lock And Key*/ Mission*
R: G-Vg. Audience. *Vg-Ex. Audience.   S: Uno
Lakefront Arena, New Orleans Jan. 23 '94. CD2
Tracks 8-12 Cornhusk Arena, Omaha, Nebraska
Apr. 2 '88.   C: ECD. Dbw. Red type.

CD - LOCK, STOCK & BARRELLED
BLUE MOON RECORDS BMCD21/22
CD1: Intro - Dreamline/ Spirit Of Radio/ Analog
Kid/ Cold Fire/ Time Stand Still/ Nobody's Hero/
Roll The Bones/ Animated/ Stick It Out/ Double
Agent/ Limelight
CD2: Bravado/ Mystic Rhythms/ Closer To The
Heart/ Show Don't Tell/ Leave That Thing Alone/
The Rhythm Method/ The Trees/ Xanadu/ Tom
Sawyer
R: G. Audience.   S: Maryland, Washington Mar.
26 '94.   C: ECD. Total time 118:43.

CD - NORTHERN HEROES
COCOMELOS RECORDS CM025/26
CD1: Dreamline (5:08)/ Spirit Of Radio (5:02)/
Analog Kid (5:44)/ Cold Fire (4:34)/ Time Stand
Still (6:06)/ Nobody's Hero (5:14)/ Roll The Bones
(6:04)/ Animate (7:18)/ Stick It Out (5:21)/ Double
Agent (5:08)
CD2: Limelight (4:44)/ Mystic Rhythms (5:52)/
Closer To The Heart (4:40)/ Show Don't Tell
(5:30)/ Leave That Thing Alone (6:00)/ Drum Solo
(6:53)/ The Trees (5:05)/ Xanadu-Prelude
Hemispheres (10:50)/ Tom Sawyer (5:00)/ Force
Ten (5:40)/ YYZ (5:25)
R: G-Vg. Audience.   S: Pensacola Civic Center,
Pensacola, FL Jan. 22 '94.   C: ECD. Dcc. Pic
CD.

S

SCREAMING TREES

CD - LIVE
HOME RECORDS HR 59193
Shadow Of Season, Alice Said (6:55)/ More Or
Less (3:15)/ The Secret Kind (3:41)/ Dollar Bill
(4:28)/ Nearly Lost You (4:42)/ Butterfly (3:46)/

Julie Paradise (6:49)/ Dollar Bill (Acoustic) (4:56)/
Winter Song (3:52)/ Before We Arise (1:57)/
Shadow Of The Season (4:23)/ Alice Said (4:17)/
Where The Twain Shall Meet (4:44)/ Winter Song
(3:59)/ Nearly Lost You (4:14)/ Uncle Anaesthesia
(3:45)/ Change Has Come (3:38)/ No One Knows
(3:03)
R: Exs. Soundboard.   S: Tracks 1-7 Birmingham,
Alabama June 11 '93. Tracks 8-9 acoustic set.
Tracks 10-18 USA '93.   C: ECD. Dcc.

CD - WINTER SONGS
HAWK 012
Before We Arise (1:55)/ Shadow Of The Season
(4:13)/ Alice Said (4:37)/ Time For Light (4:19)/
Where The Twain Shall Meet (4:33)/ Secret Kind
(3:19)/ Winter Song (4:11)/ Nearly Lost You (4:51)/
Uncle Anaesthesia (4:19)/ Change Has Come
(4:02)/ Julie Parade (5:58)/ Bed Of Roses (3:13)/
End Of The Universe (6:03)
R: Vg. Audience.   S: USA '92.   C: ECD.
Pic CD.

SEPULTURA

CD - LIVE CHAOS 93
Refuse-Resist (4:05)/ Territory (4:45)/ Innerself
(2:50)/ Slave New World (2:44)/ Amen (6:49)/
Destroy (2:07)/ Beneath The Remains (2:10)/
Mass Hypnosis (1:18)/ Under Siege (5:43)/
Instrumental (3:40)/ Nomad (5:11)/ Propaganda
(3:36)/ Antichrist (2:59)/ Murder (5:07)/ Crucifixion
(3:27)/ Biotech Is Godzilla (1:58)/ Dead Embryonic
Cells (4:44)/ Slaves Of Pain (2:13)/ Arise (3:11)
R: G. Audience.   S: Deinze, Belgium Nov. 29
'93.   C: ECD.

CD - NAILBOMB
KISS THE STONE KTS 313
Refuse-Resist (4:34)/ Territory (5:03)/ Troops Of
Doom (1:41)/ Slave New World (2:36)/
Propaganda (3:20)/ Mass Hypnosis (4:03)/ Inner
Self (4:43)/ Manifest, Nomad (8:12)/ Nomad
(reprise) (2:01)/ Kaiowas (3:16)/ Arise (3:11)/
Orgasmatron (3:38)/ Policia (2:50)
R: Exs. Soundboard.   S: Europe June 4 '94.
C: ECD. Pic CD.

CD - SAO PAOLO'S FAVOURITE SONS
SEP 002
Refuse, Resist/ Territory/ Troops Of Doom/
Antichrist/ Desperate Cry/ Amen/ Innerself/ Arise/
We Who Are Not As Others/ Propaganda/ Bio
Tech Is Godzilla/ Dead Embryonic Cells/
Crucifados Delo Systema/ Orgasmatron/ Policia
R: Vg. **G-Vg.   S: Hollywood Bowl, Los Angeles
'94. Rio De Janeiro Jan 22 '94.   C: ECD. Dcc.
*Joan Gordo (RDP) vocals. **Jan. 21 '94 with
Titas.

CD - WELCOME TO THE END OF THE WORLD
KISS THE STONE KTS 279
Intro, Refuse, Resist/ Territory/ Troops Of Doom/
Slave New World/ In The Name Of God, Inner

Self/ Altered State/ We Who Are Not As Others/
Propaganda/ Nomad/ Beneath The Remains/
Escape To The Void/ Anti Cop/ Murder, Guitar
Solo/ Clenched Fist/ Biotech Is Godzilla/ Dead
Embryonic Cells/ Crucificados Pelo Sistema/
Arise/ Policia
R: Exs. Soundboard.   S: Nov. '93.   C: ECD.
Dcc. Pic CD. Time 70:22.

SHOK PARIS

CD - METAL MAGIC
REBORN CLASSICS RC 1025
C: See listing under PANTERA.

SIMON, PAUL

CD - LATE IN THE EVENING
PERFACT 97002
Graceland (5:17)/ Bridge Over Troubled Water
(4:49)/ Born At The Right Time (5:04)/ Me & Julio
Down By The Schoolyard (3:32)/ Still Crazy After
All Those Years (3:31)/ Something So Right
(3:46)/ Homeward Bound (3:09)/ Boy In The
Bubble (5:32)/ Mrs. Robinson (3:04)/ Late In The
Evening (5:13)
R: Exs. Soundboard.   S: In concert USA '92.
C: ECD. Dcc. Michael Brecker on saxophone.

OUT OF AFRICA
PLUTO RECORDS PLR CD 9229
Born At The Right Time (5:23)/ Me And Julio
Down By The School Yard (3:52)/ Graceland
(5:08)/ Still Crazy After All These Years (3:38)/
Mrs. Hobinson (3:31)/ Bridge Over Troubled
Waters (4:45)/ Something So Right (3:39)/ The
Boy In The Bubble (5:28)/ Late In The Evening
(5:40)/ Homeward Bound (2:31)
R: Exs. Soundboard.   S: MTV Unplugged, New
York '92.   C: ECD. Dcc.

**CD - PAUL SIMON, BRUCE SPRINGSTEEN &
FRIENDS**
YELLOW CAT YC 013/14
C: See listing under various artists.

SIMON & GARFUNKEL

CD - FEELIN' GROOVY
OIL WELL RSC 033 CD
Sparrow/ Homeward Bound/ You Don't Know
Where Your Interest Lies/ A Most Peculiar Man/
Red Rubber Ball/ The Dangling Conversation/ The
59th Street Bridge Song, Feelin' Groovy/ Richard
Cory/ Benedictus/ Blessed/ A Poem On The
Underground Wall/ I Am A Rock/ Anyi/ The Sound
Of Silence/ For Emily Whenever I May Find Her/ A
Church Is Burning/ Wednesday Morning 3 A.M.
R: Ex. Soundboard.   S: Buffalo Jan. 2 '67.
C: ECD. Dcc. Time 63:15.

CD - MRS. ROBINSON
GRAPEFRUIT GRA-042-A
Mrs. Robinson (2:57)/ Homeward Bound (2:36)/

Intro (2:35)/ April Come She Will (2:02)/ Fakin' It
(3:27)/ Overs (2:16)/ The 59th Street Bridge
(Feelin' Groovy) (1:38)/ Intro (1:10)/ America
(3:31)/ A Most Peculiar Man (2:28)/ I Am A Rock
(3:12)/ At The Zoo (2:08)/ Scarborough Fair,
Canticle (3:46)/ Bye Bye Love (2:24)/ Cloudy
(2:10)/ The Leaves That Are Green (2:41)/
Punky's Dilemma (2:25)/ Intro (:33)/ The Dangling
Conversation (2:46)/ Intro (:50)/ For Emily
Whenever I May Find Her (2:39)/ A Poem On the
Underground Wall (1:59)/ Anji (instrumental)
(2:29)/ The Sound Of Silence (3:27)/ Richard Cory
(2:50)/ Old Friends (1:54)/ Bookends (1:36)/ He
Was My Brother (3:10)
R: Ex. Soundboard.   S: Los Angeles '68.
C: Australian CD. Dcc.

CD - THE SOUND OF SILENCE
GRAPEFRUIT GRA-042-B
Mrs. Robinson (4:33)/ Fakin' It (3:34)/ The Boxer
(5:30)/ So Long Frank Lloyd Wright (3:12)/ Why
Don't You Write Me (3:35)/ Silver Haired Daddy
(3:14)/ Cuba Si-Nixon No (3:30)/ Bridge Over
Troubled Water (5:45)/ The Sound Of Silence
(4:46)/ Bye Bye Love (2:35)/ Homeward Bound
(5:23)/ At The Zoo (2:15)/ America (7:24)/ Song
For The Asking (1:48)/ A Poem On The
Underground Wall (3:50)/ For Emily Whenever I
May Find Her (2:32)
R: Ex. Soundboard.   S: Ohio '69.   C: Australian
CD. Dcc.

SIMON & GARFUNKEL/PAUL SIMON

CD - MONTEREY POP
GRAPEFRUIT GRA-042-C
Intro (:23)/ Homeward Bound (2:48)/ At The Zoo
(2:23)/ Intro (1:31)/ The 59th Street Bridge Song
(Feeling Groovy) (2:14)/ For Emily Whenever I
May Find Her (2:26)/ The Sound Of Silence (4:13)/
Benedictus (3:34)/ Intro (:53)/ Punky's Dilemma
(2:22)/ Me And Julio Down By The Schoolyard
(3:03)/ Ace In The Hole (5:44)/ Something So
Right (4:15)/ One Trick Pony (4:06)/ Jonah (5:00)/
50 Ways To Leave Your Lover (4:13)/ Late In The
Evening (4:07)/ American Tune 3:33)/ Love Me
Like A Rock (3:39)/ The Boxer (5:02)
R: Exs. Soundboard.   S: Monterey Pop Festival,
CA '67/80.   C: Australian CD. Dcc.

SIMPLY RED

CD - THE RIGHT THING
GRAPEFRUIT GRA-037-A
Holding Back The Years (4:47)/ Model (3:31)/ New
Flame 94:10)/ Thrill Me (2:45)/ Stars (4:02)/ Your
Mirror (3:55)/ Money's Too Tight (To Mention)
(4:56)/ The Right Thing (4:19)/ For Your Babies
(4:23)/ Something Got Me Started (4:53)/
Grandma's Hands (3:24)/ Sad Old Red (5:51)/ It's
Only Love (4:35)
R: Exs. Soundboard.   S: New York '92.
C: Australian CD. Dcc.

SISTERS OF MERCY

Time 74:20.

CD - WELCOME TO THE TEMPLE OF LOVE
BACKSTAGE BKCD 081
Ribbons (5:43)/ Floor Show (3:38)/ Givin Ground
(4:23)/ More (6:48)/ Detonation Boulevard (3:43)/
Alice (3:34)/ Amphetamine Logic (4:11)/ Body
Electric (4:03)/ First And Last And Always (4:14)/
Temple Of Love (8:22)/ This Corrosion (7:35)/
Flood (5:48)/ Vision Thing (4:49)/ Comfortably
Numb, Some Kind Of Stranger (9:00)*
R: Ex. Audience.   S: Crystal Palace Sports
Centre, London, England Sat. July 31 '93.
*National Exhibition Centre, Birmingham, England
June 27 '92.   C: ECD. Dcc. Pic CD.

SMASHING PUMPKINS

CD - A KISS OF THIS
ROCKS 92123
Rocket (4:07)/ Quiet (3:43)/ Today (3:10)/
Rhinoceros (4:43)/ Geek USA (5:22)/ I Am One
(4:12)/ Disarm (3:15)/ Cherub Rock (4:54)/
Hummer (7:09)/ Silverfuck (12:03)/ Mayonaise
(6:45)/ Cherub Rock (4:35)/ Today (3:20)
R: Exs. Soundboard.   S: Tracks 1-11 Chicago
Metro Aug. 14 '93. Tracks 12, 13 Saturday Night
Live Oct. 30 '93.   C: ECD.

CD - ASTORIA '94
PUMPKIN MUSIC PM 054
Rocket (4:08)/ Quit (3:16)/ Today (3:21)/ Disarm
(3:16)/ I Am One (7:15)/ Hammer (4:33)/ Geek
U.S.A. (5:28)/ Spaceboy (3:45)/ Siva (4:57)/
Cherub Rock (5:08)/ Luna (3:16)/ Starla (8:50)/
Never Let Me Down Again (5:00)/ Silver Fuck
(14:35)
R: Vg. Audience.   S: The Astoria Theatre,
London, England Feb. 25 '94.   C: ECD. Dcc.

CD - DAYDREAM KISSES
HAWK 013
Rocket (4:46)/ Bury Me (4:07)/ Window Paine
(6:39)/ Snail (5:58)/ Siva (9:10)/ Drown (7:31)/ I
Am One (5:14)/ Crush (3:33)/ Silverfuck (9:25)
R: Ex. Audience.   S: Whiskey A Go Go, LA Dec.
12 '91.   C: ECD. Dcc. Pic CD.

CD - FEELING LIKE A SMASHED PUMPKIN
FLASHBACK 01 94 0226
Quiet (3:53)/ Today (3:27)/ Disarm (3:26)/ I Am
One (5:51)/ Hummer (7:13)/ Soma (8:30)/ Siva
(6:12)/ Cherub Rock (5:59)/ Starla (8:14)/ Pissant
(5:29)/ Silverfuck (10:34)/ Sweet Sweet (1:12)
R: Ex. Audience.   S: First Ave. Club,
Minneapolis Oct. 3 '93.   C: ECD. Dcc.

CD - FISHING BLUE
MIC 150
Window Panic/ Siva/ Tristessa/ Bury Me/ Honey
Spider/ Drive/ Window Panic/ Razor/ Tristessa/ I
Am One/ Waiting/ Rhinoceros/ Snail/ Hello Kitty
Kat/ Today/ Fishing Blue/ Obscured
R: G.   S: USA '90-'93.   C: ECD. Dcc.

CD - FORGOTTEN SONGS PART 1
IMPERIUM IMP 010
Spiteface/ East (version 1)/ She (live)/ Jennifer
Ever/ Nothing And Everything/ Sun (remix)/ Jackie
Blue/ La Dolly Vita/ Honey Spider (version 1)/
Terrapin/ Bullet Train To Osaka/ On My Own/ I Am
One (version 1)/ Bury Me/ Rhinoceros (version 1)
R: Ex.   C: ECD. Dcc. Time 65:15.

CD - THE GREATEST DAY
HAWK 037
Rocket (5:37)/ Cherub Rock (4:42)/ Today (3:21)/
Disarm (3:36)/ Spaceboy (3:47)/ Rudolph The Red
Nose Reindeer (1:29)/ Hummer (6:39)/ Rocket
(5:32)/ Cherub Rock (5:00)/ Today (3:25)/
Mayonaise (5:13)/ Hummer (6:47)
R: Exs. Soundboard.   S: Tracks 1-7 The
Universal, LA CA Dec. 11 '93. Tracks 8-12 Tower
Records, Chicago July 26 '93.   C: ECD. Dcc.
Pic CD.

CD - HALLOWEEN PARTY
HOME RECORDS HR 5925 31
Rocket (4:22)/ Today (3:29)/ Disarm (3:26)/ Drown
(5:14)/ Hammer (6:22)/ Soma (7:39)/ Siva (4:58)/
Cherub Rock (5:33)/ Blue (3:34)/ Today (3:27)/
Disarm (3:27)/ Cherub Rock (4:25)/ Razor (4:17)/
Tristessa (3:06)/ I Am One (4:11)/ Cherub Rock
(3:33)
R: Exs. Soundboard.   S: Crosby Auditorium, Del
Mar, CA '93. Tracks 9-12 acoustic. Tracks 13-15
live USA '93. Track 16 Grammy Awards.
C: ECD. Dcc. Pic CD.

CD - MAYONAISE DREAM
KISS THE STONE KTS 261
Cherub Rock (4:26)/ Disarm (3:19)/ Rocket (4:43)/
Spaceboy (3:02)/ Rocket (4:19)/ Cherub Rock
(4:29)/ Today (3:23)/ Disarm (3:24)/ Spaceboy
(4:07)/ Siva (4:50)/ Today (3:20)/ Disarm (3:22)/
Rhinoceros (4:36)/ Cherub Rock (4:39)/ Rocket
(4:00)/ Disarm (3:20)/ Today (3:05)/ Mayonaise
(1:50)
R: Exs. Soundboard.   S: USA & Holland '93.
Tracks 1-10 acoustic. Tracks 11-19 electric.
C: ECD. Dcc. Pic CD.

CD - RAWK
RAWK 0705
Suffer (6:03)/ Rocket (4:09)/ Bury Me (4:50)/ Snail
(6:09)/ Tristessa (3:13)/ Window Paine (7:35)/ Siva
(5:00)/ Luna (3:08)/ I Am The One (4:39)/ Crush
(3:58)/ Silverfuck (10:46)/ Rhinoceros (5:35)/ Blue
(4:42)/ Girl Called Sandoz (3:42)
R: Vg. Some distortion.   S: Den Haag, Holland
Jan. 19 '92.   C: ECD. Dcc. Time 75:35.

CD - RHINOCEROS DAYDREAMS
GOLD STANDARD 00026
Disarm/ Geek USA/ Drown/ I Am One/ Cherub
Rock/ A Silver Fuck/ Today/ I Am One/ Bury Me/
Not Worth Asking/ Rhinoceros/ Daydream/

Glynnis/ Today
R: Vg-Ex.   S: Tracks 1-7 The Lowlands Festival,
Belgium summer '93. Tracks 8-12 studio demos,
'89. Tracks 13-14 MTV '93.   C: ECD. 69:50.

CD - SOUNDS OF TURNIPS
TURNIP RECORDS
Honey Spider/ With You/ Egg/ Rhinoceros/ Stars
Falling/ Daughter/ Daydream/ Psychedelic/ My
Dahlia/ Sun/ Snap, If I Could/ Love/ East,
Alternate/ Mother/ C'Mon
R: Vg-Ex. Soundboard.   S: Demos '89.
C: Made in the USA. Orange disc. The first, and
perhaps only, release from a fan who decided to
share an early demo tape handed out by the band.
Time 59:18.

CD - SUNSHINE OF YOUR LOVE
TARANTULA TNT 010
Disarm, Sunshine Of Your Love/ Rhinoceros/
Obscured/ I Am One/ Day Dream/ Rhinoceros/
Bury Me/ On My Own/ Jennifer Ever/ East/
Nothing And Everything/ Sun/ She/ Spiteface/
Honey Spider/ Drive/ Razor/ Hello Kitty Cat
R: Exs. Soundboard.   S: Demos, outtakes and
unreleased songs.   C: ECD. Dcc. Time 77:02.

CD - 3 FEET HIGH
KISS THE STONE KTS 264
Rocket/ Quiet/ Today/ Rhinoceros/ Greek USA/ I
Am One/ Disarm/ Cherub Rock/ Hummer/
Silverfuck/ Mayonaise
R: Ex. Audience.   S: Chicago Aug. '93.
C: ECD. Dbw. Yellow type. Time 58:55.

CD - WE ARE FROM ANOTHER PLANET
MIND THE MAGIC MTM 040
Cherub Rock/ Disarm/ Rocket/ Quiet/ Today/
Drown/ Hummer/ Geek USA/ Soma/ Siva/ Window
Paine/ Offer Up/ Silverfuck/ Never Let Me Down/
Landslide
R: Ex. Audience. Tracks 14-15 soundboard.
S: Tracks 1-10 Europe '94. Tracks 11-13 Europe
'92. Tracks 14-15 radio session '93.   C: ECD.
Dcc.

SMITHS, THE

CD - ASLEEP
CHELSEA RECORDS CFC003
Wonderful Woman/ Girl Afraid/ Heaven Knows I'm
Miserable Now/ How Soon Is Now/ William It Was
Really Nothing/ The Boy With The Thorn In His
Side/ Frankly Mr. Shankly/ Bigmouth Strikes
Again/ Rusholme Ruffians/ Shakespear's Sister/
Jeane/ What's The World/ The Boy With The
Thorn in His Side/ How Soon Is Now/ Nowhere
East/ Groovy Kind Of Love/ Every Day/ There Is A
Light That Never Goes Out/ Asleep
R: Vg.   S: Track 1 unreleased Kid Jensen
session June 26 '83. Track 2 live Glasgow Mar. 2
'84. Track 3 different studio mix from Earsay Mar.
31 '84. Track 4 rare unreleased version. Track 5
John Peel Session Oct. 9 '84. Track 6-13 rare

soundcheck, Dundee Caird Hall Sept. 26 '85.
Track 14-19 rare soundcheck Oct. 1 '85.
C: ECD. Dcc. Time 70:00.

CD - THE BUTTERFLY COLLECTOR
BIG MUSIC BIG 098
Hand In Glove (2:55)/ Heaven Knows I'm
Miserable Now (3:33)/ Barbarism Begins At Home
(5:54)/ This Charming Man (2:51)/ Miserable Lie
(4:56)/ I Don't Owe You Anything (4:25)/ What
Difference Does It Make? (3:22)/ Girl Afraid (2:54)/
This Night Has Opened My Eyes (3:34)/ Still III
(3:36)/ These Things Take Time (2:41)/
Handsome Devil (3:01)/ These Things Take Time
(1:39)/ What Difference Does It Make? (3:44)/ The
Hand That Rocks The Cradle (4:20)/ Handsome
Devil (3:03)/ Jeane (3:18)/ What Do You See In
Him? (3:26)/ Hand In Glove (3:05)/ Miserable Lie
(5:10)
R: Vg. Soundboard. Tracks 13-20 G-Vg.
Soundboards.   S: Tracks 1-2 De Meervaart Hall,
Amsterdam, Holland Apr. 21 '84. Tracks 13-20
Europe Feb. 4 '83.   C: ECD. Dbw. Yellow text.
Pic CD. Time 71:40.

CD - FLOWERS
CLASSICAL CL 008
William It Was Really Nothing (2:15)/ Stretch Out
(3:03)/ That Joke Isn't Funny Anymore (3:45)/
Shakespeare's Sister (2:05)/ Headmaster Ritual
(4:26)/ Still III (2:38)/ Meat Is Murder (5:20)/
Miserable Lie (5:22)/ Barbarism Begins At Home
(7:15)/ You've Got Everything Now (4:01)/ There
Is A Light That Never Goes Out (3:45)/ How Soon
Is Now (5:30)/ London (2:09)/ Half A Person (3:34)
R: Ex. Soundboard.   S:Tracks 1-10 Apollo
Theatre, Oxford, UK '85. Tracks 11-12 National
Club, Kilburn, UK '86. Tracks 13-14 BBC Session
Dec. 17 '87.   C: ECD. Dbw.

CD - THANK YOUR LUCKY STARS
BIG MUSIC BIG 091
Please Please Please Let Me Get What I Want
(2:27)/ Still III (3:57)/ I Want The One I Can't Have
(3:55)/ There Is A Light That Never Goes Out
(4:10)/ How Soon Is Now (5:53)/ Frankly Mr.
Shankly (2:48)/ Panic (3:09)/ Stretch Out And Wait
(3:39)/ The Boy With The Thorn In His Side (3:55)/
Is It Really So Strange? (3:36)/ Cemetery Gates
(3:00)/ Never Had No One Ever (3:40)/ Rubber
Ring, What She Said (4:21)/ That Joke Isn't Funny
Anymore (4:52)/ Heaven Knows I'm Miserable
Now (4:21)/ The Queen Is Dead (5:49)/ Money
Changes Everything (4:57)/ I Know It's Over (5:59)
R: Ex. Soundboard.   S: LA Aug. 26 '86.
C: ECD. Pic CD.

SONIC YOUTH

CD - SONIC STARPOWER
COCOMELOS RECORDS CM 006
Teenage Riot (4:37)/ Dirty Boots (8:53)/ Drunken
Butterfly (3:02)/ Love Song (6:37)/ Youth Against
Fascism (4:41)/ Swimsuit Issue (3:53)/ Orange

(4:26)/ 100 Per Cent (2:40)/ Kool Thing (5:01)/ Sugar Cane (9:54)/ Express Way To Your Skull, Kill Your Idols (9:38)
R: Vg. Audience.   S: Central Park, New York Apr. 7 '92.   C: ECD. Dcc. Pic CD.

SOUL ASYLUM

CD - THE LOST ALBUM
MONTANA MO 10004
Without A Trace/ Black Gold/ Runaway Train/ New World/ Spinnin'/ Get On Out/ Sexual Healing/ Somebody To Shove/ 99%/ April Fool/ To Sir With Love/ Closer To The Stars/ Ooh Lala Song
R: Vg-Exs. Soundboard.   S: USA '93.   C: ECD. Dbw. Time 54:28.

CD - NEW WORLD
SAVE THE EARTH STE 022
Without A Trace (4:17)/ Get It On (4:10)/ New World (4:21)/ Black Gold (4:20)/ Runaway Train (4:35)/ Spinnin' (3:05)/ Somebody To Shove (3:20)/ April Fool (4:02)/ Sexual Healing (4:49)/ 99% (6:06)
R: Exs. Soundboard.   S: Ventura, CA '93.
C: ECD. Dcc.

CD - RUNAWAY CHILD
CLINTON RECORDS CL 7903
Runaway Train/ Get On Out/ Somebody Too Shove/ To Six With Love/ Closer To The Stars/ Oh Lala Song/ Somebody To Shove (different version)/ Black Gold/ Don't Stop/ April's Fool/ Runaway Train (different version)
R: Exs. Soundboard.   S: Sounds like 'Unplugged' USA '93.   C: ECD. Time 42:07.

CD - WE'RE THE OPENING BAND
HAWK 014
Veil Of Tears (3:15)/ Something Out Of Nothing (3:10)/ Cartoon (4:19)/ Keep It Up (3:48)/ Without A Trace (3:35)/ Runaway Train (4:13)/ Black Gold (4:08)/ April Fool (3:46)/ To Sir With Love (2:46)/ Sometime To Return (3:51)/ Somebody To Shove (3:21)
R: Ex. Audience.   S: USA Jan. 23 '93.
C: ECD. Pic CD.

SOUNDGARDEN

CD - BIG DUMB SEX
GRAPEFRUIT GRA-047-B
Loud Love (5:07)/ All Your Lies (3:37)/ Big Dumb Sex (4:10)/ Flower (3:23)/ Hands All Over (6:28)/ Gun (5:47)/ Loud Love (4:34)/ Get On The Snake (3:15)/ Full On Kevin's Mom (3:26)/ I Awake (4:01)/ Big Bottom (4:15)/ Beyond The Wheel (6:28)
 R: Exs. Soundboard.   S: Boston, Mass. '90.
C: Australian CD. Dcc.

CD - DIGGING THE GARDEN
RAZOR'S EDGE RZCD 0025
Searching With My Good Eyes Closed (4:53)/

Mind Riot (4:10)/ Outshined (5:08)/ Jesus Christ Pose (2:20)/ Room A Thousand Years Wide (3:50)/ Rusty Cage (3:37)/ Little Joe (5:30)/ Slaves And Bulldozers (12:51)/ Hands Over All (5:56)/ Big Dumb Sex (4:53)/ Gun (5:13)/ Beyond The Wheel (7:12)/ Somewhere (4:19)
R: Exs. Soundboard.   C: ECD. Dbw. Pic CD.

CD - THE GARDEN GROWS
COCOMELOS RECORDS CM027/28
CD1: Jesus Christ Pose (5:27)/ Spoonman (4:11)/ Let Me Drown (4:22)/ Mailman (5:09)/ The Day I Tried To Live (5:08)/ My Wave (4:50)/ Room A Thousand Eyes Wide (3:44)/ Black Hole Sun (5:21)/ Searching With My Good Eye Closed (8:14)/ Superunknown (5:09)
CD2: Rusty Cage (6:06)/ Mind Riot (4:23)/ Feel On Black Days (4:58)/ Hand All Over (5:38)/ Kickstand (2:16)/ Like Suicide (6:52)/ Face Pollution (4:57)/ Somewhere (4:56)/ Head Down (6:34)/ Limo Wreck (6:26)
R: Ex. Audience.   S: Sentrum Scene, Oslo, Norway Mar. 23 '94.   C: ECD. Dcc. Pic CD.

CD - LOUD (VOL. 1)
BANANA BAN-043-A
Hunted Down (2:43)/ All Your Lies (4:07)/ Mood For Trouble (5:07)/ Gun (5:03)/ Thank You (5:37)/ Flower (3:29)/ I Awake (4:34)/ Kingdom Of Come (2:54)/ Head Injury (3:05)/ Circle Of Power (2:19)/ Incessant Mace (9:38)/ Earache My Eye (5:16)
R: Ex.   S: USA '88.   C: Australian CD. Dcc.

CD - LOUD (VOL. 2)
BANANA BAN-043-B
Loud Love (5:07)/ All Your Lies (3:37)/ Big Dumb Sex (4:100)/ Flower (3:23)/ Hands All Over (6:28)/ Gun (5:47)/ Loud Love (4:34)/ Get On The Snake (3:15)/ Full On Kevin's Mom (3:26)/ I Awake (4:01)/ Big Bottom (4:15)/ Beyond The Wheel (6:28)
R: Ex.   S: USA '90.   C: Australian CD. Dcc.

CD - STOLEN PRAYERS
TRIBUTE TR 110
Nowhere But You*/ Spoonman*/ Fluttergirl*/ Missing*/ Stolen Prayer**/ Heartfist**/ Unholy War**/ Black Cat+/ Angel Of Fire+/ Reach Down+/ Blackhole Sun++/ Head Down++
R: Exs. Soundboard. ++Ex. Audience.   S: Studio Demos '88 - '94. *Superunknown demos. **Chris Cornell solo. +Temple Of The Dog demos. ++Live Kitsap, Wa June '94.   C: ECD. Dcc. Pic CD. Time 74:23.

SOUTHSIDE JOHNNY & LITTLE STEVEN

CD - UNPLUGGED
KISS THE STONE KTS 329
Broke Down Piece Of Man (4:19)/ The Fever (5:41)/ Little Queenie (4:17)/ Like A Hurricane (3:38)/ Wonderful Tonight (3:36)/ Better Days (4:19)/ Like A Virgin (2:40)/ Rosalita (3:29)/ I'm So Lonesome I Could Cry (4:18)/ All Night Long

(4:17)/ If I Were A Carpenter (2:53)/ Forever Young (3:19)/ Don't Look Back (3:09)/ It's Been A Long Time (4:35)/ Into The Mystic (3:48)/ Ain't Too Proud To Beg (2:15)/ I Am A Patriot (3:22)/ I Don't Wanna Go Home (4:37)
R: Exs. Soundboard. S: The K-Rock Hungerthon Rent Party, NYC Nov. 21 '93.
C: ECD. Dcc. Pic CD. Time 68:35.

SPRINGSTEEN, BRUCE

CD - A NIGHT FOR THE VIETNAM VETERAN
WINGED WHEEL 9408/10
CD1: Intro (4:50)/ Who'll Stop The Rain (3:52)/ Prove It All Night (5:08)/ The Ties That Bind (3:54)/ Darkness On The Edge Of Town (6:49)/ Johnny Bye Bye (3:13)/ Independence Day (7:45)/ Trapped (4:57)/ Two Hearts (2:52)/ Out In The Street (4:58)/ The Promised Land (5:54)/ The River (7:41)/ This Land Is Your Land (3:26)/ Badlands (5:08)/ Thunder Road (6:53)
CD2: Hungry Heart (4:34)/ You Can Look But You Better Not Touch (3:13)/ Cadillac Ranch (5:01)/ Sherry Darling (5:20)/ Jole Blon (5:13)/ Wreck On The Highway (4:22)/ Racing In The Street (7:47)/ Candy's Room (2:52)/ Ramrod (4:17)/ Rosalita Come Out Tonight (15:28)
CD3: Jungleland (11:35)/ Ballad Of Easy Rider (3:14)/ Born To Run (4:26)/ Medley: Devil With The Blue Dress, Good Golly Miss Molly, C.C. Rider, Jenny Take A Ride, I Hear A Train, You Can't Sit Down, Sweet Soul Music, Shake (14:29)/ Twist & Shout (6:46)
R: G-Vg. Audience. S: LA Sports Arena Aug. 20 '81. C: ECD. Comes in a full-color box. Full color booklet. CDs in individual paper sleeves with B&w pictures. CDs look like records.

CD - ACOUSTIC TALES
THE SWINGIN' PIG TSP149-2
CD1: Brilliant Disguise (5:44)/ Darkness On The Edge Of Town (3:56)/ Mansion On The Hill (4:58)/ Reason To Believe (5:25)/ Red Headed Woman (4:00)/ 57 Channels (And Nothin' On) (5:38)/ My Father's House (6:17)/ Tenth Avenue Freeze-Out (4:18)/ Atlantic City (3:42)/ Wild Billy's Circus Story (4:30)
CD2: Nebraska (6:05)/ When The Lights Go Out (3:55)/ Thunder Road (7:25)/ My Hometown (5:18)/ Real World (4:57)/ Highway 61 Revisited (3:53)/ Across The Borderline (5:38)/ Tougher Than The Rest (3:55)/ Soul Driver (2:23)/ State Trooper (3:03)
R: Ex. Audience. S: Shrine Auditorium, Los Angeles Nov. 16 '90. C: ECD. Box set.

CD - ACTION IN THE STREETS
UNBELIEVABLE MUSIC UM 038/39
CD1: Night (3:18)/ Rendezvous (3:24)/ Spirit In The Night (8:02)/ It's My Life (15:58)/ Thunder Road (6:20)/ Mona, She's The One (11:35)/ Tenth Avenue Freeze Out (4:32)/ Actions In The Streets (6:18)/ Backstreets (12:30)
CD2: Jungleland (11:20)/ Rosalita (Come Out

Tonight) (15:01)/ Born To Run (5:35)/ Quarter To Three (10:43)/ Something In The Night (5:58)/ Growin' Up (10:12)/ Baby I Love You (3:21)/ Walking In The Rain (4:00)/ Say Goodbye To Hollywood (3:13)/ Be My Baby (3:25)
R: G. Audience. S: Milwaukee Feb. 22 '77. CD2 tracks 5-6 Maple Leaf Garden, Toronto Feb. 13 '77. Tracks 7-10 Cleveland Feb. 17 '77.
C: ECD. Total time 144:47.

CD - ANOTHER SIDE OF SPRINGSTEEN
COLUMBUS COL CD 35D56
Held Up Without A Gun/ Be True/ Roulette/ The Big Payback/ Pink Cadillac/ Shut Out The Light/ Johnny Bye Byee/ Stand On It/ Janey Don't You Lose Heart/ Lucky Man/ Two For The Road/ I Ain't Got No Home/ Vigilante Man/ Viva Las Vegas/ Chicken Lips And Lizards Hips/ Part Man Part Monkey/ Thirty Days Out/ Streets Of Philadelphia/ Gypsy Woman
R: Exs. Soundboard. S: Studio. C: ECD. Dbw. Orange type. Time 61:21.

CD - AUSTIN 1975
WHOOPY CAT WCP-0009
CD1: Incident On 57th Street (6:03)/ Tenth Avenue Freeze Out (3:45)/ Spirit In The Night (6:45)/ It's Gonna Work Out Fine (6:06)/ Growin' Up (3:08)/ Saint In The City (5:47)/ E Street Shuffle (20:57)/ She's The One (4:32)/ Born To Run (4:07)/ Thunder Road (5:15)
CD2: Kitty's Back (17:09)/ Jungleland (8:59)/ Rosalita (10:27)/ Sandy (5:04)/ Quarter To Three (3:59)/ Twist & Shout (3:30)/ Save The Last Dance For Me (4:37)
R: Exs. Soundboard. S: Austin Coliseum, Austin, TX Sept. 12 '75. C: Japanese CD. Dcc. Pic CDs.

CD - BORDERLINE
HUMAN RECORDS 479986 3
Lucky Town/ Atlantic City/ Many Rivers To Cross/ Downbound Train/ Because The Night/ Human Touch/ Who'll Stop The Rain/ Hungry Heart/ Glory Days/ Across The Borderline/ Working On The Highway/ Rockin' All Over The World/ Bobby Jean
R: Vg. Audience. S: El Molinon Stadium, Gijon, Spain May 7 '94. C: ECD. Dcc. Time 68:47.

CD - BORN AGAIN VOL. 1
BANANA BAN-045-A
Badlands (3:33)/ Spirit In The Night (4:43)/ Prove It All Night (11:00)/ Thunder Road (5:51)/ Jungleland (9:29)/ Santa Claus Is Coming To Town (4:02)/ Fire (2:40)/ Because The Night (6:39)/ Rosalita (8:27)/ Born To Run (4:44)
R: Exs. Soundboard. S: USA '78.
C: Australian CD. Dcc.

CD - BORN AGAIN VOL. 2
BANANA BAN-045-B
Born In The USA (6:37)/ Local Hero (5:47)/ Lucky Town (4:22)/ Darkness On The Edge Of Town (5:22)/ If I Should Fall Behind (4:49)/ 57 Channels

And Nothin' On (6:55)/ The Big Muddy (4:18)/
Living Proof (6:14)/ My Hometown (6:13)/ Leap Of
Faith (4:46)/ Man's Job (5:20)
R: Exs. Soundboard.   S: USA '92 part 1.
C: Australian CD. Dcc.

CD - BORN AGAIN VOL. 3
BANANA BAN-045-C
Roll Of The Dice (12:23)/ Human Touch (8:30)/
Glory Days (7:54)/ Hungry Heart (3:38)/ Prove It
All Night (9:32)/ Rosalita Come Out Tonight
(11:14)/ Lucky Town (4:45)/ 57 Channels And
Nothin' On (3:02)/ Living Proof (5:27)
R: Exs. Soundboard.   S: USA '92 part 2.
C: Australian CD. Dcc.

CD - BRUCE SPRINGSTEEN STORY VOL. 1
E. ST. RECORDS ES 04
Purple Haze/ Get Outta My Life Woman/ Hold On
I'm Coming/ You Can't Judge A Book By Looking
At Its Cover/ Eleanor Rigby/ Suzanne/ The Break
Song/ One By One/ The Letter/ Mr. Jones/ San
Francisco Nights/ Omaha/ Hey Joe/ My
Generation/ Look Into My Window/ With A Little
Help From My Friends
S: The Left Foot, St. Peter's Church, Freehold,
New Jersey Jan. '67.   C: ECD. Time 55:00.

CD - BRUCE SPRINGSTEEN STORY VOL. 2
E. ST. RECORDS ES 05
That's What You Get/ Baby I/ Fire/ See My Friend/
Catch The Wind/ Omaha/ Unknown Song/ The
Break Song
S: The Left Foot, St. Peter's Church, Freehold,
New Jersey Jan. '67. Outtakes from acetate.
C: ECD. Time 31:25.

CD - BRUCE SPRINGSTEEN STORY VOL. 3
E. ST. RECORDS ES 06
He's Guilty/ Going Back To Georgia/ The Train
Song/ Going Back To Georgia/ The Wind And The
Rain/ Resurrection/ Garden State Parkway Blues
R: Vg-Ex.   S: Tracks 1-3 Fillmore Recording
Studios, San Francisco Feb. 22 '70. Tracks 4-7
West End, New Jersey Mar. '70.   C: ECD. Dcc.
Time 67:51.

CD - BRUCE SPRINGSTEEN STORY VOL. 4
E. ST. RECORDS ES 07
I Can't Take It No More/ Hootchie Cootchie Man/
You Mean So Much To Me/ Nothing Can Stop Me
Now/ My Baby's Natural Magic/ Down The Road
Apiece/ I'm Into Something Good/ Down To
Mexico/ I Remember/ I Just Can't Change
R: Vg-Ex.   S: Track 1 D'Scene, Sayerville, New
Jersey Jan. 18 '71. Track 2-5 '72. Tracks 6-10
Back Door Club, Richmond, Virginia Feb. 4 '72.
C: ECD. Dcc. Time 74:27.

CD - CLUBS' STORIES
WINGED WHEEL WW 9405/6
CD1: Intro - Lucille/ I Hear You Knockin'/ Wooly
Bully/ Sweet Little Sixteen/ Twist & Shout/ Louie
Louie/ Blue Suede Shoes/ Rockin' All Over The

World/ Ain't That Loving You Baby/ Jersey Girl
Carol
CD2: Money/ Medley: Johnny Bye Bye, Whole
Lotta Shakin' Going On, Shout/ Come On Let's
Go/ From Small Things Big Things One Day
Come/ Ramrod/ Lucille/ Around And Around/ The
Wanderer/ Long Tall Sally/ Twist & Shout/ Open
All Night/ On The Prowl/ Do You Wanna Dance?/
Rock Baby Rock It
R: CD1 Tracks 1-6 G. Some surface noise. Tracks
7-11 G-Vg. CD2 G. Tracks 3-10 Poor-G.   S: CD1
Tracks 1-6 Headliner Club July 16 '83 with The
Midnight Thunder. Tracks 7-11 Brighton Bar Aug.
19 '83 with John Eddie and The Frontrunners.
CD2 Tracks 1-2 Big Man's West July 17 '82 with
The Iron City Houserockers. Tracks 3-10 Stone
Pony July 25 '82. Tracks 11-14 Stone Pony Oct. 3
'82 with The Cats On A Smooth Surface.
C: ECD. Full color cardboard gatefold sleeve. Pic
CDs look like records. Time CD1 57:54.
CD2 58:51.

CD - DUETS LIVE
POST SCRIPT PSCD 1302
The Promised Land (with Jackson Browne) (4:18)/
Hungry Heart (with Crosby, Stills, Nash & Young)
(3:43)/ The River (with Sting) (6:20)/ Lean On Me
(with N. Lofgren) (4:26)/ Highway 61 (with B. Raitt
& J. Browne) (3:36)/ All The Way Home (with
Southside Johnny) (6:05)/ Great Balls Of Fire (with
J. Lewis & J. Ely) (4:04)/ Whole Lotta Shakin'
Goin' On (with J. Lewis & J. Ely) (3:59)/ It's Been
A Long Time (with Southside Johnny & Little
Steven) (5:49)/ Blowin' Down The Road (I Ain't
Going To Be Treated This Way) (with J. Ely)
(5:34)/ Lonesome Valley (with J. Ely & S. Tyrell)
(3:39)/ Settle For Love (with J. Ely) (4:35)/ Jole
Blon (with T.T. D'Arby) (4:43)/ Jumpin' Jack Flash
(with T.T. D'Arby) (6:11)/ I Ain't Got No Home
(with J. Ely) (3:49)
R: Vg-Ex.   S: Live in the USA and Europe '82-
'83.   C: ECD. Dcc.

CD - GET UP STAND UP
WINGED WHEEL WW-9407
Born In The U.S.A./ The Promised Land/ Working
On The Highway/ The River/ Cadillac Ranch/ War/
My Hometown/ Thunder Road/ Because The
Night/ Glory Days/ Born to Run/ Raise Your Hand/
Chimes Of Freedom/ Get Up Stand Up
R: Vg-Ex. Audience.   S: Turin Sept. 8 '88.
C: ECD. Dcc. Cardboard gatefold sleeve. CD
looks like a record. Time 77:08.

CD - GREATEST HITS LIVE
STENTOR STEN 91.011
Born In The USA (6:37)/ I'm On Fire (3:44)/
Because The Night (6:10)/ Dancing In The Dark
(4:44)/ Hungry Heart (3:53)/ Bobby Jean (3:50)/
Sweet Soul Music (2:27)/ Boom Boom Boom
(3:21)/ Downbound Train (3:56)/ The River (5:40)/
Cover Me (4:59)/ Brilliant Disguise (5:31)
R: G-Ex. Audience.   S: Various.   C: ECD. Dcc.
Songs fade in.

CD - HEART & SOUL
E. ST. RECORDS ES-08/09/10
CD1: Born To Run (4:56)/ Prove It All Night (6:07)/ Tenth Avenue Freeze-Out (6:10)/ Darkness On The Edge Of Town (6:10)/ Independence Day (7:18)/ Factory (3:49)/ Jackson Cage (3:44)/ Two Hearts (3:29)/ The Promised Land (6:20)/ Out In The Streets (5:46)/ Racing In The Street (8:54)/ The River (7:14)/ Badlands (5:19)
CD2: Thunder Road (6:38)/ No Money Down (3:11)/ Cadillac Ranch (5:14)/ Hungry Heart (5:02)/ Fire (5:10)/ Candy's Room (3:31)/ Sherry Darling (5:36)/ Here She Comes (4:37)/ I Wanna Marry You (5:27)/ The Ties That Bind (3:46)/ Stolen Car (4:44)/ Wreck On The Highway (4:55)/ Point Blank (8:01)/ Crush On You (5:02)/ Ramrod (4:24)
CD3: You Can Look (But You Better Not Touch) (5:05)/ Drive All Night (11:38)/ Backstreets (8:31)/ Rosalita (Come Out Tonight) (13:21)/ I'm A Rocker (4:24)/ Jungleland (10:09)/ The Detroit Medley (11:33)/ On Top Of Old Smokey (3:38)/ The Price You Pay (6:13)
R: Vg-Ex. Soundboard.   S: Complete show Tempe, Arizona Nov. 5 '80. CD3 track 8 Portland Oct. 25 '80. Track 9 Madison Square Garden, NYC Nov. 27 '80.   C: ECD. Dcc. Sticker.

CD - KNOCK ON WOOD
RAGGAMUFFIN RECORDS RR 941/2
CD1: Night/ Tenth Avenue Freeze Out/ Spirit In The Night/ It's My Life/ Thunder Road/ She's The One/ Born To Run/ Pretty Flamingo/ Incident On 57th Street
CD2: Growing Up/ (It's Hard To Be A) Saint In The City/ Backstreets/ Jungleland/ Rosalita (Come Out Tonight)/ Raise Your Hand/ Knock On Wood/ Yum Yum I Want Some/ 4th Of July (Asbury Park)/ Devil With The Blue Dress Medley/ Frankie
R: G-Vg. Soundboard.   S: Ellis Auditorium, Memphis Tenn. Apr. 29 '76. CD2 Track 11 Municipal Auditorium Mobile, Alabama May 10 '76. C: ECD. Dcc. Time CD1 73:32. CD2 70:01.

CD - LIBERTY HALL
MISTRAL MUSIC MM 9439/40
CD1: Wild Billy's Circus Days (9:53)/ N.Y.C. Serenade (14:45)/ Spirit In The Night (6:16)/ Walking The Dog (15:45)/ Saint In The City (4:15)/ E Street Shuffle (5:11)/ Blinded By The Light (10:20)
CD2: For You (10:36)/ Rosalita (10:14)/ The Fever (9:48)/ Mary Queen Of Arkansas (5:29)/ Gimme That Wine (3:02)/ Something That You Got (5:20)/ Ride On Sweet William (8:08)/ Thundercrack (13:45)
R: G-Vg.   S: CD1 tracks 1-7 and CD2 tracks 1-2 Liberty Hall, Houston, Texas Mar. 9 '74. CD2 tracks 4-8 at Liberty Hall, Houston, Texas Mar. 11 '74. CD2 track 3 at the Fever - first performance in concert ever.   C: ECD. Dcc.

CD - THE LIVE B-SIDES
SIN MUSIC 479986 2
Santa Claus Is Coming To Town/ Merry Christmas

Baby/ For You/ Incident On 57th Street/ Tougher Than The Rest/ Be True/ Chimes Of Freedom/ Born To Run/ Spare Parts/ Leap Of Faith/ Growing Up/ The Big Muddy/ Remember When The Music/ Trapped
R: Ex. Soundboard.   S: Various locations in the USA and elsewhere.   C: ECD. Dcc. Live 76:39.

CD - THE LOST RADIO SHOW
KISS THE STONE KTS 321
C: See 'The Lost Radio Show' (WCP-0011) for songs and source.

CD - THE LOST RADIO SHOW
WHOOPY CAT WCP-0011
Soundcheck (2:35)/ Satin Doll (2:30)/ Does This Bus Stop At 82nd Street (5:56)/ Growin' Up (10:16)/ Mary, Queen Of Arkansas (6:49)/ Wild Billy's Circus Story (5:40)/ Sentimental Journey (3:03)/ The Fever (8:43)/ Something You Got (7:12)/ Interview With Ed Beauchamp (18:26)
R: Exs. Soundboard.   S: KLOL FM Studios, Houston Mar. 9 '74.   C: Japanese CD. Red, white and blue cover. Yellow type.

CD - MARZ BARS 'N' GUITARS
MARS 200894
Lucky Town/ Darkness On The Edge Of Town/ Chain Smoking/ Never Be Enough Time/ Brown Eyed Girl/ Mustang Sally/ Atlantic City/ Diddy Wah Diddy/ Living Proof/ Glory Days/ Around And Around/ Bama Lama Bama Loo/ The Wanderer, Kansas City/ Special Wreck On The Highway (McCabe's Guitar Shop, Santa Monica June 18 '94)
R: Vg. Audience.   S: Tracks 1-13 Marz American Style, Long Branch, NJ Aug. 20 '94.   C: ECD. Dcc. With Joe Gruschecky and The Iron City Rockers. Time 75:47.

CD - PAUL SIMON - BRUCE SPRINGSTEEN & FRIENDS
YELLOW CAT YC 013/14
C: See listing under various artists.

CD - PRODIGAL SON
PS/1-2
CD1: Intro - Lady And The Doctor/ 4th Of July, Ashbury Park (Sandy)/ Prodigal Son/ Visitation At Fort Horn/ Growin' Up/ The Angel/ Song To The Orphans/ For You/ Hey Santa Ana/ Jazz Musician/ Camilla Horn
CD2: Seaside Bar Song/ Arabian Night/ Family Song/ New York City Serenade/ Evacuation Of The West/ Jesse/ Kitty's Back/ War Nurse/ Eloise/ Does This Bus Stop At 82nd Street?/ Marie/ Randolph Street (Master Of Electricity)
R: Exs. Soundboard.   S: Studio.   C: ECD. Time CD1 55:01. CD2 53:46.

CD - 2ND NIGHT AT THE CAPITOL THEATER
WINGED WHEEL WW-9401/2
CD1: Intro - Good Rockin' Tonight/ Badlands/ Spirit In The Night/ Darkness On The Edge Of

Town/ Independence Day/ The Promised Land/
It's My Life/ Thunder Road/ Jungleland/ Santa
Claus Is Coming To Town/ Fire/ Candy's Room
CD2: Because The Night/ Point Blank/ Kitty's
Back/ Rosalita Come Out Tonight/ Born To Run/
Tenth Avenue Freeze-Out/ Medley: Devil With A
Blue Dress, Good Golly Miss Molly, C.C. Rider,
Jenny Take A Ride
R: Exs. Soundboard.   S: Capitol Theater,
Passaic, NJ Sept. 20 '78.   C: ECD. Dcc.
Cardboard gatefold sleeve. CDs look like records.
Time CD1 70:17. CD2 64:27.

CD - THE TIES THAT BIND
TSD - TTTB
The Ties That Bind (take 8 no recording date)/
Cindy (take 3 no recording date)/ Hungry Heart
(take 2 no recording date)/ Stolen Car (take 3
recorded Sept. 24 '79)/ To Be True (take 2 no
recording date)/ The River (take 5 Sept. 3 '79)/
You Can Look...(But You Better Not Touch) (take
3 Sept. 1 '79)/ The Price You Pay (take 1 Sept. 25
'79)/ I Wanna Marry You (take 4 Sept. 24 '79)/
Loose Ends (take 2 Sept. 23 '79)
R: Exs. Soundboard.   S: Power Station Studio A,
New York. Sequenced and assembled Oct. 4 '79.
C: ECD. Power Station track sheets on front and
back. Time 38:38.

CD - UNSURPASSED SPRINGSTEEN VOL. 5: E
STREET SHUFFLE OUTTAKES
YELLOW DOG RECORDS YD 036
Hey Santa Ana (4:54)/ Evacuation Of The West -
aka 'No More Kings In Texas' (4:30)/ Kitty's Back
#1 (7:15)/ Seaside Bar Song (3:#5)/ Rosalita
(Come Out Tonight) (7:15)/ Kitty's Back #2 (7:24)/
Zero And Blind Terry (6:04)/ 4th Of July, Asbury
Park (Sandy) (5:53)/ The Fever (7:37)
R: Vg-Ex. Soundboard.   S: Studio demos,
outtakes '73 - '75.   C: ECD. Dcc.

CD - UNSURPASSED SPRINGSTEEN VOL. 6:
THE BOSS VOL. 1
YELLOW DOG RECORDS YD 037
Janey Needs A Shooter (6:04)/ The Ballad Of A
Selfloading Pistol (5:11)/ The Saga Of The
Architect Angel (4:19)/ Wintersong (6:00)/ Tonight
#1 (3:45)/ Tonight #2 (1:21)/ Wild Kisses (4:13)/
Tonight #3 (3:08)/ Tonight #4 (2:54)/ Tonight #5
(3:30)/ Tonight #6 (3:48)/ The Ties That Bind #1
(4:03)/ The Ties That Bind #2 (4:25)
R: Vg-Ex. Soundboard.   S: Studio demos,
outtakes '73 - '78.   C: ECD. Dcc.

CD - WARM AND TENDER LOVE
KISS THE STONE KTS 280
Streets Of Philadelphia (3:35)/ Warm And Tender
Love (5:38)/ Human Touch (7:07)/ Because The
Night (4:10)/ Brilliant Disguise (5:06)/ Soul Driver
(3:30)/ Who'll Stop The Rain (3:50)/ Green River
(3:11)/ Born On The Bayou (3:24)/ Glory Days
(6:23)/ Come Together (4:26)/ Curtis Mayfield
Medley (9:24)/ I Ain't Got No Home (3:11)/
Vigilante Man (4:14)

R: Exs. Soundboard except *.   S: Track 1 LA
Mar. 21 '94. *2-6 Red Bank rehearsals Mar. 23
'93. Tracks 7-9 Rock'N'Roll Hall Of Fame '93 with
John Fogerty, Robbie Robertson, Mark
Goldenberg, Roy Bitan, Benmout Tench, Don Was
& Jim Keltner. Track 10 Late Night with Letterman,
New York, June 25 '93 with Paul Shaffer. Track 11
Rock'N'Roll Hall Of Fame New York Jan. '94 with
Axl Rose, Paul Shaffer & CBS Orchestra. Track 12
New York Mar. 1 '94 with Bonnie Raitt, B. B. King,
Steve Winwood, Vernon Reid, Toni Tony Tone,
Don Was & Curtis Mayfield. Tracks 13-14
'Folkways' Woody Guthrie Tribute, NY June '88.
C: ECD. Dcc. Pic CD.

STANLEY, PAUL

CD - HEAVEN'S ON FIRE
ROCKS 92126/7
CD1: I Stole Your Love (4:19)/ I Want You (3:56)/
Tears Are Falling (4:14)/ Tonight You Belong To
Me (5:00)/ C'mon And Love Me (3:23)/ Wouldn't
You Like To Know Me (4:05)/ Heaven's On Fire
(6:03)/ Hide Your Heart (6:03)/ I Still Love You
(5:17)
CD2: New York Groove (3:44)/ Crazy Crazy
Nights (4:28)/ Reason To Live (5:51)/ Lick It Up
(5:38)/ Let's Put The X In Sex (5:01)/ Love Gun
(6:06)/ Goodbye (4:09)/ Communication
Breakdown (2:35)/ Detroit Rock City (4:21)
R: Vg.   S: Heaven, Toronto Apr. 6 '89.
C: ECD. Dcc.

STATUS QUO

CD - B'SIDES THEMSELVES
MAKE IT ALONE 9301
The Medley/ Dead In The Water/ Mysteries From
The Ball/ Heavy Daze/ Dirty Water/ Rotten To The
Bone/ Doing It All For You/ Rockin' All Over The
World/ That's Alright/ The Reason For Goodbye/
Dreamin'/ In The Army Now/ Lean Machine/
Running All Over The World/ The Power Of Rock
R: Exs. Soundboard.   S: A collection of rare B-
Sides and remixes from 1988-1991.   C: ECD.
Limited edition of 500.

CD - JUST FOR THE RECORD
SQ 00342
Joanna/ Eyes Of The World/ Intro 'Nellie The
Elephant'/ Caroline/ Mystery Medley/ Roll Over
Lay Down/ What You're Proposing/ Restless/
Caroline/ Hold You Back/ Paper Plane/ One Man
Band/ Mystery Medley
CD2: Don't Drive My Car/ Dirty Water/ Whatever
You Want/ In The Army Now/ Rockin' All Over The
World/ Don't Waste My Time/ Roadhouse Blues/
Burning Bridges/ The Anniversary Waltz/ Bye Bye
Johnny
S: CD1 tracks 1-2 from Special Guest Little Egypt.
Tracks 3-7 Wembley Arena, London Dec. 18 '93.
Tracks 8-12 Stadthalle, Braunschweig Nov. 23 '92.
CD2 tracks 1-7 Stadhalle, Braunschweig Nov. 23
'92. Tracks 8-10 Wembley Arena, London Dec. 19

'92.   C: ECD. Limited edition of 500.

CD - THE LEGEND NEVER DIES
CD 94001
Junior's Wailing/ Someone's Learning/ Umleitung/ In My Chair/ Railroad/ Roadhouse Blues/ In My Chair/ Gerdundula/ Piece Of Mind/ I'll Be Back/ You Don't Own Me/ Calling The Shot/ I Wonder Why/ Paper Plane/ The Mystery Medley
R: Tracks 1-6 Vgm. Radio broadcast. Tracks 7-15 Exs. Soundboard.   S: Tracks 1-6 Radiohurst, Stockholm Nov. 20 '71. Tracks 7-10 rare demos & studio outtakes. Tracks 12-13 rare demo & studio outtakes. Track 11 Civic Theatre, Newcastle July 18 '78. Tracks 14-15 Europe '92.   C: ECD. Limited edition of 500.

LP - LIVE IN HAMBURG
RXS 5691
S1: Junior's Wailing/ Someone's Learning/ In My Chair/ Railroad
S2: Spinning Wheel Blues/ Mean Girl/ Roadhouse Blues
Recording: G-Vgm. Audience.   S: Music Hall, Hamburg '72.   C: Eb. Limited edition of 100.

CD - RARE STATUS QUO
RSQ CD 001
Little Lady/ Paper Plane/ Jealousy/ Calling The Shots/ Jealousy/ Where Are You Now/ That's Alright/ Fakin' The Blues/ Heavy Daze/ Better Times/ It's An Illusion/ Getting Better/ Don't Waste My Time/ A Planet Called Monday/ Rain/ Need Your Love/ In My Chair
R: G-Vgs. Soundboard.   S: A collection of rare live and studio works from 1970-1991.   C: ECD. Limited edition of 500.

CD - THE PRINCES TRUST 1994
PT MUSIC CD 001/002
CD1: Intro 'Nellie The Elephant'/ Caroline/ Hold You Back/ One Man Band/ Mystery Song/ Railroad/ Most Of The Time/ Wild Side Of Life/ Rollin' Home/ Again & Again/ Slow Train/ 4500 Times/ Junior's Wailing/ Roll Over Lay Down/ Rock 'Til You Drop/ Dirty Water/ What You're Proposing/ Whatever You Want
CD2: In The Army Now/ Rocking All Over The World/ Roadhouse Blues/ Restless/ The Anniversary Waltz/ Bye Bye Johnny/ Fakin' The Blues/ No Problem/ Don't Waste My Time
R: Exs. Soundboard.   S: Royal Albert Hall, London Mar. 30 '94.   C: ECD.

CD - THIRSTY LIVE WORKS '94
Q-CD 001/002
CD1: Intro 'Mein Vater War Ein Wandersmann'/ Caroline/ Hold You Back/ Down Down/ One Man Band/ Going Nowhere/ Soft In My Head/ Mystery Song/ Railroad/ Most Of The Time/ Wild Side Of Life/ Rollin' Home/ Again & Again/ Slow Train/ Rude Awaking Time/ Queenie/ Rock 'Til You Drop
CD2: Gerdundula/ Whatever You Want/ In The Army Now/ Rockin' All Over The World/ Don't

Waste My Time/ Roadhouse Blues/ The Anniversary Waltz/ Bye Bye Johnny
R: Exs. Soundboard.   S: Stadthalle, Dornbirn Oct. 3 '94.   C: ECD.

CD - THE 12" MIXES
MAKE IT ALONE 9402
Come On You Reds/ Fakin' The Blues/ Heavy Daze/ Better Times/ In The Army Now/ Ain't Complaining/ Who Get's The Love/ Running All Over World/ Burning Bridges/ Ships In The Night/ Ol' Rag Blues/ A Mess Of Blues/ Going Down Town Tonight
R: Exs. Soundboard.   S: A collection of rare remixes and rare tracks from 1984-1994.
C: ECD. Limited edition of 500.

CD - WE PLAY ANYTHING
BLACK DEMON RECORDS XIN 9415
CD1: Breakdown (I.B.C. Studios, London '72)/ Roll Over Beethoven, Mama Weer All Crazee Now, Strange Days, Time For A Change, All That You Dream (I.B.C. Studios, London '74)/ Thunder, Come On Come On (Phonogram Studios, London '76)/ All About You (Studio Bohus, Stockholm '77)/ The Same Old Blues (Wisselord Studios, Hilversum '78)/ I Fought The Law, Because The Night, You Better Walk In, Sweet Home Alabama (Windmill Lane Studios, Dublin, Ireland '80)
CD2: Tear Drops In My Eyes, Black Rain, Revolution, Little Red Pussy (Chipping-Norton & Jacobs Studio, London '86)/ The Fighter (Take 1), The Fighter (Take 2), Die Laughing, This Is The Long Way Home, The End (Chipping-Norton & Jacobs Studio, London '87)/ Heartline, Girls Talkin', Turn On Your Radio, Don't Burn The Witch (Bray Studios '91)
R: Exs. Soundboard.   S: Different studio outtakes from '72-'91.   C: ECD. Limited edition of 200.

STEELY DAN

CD - BOOK OF LAIRS
HAWK 034/35
CD1: Royal Scam, Bad Sneakers, Aja (8:45)/ Green Earrings (5:20)/ Bodistava (5:50)/ Beautiful World (6:11)/ Josie (7:01)/ Hey Nineteen (6:18)/ Book Of Liars (4:29)/ Chain Lightening (11:23)/ Queen Flower Street (4:10)/ Home At Last (6:28)/ Black Friday (4:21)
CD2: Tesla Shadows (6:44)/ Deacon Blues (7:29)/ Tomorrow Girl (7:17)/ Babylon Sisters (6:44)/ Reelin' In The Years (7:2)/ Fall Of 1992 (6:04)/ Peg (4:40)/ Third World Man (6:31)/ Counter Moon (4:56)/ Tea House On The Tracks (6:59)
R: Vg. Audience.   S: CD1 Block Buster Pavilion, LA '93. CD2 Greek Theatre, LA Sept. 8 '93.
C: ECD. Dcc. Pic CD.

STEWART, ROD

CD - IN THE SPOTLIGHT
BIG MUSIC BIG 088/89

CD1: Intro - Hot Legs/ Cut Across Shortly/ Reason To Believe/ Handbags & Gladrags/ You Wear It Well/ Every Picture Tells A Story/ Tonight's The Night/ Maggie May/ Havin' A Party/ You're In My Heart/ Forever Young/ Downtown Train/ Infatuation/
CD2: Some Guys Have All The Luck/ The First Cut Is The Deepest/ Baby Please Don't Go, Intro/ Stay With Me/ Sweet Little Rock 'N Roller My Girl/ People Get Ready/ Have I Told You Lately/ This Old Heart Of Mine/ The Motown Song/ Da Ya Think I'm Sexy Twistin' The Night Away/ Chain Gang
R: Exs. Soundboard. S: Alamodome, San Antonio, Texas Nov. 26 '93. C: ECD. Dcc. Pic CD.

CD - LIVE IN ANAHEIM
BEST OF LIVE SERIES BOLS 001
You Wear It Well (5:13)/ Tonight's The Night (3:57)/ Sweet Little Rock & Rollers (9:03)/ Maggie May (7:22)/ Get Back (4:59)/ Georgie (6:14)/ Sailing (4:40)/ Stay With Me (7:51)
R: Exs. Soundboard. S: Anaheim '77.
C: ECD. Dcc.

CD - THAT'S ALL YOU NEED
GOLD STANDARD CES-815
Three Button Hand Me Down/ Miss Judy's Farm/ Memphis/ Too Bad/ Last Orders Please/ Devotion/ That's All You Need, Honky Tonk Woman, Gasoline Alley, That's All You Need/ I'm Losing You/ Stay With Me/ Had Me A Real Good Time/ Encore/ Around The Plynth, Gasoline Alley/ Maggie May
S: BBC radio '71-'72. C: ECD. Dcc.

STING

CD - A NIGHT IN THE LIFE OF STING
STAR 006-DoCD
CD1: If I Ever Lose My Faith In You/ Heavy Cloud But No Rain/ Love Is Stronger Than Justice/ Seven Days/ A Day In The Life/ Fields Of Gold/ Every Little Thing She Does Is Magic/ Roxanne/ It's Probably Me/ Shape Of My Heart
CD2: St. Augustine In Hell/ Straight To My Heart/ Englishman In New York/ King Of Pain/ Bring On The Night, When The World Is Running Down/ She's Too Good For Me/ Nothing 'Bout Me/ Every Breath You Take/ Fragile
R: Exs. Soundboard. S: Europe '93. C: ECD. Dcc. Tall digi-pack. CD1 Time 51:20 . CD2 49:30.

CD - AIN'T NO SUNSHINE
HAWK 022
Black Bird (2:14)/ Ain't No Sunshine (5:44)/ Childrens Crusade (6:36)/ Seven Days (4:48)/ Everything She Does Is Magic (4:21)/ Fortress Around Your Heart (4:45)/ Penny Lane (3:28)/ It's Probably Me (5:43)/ Shape Of My Heart (4:38)/ Purple Haze (3:57)/ Message In The Bottle (5:32)/ She's Too Good For Me (3:54)/ Epilogue (Nothing 'Bout Me) (5:44)/ Fragile (3:53)

R: Ex. Audience. S: Las Vegas, Nevada May 16 '93. C: ECD. Dcc. Pic CD.

CD - AN ENGLISHMAN IN BREMEN
PALAZZOGRASSI PG 03
They Dance Alone (10:45)/ Consider Me Gone (5:55)/ King Of Pain (6:02)/ Walking In Our Footsteps (5:10)/ How Fragile We Are, Little Wing (14:20)/ Too Much Information (9:15)/ Together Tonight (4:32)/ An Englishman In New York, I Got Out Of My Mind (13:15)
R: G. Audience. S: Germany '88. C: ECD. Dcc.

CD - COMPLETE CHICAGO SESSIONS
KISS THE STONE KTS 275
If I Ever Loose My Faith In You/ Love Is Stronger Than Justice/ Fields Of Gold/ Englishman In New York/ A Day In The Life/ Fortress Around Your Heart/ Medley: Epilogue (Nothing 'Bout Me), Every Breath You Take/ Mad About You/ The Wind Cries Mary/ Message In A Bottle/ The Soul Cages/ Every Breath You Take/ Be Bop A Lula/ I Miss You, Kate/ All This Time
R: Exs. Soundboard. S: Tracks 1-7 Chicago '93. 8-16 Chicago Apr. '91. C: ECD. Pic CD. 77:13

CD - LIVE VOL.1
JOKER JOK-050-A
Someone To Watch Over Me (3:25)/ Englishman In New York (4:59)/ Tempted (5:07)/ If You Love Somebody (Set Them Free) (6:15)/ Bring On The Night (2:46)/ When The World Is Running Down You Make The Best Of What's Still Around (8:02)/ The Idiot Bastard Son (2:07)/ King Of Pain (6:41)/ Don't Stand So Close To Me (11:09)/ Mack The Knife (2:53)/ Little Wing (10:26)/ Home On The Range (1:51)/ Every Breath You Take (6:55)
R: Exs. Soundboard. S: Los Angeles '88.
C: Australian CD.

CD - THE STING
ALL ABOUT FAME AAF 025 CD
A Day In The Life/ Fields Of Gold/ Every Little Thing She Does Is Magic/ Roxanne/ It's Probably Me/ Shape Of My Heart/ Straight To My Heart/ Englishman In New York/ King Of Pain/ Bring On The Night, When The World Is Running Down/ She's Too Good For Me/ Nothing 'Bout Me/ Every Breath You Take/ Fragile
R: Exs. Soundboard. S: Europe '93. C: ECD. Dcc. Digi-pack. Time 51:20.

STONE ROSES, THE

CD - ALL THE COLOURS FADE
Intro, I Wanna Be Adored/ Here It Comes/ Made Of Stone/ Waterfall/ Sugar Spun Sister/ Mersey Paradise/ Elephant Stone/ Angels Play/ Shoot You Down/ She Bangs The Drums/ Sally Cinnamon/ I Am The Resurrection
R: Ex. Audience. Problem with first song.
S: Hacienda, Manchester Feb. 27 '89. C: ECD. Time 56:39.

STONE TEMPLE PILOTS

CD - BRAND NEW LIVE
VAMPIRE VR 50011
Plush/ Sex Type Thing/ Wicked Garden/ Sin/ Dead
And Bloated/ Crackerman/ Where The River
Goes/ Creep/ Brand New Song/ Naked Sunday/
Piece Of Pie
R: G. Audience.   S: USA '93.   C: ECD. Dcc.
Time 63:05.

CD - THE GREAT PRETENDERS
BANZAI BZCD 041
Crackerman/ Wicked/ Garden/ Sin/ Plush/ Where
The River Goes/ Dead And Bloated/ Creep/ Sex
Type Thing/ Wet My Bed/ Naked Sunday/ Piece
Of Pie
R: Vg-Ex. Audience.   S: Groningen '94.
C: ECD. Dcc. Pic CD. Time 67:51.

CD - TROUBLE NO MORE
HAWK 029
Wicked Garden (4:27)/ Sin (7:41)/ Plush (7:52)/
Where The River Goes (8:05)/ Cracker Man (3:25)
R: Vg-Ex. Soundboard.   S: USA '93.   C: ECD.
Dcc. Pic CD.

STRADLIN, IZZY

CD - ROCKER
KISS THE STONE KTS 265
Bucket O' Trouble (2:48)/ Cuttin' The Rug (4:53)/
Jivin' Sister Fanny (4:23)/ Time Gone By (4:14)/
Rockin' Daddy (3:55)/ Somebody Knockin' (3:25)/
Pressure Drop (4:01)/ Little Red Rooster (4:40)/
Highway 49 (5:10)
R: Exs. Soundboard.   S: '93.   R: ECD. Pic CD.

STRAY CATS

CD - JAMMIN' WITH CATS
ALL OF US AS 34
Double Talkin' Baby (3:10)/ Rumble In Brighton
(3:39)/ Routegg (4:32)/ Rockabilly Rebel (5:43)/
Blue Cadillac (3:14)/ Runaway Boys (3:31)/ Lonely
Summernights (3:54)/ Too Hip, Gotta Go (2:32)/
Stray Cat's Strut (5:32)/ Foggy Mountain
Breakdown (2:13)/ The Raceison (1:48)/ Rev It Up
& Go (3:32)/ Blue Swede Shoes (6:35)
R: Ex. Audience.   S: Tracks 1-12, Loreley Open
Air Festival '83. Track 13 New York Bam Majestic
Theatre '88.   C: ECD. Dcc.

STYX

CD - SUNSET IN PARADISE
INTERNATIONAL BROADCAST RECORDINGS
IBR 2185
Mr. Roboto (4:34)/ Rockin' The Paradise (4:00)/
Blue Collar Man (Long Nights) (4:15)/ Fooling
Yourself (The Angry Young Man) (5:29)/
Snowblind (5:02)/ Too Much On My Hands (4:30)/
Don't Let It End (5:03)/ Suite Madame Blue (8:17)/
Cold War (8:04)/ Miss America (5:57)/ Come Sail

Away (8:04)/ Haven't We Been Here (4:38)
R: Exs. Soundboard.   S: Omni, Atlanta '83.
C: ECD. Dcc.

SUEDE

CD - PERFORMANCE
KISS THE STONE KTS 278
Pantomime Horse (7:03)/ Trashy (3:42)/ We Are
The Pigs (4:17)/ Animal Nitrate (3:15)/ My Heroine
(3:26)/ My Insatiable One (3:12)/ He's Dead
(6:47)/ Metal Mickey (3:26)/ Losing Myself (4:47)/
She's Not Dead (4:41)/ Sleeping Pills (4:46)/ Stay
Together (8:34)/ So Young (3:35)/ The Next Life
(3:32)/ My Insatiable One (3:04)
R: Ex. Audience.   S: Tracks 1-12 '94. Tracks 13-
15 '93.   C: ECD. Dcc. Pic CD.

SWEET

CD - FUNNY ADAMS
ELICH-RECORDS ER 002
Set Me Free/ Heartbreak Today/ No You Don't/
Rebel Rouser/ Peppermint Twist/ Sweet F.A./
Restless/ Into The Night/ AC-DC/ Hypnotized/
Fade Away/ You're Not Wrong For Not Lovin' Me/
The Sixteens/ Action/ The Lies In Your Eyes
R: Exs. Soundboard.   S: Studio. Tracks 10-15
live.   C: ECD. Dcc.

SWEET, MATTHEW

CD - SHAPE SHIFTER
KISS THE STONE KTS 257
Dinosaur Act/ I Wanted To Tell You/ The Ugly
Truth/ Someone To Pull The Trigger/ Girlfriend/ Do
It Again/ In Too Deep/ Day For Night/ Evangeline/
Reaching Out/ Devil With The Green Eyes/
Knowing People/ Divine Intervention/ Does She
Talk/ Time Capsule/ Crippled Inside/ I Want You
R: Exs. Soundboard.   S: Petrillo Band Shell,
Grant Park, Chicago Apr. 7 '93.   C: ECD. Dcc.
Pic CD. Time 72:59.

T

TANGERINE DREAM

CD - SONAMBULISTIC IMAGERY
BLUE MOON RECORDS BM5/6
CD1: Imagery One (44:48)
CD2: Imagery Two (41:14)/ Imagery Three (7:31)/
Imagery Four (6:50)/ Imagery Five (5:35)
R: Exs. Audience.   S: Irvine Meadows
Amphitheatre, Laguna Hills, June 6 '86.
C: ECD. Dcc.

TAYLOR, ROGER

CD – THE CROSS CROSSFIRE
SD 006
In Charge Of My Heart (6:13)/ Top Of The World
Ma (3:54)/ Penetration Guru (4:55)/ Breakdown

(4:14)/ Power To Love (4:51)/ Liar (5:11)/ Man On Fire (4:46)/ Old Man (Lay Down) (5:57)/ Sister Blue (4:24)/ Final Destination (6:49)/ Foxy Lady (5:19)/ I'm In Love With My Car (4:07)
R: Exs. Audience.   S: Milky Way, Amsterdam Holland May 29 '90.   C: ECD. Dcc. Time 59:10

CD – THE CROSS - GOSPORT FESTIVAL 1993
Q RECORDS CR CD 102
In Charge Of My Heart (5:37)/ Love Lies Bleeding (4:56)/ Ain't Put Nothin' Down (5:26)/ Band Intro (0:50)/ A Kind Of Magic (5:22)/ Power To Love (5:29)/ Life Changes (4:00)/ All The Young Dudes (3:18)/ New Dark Ages (6:31)/ Sister Blue (5:15)/ Radio Ga Ga (6:11)/ We Will Rock You (3:17)/ Top Of The World Ma (4:43)/ These Are The Days Of Our Lives (4:42)/ Final Destination (5:25)
R: Vg. Audience.   S: Gosport, England July 29 '93.   C: ECD. Dcc. The last 'The Cross' concert. Time 71:12

CD – THE CROSS - LIVE AT THE MARQUEE 22/12/92
Q RECORDS CR CD 98
Top Of The World Ma (4:28)/ Ain't Put Nothin' Down (5:17)/ New Dark Ages (6:15)/ Rock And Roll (4:31)/ Haven For Everyone (4:55)/ Man On Fire (5:16)/ Earth (with Tim Staffel on vocals, and Brian May on guitar) (5:35)/ If I Were A Carpenter (with Tim Staffel on vocals, and Brian May on guitar) (4:27)/ Too Much Love Will Kill You (with Brian May on vocal & guitar) (4:56)/ Tie Your Mother Down (with Brian May on vocals & guitar) (6:04)/ Money (3:45)/ Merry X–mas (War Is Over) (4:03)/ Radio Ga Ga (with Brian May on guitar) (6:00)/ These Are The Days Of Our Lives (with Brian May on guitar) (5:07)
R: Exs. Audience.   S: Marquee Club, London Dec. 22 '92. Special concert for 'Queen Fan Club' members only.   C: ECD. Dcc. Time 70:39

LP – THE CROSS - LIVE AT THE NEWCASTLE MAYFAIR
S1: Love Lies Bleeding/ Cowboys & Indians/ Man On Fire/ Haven For Everyone/ Love On A Tightrope/ I'm In Love With My Car/ Laugh Or Cry/ Manipulator/ Let's Get Drunk
S2: Feel The Force/ Contact/ Shove It/ Strange Frontier/ Let's Get Crazy/ Stand Up For Love
R: Vgs. Audience.   S: Mayfair, Newcastle UK March 1 '88.   C: Eb. Rare boot. Rumours are that only 25 copies where made.

10,000 MANIACS

CD - HOW YOU'VE GROWN
KISS THE STONE KTS 237
These Are Days (4:21)/ If You Intend (3:05)/ What's The Matter Here? (4:42)/ A Campfire Song (3:22)/ Like The Weather (4:20)/ How You've Grown (3:55)/ Jezebel (4:13)/ Eat For Two (3:36)/ Trouble Me (3:21)/ Gun Shy (4:43)/ Stockton Gala Days (5:10)/ Candy Everybody Wants (3:34)/ Hey Jack Kerouac (3:44)/ Few And Far Between

(3:42)/ My Sister Rose (4:19)/ Every Day Is Like Sunday (4:38)/ City Of Angels (4:32)/ Let The Mystery Be (4:37)/ Dallas (duet with David Byrne- 3:54)
R: Exs. Soundboard.   S: LA, CA, Oct. 25 '93.
C: ECD. Pic CD.

CD - IN THE GARDEN OF EDEN
NIKKO RECORDS NK009
Candy Everybody Wants (3:41)/ My Sister Rose (4:01)/ What's The Matter Here? (4:57)/ Don't Talk (5:08)/ If You Intend (3:11)/ Jezebel (4:03)/ I Beg Your Pardon (Rosegarden) (2:02)/ These Are Days (3:47)/ Hey Jack Kerouac (4:31)/ Few And Far Between (3:41)/ Everyday Is Like Sunday (3:41)/ Because The Night (3:40)/ These Are Days (4:11)/ What's The Matter Here? (5:09)/ How You've Grown (4:36)/ Jezebel (4:13)/ Stockton Gala Days (5:07)/ Candy Everybody Wants (3:28)/ Few And Far Between (2:46)/ Hey Jack Kerouac (3:20)
R: Exs. Soundboard.   S: Tracks 1-12 Kingswood Music Theater, Toronto, Canada '93. Tracks 13-20 Mountain Stage, Charleston, WV May '93.
C: ECD. Dcc. Fold-open digi-pack. Pic CD.

CD - OUT TIME AT THE GREEK
ROYAL SOUND MUSIC RSM 037
These Are Days/ If You Intend/ What's The Matter Here?/ A Campfire Song/ Like The Weather/ How You've Grown/ Jezebel/ Eat For Two/ Gun Shy/ Stockton Gala Days/ Candy Everybody Wants/ Hey Jack Kerouac/ Few And Far Between/ My Sister Rose/ Everyday Is Like Sunday/ City Of Angels/ Let The Mystery Be
S: The Greek Theatre, LA '93.   C: ECD.

THERAPY?

CD - FISTFUL OF POWER
KISS THE STONE KTS 318
Stop You're Killing Me (3:26)/ Trigger Inside (3:54)/ Isolation (3:27)/ Die Laughing (2:56)/ Femtex (2:57)/ Hellbelly (3:31)/ Nausea (3:34)/ Singing In The Rain, Brainsaw (4:11)/ Accelerator (2:32)/ Knives (2:02)/ Teenage Kicks, Screamer (3:12)/ Going Nowhere (3:00)
R: Vg. Audience.   S: Live in Europe 4-6-94.
C: ECD. Dbw. Red type. Pic CD.

CD - ISOLATION
NIKKO NKO 13
Die Laughing (2:46)/ Teethgrinder (3:14)/ Alone (3:36)/ Femtex (2:56)/ Turn (3:43)/ This One Sucks (3:48)/ Unbeliever (3:17)/ Accelerator (2:12)/ Hellbelly (3:17)/ Isolation (3:23)/ Screamager (2:41)/ Nausea (3:29)/ Going Nowhere (3:01)/ Lunacy Booth (4:47)
R: Exs. Soundboard.   S: Europe Mar. '94.
C: ECD. Digi-pack. Pic CD. Time 56:28.

CD - NO LOVE LOST
KISS THE STONE KTS 277
Innocent X (3:18)/ Opal Mantra (2:32)/ Turn (3:47)/

Neck Freak (5:58)/ Everyday (4:23)/ Accelerator (2:33)/ Screamager (2:53)/ Neck Freak (4:16)/ Meat Abstract (3:40)/ Accelerator (2:26)/ Screamager (2:40)/ Potato Junkie (3:27)/ Innocent X (3:40)/ Opal Mantra (2:26)/ Accelerator (2:14)/ Screamager (2:49)/ Potato Junkie (4:08)/ Teethgrinder (3:13)/ Skinny Pig, Fantasy Bag (10:51)
R: Exs. Soundboard.   S: '93.   C: ECD. Dcc. Pic CD.

THIN LIZZY

CD - THE IRISH DAWN
POETRY IN MOTION POET 9201
Jailbreak (4:26)/ The Boys Are Back In Town (4:46)/ Emerald (3:44)/ It's Only Money (3:15)/ Blues Boy (4:02)/ Warrior (3:57)/ Rosalie (4:55)/ Suicide (4:46)/ Angel From The Coast (2:57)/ Sha-La-La (6:42)/ Baby Drives Me Crazy (7:33)/ The Rocker (3:36)
R: G.   S: Live in Chicago '76.   C: ECD. Dcc.

THOMPSON, RICHARD

CD - ACROSS A CROWDED ROOM
HQ 04
Fire In The Engine Room (3:55)/ She Twists The Knife (4:04)/ Shoot Out The Lights (5:39)/ You Don't Say (4:08)/ Wall Of Death (3:29)/ Little Blue Number (3:06)/ When The Spell Is Broken (4:14)/ Did She Jump Or Was She Pushed (5:08)/ Wrong Heartbeat (3:42)/ Summer Rain (5:36)/ For Shame Of Doing Wrong (7:40)/ I Want To See The Bright Lights Tonight (3:00)/ Nearly In Love (4:02)/ Love In A Faithless Country (7:23)/ I Ain't Going To Drag My Feet No More (4:50)/ Withered And Died (4:19)
R: Exs. Soundboard.   S: USA '85.   C: ECD. Dcc. Digi-pack. Gold disc. Time 74:04.

CD - A RARE THING
KISS THE STONE KTS 362/63
CD1: Intro - Valerie/ Misunderstood/ Don't Let A Thief Steal Into Your Heart/ Fright Train/ Taking My Business Elsewhere/ Gonna Break Somebody's Heart Tonight/ Oh Mercy, What's Already Mine/ Don't Sit On My Jimmy Shan's/ Shoot Out The Lights/ I Can't Wake Up/ From Galway To Graceland/ '52 Black Vincent
CD2: What A Fool/ Dimming Of The Day/ Mr. Dead/ She Twists The Knife Again/ A Rare Thing/ Two Left Feet/ Blessed/ Real Gone/ Walking On A Wire/ Drinking Wine Spo-Dee O'Dee
R: Exs. Soundboard.   S: Cat's Cradle, Chapel Hill, North Carolina Aug. 13 '94.   C: ECD. Dbw. Pic CDs.

THOMPSON, RICHARD & LINDA

CD - STRANGE AFFAIR
SILVER RARITIES SIRA 145/146 2-CD
CD1: Madness Of Love/ Night Comes In/ The Bird

In God's Garden/ King Of Love/ Layla/ Jet Plane In A Rocking Chair/ The Wrong Heartbeat/ Speechless Child/ Wall Of Death/ Just The Motion/ Backstreet Slide/ Modern Woman*
CD2: House Of Cards/ Genesis Hall/ Restless Highway/ Pavanne/ Madame Soustaine/ Things You Gave Me/ Sweet Surrender/ The Gas Almost Works/ Layla/ Then He Kissed Me/ Lonely Hearts/ Strange Affair/ Sunny Vista/ Crying In The Rain/ Just The Motion/ How Many Times Do You Have To Fall/ Sweet Georgia Brown/ Modern Woman
R: CD1 Tracks 1-5 G-Vg. Audience. Hiss. Tracks 6-11 Ex. Soundboard. Track 12 Vg. Soundboard. CD2 Tracks 1-10 Ex. Audience. Tracks 11-18 Ex. Soundboard.   S: CD1 Tracks 1-5 Drury Lane May 1 '77. Tracks 6-12 Cambridge Folk Festival Aug. 1 and 2* '80. CD2 Tracks 1-10 Theatre Royal, Drury Lane Nov. 12 '78. Tracks 11-14 Richard Digence Show, Capitol Radio, London Feb. 10 '80. Tracks 15-18 Richard Digence Show, Capitol Radio, London June 22 '80.   C: ECD. Time CD1 73:29. CD2 76:04.

TOOL

CD - DRAGGING ME DOWN
HAWK 060
Intolerance/ Undertow/ Sober/ Bottom/ Prison Sex/ 4'/ Opiate/ Swamp Song
R: G. Audience.   C: ECD. Dcc. Pic CD.

CD - TALES FROM THE DARKSIDE
KISS THE STONE KTS 263
Undertow (5.42)/ Sober (5:10)/ Opiate (6:17)/ Flood (3:40)/ Prison Sex (4:50)/ Jerk-Off (4:18)/ Prison Sex (5:01)/ Bottom (6:24)
R: Exs. Soundboard.   S: '93.   C: ECD. Dcc. Pic CD.

TOWNSEND, PETE

CD - ROUGH BOY
D.T. 1001 THE GOLD STANDARD WNS-668
Rough Boys/ Eyesight To The Blind/ I'm An Animal/ Eminence Front/ You Better You Bet/ A Little Is Enough/ Heart To Hang Onto/ Let's See Action/ Let My Love Open The Door/ Face The Face/ I'm One/ Save It For Later/ Won't Get Fooled Again
R: Ex. Audience.   S: Beacon Theatre, New York July 13 '93.   C: ECD. Dcc. Gold disc. 70:19.

TRAFFIC

CD - THE PERFUMED GARDEN
GOLD STANDARD
Dear Mr. Fantasy/ Introduction/ Hole In My Shoe/ Paper Sun/ A House For Everyone/ No Face No Name No Number/ Hope They Never Find Me Here/ 40,000 Headman/ Dear Mr. Fantasy/ You Can All Join In/ Feelin' Alright/ Heaven Is In Your Mind/ Dealer/ Utterly Simple/ Coloured Rain/ Smiling Phases/ Heaven Is In Your Mind/ Pearly Queen/ Who Know's What Tomorrow My Bring?/

Colored Rain/ Dear Mr. Fantasy #2
S: Tracks 2-11 and 16-20 live on BBC Radio '67-
'68. Tracks 1, 12-15 & 21 are studio recordings
from Island Records Basing St. Studios summer
'67.   C: ECD.

TRITT, TRAVIS

CD - HOMESICK
ROYAL SOUND MUSIC RSM 027 SQ
Here's A Quarter (Call Someone Who Cares)/
Anymore/ Lord Have Mercy On The Working Man/
The Whiskey Ain't Working/ Country Club/
Outlaws Like Us/ Nothing Short Of Dyin'/ Help Me
Hold On/ Homesick/ Young Country/ Blues Man/
Burning Love
S: New York '93.   C: ECD.

U

UGLY KID JOE

CD - AMERICA'S LEAST HERO
MANIC MONSTER MUSIC MMM 009
Panhandlin' Prince (5:44)/ Come Tomorrow (4:35)/
Whiplash Liquor (3:30)/ Too Bad (5:43)/ Same
Side (4:21)/ Don't Go (4:20)/ Busy Bee (4:01)/
Neighbor (4:22)/ Sweet Leaf (2:10)/ Funky Fresh
Country Club (5:39)/ So Damn Cool (4:30)/
Goddamn Devil (4:09)/ Everything About You
(Hardcore Version) (4:21)/ Cats In The Cradle
(4:13)/ Everything About You (4:15)/ Sin City
(4:56)
R: Ex.   S: World Tour '92-'93 - various locations
throughout the USA.   C: ECD. Dcc.

CD - IN THE CRADLE
VAMPIRE VR 50008
Pan Handle Prince (5:54)/ Come Tomorrow (4:54)/
Cats In The Cradle (4:10)/ Everything About You
(4:22)/ Busy Bee (3:50)/ Neighbor (4:33)/ Sweet
Leaf (2:08)/ Funky Fresh (5:28)/ Too Bad (5:38)/
Everything About You, Megaversion (4:23)/ So
Damn Cool (3:55)/ Good Damn Devil (4:07)
R: Exs. Soundboard.   S: USA '93.   C: ECD.

UNITED KINGDOM

CD - TOUR MEMORIES
ALL OF US AS 37
Alaska, Time To Kill (8:52)/ The Only Thing She
Needs (6:57)/ Carrying No Cross (9:59)/ Thirty
Years (8:22)/ By The Light Of Day (1:48)/ Presto
Vivace (1:50)/ In The Dead Of Night (6:40)/
Danger Money (6:38)/ Wenton's Bass Solo (4:05)/
Rendezvous (6:09)/ Medley: The Only Things She
Needs (9:25)/ Waiting For You (5:00)
R: G. Audience.   S: Tracks 1-7 Boston Paradise
July '78. Tracks 8-12 Oslo July 12 '79.
C: ECD. Dcc.

URIAH HEEP

CD - BYRON'S LOST POEM
REEL TAPES RTCD 013
I Wanna Be Free (4:00)/ Easy Livin' (2:26)/ July
Morning (9:58)/ Tears In My Eyes (4:19)/
Improvisation (21:39)/ Bird Of Prey (3:54)/
Rainbow Demon (5:01)/ Look At Yourself (3:22)/
Lady In Black (6:55)/ Gypsy (10:07)
R: G. Soundboard. Hiss.   S: Munster Landhalle
3/5/72.   C: ECD. Dcc.

US 3

**CD - JAZZ IS THE TEACHER, HIPHOP IS THE
PREACHER**
MOGUL NIGHTMARE RECORDS MNR 016
I Got It Goin' On/ Make Tracks/ Knowledge Of
Self/ Just Another Brother/ Eleven Long Years/ It's
Like That/ Cantaloop/ Lazy Day/ Tukka Yoot's
Riddim
R: Exs. Soundboard.   S: Live '93.   C: ECD.
Dcc. Time 43:40.

U2

CD - BONO'S BIRTHDAY PARTY
TAKE IT OR LEAVE IT T 9302/3
CD1: Intro/ Zoo Station/ The Fly/ Even Better Than
The Real Thing/ Mysterious Ways/ One/ Until The
End Of The World/ Intro, I Need Your Love, New
Years Day/ Party Girl/ 'Bono We Love You', Tryin'
To Throw Your Arms Round The World/ Angel Of
Harlem, My Girl
CD2: I Will Follow/ Satellite Of Love/ Sunday
Bloody Sunday/ Bullet The Blue Sky/ Running To
Stand Still/ Where The Streets Have No Name/
Pride/ Crowd Noise, Video Message, Desire/
Phone Call, Martini Commercial, Light My Way/
With Or Without You/ Love Is Blindness
R: Poor-G. Audience.   S: Rotterdam May 10 '93.
C: ECD. Dcc. Time CD1 57:20. CD2 68:15.

CD - DESIRE (VOL. 3)
BANANA BAN-048-C
Where The Streets Have No Names (4:36)/ I Will
Follow (4:21)/ I Still Haven't Found What I'm
Looking For (3:57)/ Exodus (0:54)/ M.L.K. (1:53)/
One Tree Hill (4:50)/ Gloria (4:35)/ God Part II
(3:32)/ Desire (3:08)/ All Along The Watchtower
(4:16)/ All I Want Is You (0:55)/ Bad (7:33)/ Van
Dieman's Land (3:00)
R: Ex.   S: Europe '91.   C: Australian CD. Dcc.
Gold disc.

CD - DESIRE (VOL. 4)
BANANA BAN-048-D
Bullet The Blue Sky (5:30)/ Running To Stand Still
(3:14)/ Dirty Old Town (1:21)/ The Times They Are
A-Changin' (0:27)/ New Year's Day (4:46)/ Pride
(In The Name Of Love) (6:14)/ Party Girl (4:02)/
Angel Of Harlem (3:45)/ When Love Comes To
Town (5:08)/ Love Rescue Me (5:59)/ 40 (5:50)
R: Ex.   S: Europe '91.   C: Australian CD. Dcc.

CD - ENJOY

WHO AM I? WAI 018/19
CD1: Where The Streets Have No Name/ I Will Follow/ ?/ I Still Haven't Found What I'm Looking For/ Gloria/ MLK/ The Unforgettable Fire/ Sunday Bloody Sunday/ ?/ In Gods Country/ Helter Skelter/ Help/ Bad/ Ruby Tuesday/ ?/ New Years Day/ Pride (In The Name Of Love)
CD2: Star Spangled Banner/ Bullet The Blue Sky/ Running To Stand Still/ Silver & Gold/ Spanish Eyes/ With Or Without You/ Rehearsing With Daniel Lanois On The Beach In Fresno '88
R: G-Vg. Audience.   S: Denver Nov. 8 '87.
C: ECD. Dcc. Time CD1 69:15. CD2 70:55.

CD - FARAWAY, SO CLOSE...

ALTERNATIVE RECORD COMPANY ARC005-6
CD1: Mysterious Ways/ One/ Mystery Girl/ Until The End Of The World/ New Years Day/ Numb/ Satellite Of Love/ I Still Haven't Found What I'm Looking For/ I Will Follow/ Redemption Song/ Sunday Bloody Sunday/ Bullet The Blue Sky/ Running To Stand Still/ Where The Streets Have No Name/ Pride (In The Name Of Love)/ Video Box Messages
CD2: Zooropa Hymn/ Desire/ Macphisto Show/ Ultraviolet (Light My Way)/ With Or Without You/ Love Is Blindness/ I Can't Help Fallin' In Love/ 11 O'Clock Tick Tock/ The Speed Of Light/ The Magic Carpet/ Stories For Boys/ Trevor/ Another Time Another Place/ Cartoon World/ Jack In The Box/ Shadow And Tall Trees/ A Day Without Me/ Twilight/ Boy/Girl
R: Poor-G except CD2 tracks 8-19 G-Vg. Audience.   S: Rome, Stadio Flaminio July 7 '93 except CD2 tracks 8-19 National Stadium, Dublin, Ireland Feb. 26 '80.   C: ECD. Dcc. Limited edition of 1000 copies. Time CD1 70:45. CD2 74:41.

CD - THE FLY (1989-1993)

FLYING TIGERS FTBX 0039/40/41
CD1: God Part 2 (3:54)/ Desire (3:10)/ All Along The Watchtower (4:10)/ All I Want Is You (5:13)/ Where The Streets Have No Name (5:41)/ Gloria (4:44)/ I Still Haven't Found What I'm Looking For (6:12)/ M.L.K. (1:46)/ One Tree Hill (5:34)/ Van Dieman's Land (2:46)/ Pride (5:21)/ Angel Of Harlem (4:22)/ When Love Comes To Town (4:47)/ Love Rescue Me (5:34)/ With Or Without You (5:19)/ 40 (4:24)/ New Year's Day (4:20)
CD2: Bad (7:27)/ Van Diemen's Land, Bullet The Blue Sky (6:21)/ Running To Stand Still, Dirty Old Town (5:19)/ The Times They Are A' Changin', New Year's Day (5:10)/ Party Girl (3:38)/ Who's Gonna Ride Your Wild Horses (5:01)/ I Still Haven't Found What I'm Looking For (7:20)/ Satellite Of Love (3:18)/ Zoo Station (4:44)/ The Fly (5:59)/ Even Better Than The Real Thing (3:39)/ Mysterious Ways (6:59)/ One, Unchained Melody (6:10)/ Until The End Of The World (4:55)
CD3: Numb (4:10)/ Trying To Throw Your Arms Around The World (4:02)/ Angel Of Harlem (4:13)/ When Love Comes To Town (3:26)/ Stay (5:18)/

Satellite Of Love (3:42)/ Bad (6:52)/ Bullet The Blue Sky (5:27)/ Running To Stand Still (5:57)/ Where The Streets Have No Name (5:15)/ Pride (5:27)/ Desire (7:29)/ Help, Ultra Violet (Light My Way) (5:48)/ With Or Without You (3:50)/ Love Is Blindness (5:13)/ I Can't Help Falling In Love (2:20)
R: Exs. Soundboard.   S: CD1 and CD2 tracks 1-5 from 'Love Comes To Town' tour. CD2 tracks 6-8 from 'Zoo TV' tour. CD2 tracks 9-14 from 'Zooropa' tour. CD3 from 'Zooropa' tour.
C: ECD. Box set. Pic CDs. See 'Keeping The Faith', 'The New Word' and 'Rare Tracks'.

CD - GLORIA (VOL. 2)

BANANA BAN-046-B
Gloria (4:33)/ Another Time Another Place (4:45)/ I Threw A Brick Through A Window (4:43)/ Rejoice (3:23)/ With A Shout (4:20)/ The Electric Co. (5:15)/ I Fall Down (3:00)/ October (2:30)/ I Will Follow (4:19)/ An Cat Dubh, Into The Heart (6:40)/ Out Of Control (6:05)/ Twilight (4:13)/ 11 O'Clock Tick Tock (4:50)/ The Ocean (3:28)
R: Exs. Soundboard.   S: USA '81.
C: Australian CD. Dcc.

CD - GLORIA (VOL. 3)

BANANA BAN-046-C
I Threw A Brick Through A Window (4:28)/ An Cat Dubh (5:25)/ Into The Heart (1:32)/ With A Shout (4:21)/ Rejoice (3:34)/ The Electric Co. (5:02)/ I Fall Down (3;05)/ October (2:11)/ I Will Follow (3:37)/ Twilight (4:17)/ Out Of Control (4:30)/ 11 O'clock Tick Tock (4:58)/ The Ocean (3:11)/ I Will Follow (2:43)
R: Exs. Soundboard.   S: USA '81.
C: Australian CD. Dcc.

CD - GLORIA (VOL. 4)

BANANA BAN-046-D
Surrender (5:04)/ I Threw A Brick Through A Window (3:52)/ A Day Without Me (3:13)/ An Cat Dubh, Into The Heart (7:14)/ The Electric Co. (5:04)/ Sunday Bloody Sunday (5:31)/ I Fall Down (3:03)/ Party Girl (3:3)/ 11 O'Clock Tick Tock (4:33)/ The Ocean (3:00)/ '40' (3:23)/ October (2:35)/ New Year's Day (4:50)/ I Will Follow (3:37)/ Gloria (4:53)/ Fire (3:42)/ Celebration (2:45)
R: Ex.   S: Europe '93.   C: Australian CD. Dcc.

CD - HEIL MUNCHEN!

RED PHANTOM RPCD 2188-2189
CD1: Intro (5:17)/ Zoo Station (4:47)/ The Fly (6:04)/ Even Better Than The Real Thing (3:42)/ Mysterious Ways (7:15)/ One (4:38)/ Unchained Melody (1:21)/ Until The End Of The World (5:12)/ New Year's Day (5:10)/ Dirty Old Town (1:27)/ Tryin' To Throw Your Arms Around The World (5:53)/ Angel Of Harlem (4:06)/ I Will Follow (2:46)/ Satellite Of Love (4:11)/ Redemption Song (1:58)/ Sunday Bloody Sunday (4:59)/ Bullet The Blue Sky (5:16)
CD2: Running To Stand Still (6:14)/ Where The Streets Have No Name (5:13)/ Pride In The Name

Of Love (5:05)/ Zoo TV Confession Box (4:46)/ Desire, Singin' In The Rain (4:55)/ Phone Call To Mr. Helmut Kohl (3:20)/ Ultra Violet Light My Way (4:57)/ With Or Without You (4:15)/ Love Is Blindness (5:30)/ Can't Help Falling In Love (2:59)/ Mysterious Ways (4:00)/ Unreleased Instrumental Track (5:09)/ Unreleased Track (5:51)
R: G-Vg.   S: CD1 Tracks and CD2 tracks 1-17 Olympic Stadium, Munich June 4 '93. CD2 track 11 Vancouver '92 soundcheck. Tracks 12-13 El Paso 'Sun Bowl' Nov. 10 '92 soundcheck.
C: ECD. Sepia-toned cover. Pic CDs.

CD - KEEPING THE FAITH VOLUME 2 (1984-1988)
FLYING TIGERS FTBX 0035/36/37
CD1: 11 O'Clock Tick Tock (5:00)/ 2 Seconds (3:42)/ M.L.K. (2:12)/ The Unforgettable Fire (5:09)/ Wire (4:06)/ Sunday Bloody Sunday (5:27)/ The Electric Co. (8:36)/ A Sort Of Homecoming (4:59)/ Bad (10:14)/ October (2:06)/ New Year's Day (5:58)/ Pride (In The Name Of Love) (5:29)/ Knocking On Heaven's Door (4:00)/ Gloria (4:58) CD2: 40 (9:10)/ Indian Summer (3:55)/ Party Girl (3:34)/ C'mon Everybody (2:03)/ Sunday Bloody Sunday (Acoustic) (4:27)/ Maggie's Farm (6:39)/ Where The Streets Have No Name (6:26)/ I Will Follow (4:22)/ Trip Through Your Wires (3:49)/ I Still Haven't Found What I'm Looking For (5:51)/ The Unforgettable Fire (4:37)/ Bullet The Blue Sky (5:23)/ Running To Stand Still (4:25)/ Exit (4:42)/ In God's Country (3:11)/ Sunday Bloody Sunday (5:52) CD3: Bad (11:28)/ Springhill Mining Disaster (3:41)/ New Year's Day (5:18)/ Pride (In The Name Of Love) (5:25)/ Mothers Of The Disappeared (4:09)/ With Or Without You (6:39)/ Silver And Gold (6:11)/ Out Of Control (5:02)/ One Tree Hill (5:37)/ A Sort Of Homecoming (5:53)/ People Get Ready (4:50)/ All Along The Watchtower (3:20)/ Angel Of Harlem (3:37)/ When Love Comes To Town (4:15)/ Love Rescue Me (3:59)
R: CD1 and CD2 tracks 1-3 Exs. Soundboard. Rest Ex. Audience.   S: CD1 and CD2 tracks 1-3 from the 'Unforgettable' tour. CD2 tracks 4-6 from the 'Amnesty International' tour. CD2 tracks 7-16 and CD3 tracks 1-10 from the 'Joshua Tree' tour. CD3 tracks 11-15 from 'Impromptu' tour.
C: ECD. Box set. Pic CDs. See 'The Fly', 'The New Word' and 'Rare Tracks'.

CD - LE DIABLE AU CORPS
THE FLYING TIGERS HTCD 0003/4
CD1: Intro - Zoo Station/ The Fly/ Even Better Than The Real Thing/ Mysterious Ways/ One/ Until The End Of The World/ New Years Day/ Dirty Old Town/ Trying To Throw Your Arms Around The World/ Angel Of Harlem/ Love Comes To Town/ Satellite Of Love CD2: Bad/ Bullet The Blue Sky/ Running To Stand Still/ Where The Streets Have No Name/ Pride/ Desire/ Ultra Violet Light My Way/ With Or Without You/ Love Is Blindness

R: Poor-G. Audience.   S: Zooropa '93.
C: ECD. Dcc. Pic CDs. CD1 57:15. CD2 47:13.

CD - LEMON
GRAPEFRUIT GRA-006-B
Dirty Day (5:31)/ Bad, You've Got To Hide Your Love Away, All I Want Is You (7:11)/ Bullet The Blue Sky (5:02)/ Running To Stand Still (5:57)/ Where The Streets Have No Name (5:16)/ Pride (In The Name Of Love (4:16)/ I Still Haven't Found What I'm Looking For (4:19)/ Stand By Me (2:55)/ Desire (4:51)/ Help!/ Ultra Violet (Light My Way) (5:54)/ Daddy's Gonna Pay For Your Crashed Car (5:54)/ Lemon (5:14)/ With Or Without You (4:10)/ Love Is Blindness (5:10)/ Can't Help Falling In Love (2:25)
R: Exs. Soundboard.   S: Seattle, WA '93 part 2. See 'Mysterious Ways' (GRA-006-A) for part 1.
C: Australian CD. Dcc.

CD - LUCILLE
RED PHANTOM RPCD 2169
CD1: Where The Streets Have No Name (6:29)/ I Still Haven't Found What I'm Looking For/ MLK (1:62)/ Bullet The Blue Sky (4:54)/ Exit, Gloria (4:25)/ Lucille (1:51)/ I Will Follow (4:20)/ Exodus (6:44)/ The Unforgettable Fire (4:29)/ Running To Stand Still (4:16)/ In God's Country (4:07)/ Sunday Bloody Sunday (6:11)/ Bad, Candle In The Wind, Walk On The Wild Side (6:42) CD2: October (2:05)/ New Years Day (4:44)/ Pride (In The Name Of Love) (4:37)/ Party Girl (3:07)/ Spanish Eyes (3:07)/ With Or Without You, Love Will Tear Us Apart (7:57)/ 40 (6:03)/ Mothers Of The Disappeared (2:10)/ The Time Has Come (5:19)/ Mothers Of The Disappeared (5:47)/ Moving Out (4:06)/ Silver & Gold (3:15)
R: Ex. Audience. *Soundboard.   S: Glasgow, July 29 '87. *CD2 tracks 9-15 Cow Palace, San Francisco Apr. 26 '87.   C: ECD.

CD - MYSTERIOUS WAYS
GRAPEFRUIT GRA-006-A
Zoo Station (4:51)/ The Fly (5:19)/ Even Better Than The Real Thing (3:42)/ Mysterious Ways (6:55)/ One, Unchained Melody (6:05)/ Until The End Of The World (5:01)/ New Year's Day (5:04)/ Numb (4:07)/ Who's Gonna Ride Your Wild Horses (4:50)/ Tryin' To Throw Your 'Arms Around The World (6:02)/ Angel Of Harlem (3:19)/ Dancing Queen (2:51)/ When Loves Comes To Town (3:26)/ Stay (Faraway So Close!) (5:47)/ Satellite Of Love (3:56)
R: Exs. Soundboard.   S: Seattle, WA '93 part 1. See 'Lemon' (GRA-006-B) for part 2.
C: Australian CD. Dcc.

CD - THE NEW WORD VOLUME 1 (1979-1983)
FLYING TIGERS FTBX 0028/29/30
CD1: I Will Follow (3:58)/ Touch (2:43)/ An Cat Dubh, Into The Heart (7:59)/ A Day Without Me (3:05)/ Twilight (4:33)/ The Electric Co. (4:34)/ Stories For Boys (2:55)/ Boy Girl (3:24)/ Out Of Control (5:10)/ 11 O'Clock Tick Tock (4:55)/ With

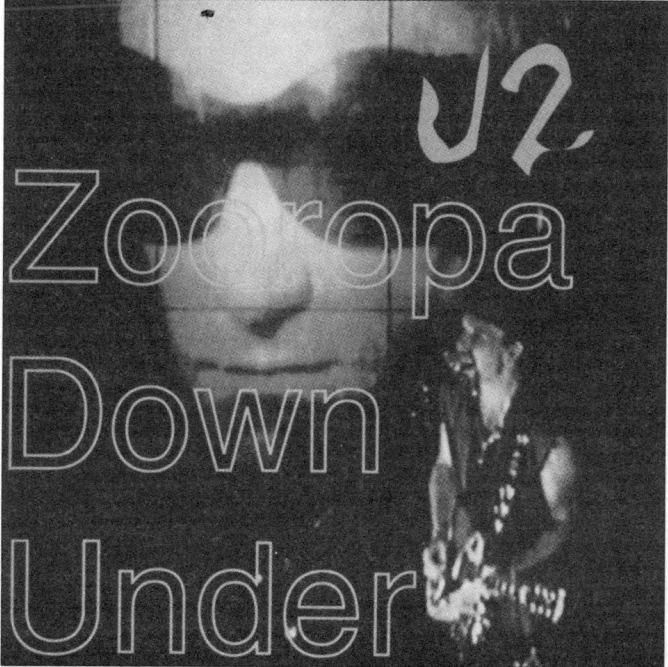

A Shout (3:53)/ The Ocean (1:53)/ 11 O'Clock Tick Tock (5:04)/ Touch (3:02)/ An Cat Dubh, Into The Heart (7:58)/ Another Time Another Place (4:33)/ The Electric Co. (4:55)/ Things To Make And Do (2:18)
CD2: Stories For Boys (3:12)/ Twilight (4:25)/ I Will Follow (4:33)/ Out Of Control (5:22)/ 11 O'Clock Tick Tock (4:53)/ The Ocean (2:16)/ Gloria (5:01)/ I Threw A Brick Through A Window (4:17)/ A Day Without Me (3:20)/ An Cat Dubh (7:52)/ Rejoice (3:40)/ The Electric Co. (5:27)/ I Will Follow (4:02)/ Out Of Control (5:02)/ 11 O'Clock Tick Tock (7:03)/ The Ocean (2:27)/ Fire (3:58)
CD3: I Fall Down (3:19)/ Intro - Surrender (5:32)/ Seconds (3:13)/ Sunday Bloody Sunday (5:47)/ October (2:09)/ New Year's Day (4:47)/ October (2:09)/ New Year's Day (4:47)/ I Threw A Brick Through A Window (3:51)/ A Day Without Me (3:04)/ Gloria (5:00)/ Party Girl (2:58)/ 11 O'Clock Tick Tock (5:05)/ I Will Follow (3:56)/ 40 (5:15)/ Two Hearts Beat As One (5:19)/ Sunday Bloody Sunday (5:28)/ October (2:07)
R: Ex. Audience and soundboard. S: CD1 tracks 1-11 from 'A Day Without Me' tour. CD1 tracks 12-18 and CD2 tracks 1-6 from the 'Boy' tour. CD2 tracks 7-17 and CD3 track 1 from the 'October' tour. CD3 tracks 2-16 from the 'War' tour. C: ECD. Box set. Pic CDs. See 'The Fly', 'Keeping The Faith' and 'Rare Tracks'.

CD - PRIDE (VOL. 1)
BANANA BAN-047-A
Out Of Control (4:36)/ Two Hearts Beat As One (5:40)/ An Cat Dubh (4:11)/ Into The Heart (3:00)/ Sunday Bloody Sunday (5:26)/ The Electric Co., Send In The Clowns (5:37)/ October (2:08)/ Gloria (4:38)/ I Threw A Brick Through A Window (3:44)/ A Day Without Me (3:20)/ 11 O'Clock Tick Tock (4:45)/ I Will Follow (3:45)/ Surrender (5:00)
R: Exs. Soundboard. S: USA '83.
C: Australian CD. Dcc.

CD - PRIDE (VOL. 2)
BANANA BAN-047-B
Where The Streets Have No Name (6:23)/ I Will Follow (4:38)/ Trip Through Your Wires (3:17)/ I Still Haven't Found What I'm Looking For (5:26)/ MLK (1:33)/ Unforgettable Fire (5:11)/ Sunday Bloody Sunday (4:52)/ Exit (4:19)/ In God's Country (3:22)/ Helter Skelter (3:22)/ Help! (1:38)/ Pride (In The Name Of Love) (4:41)/ Bullet The Blue Sky (5:58)/ Running To Stand Still (4:45)/ Silver And Gold (6:04)
R: Exs. Soundboard. S: USA '87.
C: Australian CD. Dcc.

CD - PRIDE (VOL. 3)
BANANA BAN-047-C
Running To Stand Still, Dirty Old Town (5:34)/ God Part II (3:29)/ Desire (2:57)/ All Along The Watchtower (4:30)/ All I Want Is You (5:36)/ Where The Streets Have No Name (5:45)/ I Will Follow (4:43)/ I Still Haven't Found What I'm Looking For (5:10)/ MLK (1:54)/ One Tree Hill (4:22)
R: Ex. Audience. S: Europe '89. C: Australian CD. Dcc.

CD - PRIDE (VOL. 4)
BANANA BAN-047-D
Van Dieman's Land (3:20)/ Out Of Control (4:25)/ New Year's Day (4:40)/ Pride (In The Name Of Love) (7:05)/ She's a Mystery To Me (5:50)/ Angel Of Harlem (4:10)/ When Love Comes To Town (with B.B. King - 5:10)/ Love Rescue Me (with B.B. King - 7:20)/ 11 O'Clock Tick Tock (4:50)/ With Or Without You (6:00)
R: Ex. Audience. S: Europe '89. C: Australian CD. Dcc.

CD - RARE TRACKS (1979-1993)
FLYING TIGERS FTBX 0031/38/42
CD1: Tomorrow (4:58)/ Treasure (3:25)/ The Fool (4:05)/ Out Of Control (4:18)/ Twilight (4:19)/ The Magic Carpet (3:35)/ Another Time Another Place (4:27)/ Alone In The Light (2:18)/ False Prophet (2:27)/ Scarlet (2:32)/ Tomorrow (2:21)/ Like A Song (3:53)/ The Electric Co. (5:36)/ Tonight (1:46)/ Trevor (3:10)/ Inside Out (1:45)/ With A Shout (4:01)/ Ocean (1:45)/ 11 O'Clock Tick Tock (5:03)/ Knockin' On Heaven's Door (3:53)/ New Year's Day (5:36)
CD2: Leopard Skin Pill-Box Hat (5:23)/ Blowing In The Wind (4:44)/ Southern Man (3:06)/ My Hometown (4:18)/ Womanfish (4:57)/ Sun City (3:42)/ Exit (3:36)/ In God's Country (2:49)/ Springhill Mining Disaster (3:51)/ Lost Highway (3:11)/ Rain, I Still Haven't Found What I'm Looking For, Exodus, Rain (6:21)/ Spanish Eyes (3:21)/ Helter Skelter (3:20)/ Help (2:04)/ Party Girl (2:52)/ Stand By Me (3:51)/ Maggie's Farm (4:43)/ New Gold Dream (4:52)/ Electric Co., Break On Through (4:07)
CD3: Slow Dancing (2:18)/ M.L.K. (1:45)/ One Tree Hill (4:40)/ God Part Two (3:48)/ Running To Stand Still (5:10)/ She Is A Mystery To Me (4:11)/ Hawkmoon 269 (4:46)/ One (4:15)/ Heaven And Hell (6:44)/ Fragments Of Real Thing (5:48)/ Got To Get Together (9:14)/ The Darkest Night (4:30)/ Fragments Of Wild Horses (4:20)/ How Do You Feel (7:43)/ Mercy (4:00)/ In My Dreams (3:12)
S: Rare studio outtakes, live performances and broadcasts. C: ECD. Box set. Pic CDs. Book. See 'The Fly', 'Keeping The Faith' and 'The New Word'.

CD - RIVERBOAT PRESIDENT
LORDS OF ARCHIVE L.A.R. 3
Gloria/ Another Time, Another Place/ I Threw A Brick/ A Day Without Me/ An Cat DUB/ Into The Heart/ Rejoice/ The Electric Co./ I Fall Down/ October/ Stories For Boys/ I Will Follow/ Twilight/ Out Of Control/ Fire/ 11:00 Tic Toc/ The Ocean/ New Years Day*/ A Celebration*
R: Ex. Soundboard. S: Riverboat President, New Orleans Feb. 11 '82. *Hammersmith, London.
C: ECD. Dcc. Booklet with B&w pictures from gig. Time 74:40.

CD - THROUGH THE YEARS

BLUE KNIGHT RECORDS BKR 25

I Will Follow (3:57)/ October (2:25)/ Gloria (4:55)/ Tomorrow (5:00)/ Sunday Bloody Sunday (5:50)/ New Year's Day (4:50)/ The Unforgettable Fire (4:45)/ A Sort Of Homecoming (4:20)/ In God's Country (2:55)/ Angel Of Harlem (4:15)/ When Love Comes To Town* (5:25)/ Love Rescue Me** (5:10)/ Desire (3:40)/ Van Diemen's Land (3:00)/ One (5:10)/ Until The End Of The World (4:30)/ Even Better Than The Real Thing (3:50)/ Dirty Old Town (1:01)

R: Exs. Soundboard.   S: Live '80-'92.   C: ECD. Dbw. Red/green type. *With B.B. King. **With Keith Richards & Ziggy Marley.

CD - TWO HEARTS BEAT AS ONE

ABSOLUTE RECORD PRODUCTION 945 ABS 163

Take 1 (3:47)/ Take 2 (3:46)/ Take 3 (3:39)/ Take 4 (3:36)/ Take 5 (3:36)/ Take 6 (3:36) Take 7 (3:35)/ Take 8 (3:35)/ Take 9 (3:35)/ Take 10 (3:35)/ Take 11 (3:35)/ Take 12 (3:36)/ Take 13 (3:34)

R: Exs. Soundboard.   S: Studio '83.   C: ECD. Black case with gold text.

CD - THE ULTIMATE 7" & 12" COLLECTION

Boy-Girl/ 11 O'Clock Tick Tock/ Touch/ Things To Make And Do/ Another Day/ J. Swallow/ A Celebration/ Trash, Trampoline And The Party Girl/ Endless Deep/ Treasure (Whatever Happened To Pete The Chop)/ Boomerang I/ Boomerang II/ The Three Sunrises/ Love Comes Tumbling/ Bass Trap/ 60 Seconds In Kingdom Come/ Luminous Times (Hold On To Love)/ Walk To The Water/ Spanish Eyes/ Deep In The Heart

R: Exs. Soundboard. Some surface noise.

S: '79 - '87.   C: ECD. Dbw. Red type. Pic CD.

CD - ULTRA RARE TRAX VOL 1

URU2121

The Fly, Ultra Violet (demo mix, Demo '91)/ Mercy (unreleased)/ In My Dreams (unreleased)/ Stand By Me/ Help (Self Aid Concert)/ Knockin' On Heaven's Door (with Axl Rose)/ Who's Gonna Ride Your Wild Horses (acoustic)/ Dirty Old Town (L. Mullen on vocals)/ Acrobat #1 (soundcheck '91)/ Acrobat #2 (first take '91)/ Steering Wheel (unreleased)/ Doctor Doctor (unreleased)/ Where The Streets Have No Name/ New Year's Day ('88)/ Angel Of Harlem (with B.B. King)/ Montgomery's Visit (unreleased)

R: Ex. Soundboard/Audience.   S: Various. C: ECD. Dcc. Same cover as Vol. 2 and 3. 60:50.

CD - ULTRA RARE TRAX VOL. 2

URU2122

Slow Dancing/ Spanish Eyes/ She's A Mystery To Me/ Hawkmoon/ Rain (and I Still Haven't Found What I'm Looking For)/ Exit (also Gloria)/ Bad (also Waiting For The Man)/ C'Mon Everybody/ Southern Man/ Knocking On Heaven's Door/ Maggie's Farm (also Cold Turkey)/ Womanfish/

Stand By Me/ Help/ Sun City/ Spring Hill Mining Disaster/ Mothers Of The Disappeared/ I've Got You Under My Skin (with F. Sinatra)

R: Ex. Soundboard/Audience.   S: Various. C: ECD. Dcc. Same cover as Vol. 1 and 3. 78:01.

CD - ULTRA RARE TRAX VOL. 3

URU2123

One (with R.E.M.-4:16)/ A Celebration (2:44)/ Suspicious Mind (also Angel Of Harlem - 4:09)/ Sexual Healing (also All I Want Is You - 5:41)/ My Hometown (4:11)/ All Along The Watchtower (3:56)/ I Surrender (4:48)/ I Shall Be Released (4:51)/ Jack In The Box (2:40)/ Cartoon World (4:24)/ The Speed Of Light (2:55)/ The Magic Carpet (3:34)/ I Fall Down (3:08)/ Amazing Grace (also Love Rescue Me - 4:41)/ The Unforgettable Fire (4:28)/ The King's New Clothes (3:17)/ Van Diemen's Land/ White Christmas (1:02)

R: Ex. Soundboard/Audience.   S: Various. C: ECD. Dcc. Same cover as Vol. 1 and 2.

CD - UNRELEASED ALBUM

YELLOW RECORDS U168872

Montgomery's Visit/ Get You Down/ Wake Up (part 1)/ Steering Wheel/ Feel Free!/ Did You Wanna!/ Wake Up And Take Me Down (part 2)/ Doctor Doctor!/ Don't Say Goodbye/ Heaven And Hell/ Get Together Now/ Hi As A Kite (Salome)/ Jitterbug Baby

R: Exs. Soundboard.   S: Outtakes.   C: ECD. Dcc. Time 68:54.

CD - WELCOME TO THE VIBE

HAWK 009

Zoo Station/ The Fly/ Even Better Than The Real Thing/ Mysterious Ways/ One/ Till The End Of The World/ Who's Gonna Ride Your Wild Horses/ Tryin' To Throw Your Arms Around The World/ Angel Of Harlem, Dancing Queen/ Satellite Of Love/ I Still Haven't Found What I'm Looking For/ With Or Without You/ Love Is Blindness

R: G. Audience.   S: Vancouver, Canada Apr. 23 '92.   C: ECD. Dcc. Pic CD. Time 71:33.

CD - ZOO TELEVISION - THE DRUG OF THE NATION

TAKE IT OR LEAVE IT T 9212/13

CD1: Intro (7:07)/ Zoo Station (4:48)/ Trash, Trampoline And The Partygirl (2:42)/ We Love You Bono (:30)/ Mac Phisto Phones With K.L.M. (4:24)/ Ultra Violet Light My Way (4:57)/ Are You Lonesome Tonight (:56)/ Mac Phisto Phones With Queen Beatrix (2:29)/ Slow Dancing (1:15)/ I Still Haven't Found What I'm Looking For (4:42)/ Mac Phisto Phones With Helmut Kohl (Munchen, Olympia Stadion, June 4 '93) (2:54)/ I Will Follow (2:33)/ Redemption Song (1:59)/ Sunday Bloody Sunday (5:01)/ Mac Phisto Phones With Hans Janmaat (2:23)/ Even Better Than The Real Thing (5:28)/ Until The End Of The World (5:17)/ New Year's Day (5:12)/ Stay Faraway So Close! (6:08)/ Numb (3:55)

CD2: Mac Phisto Phones With John Major (2:39)/

Rain (1:04)/ Lost Highway (1:17)/ Desire (6:20)/ Mac Phisto Phones With Salman Rushdie (4:24)/ The Fly (4:43)/ Where The Streets Have No Name (6:25)/ Mac Phisto Phones With Lady Diana (3:20)/ One (4:33)/ She's A Mystery To Me (1:30)/ Zooropa (2:54)/ Bad (6:37)/ The First Time (:34)/ Bullet The Blue Sky (5:56)/ Mac Phisto Phones With The Archbishop Of Canterbury(3:30)/ Babyface (4:31)/ Pride In The Name Of Love (4:41)/ Love Is Blindness (5:30)/ Can't Help Falling In Love With You (3:01)
R: CD1 Tracks 1-7 Poor-G. Audience. Tracks 8-20 G-Vg. Audience. CD2 G-Vg. Audience.   S: CD1 tracks 1-7 Feyenoord Studio, Rotterdam May 10 '93. Tracks 8-10 Feyenoord Stadion, Rotterdam May 11 '93. Tracks 15-20 Goffert Park, Nijimegen Aug. 3 '93. CD2 Celtic Park, Glasgow Aug. 8 '93. Tracks 5- 7 Wembley Stadium, London Aug. 11 '93. Tracks 8-14 Wembley Stadium, London Aug. 12 '93. Tracks 15-19 Wembly Stadium, London Aug. 20 '93.   C: ECD. Dcc.

CD - ZOOMERANG LIVE DOWN UNDER
BACKSTAGE BKCD063/64
C: For songs & source refer to 'Zooropa Down Under' KTS 239/40.

CD - ZOOROPA DOWN UNDER
KISS THE STONE KTS 239/40
CD1: Intro, Zoo Station (8:06)/ The Fly (7:09)/ Even Better Than The Real Thing (3:42)/ Mysterious Ways (6:41)/ Medley: One, Unchained Melody (6:00)/ Until The End Of The World (5:02)/ New Years Day (5:29)/ Numb (4:02)/ Trying To Throw Your Arms Around The World (5:02)/ Angel Of Harlem (5:15)/ Stay (Faraway So Close) (6:09)/ Satellite Of Love (3:46)
CD2: Dirty Day (5:42)/ Bullet The Blue Sky (5:23)/ Running To Stand Still (5:29)/ Where The Streets Have No Name (5:47)/ Pride (In The Name Of Love) (9:26)/ Daddy's Gonna Pay For Your Crashed Car (11:19)/ Medley: Lemon, With Or Without You (9:36)/ Love Is Blindness (5:28)/ I Can't Help Falling In Love (2:25)
R: Exs. Soundboard.   S: Sydney, Australia Nov. 27 '93.   C: ECD. Pic CDs.

CD - ZOOROPA 1993
RDSM 001/002
CD1: Introduction/ Zoo Station/ The Fly/ Zoo TV Channel Hopping/ Even Better Than The Real Thing/ Mysterious Ways/ One/ Unchained Melody/ Until The End Of The World/ New Years Day/ Zoo Interference/ Numb/ Trying To Throw Your Arms Around The World/ Angel Of Harlem/ When Love Comes To Town/ Stay (Faraway So Close)/ Satellite Of Love/ Bad
CD2: Bullet The Blue Sky/ Running To Stand Still/ Where The Streets Have No Name/ Pride (In The Name Of Love)/ Zoo Confessions/ Desire/ A Word From Mac Phisto & A Phone Call To The UN/ Help/ Ultra Violet (Light My Way)/ With Or Without You/ Love Is Blindness/ Can't Help Falling In Love With You/ Zooropa/ Baby Face/ I Will Follow

R: Ex.   S: R.D.S. Stadium, Dublin, Ireland Aug. 28 '93 except CD2 tracks 13-14 Wembley Stadium, London, England Aug. 12 '93.   C: ECD. Dcc. Pic CDs. Time CD1 75:16. CD2 64:00.

V

VAN HALEN

CD - DAYDREAMS IN DALLAS
DR. GIG DGCD 022
Poundcake/ Judgment Day/ One Way To Rock/ Runaround/ Why Can't This Be Love/ Panama/ Apolitical Blues/ Finish What Ya Started/ I Can't Drive 55/ Best Of Both Worlds/ Top Of The World
R: Exs. Soundboard.   S: Dallas, Texas '92.
C: ECD. Dcc. Time 56:20.

CD - GUITAR MAN
EVH 001
Eruption/ Hot For Teacher/ You Really Got Me/ Runnin' With The Devil/ Ain't Talkin Bout Love/ Panama/ Somebody Get Me A Doctor/ Jamie's Crying
R: Ex.   S: Studio sessions - Eddie Van Halen alone.   C: ECD. Blue/black cover. Red type. Pic CD.

CD - STAGE SHOW
SOUNDS ALIVE CD 2400120
One Way To Rock/ Hot Summer Nights/ 5150/ Panama/ Best Of Both Worlds/ Love Walks In/ I Can't Drive 55/ Ain't Talking 'Bout Love/ Why Can't This Be Love/ Rock And Roll
S: New Haven '87.   C: ECD.

VARIOUS ARTISTS

CD - ALTERNATIVE VOL.1
GRAPEFRUIT GRA-032-A
NIRVANA: Smells Like Teen Spirit (4:39)/ RED HOT CHILI PEPPERS: Give It Away (4:43)/ SONIC YOUTH: Kool Thing (4:09)/ RAMONES: Pet Sematary (3:04)/ IGGY POP: Real Wild Child (Wild One) (3:27)/ THE CLASH: Should I Stay Or Should I Go (3:42)/ PEARL JAM: Alive (5:44)/ FAITH NO MORE: Easy (2:51)/ NED'S ATOMIC DUSTBIN: Kill Your Television (3:16)/ CARTER: After The Watershed (4:03)/ THE SMITHS: How Soon Is Now? (5:12)/ BJORK: Venus As A Boy (4:36)/ L7: Pretend We're Dead (3:20)/ THE CRAMPS: Can Your Pussy Do The Dog (3:44)/ THE PIXIES: Monkey Gone To Heaven (2:56)/ THE CURE: Just Like Heaven (3:01)/ NEW ORDER: Blue Monday (6:34)
R: Vg-Ex.   S: Various live.   C: Australian CD. Dcc.

CD - ALTERNATIVE VOL.2
GRAPEFRUIT GRA-032-B
PEARL JAM: Even Flow (4:56)/ LIVING COLOUR: Love Rears It's Ugly Head (4:26)/ THE CURE: In Between Days (2:49)/ MORRISSEY: Every Day Is

Like Sunday (3:12)/ RED HOT CHILI PEPPERS: Higher Ground (3:25)/ BIG AUDIO DYNAMITE: Rush (3:52)/ SUEDE: Animal Nitrate (3:15)/ JOY DIVISION: Love Will Tear Us Apart (3:09)/ THE PIXIES: Velouria (3:21)/ SIOUXSIE AND THE BANSHEES: Kiss Them For Me (4:35)/ JESUS AND MARY CHAIN: Just Like Honey, Taste Of Cindy (4:07)/ SONIC YOUTH: 100% (3:14)/ NIRVANA: Come As You Are (3:31)/ RAMONES: Rock 'N' Roll High School, Do You Remember Rock 'N' Roll Radio (4:48)/ DEAD KENNEDYS: Too Drunk To *uck (2:31)/ PORNO FOR PYROS: Pets (4:01)/ THE SUGARCUBES: Birthday (4:30)
R: Vg-Ex.   S: Various live.   C: Australian CD. Dcc.

CD - LIVE VOL.1
GRAPEFRUIT GRA-038-A
LENNY KRAVITZ: Are You Gonna Go My Way? (3:33)/ MADONNA: Vogue (4:56)/ BILLY JOEL: River Of Dreams (3:55)/ PRINCE: Cream (4:01)/ ERIC CLAPTON: Tears In Heaven (4:45)/ STING: If I Ever Lose My Faith In You (5:28)/ BRUCE SPRINGSTEEN: Streets Of Philadelphia (3:27)/ PETER GABRIEL: Steam (4:09)/ MICHAEL JACKSON: Black Or White (4:29)/ WHITNEY HOUSTON: I Will Always Love You (4:58)/ ELTON JOHN: The One (5:13)/ PHIL COLLINS: Sussudio (6:56)/ PAUL MCCARTNEY: Coming Up (4:44)/ ELVIS COSTELLO: Oliver's Army (3:05)/ MICK JAGGER: Sweet Thing (4:30)/ JOHN LENNON: Imagine (3:17)
R: Vg-Ex.   S: Various live.   C: Australian CD. Dcc.

CD - LIVE VOL.2
GRAPEFRUIT GRA-038-B
U2: Mysterious Ways (6:21)/ THE CURE: Friday I'm In Love (3:22)/ METALLICA: Enter Sandman (4:12)/ DIRE STRAITS: Sultans Of Swing (6:11)/ VAN HALEN: Jump (4:10)/ NIRVANA: Smells Like Teen Spirit (4:34)/ BON JOVI: In These Arms (6:34)/ RED HOT CHILI PEPPERS: Give It Away (4:22)/ R.E.M.: Everyone Hurts (5:26)/ ROXETTE: Joyride (2:58)/ DEPECHE MODE: Just Can't Get Enough (4:56)/ PAUL MCCARTNEY: Hope Of Deliverance (3:26)/ QUEEN: Bohemian Rhapsody (3:58)/ KISS: I Was Made For Loving You (4:23)/ PINK FLOYD: Money (4:47)/ LED ZEPPELIN: Rock And Roll (4:03)
R: Vg-Ex.   S: Various live.   C: Australian CD. Dcc.

CD - METAL VOL.1
GRAPEFRUIT GRA-033-A
SUICIDAL TENDENCIES: I Saw Your Mommy (4:24), War Inside My Head (3:21), Possessed To Skate (2:13)/ ANTHRAX: I Am The Law (5:45), Armed And Dangerous (4:16), Antisocial (4:19)/ TESTAMENT: Apocalyptic City (5:48), Burnt Offerings (5:20), C.O.T.L.O.D. (2:29)/ MEGADEATH: Hanger 18 (4:58), Peace Sells (4:09)/ SLAYER: Medley: Mandatory Suicide, Raining Blood, Angel Of Death (11:51)/

SEPULTURA: Altered State (5:25)/ Under Siege (Regnum Irae) (4:15)/ Drug Me (2:11)
R: Vg-Ex.   S: Various live.   C: Australian CD. Dcc.

CD - PAUL SIMON - BRUCE SPRINGSTEEN & FRIENDS
YELLOW CAT YC 013/14
CD1: Intro - Boy In The Bubble (Paul Simon) (5:40)/ Crazy Love Vol. 2 (Paul Simon) (5:14)/ I Know What I Know (Paul Simon) (4:06)/ Introductions (Paul Schaefer introduces Debbie Harry and Grace Jones. Debbie and Grace introduce Lou Reed) (3:50)/ Tell It To Your Heart (Lou Reed) (6:06)/ New Sensations (Lou Reed) (7:34)/ Walk On The Wild Side (Lou Reed, Debbie Harry, Grace Jones) (7:18)/ The Wanderer (Dion) (3:59)/ Runaround Sue (Dion) (5:24)/ Teenager In Love (Dion, Ruben Blades, Lou Reed, James Taylor, Paul Simon, Billy Joel, Bruce Springsteen) (4:08)/ Homeless (Paul Simon & Ladysmith Black Mambazo) (4:58)
CD2: Graceland (Paul Simon) (5:34)/ You Can Call Me Al (Paul Simon and Chevy Chase) (6:02)/ Introduction (Ron Darling and Don Mattingly introduce Bruce Springsteen) (5:06)/ Born To Run (Bruce Springsteen) (5:36)/ Glory Days (Bruce Springsteen, Paul Simon, Billy Joel) (7:03)/ Looking For Love On Broadway (James Taylor) (2:32)/ Carolina On My Mind (James Taylor) (6:16)/ New York State Of Mind (Billy Joel) (6:36)/ Still Crazy After All These Years (Paul Simon) (4:37)/ Late In The Evening (Paul Simon) (4:01)/ Diamonds On The Soles Of Her Shoes (Paul Simon, Ladysmith Black Mamazo) (7:57)/ Rock And Roll Music (finale - all artists) (3:56)
R: Exs. Soundboard.   S: Homeless Children's Medical Benefit Concert, Madison Square Garden, New York Dec. 13 '87.   C: ECD. Dcc.

CD - PROMO 1
KISS THE STONE KTS PR 01
METALLICA: Nothing Else Matters/ DEF LEPPARD: Hysteria/ GUNS N' ROSES: Sweet Child Of Mine/ RAGE AGAINST THE MACHINE: Bullet In The Head/ KEITH RICHARDS: How I Wish/ B. SPRINGSTEEN: Big Muddy/ N. YOUNG: Harvest Moon/ K.D. LANG: Constant Craving/ J. MELLENCAMP: Paper And Fire/ R. PLANT: Ramble On/ SMASHING PUMPKINS: Today/ PEARL JAM: Baba O'Riley/ SUEDE: Metal Mickey/ SOUL ASYLUM: Sexual Healing/ STONE TEMPLE PILOTS: Plush/ U2: Stay
R: Exs. Soundboard.   S: Samples from KTS CDs.   C: ECD. Dcc.

CD - PROMO 2
KISS THE STONE KTS PR 02
THE THE: Heartland/ PEARL JAM: Daughter, W.M.A./ THE BREEDERS: Fortunately Gone/ SMASHING PUMPKINS: Dancing In The Moonlight/ 10 000 MANIACS: Everyday Is Like Sunday/ INXS: The Gift/ THE LEMONHEADS: It's About Time/ LEVELLERS: One Way/

RADIOHEAD: Creep/ BJORK: Play Dead/
JACKSON BROWNE: The Pretender/
AEROSMITH: Cryin'/ GUNS 'N' ROSES: Dead
Flowers/ LIVING COLOUR: Nothingness/ MEAT
LOAF: I'd Do Anything For Love (But I Won't Do
That)/ MARIA McKEE: East Of Eden/ MATTHEW
SWEET: Girlfriend
R: Exs. Soundboard.   S: Samples from KTS
CDs.   C: ECD. Dcc. Time 79:09.

LP - SPREADING THE VIRUS
VINYL VIRUS RECORDS
S1: GUN N' ROSES: Double Talkin' Jive/ ANNIE
LENNOX: Here Comes The Rain Again/ FRANK
ZAPPA: Cradle Rock/ QUEEN: It's A Kind Of
Magic/ THIN LIZZY: Got To Give It Up
S2: THE ROLLING STONES: Doo Doo Doo Doo
Doo/ PET SHOP BOYS: It's A Sin/ BRUCE
SPRINGSTEEN: Lucky Town/ JETHRO TULL:
Living In The Past/ AC/DC: Rocker
C: Eb. White jacket with sticker. Promo for various
Vinyl Virus releases.

CD - WOODSTOCK - THE LOST
PERFORMANCES
GREAT DANE RECORDS GDR CD 9412/ABCD
CD1: Intro/ THE BAND: The Weight (3:09)/ JOE
COCKER: Let's Go Get Stoned (7:02)/ CANNED
HEAT: Going Up The Country (3:56)/ PAUL
BUTTERFIELD: Drifting Blues (5:56)/ ARLO
GUTHRIE: Walking Down The Line (4:03)/
BLOOD SWEAT & TEARS: More And More
(2:44)/ COUNTRY JOE MCDONALD: Rockin'
Around The World (1:40)/ JOHN SEBASTIAN:
Darling Be Home Soon (3:13)/ SLY AND THE
FAMILY STONE: Love City (4:41)/ TIM HARDIN: If
I Were A Carpenter (5:21)/ MELANIE: Birthday Of
The Sun (3:58)/ JOAN BAEZ: We Shall Overcome
(4:25)/ CROSBY, STILLS & NASH: Marrakesh
Express (2:20), Black Bird (2:40)
CD2: JANIS JOPLIN: Raise Your Hand (5:19)/ As
Good As You've Been To This World (6:13)/ To
Love Somebody (5:01)/ Summertime (5:02)/ Try
Just A Little Bit Harder (4:25)/ Kozmic Blues
(4:43)/ I Can't Turn You Loose (8:49)/ Work Me
Lord (7:17)/ Piece Of My Heart (3:57)/ Ball And
Chain (6:14)
CD3: CREEDENCE CLEARWATER REVIVAL:
Born On The Bayou (4:25)/ Green River (3:01)/
Ninety Nine And A Half Won't Do (3:12)/ Bootleg
(3:21)/ Commotion (2:34)/ Bad Moon Rising
(2:02)/ Proud Mary (3:12)/ I Put A Spell On You
(4:05)/ The Night Time Is The Right Time (2:08)/
Keep On Chooglin' (8:56)/ Suzie Q (9:49)
CD4: THE WHO: Heaven And Hell (3:28)/ I Can't
Explain (2:20)/ Excerpts From Tommy I: It's A Boy,
1921, Amazing Journey, Sparks (11:33)/ Excerpts
From Tommy II: Eyesight To The Blind, Christmas,
The Acid Queen, Pinball Wizard (11:46)/ Excerpts
From Tommy III: Do You Tink It's Alright, Fiddle
About, There's A Doctor, Go To The Mirror,
Smash The Mirror, I'm Free, Tommy's Holiday
Camp, We're Not Gonna Take It (18:27)/
Summertime Blues (3:25)/ Shakin' All Over (5:00)/

My Generation (6:21)
R: Vg-Exs. Soundboard.   S: Previously
unreleased tracks from The Woodstock Music
Festival '69.   C: ECD. Book style digi-pack with
well-documented 44 page book containing color
and B&w photos. Another fine collection from
Great Dane.

VAUGHAN, STEVIE RAY

CD - BEST OF SOUL TO SOUL SESSIONS
KLONDYKE RECORDS KR 019
Chitlins Con Carne (9:30)/ Hey Motherfucker
(1:47)/ Hug You Squeeze You (Take 2 - 4:04)/
Hangnails And Boogers (3:44)/ The Sky Is Crying
(5:14)/ Boot Hill (Take 2 - 3:13)/ You Don't Wanna
Hear Me Sing That Shit (2:09)/ Testify (2:57)/
Shuffle Thing (2:34)/ Come On (Part 3, Take 2 -
6:50)/ Maudie (6:30)/ Life Without You (15:06)/
Little Wing (Take 3-6:31)/ Third Stone From the
Sun (Take 2 - 6:07)
R: Exs. Soundboard.   S: NYC '85.   C: ECD.

CD - CITY OF LIGHTS
HAWK 061
Pride And Joy (6:32)/ You'll Be Mine (5:35)/ I'm
Leaving You (7:17)/ Let Me Love You Babe (4:13)/
Leave My Girl Alone (6:24)/ Superstition (4:53)/
Willie The Whimp (5:35)/ Cold Shot (6:21)/
Couldn't Stand The Weather (12:42)/ Life Without
You (11:27)
R: Ex. Audience.   S: Greek Theater, Los
Angeles Oct. 6 '88.   C: ECD. Dcc. Pic CD.

CD - FEATHERS
NEVER END ACT 10
Empty Arms (2:43) (Austin '79)/ Wham? (2:41) (LA
'83)/ Hug You Squeeze You (3:29) (Toronto '83)/
Lenny (8:10) (Toronto '83)/ So Excited (4:19) (LA
'83)/ Tin Pan Alley (13:09) (Dallas '85)/ Change It
(4:19) (Dallas '86)/ Come On (4:23) (Dallas '86)/
Live Another Day (4:17) (Dallas '86)/ Life Without
You (11:26) (Philadelphia '87)/ Scuttle Buttin'
(2:05) (Perugia '88)/ Say What? (4:30) (Perugia
'88)/ Lookin' Out The Window (4:06) (Perugia '88)/
Scuttle Buttin' (1:51) (New York '89)/ Dirty Pool
(4:00) (New York '89)
R: Ex.   C: ECD. Dcc. Gold disc.

CD - FORCE OF NATURE
WHOOPY CAT WKP 0014/15
CD1: Boilermaker/ Close To You, Baby/ Tell Me/
Let Me Love You/ Day I'm Gone/ I'm Leaving You/
Texas Flood/ Rude Mood/ Don't Lose Your Cool/
Thunderbird
CD2: The Sky Is Crying/ I'm Crying/ Crosscut
Saw/ Shake For Me/ Wham!/ Hideaway/
Instrumental/ Pride And Joy/ Tin Pan Alley/ Love
Struck Baby/ Tell Me/ Little Wing/ Manic
Depression
R: Ex. Audience.   S: Fitzgerald's Club, Houston
Oct. 14 '81.   C: Japanese CD. Dcc. Time CD1
67:19. CD2 72:51.

CD - HELLO Y'A ALL...
HOME RECORDS HR 5912-0
House Is A Rockin (2:33)/ Tightrope (5:19)/ Little
Sister (5:20)/ Let Me Love You (3:48)/ Texas
Flood (7:17)/ Leave My Little Girl (5:48)/ Wall Of
Denial (5:48)/ Superstition (4:54)/ Cold Shot
(6:43)/ Life Without You (12:50)/ Crossfire (4:09)/
Voodoo Chile (11:32)
R: Vg. Audience.   S: Tracks 1-7 Tingley Arena,
NM Nov. 28 '89. Tracks 8-12 McNichols Arena,
CO Nov. '89.   C: ECD.

CD - LET IT HAPPEN
ROCKS 92053
Texas Flood (4:28)/ Stormy Monday Blues (8:21)/
Matchbox Blues (6:21)/ Instrumental Jam 1 (2:16)/
Instrumental Jam 2 (1:31)/ Pride And Joy (6:04)/
Ask Me No Questions (4:58)/ Outskirts Of Town
(10:45)
R: Exs. Soundboard.   S: Studio jam with Albert
King '83.   C: ECD. Dcc.

CD - MONTREAL 1989
LIVE STORM LSCD 51571
Scuttle Buttin (4:40)/ I Wanna Testify (4:19)/
Voodoo Chile (11:28)/ Honeybee (2:27)/ Can't
Stand The Weather (5:06)/ Cold Shot (4:01)/
Texas Flood (8:02)
R: Exs. Soundboard.   S: Montreal, Canada '89.
C: ECD. Dbw.

CD - OUT OF THE SHADOWS
ROCKS 92119
Voodoo Chile/ Lost Your Good Thing Now/ Honey
Bee/ Mary I Iad A Lillle Lamb/ Love Struck Baby/
Tin Pan Alley/ Cold Shot/ Couldn't Stand The
Weather/ Texas Flood/ Lenny/ Stangs Swang/
Rude Mood
R: Exs. Soundboard.   S: Davis, CA '84.
C: ECD. Dbw. Orange type. Time 74:54.

CD - TOUCH THE SKY
CAPRICORN RECORDS CR 2005
Little Wing (1:53)/ Little Wing (2:11)/ Little Wing,
3rd Stone From The Sun (14:04)/ Like Without
You (7:17)/ So Excited (3:41)/ Boiler Maker (5:44)/
Shake & Bake (2:55)/ Treat Me Right (8:05)/ The
Sky Is Crying (4:49)/ Slip Sliding Slim (1:55)/
Come On (3:35)/ Come On (4:43)/ Hug, Kiss And
Squeeze (2:01)/ Hang Nails And Boogers (4:33)/
Right Or Wrong (5:19)
R: Exs. Soundboard.   S: Power Station, NYC
Jan.-Feb. '84.   C: ECD.

CD - TRIPLE TROUBLE
ARCHIVO AR011
Testify (3:57)/ Voodoo Chile (Slight Return)
(11:29)/ Mary Had A Little Lamb (3:15)/ Couldn't
Stand The Weather (4:42)/ Cold Shot (3:59)/ Pride
And Joy (4:29)
R: Exs. Soundboard.   S: US Tour '84.
C: ECD. Dcc.

VELVET UNDERGROUND, THE

CD - LIVE IN COLUMBUS 1966 PART I
MIND THE MAGIC MTM 031
Melody Laughter/ Femme Fatale/ Venus In Furs/
The Black Angels Death Song/ All Tomorrow's
Parties
R: G. Audience.   S: Columbus '66.   C: ECD.
With Nico.

CD - LIVE IN COLUMBUS 1966 PART II
MIND THE MAGIC MTM 032
I'm Waiting For The Man/ Heroin/ Run Run Run/
The Nothing Song
R: G. Audience.   S: Columbus '66.   C: ECD.
With Nico.

CD - LIVE USA '93
VAMPIRE VR 50007
Venus In Furs (5:26)/ I Heard Her Calling My
Name (4:12)/ Sweet Jane (4:57)/ Rock And Roll
(5:27)/ We're Gonna Have A Real Good Time
Together (3:42)/ Gift (12:10)/ White Light White
Heat (3:14)/ Hey Mr. Rain (7:12)/ I Can't Stand It
(4:18)/ I'm Waiting For My Man (4:50)/ Some
Kinda Love (6:16)/ Coyote (5:20)/ Heroin (12:10)
R: Vg. Audience.   S: USA '93.   C: ECD.

CD - OSSI PARK
GERMAN RECORDS GERMAN REC. 039
Some Kinda Love/ We're Gonna Have A Real
Good Time Together/ Femme Fatale/ Venus In
Furs/ All Tomorrows Parties/ I'm Sticking With
You/ Beginning To See The Light/ I Heard Her Call
My Name/ Afterhours/ Heroin/ White Light White
Heat/ Rock 'n Roll/ I Can't Stand It/ Waiting For
The Man/ Pale Blue Eyes
R: G. Audience.   S: Live at various locations in
Holland '93.   C: ECD. Digi-pack. Time 71:58.

W

WALSH, JOE

CD - THE EAGLES HAVE LANDED
UNFORGOTTEN JEWELS UJ 94008
Going Down/ Funky 49/ Rocky Mountain Way/
Look At Us Now/ Live's Been Good/ Indian
Summer/ Ashes, The Rain And I/ Walk Away/ Two
Sides/ Ordinary Average Guy/ Turn To Stone/
Confessor/ In The City
R: Ex.   S: USA June '93.   C: ECD. Clear
fluorescent orange jewel case. Limited edition of
500. Time 71:30.

WATERBOYS, THE

CD - ALIVE ON THE INSIDE
KISS THE STONE KTS 352
Bring Em All Into My Heart/ Wonderful Disguise/ I
Am Working On My Karma/ The Return Of Pan/
Glastonbury Song/ Dublin Is A City Full Of Ghosts/
I Know She's In The Building/ Trumpets/ When

You Go Away/ Hold Me In Your Everlasting Arms/ One Sweet Step At A Time/ What Do You Want Me To Do/ Building The City Of Light/ Thank You For A Wonderful Life/ Somebody Might Wave Back/ The Whole Of The Moon
R: Exs. Soundboard.   S: Greenbelt Festival, Deene Park, Northampton, England Aug. 28 '94.
C: ECD. Dbw. Pic CD. Time 62:06.

CD - IN THE STUDIO
KISS THE STONE KTS 316
The Three Day Man (4:14)/ Whatever Happened To The West (4:29)/ Man Who Sold The World (4:25)/ Except You (4:28)/ Fire Of Unknown Origin (2:19)/ Gala (9:50)/ Red Army Blues, Dirt (9:39)/ Soul To Soul (5:04)/ Goodbye 1970's (1:19)/ Sweet Thing (4:40)
R: Vg-Ex.   S: Tracks 1 & 2 all instruments Mike Scott, Redshop Studio Dec. 23 '82. Track 3 M. Scott /Steve (bass & sax), Martin Saunders (drums) Playground Studios. Tracks 4 & 5 M. Scott (vocals & piano) Farmyard Studios May 17 '82. Track 6 M. Scott with Anthony Thistlethwaite (sax) Redshop Studio Feb. 28 '82. Track 7 rare live gig by the Red And Black - M. Scott, A. Thistlethwaite, M. Seligman, K. Wilkinson Hope & Anchor July 15 '88. Track 8 'Another Pretty Face' (dub version). Track 9 aborted demo. Track 10 demo '80.   C: ECD. Blue & white cover. Pic CD.

WELLER, PAUL

CD - ANYTIME YOU WANT ME
NIKKO RECORDS NK012
This Is No Time (4:43)/ Save Us (4:18)/ Remember How We Started (4:07)/ Above The Clouds (4:15)/ Hung Up (3:15)/ Sunflower (4:40)/ Wildwood (3:40)/ Fly On The Wall (3:55)/ Can You Heal Us Holy Man? (4:51)/ Fifth Season (5:22)/ Foot Of The Mountain (7:17)/ Ohio (3:25)/ You Do Something (3:34)/ Into Tomorrow (3:04)/ Has My Fire Really Gone Out? (3:55)
R: Exs.   S: Live in Europe & USA June '94.
C: ECD. Dcc. Digi-pack. Pic CD. Time 64:25.

CD - WALK ON BY
KISS THE STONE KTS 314
Hung Up (3:02)/ This Is No Time (6:17)/ All Pictures On The Wall (4:10)/ Bull-Rush (6:08)/ Remember How We Started (5:04)/ Above The Clouds (4:24)/ Wild Wood (3:32)/ Foot Of The Mountain (7:52)/ Can You Heal Us Holy Man? (4:42)/ You Do Something (3:30)/ Into Tomorrow (3:38)/ Has My Fire Really Gone Out? (3:37)
R: Exs.   S: Live in Europe June '94.   C: ECD. Dcc. Pic CD. Time 55:00.

WESTERBERG, PAUL

CD - GRAVEL PIT
KISS THE STONE KTS 331
Waiting For Somebody (3:27)/ Mannequin Shop (2:59)/ Achin' To Be (3:48)/ Waitress In The Sky (2:35)/ Dice Behind Your Shades (4:10)/ Merry Go Round (4:05)/ Seein' Her (3:36)/ I Will Dare (2:27)/ Whole Wide World (2:44)/ Knockin' On Mine (4:31)/ Skyway (2:06)/ Dyslexic Heart (3:35)/ Daydream Believer (2:32)/ Smokey (2:16)/ I'll Be You (3:21)/ Can't Hardly Wait (4:02)/ Here Comes A Regular (5:22)/ World Class Fad (3:12)/ Alex Chilton (3:08)/ Left Of The Dial (4:18)/ The Ledge (5:04)/ Silver Naked Ladies (4:40)
R: Ex.   S: Stone Pony, Asbury Park, NJ 7/08/93.
C: ECD. Dcc. Pic CD. Time 78:08.

CD - LUCKY'S REVENGE
HAWK 030
Waiting For Somebody (3:10) Mannequin Shop (3:13)/ Achin' To Be (4:00)/ First Glimmer (5:17)/ Waitress In The Sky (2:28)/ World Class Fad (3:32)/ Dice Behind Your Shades (4:04)/ A Few Minutes Of Silence (2:48)/ Merry Go Round (5:11)/ Someone Once Knew (2:48)/ Merry Go Round (5:11)/ Someone Once Knew (2:48)/ Knockin' On Me (4:16)/ Swingin' Party (4:28)/ Skyway (2:13)/ Things (3:42)/ Something Is Me (1:52)/ Daydream Believer (2:33)/ Can't Hardly Wait (3:11)/ Runaway Wind (4:13)/ I'll Be You (3:32)
R: Exs. Audience.   S: Whiskey A Go Go, LA July 21 '93.   C: ECD. Dcc.

WET WET WET

CD - ANGEL DUST
OCTOPUS OCTO 050
Get Ready (3:29)/ Lip Service (5:28)/ Sweet Surrender (5:20)/ More Than Love (4:51)/ Make It Tonight (4:54)/ Angel Eyes (5:15)/ Wishing I Was Looking (4:11)/ If You Only Knew (3:09)/ East Of The River (4:08)/ Goodnight Girl (3:59)/ Maybe Tomorrow (5:17)/ Holding Back The River (5:15)
R: Exs. Soundboard.   S: Europe '92.   C: ECD. Dcc.

WHITE ZOMBIE

CD - YOU ONLY DIE ONCE...
HAWK 027
Intro (1:06)/ Grindhouse A Go Go (4:31)/ Thirst! (4:48)/ Black Sunshine (5:20)/ Welcome To The Planet Motherfucker, Psycholic Slag (5:28)/ Soul-Crusher (6:20)/ Spiderbaby (Yeah-Yeah-Yeah) (4:25)/ Thunder Kiss '65 (4:12)
R: Exs. Soundboard.   S: USA summer '93.
C: ECD. Dcc. Pic CD.

WINTER, JOHNNY

CD - DERVISH BLUES
TUFF BITES T.B. 94.1007
Rock And Roll People (5:58)/ Sweet Papa John (11:29)/ Roll With It (4:29)/ Boney Moroney (6:17)/ Highway 61 Revisited (12:31)/ Jumping Jack Flash (5:03)
R: Vg-Ex. Soundboard.   S: San Bernardino, CA late Sept. '75.   C: ECD. Dcc. Digi-pack.

CD - WHOLE LOTTA LOVE
AMERICAN CONCERT SERIES ACS 042
Warm Up Blues (7:03)/ Divin' Duck (8:39)/ Goin'
Back To The Delta (9:32)/ Dust My Blues (10:31)/
Rollin' And Tumblin' (5:36)/ Leavin' Blues (7:26)/
Come On In My Kitchen (7:37)/ Roll Over
Beethoven (10:12)/ Wipe Out (8:00)
R: G.   S: Boston.   C: ECD. Dbw. Red type.

WHO, THE

CD - LIFE WITH THE MOONS
YELLOW DOG YD 052
Life With The Moons #1 (2:02)/ My Generation
('Land Of Hope And Glory' alternate) (2:00)/
Happy Jack (take 1 with studio chatter) (2:43)/
Coca-Cola Commercial (1:06)/ John Mason
Motors Jingle (:31) Jaguar (2:53)/ Life With The
Moons #2 (:30)/ Melancholia (3:01)/ Track
Records Run-Off Groove (:21)/ Life With The
Moons #3 (1:04)/ Fortune Teller (2:21)/ Cousin
Kevin, Model Child (1:24)/ Life With The Moons #4
(1:53)/ Baby Don't Ya Do It (3:27)/ Behind Blue
Eyes (alternate with false start) (4:26)/ Life With
The Moons #5 (1:50)/ Tommy's Holiday Camp
(1:33)/ I Am The See, The Real Me (alternate)
(5:42)/ The Name Game (1:20)/ Virginia (5:09)
One Life's Enough (alternate) (2:22)
R: Ex. Soundboard.   S: Upgrades from the
boxed set.   C: ECD. Dcc.

CD - THE LIVE TOMMY
GRAPEFRUIT GRA-043-A
Substitute (2:04)/ Happy Jack (2:15)/ I'm A Boy
(2:35)/ I Can't Explain (3:06)/ Overture (4:32)/ It's
A Boy (:31)/ 1921 (2:24)/ Amazing Journey (3:13)/
Sparks (4:12)/ Eyesight To The Blind (The
Hawker) (1:55)/ Christmas (3:12)/ The Acid Queen
(3:24)/ Pinball Wizard (2:44)/ Do You Think It's
Alright (:22)/ Fiddle About (1:17)/ Tommy Can You
Hear Me (1:10)/ There's A Doctor (:23)/ Go To The
Mirror (3:19)/ Smash The Mirror (1:14)/ Miracle
Cure (:17)/ Sally Simpson (4:03)/ I'm Free (2:25)/
Tommy's Holiday Camp (:58)/ We're Not Gonna
Take It (3:28)/ See Me, Feel Me (4:46)/
Summertime Blues (3:34)/ Shakin' All Over (2:52)/
Boris The Spider (2:34)/ My Generation (5:09)
R: Ex. Soundboard.   S: Europe '69.
C: Australian CD. Dcc.

CD - LOVE RAIN O'ER ME
PAST MASTERS PM 9005
Drowned (10:01)/ Bell Boy (4:50)/ Dr. Jimmy
(8:23)/ Won't Get Fooled Again (8:38)/
Summertime Blues (3:39)/ Baba O'Riley (5:35)/
Naked Eye, Let's See Action (10:48)/ My
Generation Blues (3:50)
R: Vg. Soundboard.   S: Charlton Athletic
Football Ground, London May 18 '74.   C: ECD.
Dcc. 2000 made. See 'Soccer Rock' (Past Masters
PM 9004) for part one.

CD - SOCCER ROCK
PAST MASTERS PM 9004

Young Man Blues (5:56)/ Behind Blue Eyes (4:44)/
Pinball Wizard (2:28)/ See Me Feel Me (6:00)/
Magic Bus (10:47)/ My Generation (4:47)/
Substitute (2:41)/ I'm A Boy (2:35)/ Tattoo (3:22)/
Boris The Spider (3:09)
R: Vg. Soundboard.   S: Charlton Athletic
Football Ground, London May 18 '74.   C: ECD.
Dcc. 2000 made. See 'Love Rain O'Er Me' (Past
Masters PM 9005) for part two.

WONDERSTUFF, THE

CD - LIVE AT THE ROCKFELLER
OCTOPUS OCTO 006
C: See 'On The Ropes' (KTS 289) for songs
(except last two) and source.

CD - ON THE ROPES
KISS THE STONE KTS 289
Red Berry Joy Town (2:32)/ Change Every Light
Bulb (3:23)/ On The Ropes (3:45)/ Cabin Fever
(3:48)/ Mission Drive (3:49)/ Cartoon Boyfriend
(3:11)/ Piece Of Sky (2:21)/ The Size Of A Cow
(3:01)/ Donation (4:47)/ Circle Square (3:27)/ Full
Of Life (Happy Now) (3:41)/ Radio Ass Kiss (3:06)/
Hush (4:53)/ Caught In My Shadow (3:54)/ Don't
Let Me Down, Gently (3:03)/ I Wish Them All Dead
(2:54)/ Ten Trenches Deep (5:28)/ 30 Years In
The Bathroom (4:29)/ Golden Green (3:00)/
Welcome To The Cheap Seats (2:40)/ Now For
The 13th Time (3:08)/ Good Night Though (4:29)
S: The Rockefeller, Oslo, Norway Nov. 4 '93.
C: ECD. Pic CD.

YES

CD - ENDLESS DREAM
OCTOPUS RECORDS OCTO 031/032
CD1: I'm Waiting (7:46)/ The Calling (3:06)/
Rhythm Of Love (4:59)/ Hearts (8:15)/ Real Love
(10:31)/ Changes (8:33)/ Heart Of The Sunrise
(11:16)/ Roundabout (8:41)
CD2: Cinema (2:40)/ City Of Love (6:47)/ Make It
Easy (1:54)/ Owner Of A Lonely Heart (6:21)/ And
You And I (11:59)/ Where Will You Be (8:33)/ I've
Seen All Good People (7:41)/ Walls (5:50)/
Endless Dream (18:04)
R: Exs. Soundboard.   S: Canidegua, New York
June 19 '94.   C: ECD. Dcc. Pic CD.

CD - GIMME MORE
INSECT IST 75/76
CD1: Intro - Perpetual Change, The Calling/ I Am
Waiting/ Rhythm Of Love/ Hearts/ Real Love/
Changes/ Heart Of Sunrise/ Cinema/ City Of Love
CD2: Owner Of A Lonely Heart/ And You And I/
Cord Of Life/ Eclipse/ The Preacher The Teacher/
Apocalypse/ Where Will You Be/ I've Seen All
Good People/ Walls/ Endless Dream, Endless
Dream, Talk, Endless Dream/ Round About
R: Vg-Ex. Soundboard. Some static.   S: Broome

County Arena Binghamton, NY June 18 '94
C: ECD. Dcc. Time CD1 75:16. CD2 69:37.

CD - YES
CD1: Introduction - Sound Chaser (10:00)/ Close To The Edge, The Solid Time Of Change, Total Mass Retain, I Get Up I Get Down, Season Of Man (20:02)/ To Be Over (9:49)/ The Gates Of Delirium (22:45)/ I've Seen All Good People (5:09)/ Long Distance Runaround (5:22)/ The Clap (3:15)
CD2: And You & I, Cord Of Life, Eclipse, The Preacher, The Teacher, Apocalypse (11:06)/ Ritual (24:58)/ Roundabout (8:00)/ Sweet Dreams (5:14)/ Yours Is No Disgrace (12:40)
R: Exs. Soundboard. C: ECD. Dcc. Fold-open digi-pack. Gold discs.

YOUNG, NEIL

CD - A MAN, A GUITAR AND THE HORSE
FLASHBACK 08.94. 0234
Old Laughing Lady (5:15)/ Human Highway (3:11)/ Journey Through The Past (2:56)/ Pocahontas (3:32)/ Needle And The Damage Done (2:19)/ Give Me Strength (3:22)/ A Man Needs A Maid (4:55)/ Sugar Mountain (5:28)/ Country Home (5:28)/ Don't Cry No Tears (2:48)/ Down By The River (7:03)
R: Ex. Audience. S: Boston Music Hall Nov. 22'76. C: ECD.

CD - ACOUSTIC CONCERT
SOUNDS ALIVE SA 24 006
Hey Hey My My (Into The Black) (5:06)/ Rockin' In The Free World (5:40)/ The Old Laughing Lady (5:19)/ Don't Let It Bring You Down (4:05)/ Someday (6:18)/ Crime In The City (8:09)/ Eldorado (7:16)/ Too Far Gone (3:12)/ This Note's For You (3:55)/ The Needle And The Damage Done (2:48)/ After The Goldrush (4:36)/ Hangin' On A Limb (4:48)/ Heart Of Gold (4:27)/ Ohio (2:58)/ Rockin' In The Free World (3:58)
R: Exs. Soundboard. S: Amsterdam Dec. 12 '89. C: ECD.

CD - AFTERNOON RADIO
AMERICAN FLY HF 004
Old Laughing Lady (5:36)/ Human Highway (3:37)/ Journey Through The Past (3:33)/ Pochahontas (3:41)/ Needle And The Damage Done (2:38)/ Give Me Strength (3:46)/ A Man Needs A Maid (5:17)/ Sugar Mountain (5:15)/ Country Home (6:00)/ Don't Cry No Tears (3:25)/ Down By The River (7:00)*/ Dreaming Man (6:41)*/ War Of Man (5:56)*/ Winterlong (3:44)*/ From Hank To Hendrix (3:50)**
R: Vg. Audience. **Ex. Soundboard. S: Boston Music Hall, Boston Nov. 22 '76. *Neil Young & Stray Gators At Universal Studios, Los Angeles, CA. **Grammy Awards '94. C: ECD. Pic CD.

CD - CENTRESTAGE
THE GOLD STANDARD YC-200, CY-800

CD1: Long May You Run/ From Hank To Hendrix/ Jinktown Legend/ Love Is A Rose/ Pock Hontas/ Like A Hurricane/ War Of Man/ The Needle And The Damage Done/ Tonight's The Night/ One Of These Days/ Such A Woman
CD2: Harvest Moon/ Dreaming Man/ Natural Beauty/ Don't Let It Bring You Down/ Mr. Soul/ Powderfinger/ Sugar Mountain/ You And Me/ After The Goldrush
R: Exs. Soundboard   S: WTTW, Channel 11, Chicago Nov. 17 '92.   C: ECD. Dcc. Gold discs. Time CD1 57:35. CD2 54:04.

CD - CENTRESTAGE
MISTRAL MM-9335
See 'Centrestage' (The Gold Standard YC-200, CY-800) for songs and source.

CD - DON'T BE DENIED
ZUMA 9301
On The Way Home/ Here We Are In The Years/ Harvest/ After The Goldrush/ Out On The Weekend/ Old Man/ Heart Of Gold/ Time Fades Away/ Look Out Joe/ Sugar Mountain/ Sweet Joni/ Don't Be Denied/ New Mama*/ Southern Man*/ Last Dance*/ Let's Have A Party*
R: Tracks 1-9 Ex. Soundboard. Tracks 10-16 Ex. Audience.   S: Tracks 1-9 Washington & Virginia Jan. '73. Tracks 10-16 California Mar. '73.
C: ECD. Dbw. Yellow type. *with Crosby & Nash. Time 77:33.

CD - FOREVER YOUNG (WITH BOOKER T. & THE MG'S)
THE FLYING TIGERS FTCD 0012/13
CD1: Mr. Soul (4:28)/ Loner (4:09)/ Southern Man (6:31)/ Helpless (7:08)/ Like A Hurricane (10:53)/ Motorcycle Mama (5:10)/ Love To Burn (10:40)/ Separate Ways (5:58)/ Change Your Mind (8:53)/ Powderfinger (6:06)/ Only Love Can Break Your Heart (4:17)
CD2: Harvest Moon (5:55)/ The Needle And The Damage Done (3:09)/ Live To Ride (6:07)/ Rockin' In The Free World (5:22)/ All Along The Watchtower (7:48)/ Harvest Moon (5:12)/ Unknown Legend (4:17)/ Love Is A Rose (2:23)/ War Of Man (5:16)/ You And Me (3:49)/ After The Goldrush (5:17)
R: Vg-Ex. Audience. Some soundboard.
S: European tour July '93 except CD2 tracks 7&8 Tonight Show '93 and tracks 9-12 Centerstage, Austin Feb. '93.   C: ECD. Pic CDs.

CD - FRISCO
RED PHANTOM RPCD 1184
Prime Of Life (5:24)/ Driveby (5:26)/ Sleeps With Angels (3:57)/ Hey Hey My My (Into The Black) (5:09)/ Train Of Love (4:53)/ Change Your Mind (19:35)/ Piece Of Crap (4:43)
R: Ex. Audience.   S: Bridge Benefit Concert, San Francisco, CA Oct. 1 '94.   C: ECD. Dcc. Pic CD.

CD - FUCKED UP
OHM 034

Southern Man/ Love To Burn/ Separate Ways/
Harvest Moon/ The Needle And The Damage
Done/ Charge Your Mind/ Live To Ride/ Down By
The River/ Dock Of The Bay/ All Along The
Watchtower Rockin' In The Free World
R: G-Vg. Audience.   S: Europe '93.   C: ECD.
Dcc. With Booker T. And The MG's. Time 78:24.

CD - HEART OF GOLD
GRAPEFRUIT GRA-044-B
Mr. Soul (4:33)/ When You Dance I Can Really
Love (4:08)/ Drive Back (5:41)/ My My Hey Hey
(Out Of The Blue) (5:40)/ Like A Hurricane (6:43)/
Computer Age (4:59)/ Heart Of Gold (2:53)/ Hey
Hey My My (Into The Black) (4:50)/ The Old
Laughing Lady (5:01)/ Eldorado (acoustic version)
(7:09)/ This Note's For You (3:52)/ Ohio (2:53)/
Rockin' In A Free World (3:45)/ This Old House
(4:45)/ Harvest Moon (2:24)
R: Vg-Ex. Soundboard.   S: USA'86-'92.
C: Australian CD. Dcc.

CD - LOS ANGELES 1993
RARITIES & FEW RFCD 2285
CD1: Mr. Soul/ The Loner/ Southern Man/
Helpless/ Like A Hurricane/ Rockin' In The Free
World/ Love To Burn/ Only Love Can Break A
Heart
CD2: Harvest Moon/ The Needle And The
Damage Don/ On The Way Home/ Heart Of Gold/
Powder Finger/ He Was A Friend Of Mine/ Down
By The River/ Sittin' On The Dock Of The Bay/ All
Along The Watchtower
R: G. Audience.   S: LA Sports Arena Sept. 11
'93.   C: ECD. With Booker T & The MGs.

CD - ONLY ONCE
COSMIC THRILLS CT 50006/7
CD1: Ten Men Working (6:20)/ Hello Lonely
Woman (4:24)/ I'm Going (5:24)/ Married Man
(2:41)/ Coup De Ville (4:42)/ Days That Used To
Be (4:36)/ After The Goldrush (4:07)/ Ordinary
People (12:09)/ Crime In The City (7:10)/ Life In
The City (3:34)
CD2: Bad News (7:35)/ Twilight (6:32)/ Ain't It The
Truth (5:01)/ Hey Hey (4:12)/ This Note's For You
(4:25)/ Welcome To The Big Room (6:59)/
Tonight's The Night (14:56)
R: Vg. Soundboard.   S: Jones Beach Aug. 27
'88.   C: ECD. Dcc.

CD - THE QUIET WAY
RARE RECORDING COLLECTION RRC 045
From Hank To Hendrix/ Unknown Legend/ Love Is
A Rose/ Pocahontas/ Like A Hurricane/ War Of
Man/ The Needle And The Damage Done/ Harvest
Moon/ Dreaming Man/ Mr. Soul/ Powderfinger/
Sugar Mountain/ You And Me/ After The Goldrush/
Don't Let It Bring You Down
R: Exs. Soundboard.   S: Chicago Nov. 17 '92.
C: ECD. Dcc. Time 78:00.

CD - RIDE MY MOTORCYCLE
FLASHBACK 12 93 0223

Southern Man (6:36)/ Helpless (7:53)/ Like A
Hurricane (7:53)/ Love To Burn (8:28)/ Separate
Ways (5:45)/ Powderfinger (5:21)/ Only Love Can
Break Your Heart (4:42)/ Harvest Moon (5:06)/
Dream Machine (6:23)/ Down By The River (8:27)/
All Along The Watchtower (6:35)
R: Exs. Soundboard.   S: Belgium July 3 '93.
C: ECD. Dcc.

CD - RIVERS EDGE
HAWK 018
Mr. Soul (4:03)/ The Loner (4:16)/ Southern Man
(6:43)/ Helpless (8:17)/ Like A Hurricane (8:05)/
Love To Burn (9:03)/ Harvest Moon (5:13)/ The
Needle And the Damage Done (3:01)/ Motorcycle
Mama (6:29)/ Down By The River (8:39)/ All Along
The Watchtower (6:54)
R: Ex. Audience.   S: Europe, summer '93.
C: ECD. Dcc. Pic CD.

CD - ROCK 'N' ROLL COWBOY
GREAT DANE RECORDS GDR CD 9407 A/B/C/D
CD - ROCK 'N' ROLL COWBOY
GREAT DANE RECORDS GDR CD 9407 A/B/C/D
CD1: Nowadays Clancy Can't Even Sing (Whittier
School, LA '66)/ Birds (Big Sur Folk Festival,
Easlen, CA Sept. '68)/ Cowgirl In The Sand
(Fillmore East, NY Mar. 7 '70)/ Tell Me Why, Only
Love Can Break Your Heart (Fillmore East, NY
June 3 '70)/ Everybody's Alone (during rehearsals
KQED TV Dec. '70)/ Medley: A Man Needs A
Maid, Heart Of Gold (Shakespeare Theatre,
Stratford Jan. 22 '71)/ Out On The Weekend, Love
In Mind, Dance Dance Dance (BBC TV Studio,
London Feb. 23 '71)/ Cripple Creek Ferry, L.A.,
Soldier (Carnegie Hall, New York Jan. 21 '73)/
Harvest (JFK Center, Washington Jan. 28 '73)/
Sweet Joni (Civic Auditorium, Bakersfield Jan. 20
'73)/ Tonight's The Night, Tired Eyes (Queens
College, NY Nov. 15 '73)
CD2: Pardon My Heart, On The Beach (Bottom
Line, NY May 16 '74)/ Traces, Human Highway,
Love Art Blues (Coliseum, Seattle July 9 '74)/
Hawaiian Sunrise (Roosevelt Stadium, Long
Island Sept. 8 '74)/ Like A Hurricane (Festival Hall,
Osaka, Japan Mar. 5 '76)/ Stringman
(Hammersmith Odeon, London Mar. 31 '76)/
Evening Coconut (Civic Center, Springfield June
27 '76)/ Long May You Run, Southern Man (Civic
Center, Providence July 7 '76)/ Give My Strength
(US Nov. '76)/ Comes A Time, Sail Away
(Catalyst, Santa Cruz Aug. 28 '77)/ Lady Wingshot
(Bicentennial Park, Miami Beach Nov. 12 '77)/
Shots (Boarding House, San Francisco May 24
'78)/ Downtown (Civic Center, Providence Sept.
25 '78)
CD3: If You Got Love, Transformer Man
(Scandinavium, Goteborg, Sweden Oct. 8 '82)/ My
Boy (Palmer Auditorium, Austin Jan. 14 '83)/ Old
Ways, Kinda Fonda Wanda (California Exp.
Auditorium, Sacramento July 26 '83)/ Gonna Rock
Forever, Touch The Night (Catalyst, Santa Cruz
Feb. 7 '84)/ Amber Jean, Let Your Fingers Do The
Talking, Helpless, Down By The River (Austin City

Limits TV Show Sept. 25 '84)/ Interstate, Grey
Riders, Nothin' Is Perfect (USA '85)/ Southern
Pacific (USA '85)
CD4: Mideast Vacation (Long Beach Arena, Long
Beach Aug. 28 '86)/ Eldorado (Metropolitan
Center, Minneapolis Oct. 17 '86)/ Computer Age
(Palatrussardi Milano, Italy May 5 '87)/ Bad News
(Popular Creek, Chicago Aug. 16 '88)/ Ordinary
People (Jones Beach Auditorium, Wantaught Aug.
27 '88)/ Rockin' In The Free World (Saturday Night
Live TV Show, NYC Sept. 30 '89)/ Winterlong
(Ahoy, Rotterdam, Holland Dec. 13 '89)/ Silver
And Gold (Civic Auditorium, Santa Monica Mar. 31
'90)/ Campaigner (Memorial Auditorium, Buffalo
Feb. 16 '91)/ Homefires (Orpheum Theatre,
Boston Mar. 19 '92)/ Only Love Can Break Your
Heart (Dorothy Chandler Pavilion, LA Mar. 1 '93)/
Mr. Soul (Ahoy Hall, Rotterdam, Holland July 5
'93)/ Separate Ways (Torhout Festival, Belgium
July 3 '93)/ Philadelphia (Dorothy Chandler
Pavilion Mar. 21 '94)
R: As with any set with this many sources, quality
varies. Generally speaking the set is Vg-Ex.
Audience and soundboard.   C: ECD. Book-style
digi-pack case. Excellent 44 page book. Time CD1
70:00. CD2 77:00. CD3 77:00. CD4 77:00.

CD - SILVER AND GOLD
THE SWINGIN' PIG RECORDS TSP CD 159-2
CD1: Long May You Run/ From Hank To Hendrix/
Unknown Legend/ Silver And Gold/ You And Me/
War Of Man/ Old King/ Such A Woman/ Harvest
Moon/ Heart Of Gold/ The Needle And The
Damage Done/ Too Far Gone/ Homefire Is
Burning
CD2: Dreamin' Man/ Natural Beauty/ Don't Let It
Bring You Down/ Mr. Soul/ Sugar Mountain/ After
The Goldrush/ One Of These Days/ Down By The
River/ Like A Hurricane/ Fucking Up
R: Exs. Soundboard.   S: The Tower Theatre,
Philadelphia Mar. '92.   C: ECD. Dcc. Time CD1
52:40. CD2 57:37.

CD - SOUTHERN MAN
GRAPEFRUIT GRA-044-A
Cinnamon Girl (3:24)/ Cowgirl In The Sand
(11:19)/ Wonderin' (2:10)/ Down By The River
(12:03)/ Dance Dance Dance (1:22)/ Don't Let It
Bring You Down (1:18)/ The Loner (3:18)/
Everybody Knows This Is Nowhere (3:06)/ Sea Of
Madness (3:02)/ Birds (2:38)/ Out On The
Weekend (3:55)/ The Old Man (3:21)/ A Man
Needs A Maid (3:42)/ See The Sky About To Rain
(2:53)/ Southern Man (3:22)/ Only Love Can Break
Your Heart (3:24)/ Tell Me Why (2:58)/ After The
Gold Rush (3:54)/ Harvest (2:40)
R: Vg-Ex.   S: Europe/USA '69-'76.
C: Australian CD. Dcc.

CD - THE SOUTHERN MAN
INVASION UNLIMITED IU 9307-2
CD1: Mr. Soul/ The Loner/ Southern Man/
Helpless/ Love To Burn/ Separate Ways/ Like A
Hurricane/ Powderfinger/ Only Love Can Break

Your Heart/ Harvest Moon/ The Needle And The
Damage Done/ Dream Machine
CD2: Down By The River/ All Along The
Watchtower/ Motor Cycle Mama/ Separate Ways/
Powderfinger/ Dream Machine/ Dock Of The Bay/
All Along The Watchtower/ Rockin' In The
Freeworld
R: G-Vg.   S: CD1, CD2 tracks 1-2 Belgium July
3 '93. Tracks 3-9 Finsbury Park July 4 '93. Track 9
with Pearl Jam.   C: ECD. Dcc.

CD - SPEAKIN' OUT
THE GOLD STANDARD 57179XK1
Tonight's The Night/ Mellow My Mind/ World On A
String/ Speakin' Out/ Albuquerque/ New Mama/
Roll Another Number For The Road/ Tired Eyes/
Tonight's The Night/ Flying On The Ground Is
Wrong/ Human Highway/ Helpless/ Don't Be
Denied
R: Vg-Exs. Audience.   S: The Palace Theatre,
Manchester, England Nov. 3 '73.   C: ECD. Dcc.
Time 69:54.

CD - YOUNGS HEART RUNS FREE
FREE WORLD MUSIC FWM 001/2
CD1: Mr. Soul/ The Loner/ Southern Man/
Helpless/ Like A Hurricane/ Motorcycle Mama/
Love To Burn/ Separate Ways/ Powderfinger/ Only
Love Can Break Your Heart/ Harvest Moon/ The
Needle & The Damage Done
CD2: Live To Ride/ Down By The River/ Sitting On
The Dock Of The Bay/ All Along The Watchtower/
Rockin' In The Freeworld (featuring Pearl Jam)/
I'm A Passenger/ The Road Of Plenty/ Forever
Young/ Ordinary People
R: Vg-Ex. Audience.   S: Finsbury Park, London,
England July 11 '93.

Z

ZAPPA, FRANK

CD - APOCRYPHA
GREAT DANE RECORDS GDR 9405 ABCD
CD1: Lost In A Whirpool (2:12)/ Do It In C (1:35)
(Lancaster CA '58)/ Anyway The Wind Blows
(2:36) (Pal Studio, Cucamonga, CA '63)/ Fountain
Of Love (2:16) (Pal Studio, Cucamonga, CA '63)/
Deseri (2:30) ('62)/ The Story Of Electricity (2:20)/
Metal Man Has Hornet Wings (2:56)/ I Was A
Teenage Maltshop, Status Black Baby, Ned The
Mumbler, Ned Had A Brainstorm (8:30) (Studio Z,
Cucamonga, CA '63)/ Whiskey Gone Behind The
Sun (1:18) (Broadside Bar, Pomona '64)/ Mondo
Hollywood (1:51) (Hollywood CA '65)/ Sandwich
Song (1:40) (Studio Z, Cucamonga, CA '64)/ How
Could I Be Such A Fool (1:53) ('65)/ Agency Man
(5:42) (Apostolic, NYC '67)/ Randomonium (1:31)
('67)/ Lumpy Gravy Dialogue Outtake (:45)/ In
Memoriam: Hieronymous Bosch (5:05) ('67)/ In
The Sky (2:00) (BBC-TV, London, UK '68)/
Remington Electric Razor (1:00) ('68)/ Directly
From My Heart To You (5:50)/ Twinkle Tits (10:20)

(Olympic Auditorium, LA Mar. 7 '70)
CD2: Magic Fingers (2:33)/ Studebaker (6:06)/
Interview (3:00) (London, UK '71)/ RDNZL (4:08)/
Inca Roads (3:05)/ T'Mershi Duween (2:18)/ Stink
Foot (4:06) (KCET-TV, Studio, LA Dec. '74)/ Duck
Duck Goose (3:00)/ Down In The Dew (2:56)
(Electric Lady Studios, NYC '75)/ The Purple
Lagoon (3:57)/ St. Alfonso Pancake Breakfast
(4:18) (NYC '76)/ Black Napkins (4:33)/ Heidelberg
(5:26) (Heidelberg, Germany '77)/ The Squirm
(6:06) (Palladium, NYC Oct. 31 '77)/ Dong Work
For Yuda (3:00) ('77)/ Moe's Vacations, Black
Page (7:05) (Poughkeepsie, NY Sept. 21 '78)
CD3: Suicide Chump (9:00) (Stoneybrook, NY
Oct. 15 '78)/ Nite Owl (2:15) ('80)/ Heavy Duty
Judy (4:17)/ Pick Me I'm Clean (3:32)/ Teenage
Wind (3:07)/ Harder Than Your Husband (2:32)/
Bamboozled By Love (3:04) ('78)/ Falling In Love
Is A Stupid Habit (1:56) ('80)/ This Is My Story
(1:20)/ Whipping Post (6:25)/ Clowns On Velvet
(6:17) (The Ritz, NYC Nov. 17 '81)/ Frogs With
Dirty Little Lips (2:05) (UMRK '81)/ In France
(2:35)/ Broken Hearts Are For Assholes (4:05)
(Santa Monica, CA Dec. 11 '81)/ The Texas
Medley (9:00)/ I'm The Walrus (3:40) (Springfield,
MA Mar. 13 '88)/ America The Beautiful (3:14)
(Burlington, VT Mar. 13 '88)
CD4: The Worlds Greatest Sinner (11:54) ('61)/
Gypsy Airs (1:48) ('66)/ Some Ballet Music (4:58)
(Boston, MA July 18 '68)/ The Jelly (2:10) ('67)/
The Revenge Of The Knick Knack People (6:20)
(UMRK '78)/ Spontaneous Minimalist Composition
(1:59)/ Sinister Footwear (26:00) (Zellerbach
Auditorium, San Francisco June 15 '84)/ The
Black Page No. 1 (2:02) (UMRK '86)/ While You
Where Art #1 (7:15) (UMRK '85)
R: As with any set with this many sources, quality
varies. Generally speaking the set is Vg-Ex..
C: ECD. Book-style digi-pack case.

CD - PARALIPOMENI DELLA
BATRACOMIOMACHIA
TEDDY BEAR RECORDS TB 48
Penis Dimension (11:26)/ The Air (3:53)/ The Dog
Breath - Mother People (4:23)/ You Didn't Try To
Call Me (3:34)/ King Kong (32:41)/ Who Are The
Brain Police? (6:32)
R: Ex. Soundboard.   S: Palais Gaumont, Paris,
France '70.   C: ECD. Pic CD.

CD - PUNKY'S WHIPS SHOWN OFF STAGE
TUFF BITES T.B 94.1004
CD1: Envelopes (5:29)/ I Have Been In You
(2:55)/ Tom Snyder Vs. The Red Spiders From
NBC (1:44)/ Broken Hearts Are For Assholes
(4:24)/ Stinky Finger (2:55)/ Fancy Stinky Part One

(3:20)/ Fancy Stinky Part Two (9:09)/ Punky's
Whips (11:00)
CD2: Stinkfoot Finale (4:05)/ Black Page No. 2
(2:47)/ Deadly Jaws (2:47)/ Disco Boy (5:45)/
Dinah Moe Humm (6:56)/ Bobby Brown (3:14)/
Conehead (7:53)/ Camarillo Brillo (3:26)/ Muffin'
Man (3:10)/ San Ber'Dino (4:18)/ Black Napkins
(2:18)/ Auld Lang Syne (2:55)
R: Vg-Ex. Audience. Some surface noise.
S: Los Angeles New Year's Eve '77.   C: ECD.
Dcc. Fold-open digi-pack. Pic CD.

CD - A SNAIL IN MY NOSE
TEDDY BEAR RECORDS TB 49
Intro/ Uncle Meat, 9 Types Of Industrial Pollution,
Uncle Meat (including Zolar Czakl), Interlude
(including Raindrops Keep Falling On My Head),
Sharleena (17:08)/ The Sanzini Brothers, What
Will This Evening Bring Me This Morning?, What
Kind Of Girls Do You Think We Are?, Bwana Dick,
Latex Solar Beef, Daddy Daddy Daddy (15:39)/
Little House I Used To Live In (including Penis
Dimension), Would You Like A Snack?, Holiday In
Berlin, Bull Blown (Guitar Solo By FZ), Cruising
For Burgers (18:50)
R: Ex. Soundboard.   S: Fillmore East, NYC, Nov.
'70.   C: ECD. Dcc. Pic CD.

CD - STRANGE HABITS
SPIDER GLASS SGCD 004/2
CD1: Intro (3:10)/ Stinkfoot (8:44)/ Dirty Love
(3:04)/ Filthy Habits (10:21)/ How Could I Be Such
A Fool? (3:34)/ I Ain't Got No Heart (2:36)/ I'm Not
Satisfied (1:53)/ Black Napkins (10:49)/ Advance
Romance (11:40)
CD2: Honey Don't You Want A Man Like Me
(3:35)/ The Illinois Enema Bandit (8:57)/ Wind Up
Workin' In A Gas Station (2:44)/ Tryin' To Grow A
Chin (4:06)/ The Torture Never Stops (8:00)/
Chungas Revenge, Drum Solo (15:39)/ Zoot
Allures (6:57)/ Ship Ahoy (6:52)/ I'm The Slime
(3:25)/ San' Berdino (6:25)
R: G-Vg. Audience.   S: Osaka, Japan Feb. 3 '76.
C: ECD. Dcc. Pic CD.

CD - STREAM FLASH CONSERVATIVE
CLINTON CL 7918
Prelude To Bobby Brown/ Bobby Brown/
Conehead/ Moe's Vacation/ I Have Been In You/
The Little House I Used To Live In/ Tell Me You
Love Me/ Yo Mama/ Heavy Duty Judy/
Presentation/ City Of Tiny Lights/ You Are What
You Is/ Mudd Club
R: Ex.   S: Tracks 1-6 San Francisco '78. Tracks
9-13 New York '78.   C ECD. Black jewel case
with stickers. Black CD. Time 62:38.

Appendix: Bootleg Labels

For more listings of bootleg labels see

HOT WACKS BOOK XV
The Last Wacks
and
HOT WACKS BOOK
Supplements 1 & 2

CD - ALL OF US (AS)
01 Duran Duran 'In Concert'
02 Mike Oldfield 'Tubular Bells II'
03 Pat Metheny Group 'In Concert'
04 Weather Report 'Solarization's'
05 John McLaughlin Trio 'Live'
06 R. Fripp & D. Sullivan 'The Day Before'
07 Allen Holdsworth 'Live Secrets'
08 Gathering Of Minds 'Live'
09 Steve Vai 'My Father's Place'
10 Pearl Jam 'Free World'
11/2 Neil Young 'Live'
12/2 Grateful Dead 'Live'
13/2 Cure 'High Tops N' Hairspray'
14/2 Prince 'Take This Beat'
15/2 Steve Vai 'Live'
16 Allan Holdsworth Quartet 'Live'
17 Al Di Meola 'Classic And Acoustic Guitars'
18/2 J. McLaughlin, Al Di Meola, Paco De Lucia
      'Going Rome'
19 Jeff Beck 'Live'
20 Jack Bruce 'Five Axeman'
21 V.V.A.A. 'A Guitar Night In Italy'
22 Tori Amos 'American Heartbreaker'
23 Steve Morse 'Two Faces'
24 Dixie Dregs 'Sex, Dregs & Rock 'N' Roll'
25 Weather Report 'Italian Weather'
26 Heart 'Heart 'N Zeppelin'
27 Mahavishnu Orchestra - John McLaughlin
      'The Inner Flamming Axe'
28/2 Gil Evans & John McLaughlin 'We
      Remember Jimi'
29/2 Deep Purple & Joe Satriani 'Welcome Joe'
30/2 Pink Floyd 'A Family Affair'
31 Jeff Healey Band 'Evil Blues'
32 Mick Karin Bestial Cluster 'Once Again'
33 King Crimson 'Formentera Memories'
34 Stray Cats 'Jammin' With Cats'
35 V.V.A.A. 'Jazz Explotion Superband'
36/2 Pink Floyd 'Floyd In Europe'
37 United Kingdom 'Tour Memories'
38/2 Prince 'Get Wild'
39/2 Rolling Stones 'New Voodo In New Orleans'
40 Sonny Rollins 'The Meeting'
41 Herbie Hancock 'Toys'
42/2 John Scofield & Pat Metheny 'You Speak
      My Language'
43 Steve Ray Vaughan & Buddy Guy 'See You
      Later'

CD - ARCHIVIO (ARC)
020 Texas 'First Dive'
021 Ron Wood & Keith Richards 'The Return Of
      Woody Wood Breaker'
022 Hot Tuna 'Live TV+FM'
023 Patto 'Straight To The Tempest'

CD - BABY CAPONE (BC)
001 Pink Floyd 'Meteora'
002 U2 'Zoo In The Casbah'
003/2 B. Adams 'Living In USA'
004 INXS 'Alive 'N' Kicking'
005 Def Leppard 'One Man Band'
006 Lenny Kravitz 'If 6 Was 9'
007/2 Iron Maiden 'Ecatombe'
008 Queen 'Renina Di Ipanema'
009 Black Crowes 'Stone The Crowes'
010/2 Kiss 'Death Kiss'
011 Little Village 'On The Border'
012/2 Sting 'Happy Birthday'
013 Slaughter 'Permanent Vacation'
014 Stevie Ray Vaughan 'The Hawk On Fire'
015 Men At Work 'Let's Work Together'
016 Bob Marley 'Soul Rebel'
017 Megadeth 'Rigor Mortis'
018 Joe Satriani 'The Mobster'
019/2 Sisters Of Mercy 'Echo'
020/2 Deep Purple 'Black Night In Denmark'
021/2 Rainbow 'Mixed Emotions'
022/2 Dire Straits 'High Falls'
023 Meatloaf 'The Hell On The Hill'
024 Pink Floyd 'A CD Full Of Secrets'
025 Pink Floyd 'Pompeii'
026 Pink Floyd 'Moon Walk'
027/2 Bad Company 'Crime Story'
029 Marillon 'Heaven And Hell'
030 Panthera 'Damnation'
026/2 Skid Row 'Merci Beucoup Motherfuckers'
037/2 Prince 'The Mutant'
039 R.E.M. 'Boreal Equinoxia'
045/2 Nirvana 'Pissing In Action'
046/2 Soundgarden 'Real Wild Children'
047/2 Pearl Jam 'Fear And Loathing'
048/2 Jane's Addiction 'Invitation To Dream'
050/2 Red Hot Chili Peppers 'Porno Zombie'

CD - BEST OF LIVE (BOLS)
001 Rod Stewart 'Live In Anaheim '77'
002 Palmer, Robert 'Live At The Ritz, New York'
003 Idol, Billy 'Live From L.A.'
004 Yes 'Live In L.A. Forum, '87, '74'
005 Rolling Stones, The 'Live In Detroit'
006 Foreigner 'Live In Dallas, Texas '82'
011 Cray, Robert 'Live In Springfield, Mass.'
012 Pop, Iggy 'Live In N.Y., Boston, L.A.'
013 Cocker, Joe 'Live Poglikeepslee, N.Y. '82'
014 Chicago 'Live In Lousvill, '70'
015 Mellencamp, John Cougar 'Live In Lincoln,
      Nebraska'
016 Steve Miller 'Live At The Beacon Theatre'

017 Dooble Brothers 'Live In Philadelphia'
018 McGuinn, Roger 'Live In L.A. And N.Y. City'
019 Rush 'Live In Toronto '88'
020 ELP 'Live In America'

CD - BIG RECORDS (BIG)

081 Pearl Jam 'Flashpoint'
083 Whitney Houston 'Live In New York'
084 Midnight Oil 'Blue Sky Red Earth'
085 Take That! 'Kiss This'
086/87 Guns N' Roses 'Live In Argentina'
088/89 Rod Stewart 'In The Spotlight'
090 Billy Joel 'Temptation'
091 The Smiths 'Thank Your Lucky Stars'
092 Elton John 'Fine China'
093 Kiss 'Rock And Roll All Nite'
094 Abba 'Sweet Dreams Are Made Of...'
098 The Smiths 'The Butterfly Collector'

CD - BLACK DOG (BD)

001 The Beatles 'Hodge Podge'
002 Who 'Coco Hall, Detroit '72'
003 Who 'San Francisco '71'
004 Doors 'Central Park, New York'
005 Townsend, Pete 'Quadrophenia Demos'
006 Harrison, George 'All Things Must Pass'

CD - COCOMELOS RECORDS (CM)

011 Extreme 'Take It To The Limits'
012 Nine Inch Nails 'Solid Gold Hell'
013 Disposable Heroes Of Hiphoprisy 'Political
     Technocracy'
014 Alice In Chains 'Dirty Toy Town'
015 Ice-T & Body Count 'In Your Face'
016 Ministry ?????
017 Springsteen 'Solo Acoustic'
018/19 Depeche Mode 'Mode On The Road'
020/21 Pearl Jam 'Brixton'
022/23 Van Halen 'Rocking My Hometown'
024 Pearl Jam 'The Kids Are Alright'
025/26 Rush 'Northern Heroes'
027/28 Soundgarden 'The Garden'
029/30 Coverdale - Page 'Live In Japan'
031 Pearl Jam 'New Songs'
032/33 The Eagles 'The Boys From Yesterday'
034/35 Rolling Stones 'I Can't Get Next To You'
036 Green Day 'Having A Blast'

CD - DATE (DAT)

001 Lenny Kravitz, Feat, M. Jagger 'Tattoo Me'
002 Gary Moore 'White Thunder'
003 Joe Satriani 'Europe '93'

CD - DEAD DOG (DD)

001 Depeche Mode 'The Complete Concert'
002 Front 242 'Front 242'
003 Heroes Del Silencio 'Heroes Del Silencio'
004 Metallica 'Enter The Final Show'
005 Morrissey 'Love To See Him'
006 Prince 'Intermission'
007 Psychotic Waltz 'Live'
008 Chris Rea 'Down The Road'
009 Sepultura 'Live Chaos'
010 Sisters Of Mercy 'Electric Live'

011 Waterboys 'License To Play'
012 Sting 'Nothing But Live'
013 Cure 'Dreams Come True'
020 Aerosmith 'Eat The F*ckin' Rich'
021 Cypress Hill 'Black Monday'
022 Metallica 'Enter The Final Show' Part 2
SE410 Ministry 'Jesus Built My What?'
SE420 Biohazard 'Wrong Side Of The Stage'
SE426 Faith No More 'Undressed'
SE432 Pearl Jam 'Stage Of Love And Trust'
SE436 Dinosaur Jr. 'Freakin' Live!'
SE440 Bad Religion 'Christmas Show'
SE442 Kiss 'They Are Live'
SE445 Nirvana 'The Last American Concert'
SE447 Biohazard '100% Ass-Kicking Live'
TB002 Rage Against The Machine 'Save The
       Planet-American Headlines'
TB007 Biohazard 'Wrong Side Of The Stage'
TB014 Porno For Pyros 'A Priori'

CD - DEEP RECORDS

DFCD001-92 Prince 'Play With Me Baby'
DBCD002-92 Prince 'The Sex Of It'
DFCD003-92 Prince 'Globequake'
DFCD005-92 Prince 'Funky Vibrations'
MIK003/004 AC/DC 'Fire Your Guns'
MIK012/013 Bob Dylan 'The Neverending Tour'
MIK014/015 Paul McCartney 'What A Mean
           Fiddler'
MIK016 Guns 'N Roses 'God Bless America'
MIK017 Metallica 'Don't Trad On Us'
MIK040/041 D.A.D. 'Live Craziness'
MK001/002 Metallica 'Stone Cold Crazy'
MK003 Ramones 'Halfway To Russia'
MK004 Sepultura 'They'
UM002 John Mellencamp 'John's Garage Tape'
UM004 Bruce Springsteen 'Warming Up The
       River Tour'
UM005/006 Thin Lizzy 'Sha La Live'
UM007 Rolling Stones 'Tour In Hawaii 1973'

CD - FOUR ACES (FAR)

001 Weather Report 'Live In Montreaux '76'
002 Allan Holdsworth Quartet 'Live In Japan '85'
003 Dixie Dregs 'Live In New York '81'
004 Return To Forever 'Reunion'
005 Television 'Live In San Francisco '78'
006 Miles Davis 'Miles In Paris '86'
007-2 Paul McCartney 'Out The Forum
008 Frank Zappa 'Leatherette' (1977)
009 Al Kooper & M. Bloomfield 'More Live
     Adventures From..."
010 Ossiach 'Ossiach Live'
011 Syd Barrett 'Melweg'

CD - FU (FU)

201 The Beatles 'A Paris'
202 Various Artists 'The Rock N' Roll Circus'
204 J. Mayall & The Bluesbreakers 'Milan, 1982'
205/2 Paul McCartney &The Wings 'Venezia,
       Italy Sept. 25, '76'
206/2 B.B. King & Ray Charles 'Live At
       Palatrussardi'
207 Beatles 'John, Paul, George And Sm'

CD - GRAPEFRUIT (GRA)
029-A Aerosmith 'Living On The Edge'
009-A Amos, Tori 'Cornflake girl'
001-A Beatles 'From Me To You'
001-B Beatles 'She Loves You'
001-C Beatles 'All My Loving'
001-D Beatles 'Yesterday'
001-E Beatles 'Twist And Shout'
019-A Blondie 'Heart Of Glass'
002-A Bon Jovi 'Bed Of Roses'
002-B Bon Jovi 'In These Arms'
018-A Carpenters 'Close To You'
011-A Clapton, Eric 'Tears In Heaven'
027-A Cocker, Joe 'Unchain My Heart'
030-A Cooper, Alice 'No More Mr. Nice Guy'
022-A Deep Purple 'Black Night'
031-A Def Leppard 'Let's Get Rocked'
031-B Def Leppard 'Rocket'
010-A Depeche Mode 'I Feel You'
021-A The Eagles 'Life In The Fast Lane'
024-A Flletwood Mac 'Rhiannon'
028-A Heart 'These Dreams'
014-A Houston, Whitney 'I Will Always Love You'
013-A John, Elton 'Sacrifice'
008-A Lang, K.D. 'Constant Craving'
005-A Madonna 'Vogue'
012-A Marley, Bob 'Is This Love'
023-A Meatloaf 'Anything For Love'
007-A Metallica 'Whever I May Roam'
007-B Metallica 'Fade To Black'
007-C Metallica 'Nothing Else Matters'
015-A Morrison, Van 'Gloria'
004-A Nirvana 'Come As You Are'
004-B Nirvana 'Heart-Shaped Box'
017-A Orbison, Roy 'Pretty Woman'
035-A Palmer, Robert 'She Makes My Day'
036-A Pantera 'Domination'
003-A Pearl Jam 'Daughter'
003-B Pearl Jam 'Alive'
003-C Pearl Jam 'Animal'
003-D Pearl Jam 'Jeremy'
003-E Pearl Jam 'Blood'
025-A Petty, Tom 'I Won't Back Down'
034-A Pink Floyd 'Take It Back'
034-B Pink Floyd 'High Hopes'
016-A Presley, Elvis 'Suspicious Minds'
016-B Presley, Elvis 'All Shook Up'
026-A Roxette 'It Must Have Been Love'
026-B Roxette 'The Look'
006-A U2 'Mysterious Ways'
006-B U2 'Lemon'
020-A UB 40 'I Got You Babe'
032-A Various 'Alternative Vol. 1'
032-B Various 'Alternative Vol. 2'
033-A Various 'Metal Vol. 1'

CD - HAMMERJACK (HJ)
001/2 Metallica 'Welcome To The Snakepit'
003 Guns N' Roses 'Paradiso Oct. 2 '87'
004/5 Metallica 'So Fuckin' What?'
006 Sacred Reich 'Dynamo Open Air'
007/8 Satriani, Joe 'Clysee Monmarte'
009/10 Primus 'Paridiso, Amsterdam '90'
011 Bon Jovi 'Shout'

012 Megadeth 'Peace Sells'
013 Led Zeppelin 'Bonham Sessions'
014 Plant, Robert '29 Palms & 1 Plant'

CD - HAWK DISCS
038 Rage Against The Machine 'People Of The Sun'
039/40 The Grateful Dead 'Scarlet Fire'
41 Primus 'Freak Out'
42 Doors & Eddie Vedder 'Keep The Fire Alive'
43 Smashing Pumpkins 'Out Of Focus'
44/45 Pearl Jam 'Leaving Babylon'
46 Dead Can Dance 'Exit To Eden'
47 Bjork 'The Girl From Outer Space'
48 Cream 'Long Time Commin'
49/50 Eric Clapton 'Big Blue'
51 Counting Crowes 'Children In Bloom'
52 Cranberries 'Thoughts That Linger'
53 Belly 'Sweet Ride'
54 Replacements 'Hanging It Up'
55 Porno For Pyros '100 Waves'
57 Sepultura 'Enter Chaos'

CD - HIGH QUALITY (HQ)
01/2 Various Artists 'The Spirit Of Jimi Hendrix'
02 Paul Rodgers 'Paul Rodgers & Company'
03 Tina Turner 'Rio 1988'
04 Richard Thompson 'Across The Crowded Room'
05 Neil Young 'Transworld Tour'
06 The Shadows 'Empire'
07 The Allman Brothers Band 'Off The Road'
08/2 Yes 'Live At Q.P.R. 1975'
09 Gloria Estefan 'Into The Light World Tour'
10 The Beatles 'Japan 1966+Miami 1964'
11 Phish 'Live In Stowe'

CD - HOME RECORDS (HR)
5911-1 Blind Melon 'A Sweet Slice Of Melon'
5912-0 S.R. Vaughan 'Hello Y'A All'
5913-9 Gin Blossoms 'Small Club'
5914-7 Lemonheads 'With Real Lemon Juice'
5915-8 Primus 'You Can't Party Without Me'
5916-2 Jellyfish 'California Dreaming'
5917-5 Nirvana 'Tour Over Europe '94'
5918-4 Nine Inch Nails 'Hole In Your Head'
5919-3 Screaming Trees 'Live!'
5920-6 Alice In Chains 'Tie Me Up'
5921-4 Rage Against The Machine 'F*ck The Administration'
5922-7 Counting Crowes 'Hottest Ticket In Town'
5923-9 Cracker 'Words Of Wisdom'
5924-3 Jimi Hendrix 'Jewel Box'
5925-1 Smashing Pumpkins 'Helloween Party'
5926-2 Morrissey 'New York, New York'
5927/28 Sting 'Dreaming Of U'
5929-5 Afghan Whigs 'Time For A Bavarian Death Waltz'
5930-0 Breeders 'Hello Baton Rouge'
5931-8 Tori Amos 'A Woman On A Mission'
5932/33 Pearl Jam 'And The Pearls Sweep'
5934-6 Primal Scream 'Cream De La Scream'
5935-3 Megadeath 'Black Shadows'
5936/37 Black Sabbath 'Iron Men'

5938-1 Motley Crue 'Secrets Of Tone'
5939-4 Motorhead 'Burn In Bloody Hell'
5940-7 Suicidal Tendencies 'The Art Of Suicide'
5942-5 Eric Clapton 'Jewel Box 2'
5943-2 Rolling Stones 'Jewel Box 3'
5944-6 Bjork 'Comeback'
5947-3 Pink Floyd 'Jewel Box 4'
5950/51 Pink Floyd 'And The Bell Tolls'

CD - INVASION UNLIMITED (IU)

9203 Prince 'Purple Prince In Concert'
9204 Springsteen 'Lucky London Town'
9301 McCartney 'By Invitation Only'
9302 Neil Young 'Lucky Seventeen'
9304 Brian Wilson 'Sweet Insanity'
9306 Bee Gees 'Last Minute Demos'
9307 Neil Young 'The Southern Man'
9308 Springsteen 'Cool Rockin' Daddy'
9309 Suede 'Suave and Elegant'
9410 Beach Boys 'Summer Sounds & Pet Sessions'
9414 Rollins Band 'Divine Object Of Hatred'
9415 Counting Crows 'The Ghost In Me'
T2580-2/3 Beach Boys 'Smile & Bits And Pieces'
XIL01611 Rolling Stones 'Beggar's Breakfast'
XIL01612 King Crimson 'A Weird Person's Guide To King Crimson'

CD - INSECT RECORDS (IST)

6/7 Metallica 'Damaged Justice'
8/9 Prince 'Small Club'
10 Ramones 'Blitzkrieg In Athens'
18 Rolling Stones 'In Action'
19 Robert Plant 'Promised Land'
20 Led Zeppelin 'Many More Early Times'
21/22 Rush 'Gangster Of Boats'
23 Nirvana 'Seattle Sound, Sounds Great'
24 Motely Crue 'The Red Hot Spot'
25 Japan 'Oriental Performance'
26/27 Kiss 'Peter, Paul, Gene & Ace'
28 U2 'Looking Back In The Mirror'
29 Simple Minds 'Dutch Daze'
30 Jane's Addiction 'Carnival Of souls'
31/32 Queen 'The Jewels'
33 Bob Marley 'The Last Club Tour '75'
34/35 U2 Bono Is A Dinky'
36 Primal Scream 'Purple Chain'
37 Paul Weller 'Ends Of The World'
38 Suede 'What's Your Name London Suede?'
39/40 Pink Floyd 'The 1994 West Coast Trip'
41 Frankie... 'Frankie Says Use Condoms'
42 Nine Inch Nails 'Mudstock'
43 Sigue Sigue Sputnik 'Orange Devil'
44 Elvis Costello 'Buddy Holly On Acid'
45 Sex Pistols 'Spirit Of '76'
46 Collective Soul 'Sweet Home Chicago'
47 Van Morrison 'Van The Man'
48 Jimi Hendrix 'Moons And Rainbows'
49/50 Metallica 'Candy For The Kids'
51 Suede 'Old Man's Car'
52 Blur 'Blackout'
53 Theraphy? 'I Want My Money Back'
54 Paradise Lost 'Northen Darkness'
55 Siouxsie & The Banshees 'Skreeching'

56/57 Stranglers '..And Then There Were Three'
58 Porno For Pyros 'Eccentric'
59/60 Sting '...Like A Bee'
62/63 Tori Amos 'Childhood Memories'
65/66 Rolling Stones 'Off With Our Heads'
68 Lush 'Show Us Your Tits'
69/70 Paul Rodgers & Friends 'In Bad Company'
71 Rollins Band 'Hard As Nails'
72/73 Phish 'Holiday Recording, Holiday Snap'
75/76 Yes 'Gimme More'
87 Nirvana 'Rare Tracks Vol. I'
88 Nirvana 'Rare Tracks Vol. I'

CD - KISS THE STONE (KTS)

241/42 Madonna 'Lick Me Down Under'
243 Dream Theatre 'Dream Out Loud'
244/45 Meat Loaf 'To Hell And Back'
246 Prince 'Funky Party 2Nite'
247 David Byrne 'Unplugged + More'
248 The Levellers 'Back To Nature'
249 INXS 'Empty Sun Under Clean Minds'
250 Paul McCartney 'Hey, Tokyo!'
251/52 Grateful Dead 'Dead Again'
253 Nirvana 'All Acoustically'
254 Blind Melon 'Sting Me'
255/56 Madonna 'Girlie Show Experience'
257 Matthew Sweet 'Shape Shifter'
258 Jackson Browne 'Too Many Angels'
259 Gin Blossoms 'In Bloom'
260 Radiohead 'Creepshow'
261 Smashing Pumpkins 'Mayonnaise Dream'
262 Lemonheads 'Squeeze Me Please Me'
263 Tool 'Tales From The Darkside'
264 Smashing Pumpkins '3 Feet High'
265 Izzy Stradlin 'Rocker'
266 Crowded House 'It's Only Natural'
267 The Doors 'Apocalypse Now'
268 Bjork 'Sugar Candy Kisses'
269 Duran Duran 'Acoustic World'
270/71 Elton John 'World Class'
272 Bob Mould 'The Calm Before The Storm'
273/74 Tom Petty 'Southern Gentleman'
275 Sting 'Complete Chicago Sessions'
276 Primus 'Back In The Madhouse'
277 Therapy? 'No Love Lost'
278 Suede 'Performance'
279 Sepultura 'Welcome To The End Of...'
280 Springsteen 'Warm And Tender Love'
281 Jamiroquai 'If I Like It, I Do It'
282/83 Dream Theatre 'Lords Of Sound'
284 Nirvana 'Roma'
285 Prince 'Welcome 2 The Beautiful...'
286 Allman Brohters Band 'Sweet Melissa'
287/88 Pearl Jam 'Atlanta'
289 The Wonder Stuff 'On The Ropes'
290 Rage Against The Machine 'Killing Zone'
291 Heart 'Unplugged'
292/93 Aerosmith 'Struttin' My Stuff'
294/95 Pink Floyd 'The Live Bell'
296 Cracker 'Teen Angst'
297 Counting Crows 'Carving Out Our Names'
298 Primal Scream 'Rocksucker Blues'
299 Crash Test Dummies 'Dummies At Home'
300/01 Bob Marley 'Revolution'

302 Blur 'Modrophenia'
303 Nine Inch Nails 'Coming Down Fast'
304/05 Phish 'Follow Me To Gamehenge'
306 Metallica 'No Limits - No Laws'
307 Sonic Youth 'Take Out THe Trash'
308 Bob Marley 'Downtown Trenchtown'
309 Husker Du 'Supernova'
310 Kristin Hersh 'Sparkle'
311 Pantera 'No Compromise No Sell Out'
312 Extreme 'Dreams Come True'
313 Sepultura 'Nailbomb'
314 Paul Weller 'Walk On By'
315 The Replacements 'Shit, Shower & Shave'
316 The Waterboys 'In The Studio'
317 The Cranberries 'Stories To Be Told'
318 Therapy? 'Fistful Of Power'
319 Rage Against The Machine 'Bullet Proof'
320 Grant Lee Buffalo 'Like A Shot'
322 Crowded House 'Fleadh'
323 Beastie Boys 'Seven Day Weekend'
324 The Pretenders 'Now And Then'
325 Tori Amos 'Spirit In The Sky'
326/27 Billy Joel 'After The Flood'
329 Southside Johnny/Little Steven 'Unplugged'
330 David Crosby 'Naked In The Rain'
331 Paul Westerberg 'Gravel Pit'
332 Lenny Kravitz 'Acoustic'
333 Afghan Whigs 'Flip Your Whig'
334 James 'A Strange Day'
335 Mariah Carey 'Someday'
336 Nirvana 'The Eternal Legacy'
337 Counting Crows 'Children In Bloom'
338 Blur 'Sawdust Memories'
339/40 Pink Floyd 'The Bell Gets Louder'
341/42 Grateful Dead 'Another Day In The
          Sunshine'
343 Nine Inch Nails 'When The Whip Comes
          Down'
344/45 Metallica 'Enter Mudman'
346 Rollins Band 'Alien Blueprint'
347 Hole 'Kiss Away The Darkest Day'
348 Sheryl Crow 'Run, Baby, Run'
349 Bob Marley 'Redemption'
350 The Doors 'Shattered'
351 NOFX 'Back In The Garage'
352 The Waterboys 'Alive On The Inside'
353 Tori Amos 'Fairy Tales'
354 Red Hot Chili Peppers 'Dirty Weekend'
356/57 The Rolling Stones 'The Voodoo Kiss'
358 L7 'When The Stink Hits The Fan'
359 The Offspring 'The Year That Punk Broke'
356/66 Metallica 'Pile Of Shit'
368/69 Pearl Jam 'Vortical'
370 Dead Can Dance 'Sinful Garden'
371 Pulp 'Ficton Romance'
372 Biohazard 'Run For Cover'
373 Galliano 'Down To Earth'
374/75 Pink Floyd 'Out Of This World'
376 The Black Crowes 'Taller'
377 The Rolling Stones 'Sparks Will Fly'
378 Collective Soul 'Motor City's Burnin'
379/80 Pearl Jam 'Atlanta - The Day Before'
381 Oasis 'Slide Away'
382 Eric Clapton 'Blues Rehearsals'

383 Live 'I Alive'
384/85 Whitney Houston 'Out Of Africa'
386 Elvis Costello 'Under The Influenza'
387 The Jam 'Set The Skies Ablaze'
388/89 The Rolling Stones 'Miami Dice'
390 Cathedral 'Cosmic Funeral'
391/92 Nine Inch Nails 'Slaughter In The Air'
393 Slayer 'Spirits In Black'
394 Green Day 'Spitting'
395 Nirvana 'Trick Or Treat'
396 Pantera 'Live Beyond Driven'
397 Oasis 'Black On White'
398 Pearl Jam 'Self Pollution Radio'
399 Iggy Pop 'Rock Hard'
402 The Doobie Brothers 'Reunion'
403 John Mellencamp 'Wild At Night'
404 Led Zeppelin 'Rock 'N' Roll Hall Of Fame'
405 Van Halen 'Secret Gig'

CD - LAST BOOTLEG RECORDS (LBR)
001 Pearl Jam 'Rem Jam'
002/2 Pearl Jam 'Live Force'
003/2 Sepultura 'Requiescant'
004/2 Sonic Youth 'Shoot'
005 Meatloaf 'Caught In The Act'
006 Sting 'A Day In The Life'
007/2 Bob Marley 'Official Live Bootleg'
008 10,000 Maniacs 'Theme For Imaginary
          Canyon'
009 Stone Temple Pilots 'In Stone We Trust'
010 Cranberries 'Blood Strawberries'
011 Aerosmith 'In Orbit'
012 The Jesus And Mary Chain 'Feedback'
013 Frank Marino And Mahogany Rush 'The
          Return Of The Big Two'
014 Soundgarden 'Harder Faster'
015 Tori Amos 'The Gipsy'
016/2 Pink Floyd 'The Return Of The Comet'
017 Faith No More 'No More'
018 Smashing Pumpkins 'Unbearable'
019/2 Allman 'Stone Mushroom'
020 Alice In Chains 'Rifugium Peccatorum'
021 X 'Xtraterrestral Live'
022 Take That 'It's Only Takes'
023 Pantera 'Metal Power And Walk Remixes'
024/2 Pearl Jam 'Live Studio '92'
028 Erasure 'Post Scriptum'
029 Gipsy Kings 'Pepita'
035 Jack Bruce With Blues Saraceno & Gary
          Husband

CD - MICROPHONE RECORDS (MPH)
01 Colosseum 'Valentine Live'
02 UK (With A. Holdsworth) 'Road Test'
03 Jeff Beck 'Live In Concert Collection'
04 Van Der Graff Generator 'Generators'
05 Tempest 'Live In London 1974'
06 King Crimson 'Sleepless In Japan'
07 King Crimson 'Lost Islands'
08 Gentle Giant 'The Last Giant Step'
09 Colosseum II 'Koln 1977'
10 Jack Bruce & Friends 'New York 1981'
11 Anderson, Bruford, Wakeman, Howe
          'European Tour 1989'

12 Yes 'The Age Of Buggles'
13 Strawbs 'Live In London 1977'
14 Greg Lake Band 'London 1981'
15 Brand X 'Rated X'

CD - MISTRAL MUSIC (MM)
9104 Beach Boys 'Knebworth 1980'
9105 McCartney, Paul 'London Town, Roughs & Demos'
9106 Harrison, George 'Live, Washington '75'
9107/8 Bowie, David 'Rock In Rio '90'
9112/13 Crosby, Stills, Nash & Young 'Big Sur Folk Festival'
9224 Harrison, George 'Harrisongs By George'
9225 Lennon And McCartney 'A Toot And A Snore in '74'
9226/7 Springsteen, Bruce 'Bomb Scare Show'
9228 Sting 'Midnight At Noon'
9229 Pretenders 'The American Tour '84'
9230 Genesis 'Live '81'
9231 McCartney, Paul 'The Piano Tape'
9232/33 Starr, Ringo & All Star 'Live In Copenhagen'
9234 McCartney, Paul 'Plugged And Unplugged'
9336 Starr, Ringo 'With A Little Help'
9439/40 Springsteen, Bruce 'Liberty Hall'

CD - MOVING SOUND RECORDS (labels - Flying Tigers, Neverending Sound, Razor's Edge, Tintagel)
FTCD 0055 Bryan Adams 'All For You'
HTCD 0005 Depeche Mode 'We Feel You'
FTCD 0018 R. Fripp & D. Sylvian 'Kings'
FTCD 0046 R. Fripp & D. Sylvian 'Kings Second Chapter'
FTCD 0056 Peter Gabriel 'Across The River'
T1CD 0009 Genesis 'Roma 18/4/72'
TZCD 0001/2 Guns 'N Roses 'Gathering On Stage'
T1BX 0021/24 Jimi Hendrix 'Every Way To Paradise'
T1BX 0016/17 Iron Maiden 'Face Of The Dark'
TIBX 0032/34 Led Zeppelin 'Complete Tapes 1'
TIBX 0043/45 Led Zeppelin 'Complete Tapes 2'
FTCD 0010/11 Madonna 'A Girl In Paris'
RZCD 0008 Megadeath 'Suicide Solution'
RZCD 0006/7 Metallica 'Kick It Loud'
FTCD 0050 Nirvana 'Sliver And Dumb'
FTBX 0051/53 Pearl Jam 'Deep Through The Years 1990-1994'
NSCD 0014/15 Queen 'Nihon'
RZCD 0025 Soundgarden 'Digging The Garden'
TIBX 0025/27 Springsteen 'Covers Story Vol. 1'
TIBX 0047/49 Springsteen 'Covers Story Vol. 2'
HTCD 0003/4 U2 'Le Diable Au Corps'
FTBX 0028/30 U2 'The New Word'
FTBX 0035/37 U2 'Keeping The Faith'
FTBX 0039/41 U2 'The Fly'
FTBX 0031/38/42 U2 'Rare Tracks 1979-1993)
FTCD 0019/20 'Velvet Underground'
FTCD 0012/13 Neil Young - Booker T. 'Forever Young'

CD - NIKKO RECORDS (NIK)
007/08 Bon Jovi 'Long Way From Home'
009 10,000 Maniacs 'In The Garden Of Eden'
010/11 Aerosmith 'Out Of Control'
012 Paul Weller 'Anytime You Want Me'
013 Therapy? 'Isolation'

CD - OCTOPUS (OCTO)
001 Nirvana 'XXII II MCMXCIV'
002 Rage Against The Machine
003 The Doors 'Westbury Music Fair'
004 Sepultura 'Welcome To Hell'
005 Crowded House
006 The Wonder Stuff 'Live At The Rockfeller'
007/8 Pearl Jam 'Fight (For Your Cause)'
009 Soul Asylum 'The Platinum Punks'
010 Therapy? 'Shock Treatment!'
011 Afghan Whigs 'Black Soul Gentlemen'
012 Pearl Jam 'No Fuckin' Messiah'
013/14 Elton John 'A Single Man In Moscow'
015 The Breeders
016/17 Peter Gabriel
019 Sepultura 'Castle Manifest 1994'
020 Pantera 'Castle Domination 1994'
021 Extreme 'Castle Warheads 1994'
022/23 Aerosmith 'Castle Kings 1994'
024 Meat Puppets

CD - OIL WELL RECORDS (RCS)
CD 001 Rolling Stones 'As Tears Go By'
CD 002 The Doors 'Touch Me'
CD 003 Led Zeppelin 'White Summer'
CD 004 Otis Redding 'Try A Little Tenderness'
CD 005 Cream 'Stepping Out'
CD 006 Jethro Tull 'Back To The Family'
CD 007 The Who 'Pinball Wizard'
CD 008 The Beatles 'Get Back'
CD 009 The Beatles 'Ticket To Ride'
CD 010 Pink Floyd 'Echoes'
CD 011 Rod Stewart & Faces 'Maggie Mae'
CD 012 Rolling Stones 'Jumping Jack Flash'
CD 013 Eric Clapton 'Layla'
CD 014 Jimi Hendrix 'Voodoo Chile'
CD 015 Lou Reed 'Sweet Jane'
CD 016 Santana 'Soul Sacrifice'
CD 017 David Bowie 'Starman'
CD 018 Pink Floyd 'Green Is The Color'
CD 019 Neil Young 'Winterlong'
CD 020 Bruce Springsteen 'NYC Serenade'
CD 021 David Bowie 'Rebel, Rebel'
CD 022 Elton John 'Daniel'
CD 023 Paul McCartney & Wings 'Junior's Farm'
CD 024 Van Morrison 'Moonshine Whiskey'
CD 025 John Lennon 'Come Together'
CD 026 Joe Cocker 'Shut Out The Light'
CD 027 ELP 'Pictures At An Exhibition'
CD 029 Lou Reed 'Streets Of Berlin'
CD 028 Deep Purple 'Georgia On My Mind'
CD 030 Stevie Wonder 'Higher Ground'
CD 031 The Beatles 'It's Only Love'
CD 032 The Beatles 'Across The Universe'
CD 033 Simon & Garfunkel 'Feelin' Groovy'
CD 034 The Grateful Dead 'Pain In My Heart'
CD 035 Fleetwood Mac 'Mean Old World'

CD 036 Jimi Hendrix 'Little Wing'
CD 037 Jefferson Airplane 'High Flyin' Bird'
CD 038 Neil Young & Buffalo Springfield 'Down To The Wire'
CD 039 Janis Joplin 'A Flower In The Sun'
CD 041 Led Zeppelin 'Minnesota Blues'
CD 042 The Doors 'Go Insane'
CD 043 Beach Boys 'Monster Mash'
CD 044 The Who 'Sparks On The Bay'
CD 045 King Crimson 'Talk To The Wind'
CD 046 The Byrds 'Willin''
CD 047 Velvet Underground 'The Great Banana'
CD 048 Pink Floyd 'My Uncle Is Sick...'
CD 049 Jethro Tull 'Live At The Seaside!'
CD 050 CSN & Y 'Wooden Ship'

CD - ON STAGE RECORDS (OS)

CD1   Simply Red 'Groovy Situation'
CD2   Dire Straits 'Walk Of Live'
CD3   REM 'Radio Songs'
CD4   Queen 'God Save The Queen'
CD6   Guns N' Roses 'Electric Warriors'
CD7   Iron Maiden 'What Are We Doing This For?'
CD8   Metallica 'More Than Just Metal'
CD9   AC/DC 'Thunder Boogie'
CD10 Deep Purple 'Hush'
CD11 Bruce Springsteen 'No Place Like Home'
CD12 The Doors 'The Ceremony'
CD14 Pink Floyd 'Volcanic Destruction'
CD15 Michael Jackson 'Rock With Me'
CD16 Guns N' Roses 'Welcome To The Jungle'

CD - REEL TAPES (RTCD)

001   Suzi Quatro 'Your Mama Won't Like Me'
002   Gentle Giant 'Giant Steps Forward'
003-004 Van Der Graaf Generator 'Worldly Men & Strangers. A Day In the Live Of'
005   Arthur Brown 'Cruel, Crazy, Wonderful World'
006   Ten Years After 'More Than 20 Years Later'
007   Colosseum 'Roma Caput Mundi'
008-009 Traffic 'Out Of Gridlock'
010-011 Jethro Tull The Poor Man Gets Along'
PG 1-2 Peter Gabriel 'Live To Be Loved'

CD - ROYAL SOUND MUSIC (RSM)

013SQ Charlie Daniels Band 'The Devil Went Down To Hartford'
001   Simple Minds 'The 'Real Live Tour'
003   Mellencamp 'Workingman's Rock & Roll'
004   Little Village 'Anywhere USA'
005SQ Dwight Yoakam 'Live Deluxe'
006SQ Rosanne Cash 'At The Bottom Line'
007   Neil Young 'Farmyard Connection'
008   Bad Company 'Can't Get Enough Of These Guys'
010   Paul Rodgers 'Live In New York 1993'
011   Suzanne Vega 'Short But Sweet'
012SQ Judds 'Their Sweetest Gift'
013SQ Charlie Daniels Band 'The Devil Went Down To Georgia'
014SQ Desert Rose Band 'Roses At The Ritz'
015SQ Lyle Lovett 'The Lights Of L.A. County'
016SQ Outlaws 'Riders On The Devil's Road'

017SQ McGuinn, Clarc & Hillman 'Eight Miles Live'
023   Pat Benatar 'We Belong To Pat Benatar'
024   Tori Amos 'Whole Lotta Teen Spirit'
025SQ Willie Nelson 'Home On The Road'
026SQ Kentucky Headhunters 'Dirty Picking'
027SQ Travis Tritt 'Homesick'
028SQ Carlene Carter 'Hurricane'
029SQ Patty Loveless 'That Kind Of Girl'
030   Los Lobos 'East Los Angelenos'
031SQ Trisha Yearwood 'That's What We Like About Trisha'
033SQ Mary Carpenter-Chapin 'Passionate Kisses From Austin'
036   Meat Loaf 'From Paradise To Hell'
037   10,000 Maniacs 'Our Time At The Greek'
039   INXS 'Hungry Hearts In LA'
040SQ Don Henley 'California Desperados'
041SQ Marshall Tucker Band 'Silverado'
043SQ John Hyatt 'A Thing Called Live'
045   John Mellencamp 'Junior'
046SQ Jefferson Starship 'Columbia Landing'
047-2SQ Jackson Browne 'Everyman's Alive'
048-2 Melissa Etheridge 'Bonsoir Montreal'
049   Aerosmith 'Fever'
051   Tom Petty & The Heartbreakers 'Something About Mary Jane'
053SQ Cracker 'Live Potatoes'
056   Counting Crows 'May & Nothing Before'
062SQ Suzy Bogguss 'What's The Story All About'

CD - SILVER RARITIES (SIRA)

101   Neil Young 'Separate Ways'
102/103 Robert Plant 'In The Mood'
104   Robert Plant 'Two Days In The Country'
105/106 Eric Clapton 'Tour Rehearsals'
107/108 Eric Clapton 'Kansas City Rocks'
109/110 Jimi Hendrix 'In From The Storm'
111/112 Led Zeppelin 'Complete Berlin'
113/114 Led Zeppelin 'Live On The Levee'
115/116 Van Morrison 'Wild Night'
117/118 REM 'Red Rain'
119/120/121 Grateful Dead 'Typical Daydream'
122/123 Led Zeppelin 'A Fighting Finish'
124/125 Genesis 'Before Riches'
126/127/128 Led Zeppelin 'Pleeease'
129/130 Led Zeppelin 'Two Days Before'
131/132/133 Led Zeppelin 'Kingdom Of Zeppelin'
134/135 Led Zeppelin 'For Your Love'
136/137/138 Jackson Browne 'I Am Alive'
139/140 Eric Clapton 'Carnival'
141/142 Grateful Dead 'Ain't Superstitious'
143/144 Bob Dylan 'Les Temps Changent'
145/146 Richard Thompson & Linda 'Strange Affair'
147/148 Richard Thompson 'Doom & Gloom'

CD - SPEEDBALL (SBC)

001   Blues Brothers 'Illinois BDR 529'
002/2 Rollin Stones 'Les Abbatoir'
003/2 Cure 'Accuracy'
006   Billy Idol 'Burnin' Star'
007   Robert Plant 'Green Eye'

008 Robert Cray 'Smokin' Eye'
010 Lenny Kravitz 'If Six Was Nine'
011 Pixies 'Timeless Stars'
012 R.E.M. 'Animal Attractions'
013 Sting 'Natural Acoustic'
014 Springsteen 'Bruce's Club Hopping Summer'
016 Pink Floyd 'The Knebworth Tales'
018 Prince ''87 Laments'
019 The Cure 'Acoustic Daze'
020 Molly Hatchet 'Astral Games'
021 38 Special 'Eldorado Road'
022 Point Blank 'Cold Warrior'
024 Texas 'What Goes On'
026 Eric Clapton 'Alberta, Layla & All My Love'
027 Various Artists 'The Freddy Mercury Memory Tour'
028 Carlos Santana & Jeff Beck 'Reunion'
029 Was Not Was 'Break The Wall'
031 Ringo Star Band 'Resurrection'
032 Joe Cocker 'Other Face'

CD - STAY SHARP (STS)
70501 Metallica 'Original Garage Days'
70502/2 Whitesnake 'Tokyo Bites'
70504 Sepultura 'American Devastation'
70505 Yngwie Malmsteen 'Viking Axe'
70506 Savatage 'Defenders Of The Faith'
70509 King's X 'Riding The Wind'
70514 Black Crowes 'Live In USA'
70515 Kiss 'Stranglehold'
70516 Sepultura 'Live Degration'
70517 Manowar 'Live For Glory'
70519 Megadeth 'For Fans Only'

CD - STRANGLED RECORDS (STR)
002 Smashing Pumpkins 'Smashing The Puppets'
003 Smiths 'The Hand That Rocks The Cradle'
004/5 Pearl Jam 'Glorified Daughter'
006/7 Tori Amos 'Space Doggin Bruins'

CD - TARANTURA
T2CD-3 Led Zeppelin 'Tight But Loose'
T2CD-3 Led Zeppelin 'Long Tall Sally'
TS-1 Led Zeppelin 'The Lost Geisha Tape'
T2CD-4 Led Zeppelin 'Live On Blueberry Hill'
T2CD-5 Led Zeppelin 'A 2 Last Nights'
T3CD-1 Led Zeppelin 'Hammer Of The Gods'
T4CD-1 Led Zeppelin 'Walk, Don't Run'
T4CD-2 Led Zeppelin 'Copenhagen Warm-Ups'
T3CD-2 Led Zeppelin 'Freeze!'
T2CD-6 Led Zeppelin '2nd Night In A Judo Arena'
Pb-1001 Led Zeppelin 'Pb'
T2CD-7 Led Zeppelin 'BBC Zep'
T3CD-3 Led Zeppelin 'Pretty Woman'
T3CD-4 Led Zeppelin 'Please Please Me'
T4CD-3 Led Zeppelin 'Route 66'
T6CD-1 Led Zeppelin 'The Destroyers'
TS-3 Led Zeppelin 'Complete Geisha Tape'
T1CD-001 Led Zeppelin 'One More Check!'
TM0QTCD-72007 Led Zeppelin 'Bonzo's Birthday Party'
T3CD-5 Led Zeppelin 'Blitzkrieg Over Europe'

T2CD-1 Led Zeppelin 'Front Row'
T70CD-001, 002 Led Zeppelin 'The Nobs!'
T2CD-010 Led Zeppelin 'Tulsa Hillbilly'
T2CD-8 Led Zeppelin 'Punk!'
T2CD-9 Led Zeppelin 'Loove!'
T4CD-4 Led Zeppelin 'Eye Thank Yew'
T3CD-6 Led Zeppelin 'Pussy And Cock'
T70CD-003, 004 Led Zeppelin 'The Dark Tower'
TS2CD-1, 2 Led Zeppelin 'Welcome To Cleveland'
GRECO-1-1,2 Led Zeppelin 'No Use Greco'
TARANTIC CD 1912 Led Zeppelin 'III'
TMMT 1 Led Zeppelin 'Magical Mystery Tape'
T2CD-001 Led Zeppelin 'The End'
T9CD-1-1-9 Led Zeppelin 'Get Back To L.A.'
TCD-MSG1972-0728 Led Zeppelin 'Tour-De-Force'
T4CD-5 Led Zeppelin 'Thunderstorm'
T3CD-7 Led Zeppelin 'The Jumpleg'
T3CD-8 Led Zeppelin 'The Destroyer III'
T3CD-10 Led Zeppelin 'Discover America'
T2CD-011 Led Zeppelin 'Yellow Zep'
T3CD-13 Led Zeppelin 'Zig Zag Zep'
T2CD-15 Led Zeppelin 'Who's Birthday'
TCD19CD-BOX Led Zeppelin 'A Week For Badgeholders'

LP - TAURUS LP
002 9104 Journey 'Travelling In The Universe Of Music'
004 9110 Gary Moore 'The Gold Tour'
009 9111 Y.J. Malmsteen 'I'm A Viking'
009 9114 Judas Priest 'Riding The Legend'
009 9115 David Lee Roth 'Too Hot To Handle'
009 9116 Whitesnake 'Reptile Kiss'
009 9117 Van Halen 'Van Action'
009 9118 Toto 'Live Memories'
010 901 Whitesnake 'Reptile Kiss'
010 902 Aerosmith 'Big Ten Inch Record'
010 903 Bon Jovi 'Tokyo Road'
011 9120 Guns N' Roses '44 Caliber'
012 9122 Kiss 'Scratch, Bite & Kiss'
012 9122 Kiss 'Scratch, Bite & Kiss'

CD - TAURUS ON CD (TAU)
103 Exodus 'The Great Escape'
104 New Wave Of British Heavy Metal 'The Days On Stage'
105/106 Guns N' Roses 'Welcome To The Rumour Jungle'
107 Anthrax 'Cry Of Desperation'
108 Guns N' Roses 'Out Of Time'
110/111 Metallica 'Argentina Grita'
112 H.S.A.S 'No Animation'
113 Thin Lizzy & Grand Slam 'Live'
114/115 Alcatrazz, Feat, Steve Vai 'Live'
116 Journey 'The Superjam'
117 Megadeth 'Live'
118 Phil Lynott & John Sykes 'Three Musketeers'

CD - TEDDY BEAR (TB)
01/2 Beatles 'Pop Goes The Radio #1'
02/2 Madonna 'Blond Over Japan'
03 Sonic Youth 'Energy'

04/3 Grateful Dead 'From Egypt With Love'
05 Elvis Presley 'I Was The One'
06 Lynyrd Skynyrd 'Outlaw Biker'
07/2 Guns 'n' Roses 'One More Illusion'
08/2 Beatles 'Pop Goes The Radio #2'
09 Metallica '...And Justice Is Done'
10/2 U2 'Faraway So Close'
11 Lenny Kravitz 'Lovin' Hendrix'
12/2 Prince 'My Name Is God'
13 U2 'Acoustic TV'
14 Eric Clapton 'Paper Jam'
15 Grateful Dead 'Wooden Set'
16 Miles Davis 'Nightcrawler'
17 Sepultura 'Live Chaos'
18 Pearl Jam 'Acoustic Songbook'
19/2 Janet Jackson 'Sex Is Happiness'
20 S.R. Vaughan 'Pride & Joy'
21 Jimi Hendrix 'Gone But Not Forgotten'
22 Van Morrison 'Moonlight Serenade'
23/2 Doors 'No Future'
25 Nirvana 'More Live Tits'
26/3 Grateful Dead 'Trippin' Around'
27 U2 'Rain On You'
28 Phish 'A Phishy Story'
29 Iggy Pop 'Tough Guys Do Dance'
30 Allman Brothers 'Southern Revenge'
31/2 Grateful Dead 'On The Bus'
32 Grateful Dead 'Rose Garland'
33 B. Springsteen 'Movie Of '71'
34 Pink Floyd 'Psychedelicamania'
35 Pink Floyd 'The Great Gig On The Moon'
36 Neil Young 'Hippie Dream'
37 Hot Tuna 'Tuna Fishing In America'
38 Rolling Stones 'Have A Beer'
39 Phish 'Phish On, Phishin' On'
40 Grateful Dead 'Celestial Synapse'
41 Pearl Jam 'Mesmerize'
42 Allman Brothers 'Dixie Flag'
43 Aerosmith 'Big-mammed Woman'
44 Tori Amos 'Winter'
45 Counting Crows 'Sleeping In A Perfect Blue'
46 Nine Inch Nails 'Killer Instinct'
47 Red Hot Chili Peppers 'Push To Flush'
48 Frank Zappa 'Paralipomeni Della
   Batracomiomachia'
49 Frank Zappa 'A Snail In My Nose'
50 Crowded House 'Another Time, Another
   Place'
51 Led Zeppelin 'Lighter Than Air'
52 Simon & Garfunkel 'Que Viva Barba!'
53 Black Crowes 'Soul - Soaked'
54 Nine Inch Nails 'March Of The Pigs'
55 Pink Floyd 'Sidereus Nuncius'
56 Rolling Stones 'Honky Tonk Motel'
57/2 Phish 'Crumbs Of Knowledge'
58 Pretenders 'Fifteen Hard - Ons a Day'
59 Eagles 'Hungry Cowboy'
60/3 Grateful Dead 'Thank You Uncle Bobo'
61 R.E.M. 'Wood Green'
62 Eric Clapton 'Nude Girls And Stuff Like That'
63 Pearl Jam 'Unnecessary Roughness'
64 Bob Marley & The Wailers 'Nybinghi Rastas'
65 Indigo Girls 'Days Of Wine And Roses'
66/2 Beatles 'The Acoustic Submarine'

67 Velvet Underground 'Concrete Dreams'
68 Jerry Garcia Band 'Flooded Away'
69 Elvis Presley 'Elvis Meets The Beatles'
70/3 Grateful Dead 'Funiculi Funicula'
71 Van Der Graaf Generator 'Confused Beyond
   Redemption'
72 King Crimson 'Solve Et Coagula'
73 John Mayall 'Bulldogs For Sale'
74 Lynyrd Skynyrd 'Sweet Home Tavoliere'
75 Phish 'Take Cover!'
76/2 Various Artists 'Deep In My Heart'
77 Lou Reed 'Waiting For The Glittering Man'
78 Allman Brothers Band 'Toni Brothers Band'
79 Stevie Ray Vaughan 'Alone In The Ozone'
80 Leonard Cohen 'The Housewife, The Referee
   And The Undertaker'
81 Black Crowes 'The Halloween Secret'
82 Grant Lee Buffalo 'The Great White Buffalo'

CD - VIP (VIP)

001 Kate Bush 'London 1979'
002 Brian Eno & Robert Fripp 'London
   1974+Paris 1975'
003 The Tubes 'Los Angeles 1976'
004 Eric Clapton 'Santa Monica 1978'
005 King Crimson 'Atlanta 1973+Pittsburg 1975'
006 Emerson, Lake & Palmer 'Anaheim 1975'
007 The Rolling Stones 'London 1976'
008 Led Zeppelin 'Buffalo 1973'
009 Kiss 'New York 1988'

CD - YELLOW CAT (YD)

001/2 Eric Clapton 'At The Royal Albert Hall '90'
003 McCartney, Paul 'Looking For Changes '92'
004 Cohen, Leonard 'Live In Montreaux '76'
005 Bee Gees, Barry Gibb 'Guilty Demos/The
   Wishes We Share'
006 McCartney, Paul And Band 'Saturday Night
   Live Rehearsal '93'
007/12 McCartney, Paul And The Band 'The '90
   World Tour Collection'
007/8 McCartney, Paul And Band 'Berkely
   Concert '80'
009/10 McCartney, Paul And Band '4th July '90
   Washington'
011/12 McCartney, Paul And Band 'Arizona,
   Soundcheck, Cactusclub'
013/14 Simon, P., Springsteen, B. 'Homeloss
   Childrens' Medical Benefit'
015 Morrison, Van 'Live In Edinburgh,
   Playhouse, '93'
021 Various Artists, Vol. 3 'R & R Hall Of Fame
   Superstar Jams '93'
022 Dylan, Bob 'Real Live Outtakes'
024 Meat Loaf 'Live At Naussau Coliseum 9/1/78'
025 Clapton, Eric 'Royal Albert Hall, '90 & '91'
026/27 Springsteen, Bruce 'Buenos Aires,
   Argentina '86'
028 McCartney, Paul 'One Hand Clapping'
029 McCartney, Paul 'Backyard, Plus More
   Acoustic Work'
030/31 Rolling Stones, The 'From Paris to L.A.'
032 Dylan, Bob & The Grateful Dead 'San Rafael
   Rehearsels Vol. 1'

033 Dylan, Bob & The Grateful Dead 'San Rarael
     Rehearsels Vol. 2'

CD - WANTED MAN MUSIC (WMM)
031/32 Bob Dylan 'The Streets Of Rome'
33/34/35 Bob Dylan 'Minnesota Tapes'
36/37 Bob Dylan 'Rise Again'
38 Bob Dylan 'Songs For Patty Valentine'
39 Bob Dylan 'Isle Of Wight'
40/41 Bob Dylan 'Hold The Fort'
42 Bob Dylan 'Oh Mercy Outtakes'
43/44 Bob Dylan 'Live At The Pitstop'
45/46 Bob Dylan 'Dirty Lies'
47/48 Bob Dylan 'First Supper'
49/50 Bob Dylan 'Second Supper'
051 Bob Dylan 'No Photographs Please'
52/53 Bob Dylan 'The Critics Choice Vol. 1 & 2'
54 Bob Dylan 'The Critics Choice Vol. 3'
55 Bob Dylan 'The Critics Choice Vol. 4'
56/57 Bob Dylan 'The Critics Choice Vol. 5 7 6'
58/59 Bob Dylan 'New Found Faith'
60 Bob Dylan 'Outside The Empire'

CD - WHY NOT? (WOT)
1001 U2 'Everything You Know Is Wrong'

1002 Simply Red 'Play It Again, Mick
1003 Red Hot Chili Peppers 'Tokyo Tattoo'
1004 Stevie Ray Vaughan 'Jammed Together,
     Texas Style'
1005 Janes Addiction 'Live Too'
2006/7 Genesis 'Sincerely Yours'
1008 REM 'These Days'
1009 Bon Jovi 'The Return Of The Jersey Boy'
1010 Pearl Jam 'We're Gonna Hungry'
1011 Prince & The Revolution 'An American In
     Paris'
1013 Spin Doctors 'Just Go Ahead Now'
1014 Alice In Chains 'The World Is In Chains'
2014/15 Dream Theatre 'The Dance Of Eternity'
1018 Andy Wood Vol. 1 DIGIPACK 'Words &
     Music: Communication'
1019 Andy Wood Vol. 2 DIGIPACK 'Words &
     Music: Communication'
1020 S.R. Vaughan & Double Trouble 'Live At
     L'Olympia'
1021 Stone Temple Pilots 'Hard To The Core'
1022 Suede 'Suedmania'
1023 Robert Plant 'Ramble On'
2024/25 Pearl Jam 'World Jam'
1026 Blind Melon (In Preparation)

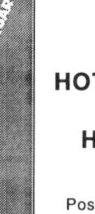

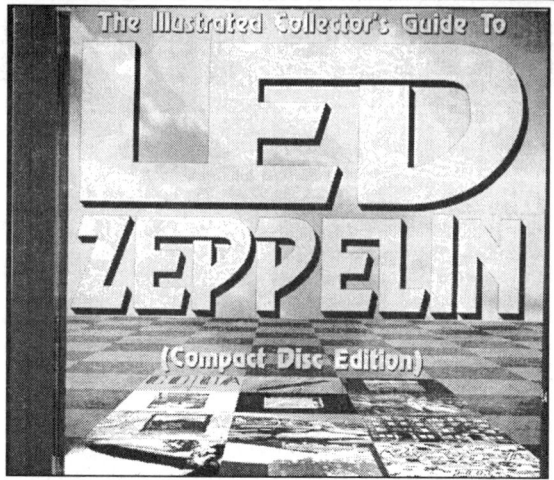

LED ZEPPELIN
LIVE

AN ILLUSTRATED EXPLORATION OF UNDERGROUND TAPES
UPDATED EDITION

This 320 page 1994 book examines over 240 Led Zeppelin concerts from 1968 to 1980.

The information-packed book is based on over 20 years of detailed analysis of tapes by author/music critic Luis Rey and was edited by noted Led Zeppelin collector and archivist Susan Hedrick.

Dates, places & track listings are all documented chronologically along with comments about each show. It also includes an extensive listing for songs played in the concerts reviewed along with a section clearing up some of the common mistakes made in dating Led Zeppelin underground tapes & bootlegs. There are also many rare and unpublished in-concert photographs from private collections.

Grant Burgess, editor and publisher of the fanzine 'The Only One', says: **LIVE** is "...an excellent source of reference...".

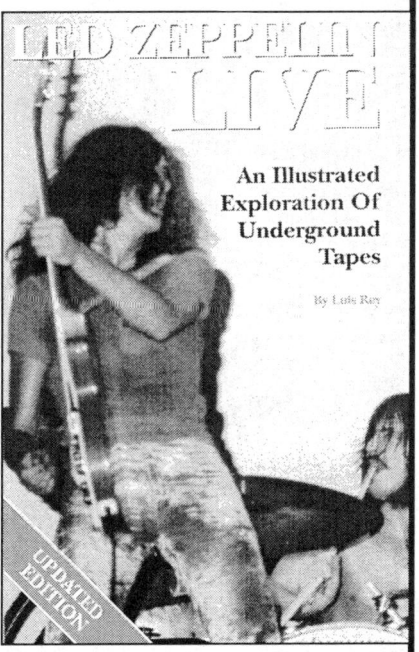

An Illustrated
Exploration Of
Underground
Tapes

By Luis Rey

Robert Godwin, author of 'The Illustrated Collector's Guide To Led Zeppelin', says:
LIVE "...deserves a tip of the hat...".

Hugh Jones, editor and publisher of the fanzine 'Proximity' says:
LIVE is "...a wealth of enjoyable reading..." and "Here is a guy that knows his stuff...".

In the USA $17.95 US FUNDS (surface mail) or $19.95 US FUNDS (air mail)
In Europe / Asia $19.95 US FUNDS (surface mail) or $22.95 US FUNDS (air mail)
In Canada $22.95 Canadian Funds.

THE HOT WACKS PRESS
PO BOX 544, OWEN SOUND, ON, N4K 5R1, CANADA
FAX 519 376 9449

GENUINE DISC TARANTURA
is now available by
sending US$18 (POSTPAID
Airmail to anywhere in
the world.)Please make
checks/money orders to:
    LEO ISHAC
P.O. BOX   400
BENTLEIGH   3204
VICTORIA AUSTRALIA

Note: All orders will
be autographed by the
author.

GENUINE DISC TARANTURA is the latest publication
by LEO T. ISHAC the author of WHOLE LOTTA ZEP
DOWN UNDER 1972 and fanzine WHOLE LOTTA ZEP.
This latest publication is a Limited Edition
Collector's issue covering the CD releases from
the stables of the Japanese TARANTURA label.
Since commencing production in early 1993 the
TARANTURA label has now released 47 titles to the
end of 1994. Many of these titles are multi-CD
sets. Most titles sell-out upon release.
The TARANTURA label has quickly become one of the
most important producing labels due to the except-
ional artwork and presentation of each unique
release. Generally audio quality is unsurpassed.
GENUINE DISC TARANTURA is a booklet reviewing all
47 titles released to date in a format similar to
that of Robert Godwin's Compact Disc Edition but
with more detail/comments regarding audio quality,
concert/studio performance and description of the
packaging.
All 47 CD covers/artwork are reproduced. The
booklet is printed on high quality glossy paper
stock and is the definitive reference source for
those collector's seeking the TARANTURA titles.
The meaning of Page's Zofo (Zoso) is explained
in this publication!

Tight But Loose – The Essential Zepp Read

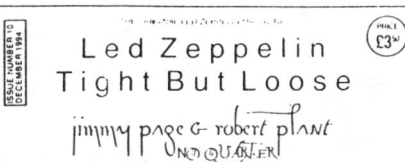

Led Zeppelin
Tight But Loose

PRICE £3^N

jimmy page & robert plant
No Quarter

Bringing the balance back

the filming project for MTV:
EXCLUSIVE in-depth coverage
PLUS: John Paul Jones Interview/The Making of Led Zeppelin 3/
60 CDs reviewed and rated + latest news update and much more inside . . .

Issue Number 10

UNLEDDED SPECIAL
featuring
JIMMY PAGE and ROBERT PLANT
THE FILMING PROJECT FOR MTV
Exclusive In-Depth Coverage

The filming – The Screening – The Album
– The Paris Conference – The Interviews –
The Complete Coverage of the No Quarter
Project
plus

John Paul Jones Interview / The Making
Of Led Zeppelin 3 / Over 60 CDs Reviewed
and Rated / Latest News Update and more.

**30,000 word 36 page 10th Issue Special.
Available from mid-December.**

Price £4.25 incl postage (Europe £5.50; USA £7;
Japan/Australia £7.50).

Cheques payable to D. Lewis, T.B.L.,
14 Totnes Close, Bedford MK40 3AX

THE LED ZEPPELIN INFORMATION SERVICE
incorporating
The Tight But Loose magazine:
The original Led Zeppelin magazine edited and researched by Dave Lewis. Packed with all the
latest news and reviews on the group and related solo projects. Informative features, exclusive
interviews, Celebration updates, collecting focus and rare visuals make the Zepp periodical the
essential companion to their music, past and present. Published twice annually.

The Information Service Newsletter
The additional interim detailed newsletter that bridges the gap between magazines. Available
to subscribers only, this update of news and views is a further aid to staying ahead of all the
latest Zepp related activity.

SUBSCRIPTION DETAILS
4 issues of the Tight But Loose magazine PLUS 4 additional Information Service
Newsletters:–

UK	– £17.00	USA/Canada	– £29.00
Europe	– £22.00	Australia/Japan	– £32.00

All prices inclusive of all postage costs.
Payment: By Cheque/Postal Order/Eurocheque/International Money Order in
UK sterling only. Payable to D. Lewis.
Send to TIGHT BUT LOOSE, 14 Totnes Close, Bedford MK40 3AX
The magazine is also available individually to non-subscribers at the following rates:
UK £4.25   Europe £5.50   USA/Canada £7.00   Japan/Australia £7.50

Tight But Loose – you know it's worth waiting for!

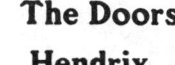

Insect Records

IST 6/7   METALLICA DAMAGED JUSTICE Los Angeles, CA, USA, February 1989
IST 8/9   PRINCE SMALL CLUB Den Hage, Holland, 18th August 1988 **Soundboard**
IST 10   RAMONES BLITZKRIEG IN ATHENS Athens, Greece, 13th March 1989 **Soundboard**
IST 18   ROLLING STONES IN ACTION Honolulu 1966 **Soundboard** & London 1964
IST 19   ROBERT PLANT PROMISED LAND Perugia Blues Festival, Italy, Summer '93 Soundboard
IST 20   LED ZEPPELIN MANY MORE EARLY TIMES Stockholm, Copenhagen & London 1969
IST 21/22   RUSH GANSTER OF BOATS Counterparts tour '94, New Orleans, LA, USA, 23rd Jan 1994
IST 23   NIRVANA SEATTLE SOUND, SOUNDS GREAT Rome, Italy, 19th November 1991 **Soundboard**
IST 24   MOTLEY CRUE THE RED HOT SPOT Milan, Italy, 16th December 1984 & Modena, Italy, September '91
IST 25   JAPAN ORIENTAL PERFORMANCE Tokyo, Japan, January 1980
IST 26/27   KISS PETER, PAUL, GENE & ACE Detroit, Washington, Long Beach, 1974 **Soundboard**
IST 28   U 2 LOOKING BACK IN THE MIRROR Hamburg, Germany, 15th February 1981
IST 29   SIMPLE MINDS DUTCH DAZE Utrecht, Holland, 7th March 1983 **Soundboard**
IST 30   JANE'S ADDICTION CARNIVAL OF SOULS Seattle, Wa, USA, 29th February 1989 Soundboard
IST 31/32   QUEEN THE JEWELS Milan, Italy, 15th September 1985 (Complete Show)
IST 33   BOB MARLEY THE LAST CLUB TOUR 75 Quite Knight Club, Chicago, IL, USA, 10th June 1975 **Soundboard**
IST 34/35   U 2 BONO IS A DINKY Austin, TX, USA, 7th April 1992 + 5 Soundcheck trax
IST 36   PRIMAL SCREAM PURPLE CHAIN Glasgow, Scotland, 2nd April 1994 **Soundboard**
IST 37   PAUL WELLER ENDS OF THE WORLD City Sq, Milan, Italy, October 1992 **Soundboard**
IST 38   SUEDE WHAT'S YOUR NAME LONDON SUEDE ? Milan, Italy fall 1993 **Soundboard**
IST 39/40   PINK FLOYD THE 1994 WEST COAST TRIP Oakland, CA, USA, 20th April 1994
IST 41   FRANKIE GOES TO HOLLYWOOD FRANKIE SAYS USE CONDOMS Royal Court, Liverpool, UK, 20th Dec. 1984
IST 42   NINE INC NAILS MUDSTOCK Saugerties, NY, USA, 13th August 1994 **Soundboard**
IST 43   SIGUE SIGUE SPUTNIK ORANGE DEVIL Q.M. Club, Glasgow, Scotland, 14th March 1986
IST 44   ELVIS COSTELLO BUDDY HOLLY ON ACID The Forum, Europe, July 1994 **Soundboard**
IST 45   SEX PISTOLS SPIRIT OF '76 Kingfish Club, Baton Rouge, LA, USA, 9th January 1978 (Shows1st ever issue)
IST 46   COLLECTIVE SOUL SWEET HOME CHICAGO Chicago, IL, USA, July 1994 **Soundboard**
IST 47   VAN MORRISON VAN THE MAN Glastonbury Festival, UK, 28 th June 1992
IST 48   JIMI HENDRIX MOONS AND RAINBOWS Live Studio recordings 1968 **Excellent Quality**
IST 49/50   METALLICA CANDY FOR THE KIDS Bicentenial Park, Miami, FL, USA, 21st August 1994 w/ Rob Halford (Judas Priest)
IST 51 ★   SUEDE OLD MEN'S CAR Rolling Stone, Milano, Italy 13th November, 1994
IST 52   BLUR BLACKOUT The Factory, Milan, Italy, 12th November 1994
IST 53   THERAPHY ? I WANT MY MONEY BACK London, UK, 27 th November 1992 **Soundboard**
IST 54   PARADISE LOST NORTHERN DARKNESS Lund, Sweden, January 1994 & Esbjerg, Denmark 28th January 1994
IST 55   SIOUXSIE & THE BANSHEES SKREECHING St Davids Hall, Cardiff, Wales, UK, 21st June 1984
IST 56/57   THE STRANGLERS ..AND THEN THERE WERE THREE Rainbow Theatre, London, UK, 4th April 1980 **Soundboard**
IST 58   PORNO FOR PYROS ECCENTRIC Saugerties, NY, USA, 13th August 1994 **Soundboard**
IST 59/60   STING ...LIKE A BEE The Coast Dome, Tampa, FL, USA, 20th February 1994 & 12 December 1985 w/ Eric Clapton
IST 62/63   TORI AMOS CHILDHOOD MEMORIES Raleigh, NC, USA, 29th July 1994 (**Fantastic**)
IST 64 ★   NIRVANA KURT'S GRAND FINALE Ice hockey stadium, Roma, Italy, 22nd February 1994 **Soundboard**
IST 65/66   ROLLING STONES OFF WITH OUR HEADS Superdome Arena, New Orleans, LA, USA, 10th October 1994
IST 67 ★   BAD RELIGION POWER POP Karen Klub, Goteborg, Sweden, 8th October 1994 **Soundboard**
IST 68   LUSH SHOW US YOUR TITS Reading Festival, UK, 26th August 1994 **Soundboard**
IST 69/70   PAUL RODGERS & FRIENDS IN BAD COMPANY The London Forum, UK, 9th February 1994 w /Brian May & Jason Bonham
IST 71   ROLLINS BAND HARD AS NAILS Montfort University, Leicester, UK, 4th May 1994
IST 72/73   PHISH HOLIDAY RECORDING, HOLIDAY SNAP Charleston, WV, USA, 26th June 94
IST 75/76   YES GIMME MORE Binghamton, NY, USA, 18th June 1994 **Soundboard**
IST 77/78 ★ MARILLION ONE OFF SHOWS Oxford Apollo, England, 8th May 1994 **Soundboard**
IST 79/80 ★ GREEN DAY GOD BLESS AMERIKA Various locations USA 93 & 94, Goteborg, Sweden, 8th October 1994 **Soundboard**
IST84/85   THE OFFSPRING PUNK'S NOT DEAD Factory Milan, Italy, 26th November & London's Astoria One, 3rd December 1994 **Soundboard**
IST 87   NIRVANA RARE TRACKS VOL. I - (1989-1994)
IST 88   NIRVANA RARE TRACKS VOL. II - (1989-1994)
IST 89 ★   NINE INCH NAILS SHALLOW GRAVE Brixton academy, London, England, 24th May 1994 **Soundboard**
IST 90 ★   JOHN CALE UNIQUE Phoenix festival, England, 15th July 1994, only 1994 UK show

PRICES:

	US$	UK£	It Lire
1 Cd	22.00	12.00	25.000
2 Cd	44.00	24.00	48.000

★ HOT OFF THE PRESS

(P&P) POSTAGE & PACKAGING:

Europe: First CD $ 3.50 - £ 2.30 - It. Lire 5.500, Each additional CD $ 1.50 - £ 1.00 - It Lire 2.000
USA and Japan: First CD $ 4.50 - £ 2.90 - It Lire 7.500, Each additional CD $ 2.00 - £ 1.30 - It Lire 3.000
International Money Order in US$, UK£, or It. Lira with your order (Sorry no credit cards)

KALEIDOSCOPIC MUSIC srl
P.O. BOX 57, CERVETERI, 00052 ROME, ITALY
☎ (39) 6. 994.1925 - Fax (39) 6. 994.1943

Hawk Discs

Distributed by

KALEIDOSCOPIC MUSIC srl

☎ (39) 6.994.1925
Fax (39) 6.994.1943

Most Trusted Name in Music

001	STONE TEMPLE PILOTS MIGHTY JOE YOUNG Los Angeles CA, USA, 2nd July 1993
002	PAVEMENT SUMMER BABE Sacramento, CA, USA, 19th May 1992 **Soundboard**
003	NINE INCH NAILS SLAVES Tipitans, New Orleans, LA, USA, 7th July 1991
004	HELMET EARTH TONES Los Angeles, CA, USA, 1992 **Soundboard**
005	SUGAR WHATEVER MAKES YOU HAPPY Athens, GA, USA, 20th February 1992
006	HOLE PRETTY PLEASE Los Angeles, CA, USA, 12th December1991 **Soundboard**
007/8	THE CURE FROM THE EDGE Seattle Coliseum, WA, USA, 1st July 1992
009	U2 WELCOME TO THE VIBE Vancouver, BC, Canada, 23th April 1992
0010/11	PETER GABRIEL SECRET WORLD TOUR Glam Slam, Los Angeles, CA, USA, 5th May 1993
012	SCREAMING TREES WINTER SONG Los Angeles, CA, USA, 1992
013	SMASHING PUMPKINS DAYDREAM KISS Los Angeles, CA, USA, 12th december 1991
014	SOUL ASYLUM WE'RE THE OPENING BAND US Tour 23rd January 1993
015	PORNO FOR PYROS PORN AGAIN Roskilde festival, Denmark, 1st July 1993
016	BABES IN TOYLAND MOCKING BIRDS Los Angeles, CA, USA, 1992
017	LEMONHEADS SECRET LIFE OF EVAN DANDO LA, CA, USA, 5th May 1993
018	NEIL YOUNG + BOOKER T RIVERS EDGE Roskilde festival, Denmark, July 1993 **Soundboard**
019	FRANK BLACK THE RETURN OF FU MANCHU US Tour, 15th July 1993
020	MONSTER MAGNET SON OF CALUGULA Los Angeles, CA, USA, 26th August 1992
021	IZZY STRADLIN SOMEBODY KNOCKIN' European Tour, 18th December 1992 **Soundboard**
022	STING AIN'T NO SUNSHINE Las Vegas, NV, USA, 16th may 1993
023	DURAN DURAN WORLD BROADCAST Tower records, Hollywood, CA, USA,15th May 1993 **Soundboard**
024	BLIND MELON HIGH TIMES Live on tour USA 1993
025	PHISH SLOTH US Tour 5th May 1992 (Set I) **Soundboard**
026	NINE INCH NAILS PUREST FEELING Cleveland, OH, USA, November 1988 **SUPERSoundboard**
027	WHITE ZOMBIE YOU ONLY DIE ONCE... US Tour, Summer 1993
028	RAGE AGAINST THE MACHINE WHO'S ON FIRST? US Tour, September 1993 **Soundboard**
029	STONE TEMPLE PILOTS TROUBLE NO MORE BBQ Mitzvah tour USA 1993
030	PAUL WESTERBERG LUCKY'S REVENGE Los Angeles, CA, USA, 21st July 1993
031	BELLY SOFT WHITE UNDER Down South, USA, 1993 **Soundboard**
032/33	PEARL JAM MANIFESTING MORRISON Indio, CA, USA, 5th November 1993 **Soundboard**
004/05	STEELY DAN BOOK OF LIARS Los Angeles, CA, USA, September 1993
036	TORI AMOS AFTER BURN Various locations USA 1992/93
037	SMASHING PUMPKINS THE GREATEST DAY LA, CA, USA, 11th December 1993 **Soundboard**
038	RAGE AGAINST MACHINE PEOPLE OF THE SUN LA, CA, USA, 11th Dec' 1993 & Mountain View 22nd June' 1993 **Soundboard**
039/40	THE GRATEFUL DEAD SCARLET FIRE Las Vegas, NV, USA, 16th May 1993
041	PRIMUS FREAK OUT LA, 11th Dec '93 & Mountain View CA, USA, 22nd June'93 **Soundboard**
042	THE DOORS w Eddie Vedder Rehearsals Power plant studio, USA, 11th January 1993
043	BLIND MELON KEEP THE OUT OF FOCUS I-Beam, San Francisco, CA, USA, 17th August 1993 **(rare encores)**
044/45	PEARL JAM LEAVING BABYLON San Diego, CA, USA, 3rd November 1993 (Usa 2nd show)
046	DEAD CAN DANCE EXIT TO EDEN Wiltern Theatre, Los Angeles, CA, USA, 15th November 1993
047	BJORK THE GIRL FROM OUTERSPACE Los Angeles, CA, USA, 19th November 1993
048	CREAM LONG TIME COMMIN' Rehearsals Power plant studio, USA, 11th January 1993
049/50	ERIC CLAPTON BIG BLUE Dodge Stadium, LA, USA, 29th August 1992
051	COUNTING CROWS CHILDREN IN BLOOM Irvine Meadowlands, Irvine, CA, USA, 11th June 1994
052	CRANBERRIES THOUGHTS THAT LINGER LA, USA, 11th & 12th December 1993 Acoustic **Soundboard**
053	BELLY SWEET RIDE LA, USA, 11th & 12th December 1993 Acoustic **Soundboard**
054	THE REPLACEMENTS HANGING IT UP Maddison, WI, USA, 4th July 1991
055	PORNO FOR PYROS 100 WAVES LA, 11th December 1993 & LA Palladium, January 1994 **Soundboard**
057	SEPULTURA ENTER CHAOS State Palace Theatre, New Orleans, LA, USA, 13th December 1992
058	BOB DYLAN STUMBLIN' ALONG Hollywood Bowl, LA, CA, USA, 2nd October 1993
059	GRATEFUL DEAD SPRING BREAK '94 Various US dates March/April 1994 **Soundboard (Excellent)**
060	TOOL SHED The Roseland NYC, NY, USA, 18th February 1994
061	STEVIE RAY VAUGHAN CITY OF LIGHTS Greek Theatre, LA, CA, USA, 6th October 1988
062	K. D. LANG LOVE SO SWEET Tupperware Theatre, Ilissamee, FL, USA, 6th September 1992
064	RAMONES MARCH OF THE PINHEADS Vogue Theatre, Indianapolis, IN, USA, 1978 **Soundboard**
065	BLACK FLAG LAST SHOW Detroit, MI, USA, 28th June 1986 **Soundboard**

PUMPKIN BROTHERS
PUMP 01/02 U2 FIRST NIGHT OF THE 1992 WORLD TOUR Florida, 29th February '1992

OCTOPUSS
OCT 001 THE BEATLES HAIL, HAIL, ROCK & ROLL Let it be Live Outtakes (Real good quality)
OCT 101 ★ GRATEFUL DEAD WINTER TOUR 1994 Madison Square Garden, NY, USA ,13 October 1994 (set I)

X RECORDS
X 001/2 DEPECHE MODE SWISS DEVOTION Zurich, Switzerland, 21st May 1993

CAPITAL
CAP 72348 FRANK SINATRA SINGS TO THE NEW YORKERS RCMH, NYC, USA, 24th April 1994

KISS THE STONE

KTS 001	THE WATERBOYS 'A GOLDEN DAY'
KTS 002	PRINCE 'PARIS AFFAIR'
KTS 003	INXS 'KICK IT IN EXCESS'
KTS 004	THE MISSION 'INTO THE BLUE'
KTS 005	REM 'IT'S THE END OF THE WORLD...'
KTS 006	VAN MORRISON 'CHURCH OF OUR LADY ST. MARY'
KTS 007	THE BLACK CROWES 'AIN'T THAT AMERICA'
KTS 008	U2 'FEEL THE NOISE'
KTS 009	THE HOTHOUSE FLOWERS 'SPIRIT'
KTS 010/11	INXS 'SOMETHING'XTRA'
KTS 012/13	BOB DYLAN 'STUCK INSIDE OF NEW YORK'
KTS 014	NEIL YOUNG 'RESTLESS'
KTS 015	NOT AVAILABLE NOW
KTS 016	ERASURE 'O L'AMOUR'
KTS 017	THE CLASH 'INTO THE 80'S'
KTS 018/19	SIMPLE MINDS 'REAL...REAL LIVE'
KTS 020	TALK TALK 'TALKING COLORS'
KTS 021	SISTERS OF MERCY 'THE NEON DREAM'
KTS 022	SIMPLY RED 'RED STARS AT NIGHT'
KTS 023	MORRISSEY 'HIGHER EDUCATION'
KTS 024	LENNY KRAVITZ 'FLOWER CHILD'
KTS 025	PIXIES 'VELOURIA'
KTS 026	THE CULT 'NEW YORK CITY BLUES'
KTS 027	U2 'THE FLAME AND THE FIRE'
KTS 028	U2 'SECOND HOMECOMING'
KTS 029	U2 'RED SUN AT MIDNIGHT'
BOX 01	U2 'BOX 579 BABY' 3 CD SET
KTS 030/31	PINK FLOYD 'A CLEAR VIEW'
KTS 032	SINEAD O'CONNOR 'BEAUTIFUL VISION'
KTS 033	PSYCHEDELIC FURS 'ROOM AT THE TOP'
KTS 034	JESUS JONES 'INFO FREAKO'
KTS 035	THE CURE 'JUST LIKE HEAVEN'
KTS 036	THE BLACK CROWES 'BLACK 'N' BLUE'
KTS 037	10,000 MANIACS 'COOL WHITE STARE'
KTS 038	ROBERT PALMER 'FEEL THE HEAT'
KTS 039	QUEEN 'A DAY AT THE STADIUM'
KTS 040	PET SHOP BOYS 'LIVE WIRES'
KTS 041	NIRVANA 'SEVENTH HEAVEN'
KTS 042/43	GENESIS 'THE INVISIBLE CAGE'
KTS 044	DEACON BLUE 'ON NEW YEARS DAY'
KTS 045	STEVIE NICKS 'CLOAKS AND DAGGERS'
KTS 046/47	STING 'THE SEAS OF SILENCE'
KTS 048	ROXETTE 'A NIGHT TO REMEMBER'
KTS 049	CARTER USM 'WHAM BAM'
KTS 050	THE WATERBOYS 'BORN TO BE TOGETHER'
KTS 051	VAN MORRISON 'SOUL LABRYNTH'
KTS 052	THE PIXIES 'ALL OVER THE WORLD'
KTS 053	LENNY KRAVITZ 'MY FLASH ON YOU'
KTS 054	IGGY POP 'METALHEAD'
KTS 055	WONDER STUFF 'INERTIA'
KTS 058	MORRISSEY 'DIGITAL EXCITATION'
KTS 059	FIELDS OF NEPHILIM 'FESTIVAL OF FIRE'
KTS 060	BILLY BRAGG 'BIG MOUTH STRIKES AGAIN'
KTS 061	PAUL YOUNG 'FOREVER YOUNG'
KTS 062	FISH 'THERE'S A GUY WORKS DOWN AT THE CHIP SHOP SWEARS HE'S FISH'
KTS 063/64	U2 'ST. STEPHENS AT THE POINT'
KTS 065	THE POGUES 'SINK THAT BOTTLE'
KTS 066	THE GODFATHER'S 'SHOOT TO KILL'
KTS 067	JANE'S ADDICTION 'DOWN IN FLAMES'
KTS 068	SISTERS OF MERCY 'TRANS-EUROPE EXCESS'
KTS 069	RIDE 'OVERDRIVE'
KTS 070	MARILLION ' GOLDEN TEARS'
KTS 071	QUEEN 'CROWNING GLORY'
KTS 072	JAMES 'LIVE AND DANGEROUS'
KTS 073	ALL ABOUT EVE 'BLESSED BY ANGELS'
KTS 074	THE MISSION 'BLOOD BROTHERS'
KTS 075	RED HOT CHILI PEPPERS 'GET THE FUNK OUT'
KTS 076	MICHAEL BOLTON 'SOUL DRIVER U.S.A.'
KTS 077/78	METALLICA 'TOTALLY DESTROY CANADA'
KTS 079	LOU REED 'MASTER CLASS'
KTS 080	PEARL JAM 'FIVE ALIVE'
KTS 081/82	THE CURE 'AND DREAMS COME TRUE'
KTS 086	SIOUXSIE & THE BANSHEES 'CASCADE'
KTS 087	THE SUGARCUBES 'HIT THE NORTH ATLANTIC'
KTS 088	JESUS & MARY CHAIN 'VENGEANCE'
KTS 089	SIMPLY RED 'RED STARS AT NIGHT VOL. 2'
KTS 090	JOHN COUGAR 'LIVE REHEARSALS'
KTS 091	L7 'MANEATER'
KTS 092	CROWDED HOUSE 'FOUR SEASONS IN ONE DAY'
KTS 093	BOB DYLAN 'SAN JOSE REVISITED'
KTS 094	RUSH 'RUN FROM THE FANS'
KTS 095	SISTERS OF MERCY 'NAPALM GODS'
KTS 096	SISTERS OF MERCY 'KISS THE BLADE'
KTS 097	SISTERS OF MERCY 'HOLOCAUST'
BOX 02	SISTERS OF MERCY 'SO DARK ALL OVER EUROPE'
KTS 098	MR. BIG 'GET BIGGER'
KTS 099	BOB DYLAN 'WANTED MAN'
KTS 100/1	U2 'ZOO TV TOUR'
KTS 102	JOHN COUGAR '4TH. OF JULY'
KTS 103	SISTERS OF MERCY 'OUT IN THE DARK'
KTS 104	RED HOT CHILI PEPPERS 'CHRISTMAS PARTY '91'
KTS 105	THE LEVELLERS 'THE FIDDLE AND THE DRUM'
KTS 106/07	GENESIS 'SUMMER NIGHTS'
KTS 108	LUSH 'KALEIDOSCOPIC HARMONIES'
KTS 109	MANIC STREET PREACHERS 'STREET PREACHING'
KTS 110/11	SOUNDGARDEN 'CROWN OF THORNS'
KTS 112	FAITH NO MORE 'LOVERS OF THEE INSANE'
KTS 113	PEARL JAM 'LOLLAPALOOZA '92'
KTS 114	LUSH/JESUS & MARY CHAIN 'LOLLAPALOOZA '92'
KTS 115	SOUNDGARDEN 'LOLLAPALOOZA '92'
BOX 003	LOLLAPALOOZA '92 VOL. 1 - 3 CD BOX + POSTER
KTS 116	MINISTRY 'LOLLAPALOOZA '92'
KTS 117	PORNO FOR PYROS/ICE CUBE 'LOLLAPALOOZA '92'
KTS 118	RED HOT CHILI PEPPERS 'LOLLAPALOOZA '92'
BOX 004	LOLLAPALOOZA '92 VOL. 2 - 3 CD BOX + TOUR PROGRAMME
KTS 110	MUDHONEY 'FUZZBUSTERS'
KTS 120	PRINCE 'DON'T CRY FOR ME ARGENTINA'
KTS 121	IRON MAIDEN 'MAIDEN EUROPE'
KTS 122	CULT 'REBIRTH OF THE PHOENIX'
KTS 123	NOT AVAILABLE NOW
KTS 124	SLAYER 'DEVIL'S DISCIPLES'
KTS 125/26	GARY MOORE 'BLUES FROM A GUN'
KTS 127/28	MICHAEL JACKSON 'LIVE AND DANGEROUS'
KTS 129/30	BOB DYLAN 'IN THE GARDEN'

Kiss The Stone

Order

KTS 133	NIRVANA 'DUMB'
KTS 134/35	ELP 'PIRATES'
KTS 136/37	MADONNA 'SOME LIKE IT HOT'
KTS 138/39	ERIC CLAPTON 'TEARS IN HEAVEN'
KTS 140	BON JOVI 'THE WILD ONES'
KTS 141	R.E.M. 'AUTOMATICALLY LIVE'
KTS 142	NEIL YOUNG 'SILVER & GOLD'
KTS 143	DON HENLEY 'AN EAGLE OUT EAST'
KTS 144	BLACK CROWES 'STARE IT COLD'
KTS 145	U2 'WATCH MORE TV'
KTS 146	BRUCE SPRINGSTEEN 'ONE WAY TICKET'
KTS 147/48	U2 'LIVE TRANSMISSION'
KTS 149	THUNDER 'SHELTER FROM THE STORM'
KTS 150	MINISTRY 'TRIP TO HELL'
KTS 151	SHAKESPEAR'S SISTER 'BACK IN YOUR OWN WORLD'
KTS 152	EMF 'ALL NIGHT RAVE'
KTS 153	UGLY KID JOE 'GET OUTTA MY FACE'
KTS 154	SONIC YOUTH 'SPLITTING THE ATOM'
KTS 155	BRYAN ADAMS 'KEEP ON RUNNING'
KTS 158	FRANK BLACK 'THE DREAM IS OVER'
KTS 158	SUEDE 'MOVIN'
KTS 159	BABES IN TOYLAND 'PLAYTIME'
KTS 160/61	BOB DYLAN 'FIFTH TIME AROUND'
KTS 162	ROXETTE 'UNCENSORED & UNCUT'
KTS 163/64	THE BLACK CROWES 'HIGH IN HOUSTON'
KTS 165	KEITH RICHARDS 'TIME IS ON MY SIDE'
KTS 166	NEIL YOUNG 'BACK TO MY ROOTS'
KTS 167	BOB MARLEY 'JAH LOVE'
KTS 168	LEMONHEADS 'SUCK ON THIS'
KTS 169	K.D. LANG 'SONGS FOR SWINGING LOVERS'
KTS 170	TOM WAITS 'COLD BEER ON A HOT NIGHT'
KTS 171	BLACK SABBATH 'BLACK BLOODY BLACK'
KTS 172	ALICE IN CHAINS 'LIVE & UNCHAINED'
KTS 173/74	SPIN DOCTORS 'HOUND AND HOUND'
KTS 175/76	U2 'THE REAL THING'
KTS 177	PANTERA 'WALK ON THE WILD SIDE'
KTS 178	RAGE AGAINST THE MACHINE 'JUSTIFY THOSE THAT DIE'
KTS 179	WORLD PARTY 'THANK YOU WORLD'
KTS 180	SCREAMING TREES 'TEN TONS OF FUN'
KTS 182	JOE SATRIANI 'MASTER OF THE ART'
KTS 183	LIONEL RICHIE 'ALL NIGHT LOVE'
KTS 184/85	METALLICA 'TEARING YOUR INSIDES OUT'
KTS 186	P.J. HARVEY 'BUILD ME A WOMAN'
KTS 187/88	VELVET UNDERGROUND 'TAKE A TRIP'
KTS 189	PORNO FOR PYROS 'PORNO FOR PERRY'
KTS 190/91	GRATEFUL DEAD 'HERE COMES SUNSHINE'
KTS 192	FRANK BLACK 'NO BIG DEAL'
KTS 193	SUGAR 'BLEEDING'
KTS 194	NEIL YOUNG 'WORLD ON A STRING'
KTS 195	SOUL ASYLUM 'BODY & SOUL'
KTS 196	BRIAN MAY 'OUT ON HIS OWN'
KTS 197/98	U2 'ZOO EUROPA'
KTS 199	ROBERT PLANT 'NO LOOKING BACK'
KTS 200/01	STING 'WALK IN THE FIELDS OF GOLD'
KTS 202/03	ERIC CLAPTON 'THECIRCUS HAS LEFT THE TOWN'
KTS 204/05	DEF LEPPARD 'THE CIRCUS COMES TO TOWN'
KTS 206	DEPECHE MODE 'ENJOY THE RUMOURS'
KTS 207	STONE TEMPLE PILOTS 'CLOSE YOUR EYES'
KTS 208	SMASHING PUMPKINS 'DROWN'
KTS 209	RAGE AGAINST THE MACHINE 'REVOLUTION'
KTS 210	MEGADEATH 'PUNISHMENT IS DUE'
KTS 211	THE THE 'SAVE ME'
KTS 212	LEONARD COHEN 'ABOVE THE SOUL'
KTS 213	TORI AMOS 'AFTER THE RAIN'
KTS 214	SPRINGSTEEN 'PLUGGED - THE REHEARSALS'
KTS 215	ELTON JOHN 'THE LAST SONG'
KTS 216	NEW ORDER 'ELECTRONIC ECSTASY'
KTS 217	WHITE ZOMBIE 'RESURRECTION DAY'

KTS 218	MOTORHEAD 'GONNA MAKE YOUR EARS BLEED'
KTS 219	PRIMUS 'MADHOUSE'
KTS 220	GUNS 'N ROSES 'UNPLUGGED'
KTS 221	PEARL JAM 'AGAINST'
KTS 223	THE BREEDERS 'DOUBLE TROUBLE'
KTS 224	SPRINGSTEEN 'FROM SMALL THINGS'
KTS 225/26	PRINCE 'DO U WANNA GO HOME'
KTS 227/28	GRATEFUL DEAD 'DAWN OF THE DEAD'
KTS 229	PRINCE 'THIS IS MY NIGHT'
KTS 230/31	BOB MARLEY 'GET UP AND LIVE'
KTS 233	LIVING COLOUR 'NOTHING LAST FOREVER'
KTS 234	JOHN MELLENCAMP 'WHEELS ARE TURNING'
KTS 235	BELLY 'GUT FEELING'
KTS 236	IGGY POP 'OUT ON THE STREETS AGAIN'
KTS 237	10,000 MANIACS 'HOW YOU'VE GROWN'
KTS 238	MARIEA MCKEE 'BREATHE'
KTS 239/40	U2 'ZOOROPA DOWN UNDER'
KTS 241/42	MADONNA 'LICK ME DOWN UNDER'
KTS 243	DREAM THEATRE 'DREAM OUT LOUD'
KTS 244/45	MEAT LOAF 'TO HELL AND BACK'
KTS 246	PRINCE 'FUNKY PARTY 2NITE'
KTS 247	DAVID BYRNE 'UNPLUGGED + MORE'
KTS 248	THE LEVELLERS 'BACK TO NATURE'
KTS 249	INXS 'EMPTY SUN UNDER CLEAN MINDS'
KTS 250	PAUL MCCARTNEY 'HEY, TOKYO!'
KTS 251/52	GRATEFUL DEAD 'DEAD AGAIN'
KTS 253	NIRVANA 'ALL ACOUSTICALLY'
KTS 254	BLIND MELON 'STING ME'
KTS 255/56	MADONNA 'GIRLIE SHOW EXPERIENCE'
KTS 257	MATTHEW SWEET 'SHAPE SHIFTER'
KTS 258	JACKSON BROWNE 'TOO MANY ANGELS'
KTS 259	GIN BLOSSOMS 'IN BLOOM'
KTS 260	RADIOHEAD 'CREEPSHOW'
KTS 261	SMASHING PUMPKINS 'MAYONNAISE DREAM'
KTS 262	LEMONHEADS 'SQUEEZE ME PLEASE ME'
KTS 263	TOOL 'TALES FROM THE DARKSIDE'
KTS 264	SMASHING PUMPKINS '3 FEET HIGH'
KTS 265	IZZY STRADLIN 'ROCKER'
KTS 266	CROWDED HOUSE 'IT'S ONLY NATURAL'
KTS 267	THE DOORS 'APOCALYPSE NOW'
KTS 268	BJORK 'SUGAR CANDY KISSES'
KTS 269	DURAN DURAN 'ACOUSTIC WORLD'
KTS 270/71	ELTON JOHN 'WORLD CLASS'
KTS 272	BOB MOULD 'THE CALM BEFORE THE STORM'
KTS 273/74	TOM PETTY 'SOUTHERN GENTLEMAN'
KTS 275	STING 'COMPLETE CHICAGO SESSIONS'
KTS 276	PRIMUS 'BACK IN THE MADHOUSE'
KTS 277	THERAPY? 'NO LOVE LOST'
KTS 278	SUEDE 'PERFORMANCE'
KTS 279	SEPULTURA 'WELCOME TO THE END OF...'
KTS 280	SPRINGSTEEN 'WARM AND TENDER LOVE'
KTS 281	JAMIROQUAI 'IF I LIKE IT, I DO IT'
KTS 282/83	DREAM THEATRE 'LORDS OF SOUND'
KTS 284	NIRVANA 'ROMA'
KTS 285	PRINCE 'WELCOME 2 THE BEAUTIFUL...'
KTS 286	ALLMAN BROHTERS BAND 'SWEET MELISSA'
KTS 287/88	PEARL JAM 'ATLANTA'
KTS 289	THE WONDER STUFF 'ON THE ROPES'
KTS 290	RAGE AGAINST THE MACHINE 'KILLING ZONE'
KTS 291	HEART 'UNPLUGGED'
KTS 292/93	AEROSMITH 'STRUTTIN' MY STUFF'
KTS 294/95	PINK FLOYD 'THE LIVE BELL'
KTS 296	CRACKER 'TEEN ANGST'
KTS 297	COUNTING CROWS 'CARVING OUT OUR NAMES'
KTS 298	PRIMAL SCREAM 'ROCKSUCKER BLUES'
KTS 299	CRASH TEST DUMMIES 'DUMMIES AT HOME'
KTS 300/01	BOB MARLEY 'REVOLUTION'
KTS 302	BLUR 'MODROPHENIA'
KTS 303	NINE INCH NAILS 'COMING DOWN FAST'
KTS 304/05	PHISH 'FOLLOW ME TO GAMEHENGE'
KTS 306	METALLICA 'NO LIMITS - NO LAWS'

The Ultimate In Quality!

KTS 307 SONIC YOUTH 'TAKEOUT THE TRASH'
KTS 308 BOB MARLEY 'DOWNTOWN TRENCHTOWN'
KTS 309 HUSKER DU 'SUPERNOVA'
KTS 310 KRISTIN HERSH 'SPARKLE'
KTS 311 PANTERA 'NO COMPROMISE NO SELL OUT'
KTS 312 EXTREME 'DREAMS COME TRUE'
KTS 313 SEPULTURA 'NAILBOMB'
KTS 314 PAUL WELLER 'WALK ON BY'
KTS 315 THE REPLACEMENTS 'SHIT, SHOWER & SHAVE'
KTS 316 THE WATERBOYS 'IN THE STUDIO'
KTS 317 THE CRANBERRIES 'STORIES TO BE TOLD'
KTS 318 THERAPY? 'FISTFUL OF POWER'
KTS 319 RAGE AGAINST THE MACHINE 'BULLET PROOF'
KTS 320 GRANT LEE BUFFALO 'LIKE A SHOT'
KTS 322 CROWDED HOUSE 'FLEADH'
KTS 323 BEASTIE BOYS 'SEVEN DAY WEEKEND'
KTS 324 THE PRETENDERS 'NOW AND THEN'
KTS 325 TORI AMOS 'SPIRIT IN THE SKY'
KTS 326/27 BILLY JOEL 'AFTER THE FLOOD'
KTS 329 SOUTHSIDE JOHNNY/LITTLE STEVEN 'UNPLUGGED'
KTS 330 DAVID CROSBY 'NAKED IN THE RAIN'
KTS 331 PAUL WESTERBERG 'GRAVEL PIT'
KTS 332 LENNY KRAVITZ 'ACOUSTIC'
KTS 333 AFGHAN WHIGS 'FLIP YOUR WHIG'
KTS 334 JAMES 'A STRANGE DAY'
KTS 335 MARIAH CAREY 'SOMEDAY'
KTS 336 NIRVANA 'THE ETERNAL LEGACY'
KTS 337 COUNTING CROWS 'CHILDREN IN BLOOM'
KTS 338 BLUR 'SAWDUST MEMORIES'
KTS 339/40 PINK FLOYD 'THE BELL GETS LOUDER'
KTS 341/42 GRATEFUL DEAD 'ANOTHER DAY'
KTS 343 NINE INCH NAILS 'WHEN THE WHIP COMES DOWN'
KTS 344/45 METALLICA 'ENTER MUDMAN'
KTS 346 ROLLINS BAND 'ALIEN BLUEPRINT'
KTS 347 HOLE 'KISS AWAY THE DARKEST DAY'
KTS 348 SHERYL CROW 'RUN, BABY, RUN'
KTS 349 BOB MARLEY 'REDEMPTION'
KTS 350 THE DOORS 'SHATTERED'
KTS 351 NOFX 'BACK IN THE GARAGE'
KTS 352 THE WATERBOYS 'ALIVE ON THE INSIDE'
KTS 353 TORI AMOS 'FAIRY TALES'
KTS 354 RED HOT CHILI PEPPERS 'DIRTY WEEKEND'
KTS 356/57 THE ROLLING STONES 'THE VOODOO KISS'
KTS 358 L7 'WHEN THE STINK HITS THE FAN'
KTS 359 THE OFFSPRING 'THE YEAR THAT PUNK BROKE'
KTS 356/66 METALLICA 'PILE OF SHIT'
KTS 368/69 PEARL JAM 'VORTICAL'
KTS 370 DEAD CAN DANCE 'SINFUL GARDEN'
KTS 371 PULP 'FICTON ROMANCE'
KTS 372 BIOHAZARD 'RUN FOR COVER'
KTS 373 GALLIANO 'DOWN TO EARTH'
KTS 374/75 PINK FLOYD 'OUT OF THIS WORLD'
KTS 376 THE BLACK CROWES 'TALLER'
KTS 377 THE ROLLING STONES 'SPARKS WILL FLY'
KTS 378 COLLECTIVE SOUL 'MOTOR CITY'S BURNIN''
KTS 379/80 PEARL JAM 'ATLANTA - THE DAY BEFORE'
KTS 381 OASIS 'SLIDE AWAY'
KTS 382 ERIC CLAPTON 'BLUES REHEARSALS'
KTS 383 LIVE 'I ALIVE'
KTS 384/85 WHITNEY HOUSTON 'OUT OF AFRICA'
KTS 386 ELVIS COSTELLO 'UNDER THE INFLUENZA'
KTS 387 THE JAM 'SET THE SKIES ABLAZE'
KTS 388/89 THE ROLLING STONES 'MIAMI DICE'
KTS 390 CATHEDRAL ' COSMIC FUNERAL'
KTS 391/92 NINE INCH NAILS 'SLAUGHTER IN THE AIR'
KTS 393 SLAYER 'SPIRITS IN BLACK'
KTS 394 GREEN DAY 'SPITTING'
KTS 395 NIRVANA 'TRICK OR TREAT'
KTS 396 PANTERA 'LIVE BEYOND DRIVEN'
KTS 397 OASIS 'BLACK ON WHITE'
KTS 398 PEARL JAM 'SELF POLLUTION RADIO'

KTS 399 IGGY POP 'ROCK HARD'
KTS 402 THE DOOBIE BROTHERS 'REUNION'
KTS 403 JOHN MELLENCAMP 'WILD AT NIGHT'
KTS 404 LED ZEPPELIN 'ROCK 'N' ROLL HALL OF FAME'
KTS 405 VAN HALEN 'SECRET GIG'

CD - BOX SETS
KTS BX 001 U2 'EIGHT 579 BABY' 3 CD SET
KTS BX 002 SISTERS OF MERCY 'SO DARK ALL OVER EUROPE'
KTS BX 003 LOLLAPALOOZA '92 VOL. 1' 3 CD BOX & POSTER
KTS BX 004 LOLLAPALOOZA '92 VOL. 2' 3 CD BOX & TOUR
         PROGRAMME
KTS BX 005 U2 'ZOO TV TOUR, 3 CD SET'
KTS BX 006 GRATEFUL DEAD 'DEAD AT THE BAY' 4 CD SET
KTS BX 007 PRINCE 'IN ROCK' 5 CD SET & BOOKLET
KTS BX 008 GRATEFUL DEAD 'OREGON' 3CD & POSTER
KTS BX 009 DOORS 'MATRIXCLUB' 4CD DIGIBOX

BIG MUSIC
BIG 001/2   JETHRO TULL 'TALES FROM THE
              CRYSTAL FLUTE'
BIG 003   UB40 'CREDIT TO THE NATION'
BIG 004   MEATLOAF 'HOT AS HELL'
BIG 005   KISS 'GODS OF THUNDER'
BIG 006   THIN LIZZY 'OUT ON BAIL'
BIG 007   ELECTRIC LIGHT ORCHESTRA
              'ROCKARIA OVERTURE'
BIG 008   THE KINKS 'ALL NIGHT STAND'
BIG 009/10   GRATEFUL DEAD 'OUT OF YOUR SKULL'
BIG 011   THE WHO 'ACCEPT NO SUBSTITUTE'
BIG 012 /13   ELVIS COSTELLO 'THIS IS TOMORROW'
BIG 014   NEIL YOUNG 'ALL NIGHT LONG'
BIG 015   THE POLICE 'CRIMEWATCH'
BIG 016   SIMPLY RED 'SIMPLY THE BEST'
BIG 017   ROD STEWART 'SKIN TIGHT'
BIG 018   THE JAM 'IT'S A MOD MOD MOD WORLD'
BIG 019   TOM WAITS 'DOWNTOWN BLUES'
BIG 020/21   VAN MORRISON 'PAGAN STREAMS'
BIG 022/23   DIRE STRAITS 'TICKET TO HEAVEN'
BIG 024   EURYTHMICS 'SWEET REVENGE'
BIG 025   STEVIE RAY VAUGAN 'COLD SHOT'
BIG 026/27   CURE 'BITE THE BIG APPLE'
BIG 028   PAUL MCCARTNEY 'A DREAM APART'
BIG 029/30   ELTON JOHN 'HEAT WAVE'
BIG 031   MADNESS 'NUTTY DREAD'
BIG 032   PINK FLOYD 'EXPLODING IN YOUR MIND'
BIG 033   ERIC CLAPTON 'BRIGHT LIGHTS IN BLUES CITY'
BIG 034/35   ROLLING STONES 'BACK IN BUSINESS'
BIG 036   LEONARD COHEN 'DIAMONDS IN THE MINES'
BIG 037   ANNIE LENNOX 'THE GIFT'
BIG 038   HANOI ROCKS 'KILL CITY BLUES'
BIG 041   BOB MARLEY 'CONQUERING LION'
BIG 042   NED'S ATOMIC DUSTBIN 'RADIO ACTIVE'
BIG 043   THE SMITHS 'LAST OF THE ENGLISH ROSES'
BIG 044/45   ROLLING STONES 'ROCKIN' AT THE FORUM'
BIG 046   THE SEX PISTOLS 'KILL THE HIPPIES'
BIG 047   VAN MORRISON 'IT AIN'T WHY, IT JUST IS'
BIG 048   S. R. VAUGHAN 'G*RAY'
BIG 049   BIG BLACK 'DEATH WISH'
BIG 050/51   ERASURE 'WELCOME TO THE GLITTER...'
BIG 052/53   PRINCE '2 LIVE 4 LOVE'
BIG 054   P.I.L. 'ROTTEN TO THE CORE'
BIG 055/56   GUNS 'N ROSES 'LIVE IN JAPAN'
BIG 057   PAUL WELLER 'GROOVE A LITTLE'
BIG 058/59   GUNS 'N ROSES 'ROCKIN' IN CHILE'
BIG 060   METALLICA 'TOWER OF STRENGTH'
BIG 061   THE SMITHS 'SAME DAY AGAIN'
BIG 062   STEVIE RAY VAUGHAN 'LET ME LOVE YOUBABY'
BIG 063   DANIEL LANOIS 'COOL WATER'
BIG 064/65   STING 'IT'S PROBABLY ME'

Kiss The Stone

Order

BIG 066	JOHN MELLENCAMP 'SOUTHERN HEMIPSHERE'
BIG 067	QUEEN 'ROCKIN' OSAKA IN 1982'
BIG 068/69	ALLMAN BROTHERS BAND 'ALL OR NOTHING'
BIG 070	LED ZEPPELIN 'ANOTHER WHITE SUMMER'
BIG 072/73	KISS 'UNCHAINED & UNMASKED'
BIG 074	ROXETTE 'BLONDE DREAMS'
BIG 075	FARM AID 6 'SOWING THE SEEDS'
BIG 076/77	METALLICA 'LIVE IN ARGENTINA'
BIG 078/079	U2 'ANYTHING IS POSSIBLE'
BIG 080	SEPULTURA 'SLAVES OF PAIN'
BIG 081	PEARL JAM 'FLASHPOINT'
BIG 083	WHITNEY HOUSTON 'LIVE IN NEW YORK'
BIG 084	MIDNIGHT OIL 'BLUE SKY RED EARTH'
BIG 085	TAKE THAT! 'KISS THIS'
BIG 086/87	GUNS N' ROSES 'LIVE IN ARGENTINA'
BIG 088/89	ROD STEWART 'IN THE SPOTLIGHT'
BIG 090	BILLY JOEL 'TEMPTATION'
BIG 091	THE SMITHS 'THANK YOUR LUCKY STARS'
BIG 092	ELTON JOHN 'FINE CHINA'
BIG 093	KISS 'ROCK AND ROLL ALL NITE'
BIG 094	ABBA 'SWEET DREAMS ARE MADE OF...'
BIG 098	THE SMITHS 'THE BUTTERFLY COLLECTOR'

CD - BOX SETS

BIG BX 001	GUNS N' ROSES 'ROCKIN' IN CHILE' 2 CD SET
BIG BX 002	LED ZEPPELIN 'THROUGH THE YEARS' 5 CD SET
BIG BX 003	ROLLING STONES 'THE FIRST DECADE' 4 CD SET
BIG BX 004	SPRINGSTEEN 'SATANS JEWEL CROWN' 4 CD SET
BIG BX 005	PRINCE 'ONLY 4 U' 4 CD SET & POSTER
BIG BX 006	THE BEATLES 'ARTIFACTS' 5 CD SET & BOOKLET
BIG BX 007	LED ZEPPELIN 'ANOTHER TRIP' 5 CD SET
BIG BX 008	THE BEATLES 'ARTIFACTS II' 5 CD SET & BOOKLET
BIG BX 009	THE BEATLES 'ARTIFACTS III' 4 CD SET & BOOKLET

COCOMELOS RECORDS

CM 001	NIRVANA 'BLIND PIG'

CM 003/4	U2 'ONE LIVE BABY'
CM 005	PIXIES 'SITUATION RED'
CM 006	SONIC YOUTH 'SONIC STARPOWER'
CM 007/08	TOM PETTY 'UNDER THE SKIES SO BLUE'
CM 009/10	'METALLICA ALL HELL BREAKS LOOSE'
CM 011	EXTREME 'TAKE IT TO THE LIMITS'
CM 012	NINE INCH NAILS 'SOLID GOLD HELL'
CM 013	DISPOSABLE HEROES OF HIPHOPRISY 'POLITICAL TECHNOCRACY'
CM 014	ALICE IN CHAINS 'DIRTY TOY TOWN'
CM 015	ICE-T & BODY COUNT 'IN YOUR FACE'
CM 016	MINISTRY 'KILL FOR KICKS'
CM 017	SPRINGSTEEN 'SOLO ACOUSTIC'
CM 018/19	DEPECHE MODE 'MODE ON THE ROAD'
CM 020/21	PEARL JAM 'BRIXTON'
CM 022/23	VAN HALEN 'ROCKING MY HOMETOWN'
CM 024	PEARL JAM 'THE KIDS ARE ALRIGHT'
CM 025/26	RUSH 'NORTHERN HEROES'
CM 027/28	SOUNDGARDEN 'THE GARDEN'
CM 029/30	COVERDALE - PAGE 'LIVE IN JAPAN'
CM 031	PEARL JAM 'NEW SONGS'
CM 032/33	THE EAGLES 'THE BOYS FROM YESTERDAY'
CM 034/35	ROLLING STONES 'I CAN'T GET NEXT TO YOU'
CM 036	GREEN DAY 'HAVING A BLAST'

CD - NIKKO RECORDS

NK 001	PEARL JAM 'BLACK & WHITE'
NK 002	U2 'OUTSIDE BROADCAST'
NK 003	BLACK CROWES 'SPECIAL DELIVERY'
NK 004	SUEDE 'STRANGE FASCINATION'
NK 005 /06	PAUL McCARTNEY 'OUT IN THE CROWD'
NK 007/08	BON JOVI 'LONG WAY FROM HOME'
NK 009	10,000 MANIACS 'IN THE GARDEN OF EDEN'
NK 010/11	AEROSMITH 'OUT OF CONTROL'
NK 012	PAUL WELLER 'ANYTIME YOU WANT ME'
NK 013	THERAPY? 'ISOLATION'

CD COSTS:

	USA$	UK£	It. Lire
1 CD	22.00	12.00	25.000
2 CD	44.00	24.00	48.000
3 CD	66.00	36.00	73.000

POSTAGE COSTS:
Europe: First CD - 5.500 It. Lire / DM 6,00 / £2.30. Each additional - 2.000 It. Lire / DM 2,50 / £1.00.
USA and Japan: First CD - $4.50. Each additional CD - $2.00.

PAYMENT:
Send complete Credit Card information or advance payment (cash or
International Money Order) with your order.
Maximum Credit Card order eight (8) CDs. Credit Cards charged in Italian Lire.
Credit Cards accepted are: Visa, American Express, Diners Club International,
Master Card and Bank Americard.
For orders above this amount, please send an International Money Order.
Full colour catalogue: $5.00 / £2 / 5.000 It. Lire.

KTS RECORDS MAIL ORDER SERVICE

VIA CANALETTO, 18 - 47046 MISANO ADRIATICO (FO), ITALY
PHONE (39) 541 610556 - FAX (39) 541 613948

The Ultimate In Quality!

WHOLESALING

MINOTAURO RECORDS srl,

VIA ACQUI, 5 - 27100 PAVIA - ITALY

PHONE:39.382.29017

FAX:39.382.530821

MUSIC FROM THE LABYRINTH

ARC 002	MUDDY WATERS-CHICAGO 81	AS	25	WEATHER REPORT- ITALY 76
ARC 003	FRANK ZAPPA-N.Y.78	AS	26	HEART - CHICAGO 76
ARC 004	ERIC CLAPTON-HAWAII 77	AS	27	MAHAVISHNU & J.MCLAUGHLIN -NY 72
ARC 006	J.CALE & C.SPEDDING-STOCKHOLM 75	AS	28/2	G. EVANS & .J.MCLAUGHLIN -ITALY 86
		AS	29/2	D. PURPLE & J. SATRIANI -ITALY 94
ARC 007	E.COSTELLO-PARIS 84	AS	30/2	PINK FLOYD - PITTSBURG 94
ARC 009	I.POP & STOOGES-STUDIO 70	AS	30/2	PINK FLOYD - PITTSBURG 94
ARC 010	AC/DC-ATLANTIC STUDIOS 77	AS	31	THE JEFF HEALEY BAND - ITALY 93
ARC 011	S.R.VAUGHAN-USA 84	AS	32	MICK KARN'S BESTIAL CLUST.-ITALY 94
ARC 012	BRIAN FERRY-AUSTRALIA 79	AS	33	KING CRIMSON-BOSTON 72
ARC 013	V.MORRISON & DR.JOHN-VARA STUD. 74	AS	34	STRAY CATS-LORELEY 83, N.Y.88
ARC 014	U2 - DENVER 83	AS	35	CLARKE/HOLDSWORTH....- MILAN 88
ARC 015	THE JEFF HEALEY BAND- TOUR 88	AS	36/2	PINK FLOYD-SWITZERLAND 94
ARC 016	THE POLICE-FRANCE 77	AS	37	UK- BOSTON 78, OSLO 79
ARC 017	THE STRAY CATS - R. BROADCAST 82	AS	38/2	PRINCE- N.Y 94
ARC 018	LOU REED-SYDNEY 74	AS	39/2	ROLLING STONES- U.S.A 94
ARC 019	L. COLE & THE COMMOTIONS-PARIS 84	AS	40	SONNY ROLLINS- HOLLAND 73
ARC 020	TEXAS- AMSTERDAM 89	AS	41	HERBIE HANCOCK- FRANCE 71
ARC 021	R. WOOD & K.RICHARDS-LONDON 74	AS	42/2	J.SCOFIELD & P.METHENY-ITALY 94
ARC 022	HOT TUNA- USA 73,75,76	AS	43	S.R.VAUGHAN & B. GUY-CHICAGO 89/PIER 84,N.Y.83
ARC 023	PATTO- ITALY 1972			
AS	01	DURAN DURAN -ARGENTINA 93	AS	44	PINK FLOYD-EUROPE 75
AS	02	M.OLDFIELD- USA 93	BLY	002	RICHARD THOMPSON -NEW HAVEN 88
AS	03	PAT METHENY- USA 92	BLY	003/4	DAVID BOWIE- RADIO, N.Y. 73
AS	04	WEATHER REPORT - LIVE 74	DAT	001	LENNY KRAVITZ-PARIS 91
AS	05	J.MACLAUGHLIN - EUROPE 91	DAT	002	GARY MOORE-FRANKFURT 91
AS	06	R.FRIPP & D.SYLVIAN- EUROPE 92	DAT	003	JOE SATRIANI-FRANCE 93
AS	07	A.HOLDSWORTH-EUROPE 92	FU	201	BEATLES-PARIS 64/65
AS	08	GATHERING OF MINDS- MONTREAUX 83	FU	202	THE ROCK N'ROLL CIRCUS-68
AS	09	STEVE VAI-MY FATHER'S PLACE 83	FU	204	J.MAYALL & T. BLUESBREAK.-ITALY 92
AS	10	PEARL JAM -USA 93	FU	205	P.McCARTNEY-ITALY 76
AS	11/2	NEIL YOUNG -USA 92,93	FU	206/2	B.B.KING & R.CHARLES- ITALY 90
AS	12/2	GRATEFUL DEAD-LAS VEGAS 93	FU	207	JOHN, PAUL, GEORGE & STU LIVERPOOL 60
AS	13/2	THE CURE- PARIS 89			
AS	14/2	PRINCE -PITTSBURG 93	HQ	01	U.J.ROTH/J.BRUCE/...-GERMANY 91
AS	15/2	STEVE VAI-ITALY 93	HQ	02	P.RODGERS -S.FRANCISCO 93
AS	16	A.HOLDSWORTH -ENGLAND 78	HQ	03	TINA TURNER -BRASIL 88
AS	17	AL DI MEOLA-AMSTERDAM 82	HQ	04	R. THOMPSON- USA 85
AS	18/2	MCLAUGHLIN/DE LUCIA/DI MEOLA- ROME 83	HQ	05	NEIL YOUNG -OHIO 83
			HQ	06	THE SHADOWS-EUROPE 89
AS	19	J.BECK-ITALY 90	HQ	07	THE ALLMAN BROTHERS- FLORIDA 82
AS	20	J.BRUCE - 92,93	HQ	08/2	YES- QPR 75
AS	21	MANZANERA/WEST/CALIFORNIA...- ITALY 89	HQ	09	GLORIA ESTEFAN -HOLLAND 91
			HQ	10	BEATLES BUDOKAN 66, MIAMI 64
AS	22	TORI AMOS - ITALY 94	HQ	11	PHISH -STOWE 92
AS	23	STEVE MORSE - KIVA 83,N.MEXICO 84	IM	01	THE BEATLES-STUDIO TRACKS
AS	24	DIXIE DREGS- N.Y. 79	IM	02	J.LENNON- ALTERNATE & OUTTAKE

        love & money

ARCHIVIO

MAIL ORDER
VINYL MAGIC 3,
VIA C.ABBA 9/R,
17100 SAVONA - ITALY
PHONE & FAX: 39.19.812081

minotauro

MUSIC FROM THE LABYRINTH

IM	03/4	BOB DYLAN - NY 67
IM	05	JEFF BECK- 67/75
LTD	18A/B	DAVID BOWIE-UK 90
LTD	20A/B	GUNS N'ROSES-ARGENTINA 93
LM	01	NIRVANA- ITALY 90
LM	02	PRIMUS-ITALY 90
LM	03	LENNY KRAVITZ-CHICAGO 90
LM	05	MR. BIG - U.S.A. 91
LM	06	NIGHT RANGER-U.S.A. 86
RTCD 001		SUZY QUATRO-ITALY 75
RTCD 002		GENTLE GIANT- ITALY 74
RTCD 003-4		V. DER GRAAF GENERATOR-ITALY 75
RTCD 005		ARTHUR BROWN- ITALY 72
RTCD 006		TEN YEARS AFTER - ITALY 71
RTCD 007		COLOSSEUM-ITALY 71
RTCD 008-9		TRAFFIC-ITALY 74
RTCD 010-11		JETHRO TULL-ITALY 72
RTCDPG 1-2		PETER GABRIEL-STOCKHOLM 93
SBC	001	BLUES BROTHERS-WINTERLAND 79
SBC	002/2	ROLLING STONES-PARIS 76
SBC	003/2	THE CURE-FRANCE 81
SBC	006	BILLY IDOL-U.S.A. 82
SBC	007	ROBERT PLANT-WEMBLEY 85
SBC	008	ROBERT CRAY-U.S.A. 89
SBC	010	LENNY KRAVITZ-U.S.A. 90
SBC	011	THE PIXIES-ENGLAND 88, 89
SBC	012	R.E.M.-AMERICAN ACOUSTIC TOUR 91
SBC	013	STING - AMERICAN ACOUSTIC TOUR 91
SBC	014	BRUCE SPRINGSTEEN-FROM1987 TO 91
SBC	016	PINK FLOYD-HERFORSHIRE 90
SBC	018	PRINCE-PARIS 87
SBC	019	THE CURE-LONDON 91
SBC	020	MOLLY HATCHET-FLORIDA 80
SBC	021	38 SPECIAL- TEXAS 84
SBC	022	POINT BLANK- ATLANTA 79
SBC	024	TEXAS-SWITZERLAND 92
SBC	026	ERIC CLAPTON-U.K. 92
SBC	027	THE FREDDIE MERCURY MEMORIAL CONCERT 46/91-WEMBLEY ARENA 92
SBC	028	C. SANTANA & JEFF BECK-JAPAN 86
SBC	029	WAS NOT WAS-MONTREAUX 92
SBC	031	RINGO STARR- MONTREAUX 92
SBC	032	JOE COCKER-MONTREAUX 92
STR	002	SMASHING PUMPKINS-USA 93
STR	003	THE SMITHS-EUROPE 83/84
STR	004/5	PEARL JAM-ATLANTA 94
STR	006/7	TORI AMOS-UCLA CAMPUS 94

TAU	103	EXODUS-DYNAMO OPEN AIR FES. 88
TAU	104	VV.AA-READING FESTIVAL 80, 81
TAU	105/6	GUNS N'ROSES-ARGENTINA 92
TAU	107	ANTHRAX -DALLAS 89
TAU	108	GUNS N'ROSES-DUSSELDORF 87
TAU	110/11	METALLICA-BUENOS AIRES 93
TAU	112	H.S.A.S.- U.S.A. 84
TAU	113	THIN LIZZY & GRAND SLAM -78/BBC 84
TAU	114/15	ALCATRAZZ & STEVE VAI-JAPAN 84
TAU	116	JOURNEY-LOS ANGELES 78
TAU	117	MEGADETH-SAN FRANCISCO 92
VIP	001	KATE BUSH-LONDON 79
VIP	002	FRIPP & ENO-LONDON 74, PARIS 75
VIP	003	THE TUBES-LOS ANGELES 76
VIP	005	K. CRIMSON-ATLANTA 73,/PITTS.75
VIP	007	ROLLING STONES-LONDON 76
VIP	008	LED ZEPPELIN-BUFFALO 73
VIP	009	KISS-NEW YORK 88
BCB	01	BLACK CAT BONES-MARQUEE '68
BGS1992		QUEEN-JAPAN 82
BM	063/2	JIMI HENDRIX -FILLMORE EAST 69
BMCD 13		NINE INCH NAILS-DEMOS
CA	1111	ROLLING STONES-DETROIT 69
JH	01/2	JIMI HENDRIX-VARIOUS JAM AT RECORD PLANT, N.Y.67/70, PARIS, 67, ENGLAND 70, ZURICH 68 (UNRELEASED CONCERT)
JT	01	JETHRO TULL-EUROPEAN TOUR 73
KUK	01	KRAFTWERK-ITALY 91
LOTUS01		PRINCE-SPAIN 93
LZ	01/2	LED ZEPPELIN-FILLMORE WEST 69
MD	1/4	MILES DAVIS-VARIOUS LOCATIONS 1970 TO 73
NC	01	KISS-SHEFFIELD/GLASGOW 92
NR	02/2	KISS-ARGENTINA 94
NU	1	I NUMI-PAVIA 75
PLS79921		PEARL JAM-CBGB 91
PLS79923/2		AEROSMITH - L.A. 93
PRC	01	PRINCE-BRAZIL 91
RA	01	EMERSON, LAKE & PALMER-TALY 92
RS	01/8	ROLLING STONES-VARIOUS LOCATIONS U.S. TOUR 75
VAR	01	NIRVANA-UNRELEASED TRACKSDEMO
YFR	001	FRANK ZAPPA-BOLOGNA 74
YYM	002	LES CHAUSETTES NOIRES & E. MITCHELL-OLYMPIA 63
YYM	008	MICHELM POLNAREFF - LAUSANNE 67

Australian Compact Disc Catalog

Grapefruit • Joker • Kiwi •
Australian Fan Club • Australian Gold

- Now, the best and rarest compact discs are available from Australia. When you think quality, you think Japan or Australian Import!
- For the first time Australian Imports are available under one roof!
- To order, call or fax to the number below or contact your local dealer!
- MC/Visa Only.
- Single CD's =$20.00 Double CD's=$40.00 Box Sets =$90.00
- Add $5.00 for the first CD and $1.00 for each additional CD for Shipping.

Call us or Fax us for more 1995 shows from all over the world from your favorite artists. Look for our ads in *Live Music Review*.
• Dealers • Stores • Distributors •
Wholesale Inquiries Welcome! Call for prices!

011-613-429-7012

Woodstock '94

The complete 22 set library of 30 CD's direct from Woodstock '94 Soundboard tapes in their entirety. These CD's are the official Authorized Woodstock CD's Released in Australia only. Available for the first time for export. These high quality CD's are in very limited release. First come, first serve.

Aerosmith (2 CD's)	Cypress Hill/Salt N Pepa	Primus + Candlebox
Allman Brothers (2CD's)	Bob Dylan (2 CD's)	Red Hot Chili Peppers
Arrested Dev./Salt N Pepa	M. Etheridge/Cranberries	Paul Rodgers and Slash
The Band (2 CD's)	Peter Gabriel	Henry Rollins Band
Blind Melon	Green Day + Fri. Hilights	Santana (2 CD's)
Joe Cocker	Metallica (2 CD's)	Spin Doctors
CSN (2 CD's)	Nine Inch Nails (2 CD's)	Traffic
	Porno for Pyros	

Other Australian Rarities Available Now!

Aerosmith -	Mama Kin's (Soundboard at Mama Kin's Boston MA 12-19-94)	1CD
Alice in Chains -	Them Bones (Recorded live in Boston on 11/27/92)	1CD
Tori Amos -	I'm on Fire (Recorded from soundboard on 10-26-94)	2CD's
Tori Amos -	Cornflake Girl (Recorded all over the world in 1992)	1CD
Beatles -	Texas 66 (Recorded live in Texas in 1966)	1CD
Beck -	Suicidal Jerk (Recorded live on 10-28-94)	1CD
Biohazard -	Last Night (From soundboard 12-22-94)	1CD
David Bowie -	BBC Bowie - Every BBC Appearance from 1969 - 1972	1CD
Candlebox -	A Light You'll Never Forget (Recorded Live on 11-10-94)	2 CD's
Eric Clapton -	We All Came Down to Montreaux (Live in Montreaux 12-7-86)	2 CD's
Elvis Costello -	No Dancing - (Recorded in the UK in 1979)	1CD
The Cranberries -	Fruits of our Labor (Live from soundboard NYC 12-17-94)	1CD
Sheryl Crow -	Las Vegas (Recorded Live from soundboard on 10-17-94 pt. 1)	1CD
Sheryl Crow -	All I Wanna Do (Recorded from soundboard on 10-17-94 pt. 2)	1CD

Cult -	Coming Down Live (Recorded from soundboard on 10-29-94)	1CD
Depeche Mode -	I Feel You (Recorded live in the USA 1992)	1CD
The Doors -	Somewhere in America - (Recorded in the USA in 1967)	1CD
Green Day -	Fuck You (Recorded Live at UMASS 11-28-94)	1CD
Green Day -	The Greenest Hits (Sndbrd. Chicago 1994+unreleased tracks!)	1CD
Guns N Roses -	Sweet Cow O' Mine (Live in Wisconsin in 1987)	1CD
Guns N Roses -	Welcome to the Horizon - (Horizon 10-31-87)	2CD's
Helmet -	Live Biscuits (Live from soundboard on 12-16-94)	1CD
Hole -	Dissed (Live from soundboard on 10-8-94)	1CD
Melissa Etheridge -	Melissa Part 1 (Recorded live on 12-11-94)	1CD
Melissa Etheridge -	Melissa Part 2 (Recorded live on 12-11-94)	1CD
Melissa Etheridge -	Melissa Part 3 (Recorded live on 12-11-94)	1CD
Elton John -	Sacrifice - (Recorded at Foxboro, Mass. 9-6-93)	1CD
Lenny Kravitz -	Flowerchild - (Recorded in Amsterdam 1993)	1CD
K.D. Lang -	Constant Craving - (Recorded live in Toronto, 1993)	1CD
Led Zeppelin -	Wizardry - (Recorded at Madison Square Garden, NY 7-28-73)	1CD
Led Zeppelin -	Stormy Blues - (recorded at Vancouver Canada 1970)	1CD
Led Zeppelin -	Dazed & Confused (recorded in London 6-24-69)	1CD
Led Zeppelin -	Tour Over Europe - (recorded in Switzerland 6-29-80)	1CD
Live -	Shit Town (Recorded live on 10-6-94)	1CD
Madonna -	Clowning Around - (Recorded in Europe 1990)	1CD
Madonna -	Vogue - (Recorded live in London 1993)	1CD
Metallica -	To Russia With Metallica (Recorded live in Europe 1993)	1CD
Moody Blues -	Question - (Recorded in Hollywood,CA 1986)	1CD
Nine Inch Nails -	Nassau '95 (Recorded at Nassau Coliseum 1-6-95)	1CD
Nirvana -	Heart Shaped Disk Volume 1,(Disk 1 of Box set Volume 1)	1CD
Nirvana -	Heart Shaped Disk Volume 2,(Disk 2 of Box set Volume 1)	1CD
Nirvana -	Heart Shaped Disk Volume 3,(Disk 3 of Box set Volume 1)	1CD
Nirvana -	Heart Shaped Disk Volume 4,(Disk 4 of Box set Volume 1)	1CD
Nirvana -	Heart Shaped Disk Volume 5,(Disk 1 of Box set Volume 2)	1CD
Nirvana -	Heart Shaped Disk Volume 6,(Disk 2 of Box set Volume 2)	1CD
Nirvana -	Heart Shaped Disk Volume 7,(Disk 4 of Box set Volume 2)	1CD
Offspring -	Live (Recorded at Roseland NYC on 10-25-94)	1CD
Page & Plant -	Live 95(Complete Rockline Interview+Rock N Roll Hall of Fame)	1CD
Pearl Jam -	Self Pollution Pt. 1(1-8-94 FM Broadcast - over 2 hours of Pearl Jam, Alice in Chains, Mud Honey & Fastbacks from Eddie's house.)	2CD's
Pearl Jam -	Self Pollution Pt. 2(1-8-94 FM Broadcast - over 2 hours of Pearl Jam, & SoundGarden live from Eddie Vedder's house.)	2CD's
Pearl Jam -	Best of Self Pollution (1-8-94 FM Broadcast- Best of Pearl Jam)	1CD
Pearl Jam -	Roseland (Recorded at Roseland on 11-12-91 &11-15-91)	1CD
Pearl Jam -	Rough Mixes - (The Rough Mixes for "Ten" CD 4-26-91)	1CD
Pearl Jam -	Alive - (Recorded live in Springfield, Mass. 4-6-94)	2CD's
Phish -	Good Times Bad Times (Live in Providence RI 12-29-94)	2CD's
Pink Floyd -	By Light of the Silvery Moon (Giants Stad. 7-18-94)	2CD's
The Pretenders -	Kid - (Recorded live in Chicago 1984)	1CD
Prince -	World Tour 1990	1CD
REM -	Old Man Kensey - (Recorded live in Utrecht 9-19-87)	1CD
REM -	Carnival of Sorts - (Recorded in Washington, DC 3-18-87)	1CD
REM -	Pilgrimage - (Recorded live in Los Angeles, CA 1989)	1CD
REM -	1994 (All new REM Live from soundboard in 1992,1993,1994!)	1CD
Rolling Stones -	VooDoo You (Live at Foxboro Stadium, MA 9-5-94)	2CD's
Rush -	Tom Sawyer - (Recorded live on the USA 1989)	1CD

Sound Garden -	Live at the Armory (New York City 6-17-94)	2CD's
Sting -	Little Wing - (Recorded live in the USA 1988)	1CD
Veruca Salt -	Live at the Chocolate Factory (Live in Seattle on 11-14-94)	1CD
Weezer -	Geezer (Recorded live on 12-4-94)	1CD
Neil Young -	Work Songs - (Live in Hamburg, Germany 12-8-89)	1CD

Box Sets Available Now!

Nirvana -	Heart Shaped Box Vol.1 Includes 4 CD's, 32 page photo booklet & 32 page song biography. Nirvana stickers! Comes in a Heart Shaped Box!
Nirvana -	Heart Shaped Box Vol. 2 Includes 4 CD's, 32 page photo booklet & 32 page song biography. Nirvana stickers! Comes in a Heart Shaped Box! Completely different than Volume 1.Both are a must for the serious collector!

Pearl Jam Coming Soon!!!

Exclusive Australian only fan club releases Featuring different and unreleased mixes from the Vitalogy sessions and unreleased recording of Pearl Jam from their rare and unreleased 1995 performances in Seattle, Montana & Washington, DC. Very rare & limited!

*Pearl Jam -Seattle 2-5-95	Pearl Jam - Last Exit	Pearl Jam - Betterman
*Pearl Jam -Seattle 2-6-95	Pearl Jam - Not For You	Pearl Jam - Aye Davanita
*Pearl Jam -Montana 2-8-95	Pearl Jam - Tremor christ	Pearl Jam - Immortality
*Pearl Jam -Osaka 2-21-95	Pearl Jam - Nothing Man	Pearl Jam - Hey foxymo-
*Pearl Jam -Melbourne3-16-95	Pearl Jam - Whipping	phandlemama, that's me
*Pearl Jam -Melbourne3-17-95	Pearl Jam - Bugs	
*Pearl Jam -Melbourne3-18-95	Pearl Jam - Corduroy	*=2 CD Set. These are Kiwi
*Pearl Jam -Tokyo 2-20-95	Pearl Jam - Satan's Bed	Releases. All others are 1CD.

Look for the rest of the Pearl Jam 1995 World Tour on CD — Only from Kiwi!!!!

Also Coming Soon!!!

Adam Ant -	(Recorded live on 5-18-95)	1CD
Beastie Boys -	(Recorded live in NY on 5-95)	1CD
Big Head Todd -	(Recorded live at the Palace on 2-5-95)	1CD
Blues Traveler -	(Recorded live from the soundboard 1994	1CD
Bush -	Now & Zen (Recorded Live at Club Babyhead, Providence, RI on 2-27-95)	1CD
The Cranberries -	Mother's Day 1995- (Recorded live on Mother's Day 5-15-95)	1CD
Sheryl Crow -	Unplugged, Plugged, & In the Studio	1CD
Sheryl Crow -	(Recorded live at The Beacon Theatre, NYC On St. Patrick's Day 3-17-95)	1CD
Sheryl Crow -	(Live at The Beacon Theatre, NYC 3-17-95 & The Palace 3-18-95)	1CD
Sheryl Crow -	(The Palace in New Haven 3-18-95)	1CD
Danzig -	(Recorded live from the soundboard 1995)	1CD
Dinosaur Jr. -	Homeboy (Recorded live from the soundboard 9/94)	1CD
Melissa Etheridge	The Complete Melissa Etheridge (1995 unplugged+Live soundboard Bonuses)	1CD
Extreme -	Extraordinary (The only 1995 club show of Extreme recorded on 3-15-95)	1CD
Fu Fighters -	(Features ex-Nirvana members Dave Grohl & Pat Smear) (Live in 1995)	1CD
Helmet -	Always Last (Recorded live on 2-11-95)	1CD
Hole -	Roseland Vol. 1 (Recorded live & loud at NYC's Roseland on 2-15-95)	1CD
Hole -	Roseland Vol. 2 (Recorded live at NYC's Roseland on 2-15-95 & 2-16-95)	1CD
Hole -	Roseland Vol. 3 (Recorded live & loud at NYC's Roseland on 2-16-95)	1CD
Jefferson Starship	(Recorded live on 2-18-95 at The Sting in New Britain)	1CD
King Krimson -	(Recorded live in NY on 6-95)	1CD
Lemon Heads -	Ugly Like Me (Recorded live in 1994)	1CD
Letters to Cleo -	Outtakes and Demos (Rare & Unreleased outtakes and demos)	1CD
Little Feat -	(Recorded live on 5-19-95)	1CD
Live -	Live (Recorded live on 2-11-95 at UMASS in Amherst, MA)	1CD

Live -	(Recorded Live at Western Conn. University, Danbury, CT on 2-12-95)		1CD
Love Spit Love -	Live Spit Live (1-13-95 a rare club performance)		1CD
Dave Matthew's Band -	Electric in New York (Recorded live in New York 1994)		2CD's
Dave Matthew's Band -	Acoustic in New York (Recorded live in New York 1995)		2CD's
Ned's Atomic Dustbin -	(Recorded live in 1995)		1CD
Nine Inch Nails -	(Recorded live in Worchester, MA 1995)		1CD
Nirvana -	Unedited Unplugged (The Complete 70 min performance—includes the 15		
	minutes of stage banter not included in the DGC release.)		1CD
Oasis -	(Recorded Live at Lupos in Providence, RI. 3-10-95)		1CD
Offspring -	Roseland (Recorded live on 3-3-95 at NYC's Roseland)		1CD
Offspring -	Roseland Revisited (Recorded live on 3-4-95 at NYC's Roseland)		1CD

Look for the **ENTIRE** Page/Plant 1995 American Tour on CD — Only from Kiwi!!!! All are 2CD's

Atlanta 2-28-95,3-1-95	Austin, TX	Philadelphia, PA	Memphis, TE
Miami, FLA	Dallas, TX	Meadowlands, NJ	Knoxville, TE
Orlando, FLA	Houston, TX	Boston, MA	New Orleans,LA

Pavement -	(Recorded live in 1995)		1CD
Pearl Jam -	Acoustic 1995 (Featuring a rare Australian Interview & the only acoustic		
	performance of 1995)		2CD's
Tom Petty -	Unplugged (The complete unplugged performance recorded on 2-95)		1CD
Tom Petty -	April Fools (Recorded live on 4-1-95)		1CD
Liz Phair -	(A rare & exclusive electric performance at NYC's Town Hall Theatre on 4-24-95) 1CD		
Matthew Sweet -	(Recorded live in 1995)		1CD

The **REM** 1995 American Tour on CD — Only from Kiwi!!!! All are 2CD's

Madison Square Garden 6-22-95	Madison Square Garden 6-23-95
Madison Square Garden 6-24-95	Great Woods, MA 6-16-95
Great Woods, MA 6-17-95	Great Woods, MA 6-18-95

Slash's Snakepit - (Slash from GNR's band. Recorded live in Providence, RI on 4-17-95)		1CD
Slayer/Biohazard/Machinehead - Valentine's Day Massacre (Recorded live on 7-14-95)		2CD's
Spin Doctors - New Stuff (Recorded live 3-9-95 features songs from the upcoming '95 CD!) 1CD		
STP	Vaseline (Recorded live in 1994)	1CD
Sugar -	Sweet (Recorded live in 1994)	1CD
Toad the Wet Sprocket - (Recorded live in 1995)		1CD
Throwing Muses - Recorded live in 1995)		1CD
Van Halen -	(Live in Jacksonville, FLA)	2CD's
Velocity Girl -	(Recorded live in 1995)	1CD
Veruca Salt -	(Recorded live at the New York Academy 3-24-95)	1CD
Violent Femmes - I Got a Machine (Recorded live in 1994)		1CD
Violent Femmes - This Side of Paradise (Recorded live in 1994)		1CD
Mike Watt -	Big Train (Recorded live in 1995)	1CD
Weezer -	Sneezer (A new 1995 show featuring new tunes! Roseland, NYC 2-28-95)	1CD

Box Sets Coming Soon!!!

Pearl Jam -	Voters for Choice Vol.I (Recorded on 1-14-95. Complete performances of Pearl Jam,
	Neil Young, L7 & Lisa Germano on audio. Neil Young +Pearl Jam on Video (3CD's +1 VHS+poster)
Pearl Jam -	Voters for Choice Vol.I (Recorded on 1-15-95. Complete performances of Pearl Jam,
	Neil Young, L7 & Lisa Germano on audio. Neil Young +Pearl Jam on Video (3CD's +1 VHS+poster)
Grateful Dead -	3 from the Vault (4 CD+ Poster) Four hours at the Lyceum, London 5-26-72
Phish -	The White Album (4 CD)Their complete performance on 10-31-94. 4.5 Hours of
	Phish and the entire Beatles' White Album + Cool Poster!)
Nirvana -	Heart Shape Box 3 (4CD) color booklet vol. 3, vol. 1 of Lyrics to every Cobain song,
	Soundboard concerts spanning their entire career, more cool stickers!
Nirvana -	Heart Shape Box 3 (4CD) color booklet vol. 4, vol. 2 of Lyrics to every Cobain song,
	More soundboard concerts spanning their entire career, more cool stickers!

R A R E   V I D E O
S A L E

Hello Collectors! Welcome to P. Grant's latest Video Offering. All tapes are VHS (American System-NTSC). Foreign customers, if you need PAL or SECAM conversions, add $10. 00 per tape extra. All tapes are fully guaranteed. If you have a problem, please return it within 7 days for an exchange.

When writing to us, if you would like a reply, please include a self-addressed, stamped envelope. We ship a.s.a.p. but please allow 2-4 weeks delivery.

Payment for all tapes is $30.00 each, postal money orders only, in U.S. funds only. Postage is as follows: U.S. postage $3.00 1st Class + $1.00 each additional tape; Canada $5.00 + $2.00 each additional tape; Europe Airmail $12.00 + $5.00 each additional tape; Japan $15.00 + $7.00 each additional tape. We do not accept personal checks any longer. We will, however, accept payment in cash. Postal Money Orders can be purchased at your local Post Office for 75 cents in the U.S. and Canada. Hot Wacks customers, mention Hot Wacks and deduct $2.00 from your order. Thank you.

P. Grant - 332 Bleecker Street, #E28, New York, NY 10014 USA - TEL (212) 330-8149

ABBA COMPILATION 1976-79 PRO 110 MIN
ABBA BIOGRAPHY 74-82 PRO 60 MIN
ABBA REBOJNE 2HRS PS
AC/DC CLEVELAND 1978 PRO 30 MIN.
AC/CD TORONTO 1990 2 HRS.
AC/DC JAPAN 81 PRO 50 MIN
AC/DC LONDON 78 PRO 90 MIN
ACOUSTIC SET W/C CROW/B DIDDLEY/R CRAY 160 MINPS
AEROSMITH NEW YORK 1990 100 MIN.
AEROSMITH NEW HAVEN CT. 1989 100 MIN.
AEROSMITH LARGO 1980 PRO 90 MIN
AEROSMITH HOUSTON 1977 PRO 2 HRS.
AEROSMITH SAN FRANCISCO '88 & PHILLY '90 PRO 2 HRS.
AEROSMITH NJ 9/11/93 110 MIN.
AEROSMITH RIO 1994 PRO 120 MIN
AEROSMITH HOUSTON 7/24/77 PRO 75 MIN
AEROSMITH HOUSTON 7/25/77 PRO 75 MIN
AEROSMITH JONES BEACH 9/4/93/110 MIN
AEROSMITH WOODSTOCK '94 115 MIN PS
AFGAN WHIGS SAN DIEGO '94 75 MIN HH
ALICE IN CHAINS RIO 93/OAK 92 PRO 2HRS
ALICE IN CHAINS SEATTLE 90 PRO 60 MIN
ALICE IN CHAINS WASH. 89 2 HRS
ALICE IN CHAINS MICH. 91 70 MIN
ALICE IN CHAINS ROTTERDAM '93 90 MIN
ALIEN SEX FIEND LONDON 1983 PRO 45 MIN.
G.G. ALLIN BLEEDIN' STINKIN' & DRINKIN' TAMPA 1991 60 MIN PS
G.G. ALLIN TEXAS 92 110 MIN.
G.G. ALLIN ASBURY PARK 1991 90 MIN
GREG ALLMAN -ONE WAY OUT- NASHVILLE '88 PRO 1 HR.
ALLMAN BROTHERS JONES BEACH NY '90 2 HRS. 20 MINS.
ALLMAN BROTHERS FILLMORE EAST 1970 PRO 45 MINS.
ALLMAN BROTHERS MT. VIEW CA. 1989 PRO 90 MIN.
ALLMAN BROTHERS JONES BEACH 9/4/'91 2 HRS. 20 MINS.
ALLMAN BROTHERS RARITIES 72-82 PRO 1 HR.
ALLMAN BROTHERS JAPAN 1992 PRO 65 MINS.
ALLMAN BROTHERS CRESTED BUTTE, COLORADO 2/23/'91 FULL SHOW 2 HRS. 30 MINS.
ALLMAN BROTHERS UNPLUGGED NY UNCUT PRO 90 MIN.
ALLMAN BROTHERS BEACON THEATRE NYC 3/'92 2 HRS.
ALLMAN BROTHERS BEACON, NYC 4/1/94
ALLMAN BROTHERS WOODSTOCK '94 90 MIN PS
TORI AMOS PALM BEACH, FL 8/16/92 90 MIN
TORI AMOS ALBANY 92 100 MIN.
TORI AMOS DAVID LETTERMAN REHEARSALS 40 MIN PS
TORI AMOS SYMPHONY SPACE NYC 3/30/94/91 MIN
TORI AMOS WASHINGTON D.C. 4/27/94 90 MIN HH
ANDERSON, WAKEMAN, BRUFORD, HOWE -JONES BEACH '89
JOHN ANDERSON CHILE '94 60 MIN PS
ANDERSON, WAKEMAN, BRUFORD, HOWE -'89 REHEARSALS ANTHRAX
ALBANY & PHILLY 1991 2 HRS.
ANTHRAX HOUSTON, TX 5/5/94 90 MIN
BABES IN TOYLAND MILWAUKEE 91 60 MIN
BAD BRAINS LONG BEACH, CA 11/22/89 90 MIN
BAD BRAINS LONDON 1989 60 MIN.
BAD BRAINS THE EDGE, FT. LAUDRDL, FL 11/30/93 71 MIN
BAD RADIO W/EDDIE VEDDER SAN DIEGO 89 60 MIN
BAND JAPAN 1984 PRO 2 HRS.
BANGLES COLLECTION PRO 2 HRS
BAUHAUS LONDON 1983 PRO 75 MINS.
BAUHAUS SHADOW OF LIGHT PRO 40 MINS.
BAUHAUS ARCHIVES PRO 40 MINS.
BEACH BOYS WASHINGTON, D.C. 1976 PRO 1HR
BEASTIE BOYS MIAMI 5/29/92 90 MIN

BEASTIE BOYS LAS VEGAS '94 70 MIN HH
BEASTIE BOYS WASHINGTON D.C. 5/28/94 90 MIN HH
BEATLES BEST OF 1963 PRO 30 MINS.
BEATLES BEST OF 1964 PT. 1 PRO 1 HR.
BEATLES BEST OF 1964 PT. 2 PRO 1 HR.
BEATLES BEST OF 1965 PRO 1 HR.
BEATLES BEST OF 1966 PRO 1 HR.
BEATLES BEST OF 1967 PRO 1 HR.
BEATLES BACKTRAX - THE VIDEO! (FAB BOX) PRO 1 HR.
BEATLES BACKTRAX 2 PRO 1 HR.
BEATLES JUDO ARENA PRO 45 MINS.
BEATLES LET IT BE (ORIGINAL FILM)
BEATLES LET IT BE OUTTAKES PRO 1 HR.
BEATLES LET IT BE OUTTAKES VOL. 2 PRO 60 MIN
BEATLES ED SULLIVAN PRO 90 MIN.
BEATLES UNSURPASSED VIDEOS PRO 90 MINS.
BEATLES UNSURPASSED VIDEOS VOL. 2 PRO 90 MINS.
BEATLES UNSURPASSED VIDEOS VOL. 3 PRO 90 MIN
BEATLES MAGICAL MYSTERY TOUR PRO 60 MIN.
BEATLES LET IT BE OUTTAKES VOL. 2 PRO 60 MIN.
AROUND THE BEATLES AND BIG NIGHT OUT PRO 40 MINS.
JEFF BECK MILAN, ITALY 1 HR. 1989
JEFF BECK & SANTANA JAPAN 1987 PRO 1 HR.
JEFF BECK COLLECTION 2 HRS
BELLY LONDON '92-'93 110 MIN
BIG BLACK COLLECTION 2 HRS
BIG BLACK PIG PILE 80 MIN PS
BIOHAZARD L'AMOURS 1993 PRO 60 MIN
BLACK CROWES HARTFORD CT./NASSAU NY 1990 90 MINS.
BLACK CROWES BEACON THEATRE NYC 8/'92 2 HRS.
BLACK CROWES COMPILATION PRO 100 MIN
BLACK CROWES GERMANY 93 PRO 70 MIN
BLACK FLAG SAN FRANCISCO 84 PRO 1HR
BLACK SABBATH COLLECTION PRO 90 MIN.
BLACK SABBATH PARIS 70/BEAT CLUB '70-72 PRO 70 MIN.
BLACK SABBATH NEVER SAY DIE 1978 PRO 1 HR.
BLACK SABBATH BEACON THEATER NYC AUGUST 1992
BLACK SABBATH CAL 92 100 MIN
BLACK SABBATH RARITIES VOL. 1 PRO 2 HRS
BLONDIE COLLECTION PRO 2 HRS.
BLIND MELON WOODSTOCK '94 70 MIN PS
BODY COUNT CBGB'S NY 8/14/91 2 HRS
BODY COUNT CHICAGO 92 100 MIN
BON JOVI BUFFALO, NY 140 MIN PS
BON JOVI JAPAN 1985 PRO 45 MIN.
BON JOVI TOKYO 12/31/88 PRO 2 HRS.
BOOTSY'S NEW RUBBER BAND JAPAN '93 80 MIN PS
DAVID BOWIE MARQUEE 1973 PRO 1 HR. (1980 FLOOR SHOW)
DAVID BOWIE JAPAN 1990 PRO 2 HRS.
DAVID BOWIE VANCOUVER 1990 PRO 90 MIN.
DAVID BOWIE BRAZIL 1990 PRO 1 HR.
BREEDERS READING FESTIVAL 1993 45 MIN
BREEDERS NEW ORLEANS 93 + FL 93 90 MIN
KATE BUSH THE COLLECTION (FAB BOX) PRO 75 MIN.
KATE BUSH HAMMERSMITH 79 PRO 60 MIN
BUTTHOLE SURFERS DETROIT 2/22/85 PRO 70 MINS.
BUZZCOCKS LIVE LEGENDS 50 MIN PS
BUZZCOCKS GERMANY 81 PRO 60 MIN
BYRDS COLLECTION VOLUME 2 PRO 90 MIN
BYRDS COLLECTION PRO 90 MIN.
CHEAP TRICK CHICAGO 1993 PRO 1 HR.
CHEAP TRICK DKRC 76 PRO 30 MIN.
CINCINNATI POP FESTIVAL 1970 W/GRAND FUNK, TRAFFIC & IGGY AND THE
STOOGES & ALICE COOPER 90 MIN PS

RARE VIDEO SALE

CLAPTON NASSAU NY 8/'90 2 HRS. 15 MIN.
CLAPTON OGWT 1977 PRO 1 HR.
CLAPTON M.S.G. 1990 1 HR. 45 MIN.
CLAPTON SAT. NIGHT LIVE REHEARSALS '90 PRO 70 MIN.
ERIC CLAPTON S.N.L. REHEARSAL 1990 120 MIN PS
ERIC CLAPTON CRADEL REHEARSALS 9/28/94 60 MIN PS
CLAPTON RIO '89 & ROYAL ALBERT HALL '91 PRO 1 HR.
CLAPTON ROYAL ALBERT HALL 1990 PRO 1 HR.
CLAPTON PHILADELPHIA 5/4/'92 2 1/2 HRS.
CLAPTON'S ROLLING HOTEL (RARE) PRO 1 HR.
CLASH NEW JERSEY 1979 B/W PRO 75 MIN.
COVERDALE-PAGE OSAKA, JAPAN 12/21/93 120 MIN
COVERDALE/PAGE JAPAN 12/20/93 120 HH
CONCRETE BLONDE TORONTO 1993 100 MIN
CONCRETE BLONDE MAINE 89/MILW 87 140 MIN.
COUNTING CROWS ROME 4/18/94 90 MIN.
ALICE COOPER LIVE TRASH NEW YORK 1990 90 MIN.
ALICE COOPER A STRANGE CASE 1978 PRO 75 MIN.
ELVIS COSTELLO ROCKPALAST 1983 PRO 90 MIN.
ELVIS COSTELLO C.W. POST NY 1989 2 HRS. 15 MIN.
ELVIS COSTELLO JAPAN 1987 & UNPLUGGED PRO 80 MIN.
COSTELLO JONES BEACH 6/11/94 120 MIN HH
ELVIS COSTELLO UNPLUGGED UNEDITED PRO 1 HR.
GEORGE CLINTON/PINK FLOYD RITZ NYC '89 120 MIN PS
CRACKER CARBONDALE, IIL. 2/26/94 85 MIN
CREAM'S FAREWELL CONCERT PRO 50 MIN.
CREAM FRESH LIVE CREAM PRO 74 MIN.
CREEDANCE CLEARWATER LONDON PRO 30 MIN.
JOE CROCKER WOODSTOCK '94 75 MIN PS
CROSBY, STILLS & YOUNG SAN FRANCISCO 1991 1 HR.
CROSBY, STILLS, & NASH WOODSTOCK '94 90 MIN PS
CULT TORONTO 1990 100 MIN.
CULT LYCEUM 1987 PRO 60 MIN
CULT MEXICO '91 90 MIN PS
CURE LIVE IN JAPAN 1984 PRO 90 MIN.
CURE RIO 1987 PRO 45 MIN.
CURE BELGIUM 1990 2 HRS.
CURE LONDON 1991 2 HRS.
CURE ON STAGE OFF STAGE PRO 2 HRS.
CURE NEW ORLEANS 6/8/'92 2 HRS.
CURE KILBURN 92 PRO 65 MIN
CYCLE SLUTS FROM HELL NEW YORK 88 30 MIN
DANCE CRAZE SKA MOVIE PRO 90 MIN.
DANZIG ENGLAND 1988 40 MIN.
DANZIG MILAN 92 85 MIN
DANZIG SACRAMENTO 1992 90 MIN
DANZIG THE RITZ, NYC 5/21/93 85 MIN
DEAD KENNEDYS SAN FRANCISCO 84 PRO 2 HRS
DEEP PURPLE DENMARK 1972 PRO 2 HRS.
DEEP PURPLE LIVE 1970 COLOR PRO 30 MIN.
DEEP PURPLE ROYAL ALBERT HALL 1969 PRO 1 HR.
DEEP PURPLE CAL JAM 74/JAPAN 75 PRO 100 MIN
DEEP PURPLE CZECHOSLOVAKIA 92 PRO 2 HRS.
DEF LEPPARD GERMANY 1992
DEF LEPPARD THE INTERVIEWS PRO 1 HR.
DEPECHE MODE PHILLY 1990 2 HRS.
DEPECHE MODE ROTTERDAM 1990 100 MIN.
DEPECHE MODE ST. PETE, FLA. 10/3/93 60 MIN.
DEPECHE MODE ORLANDO 10/5/93 115 MIN.
DEPECHE MODE MIAMI 10/2/93 115 MIN
DEPECHE MODE MIAMI 5/31/90 106 MIN.
DINOSAUR JR U-MASS 1986 PR0 30 MIN
DINOSAUR JR AUSTIN, TX 2/8/92 75 MIN.
DINOSAUR JR ENGLAND 10/4/91 75 MIN HH
DINOSAUR JR READING FESTIVAL 1993 60 MIN
DIRE STRAITS NY 1992 2 HRS. 15 MIN.
DISCHARGE LIVE IN JAPAN 30 MIN PS
D.O.A SANFRANCISCO 11/20/90 90 MIN PS
DOORS DANISH TV SPECIAL PRO 30 MIN.
DOORS CRITIQUE PRO 30 MIN.
DOORS FEAST OF FRIENDS PRO 40 MIN.
DOORS EUROPEAN DOCUMENTARY 120 MIN PS
DREAM THEATER SAN FRANCISCO 6/5/93 90 MIN.
D.R.I. MIAMI BEACH THEATER 12/3/94 45 MIN
DURAN DURAN SING BLUE SILVER PRO 90 MIN
DURAN DURAN MIAMI 11/20/93 110 MIN.
DURAN DURAN CHILE '93 PRO 60 MIN
DURAN DURAN RARITIES PRO 2 HRS.
BOB DYLAN WEST POINT 1990 90 MIN
BOB DYLAN WEST POINT '94 80 MIN HH
BOB DYLAN WOODSTOCK '94 90 MIN PS
BOB DYLAN HARD RAIN LIVE 1976 PRO 1 HR.
BOB DYLAN HARD RAIN ALTERNATE VERS.PRO 1 HR.
BOB DYLAN CANADA 1964 PRO 30 MIN.
BOB DYLAN EAT THE DOCUMENT PRO 75 MIN.
BOB DYLAN RENALDO & CLARA PT. 1 PRO 2 HRS.
BOB DYLAN RENALDO & CLARA PT. 2 PRO 2 HRS.
BOB DYLAN BALTIMORE 1990 90 MIN.
BOB DYLAN JONES BEACH 1989 90 MIN.
BOB DYLAN JONES BEACH 1991 90 MIN.
BOB DYLAN UNSURPASSED VIDEOS VOL. 1 PRO 90 MIN.
BOB DYLAN UNSURPASSED VIDEOS VOL. 2 PRO 90 MIN.
BOB DYLAN MIAMI 9/22/93 60 MIN
BOB DYLAN W. PALM BEACH 9/23/93 99 MIN
BOB DYLAN PEORIA, IL 4/13/94 110 MIN
BOB DYLAN/G. DEAD BUFFALO, NY 7/12/87 PRO 60 MIN
BOB DYLAN/GRATEFUL DEAD FOXBOR 1987 60 MIN PS
BOB DYLAN/GRATEFUL DEAD WASHINGTON 1987 60 MIN PS
EAGLES DENVER 6/14/94 120 MIN HH
EAGLES MTV CONCERT CALIF '94 120 MIN PS

EAGLES SEATTLE 76 PRO 100 MIN
ECHO AND THE BUNNYMEN COLLECTION PRO 1 HR.
EINSTURZENDE NEUBAUTEN CHICAGO 84 PRIV. 60 MIN
ELP PICTURES AT AN EXHIBITION PRO 75 MIN.
ELP MANTICORE TOUR 1973 PRO 50 MIN.
ELP MEXICO 4/20/93 90 MIN HH
ELP JONES BEACH NY 7/92 2 HRS.
ELP CAL JAM 1973 AND U.K. 1971 PRO 2 HRS
ELP MONTREAL 1977 PRO 2 HRS.
ELP JAPAN 7/22/72 PRO 90 MIN.
ELP ITALY 1993 PRO 60 MIN.
ELP CAL JAM 1973 & UK PRO 2 HRS.
ELP RADIO CITY, NY 2/93 2 HRS.
ELP VERONA, ITALY 9/26/92 2 HRS
ELP BEACON THEATRE, NYC 6/1/92 60 MIN & T.V. INTERVIEW &
PERFORMANCE REGIS & KATHY LEE SHOW
BRIAN ENO 72-89 PRO 120 MIN
ERASURE INNOCENTS (COLLECTION) PRO 60 MIN
EXPLOITED LIVE 1983-1987 45 MIN PS
EXPLOITED SEXUAL FAVOURS 60 MIN PS
MELISSA ETHERIDGE SPAIN 1990 PRO 1 HR.
MELISSA ETHERIDGE COLLECTION PRO 75 MIN.
MELISSA ETHERIDGE NYC 2/19/92 I HR. 30 MIN.
MELISSA ETHERIDGE GERMAN TV 1993 PRO 60 MIN.
MELISSA ETHERIDGE JONES BEACH 7/10/94 120 MIN HH
MELISSA ETHERIDGE WOODSTOCK '94 60 MIN PS
EXODUS MIAMI BEACH THEATER 12/3/92 39 MIN
EXTREME MIDDLETOWN NY 9/11/91 1 HR.
EXTREME RIO 92 PRO 90 MIN
FAITH NO MORE RIO 1991 PRO 40 MIN.
FAITH NO MORE SAN FRANCISCO '93 100 MIN HH
FIGHT LIMELIGHT, NY 1/16/94 80 MIN
FIGHT JAPAN '94 85 MIN PS
FISHBONE SAN FRANCISCO 92 PRO 90 MIN
FISHBONE MIAMI, FL 11/29/91 75 MIN
FLEETWOOD MAC NEW YORK 1990 100 MIN.
FLEETWOOD MAC COLLECTION '73-80 PRO 1 HR.
ACE FREHLEY LIVE 1990 75 MIN.
ROBERT FRIPP STRING QUARTER JAPAN '92 PRO 100 MIN
FRIPP/SYLVIAN JAPAN 10/26/93 120 MIN
FUGAZI MILWAUKEE 1989 75 MIN.
FUGAZI WASHINGTON 7/25/92 70 MIN
PETER GABRIEL ROCKPALAST 1977 PRO 90 MIN.
PETER GABRIEL NEW YORK 93 70 MIN
PETER GABRIEL JAPAN 86 PRO 2 HRS
PETER GABRIEL ROME 5/18/93 2 HRS
PETER GABRIEL ITALY 6/1/94 105 MIN PS
PETER GABRIEL GERMANY 4/20/93 2 HRS.
PETER GABRIEL WOODSTOCK '94 50 MIN PS
JERRY MSG 11/15/91 135 MIN.
JERRY GARCIA PROVIDENCE 11/1193 115 MIN HH
GASLIGHT SPECIAL W/PHIL LYNOTT & RICK WAKEMAN '83 PRO GENESIS
MONTREAL 1974 PRO 1 HR.
GENESIS PROMOS 1971 - LIVE 1973 PRO 1 HR.
GENSIS NASSAU 81 PRO 60 MIN
GENSIS RARITIES VOLUME 1 PRO 90 MIN
GO'S GO'S GERMANY '81 60 MIN
GONG LIVE 50 MIN PS
GRAND FUNK LA 1974 PRO 50 MIN.
GRATEFUL DEAD ALPINE VALLEY 7/19/89 90 MIN PS
GRATEFUL DEAD MADISON SQ GARDEN 9/18/93 90 MIN HH
GRATEFUL DEAD NEW YEAR'S 85-86 PRO 2 HRS.
GRATEFUL DEAD NASSAU NY 1990 PART 1 100 MIN.
GRATEFUL DEAD NASSAU NY 1990 PART 2 100 MIN.
GRATEFUL DEAD OREGON 8/27/72 80 MIN PS
GRATEFUL DEAD OAKLAND 12/31/87 120 MIN PS
GRATEFUL DEAD HARTFORD 1990 150 MIN.
GRATEFUL DEAD ROCKPALAST 1981 PRO 100 MIN.
GRATEFUL DEAD MSG 9/14/90 100 MIN.
GRATEFUL DEAD MSG 9/15/90 100 MIN.
GRATEFUL DEAD MSG 9/19/90 100 MIN.
GRATEFUL DEAD MSG 9/20/90 100 MIN.
GRATEFUL DEAD STOCKHOLM SWEDEN 1990 110 MIN.
GRATEFUL DEAD WEST GERMANY 1990 2 HRS.
GREATEFUL DEAD ROOSEVELT STADIUM NJ1976 90 MIN.
GRATEFUL DEAD PARIS 1990 2 HRS.
GRATEFUL DEAD VIRGINIA 1989 2 HRS.
GRATEFUL DEAD WEMBLY 1990 2 HRS.
GRATEFUL DEAD NASSAU COLISEUM 3/91 100 MIN.
GRATEFUL DEAD GIANTS STADIUM 6/17/91 1 110 MIN.
GRATEFUL DEAD GIANTS STADIUM 6/17/91 2 110 MIN.
GRATEFUL DEAD MOUNTAIN VIEW CA 1989 PRO 100 MIN.
GRATEFUL DEAD PHILLY 1990 2 HRS.
GRATEFUL DEAD MSG 9/91 PT. 1 2 HRS.
GRATEFUL DEAD MSG 9/91 PT. 2 2 HRS.
GRATEFUL DEAD NASSAU NY 3/92 PART 1 1 HR.
GRATEFUL DEAD NASSAU NY3/92 PART 2 2 HRS.
GRATEFUL DEAD/STEVE MILER LAS VEGAS 5/3/92 2 HRS.
GRATEFUL DEAD TEMPE, AZ 92 90 MIN
GRATEFUL DEAD DENVER 92 90 MIN
GRATEFUL DEAD TEMPE AZ 92 90 MIN
GRATEFUL DEAD COLLECTION 69-72 PRO 2 HRS.
GRATEFUL DEAD OAKLAND 7/24/84 PRO 100 MIN
GREEN DAY TAMPA '91 90 MIN
GREEN DAY WOODSTOCK '94 40 MIN PS
GUNS N' ROSES 1988 UNCENSORED RITZ PRO 75 MIN.
GUNS N' ROSES FELT FORUM 1988 100 MIN.
GUNS N' ROSES RIO 1/20/91 PRO 100 MIN
GUNS N' ROSES RIO 1/23/91 PRO 65 MIN

MORE RARE VIDEO —>

RARE VIDEO SALE

GUNS N' ROSES RIO 1991 SECOND SHOW PRO 1 HR
GUNS N' ROSES THE ROXY LA 1986 PRO 2 HRS.
GUNS N' ROSES INDIANA 1991 PRO 2 HRS. 15 MIN.
GUNS N' ROSES NASSAU COLISEUM NY 1991 110 MIN.
GUNS N' ROSES PARIS 1992 PRO 2 1/2 HRS.
GUNS N' ROSES ARGENTINA (12/92 PRO 2HRS 30 MIN)
GUNS N ROSES ARGENTINA 7/93 PRO 100 MIN.
GUNS N' ROSES RITZ, NY 1991 90 MIN
GUNS N' ROSES OKLAHOMA 92 PRO 3 HRS
GUNS N' ROSES CHICAGO 92 PRO 3 HRS
GUNS N' ROSES CHILE 1993 PRO 110 MIN
GUNS N' ROSES HARTFORD 3/9/93 110 MIN
GWAR NY 88/WASH 88
HANOI ROCKS 'ALL THOSE WASTED YEARS LIVE AT THE MARQUEE CLUB
'90 MIN PS
GEORGE HARRISON & ERIC CLAPTON JAPAN 91 2 HRS 30 MIN
JULIANA HATFIELD PHILA. 8/4/93 50 MIN
HEART NEW YORK 1990 100 MIN.
HEART COLLECTION PRO 2 HRS.
HEART COLLECTION VOL. 2 PRO 2 HRS.
HEART STUDIO REHEARSALS 1985 PRO 90 MIN.
HEART STUDIO REHEARSALS PT. 2 PRO 90 MIN.
HEART N.Y.C. 11/20/93 BEACON THEATER 95 MIN
HEART WASHINGTON '76 70 MIN PS
HEAVY METAL THE MOVIE
HELMUT HOUSTON 5/16/93 100 MIN
JIMI HENDRIX RARITIES PRO 1 HR.
JIMI HENDRIX RARITIES VOL. 2 100 MIN
JIMI HENDRIX SWEDEN 1969 PRO 1 HR.
JIMI HENDRIX ISLE OF WIGHT 1970 PRO 1 HR.
JIMI HENDRIX SEE MY MUSIC TALKING PRO 2 HRS.
JIMI HENDRIX BAND OF GYPSIES NY '69 PRO 2 HRS.
JIMI HENDRIX ATLANTA POP FESTIVAL 1970 PRO 1 HR.
JIMI HENDRIX COMPLETE WOODSTOCK PRO 90 MIN.
JIMI HENDRIX ROYAL ALBERT HALL 1969 PRO 1 HR.
ROBYN HITCHCOCK MARQUEE 1986 PRO 70 MIN.
ROBYN HITCHCOCK DETROIT 88 2 HRS
HOLE TORONTO/NY '91 70 MIN HH
IAN HUNTER & MICK RONSON ROCKS COLLECTION PRO
IAN HUNTER & RONSON STOCKHOLM & NYC '81 PRO 100 MIN.
IT'S CLEAN IT JUST LOOKS DIRTY VARIOUS ARTISTS (HUSKERDU, PTV,
SWANS) 60 MIN PS
HUSKER DU PATIO CLUB 85 70 MIN
BILLY IDOL WEMBLY 1990 PRO 90 MIN
ICE T & BODY COUNT CHICAGO 92
BILLY IDOL WEMBLEY 1990 PRO 90 MIN.
IRON MAIDEN ALBANY 1991 2 HRS.
IRON MAIDEN LONDON 1980 PRO 30 MIN.
IRON MAIDEN MEXICO '91 90 MIN PS
IRON MAIDEN NEW HAVEN 1991 90 MIN.
IRON MAIDEN ITALY 92 PRO 85 MIN.
JANET JACKSON JAPAN 1990 PRO 75 MIN.
JANET JACKSON JONES BEACH 6/27/94 120 MIN HH
JANET JACKSON JONES BEACH 6/28/94 120 MIN HH
JANET JACKSON PEORIA, IL. 2/8/94 110 MIN
MICHAEL JACKSON GERMAN TV SPECIAL '92 PRO 70 MIN.
JANES ADDICTION AMSTERDAM 3/17/91 80 MIN HH
JANES ADDICTION SANTA BARBARA CA '89 75 MIN.
JANES ADDICTION SANTA BARBARA CA 89 75 MIN
JANES ADDICTION DETROIT 1989 PRO 70 MIN.
JANES ADDICTION RITZ 1990 1 HR
JANES ADDICTION NEW YORK 1990 1 HR.
JANES ADDICTION HOUSTON 1989 70 MIN.
JANES ADDICTION ITALY 1991 PRO 80 MIN.
JANES ADDICTION MILWAUKEE 1990 90 MIN.
JANES ADDICTION TROY, NY 1992 2 HRS.
JANES ADDICTION HAWAII 1991 1 HR. (LAST EVER)
JAPAN COMPILATION PRO 120 MIN
JELLYFISH GERMANY 1992 PRO 60 MIN
JEFFERSON AIRPLANE SAN FRANCISCO 70 PRO 2 HRS
JEFFERSON STARSHIP "DEEP SPACE 94" 1/4/94 CHURCH ST. STA.
ORLANDO, FL 83 MIN
JESUS LIZARDWASHINGTON, DC 92 1 HR
JESUS MARY CHAIN ITALY '92 PRO 60 MIN
JETHRO TULL ALBANY NY 11/91 90 MIN
JETHRO TULL NYC 10/'92 90 MIN.
JETHRO TULL ENGLAND 5/26/93 100 MIN.
JETHRO TULL TURKEY 7/13/91 PRO MIN
JESUS AND MARYCHAIN ITALY 4/92
JOAN JETT LIVE ON BROADWAY 75 MIN.
JOAN JETT COLLECTION PRO 2 HRS.
JOAN JETT DU BEAT E.O. RARE PUNK FILM 90 MIN PS
JOAN JETT WEST POINT, NY 3/3/'90 75 MIN.
JOAN JETT MIDDLETOWN, NY 11/23/'91 80 MIN.
JOAN JETT MEXICO 12/12/91 90 MIN PS
JOAN JETT BALTIMORE 1/'92 90 MIN
JOAN JETT JETT AGE JAPANESE COLLECTION PRO 1 HR.
JOAN JETT TORONTO, CANADA 7/10/93 90 MIN
JOAN JETT T.V. SPECIALS AUG. '94 60 MIN PS
BILLY JOEL JAPAN 1991 PRO 1 HR.
BILLY JOEL MSG 10/14/93 100 MIN.
BILLY JOEL MSG 10/4/93 100 MIN
BILLY JOEL GERMANY '94 120 MIN PS
BILLY JOEL NASSAU COLISEUM '94 100 MIN
ELTON JOHN NYC 1992 2 HRS.
ELTON JOHN COLLECTION PRO 2 HRS.
ELTON JOHN CRAZY WORLD 60 MIN PS
ELTON JOHN BEST OF PRO 2 HRS.
ELTON JOHN/BILLY JOEL WASH. D.C. 7/20/94 I 120 MIN HH

ELTON JOHN/BILLY JOLE WASH. D.C. 7/20/94 II 120 MIN HH
JANIS JOPLIN COLLECTION (JAPAN)
JOURNEY SOUNDSTAGE 1978 PRO 1 HR.
JOURNEY HOUSTON 82 PRO 90 MIN
JOURNEY COMPILATION PRO 90 MIN
JOY DIVISION COLLECTION PRO 1 HR.
JOY DIVISION HERE ARE THE YOUNG MEN PRO 60 MIN
JUDAS PRIEST TORONTO 1990 2 HRS.
KING CRIMSON JAPAN PRO 90 MIN.
KING DIAMOND HOUSTON 1989 90 MIN.
KINGS OF INDEPENDENCE PRO 40 MIN.
KINKS COMPILATION #1 PRO 90 MIN.
KINKS OGWT 1977 PRO 75 MIN.
KINKS BIOGRAPHY 1964-1984 PRO 75 MIN.
KISS BRAZIL 8/27/94 105 MIN HH
KISS BRAZIL 8/26/94 100 MINHH
KISS BRAZIL, SO. AMER. '94 PS
KISS THOSE COMP. 120 MIN PS
KISS THE COLLECTION PRO 90 MIN.
KISS THE COLLECTION VOL. 2 PRO 75 MIN.
KISS THE COLLECTION VOL. 3 PRO 1 HR.
KISS THE COLLECTION VOLUME 4 2 HRS.
KISS JAPAN 1977 PRO 45 MIN.
KISS DETROIT 1975 PRO 45 MIN.
KISS NASHVILLE, TN '94 90 MIN HH
KISS NEW YORK 1990 100 MIN.
KISS THE INTERVIEWS PRO 1 HR.
KISS DETROIT 1990 PRO 100 MIN.
KISS ANAHEIM CA 1976 PRO 70 MIN.
KISS THE DYNASTY FILE 2 HRS.
KISS CREATURES OF THE NIGHT FILE 2 HRS.
KISS THE ELDER FILE 2 HRS.
KISS UNMASKED FILE PRO 2 HRS.
KISS BOSTON, MA 1992 1 HR.
KISS THE RITZ NYC 5/'92 90 MIN.
KISS WEMBLEY 1992 90 MIN.
KISS A VISUAL EVOLUTION PRO 1 HR.
KISS SYDNEY AUSTRALIA '90 PRO 2 HRS.
KISS WINTERLAND 74 PRO B/W 75 MIN
KISS COLLECTION VOL. 5 PRO 2 HRS
KISS COLLECTION VOL. 6 PRO 2 HRS
KISS OAKLAND 92 2 HRS
KISS SAN BERNANDINO 92 2 HRS.
KISS LOS ANGELES 93 40 MIN.
KISS LARGO 7/8/79 PRO 100 MIN.
KISS HOUSTON 9/2/77 PRO 100 MIN.
KISS DETROIT 1992 PRO 120 MIN
KISS CHICAGO 1994 75 MIN
KISS KISS THIS PRO 120 MIN
KISS KISS THESE PRO 60 MIN
KISS ME SPECIAL VOLUME 1 PRO 120 MIN
KISSTORY VOLUME 1 PRO 120 MIN
KIX BALTIMORE, MD 7/4/'91 90 MIN.
KMFDM DALLAS 1/28/90 60 MIN PS
KMFDM MILWAUKEE 4/13/91 80 MIN.
LENNY KRAVITZ ITALY 91 PRO 90 MIN
LENNY KRAVITZ ESSEN, GERMANY '93 100 MIN
LENNY KRAVITZ PINK POP FESTIVAL 1993 PRO 60 MIN
L7 COLLECTION 2 HRS.
L7 ITALY 6/91 PRO 1 HR.
K.D. LANG UK 1990 PRO 60 MIN.
LED ZEPPELIN ROYAL ALBERT HALL (FAB BOX) PRO 1 HR.
LED ZEPPELIN CHICAGO '75 - COLLECTION (FAB BOX) PRO 1 HR.
LED ZEPPELIN DANISH TV 1969 (FAB BOX) PRO 30 MIN.
LED ZEPPELIN VIDEO DAZE PT. 1 PRO 140 MIN.
LED ZEPPELIN VIDEO DAZE PT. 2 PRO 100 MIN.
LED ZEPPELIN VIDEO DAZE PT. 3 PRO 50 MIN.
LED ZEPPELIN VIDEO DAZE PT. 4 (1975) SUPER 8 1 HR.
LED ZEPPELIN VIDEO DAZE VOL. 5 (RARE FOOTAGE) 80 MIN PS
LED ZEPPELIN LA 1975 PRO 30 MIN.
LED ZEPPELIN NY MSG 1977 PRO 1 HR.
JIMMY PAGE ARIZONA 1988 PRO 100 MIN
PAGE/PLANT JAPAN TV '94 STAIRWAY TO HEAVEN 15 MIN PS
LED ZEPPELIN PARIS 1969 (RARE) + SONG REMAINS THE SAME OUTTAKES
PRO 50 MIN.
LED ZEPPELIN KNEBWORTH '79 PRO 2.5 HRS. (FAB BOX)
TEXAS POP FESTIVAL '69 PRO 90 MIN (WITH ZEP FOOTAGE)
THE LOST LENNON TAPES VOL. 1 PRO 90 MIN.
THE LOST LENNON TAPES VOL. 2 PRO 2 HRS
THE LOST LENNON TAPES VOL. 3 PRO 100 MIN
THE LOST LENNON TAPES VOL.4 PRO 120 MIN
THE LOST LENNON TAPES VOL. 5 PRO 120 MIN
JOHN LENNON TRIBUTE PRO 2 HRS
LIVING COLOR TORONTO 1990 PRO 75 MIN.
LIVING COLOUR ITALY '93 100 MIN PS
LOLLAPALOOZA TOUR CHICAGO 1992 2 HRS. (INCLUDES: SOUNDGARDEN,
PEARL JAM & CHILI PEPPERS)
LUSH SAN FRANCISCO '92 60 MIN HH
LUSH PROVIDENCE 91 65 MIN.
LYNYRD SKYNYRD SAN FRANCISCO 1975 B/W PRO 75 MIN.
LYNYRD SKYNYRD JONES BEACH NY 1991 90 MIN.
LYNYRD SKYNYRD BBC- OGWT 1975 B/W 75 I HR (RARE!)
LYNYRD SKYNYRD COMPILATION PRO 90 MIN
LYNYRD SKYNYRD ATLANTA 2/19/93 160 MIN
LYNYRD SKYNYRD COW PALACE '75 (B/W) PRO 80 MIN
MADNESS MADSTOCK, ENGLAND '92 PRO 90 MIN.
MADONNA JAPAN 1990 PRO 100 MIN.
MADONNA COLLECTION PRO 100 MIN.
MADONNA COLLECTION VOL. 2 PRO 90 MIN.
MADONNA COLLECTION VOLUME 3 PRO 100 MIN

RARE VIDEO SALE

MADONNA SPAIN 1990 PRO 100 MIN.
MADONNA UNAUTHORIZED BIOGRAPHY PRO 2 HRS.
MADONNA JAPAN 1987 PRO 90 MIN.
MADONNA THE INTERVIEWS PRO 1 HR.
MADONNA NICE, FRANCE 8/'90 PRO 2 HRS.
MADONNA INTIMATE INTERVIEWS
MADONNA MSG 10/14/93 110 MIN.
MADONNA PHILLY 1993 100 MIN
MADONNA PROMO REEL PRO 100 MIN
MADONNA JAPAN 12/8/93 PRO 120 MIN
MADONNA AUSTRALIA 93 PRO 100 MIN
MARILLION HAMMERSMITH 1983 PRO 50 MIN.
MARILLION STOKE 1990 PRO 90 MIN
MARILLION LORELY 87 PRO 80 MIN
BOB MARLEY RAINBOW 1979 PRO 60 MIN.
BOB MARLEY TIME WILL TELL 90 MIN PS
BRIAN MAY HARTFORD 1993 60 MIN
BRIAN MAY LONDON 1993 PRO 95 MIN
MCCARTNEY BROADWAY & NY '89 (FAB BOX) PRO 1 HR.
PAUL MCCARTNEY VIDEO PACK PRO 1 HR.
PAUL MCCARTNEY LIVE IN RIO 1990 PRO 1 HR.
PAUL MCCARTNEY ONE HAND CLAPPING PRO 2 HRS.
PAUL MCCARTNEY JAPAN 1990 PRO 2 HRS. 15 MIN.
MCCARTNEY LONE STAR ROADHOUSE NY 1990 PRO 1 HR.
PAUL MCCARTNEY VIDEOPHILE '89-90 PRO 90 MIN.
PAUL MCCARTNEY CHICAGO 1990 2 HRS.
MCCARTNEY UNPLUGGED UNEDITED PRO 1 HR. 40 MIN.
PAUL MCCARTNEY VIDEO PORTRAIT PRO 1 HR.
MCCARTNEY ED SULLIVAN THEATRE 12/10/'92 PRO 90 MIN.
PAUL MCCARTNEY CHILE 1993 PRO 110 MIN
PAUL MCARTNEY SNL REHEARSALS 2/20/93 75 MIN
PAUL MCCARTNEY ROCK SHOW
PAUL MCCARTNEY JAPAN 86 PRO 60 MIN
PAUL MCCARTNEY INTRO TO GET BACK (JAPAN & BUDAKON)
PAUL MCCARTNEY JAPAN, 122493 LIVE CONCERT & REHEARSALS JAMES
PAUL MCCARTNEY SHOW PRO 1 HR.
M.C. HAMMER TOKYO 1991 PRO 1 HR
MEGADEATH NEW HAVEN,CT. 1990 45 MIN.
MEGADEATH LARGO 1986 1 HR.
MEGADEATH FAIRFAX, VA 11/5/92 90 MIN
JOHN MELLENCAMP PHILADELPHIA 1992 2 HRS. 15 MIN.
JOHN MELLENCAMP INDIANA 92 PRO 90 MIN
JOHN MELLENCAMP COMPILATION PRO 2 HRS
MENTORS MINNEAPOLIS 1991 60 MIN PS
MERCIFUL FATE FT. LAUDERDALE 1983 90 MIN
METALLICA RARITIES 120 MIN PS
METALLICA WOODSTOCK '94 105 MIN PS
METALLICA ENGLAND 1988 PRO 30 MIN.
METALLICA HARTFORD, CT. 1989 2 HRS.
METALLICA NEW YORK 1989 100 MIN.
METALLICA QUEBEC 1986 100 MIN.
METALLICA REHEARSAL SHOW 8/1/'91 2 HRS.
METALLICA REHEARSAL SHOW 8/2/'91 2 HRS.
METALLICA MILWAUKEE 11/'91 150 MIN.
METALLICA NASSAU, NY 12/20/'91 2 HRS. 40 MIN.
METALLICA CAMPAIGN, IL. 1992 2 HRS. 40 MIN.
METALLICA BINGHAMTON, NY PT. 1 1992 90 MIN.
METALLICA BINGHAMTON, NY PT. 2 1992 90 MIN.
METALLICA ALBANY, NY PT. 1 1992 90 MIN.
METALLICA ALBANY, NY PT. 2 1992 90 MIN.
METALLICA HARTFORD, PT. 1 1992 90 MIN.
METALLICA HARTFORD, PT. 2 1992 90 MIN.
METALLICA PROVIDENCE, RI 2/29/92 2 HRS.
METALLICA CHATTANOOGA, 3/12/92 PRO 2 HRS. PART 1
METALLICA CHATTANOOGA, 3/12/92 PRO 1 HR. PART 2
METALLICA STUDIO OUTTAKES 1993 PRO 60 MIN
METALLICA SAN FRANCISCO 83 60 MIN
MINISTRY DALLAS 1990 PRO 75 MIN.
MINISTRY DENVER 92/CINEY 92 2 HRS.
MINISTRY ORLANDO 12/11/92 80 MIN.
MISFITS COMPILATION PRO 2 HRS.
MOODY BLUES JONES BEACH, NY 1990 2 HRS.
MOODY BLUES JONES BEACH, NY 1991 2 HRS.
MOODY BLUES ALLENTOWN, PA 1992 2 HRS.
MOODY BLUES RADIO CITY, NY 1993 2 HRS.
MOODY BLUES NEW ORLEANS 2/25/94 W/ORCH. 120 MIN
MOODY BLUES BATON ROUGE 2/26/94 W/ORCH. 120 MIN
MOODY BLUES ORLANDO, FL 6/12/94 ORCH. 120 MIN
MOODY BLUES PENSACOLA, FL 1/27/94 120 MIN
GARY MOORE & THIN LIZZY AUSTRALIA PRO '78
VAN MORRISON IRELAND PRO 1979
MORRISSEY COLLECTION 1991 PRO 2 HRS.
MORRISSEY LONDON 1991 PRO 80 MIN.
MORRISSEY HEAVEN KNOWS I'M MISERABLE NOW VIDEO RETROSPECTIVE
PRO 2 HRS.
MORRISSEY THE MALADY LINGERS 30 MIN PS
MORRISSEY ST. LOUIS 9/29/'92 90 MIN.
MORRISSEY VIDEO ARSENAL PRO 2 HRS.
MOTLEY CRUE NEW YORK 1990 100 MIN.
MOTLEY CRUE KANSAS CITY 1990 PRO 100 MIN.
MOTLEY CRUE TACOMA 1987 PRO 75 MIN
MOTLEY CRUE AUBURN HILLS, MI 1990 PRO 2 HRS.
MOTORHEAD TORONTO PRO 1 HR.
MR. BUNGLE SAN FRANCISCO 4/20/92 100 MIN
MR. BUNGLE TORONTO 92 PRO 90 MIN
BOB MOULD MAXWELL'S NJ 3/12/91 120 HH
BOB MOULD IRVING PLAZA 10/14/93 75 MIN HH
HONEY ITALY 1989 1 HR.
PETER MURPHY VANCOUVER 92 95 MIN.
MY LIFE WITH THRILL KILL KULT TEXAS 90 1 HR.

NALPALM DEATH MONTREAL 1992 50 MIN
NEW ORDER FACT 77 LIVE NY 1981 PRO 1 HR.
NEW ORDER JAPAN 1985 PRO 1 HR.
NEW YORK DOLLS FORBIDDEN DOLLS 30 MIN PS
NEW YORK DOLLS LIVE IN A DOLL'S HOUSE PRO 30 MIN.
NEW YORK ROCK N SOUL REVUE PHILADELPHIA 92 2 HRS.
STEVIE NICKS AUSTRALIAN COLLECTION 77-94 120 MIN PS
STEVIE NICKS US FESTIVAL 1983 PRO 100 MIN.
STEVIE NICKS COLLECTION PRO 2 HRS.
STEVIE NICKS PHILADELPHIA 1991 100 MIN.
STEVIE NICKS JONES BEACH, NY 1991 EXCELLENT 2 HRS.
STEVIE NICKS CALIFORNIA 8/'91 PRO 90 MIN.
STEVIE NICKS SAN JOSE 1989 PRO
NINE INCH NAILS DALLAS, TX 6/26/90 50 MIN PS
NINE INCH NAILS MIAMI '90 & NEWARK '89 90 MIN.
NINE INCH NAILS POUGHKEESIE, NY 8/3/94 90 MIN HH
NINE INCH NAILS WOODSTOCK '94 90 MIN PS
NIRVANA KURT COBAIN TRIBUTE 40 MIN PS
NIRVANA DETROIT 12/'91 EXCELLENT 1 HR.
NIRVANA MEXICO '89 35 MIN PS
NIRVANA NEW JERSEY & DALLAS 1991 2 HRS.
NIRVANA ROME, ITALY 1991 PRO 1 HR.
NIRVANA ROME 2/25/94 120 MIN HH
NIRVANA S.N.L. REHEARSALS 45 MIN PS
NIRVANA HOLLAND 12/'91 PRO 1 HR.
NIRVANA 'IN SCOPE' '91-'94 90 MIN PS
NIRVANA PHILADELPHIA 93 HH 90 MIN
NIRVANA RIO 1993 PRO 75 MIN.
NIRVANA KOLN '90 & ROTTERDAM '91 80 MIN
NIRVANA TRIBUTE PRO 120 MIN
NO NIRVANA COMP INCLUDES: SUGAR, BELLY, PUMPKINS RAGE, PEARL,
REM PRO 60 MIN
TED NUGENT ROCKPALAST 76 PRO 30 MIN.
OVERKILL HOUSTON 1989 1HR
OZZY SEATTLE 6/11/92 PRO 100 MIN.
OZZY OSBOURNE POUGHKEEPSIE, NY 1/21/'92 110 MIN
OZZY OSBOURN PHILADELPHIA NY PRO 2 HRS
OZZY OSBOURNE IRVINE 82 PRO 100 MIN
OZZY AND RANDY AFTER HOURS 1981 PRO 1 HR
JIMMY PAGE ARIZONA 1988 PRO 100 MIN.
PARLIAMENT FUNKADELIC HOUSTON 78 PRO 2 HRS.
PANTERA DAYTONA 7/94 90 MIN HH
PANTERA DENMARK 93 2 HRS.
PANTERA HOLLYWOOD 94/CHICAGO 93 100 MIN
PANTERA SAN DIEGO 7/19/94 80 MIN HH
PARLIAMENT FUNKADELIC HOUSTON 75/76 PRO
PARLIAMENT FUNKADELIC ALL STARS WASH. 83 PRO 2 HRS
PARLIAMENT FUNKADELIC ALL STARS HOUSTON 84 PRO 2 HRS
PARLIAMENT FUNKADELIC CAP CENTER 78 PRO 2 HRS
PARLIAMENT FUNKADELIC HOUSTON 78 PRO 2 HRS
PARLIMENT FUNKADELIC PART 1 MIAMI, FL 6/28/93 120 MIN
PARLIAMENT FUNKADELIC PART 2 MIAMI, FL 6/28/93 100 MIN
PEARL JAM BOSTON 4/11/94 90 MIN HH
PEARL JAM FAIRFAX, VA 4/8/94 105 MIN HH
PEARL JAM SEATTLE 1991 1 HR.
PEARL JAM LIMELIGHT NY 1992 1 HR.
PEARL JAM MILWAUKEE '92 & SNL '92 EXCELLENT 90 MIN.
PEARL JAM MILAN 1992 PRO 2 HRS.
PEARL JAM VIDEO COLLECTION 2 HRS.
PEARL JAM RARITIES VOL. 2 2 HRS.
PEARL JAM MIAMI 8/22/92 75 MIN.
PEARL JAM SAN JOSE '93 90 MIN
PEARL JAM SAN FRANCISCO 5/15/92 100 MIN HH
PEARL JAM REHEARSALS 45 MIN PS
PEARL JAM NEW ORLEANS 11/16/93 82 MIN.
PEARL JAM VERONA, ITALY 1993 & TORONTO 1993 90 MIN.
PEARL JAM JONES BEACH 8/9/92 45 MIN HH
PEARL JAM HOLLAND 3/2/92 120 MIN HH
PEARL JAM ROTTERDAM 3/6/92 120 MIN HH
PEARL JAM PHILADELPHIA 4/10/92 100 MIN HH
PEARL JAM CHICAGO '92 & CALIFORNIA '92 120 MIN HH
PEARL JAM RARITIES VOL. 3 120 MIN MIN
PEARL JAM RARITIES VOL. 4 120 MIN PS
PEARL JAM WINNIPEG CANADA '93 & JAPAN '92 120 MIN PS
TOM PETTY BEACH PARTY 1977 PRO 100 MIN.
TOM PETTY NASSAU, NY 1991 90 MIN.
TOM PETTY NASSAU COLISEUM 1991 90 MIN.
PHISH MOUNTAIN VIEW, CA 93 PRO 1 HR.
PHISH NEW HAVEN, CT '93 160 MIN
PHISH WATERBURY '93 90 MIN
PHISH WOODBURY, CT 60 MIN PS
PHISH CAMEO THEATER, MIAMI BCH 2/25/93 96 MIN
PIGFACE MILWAUKEE 91 80 MIN
PIL JAPAN 1983 PROM 40 MIN.
PIL NEW YORK 10/4/'89 90 MIN.
PINK FLOYD EARL'S COURT '94 120 MIN PS
PINK FLOYD SAN DIEGO 4/14/94 150 MIN HH
PINK FLOYD FILLMORE WEST 1971 PRO 2 HRS.
PINK FLOYD LONDON 66-67 W/SYD 30 MIN PS
PINK FLOYD MIAMI 3/30/94 150 MIN HH
PINK FLOYD NEW YORK MSG 1987 150 MIN.
PINK FLOYD NASSAU 1988 2 HRS.
PINK FLOYD RARITIES VOL. 2 PRO 2 HRS.
PINK FLOYD NASSAU COLISEUM NY 2/27/80 PRO 115 MIN
PINK FLOYD DALLAS, TX 4/94 150 MIN
PINK FLOYD OAKLAND, CA 4/22/94 120 MIN
PINK FLOYD VENICE '88 110 MIN PS
SYD BARRETTS FIRST TRIP 8mm SILENT
THE PIXIES U.K. 1991 PRO 90 MIN.

MORE RARE VIDEO —>

RARE VIDEO SALE

THE PIXIES COLLECTION PRO 2 HRS
ROBERT PLANT NEW YORK 1990 100 MIN.
ROBERT PLANT FRESNO 1990 REHEARSALS PRO 30 MIN.
ROBERT PLANT DALLAS, TX REHEARSALS 1988 PRO 65 MIN.
ROBERT PLANT WITH FAIRPORT CONVENTION & GERMANY '90
ROBERT PLANT JACKSONVILLE, FLA 9/18/93 105 MIN.
ROBERT PLANT SUNRISE, FLA 9/15/93 100 MIN.
ROBERT PLANT MONTREAUX 1993 PRO 50 MIN
ROBERT PLANT THE PARAMOUNT, NYC 11/30/93 110 MIN
ROBERT PLANT RIO 1/22/94 PRO 120 MIN
POGUES POUGEVISION PRO 1 HR.
POISON NEW YORK 1988 75 MIN.
POLICE ROCKPALAST 1/11/80 60 MIN PS
POLICE ROCKPALAST 10/18/80 & GERMANY 7/31/82 90 MIN PS
POLICE ROCK CONCERT '78 JAPAN 1980 PRO 90 MIN.
POLICE MONTREAL 83/LONDON 79 PRO 2 HRS
IGGY POPTORONTO 1982 PRO 60 MIN
IGGY POP PARIS 1991 PRO 1 HR
IGGY POP SAN FRANCISCO 1981 PRO 45 MIN
PORNO FOR PYROS CAL 93 50 MIN.
PORNO FOR PYROS TAMPA 93 & MIAMI 93 120 MIN
PORNO FOR PYROS WOODSTOCK '94 60 MIN PS
PRIMUS WOODSTOCK '94 40 MIN PS
PRIMUS SAN JOSE, CA 3/21/92 75 MIN
PRIMUS PHILADELPHIA 1993 70 MIN
PRIMUS MIAMI, FL 11/29/91 75 MIN
PRIMUS LOLLAPALOOZA 7/18/93 70 MIN HH
PRINCE NEW YORK CITY 7/13/94 120 MIN HH
PRINCE MUNICH GERMANY 1992 2 HRS.
PRINCE ROTTERDAM 1992 2 HRS
PRINCE GERMANY 1988 PRO 2 HRS
PRINCE PROMO REEL PRO 2 HRS.
PRINCE JAPAN 1990 PRO 100 MIN.
PRINCE BARCELONA, SPAIN 1990 PRO 100 MIN.
PRINCE MIAMI '94 GLAM SLAN 2 SHOWS 140 MIN PS
PRINCE MINNESOTA 1983 PRO 75 MIN.
PRINCE BRAZIL 1991 PRO 40 MIN.
PRINCE MINNESOTA 1987 PRO 75 MIN.
PRINCE ARSENIO HALL '91 & HOUSTON '81 PRO 2 HRS.
PRINCE COLLECTION RARE TV PRO 90 MIN.
PRINCE COLLECTION VOL. 2 MORE RARE PRO 2 HRS.
PRINCE COLLECTION VOLUME 3 PRO 100 MIN
PRINCE HOUSTON 1983 PRO 90 MIN.
PRINCE MOUNTAIN REHEARSALS PRO 2 HRS.
PRINCE BBC TV 1991 PRO 2 HRS.
PRINCE GERMANY 1992 2 HRS30 MIN
PRINCE COLLECTORS EDITION MINT PRO2 HRS.
PRINCE DETROIT 1986 PRO 1 HR.
PRINCE RADIO CITY 3/24/93 2HRS 30 MIN
PRINCE RADIO CITY 3/25/93 2 HRS 30 MIN
PRINCE IN CONCERT 92 PRO 2 HRS
PRINCE FAIRFAX, VA 93 2 HRS
PRINCE PARIS, FRANCE 8/31/93 2 HRS.
PRINCE TORONTO 1993 135 MIN
PRINCE WERSTER, GERMANY 1993 90 MIN
PRINCE PAISLEY PARK JAPAN 94 PRO 90 MIN
PSYCHIC TV JOY PRO 1 HR.
QUEEN THE INTERVIEWS PRO 1 HR.
QUEEN RARE AND LIVE (IMPORT) PRO 1 HR.
QUEEN WEMBLEY PRO 75 MIN.
QUEEN FLIXX VOL. 1 PRO 1 HR
QUEEN FLIXX 2 PRO 90 MIN
QUEEN RAINBOW THEATER ENGLAND 1974 & MORE PRO 70 MIN
QUEEN MILTON KEYNES, ENGLAND 82 PRO
QUEEN HYDE PARK 1976 1976 PRO
QUEEN JAPAN 1985 PRO
QUEEN JAPAN 1979 PRO
QUEEN OSAKA, JAPAN 1982 PRO
QUEEN HAMMERSMITH 1979 PRO
QUEEN LIVE AID AND REHEARSALS '85 PRO
QUEEN FREDDIE MERCURY TRIBUTE '74-84 PRO
QUEEN HAMMERSMITH 1979 PRO NY '89 & RIO '91 PRO 2 HRS.
QUEENSRYCHE RARITIES 120 MIN PS
QUEENSRYCHE JAPAN 1991 2 HRS.
QUEENSRYCHE BINGHAMPTON N.Y. 7/20/'91 2 HRS.
QUEENSRYCHE JAPAN 1984 PRO 1 HR.
RAGE AGAINST MACHINE WASHINGTON DC '93 60 MIN.
RAGE AGAINST MACHINE GERMANY 2/7/93 PRO 90 MIN.
RAINBOW GERMANY 1977 PRO 100MIN
RAINBOW JAPAN 84 PRO 120 MIN
BONNIE RAITT GERMANY '94 60 MIN PS
RAMONES HOUSTON '76 & NY '88 90 MIN.
RAMONES LIVE 77 PRO 60 MIN
RAMONES ITALY 6/92 PRO 1 HR.
RAMONES RITZ NY 89 PRO 1 HR.
RAMONES SAN FRANCISCO 78 PRO 60 MIN B/W
RAMONES ENGLAND 92/ GERMANY 92 PRO 75 MIN.
RAMONES SAN FRANCISCO 78 PRO 60 MIN. B/W
READING FESTIVAL READING 1972 120 MIN PS
RED HOT CHILI PEPPERS WOODSTOCK '94 70 MIN PS
RED HOT CHILI PEPPERS GERMANY 1987 PRO 90 MIN.
RED HOT CHILI PEPPERS JAPAN 1990 MINT PRO 100 MIN.
RED HOT CHILI PEPPERS TROY ,NY 1992 90 MIN
RED HOT CHILI PEPPERS MILWAUKEE 1991 40 MIN
RED HOT CHILI PEPPERS RIO 93 PRO 100 MIN
RED HOT CHILI PEPPERS HOLLAND 90 AND ITALY 92 PRO 2HRS
LOU REED HOUSTON 1974 B/W PRO 30 MIN.
REM GERMANY 1985 PRO 1 HR.
REM GERMANY 1989 100 MIN.

REM COLLECTION PRO 90 MIN.
REM COLLECTION VOL. 2 PRO 60 MIN.
REM TIME PIECE & UNPLUGGED (RARE PROMOS) PRO 75 MIN
REM MILAN ITALY 1991 PRO 90 MIN
REM SAT. NIGHT LIVE REHEARSALS '91 60 MIN PS
REPLACEMENTS NEW YORK 1989 75 MIN.
REPLACEMENTS NEW YORK 1991 90 MIN.
REPLACEMENTS ROTTERDAM '91 75 MIN
RESIDENTS THE MOLE SHOW PRO 1 HR.
RESIDENTS HISTORY OF PRO 1 HR.
REVOLTING COCKS HOUSTON 9/15/90 65 MIN
KEITH RICHARDS GERMANY 1992 PRO 2 HRS
KEITH RICHARDS BEACON THEATER, NY 2/20/93 2 HRS
KEITH RICHARDS BEACON THEATER, NY 2/22/93 2 HRS
KEITH RICHARDS BEACON THEATER, NY 2/24/93 2 HRS
KEITH RICHARDS COLLECTION '89-92 PRO 90 MIN
KEITH RICHARDS BEACON THEATER NY 88 90 MIN
KEITH RICHARDS CHICAGO 93 PRO 120 MIN
KEITH RICHARDS BOSTON 93 PRO 2 HRS
RIP PARTY W/GNR, METALLICA, SKID ROW 11/16/90 PRO 35 MIN
ROCK N' ROLL CIRCUS B/W PRO 1 HR.
ROCK N' ROLL CIRCUS HIGH SCHOOL (JAPANESE EDITION)
ROCK N ROLL HALL OF FAME 93 PRO 80 MIN
ROLLING STONES AUSTRALIA '73 B/W VERY RARE 60 MIN PS
ROLLING STONES NEW JERSEY 8/12/94 120 MIN HH
ROLLING STONES GIANT STADIUM 8/12/94 120 MIN HH
ROLLING STONES C.S. BLUES (FAB BOX) PRO 90 MIN.
ROLLING STONES MARQUEE '71 (FAB BOX) PRO 1 HR.
ROLLING STONES MIAMI 11/25/94 - SUPER!! 160 MIN PS
ROLLING STONES HYDE PARK 1969 PRO 1 HR.
ROLLING STONES ED SULLIVAN SHOWS PRO 75 MIN
ROLLING STONESLADIES & GENTLEMEN OUTTAKES PRO ROLLING
STONES ROLLING STONES COLLECTION VOL. 1 PRO
ROLLING STONES COLLECTION VOL. 2 PRO 2 HRS.
ROLLING STONES COLLECTION VOL. 3 PRO 80 MIN.
ROLLING STONES HAMPTON, VA. 1981 PRO 140 MIN.
ROLLING STONES ATLANTIC CITY 1989 PRO 140 MIN.
ROLLING STONES TOKYO 1990 PRO 140 MIN.
ROLLING STONES ATLANTA 1978 PRO 45 MIN
ROLLING STONES PARIS 1976 PRO 1 HR.
ROLLING STONES PHILA. PA 9/23/94 120 MIN HH
ROLLING STONES 'PRO SHOT' -NJ '94 120 MIN PS
ROLLING STONES SPAIN 1990 PRO 90 MIN.
ROLLING STONES THE INTERVIEWS PRO 1 HR.
ROLLING STONES WITH MUDDY WATERS '81
ROLLING STONES WITH LIVE CONCERT FOOTAGE 60 MIN PS
ROLLING STONES TORONTO 1989 PRO 90 MIN.
ROLLING STONES TORONTO 8/19/94 120 MIN HH
ROLLING STONES TORONTO RPM CLUB = 3 SONGS AND NEWS
ROLLING STONES VINTAGE STONES '64-74 PRO 90 MIN.
ROLLING STONES CHARLIE IS MY DARLING PRO 1 HR.
ROLLING STONES BLACK & BLUE 1976 PRO 1 HR.
ROLLING STONES SNL REHEARSALS & MORE PRO 70 MIN.
ROLLING STONES HOUSTON 1981 PRO 2 HRS.
ROLLING STONES DALLAS 1989 PRO MINT 1 1/2 HRS.
ROLLING STONES KNEBWORTH 1976 PRO 1 HR.
ROLLING STONES JAPAN ALTERNATE SHOW 2/24/90 OSAKA PRO
ROLLING STONES UNSURPASSED VIDEOS VOL. 1
ROLLING STONES UNSURPASSED VIDEOS VOL. 2
ROLLING STONES SEATTLE 81 PRO 2 HRS
ROLLING STONES LOS ANGELES 75 PRO 135 MIN
ROLLING STONES NEW ORLEANS 7/13/78 PRO 100 MIN
ROLLING STONES R.F.K. WASH. D.C. 8/3/94150 MIN HH
MICK JAGGER WEBSTER HALL, NY FEB.9, 1993 PRO 1 HR
MICK JAGGER SNL REHEARSALS 2/13/93 50 MIN
NEW BARBARIANS LARGO 79 PRO 2HRS 30 MIN
CHARLIE WATTS BIG BAND JAPAN 1991 PRO 1 HR.
ROLLINS BAND NEW YORK 92 100 MIN
ROLLINS BAND 1992 2 HRS.
ROLLINS BAND ITALY 6/92 PRO 1 HR.
ROLLINS WASHINGTON D.C. 5/14/94 45 MIN HH
ROLLINS BAND WOODSTOCK '94 35 MIN PS
ROXY MUSIC FRANCE 1982 PRO 1 HR.
RUNAWAYS JAPAN 77 PRO 75 MIN
RUNAWAYS CHICAGO 78 PRO 40 MIN. B/W
RUSH '75-76-77 PRO 30 MIN.
RUSH PHILADELPHIA 1990 110 MIN.
RUSH ALBANY NY 1990 2 HRS.
RUSH ALBANY NY 12/12/'91 2 HRS.
RUSH NASSAU COLISEUM 1992 2 HRS
RUSH NYC 12/6/'91 2 HRS.
RUSH DETROIT 90 PRO 2 HRS
RUSH FRESNO '94 100 MIN
RUSH MADISON SQ. GARDEN 3/8/94 115MIN
LEON RUSSEL & E. WINTER MURFREESBORO '88 90 MIN PS
SAMHAIN LIVE 1984 2 HRS.
SANTANA CHILE 92 PRO 2 HRS.
SANTANA JAMES L KNIGHT CTR. MIAMI 9/22/93 89 MIN
SANTANA WOODSTOCK '94 60 MIN PS
JOE SATRIANI MONTREUX 1988 PRO 60 MIN
SEPULTURA HOLLAND & PHILLY '89-90 2 HRS.
SEPULTURA LAMOURS, NY 1989
SEPULTURA RIO 1/22/94 PRO 60 MIN
SEX PISTOLS DECADE 30 MIN PS
SEX PISTOLS BURIED ALIVE 30 MIN PS
SEX PISTOLS DOA PRO 100 MIN.
SEX PISTOLS WINTERLAND 1978 PRO 1 HR.
SEX PISTOLS BULLOCKS TO EVERYONE (RARE CONCERT FOOTAGE) PRO
90 MINS.
SICK OF IT ALL PHILADELPHIA 1993 6 MIN

RARE VIDEO SALE

SIOUXSIE AND THE BANSHEES LONDON 1981 PRO 30 MIN
SISTERS OF MERCY COLLECTION PRO 2 HRS.
SISTERS OF MERCY SAN FRANCISCO 1991
SISTERS OF MERCY CHICAGO 1984 PRO 1 HR.
SISTERS OF MERCY LONDON 1985 PRO 1 HR.
SKINNY PUPPY HOLLAND 88 1 HR.
SKINNY PUPPY MIAMI 6/18/92 70 MIN.
SKREW TEXAS 93 2 HRS.
SLAUGHTER NEW YORK 1990 1 HR.
SLAYER JAPAN 1990 2 HRS.
SLAYER NEW YORK 1988 100 MIN.
SLAYER 1994 90 MIN PS
SLAYER TROY, NY 2/11/'91 85 MIN.
SMASHING PUMPKINS MUNICH 1994 70 MIN PS
SMASHING PUMPKINS SAN FRANCISCO 91 100 MIN
SMASHING PUMPKINS S.N.L. REHEARSALS 45 MIN PS
SMASHING PUMPKINS NEW YORK 91/FLORIDA 92 2 HR
SMASHING PUMPKINS CHICAGO 8/19/93 PRO 30 MIN.
SMASHING PUMPKINS GERMANY 9/4/92 PRO 75 MIN
SMASHING PUMPKINS LAS VEGAS '94 75 MIN HH
SMITHS VIDEOGRAPHY VOL. 1 PRO 100 MIN.
SMITHS VIDEOGRAPHY VOL. 2 PRO 100 MIN.
SMITHS SPAIN 1985 PRO 90 MIN.
SMITHS PARIS 1986 PRO
SONIC YOUTH NY 1991 2 HRS
SONIC YOUTH NEW YORK 92 75 MIN.
SOUNDGARDEN LA 2/11/88 1 HR.
SOUNDGARDEN SAN FRANCISCO 92 2 HRS.
SOUNDGARDEN SEATTLE '92 PRO 60 MIN
SOUNDGARDEN JAPAN 94/HOLLAND 92 PRO 60 MIN
SPIN DOCTORS BEACON THEATRE NYC '92 2 HRS. 40 MIN.
SPIN DOCTORS ITALY 93 PRO 80 MIN.
SPIN DOCTORS WOODSTOCK '94 70 MIN PS
BRUCE SPRINGSTEEN PLUGGED REHEARSALS 92 PRO 90 MIN
BRUCE SPRINGSTEEN HARTFORD PART 1 11/92 2 HRS
BRUCE SPRINGSTEEN PART 2 11/92 90 MIN
BRUCE SPRINGSTEEN SATERDAY NIGHT LIVE REHEARSALS & BBC TV 1992
PRO 2 HRS
BRUCE SPRINGSTEEN NEW JERSEY 1978 PRO
BRUCE SPRINGSTEEN ARGENTINA 1988 PRO
BRUCE SPRINGSTEEN BERLIN 1988 PRO 90 MIN.
BRUCE SPRINGSTEEN LARGO 1978 PRO 2 HRS.
BRUCE SPRINGSTEEN BENEFIT CONCERT LA '90 80 MIN.
BRUCE SPRINGSTEEN PHOENIX 1978 PRO 35 MIN.
BRUCE SPRINGSTEEN RARITIES VOL. 1 PRO 2 HRS. (UNRELEASED VIDEOS
AND CONCERT FOOTAGE)
BRUCE SPRINGSTEEN LARGO 1980 PRO 2 HRS.
BRUCE SPRINGSTEEN LARGO 1980 PRO PT. 2 1 HR.
BRUCE SPRINGSTEEN ITALY 6/20/'92 2 HRS.
BRUCE SPRINGSTEEN ITALY 6/20/'92 PT. 2 90 MIN.
BRUCE SPRINGSTEEN NEW JERSEY 7/26/92 2 HRS 40 MIN
BRUCE SPRINGSTEEN NJ AUGUST 10, 1992 PART 1 2 HRS
BRUCE SPRINGSTEEN NJ AUGUST 10, 1992 PART 2 2 HRS
BRUCE SPRINGSTEEN NJ 93 PT 1 2 HRS
BRUCE SPRINGSTEEN NJ 93 PT 2 2 HRS
BRUCE SPRINGSTEEN MSG 93 90 MIN
BRUCE SPRING STEEN COUNT BASIE THEATER, NJ PRO 70 MIN
REHEARSALS & INTERVIEW
PAUL STANLEY NEW YORK 1989 PRO 75 MIN.
PAUL STANLEY NEW HAVEN 1989 100 MIN.
STEELY DAN ALBANY 9/23/93 135 MIN.
ROD STEWART & FACES BIOGRAPHY '69-74 PRO 1 HR.
ROD STEWART GERMANY 1991 PRO 90 MIN.
ROD STEWART & FACES BBC 1971 PRO 60 MIN
ROD STEWART UNPLUGGED UNEDITED PRO 105 MIN
STEELY DAN ALBANY 93 135 MIN
STING NASSAU COLISEUM 1991 100 MIN.
STING PARAMOUNT THEATER, NY 6/93 2 HRS.
STING OLSO, NORWAY 9/28/93 PRO 120 MIN
STONE TEMPLE PILOTS HARTFORD, CT '94 100 MIN HH
STONE TEMPLE RARITIES 120 MIN PS
STONE TEMPLE S.N.L. REHEARSALS 45 MIN PS
STONE TEMPLE PILOTS ILLINOIS 93 80 MIN.
STONE TEMPLE PILOTS TORONTO/93 60 MIN
IZZY STRADLIN AMSTERDAM 1993 90 MIN
STRANGLERS COMPILATION 1977-1982 PRO 1 HR.
STRANGLERS THE OLD TESTAMENT
SUEDE ITALY '94 60 MIN PS
SUEDE LONDON 93 90 MIN.
SUGAR NORWICH '92 60 MIN HH
SUGAR ACADEMY OF MUSIC, NYC 10/23/92 60 MIN
SUPERCHUNK WASHINGTON, CD 93 2 HRS
SUGARCUBES ALABAMA 89 PRO 75 MIN
SUPREMES COLLECTION PRO 75 MIN.
10,000 MANIACA LONG ISLAND NY 1990 2 HRS
10,000 MANIACS CARNEGIE HALL NYC 9/92 2 HRS
10,000 MANIACS ST. LOUIS 1993 PRO 100 MIN
10,000 MANIACS VIDEO COMPILATION PRO 2 HRS
10,000 MANIACS UNPLUGGED UNEDITED PRO 120 MIN
10,000 MANIACS N.Y.C. 7/29/93 60 MIN
TEMPLE OF THE DOGS SEATTLE 90 60 MIN
THIN LIZZY AUSTRALIA 78 PRO 45 MIN
RICHARD THOMPSON BALTIMORE '92 75 MIN
T-REX COLLECTION PRO 1 HR.
T-REX REMAS PRO 1 HR.
JOHNNY THUNDERS DEAD OR ALIVE LONDON 1984 PRO 45 MIN.
JOHNNY THUNDERS ST. LOUIS 1985 PRO 90 MIN
JOHNNY THUNDERS NEW YORK 1989 90 MIN
JOHNNY THUNDERS LOS ANGELES 1985 80 MIN
PETE TOWNSEND BEACON THEATER, NY 93 2 1/2 HRS.

PETE TOWNSEND BROOKLYN, NY 93 135 MIN.
TRAFFIC WOODSTOCK '94 90 MINPS
UKIDK PUNK FILM PRO 60 MIN
URGE OVERKILL NEW ORLEANS 11/11/93 40 MIN
U2 NY, CA, PONTIAC, MI PRO 90 MIN
U2 SAVE THE YUPPIES FRISCO (FAB BOX) PRO 1 HR.
U2 AUSTRALIAN TV 1990 PRO 30 MIN.
U2 ROCKPALAST 1983 PRO 90 MIN.
U2 RITZ NY 1981 PRO 45 MIN.
U2 US FESTIVAL 1983 PRO 100 MIN.
U2 ROCKPOP 1984 GERMANY PRO 1 HR.
U2 LAKELAND, FLA. 2/29/'92 110 MIN.
U2 LA AND NY 1987 PRO 90 MIN.
U2 MEADOWLANDS ARENA NJ 1992 110 MIN.
U2 NASSAU COLISEUM NY 3/9/'92 110 MIN.
U2 ALBANY NY 3/'92 2 HRS.
U2 REHEARSALS - SOUNDCHECK 1992 50 MIN.
U2 PARIS 87/PARIS 82 PRO 90 MIN
U2 DUBLIN 92 PRO 100 MIN
UA IN CONFERENCE PRO 60 MIN
U2 ZOO TV COLLECTION PRO 2 HRS.
STEVE VAI VINTAGE COMPILATION PRO 90 MIN
VAN HALEN US FESTIVAL 1983 PRO 2 HRS.
VAN HALEN VINTAGE COMPILATION PRO 90 MIN.
VAN HALEN VINTAGE COMPILATION VOL. 2 PRO 90 MIN.
VAN HALEN JAPAN 1989 PRO 90 MIN.
VAN HALEN VENEZUELA 1/16/'83 PRO 90 MIN.
VAN HALEN ALBANY NY 1991 110 MIN.
VAN HALEN VINTAGE COLLECTION VOL. 3 PRO 1 HR.
VAN HALEN COLLECTION VOL. 4 PRO 2 HRS.
VAN HALEN DALLAS, TX 12/4/'91 PRO 1 HR.
VAN HALEN CLUB CABO WABO, MEXICO MAY 1992 2 HRS.
VAN HALEN MONTREAL 84 100 MIN
VAN HALEN JONES BEACH, NY 7/93 2 HRS.
VAN HALEN VINTAGE VOLUME 5 1984-86 PRO 90 MIN
VAN HALEN 5150 STUDIOS PRO 60 MIN
STEVIE RAY VAUGHN JAPAN 1985 PRO 90 MIN.
STEVIE RAY VAUGHN TROY, NY 1989 100 MIN.
STEVIE RAY VAUGHN VIDEOFILE PRO 90 MIN
STEVIE RAY VAUGHN ROCKPALAST 1985 PRO 90 MIN.
STEVIE RAY VAUGHN NEW ORLEANS 1989 PRO 100 MIN.
STEVIE RAY VAUGHN MONTREUX & HAWAII 1984 WITH BECK
STEVIE RAY VAUGHN LAST VIDEO TAPED SHOW ST. LOUIS
STEVIE RAY VAUGHN DAYTONA '87 PRO 90 MIN.
STEVIE RAY VAUGHN AUSTIN CITY LIMITS-UNPLUGGED 2 HRS.
STEVIE RAY VAUGHN AMARILLO, TEXAS 9/27/89 PRO 60 MIN
STEVIE RAY VAUGHN CAPITOL THEATRE, NJ 1985 PRO 60 MIN
STEVIE RAY VAUGHN RARITIES VOL. 1 PRO 120 MIN
VELVET UNDERGROUND DOCUMENTARY PRO 1 HR.
TOM WAITS CHICAGO 75 PRO 60 MIN
TOM WAITS ITALY 86 PRO 60 MIN.
WARRANT JAPAN 1990 PRO 90 MIN.
WELCOME TO THE FILLMORE W/BYRDS 1970 PRO 60 MIN
PAUL WESTERBURG ST. PAUL 1993 100 MIN
PAUL WESTERBURG LIVE IN THE MIDWEST 1993 1 HR.
WHITE ZOMBIE CALIFORNIA 92 90 MIN
WHITE ZOMBIE NORWALK 1993 60 MIN
WHO CLEVELAND 1975 PRO 75 MIN.
WHO COLLECTION PRO 100 MIN.
WHO COLLECTION VOL. 2 PRO 100 MIN.
WHO GLEN FALLS NY 1989 PRO 75 MIN.
WHO PONTIAC 1975 PRO 90 MIN.
WHO CHARLTON, ENGLAND 1974 PRO 50 MIN
WHO KIDS ARE ALRIGHT JAPANESE VERSION PRO 100 MIN.
ROGER DALTREY CARNEGIE HALL 2/26/94 PRO 160 MIN
XTC COLLECTION PRO 45 MIN.
XTC ROCKPALAST PRO 2 HRS.
YES BELGIUM TV SPECIAL 1971 PRO 30 MIN.
YES NASSAU COLISEUM NY 1991 160 MIN.
YES PHILADELPHIA 1979 PRO 1 HR.
YES ALBANY NY 1991 2 HRS. 30 MIN.
YES LARGO 1984 PRO 150 MIN.
YES DENVER & PHILADELPHIA 91 PRO 2 HRS. (JAPANESE TV)
YES QUEENS PARK, ENGLAND PRO 2 HRS 30 MIN
YES MONTREAUX 1977 PRO 60 MIN
NEIL YOUNG CENTERSTAGE/FARM AID PRO 100 MIN
NEIL YOUNG NEW YORK CITY 1991 100 MIN
NEIL YOUNG ORLANDO, FLA. 1991 2 HRS.
NEIL YOUNG SNL REHEARSALS & RITZ NY 1979 PRO 1 HR.
NEIL YOUNG NYC 2/15/'92 70 MIN.
NEIL YOUNG AUSTIN CITY LIMITS PRO 1 HR.
NEIL YOUNG RALEIGH, NC 93 2 HRS.
NEIL YOUNG HUSTON 1992 PRO 110 MIN
ZAPPA LA 1974 PRO 1 HR.
ZAPPA NEW YORK 1981 PRO 90 MIN.
ZAPPA STOCKHOM 73 PRO 70 MIN.
FRANK ZAPPA TRIBUTE 90 MIN PS
WARREN ZEVON ITALY '93 90 MIN HH
ZZ TOP TORONTO 1990 100 MIN.
ZZ TOP MADISON SQ. GARDEN 6/6/94 120 MIN HH
ZZ TOP ST. LOUIS 5/7/94115 MIN HH

P. Grant Video - 332 Bleecker Street, #E28,
New York, New York 10014 USA
TEL (212) 330-8149

ARE YOU A BOOTLEGGER?

Do you make bootlegs?
How are changes in laws affecting you?

Are you a taper?
What kind of equipment do you use?

Tell us all about it.
Let the fans hear it right from the source.

Write a few paragraphs or a full article. All submissions will be considered for publication in

THE ULTIMATE WACKS

(An upcoming in-depth look at the world of boots)

Send your thoughts by letter or FAX to:

THE HOT WACKS PRESS

PO BOX 544, OWEN SOUND, ON, N4K 5R1, CANADA
FAX 519 376 9449

We ask that all submissions be sent with samples of your product and a full catalogue of releases. We would also like a contact number (phone or fax) or address that allows us to ask any questions that may come up regarding your comments. Anonymous submissions will be considered with proof in the form of product and a full catalogue of releases.

WHAT DO BOOTLEGS MEAN TO YOU?

Are you a fan or foe of bootlegs? Tell us what you think about bootlegs and bootleggers.

Write a paragraph or a full article. All submissions will be considered for publication in

THE ULTIMATE WACKS

(An upcoming in-depth look at the world of boots)

Send your thoughts by letter or FAX to:

THE HOT WACKS PRESS

PO BOX 544, OWEN SOUND, ON, N4K 5R1, CANADA
FAX 519 376 9449
We ask that all submissions be sent with a contact
number (phone or fax) that allows us to ask any questions that
may come up regarding your comments.

EARLY DAYS & LATTER DAYS

The LED ZEPPELIN Collectors Magazine

If you collect ZEP, this magazine is for you!!

Each Issue of this 36 page A4 size publication is packed with detailed and accurate info on every aspect of collecting ZEP.

Whether you collect Live CD's, Vinyl, Tapes, Videos, Worldwide Pressing Variations, Photo's, Books, Programmes, Memorabilia, Promo Items, or just listen to the music, **"Early Days & Latter Days"** is indispensable.

More than 2,000 Readers in 27 countries around the world read the only ZEP magazine for the collector. So, why don't you join this ever growing number and subscribe now!!

SUBSCRIPTION RATES - 4 Issue - including Postage.
UK - £14.00   EUROPE - £16.00   USA - £18.00   REST OF WORLD - £20.00

SINGLE ISSUES including Postage.
UK - £3.00   EUROPE - £3.50   USA - £4.00   REST OF WORLD - £4.50

Payment by UK sterling or US Dollars in cash by registered post.
All cheques/Money Orders/P.O.'s payable to A.ADAMS. Available from'

EARLY DAYS & LATTER DAYS
The LED ZEPPELIN Collectors Magazine
111, SUSSEX ROAD,
SOUTH CROYDON, SURREY, CR2 7DD U.K.

NEXT ISSUE, NUMBER SIX, DUE MAY 1995 - £4.00

These back issues are also available - at the above rates.

ISSUE FIVE - 1977 USA Tour Special including full Boot listing, Collecting Coverdale/Page, Uncensored 5-CD Box unravelled, BBC Vaults Video's, Robert '93 Collectables, The Rare Boot CG series under the microscope, Jimmy at Battersea '84, loads of rare shots, up to date news, Collectors Corner and much much more......

ISSUE FOUR - CD Frenzy - the Ghost series unravelled, Remasters 2, Australia '72 Update, Paris '69 Video, Film Outtakes Video, Trouser Press Intv, Zep books special, Studio Daze 2 - Olympic Gold examined, Collectors Corner and much more......

ISSUE THREE - Earls Court Special incl Prog reprint, unseen photo's and all Boots examined, ZEP 3 sessions, It's Been A Long Time US CD Promo, 1969 Videos, Trouser Press Intv, Collectors Corner and more......

ISSUE FIVE - Bath '70 special incl Programme reprint, unseen photo's and report/Boots examined, USA '75 Video footage, James Patrick Page Session Man, Robert T & C '91 Special, Lost & Found - the "Studio Daze" & "Jennings Farm Blues" source material examined, plus collectors corner and loads more......

ISSUE ONE - SORRY, COMPLETELY SOLD OUT!!

What most
bootleg collectors think
when they come across a
rare item...

Nunc
hic
aut
numquam

Latin for... "It's now or never."